Spontaneous Spoken Language

Spontaneous Spoken Language

Syntax and Discourse

JIM MILLER
 and
REGINA WEINERT

CLARENDON PRESS · OXFORD
1998

Oxford University Press, Great Clarendon Street, Oxford OX2 6DP
Oxford New York
Athens Auckland Bangkok Bogota Bombay
Buenos Aires Calcutta Cape Town Dar es Salaam
Delhi Florence Hong Kong Istanbul Karachi
Kuala Lumpur Madras Madrid Melbourne
Mexico City Nairobi Paris Singapore
Taipei Tokyo Toronto Warsaw
and associated companies in
Berlin Ibadan

Oxford is a trade mark of Oxford University Press

Published in the United States
by Oxford University Press Inc., New York

© Jim Miller and Regina Weinert 1998
The moral rights of the authors have been asserted

All rights reserved. No part of this publication may be reproduced,
stored in a retrieval system, or transmitted, in any form or by any means,
without the prior permission in writing of Oxford University Press.
Within the UK, exceptions are allowed in respect of any fair dealing for the
purpose of research or private study, or criticism or review, as permitted
under the Copyright, Designs and Patents Act, 1988, or in the case of
reprographic reproduction in accordance with the terms of the licences
issued by the Copyright Licensing Agency. Enquiries concerning
reproduction outside these terms and in other countries should be
sent to the Rights Department, Oxford University Press,
at the address above

British Library Cataloguing in Publication Data
Data available

Library of Congress Cataloging in Publication Data
Spontaneous spoken language: syntax and discourse
Jim Miller and Regina Weinert.
Includes bibliographical references.
1. Colloquial language. 2. Grammar, Comparative and general—
Syntax. 3. Discourse analysis. 4. Typology (Linguistics)
5. Language acquisition. I. Weinert, Regina. II. Title.
P408.M55 1997 415–dc21 97-39156
ISBN 0-19-823656-5
10 9 8 7 6 5 4 3 2 1

Typeset by Joshua Associates Ltd., Oxford
Printed in Great Britain on acid-free paper by
Biddles Ltd., Guildford and King's Lynn

For Margaret
In Erinnerung an Josef Weinert

Preface

THIS book has taken longer to write than we expected. It began as an account of the syntactic structures and discourse devices to be found in spontaneous spoken language. It gradually developed into a comparison of syntax and discourse in spontaneous spoken English, Russian, and German. One motive was to make linguists in English-speaking countries aware of the work that has been carried out elsewhere; another motive was to gather cross-language evidence to support the view that we were dealing with regular structures and not with performance errors. The book also developed into an attempt to demonstrate that the growing body of analyses of spontaneous spoken language was relevant to a number of areas in theoretical linguistics: received views of constructions in particular languages, to theories of the on-line processing of spoken language by humans, to theoretical work in typology, and, perhaps most crucially, to theories of first language acquisition.

The book has its roots in two research projects. The first is a project on the syntax of Scottish English carried out by Jim Miller and Keith Brown in the Department of Linguistics at the University of Edinburgh, between 1977 and 1980. That project was supported by the UK Social Sciences Research Council. The second project is part of the work being carried out in the Human Communication Research Centre at the University of Edinburgh. The HCRC is supported by the UK Economic and Social Research Council. The University of Hull Research Support Fund made possible the collection of additional German data. We thank Gillian Razzaki, who collected and transcribed the German Map Task dialogues.

Numerous colleagues and friends have helped us along the route. Phil Carr discussed various issues at length and commented in detail on an earlier version of Chapter 8, as did Henry Thompson and Nigel Vincent. John Anderson, Ellen Bard, and Bob Ladd provided salutary comments on an earlier version of Chapter 2. Jim Hurford and Caroline Heycock gave us thorough critiques of what is now Chapters 7 and 8. Gill Brown read an earlier paper which was a summary of Chapters 3 and 8 and furnished data and comments from her own work on spoken English. Ronnie Cann was always willing to answer questions and discuss points in the middle of Head-of-Department business. Lesley Milroy read the entire manuscript and her critique enabled us to considerably improve the text. Julie Read of the Department of Linguistics, Latrobe University, Melbourne discussed the relative clause structures presented in Chapter 3 and e-mailed papers dealing with her own work on similar constructions in spoken Australian English. The observations of two anonymous referees persuaded us that the original versions of Chapters 1 and 4 had to be totally revised. The Eurotype project, funded between 1990 and 1994, led us to the interesting work of Jocelyne Fernandez-West at the CNRS in Paris. It also led to discussions with Rosanna Sornicola of the University of Naples. She supplied encouragement, and inspiration too via her classic work on spontaneous spoken Neapolitan, *Sul parlato*. Lynn Childress did magnificent work on a less than perfect manuscript, saving us from errors and omissions.

Many readers will have noticed the split infinitive above. Hopefully the controversy over split infinitives will gradually pass, but there are two items that we would mention in connection with approved usage. Throughout we have used the plural form *corpuses* and not *corpora*. The latter, along with *consortia*, *stadia*, and so on, strikes us as overly Latinate even in an academic text full of Greco-Latinate vocabulary. *Data* is sometimes treated as a plural noun and sometimes as a singular mass noun.

J.M. and R.W.

Contents

Abbreviations		xiii
1 Introduction		1
1.1	Introduction	1
1.2	Spoken and written language in linguistics	4
1.3	The data	6
	1.3.1 Data from English, German, and Russian	7
	1.3.2 Adequacy of the data	10
1.4	Genres: dimensions, individuals, and education	14
1.5	Spontaneous spoken language	22
2 Sentences and Clauses		28
2.1	Introduction	28
2.2	Sentences in spontaneous spoken language: an overview	29
2.3	Sentences in spoken texts	32
2.4	Text-sentences in spoken language	34
	2.4.1 Intonational criteria	34
	2.4.2 Intuitions about sentences in spoken language	35
	2.4.3 The sentence: a changing concept	41
2.5	The sentence as a unit of analysis	46
	2.5.1 Sentences and clauses in spontaneous dialogue	46
	2.5.2 Sentences and syntactic analysis	49
	2.5.3 Sentences, clauses, and distribution	56
	2.5.4 Spoken language with fragmented syntax	58
	2.5.5 Fragmented syntax in spoken Russian	61
2.6	Conclusion	71
3 Clauses: Type, Combination, and Integration		72
3.1	Introduction	72
3.2	Clauses	76
	3.2.1 Definition of clause	76
	3.2.2 Clauses and situations	78
3.3	Constraints on complexity in spontaneous spoken language	79
3.4	Main and subordinate clauses	80
	3.4.1 Finite constructions missing from the corpus of spoken language	81
	3.4.2 Non-finite constructions missing from the corpus of spoken language	85

x *Contents*

		3.4.3	Passives	88
		3.4.4	Proportion of main and subordinate clauses	89
	3.5	Form and function: when a subordinate clause is not a subordinate clause		94
		3.5.1	English	94
		3.5.2	Spoken Russian	95
	3.6	Order of main clause and subordinate clause		100
	3.7	WH constructions		104
		3.7.1	Relative clauses	105
		3.7.2	WH clefts	120
		3.7.3	Headless relative clauses in Russian	130
	3.8	Conclusion		132
4	Noun Phrases: Complexity and Configuration			133
	4.1	Introduction		133
	4.2	Complexity of noun phrases		135
		4.2.1	Noun phrases in written English	135
		4.2.2	Noun phrases in spontaneous speech	139
	4.3	Spontaneous spoken English		143
		4.3.1	The data and its coding	143
		4.3.2	The spontaneous spoken narrative	145
		4.3.3	Extract from spontaneous conversation	153
		4.3.4	A newspaper text	153
	4.4	Spoken and written Russian		159
		4.4.1	Russian conversation and Russian newspaper text	160
		4.4.2	Split noun phrases	164
	4.5	Noun phrases in spoken German		169
	4.6	Split NPs: a problem for constituent structure		176
		4.6.1	'Split' NPs in Russian	177
		4.6.2	'Split' NPs in Australian languages	180
	4.7	Theoretical implications		182
		4.7.1	Configurational languages and spoken language	182
		4.7.2	Scrambling and 'split' NPs	183
		4.7.3	Functional constituents as heads	186
5	Focus Constructions			190
	5.1	Introduction		190
	5.2	Concepts for the analysis of discourse		193
		5.2.1	Focus (1)	193
		5.2.2	Deixis	194
		5.2.3	Theme and thematization	195
		5.2.4	Given and new information	195
	5.3	Results		196
	5.4	Focus (2)		198

Contents xi

		5.4.1	Overview	198
		5.4.2	Halliday	198
		5.4.3	Chafe: components of contrastiveness	200
		5.4.4	Dik: extended notion of focus	200
		5.4.5	Vallduví	202
		5.4.6	Grosz and Sidner: focus space and transition	202
	5.5	Macro- and micro-focus		203
		5.5.1	A text schema	203
		5.5.2	Transitions and contrasts	205
		5.5.3	Macro- and micro-focus in a spoken Russian text	206
	5.6	Given		209
		5.6.1	Ellipsis	209
		5.6.2	Ellipsis in Russian	212
	5.7	Highlighting devices		229
		5.7.1	Knowledge stores and focus spaces: highlighting entities	230
		5.7.2	Existential and existential-possessive constructions	230
		5.7.3	New entities in written texts	231
		5.7.4	New entities in the Map Task dialogues	232
		5.7.5	SEE and KNOW	233
		5.7.6	Highlighting constructions in German	236
		5.7.7	NP-Clause	237
		5.7.8	Highlighting new propositions	242
	5.8	Russian word order		259
	5.9	Conclusion		262
6	Focus Constructions: Clefts and *like*			263
	6.1	Introduction		263
	6.2	An overview of the clefts		263
		6.2.1	Cleft types	263
		6.2.2	The main points in the analysis	264
		6.2.3	Distribution of clefts in the data	265
		6.2.4	Theoretical preliminaries	267
		6.2.5	RWH clefts	274
		6.2.6	WH clefts	291
		6.2.7	IT clefts	300
		6.2.8	Conclusions	305
	6.3	LIKE		306
		6.3.1	Previous accounts of LIKE	307
		6.3.2	Why LIKE is not a pause filler	312
		6.3.3	Non-contrastive focus	315
		6.3.4	LIKE as a non-contrastive focuser	317
		6.3.5	LIKE in the spontaneous conversations	328
		6.3.6	Conclusion	334

xii *Contents*

7	Historical Linguistics and Typology	335
	7.1 Introduction	335
	7.2 Historical Linguistics	335
	7.3 Typology	338
	7.3.1 English conditional constructions	338
	7.3.2 Participles and gerund	340
	7.3.3 Negation	341
	7.3.4 Relative clauses	342
	7.3.5 Clause combining	353
	7.3.6 Subject-prominent and topic-prominent languages	363
	7.3.7 Noun phrases	366
	7.3.8 Word order	369
	7.4 Conclusion	372
8	Written Language, First Language Acquisition, and Education	373
	8.1 Introduction	373
	8.2 Chomsky's theory of language acquisition	373
	8.3 A critique of Chomsky's theory	375
	8.3.1 Introduction	375
	8.3.2 Magnasyntax vs. the syntax of spontaneous spoken language	376
	8.3.3 Magnasyntax and the goals of generative grammar	378
	8.3.4 Misuse of magnasyntax in discussions of first language acquisition	381
	8.3.5 The non-degenerate nature of written language	383
	8.3.6 Computationally complex structure-dependent rules, formulas, and imitation	384
	8.3.7 Creativity	394
	8.3.8 How long do children take to acquire their native language?	396
	8.3.9 Degrees of competence and literacy	400
	8.3.10 Grammaticality judgements	403
	8.3.11 Mechanisms of language acquisition	406
	8.4 Language processing by humans and by computer	419
	8.5 Literacy and education	421

Epilogue 426

References 427

Index 443

Abbreviations

ABS	Absolutive Case
ACC	Accusative Case
ALL	Allative Case
ANAPH	Anaphoric
AUX	Auxiliary
COMP	Complementizer
DAT	Dative Case
DEM	Demonstrative
DEMPRO	Demonstrative Pronoun
ERG	Ergative Case
EXCL	Exclusive
FEM	Feminine
FUT	Future
GEN	Genitive Case
IMPERF	Imperfective
INF	Infinitive
IRREAL	Irrealis
LOC	Locative Case
M	Masculine
NOM	Nominative Case
Part.	Particle
PFV	Perfective
PL	Plural
PRO	Pronoun
sep.	separable
SG	Singular
SUB	Subordinate
WH	WH pronouns (e.g. *which*) and their equivalents in other languages

1 Introduction

1.1. Introduction

What is the topic of this book? The answer 'spontaneous spoken language and written language' is brief but unhelpful, because the major topic encompasses a number of independent but interlocking themes. The descriptive and analytical chapters are devoted to the syntactic structure of clauses and phrases in spontaneous speech and to the grammatical devices that play a central role in the organization of spontaneous spoken discourse. Excluded from direct investigation are the central phenomena of intonation, rhythm, voice quality, and non-verbal communication.

The central thesis of the book is that the syntactic structure of phrases and clauses in spontaneous spoken language is very different from the structure of phrases and clauses in written language. The differences reside in the complexity of such constructions—what is meant by complexity will be explained in Chapters 3 and 4—and in the types of constructions. There are many types of phrase and clause construction that occur frequently in writing but very rarely in speech and other types that occur frequently in speech but never in writing. A secondary thesis, which forms the subject matter of Chapters 5 and 6, is that the organization of spontaneous spoken discourse is very different from the organization of written discourse, and has its own discourse-organizing devices.

Since the early 1980s articles and books on spoken and written language have been appearing—not in large numbers but steadily. This book, we believe, makes various new contributions to the field. With respect to the debate on whether a genre of spoken English can be established, we take the view that it is important to pay attention not just to properties of texts (e.g. monologue or dialogue, collected in formal or informal circumstances) but to characteristics of the informants. In particular, the effect of formal education, especially higher education, on spoken language, even spontaneous spoken language, has not been properly taken into account.[1] Much of the English data on which the analyses are based consists of spontaneous conversation collected in relaxed circumstances from speakers who have no

---

[1] G. Brown, Currie, and Kenworthy (1980: 15 n.) comment that members of the academic staff and postgraduate students at Edinburgh University were excluded from their study because 'it seems possible that the speech of those who spend a large proportion of their time immersed in written language may be quite untypical of the speech community as a whole'.

higher education, and in some cases just the minimum of formal education. (See § 1.3 on data.) We recognize of course that there are different genres of spoken language and that degree of formality and length of planning time are crucial factors. Let us also make it quite clear that proposals to recognize a genre of spoken English (or spoken French/Russian etc.) are not on the agenda; it is however evident from bodies of spontaneous spoken English, Russian, French, and German that spontaneous speech does have specific syntactic properties.

The data is taken not just from English but from corpuses of spontaneous Russian, German, and French. The different languages are brought into play in order to demonstrate that certain structures and properties characterize clauses in spontaneous speech across languages. (The above-mentioned languages are all Indo-European, but the data from Australian languages cited in Chapter 3 give grounds for thinking that the structures and properties are not confined to Indo-European.) Cross-language material apart, the book does offer new and more detailed analyses of clause structure and the relationships between clauses in spontaneous spoken English.

While the data is interesting in itself, Chapters 7 and 8 expound a crucial but neglected argument, that the syntactic differences between spontaneous spoken language and written language have direct consequences for various areas of linguistics; typology, psycholinguistics, and sociolinguistics, not to mention certain assumptions lying behind generative grammar. Chapter 7 deals with typology; the bulk of Chapter 8 is devoted to the current Chomskyan theory of first language acquisition vis-à-vis the syntactic properties of spontaneous spoken language and the special way in which written language is learned. The final part of Chapter 8 relates the data and its analysis to sociolinguistics, in particular education in relation to the perennial problem of standard and non-standard varieties of languages.

It is worthwhile drawing out what is implicit in the above paragraphs. We do not attempt to give a complete description of the syntactic constructions in any one corpus of data. Rather our concern is to analyse some data in detail, point out the cross-language parallels, and draw out the theoretical consequences of the analysis. (See the discussion in § 1.3 below.) We do not attempt to establish criteria enabling computers to recognize a genre of English called 'spontaneous speech', but we do suggest that there is a range of syntactic constructions typical of spontaneous spoken English and with parallel constructions in the spontaneous speech produced by speakers of other languages. Conversely, there is a range of syntactic constructions typical of written English. The constructions typical of spontaneous speech do not occur in written texts except in the representation of conversation. The constructions typical of written English are very rare in spontaneous speech and indeed are usually found only in the spontaneous speech of people who have passed through both secondary and higher education. As Chapters 2–4 demonstrate, the syntactic differences between spontaneous speech and writing have to do with type of construction but also with complexity of construction.

The book is neither formalist nor functionalist, taking these terms as referring to the on-going debate as to whether constituent-structure and dependency relations or functions are to be taken as basic in models of syntax. We take the view that such debates are ultimately sterile, that adequate accounts of syntax and discourse require both form and function and that, while reductionism might seem attractive in the context of biology, chemistry, and physics, it is deadening when applied in linguistics. In all our analytical work on spoken language we have had to pay attention both to formal properties of constituent structure and dependency relations and to functional properties, ranging from the traditional grammatical functions and participant roles to the larger functions served by particular syntactic constructions in discourse.[2]

One further statement of position can usefully be made at the outset: this book is neutral in the debate as to whether a sharp divide can be drawn between literate and oral societies. Our research leads us to believe that the syntax of spontaneous language is far less complex than the syntax of formal written language; the former possesses constructions that do not occur in the latter, and vice-versa. (See Chapters 2–4.) Furthermore, the two different varieties of language have different devices for organizing discourse. As suggested by Akinnaso (1982) and demonstrated by Biber (1988)—see §1.3 below—major differences in syntax and vocabulary are associated with formality as opposed to informality. Spoken language can be formal as well as informal and oral societies have formal spoken texts such as the language of religious and social ceremonies. We have no views on how complex the language of such ceremonies might be relative to the spontaneous speech of a given oral society and as Chapter 8 makes clear, we do not associate the capacity for logical thought or the manipulation of abstract concepts solely with the ability to use complex written language. (See Denny 1991.)[3]

---

[2] Of course, since we do not attempt to develop a generative (formal and explicit) grammar of the data we deal with in this book, we are not required to translate our assumptions into an adequate model. Were we to make such an attempt, our sympathies would lie in the direction of HPSG.

[3] Our position is quite compatible with the theory argued by Goody (1977: 74–111) that possession of written language enables previously oral societies to control and manipulate much larger amounts of information and to increase the stock of knowledge available to them.

1.2. Spoken and Written Language in Linguistics

It is hardly novel to recognize a distinction between spoken and written language. After all, a central tenet of twentieth-century linguistics is that spoken language both differs from written language and has priority over it. Earlier this century certain linguists dismissed writing. Bloomfield (1935: 21) stated that writing was not language but merely a way of recording language. He appealed to various facts; writing is a relatively recent development in human history; throughout the history of written language literacy was confined to a very few people, mass literacy being a goal of twentieth-century societies; the study of writing requires a knowledge of language but not vice-versa; and written records are related only indirectly to the history of the languages in which they are written.

Bloomfield's position was doubtless influenced by the need to combat the concentration of research on written texts and the widespread perception that written language is the measure of all things linguistic. Contemporaries of Bloomfield in other theoretical schools took a broader view; for example, linguists of the Prague School, mindful of the need to describe and stabilize literary Czech, kept both spoken and written language in view. (See Havránek 1932; Vachek 1939.)[4]

The approach set by Bloomfield has been continued in theoretical linguistics, especially in all theories of syntax, whether generative or not. It is significant that, for example, Chomsky talked of an ideal speaker-hearer but not of the ideal writer-reader, although, as we will see, there is a mismatch between declaration and practice throughout theoretical syntax. One exception is Lyons (1968: 39–42), who draws attention to the differences of grammar and vocabulary that distinguish spoken and written language and points out that in literate societies the relationship between spoken and written language is complex, to the extent that the spoken and written varieties of a given language may be partially independent. This does not undermine the principle that spoken language is prior; not only do the reasons cited by Bloomfield still hold good but spoken language is still the principal means of communication for most members of even highly literate societies, and children, acquiring spoken language first and with apparent ease, typically acquire/learn written language over a number of years, often under stress and not always successfully.[5]

The terms 'spoken language' and 'written language' do not refer merely

---

[4] There is no suggestion that there was no interest in written language elsewhere, since any literate society has a large group of people interested in questions of style and correct usage. What is of interest here is the attitude of theoretical linguists towards the question of spoken and written language.

[5] See § 8.3 for a discussion of the acquisition of spoken language and the acquisition/learning of written language.

to different mediums but relate to partially different systems of morphology, syntax, vocabulary, and the organization of texts. These facts are crucial for investigations of language but are generally ignored in theoretical syntax once the initial declaration about the priority of spoken language has been made. The neglect of these facts may have no significant consequences, say in a formal model where the development of the formal theory is such that the examples taken into consideration are neutral between spoken and written language.The consequences become important when a given formal theory is applied to complex data and when its proponents devise complex examples in order to demonstrate the superiority of their theory over some rival. Such complex examples are always typical of formal written language—see the discussion and examples in Chapter 8. When the formal theory gives rise to a theory of first language acquisition the problems become even worse, because the essential principles and parameters of the theory, developed on the basis of written language, are applied to the acquisition of spontaneous spoken language.

The neglect of the distinctions between spoken and written language is peculiar to theoretical syntax of all schools but elsewhere the distinctions have been investigated in some detail. (The scholars and groups cited in this paragraph are taken merely as examples to show that we are not labouring in a deserted field.) In the English-speaking world interest has been focused on text organization, e.g. in Tannen's classic paper (Tannen 1982) and in the work of Chafe (see Chafe 1980, 1982 and Chafe and Danielewicz 1987). Clause constructions have typically been examined by researchers into nonstandard English who are perforce looking at spoken language and have to deal with extensive morpho-syntactic differences inside clauses but there are English language scholars such as Enkvist (1982) who have taken up the problem of how to analyse the loosely integrated and even fragmentary syntax of spoken language. (Cf. also the pioneering work of Sornicola 1981 on Neapolitan Italian.) In Europe much work has been and is being carried out on both the syntax and discourse organization of spoken language. The Prague School continues to be active (cf. Müllerová, Hoffmannová, and Schneiderová 1992); French linguists, such as the groupe Aixois directed by Blanche-Benveniste, have collected many texts of spoken French and analysed their phrase and clause syntax (cf. Blanche-Benveniste 1991) and the group at LACITO in Paris under the direction of Fernandez are investigating French and other languages (cf. Fernandez 1994*a* and 1994*b*); Russian linguists have collected and analysed the syntax and discourse organization of large quantities of spoken Russian (cf. Zemskaja 1973; Lapteva 1976; Krasil'nikova 1990); observations in relation to spoken German date back to Wunderlich (1894) and Behagel (1927). The Institut für Deutsche Sprache in Freiburg collected a major spoken language corpus, subsequently analysed in relation to text type and various formal and functional features (e.g. Steger 1967, 1970; Texte 1971, 1974, 1975; Gesprochene 1973; Schank and Schoenthal 1983; Forschungen 1970). Many additional spoken language corpuses have since been collected and analysed (Leska 1965; Schulz 1973; Wackernagel-Jolles 1971; Weiss 1975; Heinze 1979; Brons-Albert 1984). Findings of these early studies are largely quantitative and more recent linguistic approaches are rare (e.g. Günthner 1993). Conversely, many theoretical linguists, generative or not, remain unaware of this research and of its implications for various areas of linguistic theory.

What does this book have to add? The principal contributions are the discussion of the sentence and the analysis of spoken language, the investigation of the constituent structure of clauses and clause complexes, and the account of why it is important for linguistic theory to recognize the syntactic and discourse differences between spoken and written language, especially in relation to language acquisition. The book attempts to bridge a gap between linguists concerned with collecting bodies of spoken language and linguists concerned with theoretical issues. The two groups seldom come into contact and neither group shows any sound knowledge of or interest in the concerns of the other. Investigators of spoken language have demonstrated little awareness of relevant theoretical issues. For example, with the exception of, e.g. Blanche-Benveniste (1991) and Zemskaja (1973), accounts of spoken language typically do not concern themselves with questions of constituent structure or dependency relations nor with the structure appropriate to arrangements of more than one clause, and certainly not with issues relating to first language acquisition.

The book is unusual in drawing on data from three languages, English, German, and Russian. The cross-language data is important because it enables us to show that similar syntactic structures occur in different spoken languages, which provides a strong argument against the all too-familiar propensity to dismiss this or that construction as a product of performance difficulties. When the same construction occurs regularly in one language and has direct counterparts in other languages, explanations in terms of performance difficulties are not defensible. Finally, much of the English data is unfamiliar, while outside Russia and Eastern Europe the spoken Russian data collected by Zemskaja and others is known only to Russianists.

1.3. The Data

In this section we specify the data on which our account of spontaneous spoken language is based, discuss the adequacy of the data, and situate our work with respect to corpus linguistics.

1.3.1. *Data from English, German, and Russian*

i A computerized corpus of 50,000 words of spontaneous conversation produced by speakers of Scottish English from Lothian (including the research assistants who recorded the conversations). It was collected in between January 1978 and March 1979 as part of a project on the syntax of Scottish English.[6] The majority of the speakers were 17- or 18-year-old school pupils, male and female, but there are substantial contributions from three male speakers in their early sixties, two female speakers in their early twenties, four first-year university undergraduates aged 19 and one male in his early thirties. The conversations contain dialogue, reminiscences and narratives, jokes and banter. The conversations are coded so that it is possible to work out which participants use which syntactic structures and discourse devices. For example, anticipating Chapter 6, we can say that the participants split into those who made heavy use of the discourse particle LIKE and those who used it rarely or not at all.

The conversations with the school pupils were collected in school, the research assistant going once a week to talk to the same senior pupils. The setting was not very informal but the method did produce a rapport between some of the pupils and the researcher which resulted in excellent, unforced conversation, the slightly scurrilous nature of some of the material indicating the relaxed attitude of the informants. The initial conversations are stiff, with the research assistant playing a large part but the later conversations are full of comment and narrative from the pupils. The early conversations incline towards interviews but the later ones are genuine conversations with the pupils taking an active role. The 60 year olds were recorded in a social club and the undergraduates during a meal. With respect to the crucial syntactic properties described in Chapters 3 and 4, there was no difference between the 18-year-old pupils, the undergraduates, and the 60 year olds.

The original version of the corpus was left unpunctuated and all in lower case, apart from the initial letters of proper names. This was done in order to avoid imposing syntactic analysis on other users. The entire corpus does have minimal syntactic coding—for different types of relative clause and complement clause. Since the original research project focused on relative clauses, modal verbs and negation, a concordance program was used to collect the relevant data by picking out the actual forms, e.g. *didn't* vs. *did not*. The original corpus was also analysed for passive constructions and the use of the definite article. For the research reported here, a subset of 10,000

---

[6] The project was carried out by Keith Brown and Jim Miller on a grant from the then Social Sciences Research Council (now the Economic and Social Science Research Council). The data was collected by Martin Millar and William Campbell and the transcriptions were done by Sue Polson, Martin Millar, and William Campbell.

8 *Spontaneous Spoken Language*

words was coded for clause type, types of noun phrase, and features of discourse organization. The analysis of the computerized corpus was supplemented by data obtained from informants using elicitation techniques. The data relates to relative clauses, modal verbs, prepositions, infinitives, and gerunds (see E. K. Brown and Miller 1982).

ii A 12,000 word subset of 36,000 words of dialogue produced by speakers of Scottish English in connection with the performance of a task. The speakers were from the West of Scotland, mostly from Glasgow. This body of data is called the HCRC Map Task Corpus because the task was based on a map and this version of the task was developed and administered by the Dialogue Group in the Human Communication Research Centre at the Universities of Glasgow and Edinburgh. Two participants cooperated in each performance of the task. Both had maps with various landmarks. The two sets of landmarks largely overlapped, but there were landmarks present only on one map and landmarks that were present on both maps but in different places. One map had a route going from a starting point to a finishing point, while the other map only had a starting point. The participant with the route had to instruct the other participant in how to draw the route. The corpus is coded for the same syntactic and discourse features as the subset of conversations described in the previous paragraph but also has coding for information structure, game structure, and phonetic features (cf. A. Anderson *et al.* 1991).[7]

iii The Glasgow Map Task Corpus, a set of 144 dialogues collected from pupils of different ages at primary and secondary schools in Glasgow by Anne Anderson and Simon Garrod in 1987–1989 as part of a project funded by the Economic and Social Research Council. We will make little reference to this body of data, but it served the valuable purpose of demonstrating that the discourse devices found in adult spontaneous spoken language are not present in the language of younger speakers (7–10 year olds), being acquired only with maturation.

iv Macaulay (1991) is a valuable source of information about Scottish English as it presents an analysis of 110,000 words of what Macaulay describes as interviews. Macaulay (1991: 18) observes that half of the topics discussed in the interviews were raised by the respondents and that half of

---

[7] The geographical distance between Lothian and Glasgow is only fifty to seventy miles (depending on what part of Lothian is taken as the point of departure) but is important linguistically. If we were concerned with varieties of non-standard English rather than spoken language, the differences would prevent the two corpuses of data from being used in the same study. The phonetic differences are enormous. With respect to clause structure and discourse organization, there is fortunately no difference that we have been able to discern apart from those that are associated with performing a task as opposed to taking part in a conversation.

the time was spent on these topics; that is, the respondents were not waiting passively for the next question but actively participating. Much of his data consists in fact of narratives by his respondents about their working lives. Macaulay's data was especially valuable as a cross-check on the analysis of clause types in our corpus of conversations.

v   The Russian data is taken from the major collection of data described in Zemskaja (1973); the transcripts are printed in Kapanadze and Zemskaja (1979). Other important sources of information about spoken Russian are Lapteva (1976), Sirotinina (1974), and Krasil'nikova (1990). Zemskaja and Šmelev (1984) was consulted, although it deals with a specific urban variety of spoken Russian. Zemskaja's corpus, judging by the transcripts in Kapanadze and Zemskaja (1979), contains approximately 50,000 words.

It is essential to specify the use that we have made of Zemskaja (1973) in order to scotch suspicions that we have simply pillaged a corpus that is inaccessible to most linguists outside Russia and Eastern Europe. Briefly, Zemskaja (1973) serves as a source of data while the bulk of the analysis is ours. There are two reasons for using Zemskaja's data. One is simply to inform non-Slav readers that the Russians have been engaged in corpus collection and analysis for a long time; Zemskaja's corpus certainly goes back at least to the late 1960s. The second reason is that, for political and cultural reasons (even after the collapse of Communism), there is no easy way for foreigners to collect samples of spontaneous spoken Russian. The Essex Project, which ran from 1963 to 1970, collected examples of spoken Russian, but none of the relaxed conversations in informal circumstances that make Zemskaja's work so valuable.

As far as the analysis is concerned, we must emphasize that the technical vocabulary used by Zemskaja is not the technical vocabulary used in Britain and North America; we provide our own analyses of certain constructions in terms of definite or indefinite deictics, our own proposals about a parallel between Russian constructions and WH and reverse English clefts, and our own proposal linking referential expressions containing just a prepositional phrase with the occurrence of zero NPs. (See the discussion in Chapters 3 and 4.) In order to investigate certain phenomena in detail, including clause types, noun phrase types, and the occurrence of pronominal and zero anaphoric and non-anaphoric referring expressions, we entered on computer some 10,000 words of Kapanadze's and Zemskaja's transcripts and coded them for the same syntactic and discourse features as the Map Task Dialogues and the subset of conversations. Samples of various types of written text were also examined—a novel, dialogue in a play, and newspaper articles. The research would not have been possible without the original Russian corpus and analyses of it by Zemskaja, Lapteva, and others, but we have collected data of our own and carried out a great deal of analysis.

vi The German data comes from various sources. The conversation data was extracted from two corpuses collected by the Institut für Deutsche Sprache, Mannheim and Freiburg, Germany. They are the Dialogstrukturenkorpus (DSK, *c.*225,000 words) and the Freiburger Korpus (FKY, *c.*475,000 words). The data is semi-informal, or semi-formal, involving television programme discussions, radio telephone conversations, general discussions between student and lecturer about courses, etc.

Regina Weinert collected and coded a German Map Task Corpus containing 14 dialogues, *c.*30,000 words. Subjects were 22–29-year-old university students who had just arrived in the UK on an exchange programme, with the exception of two speakers in their thirties who had been in the UK for about two years. Subjects came from a number of regions, including both northern and southern Germany.

1.3.2. *Adequacy of the data*

A central question pertaining to our databases is: how big should they be? The answer to this question is in two parts, one relating to size and the other relating to quality of analysis. The question of size was the subject of an exchange between Biber and Oostdijk (Oostdijk 1988; Biber 1990). One of Oostdijk's concerns, the concept of genre and the fact that it is not well defined, is not relevant here, since we do not attempt to define any particular genre. Oostdijk's other concern was the appropriate size of samples of a corpus. But appropriate for what? Oostdijk has in mind the statistical analysis of corpuses, and in particular statistical analysis in order to isolate different types of text on the basis of linguistic criteria. He maintains that 'samples of 20,000 words each are sufficiently large in order to yield reliable information about the frequency of occurrences of most syntactic structures' (Oostdijk 1988: 20). Biber (1990: 258) carried out tests on four samples of 1,000 words each, on the assumption that, if his tests for different genres were successful on 1,000 words, they would also be successful on samples of 2,000 or 5,000 words. The bulk of his paper is devoted to a demonstration that his factor-analysis was successful even on his tiny samples.

There is no statistical analysis in this book but we do claim that the syntax of spontaneous speech is different from the syntax of written English. Even by Oostdijk's standards the data available to us is numerically sufficient. The samples of text that have been coded in detail for syntax consist of 10,000 words (spontaneous conversation), 12,000 words (Map Task), 10,000 words (Russian) and 30,000 words (German). Spontaneous conversation and task-related dialogue would probably count as different genres for the creators of the London-Lund Corpus (see Svartvik and Quirk 1980), but we treat them just as spontaneous spoken English.

The syntactic structures that occur in the conversation also occur in the task-related dialogues and our goal is to demonstrate the syntactic differences between spontaneous speech and writing, not to isolate all the characteristic grammatical properties of one or other genre. From this perspective, our sample of spontaneous spoken English has 20,000 words. The sample of Russian has 10,000 words but our analysis is backed by the work of Russian scholars on the whole 50,000 words. Our sample of spoken English is backed by the work of Macaulay on his spontaneous narratives and by the work of Chafe and others on (American) English dinner-table conversations and narratives. That is, our analyses of syntax and discourse are valid for our data, which constitutes a particular and limited corpus; however, our analyses are broadly compatible with the analyses of other bodies of data and it is this compatibility which justifies the assumption that our analyses are generally applicable to spontaneous spoken language.

The balance between corpus size and quality of analysis is crucial, a point that is made by Leech (1991: 9–14). He argues that size is not all-important (but with the counterpoint that large corpora have a role in training and testing models of language, particularly probabilistic models, which is not relevant here). He puts forward various arguments, three of which are important for our purposes. First, a large but haphazard collection of material does not constitute a corpus, which he defines loosely as material designed or required for a particular representative function (Leech 1991: 11). The Brown Corpus is a collection of different types of text and could be described as a general-purpose corpus, but there are corpora representing only one domain, e.g. the language of the oil industry. Leech suggests that recent large corpora such as the Oxford Text Archive are indeed an archive and not a corpus, since texts of any sort are collected as and when they become available. Our data counts as a corpus by this criterion, since it belongs to one type, spontaneous spoken English.

Leech's second argument is right at the centre of our concerns and is one that we wish to elaborate with respect to other corpora. The transcription of spoken discourse, says Leech, is a time-consuming process fraught with problems and the collection of spoken discourse on the same scale as written text will remain a dream of the future (Leech 1991: 18). Everyone who has done transcription knows that nine hours of transcription time are required for an accurate but basic transcription of one hour of dialogue—excluding pitch, rhythm, pauses, sighs, and other non-linguistic noises. Leech's third argument is that tools for linguistic analysis are still relatively primitive, which limits the extent to which large corpora can be exploited for linguistic purposes (Leech 1991: 12).

The last two points bear on our answer to a question that has been asked; why the small corpora of English listed above and not the large corpora such as the London-Lund Corpus of spoken English or the recent corpus of

London Teenager Language? An important point is that the corpuses listed above are not just transcriptions but transcriptions together with tape recordings. As will be argued in detail in Chapters 2 and 3, the assignment of syntactic structure to spontaneous speech is far from straightforward—it is one of the problems besetting transcription. There are difficulties in establishing sentence boundaries, for which reason Chapter 2 argues for the abandonment of the sentence as a unit of analysis for spontaneous speech. (This view has been advanced by other linguists working on spontaneous speech.) The cores of clauses can be established on the basis of what constituents are complements of a given verb, but the placement of adjuncts is not obvious. For example, suppose a speaker produces the utterance *the garage is in Broughton Place Lane just round the corner from Broughton Place*. Suppose the phrase *just round the corner* is separated from *Lane* by a long pause, so long that it has clearly been added as an afterthought. Does *just round the corner from Broughton Place* belong in the clause *the garage is in Broughton Place* or is it outside the clause, although it modifies *garage*? In Chapter 2 we appeal to the notion of rhetorical relations that hold across sentence and clause boundaries and propose that in such examples the afterthought is not in fact a constituent of the clause. We also propose, along with other analysts of spontaneous speech, to recognize that clauses may fall into clause complexes in which the clauses are interrelated but that this does not constitute a good reason for assuming that such groups of clauses are organized into a sentence. Sentences are units of written language and reflect (more or less) conscious decisions taken by writers.

As observed in the introduction to Leech, Myers, and Thomas (1995), Ochs (1979) drew attention to the fact that transcription becomes data; they add that nowadays both transcription and coding become data. It is very convenient to have transcriptions of spontaneous speech but also dangerous, for the simple reason that the analyst is prisoner of the transcribers' (possibly incorrect) decisions. This is why our corpus of spontaneous conversation, as specified in (i) and (ii) above, was transcribed without capital letters and without punctuation. The corpus has been made available to other researchers but to exploit it to the full they have to listen to the recordings, not just consult the transcriptions. Anyone concerned by these points (readers are asked to read Chapters 2 and 3 before making a decision) must be alarmed by the assertion in Greenbaum (1991: 91) that the spoken material in the International Corpus of English is to be divided into sentence units—although Greenbaum is justified in his expectation that major parsing problems will arise.[8]

To sum up the above paragraphs, this work is based on the corpuses of

---

[8] The difficulties have long been known. See e.g. the discussion in Brown, Currie, and Kenworthy (1980: 40–4) about the problems in assigning tone groups in a substantial number of the clauses in their data and in determining the clauses to which adjuncts belonged.

spoken English specified in (i) and (ii) above because both transcripts and recordings were available. Another important reason is that the people who provided the utterances were either just at the beginning of their higher education or had not yet entered higher education or had left school with the minimum of formal education. (Readers are reminded of the comments in §1.1 and n. 1.) We agree entirely with Greenbaum's comment (Greenbaum 1991: 89) that the researchers did not select the language for the corpus but selected the people and left them to produce the language. Our corpuses were produced by a very different set of people from those who produced the data in the London-Lund Corpus (middle-class, male academics) and the intention was to investigate spontaneous speech produced by people with no higher education. There were good reasons for this approach. Svartvik (1966) analysed the passive clauses in the spoken part of the London-Lund Corpus. On the basis of the analysis, he claimed that the GET Passive is so infrequent in Modern English as to be almost extinct. This claim was correct for his data, but it is hardly surprising that the GET Passive was missing, given that it was at that time proscribed from formal written English and banned from school and university classroom. The GET Passive is still infrequent in writing but in our corpus it is the major passive construction; from the fact that schoolteachers wage an unceasing battle to persuade pupils to abandon the GET Passive in writing it is clear that it is the major passive construction in spontaneous spoken English in general.

A third reason for working with our corpuses is that the syntax of subsets of both corpuses has been analysed. During 1990 the Map Task Corpus was analysed and coded with respect to clause type: main clauses and subordinate clauses; different types of main clause, relative clause, complement clause and adverbial clause; finite and non-finite clauses—infinitives, participles, and gerunds; cleft clauses and other focusing devices. This analysis was done by hand because the software for doing it automatically does not exist. There are tools that will parse and tag individual words, but this exercise would not have yielded the information we needed concerning clause type. Even if software had been available, its output would have been another layer of analysis between the investigator and the original data. In any case, without recordings it would have been impossible to carry out this sort of syntactic analysis reliably on other corpuses of transcribed utterances. The business of analysis is slow and delicate, particularly in the initial stages. The syntactic analysis of the subset of the Map Task Corpus was part of a larger project for which funds were available to pay research assistants to code the data for syntax, information structure (first and second mentions and type of referring expression), game structure (treating the dialogues as a game consisting of sub-games), and certain phonetic properties. The subset of spontaneous conversation was syntactically coded by Jim Miller at a later date, but with a coding system that had been extended and refined as a result of the Map Task project and the experience of applying the coding. Other corpuses were in existence, but for the reasons outlined above they were not appropriate.

Implicit in the above discussion is the reason for the modest number of words in our corpuses. It would have been physically impossible to code up any more data and write this book within a reasonable time. The task of analysing clause syntax and discourse organisation is very different from the task performed by Biber—counting the occurrences of fifty properties and carrying out a factorial analysis of the results. Of course, such a task is laborious and time-consuming, but software is available for the laborious statistical analysis and the properties are relatively superficial. These comments are not to be interpreted as depreciative; the crucial point is that the discussion in this book rests on a deeper and richer analysis of syntax and discourse than Biber required, and the type of analysis both restricts the amount of data that can be covered in a given time and can yield interesting results on a much smaller body of data than the one examined by Biber. A decision had to be taken as to when enough data was available for respectable analyses to be put forward. This is in line with good scientific practice. A balance has to be struck between data and theory. An initial theory is necessary if interesting data is to be picked out and analysed in the first place, but the analysis in turn has to be tested against further data and thereby serves as an instrument for locating interesting, relevant data, and so on. Describing a large corpus of data would not only have taken a very long time but, with respect to our aims, would have been sterile.

1.4. Genres: Dimensions, Individuals, and Education

An important distinction is drawn between language as product and language as process. In Chapters 5 and 6 on the organization of spoken texts, the notion of process will play an important part as we look at what speakers aim to achieve by the use of different constructions. Our immediate concern is with products, that is, different types of text. Although no attempt is made here to establish a list of criterial properties for a particular genre, a key claim is that spontaneous spoken language possesses interesting properties; the type of clause and phrase constructions that occur, the complexity of such constructions—or the lack of it, the loose integration of clauses into clause complexes, and the devices used for the organization of discourse. Since this claim is controversial against the background of other pronouncements on spoken language, it is necessary briefly to discuss the concept of genre and the collection of texts. (Oostdijk's view that genre is not a well-defined concept will not be addressed.)

It is controversial to claim that spontaneous spoken language has its own syntactic properties. Previous work on spoken language (Poole and Field 1976 and Kroll 1977) produced contradictory findings, and one account (Halliday 1985, 1989) offers yet another analysis. The most detailed recent statistical work on a computerized database (Biber 1988) demonstrates how delicate is the task of establishing individual relevant properties and finding sets of properties that distinguish one type of text from another. We will first examine the different views just cited, then look briefly at Biber's work and finally describe why we are confident that our data provides a new and clearer perspective.

It will be helpful to examine examples of different text types before looking at the conflicting analyses of spoken language.

Text 1

A: we had a laugh yesterday   we were away on Wednesday   we were out at Dean Centre   and em we were making a magazine   and we were doing a lot of adverts and that   so there was this notice pinned on the common room notice board when I walked in earlier in the morning   it was for Louise   and it was from a member of the mag committee   and it was   'a Mr C. Lyon had phoned   and would you phone him back'   it was about an advert   and it gave two numbers his home number and his office number   so he says   'Louise you better phone it you know'   but she says   'who would write it?   It must have been somebody who took a message'.

Text 1 is typical of the spontaneous spoken language in our database. It is a spontaneous narrative about an event that happened the day before the recording. It may have been recited before the recording—given that it involves a joke successfully played on A's best friend, it had probably been recounted to friends and parents. The text has been arranged for present purposes with each main clause separated from the preceding and following main clauses by two spaces. The reported speech is inside single quotes. The main features of the syntax are the series of main clauses. There is one subordinate adverbial clause of time—*when I walked in earlier in the morning*—and one reduced relative clause *pinned to the common room notice board*. There is no indirect speech; instead all the reported speech is conveyed as though directly reproducing the reported speaker, and in some cases A changes her voice quality to signal reported speech. Thus, A says *he says 'Louise you better phone it you know'* and not *he said that Louise should phone it*. Note that the reporting of the wording on the notice is mixed. *A Mr C. Lyon had phoned* is classic oratio obliqua whereas *would you phone him back* is straight reproduction of the actual words. Untypical of our spontaneous spoken language is the compound noun *common room notice board*. Two-element compound nouns are not frequent, far less four-element compounds. A plausible explanation is that this compound consists of two compounds *common room* and *notice board*, which both occur frequently in schools, and in any case the four-element compound itself probably occurs frequently and can be considered as a technical term that pupils learn in order to understand and talk about routine events in the school day.

Text 2
However defective our knowledge may be, we have ample evidence to show that great empires rose and fell in India, and that, as in religion, art, literature and social life, so in political organisation, India produced her own system, distinctive in its strength and weakness.

Text 2, from Basham (1971), is typical of the formal language of monographs. The sentence has one main clause running from *we have ample evidence* to *strength and weakness*. The main clause is preceded by an adverbial clause, which is in itself highly unusual in spontaneous spoken language, but the adverbial clause is rare even in written language. It is a clause of concession, but the concession is expressed by *however* modifying *defective*. The main clause contains, not just two conjoined complement clauses, *that great empires rose and fell in Indian* and *that . . . India produced her own system, distinctive in its strength and weakness*, but a correlative construction inside the second complement clause—*as in religion . . . so in political organisation*, and the noun *system* is modified by an adjective phrase following it—*distinctive in its strength and weakness*.

Text 3
He has no answer. All he is pointing out is the structure of human existence as the framework within which the questions have to be posed. He is showing that this is a dimension of human existence which simply has to be faced. The particular answer given to the question 'What meaning does my life have?' will depend on the individual.

Text 3 has no one sentence as complex as that in Text 2, but there are plenty of subordinate clauses—*within which the questions have to be posed, that this is a dimension of human existence which simply has to be faced*. The first relative clause has Preposition + WH at the beginning, a type which is absent from our corpus of spoken language, and the second relative clause, *which simply has to be faced*, is embedded inside a complement clause. These features alone indicate that this is not an example of spontaneous spoken language. On the other hand, the content of the question is reported by means of a direct interrogative—*the question 'What meaning does my life have'* as opposed to *the question as to what meaning the life of a human being has*' and the text is introduced by a very short sentence—*He has no answer*. The text could be deliberately written this way to hold the reader's interest or to hold the attention of listeners to a serious programme. It is in fact the text of a radio talk.

These three texts were carefully chosen for the demonstration but, as Biber's work shows so clearly, working out criteria for assigning any given text to a given genre is far more complex and does not come with a cast-iron guarantee. In addition, within the broad genre of spoken language many different sub-genres can be recognized differing in formality, purpose, and setting: lectures, sermons, legal speeches, news broadcasts, Radio 3 talks, story-telling; within the genre of written language there are sub-genres such as literature (!) (including sub-sub-genres such as novel, play, poetry, autobiography, and diary), business correspondence, company reports, academic books. (Invoking genre in this way is doubtless as theoretically misguided as thinking of phonemes as indivisible atoms instead of bundles of properties—indeed, in the latest theoretical work on phonology even the latter view is held to be prehistoric. None the less, it is convenient for present purposes.) At a certain level within say the sub-sub-sub-sub-genre of the literary novel different types of texts appear: the texts of Jane Austen, the texts of Charlotte Brontë, the texts of Margaret Forster, and so on. Within the sub-sub-genre of informal conversation different types of text appear too: the informal conversation of Susan Sontag, John Major, an electrician, or a shop assistant.[9] Note that the situation is made even more complex by the existence of non-standard varieties of many languages. The spontaneous speech of a child in Edinburgh has different syntax and vocabulary from that of a child in Sheffield or Exeter or London, and further complications are introduced by other sociolinguistic factors.

Analysts of spoken language have come to different conclusions as to its syntax. Kroll (1977) found that written narratives contained more subordinate constructions than spoken ones: 35% vs. 14%. For coordinate constructions the position was reversed: 40% in spoken narrative but only 25% in written narrative. Chafe (1982) emphasized the fragmented syntax of spoken language as opposed to the highly integrated syntax of written language. (See the discussion in Chapter 3.) In contrast, Poole and Field (1976) found spoken discourse to have a significantly greater degree of

---

[9] It is not always easy to determine what a given speaker/writer is doing with a particular chunk of product, though there is often agreement among members of the same 'speech community' (a convenient term but a slippery concept) as to what a speaker or writer is doing. But note that different listeners/readers can react quite differently to the same product. A major advantage of analysing dialogues produced in connection with the performance of a specific task is that the analysts know what speakers and hearers are trying to achieve, what information is objectively given, what speakers treat as given even though it is in fact not. These advantages attach to the Map Task dialogues described in § 1.3.1 and will be exploited in Chapters 5 and 6 on the organization of discourse.

subordination, elaboration of syntactic structure, and use of adverbs; and Halliday (1989: 76–91) maintains that written language is complex in that highly compact and simple syntactic constructions are loaded with many lexical items. Spoken language is complex in a different way, having intricate syntactic structure with a considerable proportion of subordinate clauses. Lexical items are spread over a larger number of clauses, whereby the lexical density of each clause is reduced. These distinctions are exemplified by the written sentence *The use of this method of control unquestionably leads to safer and faster train running in the most adverse weather conditions* and a possible spoken variant /// *If this method of control is used // trains will unquestionably (be able to) run more safely and faster // (even) when the weather conditions are most adverse* /// (Halliday 1989: 79).

Can the discrepancy be resolved? Beaman (1984: 51) suggested that different analysts arrived at different conclusions because they had different types of data. In particular, the analysts confounded different features of discourse: the modality (spoken vs. written) and register (formality). Beaman proposed that what have been treated as differences between spoken and written discourse may in fact reflect differences in formality or planning time. The correctness of her suggestions is demonstrated by Biber's work, since formality and planning time are important factors, though only two among many.

Beaman, following Tannen (1982), regards narrative as a distinct genre. She claims that the spoken and written narratives in her study (the Pear stories) are all 'relatively informal, spontaneous, generally empathic and of a relatively inconsequential nature' (Beaman 1984: 52). Two further points can be made. The first is that narrators, having the floor and not having to manage turn-taking or adjust to contributions from other speakers, can concentrate on the form and content of the narrative. It would not be surprising to find that narratives have more subordinate clauses and more lexical variety than impromptu conversation. The second point is that even in pre-literate societies we can expect narrative discourse to differ from everyday conversation: the more experienced and skilled the narrator, the more striking the difference.

Biber (1988) summarizes the contradictory findings of different researchers and proposes a more subtle approach. He draws up a list of grammatical constructions and categories: e.g. yes–no questions, IT clefts, WH questions, agentless passives, 3rd person pronouns, adjectives. The list is established on the basis of what properties co-occur with a high frequency in texts. Each factor is assigned a weighting on the basis of its frequency in types of text. The weighting is on a scale from +1 to −1. For instance, THAT-deletion, as in *I heard (that) you were leaving* and *the book (that) I read*, is frequent in conversations—what Biber characterizes as highly interactive texts produced under conditions of high personal involvement and real-time constraints (1988: 135). It is assigned a weighting of .91. Features that are not so salient are assigned a low weighting: for the same type of text, WH clauses and word length have weightings of .47 and −.58, respectively. (See Biber 1988: 102.)

On the basis of the factors and their co-occurrence, Biber (1988: 79–120) distinguishes various general dimensions such as 'Involved vs. Informational Production', 'Narrative vs. Non-Narrative Concerns', 'Explicit vs. Situation-Dependent Reference', and 'On-Line Informational Elaboration'. Let us consider the first dimension in the list. Texts at the 'Informational Production' end contain full nouns (as opposed to pronouns), prepositions, long words, varied vocabulary, and attributive adjectives. Texts at the 'Involved Production' end lack these items but contain private verbs such as FEEL, GUESS, THINK, second person pronouns, contractions—*I'm, they're*, and so on, present-tense verbs, and contact complement clauses—*I think she's left* vs. *I think that she's left*. The latter texts result from highly affective interactions and are subject to constraints on the production of utterances in real-time; the former have high information content and are produced with time for editing. (For the lack of nouns, prepositions, and attributive adjectives in noun phrases in spontaneous spoken language, see Chapter 4.) At the 'Involved Production' end of the dimension are face-to-face conversation and telephone conversation; in the middle are personal letters, spontaneous speeches, interviews; and at the 'Informational Production' end are academic prose, press reportage, and official documents. Biber draws attention to the occurrence of spoken and written texts on each dimension and uses this fact as an argument against the centrality of the division between speech and writing.

The problem highlighted by Biber is that different text types line up differently with respect to each dimension; not only does no clear-cut distinction between written and spoken language emerge but Biber found more variation inside the set of written texts and inside the set of spoken texts than between the two sets. We will argue here that Biber's results are not surprising given the source of his spoken data, the London-Lund Corpus commented on in §1.3.2 above. In an earlier paper Biber (1986: 389 n. 4) observes that the spoken language consisted of conversations among middle-class, middle-aged, university-educated male adults. The Map Task dialogues and the Scottish-English conversations are from people who are not university-educated, either because they are too old to have benefited from the availability of further and higher education or because they are too young and are still at school or are first-year undergraduates.

The type of participants is crucial, because, as mentioned briefly in §1.3.2, one essential factor in this discussion is exposure to written language and formal education. Children in a literate society learn informal spoken conversational language as their native tongue. A proportion of children in Britain, for example, listen to nursery rhymes, then short stories, then longer stories. From the age of 5 they are taught to read and write—not just to realize linguistic units as marks on paper but to understand and use the structures and vocabulary of written English. This process lasts from age 5 to age 16 at the very least and covers the language of personal narrative, description of scenes, reports of important public events, the language of modern and classical English literature, the description of experiments in science classes, the technical vocabulary and phraseology of mathematics, the sciences, modern studies, and so on. While full participation in secondary education affects the written language of speakers and to some extent their spoken language, we advance the plausible hypothesis, based on our experience of school pupils and university students, that the greatest effect of written on spoken language comes from higher education.

For some speakers, the process of learning to use (as opposed to understand) all these different types of written English continues until they are 18, and through their years in higher education. Not everybody is equally capable of combining clauses into a well-integrated sentence with subordinate adverbial clauses, participial phrases and relative clauses introduced by a preposition plus a WH word. Not everybody possesses the same range of vocabulary and the same skill at using their vocabulary accurately and effectively. (NB: 'Not everybody' can apply to the set of university graduates, to the set of people who have had any kind of further education, to the set of people who have stayed at school till 18, or to the entire population of the UK.)

The variation in knowledge and skill is important, because speakers with knowledge and control of written language use written structures in their speech, whether narrative or informal conversation. The informants recorded by Beaman, Chafe, and Poole and Field were university undergraduates, by definition people with a knowledge of written language. The example of spoken language from Halliday (1989) quoted above, is typical of very literate speakers: note the two subordinate adverbial clauses, the nominalization *the use of this method of control*, the adverb *unquestionably*, and the adjective *adverse*. Halliday (1989: 79) gives what he calls a more natural spoken version which contains sequences such as *you can be quite sure that* . . . , *no matter how bad the weather gets,* . . . *than they would otherwise*. The *quite* in the first sequence, equivalent to *completely*, is literary, as is the second sequence and *otherwise* in the third sequence.

The speakers who supplied Biber's spoken language—Biber used the spoken language data in the Survey of English Usage—are precisely from the segment of the population most affected by formal written language and this is, for us, the reason why he found, correctly with respect to his data, that a clear-cut distinction between spoken and written language cannot be established. We accept that claim but add the qualification that spontaneous spoken language from speakers of English who have not had higher education provides data that is clearly different from the language of formal written English—the language of academic monographs and textbooks, heavyweight newspapers, official documents, and serious literature. The data reported and analysed in Chapters 2–6 constitute the core of the supporting argument. It must be emphasized that investigators of spontaneous spoken language in a number of countries have discovered that such language has syntactic structures that are not just less complex but different. The Russian data collected by Zemskaja and her colleagues and described in Chapters 3–4 is an excellent example, in spite of having been collected from Russians in the most highly educated professions—academics, doctors, lawyers, and so on. Our claim that the language in our corpus of spoken language allows a clear distinction to be established between spontaneous spoken language and the language of formal written texts is consistent with acceptance of Biber's dimensions; after all, the constructions that occur in spontaneous speech reflect the properties that characterize one pole of each of Biber's dimensions—situation-dependent reference, real-time constraints on language production, affective interaction, and so on.

To sum up: it is correct that written language in general and spoken language in general cannot be clearly differentiated, since it is not just the medium that is important but the factors listed by Biber. To these must be added the fact that even in spontaneous speech individual speakers can and do use syntax and vocabulary that is normally found only in formal written texts, though the ability to do this correlates in large measure with exposure to higher education. This makes it impossible to assert that a given construction or word never occurs in spontaneous speech; we are entitled to claim only that the construction or word typically occurs in spontaneous speech. None the less, the spontaneous speech of people who have not been exposed to higher education (and a fortiori of people who have had only legal minimum of secondary education) displays large differences from formal written language, and Zemskaja demonstrated the existence of such differences in the spontaneous speech of educated Russians.

It is possible to react pessimistically to the use of words such as *typically* and *generally*. For instance, Barton (1994: 85) talks of the slight structural differences even between the extremes of conversation and literary text—by conversation is meant the conversation of academics analysed by Biber, and asserts that no structure is found only in written language or only in spoken language. This reaction is unreasonable. Anybody who has worked in depth on some area of a natural language knows that syntactic patterns and the distribution of lexical items therein are rarely absolute. The most one can hope for is that a given pattern will turn out to be typical of a particular set of texts or speakers of a given language. Indeed, if we exclude highly educated people who use complex language even in informal speech or, conversely, people who insist on writing constructions and lexical items that are recognized as colloquial, it is striking how many syntactic and lexical differences there are between literary English texts and spontaneous spoken English (or Russian or German, and so on). A good number of structures occur only in spontaneous spoken English; some syntactic structures occur only in formal written English along with a vast range of Greco-Latinate vocabulary.

1.5. Spontaneous Spoken Language

Spontaneous spoken language has certain key properties.

i Spontaneous speech is produced in real time, impromptu, and with no opportunity for editing, whereas written language is generally produced with pauses for thought and with much editing.
ii Spontaneous speech is subject to the limitations of short-term memory in both speaker and hearer: it has been said (by the psycholinguist George Miller) that the short-term memory can hold $7 +/-2$ bits of information.
iii Spontaneous speech is typically produced by people talking face-to-face in a particular context.
iv Spontaneous speech, by definition, involves pitch, amplitude, rhythm, and voice quality.
v Spontaneous face-to-face speech is accompanied by gestures, eye-gaze, facial expressions, and body postures, all of which signal information.

Properties (i)–(v) are reflected in certain linguistic properties.

a Information is carefully staged, a small quantity of information being assigned to each phrase and clause.
b Spontaneous spoken language typically has far less grammatical subordination than written language and much more coordination or simple parataxis.
c The syntax of spontaneous spoken language is in general fragmented and unintegrated; phrases are less complex than phrases of written language; the clausal constructions are less complex. A central role in signalling relationships between chunks of syntax is played by deictics. (See Chapter 3.)
d The sentence is not a useful analytical unit for informal spoken language.

e The patterns of constituent structure and the arrangement of heads and modifiers do not always correspond to the patterns recognized by syntactic theory.
f The range of vocabulary in spontaneous language is less than in written language.
g A number of constructions occur in spontaneous spoken language but not in written language, and vice-versa.

The linguistic properties spring from the various general properties of spontaneous spoken language—but the pragmatic nature of the general properties does not mean that the syntax of spontaneous spoken language is to be treated as resulting from performance error. The properties of spontaneous spoken language and the properties of formal written language both reflect the conditions under which they are produced. This does not mean that the properties of the former result from attempts to use the structures typical of the latter—attempts which fail because of the time constraints and the different tasks that claim attention in any fact-to-face interaction. Rather, the structures of spontaneous spoken language have developed in such a way that they *can* be used in the circumstances in which conversation, for example, usually takes place.

The simple nature of phrases, the unintegrated nature of the syntax and the smaller range of vocabulary are all made possible by (iii), since typically a lot of information is shared or present in the situation of utterance and does not need to be articulated. This also leads to the occurrence of relatively simple referring expressions. Spoken language is characterized by frequent pronouns and also, especially in the case of languages such as Russian, the regular occurrence of zero noun phrases, both subject and object. (See Chapter 4 on noun phrases and Chapters 3 and 5 on zero noun phrases.) Furthermore, a certain quantity of information can be signalled by the ancillary systems mentioned in (iv) and (v).

Since the unintegrated nature of the syntax is so striking, it is worthwhile pointing out that the lack of conjunctions or subordinating links does not mean that relationships among clauses are not signalled at all. Both Schulz (1973: 19–50) and Fernandez (1994: 95–6) demonstrate that the relationships between clauses can be signalled either by particles, as in (1) and (2) or by intonation, as in (3).

(1) Meistens, nachmittags,   geh ich dann mit die [sic] Kinder raus, ...,
    mostly   in-the-afternoon go I   then with the   children out
    die   müssen ja   auch   frische Luft haben
    they must   Particle Particle fresh air   have
    'I usually go out with the children in the afternoon ... because after all they must have fresh air'

(2) Da   haben die nichts   mit verdient Die Kumpels,   die hierher
    There have they nothing with earned   the fellow workers who here
    kamen, die hatten doch   wenig Geld
    came   they had   Particle little money
    'They earned nothing from that because the fellow workers who came here
    had little money'

Schulz glosses both examples by means of clauses introduced with *weil* (because) and with the finite verb in clause-final position, the classical mark of subordinate clauses in German: *Meistens gehe ich nachmittags mit den Kindern nach draußen . . ., weil sie frische Luft haben müssen* and *Damit verdienten sie nichts, weil die Kumpel, die hierher kamen, wenig Geld hatten.* In the actual spoken examples the particles *auch* and *doch* signal that there is a relationship between the two clauses.

Fernandez (1994a: 95–6) points out that intonation signals the integration of two clauses as opposed to simple coordination or juxtaposition. Consider the French examples in (3):

(3) (a) T'auras pas   de dessert   t'es pas venu   avec nous
        You won't have any dessert (because) you didn't come with us
    (b) Il n'a pas plu   le linge   est sec
        It hasn't rained (since) the washing is   dry

A special pitch pattern signals that *t'es pas venu avec nous* and *le linge est sec* are not free-floating clauses but are linked to the first clause in each example. Of course, the type of link—time, reason, concession—does have to be reconstructed by the addressee. Fernandez (1994a: 124–5) draws attention to the use of repetition and inversion of word order in spontaneous speech as strategies of persuasion (and, we might add, attention-holding). She gives a good example from Sami, reproduced here as (4).

(4) In Alavieska and in Taivalkoski I have been. I have been in Nuorgam . . . in Palokoski

    Karigasnieme-ssä   olen ollu
    Kariganieme - LOC I-am having-been

    Rautuskaiji-ssa   olen ollu
    Rautuskaiji-LOC I-am having-been

    ja   joka   paika-ssa   olen ollu
    Particle every place-LOC I-am having-been

The first clause contains coordinated NPs in the locative case, glossed above as *in Alavieska* and *in Taivalkoski*. In the second clause the locative case NPs are in final position, simply juxtaposed *in Nuorgam . . . in Palokoski*. The remaining three clauses all have the order locative case NP—verb; the NP in the final clause sums up and generalizes the locative case NPs—*joka paika-ssa* 'in every place'. The boundary between the locative case NPs and the verb is further marked by two non-verbal signals. The first is gestural—a slap of the speaker's hand on the table. The second is intonational: in each utterance the portion to the left of the / carries falling pitch, whereas the portion to the right carries level pitch. The portions with the falling pitch are part of the rheme of the clause *I have been in Nuorgam* . . . and the portions with the level pitch are analysed as post-rheme elements or 'mnémèmes'.

Consider the following two English texts.

(5) then he said why was I always trying to CHANGE him and I said probably because he's such an obnoxious thoughtless selfish overbearing self-righteous hypocritical arrogant loudmouthed misogynist bastard

(6) Mr X was tall   bald hair to here   and a beard   he looked like Jesus   he liked to think he did   he liked to think he was Jesus   he was horrible   the most horrible man

Example (5) is taken from a humorous postcard (the words are spoken by one woman to another—both are enjoying a glass of wine and a cigarette) and the humour comes precisely from the fact that even in formal circumstances, never mind the relaxed atmosphere that is engendered by drinking wine with friends, most people cannot produce a string of nine well-chosen adjectives off the cuff, and even the most fluent speakers are hard pressed to produce complex syntax at the right moment in stressful situations. Most of us suffer from *l'esprit de l'escalier*.

Example (6) is taken from our corpus of spontaneous conversation. It illustrates the combination of verbal and non-verbal communication. The speaker begins with the simple clause *Mr X was tall*. There is a pause before the next adjective, *bald*, which probably does not belong to the first clause. *Hair to here* certainly does not belong to the first clause via ellipsis, since *Mr X was hair to here* is not a possible clause. Likewise *and a beard* does not belong to any clause. The syntactic structure consists of a clause that establishes a referent and one property of the referent, and the other chunks of syntax are simply syntactically independent phrases that in the text must be interpreted as expressing properties of the initial referent.

The phrase *hair to here* is clearly accompanied by a gesture specifying the reference of *here*. There is no contradiction; the speaker is saying that Mr X is bald on top but his remaining hair is almost down to his shoulders. The next clause carries the assertion that Mr X looked like Jesus but the next two clauses reduce the speaker's commitment to the truth of the assertion—*he liked to think he did, he liked to think he was Jesus*. The last clause is the culmination of the description—*he was horrible*. The final phrase is not by its intonation part of the final clause, but again conveys a property that can only be assigned to the entity introduced at the beginning as Mr X. It does not just repeat the information expressed by *horrible* but increases the degree of horribleness and drives home the speaker's disgust. The description is very effective, but is not conveyed in the integrated syntax we would expect in formal written English.

Sornicola (1981), working on Neapolitan Italian, and Enkvist (1982) argue strongly that even apparently fragmented syntax should be treated on its own terms and not as the degraded realization of an ideal clause or clause complex, particularly as it is not always obvious what the ideal structure might be. Consider (7), also from our corpus of spontaneous conversations, which poses more severe problems than (6).

(7) A   whose idea// was it
    B1 X's
    C   uhuh
    B2 they got one of the teachers that we always play jokes
        on/one of the young
        women/ they got her to write it

The sequence *one of the young women* is spoken on a much lower pitch than the surrounding material and there is a clear tonic on *we* and *write* in B2. What syntactic structure in her competence was the speaker aiming at? It might have been *they got one of the teachers that we always play jokes on to write it*, but the inserted explanatory material *one of the young women* has disturbed the flow of the surface syntax. An alternative is that *they got one of the teachers that we always play jokes on* corresponds to one originally complete syntactic structure and that *they got her to write it* corresponds to another complete piece of syntax. That is, although the inserted material can be seen as interrupting the syntactic performance, it is equally possible that the text clauses correspond to the original abstract syntactic structures that the speaker had in mind.

A further example of unintegrated syntax typical of spontaneous spoken English is given in (8) from the Map Task dialogues.

(8) what you're going to do—you're going to go up past the allotments

Weinert and Miller (1996) were taken to task by one referee for confusing competence and performance in their discussion of the structure of WH clefts in English. According to the referee, (8) is the result of performance factors. But what would be the structure shared by (8) and the integrated WH cleft of written English in (9)?

(9) What you are going to do is go up past the allotments

The written construction has a copula but the spoken construction has not. The spoken construction has a second main clause with progressive aspect but the written construction has not. The spoken construction has an overt subject NP in the second clause but the written construction has not. A single integrated source structure would require a large number of unusual empty categories. Of course, perhaps the referee meant simply that speakers start to produce an integrated WH clause, run into planning problems, cut the construction short after the WH clause, and produce a main clause *faute de mieux*. This interpretation does not square with the fact that the context surrounding the WH clefts in the Map Task dialogues and the spontaneous conversations displays no symptoms of planning problems such as hesitations or repetitions. It also ignores the fact that the structure in (8) is easily analysed as an information packaging construction in the sense of Vallduví (1993). The WH clause encodes an instruction to the listener to erase the information in the file 'next action' and to prepare to enter fresh (and correct) information. (For the arguments supporting this analysis, see Weinert and Miller (1996) and Chapter 6 in this volume.) The WH word points forward to some entity, whether proposition or concrete individual, which the speaker specifies in the second clause.

Fernandez (1994*b*: 20) observes that discourse particles play an important role in the presentation of disconnected phrases as a coherent message. In the Finnish example in (10) the particles connect chunks of syntax that do not by themselves make up a clause conveying a proposition. (The particles are in bold.)

(10) **Nii mut** se   oli **nys** se   PIRtuaika   **sitte**   joka paikas
     OK but THAT was now THAT time of moonshine afterwards all   sides
     'After that there was illicit alcohol everywhere'

The perspective advocated by Sornicola, Enkvist, and Fernandez, and this book, is beautifully captured in a passage from Heath (1985: 108) talking about the phenomena that are typical of Australian languages in terms that are appropriate to the study of spoken language in general:

There has been a recurrent tendency in much syntactic research to distinguish between an underlying, rather crystalline 'grammar', which then interacts in real speech with a distinct outer 'psycholinguistic' component, the latter being especially concerned with short-term memory limitations, linear ordering of major clause constituents, resolution of surface ambiguities, etc. My view is that these two aspects of language are far more tightly welded to each other than it seems at first sight.

We share Heath's view, which in particular informs the discussion of sentences in Chapter 2 and of clauses in Chapter 3.

2 Sentences and Clauses

2.1. Introduction

This first chapter on syntax asks a central question: what are the appropriate analytical units for the syntax of spontaneous spoken language? This important question has received different answers: either the same units apply as in the syntactic analysis of written language or a different but overlapping set is required. The position defended here is that the sentence should be regarded as a low-level discourse unit of written language, that clauses and phrases are units of both spoken and written language, and that sequences of clauses in spoken language may form clause complexes. The last section of the chapter argues that much spontaneous language does not even have a syntactic structure in which phrases combine into clauses or clauses into integrated clause complexes. Rather, the structure consists of blocks of syntax with little or no syntactic linkage and requiring from the listener a larger than usual exercise of inference based on contextual and world knowledge.

None of the above ideas is new. For instance, Halliday (1989) assumes that sentences are inappropriate for the analysis of spontaneous spoken language and works with clause complexes, but he does not state explicitly what he takes a sentence to be and he does not argue for his approach but simply adopts clause complexes. Here we will define the sentence and present arguments for taking the clause as the central unit of syntax, spoken or written. Sornicola (1981) presents data from Neapolitan Italian demonstrating that spontaneous spoken language may have a very fragmentary syntax and opposes any approach in which such fragmentary syntax is analysed in terms of underlying integrated clauses and phrases which have been distorted by performance error. We will extend and reinforce her argument with data from our corpus of spontaneous Scottish English conversation and with data from Zemskaja's corpus of spoken Standard Russian. The latter is particularly interesting, as it comes from informal spontaneous conversation from highly educated speakers but offers a range of regularly occurring structures in which the various phrases or clauses are not integrated with the other clauses and phrases in the clause complex but retain a large degree of syntactic independence. Their syntax (though not their content) looks inward rather than outward.

2.2. Sentences in Spontaneous Spoken Language: An Overview

Many linguists working on spoken language abandon the sentence as an analytic unit as a result of data like the text in (1), which is the transcription of a conversation.[1] The '+' signs mark brief pauses.

(1) I used to light up a cigarette + you see because that was a very quiet way to go + now when I lit up my cigarette I used to find myself at Churchill + and the quickest way to get back from Churchill was to walk along long down Clinton Road + along + Blackford something or other it's actually an extension of Dick Place but it's called Blackford something or other it shouldn't be it's miles away from Blackford Hill + but it's called Blackford Road I think + uhm then along to Lauder Road and down Lauder Road—

As Crystal (1987: 94) observes about another, but similar, text, it is not easy to decide whether the pauses mark sentence boundaries or whether the whole text is one loosely constructed sentence. An additional problem in (1) is that one stretch uninterrupted by pauses appears to consist of what would be several sentences in writing: *It's actually an extension of Dick Place, but it's called Blackford something or other, It shouldn't be, It's miles from Blackford Hill.* Two of the clauses are conjoined by *but*, but two are simply adjacent to the preceding one. To make matters worse, the pause marking the beginning of the stretch—+ *Blackford something or other*—precedes the phrase *Blackford something or other*, which is the complement of *along*, a constituent of a clause that crosses the pause boundary.

Of course the text in (1) is taken from conversation, although (1) itself is strictly speaking a narrative which is part of a conversation, and both conversation and narrative are special genres with their own conventions and properties. None the less, it is spontaneous conversation and narrative that children are exposed to when they learn their first language and that most adults use most of the time. These facts are good reasons for regarding spontaneous conversation and narrative as basic in the human linguistic repertoire. Since it is still controversial to suggest that sentences are foreign to spontaneous conversation and narrative, the different opinions are summarized and further arguments presented. Rhetorical structure and discourse representation are pinpointed as offering resources for an alternative analysis.

Throughout this book we will take for granted a major distinction between language system and language behaviour. The language system consists of the syntactic, morphosyntactic, semantic, phonological, and graphological

---

[1] This example is taken from a tutorial exercise prepared by Gill Brown and George Yule in the Department of Linguistics, University of Edinburgh in 1980. The exercise consisted of a tape recording of the original conversation and a transcription.

principles controlling the generation of semantic and syntactic structures, the insertion of lexical items into the syntactic structures, and the realization of the structures as speech or writing.[2] The products of speaking and writing are texts, which may be spontaneous or deliberately elicited by investigators.

Hypotheses about particular language systems or the general nature of language systems are based on texts and intuitions. It is essential to distinguish units that can be recognized in texts from units belonging to the hypothesized language system. Strictly speaking, the different units should be clearly kept apart by means of different terms, such as 'text-sentence', 'system-sentence', 'text-clause', 'system-clause', etc., as in Lyons (1977). In this book, 'sentence' and 'clause' will be used *tout court* where it is clear from the context whether the unit belongs to text or to the language system.

Part of the current controversy reviewed in §2.3 revolves round the question of what text units can be recognized in spoken language. In written language, sentences and clauses (and phrases, paragraphs, etc.) are obvious in any text laid-out according to the conventions of the society in which it was written. The relevant conventions differ from society to society and from one period of time to another in the same society—cf. §2.4.3. It is not easy to establish what units can be recognized in spoken language and are useful for its analysis. Some analysts maintain that sentences are not recognizable in spoken language, others—that they are.

The central problem is that it is far from evident that the language system of spoken English has sentences, for the simple reason that text-sentences are hard to locate in spoken texts. Clauses are easily recognized: even where pauses and a pitch contour with appropriate scope are missing, a given verb and its complements can be picked out. Of course, one reply to the objection is that the system-sentences employed by linguists need not correspond to text-sentences. System-sentences are postulated by linguists in order to handle distribution and dependency relations, and should be retained if this goal is achieved. Against this, it can be argued that system-sentences do not map onto text-sentences in spontaneous language because system-sentences are based on the prototype concept of a sentence as containing at least one main clause and possibly other coordinated main clauses and/or subordinated clauses.[3]

It can also be argued that the language-system unit that is the essential locus of both dependency relations and distributional properties is in fact the clause. (Cf. §2.5.2.2.) And one can ask why, for example, the text in (1) should be thought of just as a collection of sentences or as one sentence; a

---

[2] The term 'semantic' is intended to apply to the set of principles that are divided by many linguists into 'semantic' and 'pragmatic'.
[3] That this is the prototype concept is easily verified by examining popular manuals such as Burton (1986), the literature in any generative framework or the training offered to school pupils.

third possibility is that it is a collection of clauses constituting a coherent discourse by virtue of certain rhetorical relationships.

The above remarks apply only to spontaneous spoken English. For written English (and probably all other modern written languages) it does seem self-evident that the language system has sentences and clauses, since text-sentences are easily located in written texts through the use of capital letters and full stops. The one proviso is that sentences are learned through the process of reading and writing, and are taught to the majority of language-users, whereas clauses are acquired without specific teaching. Children in the early stages of primary school typically produce single-clause sentences and have to acquire the ability (partly by instruction, partly by reading) to combine a number of clauses into a sentence.

These characteristics of clauses and sentences bear on other issues, such as whether a given language system is independent of the medium in which it is realized. If sentences are to be admitted as units of written but not spoken language, the next step is to analyse written and spoken language as having different language systems. To some extent this analysis is unavoidable anyway, since even within single clauses it is clear that written English (and other languages) permits more complex phrasal and clausal constructions, and more complex vocabulary, than occur in spoken English. In addition, written English has constructions that do not occur in spontaneous spoken English, and vice-versa. (See e.g. Biber (1988) and Chafe (1982) for English; Zemskaja (1973) and Lapteva (1976) for Russian; and Blanche-Benveniste (1991) for French.) The question is whether the differences can reasonably be hypothesized to include different units as opposed to the same units but with different degrees of complexity.

If spoken texts lack sentences, the language system must be analysed as having clauses combining into clause-complexes, as suggested by Halliday (1989). There are two major types of syntactic relationship, embedding and combining. Adverbial clauses only combine, that is, are not part of any constituent in a matrix clause. Only relative and complement clauses can be embedded, since relative clauses are regularly part of an NP and complement clauses function as arguments of verbs. However, many occurrences of relative clauses cannot be treated as embedded, especially if, as in (18) in §2.5.1, they occur in a different turn from the head noun and come from a different speaker. Of course, even without sentences, it would be possible to handle such examples by postulating a system-clause in which the relative clause is embedded inside an NP and is adjacent to the head noun. The system-clause would then be mapped onto the actual arrangement of text-clauses.

This treatment of (18) is rejected here on the ground that what must be captured is the relationship between the relative clause and the relevant NP in the main clause. This is just one of various relationships between clauses, and between separate text-sentences in written language, which cannot be handled by ordinary syntactic theory and analysis, which confines itself to what occurs between sentence boundaries in writing. It does not handle relationships that cross sentence boundaries and certainly not relationships between non-adjacent clauses in speech. Analysts can either develop rules mapping integrated system-structures onto unintegrated text-structures or devise discourse rules handling both the relationships among spoken clauses and the relationships among written sentences. It is the discourse rules that are advocated here.

Of course readers are entitled to ask why they should give up a well-developed system of sentential syntactic analysis in return for a system that exists only in the form of a promissory note. The answer is in several parts. First, the analysis of written language still needs sentential syntactic analysis. There is no demand that such analysis be given up altogether, merely that limitations on its scope be recognized. Second, written language cannot be completely analysed without discourse rules specifying the relationships between separate sentences—relationships that also hold between the clauses of speech. The relationships range from coreference to rhetorical structure ones such as condition, elaboration, and concession (Cf. Matthiessen and Thompson 1988.) Third, the alternative to discourse rules is a set of rules mapping tightly integrated arrangements of system sentences onto loose arrangements of sentences (in writing) and clauses (in speech). Such a system of rules has not even been foreshadowed, far less explicitly proposed.

Fourth, the absence of any sentence marking in speech compared with an abundance of clear sentence marking in writing raises questions as to the validity of the sentence in the analysis of spoken language. Finally, the sort of discourse rules called for already exist in prototype form in the work of Mann, Thompson, and others. (See Matthiessen and Thompson 1988; Mann and Thompson 1987; Hovy 1990.) Matthiessen and Thompson (1988: 300) demonstrate two essential points: the same general relationships hold among clauses in clause combinations as among higher-level units of text, and clauses have the same combinatory structure as higher-level text-units, namely as members of a list or as nucleus with satellite.

2.3. Sentences in Spoken Texts

This section briefly surveys the arguments for and against the sentence as a unit in spoken texts and as an analytical unit in accounts of spoken language. The task is made easier by the limited amount of argument in favour of the sentence; it has simply been taken for granted that the sentence has a place in the analysis of spontaneous spoken language. The case against has been stated most clearly by Halliday (1989: 66), who argues that the basic unit of syntax is the clause. Clauses occur singly and in complexes, and clause and clause-complex are indispensable concepts for the study of both spoken and written syntax. Sentences in written language developed from the desire to mark clause-complexes; the initial capital letter of the first word in a clause-complex and the full stop following the final word signal which clauses the writer wants the reader to construe as interconnected. Of course, clauses are also interconnected in spoken language, as argued at the end of Chapter 1; the difference is that interconnectedness is not signalled by adjacency nor even by the relevant clauses occurring in the same turn (in conversation) or under the same intonation contour (in narrative).

A number of researchers recognize the problematic nature of the sentence in spoken language. Quirk *et al.* (1985: 47) state that the sentence boundaries can be difficult to locate 'particularly in spoken language' and point out that the question 'What counts as a grammatical English sentence?' does not always permit a decisive answer.[4] They deal with the difficulty by avoiding any definition of sentence while continuing to use the term for a unit greater than the clause. Linell (1988: 54) reaffirms the lack of clear-cut sentences in spoken language and adds that talk consists of phrases and clauses loosely related to each other and combining into structures less clear and hierarchical than the structures dealt with in grammar books. Similar points had been made earlier by G. Brown *et al.* (1984: 16–18). Brown *et al.* and Linell are satisfied to work with phrases and clauses and so are we. Some analysts propose a thorough clearing-out of concepts. For instance, Crookes (1990) surveys a range of work whose goal is to develop an alternative basic unit for work on oral texts. His survey includes the *idea unit* of Kroll (1977), the *turn unit* of conversational analysis, the *tone unit* of Quirk *et al.* (1985), *inter alias*, the *t-unit* of Hunt (1966), and the *utterance* as defined by Crookes and Rulon (1985: 9). The details of these various alternative units need not concern us here, as none of them relates directly to syntactic structure. *Pace* Crookes, the analysis of dialogue requires turns and phrases and clauses, since it is quite unclear how syntactic structure could be analysed without the latter. Crookes is however quite correct in describing tone groups as controversial. Indeed, G. Brown and Yule (1983) and their phonetician colleagues found it so difficult to apply the concept of tone groups to spontaneous conversation and narrative that they abandoned tone groups and worked instead with units delimited from each other by pauses, which could be short, medium, or long.

Sentences in spoken language are defended by Chafe and Danielewicz (1987: 94–6), who appeal to both clause and sentence in their analysis of

---

[4] The phrase 'particularly in spoken language' invites the inference that it is sometimes difficult in written language too. It is not clear why it should be difficult to recognize sentences in written English, provided a given writer has used capital letters and full stops according to convention. Whether readers find that writer's usage stylistically acceptable is quite another question.

spoken language. For spoken language they emphasize the central place of what they call 'prototypical intonation units', consisting of a single coherent intonation contour, possibly followed by a pause and stretching over a maximum of six words, which often coincide with clauses but which may also coincide with phrases or simply fragments of syntax. Chafe and Danielewicz (1987: 103) further say that, although the sentence is a controversial unit in the analysis of spoken language, speakers appear to produce sentence-final intonation when they judge that they have come to the end of some coherent content sequence.

2.4. Text-Sentences in Spoken Language

2.4.1. *Intonational criteria*

One difficulty with Chafe and Danielewicz's (1987) account is that their sentences correspond more to short paragraphs than to the prototypical written sentences. The intonation contours they describe may encompass one or more main clauses, not conjoined but simply adjacent to each other. Conversely, the same type of intonation contour may encompass a mere phrase. Interestingly, similar difficulties occur in Russian. The transcripts of spoken Russian in Kapanadze and Zemskaja (1979) are coded for what they call completed and uncompleted intonation. The latter occurs when speakers signal that they have not completed their utterance but are merely pausing, while the former signals completion of the utterance. What Kapanadze and Zemskaja call signalling completion of an utterance appears to be equivalent to speakers signalling that they have come to the end of a coherent content sequence, as Chafe and Danielewicz put it. Consider the example in (2), where single obliques mark uncompleted utterance intonation, and double obliques mark completed utterance intonation. Sequences of three full stops indicate a pause. The capital letters and punctuation are taken from the original. The lines are assigned letters for ease of reference.

(2) (*a*) // Potom iz   drugoj   gruppy kievljan   tože/ nu kak re . . .
          then   from (the) other group   of Kievans also/ [interpretation unclear]
    (*b*) žalko vse-taki . . . rebjat/   oni ne znajut dorogu
          sorry however   (for) them/ they not know (the) road
    (*c*) i   pojdut/   i   eti   tože vstajut
          and   will-set-off / and these-ones too   get-up //
          i.e. 'then people from the other group of Kievans also [broken syntax]—
          anyway I was sorry for them [lit. the children]—they didn't know the
          route and were about to set off—these ones too were getting up'

(Kapanadze and Zemskaja 1979: 95)

As the double obliques show, the speaker treats the whole sequence in (2) as a complete utterance. The sequence contains a prepositional phrase and a fragment in line (*a*), two main clauses in line (*b*), and two more main clauses in line (*c*). Of course, speakers can use coordinating and subordinating devices to combine a number of clauses into a single written sentence, but there is no justification for postulating one or more sentences here apart from the reader's/listener's intuition—and different readers or listeners have different intuitions, as will be demonstrated shortly.

2.4.2. Intuitions about sentences in spoken language

Wackernagel-Jolles (1971: 148–69) demonstrated that speakers do not share intuitions about what counts as a sentence in spoken language. She got groups of thirty to fifty final-year undergraduate students at a German university to listen to recordings of narratives by native speakers of German. The narratives were prompted by questions from an interviewer. Each text was played through once to allow the students to accustom themselves to the speaker's voice. They were then issued with a transcription of the recording, without punctuation. The text skipped to a new line only where there was a change of speaker. The recording was then played through a second time and the students were asked to draw a line in the text wherever they thought a sentence ended. Agreement as to sentence-endings ranged from 13 out of 20 in one text to 6 out of 29 in another. The former text was the telling of a fairy-tale; the latter—a panel-beater recounting his early life and his war experiences.

Wackernagel-Jolles (1971: 149) comments that uninterrupted story-telling was especially conducive to clear intonation signals but that the factors governing the recognition of sentence boundaries are far from obvious. The students were agreed on 20.6% of the sentence boundaries in a text produced by a slow-speaking man but agreed on 42.8% of the boundaries in a text produced by a male student with fast and 'lazy' pronunciation. They agreed on 41% of the boundaries in a text produced by a non-academic female student who failed to complete many syntactic constructions but only on 30% in a text from a clergyman with very expressive intonation. Ignoring the differences between the various text types, we see that the essential point is that naive speakers/writers, who as university students can doubtless organize their own written texts into acceptable sentences, were unanimous about the final boundary for less than half of the sentences in the texts.[5] For these subjects the sentence is a relatively fluid unit.

---

[5] The data from Wackernagel-Jolles not having been subjected to statistical analysis, it is impossible to state whether the students were in greater agreement on the sentence boundaries than chance would permit. For present purposes that question is not directly relevant, since the point being made is that even with a transcript there was a conspicuous lack of agreement

The investigation by Wackernagel-Jolles has been followed by a large number of studies on German, the majority of which, being concerned with the relative complexity of written and spoken language, regard it as essential to first define the units of analysis which can be applied to both. While intonation is considered an important factor, most studies acknowledge that it is not a reliable indicator of sentence/unit boundaries. Solutions focus on syntactic and functional features and their weaknesses demonstrate the importance of the experimented work by Wackernagel-Jolles.

Let us note first that German does not have the exact equivalent of the distinction *sentence* and *clause*. The term *Satz* generally refers to both in non-specialist and specialist contexts. In the discussion of the problem of segmentation the use of *Satz* becomes two issues: (*a*) is it possible to segment speech into sentences, i.e. larger syntactic units beyond the simple main clause?; (*b*) should units which do not include a subject and predicate be included in the analysis and be labelled *Satz* on the basis of their communicative function? In order to distinguish clause and sentence, the terms *Satz* and *Satzgefüge* are usually used. The problem of syntactic vs. functional units is not disentangled in these early studies, although there is clearly an appreciation of the problem (see especially Heinze 1979). The result of the reluctance to abandon the sentence as the minimal unit of analysis for spoken language results in a straitjacket compromise, whereby neither the structure of shorter phrases and fragments, nor the discourse-connectedness within larger units are characterized appropriately in their own terms.

Different solutions have been adopted depending on a given analyst's focus of interest. Leska (1965) argues that there is no coherent way of determining the number of sentences contained in spoken language. She decides to operate with a broad notion of sentence (or clause) as a unit which has an independent communicative function and does not consider how strings of such units might be combined into larger units. The notion of *independent communicative function* also features in the analysis by Jäger (1976). The problem with this analysis is that it includes units which do not correspond to complete clauses or sentences on the basis that otherwise much of spoken language would remain uncategorized, e.g. sequences commonly referred to as elliptical utterances, sentence fragments, and the like. Heinze (1979) similarly attempts to widen the concept of sentence to accommodate spoken language phenomena which would be considered defective in terms of the written language. His reasons are that (*a*) they have to be included in a characterization of spoken language and (*b*) quantitative comparison between written and spoken language is otherwise

about the location of the sentence boundaries. It would be surprising if listeners were to disagree about the boundaries and the constituents of individual clauses, though admittedly the relevant results must come from an experiment that is yet to be conducted.

not possible. These arguments are not convincing, since making the class of sentences more inclusive simply obscures central differences between its members. As Halford (1990) suggests, quantitative comparison of complexity between written and spoken language sentences becomes somewhat meaningless, i.e. such as analysis does not necessarily compare like with like.

There are also problems with sentence boundaries. These are apparent in the criteria used by the Forschungsstelle Freiburg for determining dependent clauses in the analysis of their spoken language corpus. They adopt a criterion of substitutability which is used to determine, for instance, the dependence of questions which do not have the verb-final order of indirect questions, and also the dependence of clauses which may be substituted by a *daß* complement clause. This would lead to a sequence such as *ich frage Sie was haben Sie erreicht* ('I ask you what have you achieved') being considered one sentence, in analogy with the indirect question *ich frage Sie was Sie erreicht haben* ('I ask you what you achieved have'). Similarly the sequences *Sie sagen es ist eine Schande* ('You say it is a disgrace') and *Sie sagen daß es eine Schande ist* ('You say that it a disgrace is') are both considered to constitute a single sentence. This analysis misses the important difference in terms of *syntactic* vs. *discourse* dependence. The two clauses *Ich frage Sie* ('I ask you') and *was haben Sie erreicht* ('what have you achieved') are interdependent with respect to the discourse, but there is no syntactic evidence that the second clause is embedded in the first. The problem becomes even more obvious in longer sequences which are considered one sentence and which often, as in the case of Chafe and Danielewicz (1987), resemble paragraphs more than written language sentences. Since the sequences are not even based on intonation contours, they become highly arbitrary. For instance, sequences introduced with *und* or *aber* which contain both subject and predicate (the Freiburg criterion for a main clause) are sometimes analysed as belonging to the same sentence as the preceding clause and sometimes as constituting a new sentence. Again, this casts doubt on conclusions drawn with regard to the complexity of written and spoken language on the basis of quantitative comparisons. For instance, Heinze (1979), who adopts the criteria of the Forschungsstelle Freiburg, argues that his data show spoken language to be just as complex as written language. In both types of data he found more complex than simple sentences (54%–42% and 55%–43% in spoken and written data, respectively). Spoken language also contained more complex sentences with more than one dependent clause (*c.*4% more). These findings need to be considered, however, in the light of two related factors. First, as argued above, the segmentation criteria do not clearly differentiate syntactic from discourse dependence. Second, main clauses with multiple dependent clauses are often of a very specific type, as pointed out by Heinze himself. The most frequent dependent clauses are *daß* complement clauses which appear to be more co-ordinated clauses with a long distance discourse dependency on a main clause which may indeed become very loose. (3*i–viii*) below illustrate both the problem with Heinze's segmentation and the function of *daß* complementation.

(3) (*i*) das heißt
         that is
    (*ii*) wir haben in diesem Jahr neunzehn hundert ein und siebzig
         we have in this   year nineteen-hundred-and-seventy-one
         nicht damit   rechnen können
         not   with-it count   been-able-to
         'we have in this year 1971 not been able to foresee'
    (*iii*) daß die Geldentwertung so schnell vor   sich geht
         that the devaluation   so quickly before self goes
         'that devaluation would happen so quickly'
    (*iv*) und haben die Werte so angepaßt
         and have the values so adjusted
         'and have adjusted the figures in such a way'
    (*v*) daß sie hier reinpassen den jeweiligen Entwertungsraten gemäß
         that they here fit-in   the specific   rates-of-devaluation relative-to
         'that they fit in here relative to the specific rates of devaluation'
    (*vi*) und daß sie aufkommensneutral bleiben
         and that they revenue-neutral   remain
         'and that they remain revenue neutral'
    (*vii*) das heißt
         that is
    (*viii*) daß sie einen entlastenden Effekt haben in ihrer Gesamtheit
         that they a   beneficial   effect have in their togetherness
         'that their effect is beneficial as a whole'

Heinze considers the above example one complex sentence, illustrating how complex spoken language sentences can be. (This example is a useful reminder of the need to distinguish informants and also topics. The speaker is a highly educated politician discussing a complex technical topic that he has undoubtedly discussed before in his political career.) Heinze also considers this complex sentence as both asyndectic and syndectic, offering both speaker and hearer a way into the idea units, yet he does not explore the implications of this analysis. We may for instance consider the use of *daß*-clauses paratactic, especially in (3*v*)–(3*viii*), where *daß* is more of a discourse marker than a complementizer—a written version would omit *daß* in (3*vi*) and (3*vii*).

Schlobinski (1988) observes the use of syntactically non-embedded *daß* clauses in psychotherapy discourse where the dependence relates to the general discourse context and not even necessarily to any one specific discourse utterance. He gives (4) as an example.

(4) K ich glaub, also, ich geb erstmal klein bei
    I think, well, I give first small in
    um... wenn ich jetzt noch mal was dagegen sage,
    to ... when I now once again something it-against say,
    'I think, well, I'll give in to him for the moment (in order to . . .), if I contradict him yet again'
    kann ich mir einfach nicht erlauben,
    can I me simply not allow
    dann wird er wieder laut.
    then becomes he again loud.
    Also muß ich schon mal klein beigeben
    So must I Particle Particle small give-in
    'I just can't afford to do that, then he'll start to shout again. So I'll just have to give in to him'
  T Daß sie doch jetzt das Gefühl haben, sich ducken zu müssen
    That you Particle now the feeling have, yourself duck to have
    'that you get the feeling, you have to duck'

Such *daß* constructions always refer back to the content of the client's utterance, formulating the feelings for him/her. They are not integrated syntactically, however. Notice that the connection between K's contribution *So I'll just have to give in to him* and T's *daß* clause is not to be interpreted straightforwardly as a relation of result. In other words it is not a continuation, but a parallel formulation of the *same* content expressed in the whole of K's contribution, aimed at helping the client to understand his/her feelings; it relates to the general, overarching discourse schema and the therapist's role in it. It may be a high-level notion such as 'you feel that' or 'you mean that' etc.; that is, we may be able to construct an expression which explains the use of the *daß* construction. However, these expressions are not present linguistically. It is possible that there is a scale of syntactic integration and that different *daß* complement clauses may occupy different positions on that scale.

Heinze's analysis frequently shows up the difference between syntactic and discourse dependencies, without this difference being clarified (e.g. in his comments on (3) above). The need for clarification may partially be hidden by the high degree of formality of his data and hence its relatively easy segmentation in terms of his criteria. His approach to segmentation is not possible for many other types of spoken language text, however, as shown by the above examples.

Halford (1990) also argues against an analysis of spoken syntax in terms of written language sentences. Her discussion of the distinction between syntactic and parasyntactic phenomena, syntagms and sentences, contains however some theoretical and terminological confusion. For instance, her adoption of the term 'sentence' for what is apparently a discourse unit does not leave room for the structural unit 'sentence' for written language. She also, somewhat confusingly, includes speech-act distinctions under parasyntactic phenomena. However, we agree with her basic premise that spoken language is organized into discourse units which cannot always be captured syntactically. We cite here two of her examples which do not allow a clear decision as to where a sentence boundary might fall. For (5) Halford (1990: 34) argues that the unit highlighted in bold belongs to both the preceding and the following unit. The intonation does not help to disambiguate the clausal structure. Halford (1990: 37) uses (6) to illustrate topic movement, but we believe that it is indeed a similar phenomenon of bi-directional attachment, although more complex and also explicitly signalled by the copula. (7a,b) are additional examples of our own taken from radio interviews.

(5) I hate sitting around here **because I'm in a bad mood** I'll go home
(6) but what I want to get into is Canadian Raising which is probably the most distinctive feature in Canadian English is the thing called Canadian Raising which is a historically inaccurate term . . .
(7) (a) that's why we do it is because we want to make sure
   (b) that's the other thing about ivy is that it is an evergreen

Such examples which cannot readily be analysed in terms of sentences occur regularly in spoken language. (6) starts out as a WH cleft. (See the detailed discussion of WH clefts in Chapters 3 and 6.) This construction consists of a WH clause, here *what I want to get into*, a copula—*is*, and a noun phrase or non-finite verb phrase. Here the third constituent is the noun phrase *Canadian Raising. Canadian Raising* is modified by the non-restrictive relative clause *which is probably the most distinctive feature in Canadian English*. The only comment we would make here is that non-restrictive relative clauses have proved difficult to analyse; they do not appear to be embedded in a single noun phrase with the noun they modify and it has even been proposed that in transformational models they be derived from a conjoined main clause. For (6) the clause would be *and that is probably the most distinctive feature in Canadian English*. The non-restrictive relative clause is followed by a clause that has no subject—*is the thing called Canadian Raising which is a historically inaccurate term*. With respect to the discourse this clause provides further clarification of the entity referred to by *what I want to get into* but its syntactic status is quite unclear. It is not obviously conjoined to *is Canadian Raising which is probably the most distinctive feature in Canadian English* although it does run parallel to it.

In (7a,b) *that's why we do it* and *that's the other thing about ivy* are instances of the reverse WH cleft construction. This structure consists of *this* or *that* plus a copula, here *'s*, plus a WH clause—*why we do it*—or a noun phrase—*the other thing about ivy*. (7a) is completed by another copula *is* and the clause *because we want to make sure*; that is, (7a) could be analysed as a coalescence of a reverse WH structure *that's why we do it* and a WH cleft *why do we do it is because we want to make sure*. Similarly (7b) could be analysed as a coalescence of the reverse cleft *that's the other thing about ivy* and a 'WH' cleft *the other thing about ivy is that it is an evergreen*. It is equally possible that for the speakers the whole sequence *that's why we do it* is a single WH clause with *that's* functioning not as a clause but simply as a highlighting or focusing element. Whatever the appropriate analysis, the central point is that examples such as (5)–(7), together with our other examples, form an ever-growing body of data which cannot readily be explained in terms of performance errors and corrections without seriously distorting our view of the nature of spoken language.

2.4.3. The sentence: a changing concept

It was remarked in §2.2 that young children in general appear not to have a clear notion of sentence but learn to write complex sentences at school. In this connection it is interesting that in written English text-sentence boundaries vary from one historical period to another, from one genre to another, and from one individual to another. A broader perspective shows that they vary from one culture to another. This variation can be interpreted as evidence that the text-sentence is not a stable unit of syntax but a discourse unit whose composition and complexity is subject to cultural variation and rhetorical fashion. Clauses (and phrases) are not subject to such variation and fashion. Unstable text-sentences indicate that even for written language system-sentences do not map onto text-sentences in any straightforward fashion, and they throw doubt on the text-sentence as a unit in spoken language and on the system-sentence as a useful unit in the analysis of spoken language.

Changing rhetorical fashion can be seen from (8), from Pepys's Diary. The editor (see Latham 1978) explains that Pepys used full stops to mark the final boundary of both sentences and phrases and dashes to mark some boundaries inside sentences. Latham has replaced Pepys's dashes with semicolons. Example (8), which is typical of Pepys's writing, shows an awareness of phrases and clauses and of larger discourse units, but not of the prototype sentence as described in §2.1 above, with a main finite clause and possibly coordinated and subordinated final clauses.

(8) to Whitehall to the Duke, who met us in his closett; and there he did desire of us to know what hath been the common practice about makeing of forrayne ships to strike sail to us: which they did all do as much as they could, but I could say nothing to it, which I was sorry for; so endeed, I was forced to study a lie; and so after we were gone from the Duke, I told Mr Coventry that I had heard Mr Selden often say that he could prove that in Henry the

7ths time he did give commission to his captains to make the King of Denmark's ships to strike to him in the Baltique.

(Latham 1978: 34)

The arrangement of clauses in (8) is not peculiar to Pepys or to diary writing but is found in other authors and other genres, such as Jane Austen's novels. The example in (9) is from *Emma* (Austen 1953: 129).

(9)   (*i*) Mrs and Miss Bates occupied the drawing-room floor; and
      (*ii*) there, in the very moderate-sized apartment, which was
      (*iii*) everything to them, the visitors were most cordially and even
      (*iv*) gratefully welcomed; the quiet neat old lady, who with her
      (*v*) knitting was seated in the warmest corner, wanting even to
      (*vi*) give up her place to Miss Woodhouse, and her more active,
      (*vii*) talking daughter almost ready to overpower them with care
      (*viii*) and kindness, thanks for their visit, . . . and sweet-cake from
      (*ix*) the beaufet: 'Mrs Cole had just been there, just called in for
      (*x*) ten minutes . . . and been so kind as to say she liked it very much;
      (*xi*) and, therefore, she hoped Miss Woodhouse and Miss Smith
      (*xii*) would do them the favour to eat a piece too.'

Example (9) is a single sentence in that it begins with a capital letter in line (*i*) and ends in a full stop in line (*xii*). A modern writer might well have no semi-colon in line (*i*) and replace the semi-colon in line (*iv*) with a full stop, converting the participial phrase *the quiet old lady . . . beaufet* into a separate sentence. Both Pepys and Jane Austen use the sentence as a holder for a number of clauses that are closely connected with respect to the setting and the events they describe or the topic they deal with.

Even modern authors can produce paragraph-like sentences, though rather shorter than (9). Cf. (10).

(10) When Homer got close to the carton, he saw that it was not empty; David Copperfield, Junior, was in the bottom of the carton—Curly Day was giving him a ride.

(John Irving, *Cider House Rules* (Black Swan, 1991) 217)

The concept of text-sentence is not stable across cultural boundaries. The French weekly *L'Express* has a house style that encourages phrases and subordinate clauses of all types to be presented as single text-sentences, as exemplified in (11).

(11) (*a*)   (*i*) Ils   sont de bonne foi.
               They are of good faith (i.e. sincere)
         (*ii*) Comme étaient de bonne foi ces   ménagères engueulant
              As   were   of good faith these housewives shouting-at
              les refuzniks
              the refuseniks

(b) (i) Certains . . . ont invité les contestataires à aller se plaindre
       Certain ones invited   the objectors   to go to-complain
   (ii) auprès de Raissa Gorbatchev.
        to   Raisa Gorbachev
   (iii) Avec quelques commentaires grossiers sur la femme
         With some   comments   coarse   on the wife
   (iv) du   secrétaire général.
        of the secretary general
   (v) Ce qui n'était pas très   difficile
       Which was not   very difficult

(11*a.ii*) contains a subordinate adverbial clause of comparison constituting a complete sentence, namely *Comme étaient de bonne foi ces ménagères engueulant les refusniks*. (11*b.iii*) has a prepositional phrase as a separate sentence, while (11*b.v*) has a relative clause as a separate sentence. Relative clauses as separate sentences are not unusual and not modern. Classical Latin texts offer many examples, such as the one in (12).

(12) (i) ergo telis   undique   obruitur;
         then with-weapons from-everywhere it-is-showered
   (ii) confossoque   eo, in vehiculum Porus imponitur.
        having-been-transfixed it, in carriage   Porus is-placed
   (iii) Quem rex   ut   vidit . . . miseratione commotus . . . inquit
         whom the-king when he-saw . . . by-pity   moved . . . he said
   (iv) Quae amentia te   coegit . . . belli   fortunam   experiri;
        What madness you moved . . . of-war the-fortune to-try
   (v) cum Taxilis esset . . . tibi   exemplum?
       when of-Taxiles was . . . to-you the-example

   'Then it [elephant] was showered with weapons from all sides. When it was dead, Porus was placed in a carriage. When the king saw him . . . moved by pity . . . he said: 'What madness made you try the fortunes of war when you had the example of Taxiles?'

   (Quintus Curtius Rufus)

The syntactic structure in question is on line (*iii*) of (12). *Quem* is listed in Classical Latin grammars as one of the forms of the relative pronoun, and relative clauses in fact occur frequently as part of NPs. However, the structure on line (*iii*) is not only a regular feature of Classical Latin texts but is recommended as a feature of good style. The view taken here is that whether in an embedded or an independent clause *quem*, and all the other forms of the relative pronoun, is an indefinite deictic that can point to relevant referents across both clause and sentence boundaries. (For further discussion, cf. §2.5.)

The Russian weekly *Argumenty i Fakty* offers the examples in (13).

(13) (a) Komandir soznatel'no idet na risk.
    (the) captain consciously goes on risk.
    'The captain knowingly takes a risk'
 (b) Nadejas', čto peregruzki ne budet.
    hoping, that overloading not will-be

In (13b) *nadejas'* is a non-finite verb form, a gerund. An equally interesting example is (14).

(14) (a) Tol'ko za poslednij god ob"em aviaperevozok v obščem
    Only in (the) last year the volume of air-journeys in general in
    po SNG sokratilsja na 30%.
    the CIS has fallen by 30%
 (b) Na Ukraine i v Rossii—na tret', v Tadžikistane—na polovinu.
    In (the) Ukraine and in Russia—by (a) third, in Tadjikistane—by (a) half

The interesting point about (14b) is that it is a complete text-sentence consisting of a gapping construction, and the constituent required in order to interpret the gap, *sokratilsja*, is in the previous sentence. (14b) is relevant not only as an example of a verbless sequence functioning as a sentence in a text but as an example of a dependency carrying over from one sentence to another. This property means that in a generative analysis the gap must be handled by a mechanism that can operate across sentence boundaries as well as across clause boundaries and the example is another piece of evidence in support of the view that the abandonment of sentences as analytical units with respect to spoken language, far from creating new problems, requires mechanisms already required by existing problems.

Farther afield, the Quran is said to have no unit between the clause and a unit corresponding roughly to the paragraph in the European literary tradition. In Turkey sentence-writing conventions have been consciously changed in recent times. Lewis (1953) talks of traditional Turkish prose writers rambling happily on adding participial phrase after participial phrase but observes that modern writers try to keep their sentences short, a practice now being taught in Turkish schools.

The elaboration of clause sequences into complex sentences has been traced for various languages. For example, Palmer (1954: 119), discussing the development of prose style in Latin, comments on how progression from the earliest to later Latin texts shows how 'the naive juxtaposition of simple sentences is gradually built up into the complex period with careful subordination of its constituent parts.' That is, the earliest written texts had text-sentences consisting of a small number of clauses, and over time more complex written text-sentences were elaborated by Latin writers. This development resulted from conscious effort, unlike changes in spontaneous spoken language; the development did not take place in the spoken language; and the resulting written text-units had to be taught. (NB: Palmer is not talking about the development of subordinate clauses, which were present in the earliest stages of Latin, but about the organization of main and subordinate clauses into highly integrated and complex sentences.)

The same sort of development had to take place independently for the modern descendants of Latin once the connections with Latin had been broken. This rupture did not affect the Church, which continued to speak and write Latin, but it did affect the vast majority of the population. The organization of clauses into sentences had to be established for each vernacular Romance language once it began to be used as a vehicle for prose literature. For French, Price (1971: 161) cites (15) as examples of clauses that are closely connected in meaning without the connection being signalled by a conjunction.

(15) (*a*) Dunc ad tel doel, pur poi d'ire ne fent
 then has such grief for little from anger not bursts
 'Then he feels such grief that he nearly bursts with rage'
 (*b*) Guardez de nos ne turnez le curage
 take care from us not turn the heart,
 i.e. 'Take care that you do not turn your hearts away from us'

The poorly developed sentence structure is also indicated by the fact that the single conjunction *que* expressed a variety of relationships—purpose, result, cause, time—where Modern Written French has a range of different conjunctions each of which is specific to a particular relationship. Guiraud (1963: 113) observes that the Old French literary language was very close to the spoken language, having an essentially paratactic organization of clauses into larger units. Such a syntax 'n'a jamais eu l'entraînement ou la pratique qui l'auraient pliée à l'expression d'une pensée élaborée; elle ignore l'articulation logique de la démonstration scientifique ou les méandres de l'argumentation philosophique' ['has never had the training or practice that would have formed it to the expression of elaborated thought; it is unaware of the logical structure of scientific argument or the meanderings of philosophical discussion'—Jim Miller]. It is significant that Guiraud mentions the uses to which language is put by literate human beings; French syntax did not develop a complex, hypotactic organization of clauses by some mysterious process but through the conscious efforts of certain literate people to convert French into an instrument suitable for the purposes served by Classical Latin. Olson (1991) refers to similar efforts on the part of the Royal Society of London when it was founded in the seventeenth century.

2.5. The Sentence as a Unit of Analysis

We turn now to sentence and clause in linguistic analysis. The burden of the preceding discussion is that the sentence is not a unit that can be recognized in spoken texts or applied in their analysis. In contrast, the sentence is a prominent unit in written texts and requires a corresponding analytical unit. Interestingly, there is evidence that the clause should be taken as the major locus of distributional and dependency relations and not the (system) sentence.

2.5.1. *Sentences and clauses in spontaneous dialogue*

We can usefully begin by returning to the problems discussed in §2.2 in connection with the text in (1). Consider the examples in (16)–(19).

(16) B right if you go from the front giraffe's foot about
hold on let me see—
if you go down about straight down about 6 cms
you find the waterhole
and it's a big hole ... with reeds round the side of it ... and animals drinking out of it
and it's about
it's a an oval hole
it's about 2 cms wide north to south
and from the side to side it's about—3 cms wide ...

(17) A you go down to the bridge
B uhuh to the left of the swamp?
A to the left of the swamp—taking a gentle curve south west

(18) A ... the first day we went canoeing
L where I capsized

(19) A1 eh you've got an East Lake haven't you
B1 aye away at the top?
A2 uhuh
B2 of the page?

(16) illustrates how in spontaneous spoken language information is carefully staged, in the sense of being spread out over different clauses. Most of the clauses are simple clauses and are simple in structure, though one clause has two prepositional phrases with a participial phrase inside one of the latter— *with reeds round the side of it* and *(with) animals drinking out of it*. It would be possible to gather the clauses into sentences, but various possibilities are open. For example, we might decide to have *You find the waterhole and it's a big hole ... [and it's about]. It's an oval hole. It's about 2 cms wide north to south. And from...* Another possible version is *You find the waterhole. And it's a big hole... It's about 2 cms wide north to south and from ...*

The basic difficulty is that in collecting the clauses into sentences we rely on recognizing clauses and on our knowledge of the stylistic conventions for written dialogue. As in (1), the intonation and pause boundaries do not coincide with the possible sentence boundaries, and to add to the difficulties the prepositional phrases *with reeds round the side of it* and *(with) animals drinking out of it* are separated from the initial part of the clause and from each other by a long pause. It is in fact unclear whether these chunks should be analysed as combining into a single clause. The analyst can combine the clauses into sentences, but the combining process is arbitrary and the sentences would not contribute to the analysis of the data as a coherent text. Coherence relations (say, as part of a discourse representation theory) must apply to clauses and indeed phrases, and sentences are not necessary.

Of course, the interplay between theory and the analysis of data is subtle. It would be legitimate to argue that the relationships between the various pieces of syntactic structure are just what generative sentence grammars are designed to handle, and that the pieces of syntactic structure should be treated as deriving from a single system-sentence in which the relationships are specified before the system-sentence is mapped on to the smaller pieces of text structure. This approach would be open to the objection that there is no mechanism for such mappings, that when applied to written language it would pay no attention to the boundaries of text-sentences as signalled by authors, and that it ignores the syntactic and discourse structure of spoken texts. A further objection is that a model of rhetorical relations in text is in the course of development, and this model will allow analysts to keep closely to the surface organization of texts and to bring out the relationships among the phrases and clauses.

The same problem arises in (19), where B2 modifies B1, but B1 has a completed intonation contour, and is separated from B2 by A2. A2, part of the conversation management, does not overlap with B1 or B2. While the speaker could have uttered B1 and B2 as part of the same pause and intonation unit, he did not, and there are no criteria to justify treating them in any way except as two separate but discourse-related phrases. The fact that the speaker might well have written the two phrases as part of a single sentence, given planning time, is irrelevant. Similarly, (16) could have been *written* as the compact, dense, syntactically integrated piece of prose in (20), but the characteristics of (20) cannot be invoked as criteria in the analysis of (16). It would be rather like taking a piece of written language, rewriting it, analysing the rewritten piece, and presenting the analysis as pertaining to the original passage!

(20) It's a big oval waterhole about 2 cms wide north to south and about 3 cms wide from side to side, surrounded by reeds and with animals drinking out of it.

(17) and (18) exemplify other relationships that cannot reasonably be analysed by invoking a single sentence. (17) presents a free participial

phrase *taking a gentle curve south west*, modifying the clause produced in a previous turn by the same speaker, and (18) presents a relative clause *where I capsized*, modifying a constituent in the clause produced by the previous speaker. Participial phrases are discourse-dependent in the sense that the listener cannot interpret them without reference to a previous piece of text; at the very least, a subject has to be found for the participle itself. The nearest candidate for the subject is in the first line of (17), but this is not a reason for analysing the participial phrase as belonging to one and the same sentence as *you go down to the bridge*. Note that speaker A was not interrupted in the process of producing a single sentence. *You go down to the bridge* is a completed utterance, with appropriate intonation. B signals acceptance of the instruction with *uhuh*, looks at the map and realizes that he needs more information: *to the left of the swamp?* A produces the participial phrase in response to B's question.

The relative clause in (18), *where I capsized*, is an example of a non-restrictive relative clause. In examples such as *Show me the essay which was submitted late* there is no pause between *essay* and *which* in speech and no comma in writing and the relative clause helps the listener to pick out the appropriate referent. In *This essay, which was submitted late, is terrible*, the relative clause is separated from *essay* by a pause in speech and by a comma in writing. It has no referential function but merely adds information about the essay. Such non-restrictive clauses may be produced after very long pauses or in a different turn from the head noun, and may even be produced, as in (18), by a different speaker.

The key to the behaviour of non-restrictive relative clauses and to the interpretation of (18) is that they are introduced by WH items which are indefinite deictics, used for pointing at entities not in the immediate situation of utterance because not yet mentioned. Speakers either ask for a specification of an entity, as in *Who is going to drive the car?* or provide the specification, as in *I tell you what—you drive the car and I'll take the train* or *I remember what he bought for our first anniversary—a beautiful Chinese watercolour*. In the first example where the speaker provides the specification, the speaker knows what he or she wants to say; the *what* is specific for the speaker but non-specific for the listener, for whom it points forward. The speaker's message is 'I'm about to tell you something'. In the first example, *what* is specified by *You drive the car* and in the second example—by *a beautiful Chinese watercolour*. With respect to the first example, the speaker can be thought of as saying 'Someone is going to drive the car—specify the person.' In relative clauses, restrictive or non-restrictive, WH items function in the same fashion. They signal that the listener is to look for an entity possessing the property conveyed by the relative clause. That is, the listener is given the information that a non-specific entity has the relevant property and the listener has to seek out further specification by locating the NP referring to the entity. *Where* in (18) signals that the listener has to find the place that is pointed to.

This interpretation of WH words gains support from the fact that other languages offer analogous constituents and structures. For example, the Russian equivalents of the English WH words are instructive. *Kto* corresponds to *who* in interrogatives but to *anyone* in conditional clauses: *esli kto pridet* = *if anyone comes*. To *kto* can be added the deictic *to* (= *that*), yielding *kto-to*. A speaker saying *kto-to zvonil* (= Someone phoned) is conveying that he or she can specify the someone, even in vague terms such as *It sounded like a woman of 30 or so*. The addition of another affix *-nibud'*, as in *kto-nibud'* yields a vaguer deictic: *kto-nibud' ukral mne portfel'* (= *Someone has stolen my briefcase*). The speaker cannot specify any properties of the someone. *Kto* also functions as a relative pronoun, but only when the head noun is TOT. However, the usual relative pronoun is *kotoryj*, and there is general agreement among Slavists that it consists of the indefinite *ku* plus and element *tor-*. We can thus see formal and semantic relationships among Russian interrogative, indefinite, and relative pronouns.

2.5.2. Sentences and syntactic analysis

2.5.2.1. Bloomfield's definition

It will be useful to consider the role of the sentence in syntactic analysis. Bloomfield (1935: 170), having discussed an invented text *How are you? It's a fine day. Are you going to play tennis this afternoon?* makes the declaration in (21).

(21) It is evident that the sentences in any utterance are marked off by the mere fact that each sentence is an independent linguistic form, not included by virtue of any grammatical construction in any larger linguistic form.

Crystal (1987: 94) puts it more concisely: a sentence is the largest unit to which syntactic rules apply. While representing an enormous advance over statements about sentences expressing complete thoughts, this sort of definition is itself open to objection. One self-evident fact about (21) is that Bloomfield's sentences each consist of a single finite clause. Bloomfield does treat the problem of parataxis—two or more main clauses juxtaposed with no pauses or intonation breaks to mark the putative sentence boundaries, as in (1) above—by invoking a set of pitch phonemes. This treatment is decisively countered by Matthews (1981: 30–4), on the grounds that intonation is continuous, the phonemic principle of sameness/distinctness does not apply and there are no rules governing parataxis. Matthews (1981: 35–8, 46), on the basis of Tag Questions and the distribution of *please*, further points out that not all phenomena in a given language lend themselves to a rigorous rule-based account, for the simple reason that any natural language has areas of indeterminacy.

2.5.2.2. Sentences, clauses, and dependency relations

Matthews's objection can be restated thus: What units of syntax (in spoken or written language) are affected by the rules of distribution and dependency relations? The answer to be offered here is that the clause is the locus of the densest dependency and distributional properties, although a few dependency relations cross clause boundaries, and although, in written language, a few dependency relations cross sentence boundaries. The first part of the answer will be used to support the view that the sentence is not required as an analytical unit in spoken language (and may be less central in written language than previously thought). The second part of the answer, dependency relations crossing clause boundaries, could be interpreted as supporting the sentence as an analytical unit even in spoken language, but this potential argument is counteracted by the third part, dependency relations crossing text-sentence boundaries in written language. Because dependency relations cross text-sentence boundaries, a complete grammatical theory must have a mechanism for specifying such dependencies, and whatever the mechanism is, it will undoubtedly be able to specify dependencies from clause to clause when the clauses are gathered, not into a sentence but into a text.

Let us consider first the dependency relations in the Russian examples in (22).

(22) (a) Molodaja devuška verila   materi
       young   girl   believed (her) mother
   (b) Molodaja devuška verila, čto mat'   pomogaet ej
       young   girl   believed that (her) mother is-helping her
       'The young girl believed that her mother was helping her'

(22a) consists of a single main clause which can stand on its own (and constitutes a sentence in written Russian). Within that clause there is a dense network of dependencies. *Verila* has the two NPs as complements—it requires both a subject and an object NP.[6] Having singular number and feminine gender, *verila* requires its subject noun to be singular and feminine, and also in the nominative case. *Devuška* has all these properties. *Verila* requires its direct object to be in the dative case—most transitive Russian verbs govern their direct object in the accusative case. *Materi* is a dative case form. The adjective *molodaja* agrees in number, gender, and case with its head noun. In copula clauses with BYT' (BE), the subject noun agrees

---

[6] Whether dative complement NPs are direct objects is open to question. Since nothing in this account depends on a decision one way or the other, the term 'direct object' is used for convenience.

with adjective complements of BYT' in gender and number: *Vrač byl simpatičnyj* ('(the) doctor—was—nice'), where *vrač* and *simpatičnyj* are both nominative case, singular number, and masculine gender.

(22*b*) demonstrates another property of VERIT' (BELIEVE). Verbs control how many constituents co-occur with them in clauses, and what type. VERIT' allows direct object NPs as its complement, but it also allows clauses. This is an important property, since many verbs exclude clauses and some verbs allow only clauses. Only one property of rection crosses the clause boundary, the mood of the clause. In Russian this is signalled by the complementizer—*čto* with *verila*, but some verbs require *čtoby* and a past tense verb—as in *Devuška xotela, čtoby mat' pomagala ej* ('(the) girl—wanted—that—(her) mother—help—her'), where *pomagala* is a past tense form. All the other dependencies in the complement clause are controlled by the verb in that clause.

Cross-clause dependencies are thick on the ground in Classical Greek complement structures, as exemplified in (24)–(27). Let us note first that, as in Russian, the densest network of dependencies is inside the Classical Greek clause. This is demonstrated in (23*a*), where the verb *akouousi* assigns nominative case to its subject noun and accusative case to its direct object noun. (In contrast, in (23*b*) the verb *xratai* assigns dative case to its object noun, and the very assignment of dative case raises the question whether that verb takes a direct object or an oblique object.) In turn the nouns spread case, number, and gender to any dependent articles and adjectives: *andres* assigns nominative, plural, and masculine to *hoi* and *kakoi* and *logous* spreads accusative, plural, and masculine to *tous*. *Gunaikos* (of the woman) is a feminine noun in the genitive case because of its relationship to *logous*. *Gunaikos* spreads genitive, singular, and feminine to *te:s* and *sofe:s*.

(23) (*a*) hoi kakoi andres ouk akouousi
        the evil   men   not are-listening-to
        tous te:s   sofe:s gunaikos logous
        the of-the of-wise of-woman words
        'The evil men are not listening to the words of the wise woman'
    (*b*) he gune: xratai tois bibliois
        the woman is-using the books

As in English, complement-taking verbs in Classical Greek control the complementizer in the complement clause. Verbs of saying take *hoti* (that), as in (24), verbs of movement take *hina* (in order to), as in (25), verbs of enquiring take *ei*, as in (26), and certain specific verbs take *hopo:s* as in (27).

(24) (*a*) legei   hoti grafei
        He/she-says that he/she-is-writing
    (*b*) eipen   hoti grafoi
        He/she-said that he/she-was-writing

(25) (a) erxetai   hina   ide:
is coming in-order-that sees
i.e. 'He/she is coming to see'
(b) elthen hina   idoi
came in-order-that sees
i.e. 'He/she came to see'

(26) (a) punthanetai ei akouousi tous logous
asks   if hear   the   words
'He/she is asking if they hear the words'
(b) eputheto ei akouoien tous logous
asks   if hear   the   words'
'He/she asked if they heard the words'

(27) (a) spoudaze hopo:s akousetai tous logous
hurries to   hear   the words
'He/she is hurrying to hear the words'
(b) espoudase hopo:s akousetai tous logous
hurried to   hear   the words
'He/she hurried to hear the words'

Note that although *hopo:s* in (27a,b) has been translated by *to*, the complement clause is finite, *akousetai* being third person singular future. In addition to verbs selecting complementizers, there is another dependency crossing the clause boundary. When the verb in the matrix clause is past tense, the verb in the complement clause is in the optative mood. When the verb in the matrix clause is present tense, the verb in the complement clause is either indicative, after *hoti* in (24a) and *ei* in (26a), or subjunctive, after *hina* in (25a). When the verb in the matrix clause is aorist, the verb in the complement clause is in the optative mood.[7] The exception to these changes in mood is *hopo:s* in (27a,b), which requires the verb to be future tense. In the last case it is *hopo:s* and not the verb in the matrix clause that governs the occurrence of future tense.

Another example of cross-clause dependency is found in Russian (and Greek) relative clauses, exemplified in (28).

(28) Nekotorye   bojalis' politiki,   kotoruju vvel   Stalin
Certain (ones) fear   (the) policy which   introduced Stalin

The relative clause in (28) is *kotoruju vvel Stalin. Kotoruju* is a relative pronoun with feminine gender, singular number, and accusative case. The accusative case is assigned by *vvel* ('introduced'), which also assigns nominative case to the subject noun *Stalin* and agrees with it in number. In the main clause *bojalis'* ('fear') is third person plural, as is the subject

---

[7] Optative verb forms were used to express wishes (*he:mas sozoi*—us he-save, i.e. 'If only he would save us') and occur in various irrealis constructions, such as the protases of conditional structures, expressing greater remoteness from reality than is expressed by subjunctive forms.

noun *nekotorye*. *Politiki*, the object of *bojalis'*, is in the genitive case, which is required by that verb. In addition, *politiki* is feminine gender and singular number, the very properties that turn up in the relative pronoun. That is, the case of the relative pronoun is determined by the verb in the relative clause and by whether the pronoun is the subject or object of the verb, but the gender and number of the relative pronoun are determined by the noun modified by the relative clause.

Dependencies typically do not cross clause boundaries into adverbial clauses. Certain combinations of adverbial clause and main clause appear to involve cross-clause dependencies, such as the rules in Classical Greek governing clause combinations expressing fulfilled or unfulfilled conditions as in (29).

(29) (a) ei touto epoioun, edikoun
        if this they-were-doing, they-were-wrong
    (b) ei touto epraxen, edikesan an
        if this they-had-done, they-would-have-been-wrong

The English copula + adjective structure *were wrong* corresponds to a single verb in Greek, *edikoun*. (29a) expresses a fulfilled condition; the conditional clause contains an Imperfect verb, *edikoun*. (29b) expresses a remote, unfulfilled condition. The conditional clause contains an aorist tense form, *epraxen*, and the main clause contains an aorist form and the particle *an*. Such examples, however (both the Classical Greek ones and their English equivalents), are not instances of dependencies crossing from one clause to another. The syntactic constraints affect both the main and adverbial clauses, and the dependencies appear to be associated with the entire combination, rather than flowing from the main clause to the adverbial clause.

The above examples of cross-clause dependencies do not vitiate the proposition that the clause is the site of the densest network of dependencies. In each of the above examples, at most two dependencies cross the clause boundary, the selection of complementizer by the verb and the selection of mood in the complement clause. Inside each clause is a much greater number of dependencies. The verb controls the type of constituents it requires; some verbs allow two NPs, others allow three, and yet others allow only one; some verbs allow adjective phrases or PPs. In a given clause the verb assigns case to the dependent nouns and controls the choice of preposition in the PPs. Inside the phrasal constituents the head, N, A, or P, assigns case to its dependent constituents, and a head N also assigns gender and number. And there may be further PPs inside the NP and AP. Not all these dependencies flow directly from the verb, but they are all sited inside a given clause.[8]

---

[8] Note that the recent major works based on fieldwork on 'exotic' languages focus exclusively on the clause—Nichols and Woodbury (1985) and Foley and Van Valin (1984).

Relative clauses and complement clauses differ from adverbial clauses in being embedded, relative clauses occurring inside NPs and complement clauses functioning as arguments of verbs. Given these close relationships, the cross-clause dependencies are not surprising, but note that for relative clauses it is only agreement in number and gender (which applies to full NPs and succeeding pronoun anaphors in different sentences), while for complement clauses it is only mood—but cf. the comments below on the type of constructions that are common in spoken language.

Relative clauses are interesting in another respect. Non-restrictive relative clauses are often separated from their antecedent NP by a long pause, or a break in intonation or a change of conversational turn. Compare the change of turn in (18) and the break in intonation in (30).

(30) on zastavil [ego] nam čitat'   kurs   tureckogo jazyka//
    he made   him   to-us to-read course of-Turkish of-language
    Očen' interesnyj// Iz kotorogo   ja massu vynes
    very interesting (one) from which   I   a-mass took-out
    'he made him teach us a course on Turkish—very interesting—from which I learned a lot'

(Kapanadze and Zemskaja 1979: 2–3)

Kapanadze and Zemskaja use double obliques to mark the end of a completed utterance intonation contour and the beginning of a new contour. In (30) the relative clause *iz kotorogo ja massu vynes* is separated from the previous phrase by a double oblique.

The close relationship between complement clauses and the matrix clauses in which they are embedded is undeniable, but one phenomenon must be mentioned here: constructions that are quite regular and frequent in written language simply do not occur, or are very rare, in spontaneous speech. For instance, what would be a complement clause in writing is typically expressed in speech as though a speaker's exact words were being reported direct, as in (31)–(33).

(31) (*a*) So I asked what are you doing
    (*b*) I asked what he was doing

(32) (*a*) I said we'll help
    (*b*) I said that we would help

(33) (*a*) Then she explained—the baby was ill and she had to stay at home
    (*b*) Then she explained that the baby was ill and she had to stay at home.

In (31*a*) and (32*a*) the speaker purports to repeat the words used in the original utterance of the message, while in (33*a*) the report of the speech is embodied in clauses with past tense verbs, *was* and *had*, but the clauses are not embedded complement clauses, as indicated by the dash. In spontaneous spoken language not only is reported speech embodied in main clauses with present tense verbs and with first or second pronouns as in (31*a*) and (32*a*) but these clauses are marked off from the surrounding text by a change in voice quality and/or amplitude and/or pitch.

Admittedly, the frequency of the different constructions in a large body of spontaneous speech has yet to be rigorously calculated, but a sample of the corpus of spontaneous conversation showed no occurrences of verbs of saying followed by a complement clause as opposed to ten occurrences of verbs of saying followed by the purported words of the person being talked about.

2.5.2.3. *Dependencies crossing sentence boundaries*

To close this discussion of dependencies, let us consider (34) and (35), which exemplify dependencies crossing text-sentence boundaries.

(34) **Etot portnoj** byl krasivo starejuščij mužčina
This tailor was handsomely growing-old man
šest' večerov v nedelju stojal **on** za stolom
Six evenings in week stood he at table
rezal šil proglažival švy utjugom
cut sewed smoothed seams with-iron
Zarabatyval den'gi. Voskresen'je provodil na ippodrome
Earned money. Sunday spent at racecourse
'This tailor was growing old but keeping his good looks. Six evenings in the week he stood at the table cutting, sewing, and ironing seams. He earned good money. Sunday he spent at the racecourse.'

(Rybakov 1988: 25)

(35) A ona molčit. Idet, ladoški v rukava svitera sprjatala
But she is-silent. Walks, hands in sleeves of-sweater has-hidden
i molčit
and is-silent
'But she says nothing. She walks along with her hands in the sleeves of her sweater and says nothing.'

(Ivanov and Karelov 1986: 11)

In (34) the first sentence has the full masculine singular NP *etot portnoj*, the second sentence has the masculine singular pronoun *on*; and the third and fourth sentences have the subject-less masculine singular verbs *zarabatyval* and *provodil*. The properties 'masculine' and 'singular' are projected by *etot portnoj* into the pronoun in the second sentence and then into the verb forms in the third and fourth sentences. In (35) the Agent is referred to by the feminine singular pronoun *ona*, which itself refers back to a full NP omitted here. In the second sentence the verb *idet* has the properties 'singular' and 'third person' (but not 'feminine') and the verb *sprjatala* has the properties 'feminine', 'singular', and 'third person'.

2.5.3. Sentences, clauses, and distribution

With respect to distribution it is equally obvious that the classic distributional criteria apply within clauses rather than sentences. For example, in Radford (1988: 69–75), the vast bulk of the distributional evidence relates to single main clauses. Where there is more than one clause, one reason is that the additional material is needed to provide a convincing linguistic context; e.g. in *Down the hill John ran, as fast as he could* the adverbial clause of manner, *as fast as he could*, lends naturalness to the fronted prepositional phrase, *down the hill*. A second reason is that the extra clause is a relative clause or a complement clause, i.e. clauses that are embedded inside arguments of the verb in the main clause. One example, from a discussion of how heavy noun phrases are shifted to the end of sentences, is *He explained to her all the terrible problems that he had encountered*, where the relative clause gives the necessary weight to the shifted noun phrase *all the terrible problems that he had encountered*. In any case, distributional analysis runs into the same problem as verbs and complement clauses; complex sentences of the sort appealed to in the literature on syntax are missing from spontaneous spoken language.

The only clauses that have distribution inside a unit bigger than the clause are adverbial clauses. In written English and in relatively formal spoken English adverbial clauses of time and reason, for example, can precede or follow the main clause with which they combine, but in informal spoken English they tend to follow the main clause. That is, since their distribution even in written English is limited, they are no more than mild exceptions to the rule that the clause is the main focus of distributional properties. In any case, it is not clear that even adverbial clauses can be moved inside a sentence in written English.

The difficulty is that not all subordinate clauses are equally subordinate, where subordination is measured in terms of possible constructions and word orders. Main clauses permit a large range of constructions—declarative, interrogative, imperative, tag questions—and a large range of word orders, whereas subordinate clauses vary in the extent to which they allow constructions other than declarative and word orders other than subject–verb–direct object. Consider the examples in (36).

(36) (*a*) Because Aunt Norris came into the room, Fanny stopped speaking
    (*b*) Fanny stopped speaking because Aunt Norris came into the room

In (36*a*) the adverbial clause of reason *because Aunt Norris came into the room* is at the front of the sentence and has limited structural possibilities. *Into the room*, for example, cannot be moved to the front of the clause, and the subject NP and the verb cannot be transposed, but these changes can be carried out in the *because* clause in (36*b*). Cf. (37*a*,*b*).

(37) (a) *Because into the room came Aunt Norris, Fanny stopped speaking
(b) Fanny stopped speaking, because into the room came Aunt Norris

It has been suggested that *because* clauses have a different discourse function in sentence-initial and sentence-final positions (Chafe 1984). In sentence-initial position, *because* clauses (indeed, adverbial clauses in general) function as a guide to information flow. As Chafe puts it, 'the adverbial clause . . . [signals] a path or orientation in terms of which the following information is to be understood'. The devised example given by Chafe is *Because it has such a big memory, I decided to buy it*, where the information that the computer in question has a large memory is the background against which the listener or reader is to assess the information that the speaker decided to buy it. In sentence-final position adverbial clauses are used by speakers simply to add something to the assertion conveyed by the main clause.

Chafe points out that *because* clauses following the main clause can typically be paraphrased by *and the reason was that*, and maintains that sequences of 'main clause'–'*because* clause' come close to sequences of coordinate clauses, that is, clauses of equal status. The *because* clause may relate to one particular constituent in the main clause or may not relate directly to the main clause at all. That is, the un-subordinate nature of such *because* clauses, as evidenced by their syntactic flexibility, is accompanied by semantic flexibility. For instance, in *Fiona isn't coming to work today because her husband phoned up to say she was ill*, the *because* clause is presenting, not the reason for Fiona's absence, but the reason for the speaker being able to state that Fiona is not coming in to work. For some speakers adverbial clauses of reason following the main clause can even contain interrogative structures: e.g. *I'm not going to the party because who's going to be there?* The question may be one to which the speaker already knows the answer, but it is none the less a piece of interrogative syntax. Analogous remarks apply to adverbial clauses in general, although clauses of reason probably enjoy the greatest amount of syntactic freedom. The essential point is that the moving of adverbial clauses may be a mirage: it is not one and the same type of clause occurring in two different positions but a different, albeit related, type of clause in each position. In any case, the analysis advocated here for informal spoken English is that adverbial clauses combine with main clauses to form a clause complex, and that the relationships between the clauses in clause complexes should be handled by discourse rules. (Cf. § 2.2.)

Complement clauses might appear to be better examples of distribution inside the sentence, given that there appears to be no major difference in meaning between a sentence such as (38*a*), with a complement clause in sentence-initial position, and (38*b*), with the complement clause in sentence-final position.

(38) (a) That the enemy was approaching the town apparently did not worry the inhabitants
(b) It apparently did not worry the inhabitants that the enemy was approaching the town

For written English it is indeed correct that complement clauses can occur at the beginning or end of sentences, but in spontaneous spoken English such examples as (38a) are practically unknown. There are none in the corpuses of Conversation and Map Task dialogues and they are very rare even in the formal spoken language heard in serious discussion programmes on radio and television. That is, in spontaneous spoken English, complement clauses are not mobile but fixed.

2.5.4. *Spoken language with fragmented syntax*

The above considerations demonstrate how inappropriate the sentence is as a unit of analysis with respect to spontaneous spoken language but the data at least consists of phrases organized into clauses, the syntagmatic relations between the phrasal constituents can be specified unambiguously, and the text-clauses can be analysed by means of constituent structure diagrams. Sornicola (1981: 20–34) observes that many instances of spontaneous spoken data do not allow syntagmatic relations to be established. In some cases this is because of changes in planning, as in (39).

(39) programmi   che/   per   i   bambini/ingiommi/   a   l'indomana /
     programmes   that/ for   the children/   /for tomorrow
     vedono/   guardono/   per la   scuola
     they-see/ they-watch/ for the school

Sornicola suggests that (39) could be assigned the semantic interpretation and possibly even the syntactic structure of the tidied-up version in (40).

(40) programmi   che [i bambini]   vedono [perché sono   loro   utili]
     programmes that [the children] see   [because they-are to-them useful]
     per la   scuola il   giorno dopo
     for the school the day   after

(40) contains an ideal NP–Relative Clause structure and an explicit statement of background information, *perché sono loro utili*, which is missing from the original example (39). The difficulty is, as Sornicola remarks (1981: 23), that to apply the semantic and syntactic structures of (40) in the analysis of (39) would be to pay scant respect to the facts of constituent order and interpolations in the latter. The background information has to be inferred by the listener to (39): that is, the listener has to ask why the speaker talks of the children watching the programmes for school and should be able to hypothesize that the programmes contain items of

general knowledge, or perhaps even items relating to arithmetic and language, that the children will enjoy and that improve the children's knowledge of the world, and so on. It seems right to see a semantic link between *la scuola* and *il giorno dopo*, and we might believe that a well-constructed piece of syntax would have these two phrases adjacent. It also seems right to see *i bambini* as the grammatical subject of *vedono* and *guardono*, and we would expect to find the noun phrase and the verb adjacent in our well-constructed piece of syntax.

The fact is however that in the original utterance (39) *i bambini* is the object of the proposition *per* and the listener has to infer the subject of the verbs on the basis of the available syntax and lexical items—is there a plural noun that might be linked with the plural verb?—and relevant world knowledge—children go to school and there are special children's programmes that provide both entertainment and information. *A l'indomana* and *per la scuola* are likewise linked semantically, but they are not adjacent. Within many formal models of syntax (39) might be analysed as corresponding to a well-formed NP–Relative Clause structure, with the untidy syntax arising as a result of performance errors. But what grounds are there for supposing that the speaker, having abandoned the apparent relative clause beginning with *che*, continued to aim at the same construction? *Programmi per i bambini* is a respectable noun phrase and the sequence *vedono/ guardono / per la scuola* is a respectable main clause. The subject and direct object of the verbs have to be inferred, but the inference is hardly difficult if *programmi per i bambini* is taken as presenting the topic of this section of discourse and given that the verbs require human subjects.

(41) is an example from spontaneous spoken English already mentioned in Chapter 1 but directly relevant to the current point.

(41) A   whose idea// was it
     B1 Charlie Richardson's
     C   uhuh
     B2 they got one of the teachers that we always play jokes on/one of the young women/ they got her to write it

The sequence *one of the young women* is spoken on a much lower pitch than the surrounding material and there is a clear tonic on *we* and *write* in B2. What syntactic structure in her competence was the speaker aiming at? It might have been *they got one of the teachers that we always play jokes on to write it*, but the inserted explanatory material *one of the young women* has disturbed the flow of the surface syntax. An alternative is that *they got one of the teachers that we always play jokes on* corresponds to one originally complete syntactic structure and that *they got her to write it* corresponds to another complete piece of syntax. That is, although the inserted material can be seen as interrupting the syntactic performance, it is equally possible that the text clauses correspond to the original abstract syntactic structures that the speaker had in mind.

Sornicola suggests that many spontaneous spoken utterances are to be analysed, not as coherently organized pieces of syntax but as resulting from the juxtaposition of information blocks. Such sequences of information blocks can only be interpreted by discourse interpretation mechanisms that are designed to handle separate chunks of syntax, beginning with separate sentences. (See the comments in §2.2. above.)

Equally important is the fact that from time to time listeners are required to interpret sequences whose syntax is, from the standpoint of written language, quite unsatisfactory. Consider (42), from the corpus of spontaneous conversation.

(42) no if we can get Louise/ I mean her mother and father/ Louise's parents would give us/they've got a big car and keep the mini for the week// but Louise isnae too keen on the idea so . . .

A written version of (42) might be as in (43)

(43) No. Louise's parents have got a big car. If we can get them to give us the big car and if they would take the Mini for the week [we could all travel by car together]. But Louise is not too keen on the idea, so [we will not be travelling in the big car].

The written version differs from the original spoken version in several respects. It has complete and coherent syntax, the information is well organized, with the fact about Louise's parents' car presented first, and information that was left for the listener to infer in the actual conversation is made explicit—cf. the clauses inside the square brackets. From a comparison of the written and spoken versions it is only too easy to conclude that the spoken text is a hopeless piece of communication with fragmented and incomplete syntax and a badly organized sequence of information. The fact is that none of the participants in the conversation appeared to notice anything amiss, the field-worker did not hesitate or ask the speaker for clarification and the conversation continued smoothly. Even more interestingly, groups of students who have been asked to listen to the section of conversation containing (42) have also failed to notice the syntactic problems until they saw the transcription and were asked to analyse its syntax.

Let us consider (42) more closely. The first item, *no*, answers a question from the interviewer as to whether the speaker and her friends would go on holiday in Louise's Mini. The first clause *if we can get Louise* could be considered complete in isolation but in the context it is reasonable to suppose that the speaker intended to continue with an infinitive. However that may be, the listener has the information that the speaker is thinking of getting Louise to do something, and in the context of holidays and Louise's Mini, the range of inferences will be confined to the frame of going on holiday by car. The next piece of syntax, *I mean her mother and father*, introduces Louise's parents as important players in the frame. The third piece of syntax is more puzzling—*Louise's parents would give us*. The puzzle is whether it is to be seen as a main clause or as the bulk of a conditional clause linked to the subordinating conjunction *if* right at the beginning of the excerpt. The modal verb *would* lends support to the latter interpretation. The fourth piece of syntax consists of a main clause, *they've got a big car*, which conveys a necessary piece of background information, and the fifth piece, *and keep the mini for the week*, can most obviously be analysed as depending on the modal verb *would*.

The missing direct object of *give* in *Louise's parents would give us* does not cause difficulties for the listeners. The explanation that seems most plausible is that the listeners know that GIVE requires a direct object and infer the intended direct object from the statement of background information *they've got a big car*. Further support for that inference comes from *and keep the mini for the week*, which only makes sense if the speaker is talking about a possible exchange of cars. The important point is that listeners can interpret the whole of (42) by treating each piece of syntax as an information block, extracting the information and linking the separate chunks of information using syntax and world-knowledge. This is not a simple task but it is quite feasible for the participants in a situated language interaction, granted assumptions about the speaker's intentions and willingness to follow the usual convention that a discourse topic is not changed without adequate notice. That is, as with Sornicola's data, it is not necessary to suppose that language-users relate utterances to complete syntactic trees as employed in the theoretical linguistic world of idealized data.

2.5.5. *Fragmented syntax in spoken Russian*

The idea that much spoken language has to be analysed in terms of syntactic blocks that do not fit together into organized clause complexes receives strong support from work on spoken Russian carried out many years ago by Zemskaja and her colleagues in Moscow. (Cf. Zemskaja 1973.) Zemskaja's work is extremely valuable because her data consists of spontaneous spoken Russian produced in relatively informal conditions by professional Russians—lawyers, doctors, academics—and because her data contains block structures that are uninterrupted by long pauses or changes of intonation.

2.5.5.1. Reference by means of phrases and clauses without nouns

Zemskaja (1973: 227 ff.) provides examples of referring expressions without nouns, as in (44).

(44) (*a*)   s   zelenymy balkonami/ eto vaš?
       with green   balconies/   that yours?
   (*b*)   moloko raznosit/   ne   prixodila ešče?
       milk   she-delivers/ not came   yet?
       'the woman who delivers the milk, has she not come yet?'
   (*c*)   u okna   ležala/ kapriznaja očen'
       at the-window she-lay/ moody   very
       'the woman in the bed by the window was very moody'

Instead of (44*a*) we might have expected *dom/dača/kvartira s zelenymi balkonami*, but since the speaker is clearly referring to an entity present in the immediate context of utterance, the noun can be omitted. Of course, the omission of the noun is a property of Russian and not of English. The corresponding English utterance would have to be along the lines of *the flat with green balconies, is it yours?* or *the one with green balconies, is it yours?* (44*b*,*c*) are more complicated because the 'missing' syntax is not just a noun but a noun and a relative pronoun. By 'missing' is meant that in writing (44*b*,*c*) have to be converted to (45) and (46).

(45) ženščina, kotoraja moloko raznosit, ne   prixodila ešče?
     Woman who   milk   delivers not came   yet?
(46) ženščina, kotoraja u   okna   ležala, kapriznaja očen'
     Woman who   at window lay   moody   very

The essential point is that (44*b*,*c*) must on no account be thought of as reduced versions of (45) and (46). Rather, the written examples have a very different clausal structure from the spoken ones. (45) and (46) consist of a main clause in which the subject NP contains a relative clause: *ženščina, kotoraja moloko raznosit* and *ženščina, kotoraja u okna ležala*. (44*b*,*c*) consist of two main clauses juxtaposed: *moloko raznosit* and *ne prixodila ešče* in (44*b*) and *u okna ležala* and *kapriznaja očen'* in (44*c*). From the perspective of English, one possibility that suggests itself is a headless relative construction. Could the Russian examples be equivalent to *Has who delivers the milk come yet?* and *Who was in the bed by the window was very moody*. The attraction of the English examples is that, in spite of their infelicitous syntax, they provide subject NPs for the main clauses. This attraction does not transfer to the Russian examples, principally because the Russian equivalents of English headless relatives involve either a general noun such as *čelovek* (person) followed by a relative clause, or a correlative construction: *I will live where you live*, with the headless relative *where you live*, corresponds to the Russian *Ja budu žit' tam, gde ty budes' žit'*, with a correlation between *tam* and *gde*. The Russian equivalent of *the one who* is *tot, kto* (that-one, who). In order to analyse (44*b,c*) as headless relatives we would have to postulate a process whereby the relative pronoun is deleted from the relative clause and the noun modified by the relative pronoun is also removed. This is a peculiar type of deletion not to be observed elsewhere in Russian syntax and objectionable on theoretical grounds— deletion causes major problems for generative models. Headless relatives must be excluded from consideration.

The analysis proposed above—that (44*b,c*) consist of two juxtaposed main clauses—is made possible by the frequent lack of subject NPs in spoken Russian. One of the striking features of Zemskaja's data is the frequency of zero subject NPs and zero direct object NPs, especially in conversation. Even in written Russian an entity introduced by an overt NP in one clause can be referred to by zero subject NPs over five or six clauses, and even across sentence boundaries.

It is clear that the speakers of (44*b*) and (44*c*) were referring to entities already mentioned or were treating the entities as highly given; in this context the absence of overt subject NPs is normal. For (44*b*) an appropriate gloss is *she delivers milk—has she come yet*, and for (44*c*)—*she was in bed by the window—she was/is very moody*. The occurrence of the feminine verb forms *prixodila* and *ležala* indicates that the speakers were referring to specific persons, women in both cases.

Should (44a) be handled differently from (44*b,c*)? After all, it differs from them in involving the absence of NP from a PP as opposed to a clause and in having a PP with no deictic items. In contrast, clauses contain finite verbs with personal (deictic) inflexions, and the occurrence of zero subject NPs in particular is frequent in Russian texts. Many analysts, including the writer, would answer affirmatively, but those analysts who believe that PPs have subject NPs would probably say that all three examples are instances of the same phenomenon. (As it happens, with respect to discourse they do not constitute quite the same phenomenon, because the omission of the NP modified by the PP is not controlled by principles of discourse coherence, whereas the omission of subject NPs from clauses is so controlled.) What is shared by the examples is that the speakers referred to entities, not by picking an appropriate lexical item but by picking a VP or PP denoting a property of the entity. In this respect they are equivalent to Nunberg's examples with *the ham sandwich*, where that NP is used to refer to the person eating the ham sandwich. Presumably a Nunbergian speaker would have said *the green balconies—is that your flat* and *the bed by the window was very moody*, but it is not obvious what would be the Nunberg equivalent of (44*b*).

2.5.5.2. Infinitive constructions with 'condensed relative pronouns'

Zemskaja does present examples that she analyses as containing 'condensed relative pronouns'. These examples contain clauses that are at least reminiscent of relative clauses and Zemskaja's term indicates that she views the construction much as analysts of English have viewed headless relatives. However, the constructions are not identical. Consider (47a–e).

(47) (a) u tebja net čem pisat'
    at you not with-which to-write
    'you have nothing to write with'
 (b) voz'mi na čem sidet'
    take on which to-sit
    'take something to sit on'
 (c) daj vo čto zavernut'
    give into which to-wrap
    'give me paper to wrap them in'
 (d) ona živet gde muzej
    she lives where museum
    'she lives where the museum is'
 (e) prixodi kogda saljut
    come when parade
    'come when the parade is taking place'

(47d,e) can be seen as correlative structures from which the first member of the correlation has been deleted: for (47d) read *ona živet tam, gde muzej* ('she lives there where museum') and for (47e)—*prixodi togda, kogda saljut* ('come then when parade'). Zemskaja seems to analyse these examples not as involving a deletion of *togda* ('then') or *tam* ('there') but as resulting from a coalescence of, for example, *tam* and *gde* ('where') into *gde*. What is clear is that both of these examples contain an item that occurs in a complete correlative structure, namely *gde* and *kogda*.

The other three examples are more complex. Consider (47a). What kind of structure is *čem pisat'* ('with-which to-write')? Let us note first that it is an unlikely candidate for a relative clause because, like *kto* (who), *čto—čem* is the instrumental case form—functions as a relative pronoun only in relative clauses modifying *tot, to*, etc.: cf. *To, čto ona skazala, ponravilos' vsem* ('that, which she said, pleased to-everyone') and *te, kto prišli, ne očen'- to pomagali* ('those, who came, not very-much helped'). *Tot* ('that one'), of course, can only be used to refer to specific given entities, and since (47a) does not relate to a specific writing instrument that interpretation is ruled out. On the other hand, *čto* ('what') and *kto* ('who') can be analysed as indefinite deictics, that is, as deictics used by speakers to point at entities that are non-specific for the listeners but may or may not be specific for the speakers—see the discussion in §2.5.1. When they are specific for the speaker, the latter can proceed to specify the entity for the listener. Cf. *Vot čto vam skažu: ja ne budu* . . . ('here what to-you I-will-say: I not will', i.e. 'Here's what I've got to say to you: I'm not going to . . .') or *Ona vot čto sdelala: zvonila včera i* . . . ('she here what did: phoned yesterday and', i.e. 'Here's what she did: she phoned yesterday and . . .').

Another complexity is the analysis of the infinitives. In formal written English examples occur such as *We bought a notebook in which to make notes about our travels*. The infinitive sequence in such examples can be analysed as a type of relative clause; indeed this example contains the relative pronoun (*in*) *which*. Spoken Russian does possess a construction in which an infinitive, to use Russian linguistic terminology, extends (*rasprostranjaet*) the noun it modifies. Examples are given in (48).

(48) (*a*) Pape   nado   kreslo sidet'
    to-Daddy necessary chair to sit
    'Daddy needs a chair to sit in'
  (*b*) Gde zdes' kassa   platit'
    where here cashdesk to-pay
    'Where's the cashdesk for you to pay for your purchases?'
  (*c*) Tebe   nužen   partner exat'?
    to-you necessary partner to-travel
    'Do you need someone to travel with?'

Zemskaja (1973: 265) suggests that in spoken Russian (48*b*) and (48*c*) have synonymous equivalents in *kassa čtoby platit'* ('cash-desk in-order-to pay') and *partner čtoby exat'* ('partner in-order-to travel'). As written Russian equivalents she proposes *kassa dlja oplaty* ('cash-desk for payment') and *partner dlja poezdki* ('partner for the-journey'). That is, the relationship between the infinitive and the noun it modifies seems closest to one of purpose. The purpose interpretation causes no problems with the intransitive verbs *sidet'* ('sit'), *platit'* ('pay'), and *exat'* ('travel') but is problematic with other examples containing transitive verbs, as in (49).

(49) (*a*) U vas novaja kleenka v kuxne   stelit'
    at you new   oilcloth in kitchen to-spread
    'have you a new oilcloth to spread on the kitchen table?'
  (*b*) U   tebja est' vaza na škaf   postavit'?
    at you is   vase on the-cupboard to-put
    'have you a vase to put on the cupboard?'

A straightforward rephrasing with *čtoby* ('in-order-to') is not possible—or at most is on the margins of acceptability—and only a relative clause structure is possible: *u nas novaja kleenka, kotoruju my budem stelit' v kuxne* ('at us new oilcloth which we will spread in (the) kitchen') and *U tebja est' vaza, kotoruju možno na škaf postavit'?* ('at you is (a) vase which (it is) possible on (the) cupboard to-place'). The fact that a relative clause version is possible does not justify us in treating the infinitive as a reduced relative clause construction. Given the general flexibility of inter-clause relations in spoken Russian (about which more in Chapter 3) a more appropriate treatment is to analyse the infinitive as denoting an event in which the entity denoted by the relevant noun is to be involved. The exact role of the entity is determined by a mixture of semantic and pragmatic information. For instance, oilcloths are typically spread on tables and vases are typically placed on suitable surfaces and have flowers put in them. Note that although the only acceptable syntactic paraphrase involves a relative clause, purpose and intention are present and can be inferred by the listener.

In (49a,b) the infinitives are modified by PPs, *v kuxne* ('in kitchen') and *na škaf* ('on wardrobe'). (47a–c) can be seen as parallel except that the modifier of the infinitive is the indefinite deictic. The other major difference is that the infinitive plus modifier sequence, *čem pisat'* ('with-which to-write'), *na čem sidet'* ('on which to-sit'), *vo čto zavernut'* ('into which to-wrap') function as non-specific referring expressions. Zemskaja's analysis in terms of a condensed relative pronoun does not appear helpful or defensible, but an analysis as infinitive phrases does. They can be seen as pragmatically parallel to (44a) in that they are used to refer to a property of an entity. The infinitive phrases in (47a–c) differ from the extending infinitives in (48) and (49) in bearing a grammatical function relating to the finite verb. In (47b) *na čem sidet'* is the direct object of *voz'mi* ('take') and in (47c) *vo čto zavernut'* is the direct object of *daj* ('give'). The appropriate responses to the questions *Voz'mi čito* ('take what?') and *daj čto* ('give what') are (allowing for ellipsis) *na čem sidet'* ('on what to-sit') and *vo čto zavernut'* ('into which to-wrap'). In (47a) *čem pisat'* is the complement—or direct object, depending on the analysis—of *net*. (50a,b) show the infinitive phrases as subject and oblique object, respectively.

(50) (a) čem   pisat'   na stole
        with-which to-write (is) on the-table
        'there's something to write with on the table'
    (b) pozabot'sja   čem   pisat'
        take-trouble (about) with-which to-write
        'make sure you've got something to write with'

Note that in (50a) *čem* gets its instrumental case from *pisat'* and the clause/phrase *čem pisat'* is self-contained in that its subject function is not signalled. *Pozabot'sja* normally takes the preposition *o* governing a noun in the prepositional case, but in (50b) there is no marking signalling the relationship of *čem pisat'* to *pozabot'sja*.

2.5.5.3. Finite constructions with 'condensed relative pronouns'

We have seen that infinitive sequences containing indefinite deictics can occur as subjects, direct objects and indirect/oblique objects. Finite clauses containing indefinite deictics also occur as direct objects, as in (51) and as indirect/oblique objects as in (52).

(51) daj   mne   na čem   ty   gladila
    give to-me on what you   were-ironing
    'give me what you were ironing on'

(52) (a) vy   spravku daete tol'ko kto ležit
        you   give   note only   who is-lying
        'you give a certificate only to someone who is ill'
    (b) kto   vyigral dadut   priz
        who   won   they-will-give (a) prize
        'to the person who wins they will give a prize'
    (c) kto zapisalsja včera/sejčas   bilety   davat' budut
        who subscribed yesterday/now tickets   give   they-will
        'to people who subscribed yesterday they will now give tickets'

Na čem ty gladila in (51) is the direct object of *daj* and in (52a) *kto ležit* is the indirect/oblique object of *daete*. In (52b,c) *kto vyigral* and *kto zapisalsja* could be analysed as the indirect/oblique object. Another possibility is that these are theme NPs standing outside the rest of the clause and that *dadut* and *davat' budut* simply lack an indirect/oblique object. Note that, although it normally assigns dative case to its indirect object, the finite verb in (52a–c) does not assign dative case to *kto*. (*Kto* is the nominative form.) This might be taken as indicating the need to postulate an ellipted *tomu*, given the typical valency of DAT', but another analysis would see the nominative case of *kto* as justified not only by its relation to *ležit*, *vyigral*, and *zapisalsja* but also by the widespread phenomenon of nouns occurring in the nominative case where we would expect an oblique case. (Such constructions have been described by Lapteva 1976). These examples are but another illustration of how difficult it can be to propose a single well-motivated analysis for spontaneous spoken data.

The nominal nature of the finite clauses with indefinite deictics is further demonstrated by the fact that they can be coordinated with ordinary phrases. (A central fact of syntax is that typically only constituents of the same type can be coordinated.) Cf. (53).

(53) ne   zabud' mylo i   čem   vytirat'sja
    not forget soap and with-which to-dry-self
    'don't forget soap and something dry to yourself with'

They can occur as subject, as in (54).

(54) (a) kto u vas živet/ včera   k nam zaxodila
         who at you lives/ yesterday to us   called on
         'the person who is living at your flat called on us yesterday'
    (b) kto tebe cvety   prinosit/ opjat' pod oknami xodil
         who to-you flowers brings/ again under windows was-walking
         'the person who brings you flowers was walking up and down underneath the windows of the flat again'

Note that although *kto* itself is neutral with respect to gender the verb in the main clause has to be feminine or masculine depending on the entity referred to.

The sequences can occur as the complement of EST' or NUŽNO, as in (55).

(55) (a) est' kuda   cvety   postavit'?
         is whither flowers to-put
         'Is there something to put the flowers in?'
    (b) u nego ne bylo čto   podstelit'
         at him not was what to-put-under
         'he had nothing to put under it'
    (c) emu nužno   čem   zavjazat'
         to-him necessary with-which to-tie
         'he needs something to tie it with'
    (d) tebe nado   vo čto zavernut'
         to-you necessary into what to-wrap
         'you need something to wrap it in'

est' in (55a) and *nužno* in (55c) normally take subject nouns in the nominative case. The negative existential construction in (55b) normally requires a complement noun in the genitive case, as in *u nego ne bylo deneg* ('at him not was money'), where *deneg* is the genitive form of DEN'GI ('money'). In the construction in (55d) *nado* would normally govern a complement noun in the accusative case. Instead of a noun in the typical case, (55a,d) have prepositional phrases, (55b) has a 'headless relative' containing *čto*, which probably has to be described as being in the accusative, since it is in the direct object of *podstelit'*, and (55c) has a 'headless relative' with *čem*, which is in the instrumental case and is the oblique object of *zavjazat'*.

The sequences can occur as the oblique object. In (56) *čto svarju* can only be replaced by a noun in the instrumental case.

(56) kormimsja čto   svarju
    let's-eat what I-will-make
    'Let's have what I'm going to make'

The sequences are never preceded by prepositions, as exemplified in (57). The fact that they cannot be governed by prepositions and cannot be assigned case by the verb in the main clause can be interpreted as indicating that the syntactic connection between the *čto* clause and the finite verb in the main clause is loose.

(57) (*a*) eto zavisit ne ot studentov/ a kto stroit zdanie
that depends not from students/ but who builds building
'that depends not on the students but on who is doing the building'
(*b*) eto zavisit kogda brosiš' kurit'
that depends when you-will-give-up smoking
'that depends on when you give up smoking'

In written Russian (57*a,b*) would be recast thus: *eto zavisit . . . ot togo, kto stroit zdanie* ('that depends . . . on that-one who builds (the) building') and *eto zavisit ot togo, kogda brosiš' kurit'* ('that depends on that when you-give-up smoking'). It is tempting to see the spoken examples as reduced versions of the written examples, but another view is that the written construction is an elaborated version of the spoken one. The latter view is consonant with the generally looser syntactic organization of spoken language and the tighter organization of written language, and is further supported by the fact that the ellipting of *ot togo* is not part of a general principled process of ellipsis in Russian.

A clause containing an indefinite deictic can have a noun phrase in apposition, the connection between the clause and the NP being called by Zemskaja 'svjaz' sopodčinenija'. Examples are given in (58).

(58) (*a*) kupi čem zapisyvat'/ ručku šarikovuju
buy with-which to-take-notes/ (a) pen ballpoint
'buy something to take notes with—a ballpoint pen'
(*b*) u nas est' vo čto smotret'/ apparatik takoj
at you is into what to-look/ (an) instrument such
'you've got a thing for looking into, some kind of instrument'
(*c*) daj čem vyteret'sja/ nosovoj platok ili trjapočku čisten'kuju
give with-which to-dry-self / nose cloth or cloth clean
'give me something to dry myself with, a handkerchief or a piece of clean cloth'

The significance of (58) is that normally noun phrases are in apposition to other noun phrases. Zemskaja does not have much to say about constituent structure but we can at the very least treat *čem zapisyvat'*, *vo čto smotret'* and *čem vyteret'sja* as nominal, since they carry grammatical functions—respectively, direct object of *kupi*, subject of *est'*, and direct object of *daj*. The nouns they are in apposition to are in the appropriate case, the accusative: *ručku, apparatik,* and *trjapočku*. The evidence of the NPs in apposition, together with the other evidence, leads us to analyse these clauses as the sole constituents of NPs.

Interestingly, NPs can have clauses in apposition to them containing indefinite deictics, although the examples given by Zemskaja contain only *kak* and *gde*, as in (59). Zemskaja observes that the clause in apposition contains a verb from the same root as a preceding noun but is merely a paraphrase of the noun, bringing no new information.

(59) (*a*) posmotrite na ee povedenie/ kak ona vedet sebja
 look at her behaviour/ how she behaves herself
 (*b*) posledi za ego progulkami/ gde on guljaet
 follow behind his walks/ where he walks
 (*c*) imenno ispolnenie/ kak on ispolnjaet/ mne očen' nravitsja
 namely playing/ how he plays/ to me much pleases,
 'it's his playing, how he plays, that I really like'

The clauses with indefinite deictics can function as vocatives, as in (60).

(60) (*a*) kto pal'to snjal/ proxodite v zal
 who coat has-removed/ go-through into room
 'Those who have taken their coats off, go through into the room'
 (*b*) komu vyxodit'/ ne tolpites' v proxode
 to-whom to-go-out/ not crowd in corridor
 'those who have to go out, do not crowd the corridor'

As in the previous examples, the clauses are self-contained, *kto* and *komu* being assigned nominative and dative case, respectively, by the verb in the clause. English offers parallel examples: *whoever has got their coat off, go through into the room* and *whoever has to go out, don't push and shove*.

Finally in this section we look at examples in which nouns are modified by indefinite deictic clauses and by indefinite deictic infinitives. Consider (61).

(61) (*a*) a u vas est' apparatik (vo čto smotret')
 and at you is instrument (in what to look)
 'Have you got an instrument, something to look into?'
 (*b*) ja ne znaju dorogu (kak exat')
 I not know road (how to-go)
 'I don't know the road (how to get there)'
 (*c*) A kto u vas delaet dekoracii?
 who at you does decoration?
 'Who does your decorating?'
 B dekorator/ kto xorošo risuet
 decorator/ who well paints
 'a decorator, someone who paints well'

The indefinite deictic clauses and phrases in (61) would in written Russian be replaced by relative clauses: say, *v kotoryj možno smotret'* ('in which is-possible to-look') in (61*a*), *po kotoroj nado exat'* ('along which is-necessary to-go') in (61*b*) and *kotoryj xorošo risuet* ('who paints well') in (61*c*). The clauses and phrases in the spoken examples cannot be handled as relative clauses because *čto* and *kto* do not function as relative pronouns except in the combinations *tot, kto,* and *to, čto*. Rather they modify the nouns *apparatik, dorogu,* and *dekorator* but are not integrated with them into a noun phrase.

2.6. Conclusion

The central argument of this chapter has been that there is practically no evidence to support the use of text-sentences and system-sentences in the analysis of spontaneous spoken language. In contrast, text- and system-sentences are indisputable units in written language. There is a large body of evidence, of which only samples have been given, to support the idea that text- and system-sentences are low-level discourse units relating to the organization of clauses into larger texts. These units are culture-dependent; what counts as an acceptable sentence varies across different cultures and across time within one culture. Planned or semi-planned spoken language is different, but typically is heavily influenced by the units and organization of written language.

The sentence being inapplicable in the analysis of spontaneous spoken language is part of a larger phenomenon, the general unintegrated nature of the syntax of spontaneous speech. Zemskaja provides many instances of syntactic structures from speech which do not occur in writing and cannot be tidied up by being derived from constructions that do occur in writing. Sornicola argues strongly that any such analytical moves could only be interpreted as gross disrespect for the data. She provides examples of spontaneous speech in which the syntax can only be analysed as a succession of phrases, not as clauses. Chapter 1 closed with a passage from Heath (1985) on the danger of assuming that the syntactic structures of spontaneous speech are deep down the highly organized structures of written language which come to the surface distorted by the stresses of on-line, instant, unplanned communication. This chapter has spelt out some of the implications of taking seriously the view that spontaneous speech is organized round unintegrated syntactic structures. Chapter 3 will explore in some detail the notion of clause complexes and the lack of integration in the organization of clauses into larger groupings and it will be shown that Heath's concise wording conceals rather large implications for the study of syntax.

3 Clauses: Type, Combination, and Integration

3.1. Introduction

In Chapter 2 it was argued that the sentence be abandoned as a unit of analysis for spontaneous spoken language and that Halliday's notion of clause complex be applied instead. We now turn to units smaller than the sentence—the clause and the phrase. The clause is the topic of this chapter while Chapter 4 deals with noun phrases. The discussion of clauses includes infinitives and gerunds, traditionally treated as phrases but now generally regarded as non-finite clauses. This chapter will present a large amount of data from English and Russian in order to demonstrate three general points. Two relate to the constructions of spontaneous spoken language: (1) clause constructions occur in spoken language which are excluded from written language, and many clause constructions which are typical of writing are quite untypical of spontaneous speech; (2) clauses combine and interconnect differently in spontaneous spoken language and in written language. The third point is that similar (but not completely identical) constructions occur in spontaneous speech across languages. This point is important because it makes it more difficult to dismiss the structures of spontaneous speech as mere performance errors.

The data is drawn from the bodies of spoken English described in Chapter 1. Supporting data comes from Russian, French, and German. Examples of subordinate clauses in Australian Aboriginal languages will be examined in order to see what phenomena are presented by languages which are both oral and very different in grammatical structure from what Whorf called 'Standard Average European'.

The language we are most conscious of is written language, simply because, being relatively permanent, it can be scrutinized, edited, and pored over in the search for possible interpretations. The writer typically has time to consider choice of words, the best way of combining clauses into sentences, and the best way of spreading information over paragraphs, sections, and chapters. A major task of schools is to teach pupils to produce well-organized prose employing a wide range of vocabulary and syntactic structures in which clauses are elegantly combined into sentences. Spontaneous spoken language is not the concern of schools nor indeed of most university departments of Linguistics. Consequently the student's first brush with the syntax of spontaneous spoken language typically induces surprise followed by a refusal to accept that the syntax follows patterns and that the patterns are regular and frequent.

That the patterns are regular can be demonstrated from any corpus of spontaneous spoken language, as can the type of pattern. We argue here that similar patterns are to be found in bodies of spontaneous speech from different languages. Why are the patterns surprising at first sight? One salient property is that constructions quite typical of written language are missing from spontaneous speech. These include certain kinds of adverbial clause, full gerunds (*their being unaware of the situation*), free participial phrases (§3.4.2.3), certain relative clause constructions (§3.7.1), and a number of others. (See §3.4.) Some constructions do occur in both writing and spontaneous speech but with a different distribution. For instance, complement clauses such as *that they had left* occur as direct objects but not as subjects. Thus *I knew that they had left*—rather, *I knew they had left*, without the complementizer *that*—is unexceptional in speech, whereas the analyst will be hard put to find instances of examples in which the complement clause is subject, as in *That they had left was very surprising*.

A second salient property is the degree to which clauses are integrated into clause complexes. Consider the following utterance produced by a colleague of Jim Miller's during a discussion about the installation of a ventilator fan in a computer room: *OK we install it there's no guarantee it'll work*. There are three clauses, each recognizable by its finite verb: *we install it*, *there's no guarantee*, and *it'll work*. The last clause is the complement of *guarantee* but is not connected to it by a complementizer. A formal written version would be *There is no guarantee that it will work*. More interestingly, the first clause, *we install it*, bears a relationship to the second clause. This relationship belongs to the set of what are called rhetorical relations (see Mann and Thompson 1987 and Matthiessen and Thompson 1988). In this case the first clause is equivalent to *suppose we install it*, and in uttering it the speaker is both making a concession and laying down a condition. His concession is to accept as possible a proposal to install a new ventilator fan and the condition is that even with the new fan installed there is no guarantee that the system will run successfully.

The interpretation of the spoken text involves (at least) an inference that the event described by *we install it* precedes the situation described by *there's no guarantee it'll work*. This inference is partly sanctioned by the knowledge that the proposed new fan is not yet in place and partly by the regular pattern whereby, given a clause x directly followed by clause y, the situation described by clause x precedes in time the situation described by clause y. The formal written version of this text would run thus: *Even if we install it, there is no guarantee that it will work.* The concession and the condition are signalled by *even if*. The Russian data reported in §3.5 exemplify a number of different adverbial clauses that merely follow the main clause without any overt linking.

The syntactic integration of two clauses may be achieved by one clause being reduced. In the English WH cleft construction exemplified by *What they do is ignore minor crimes* two clauses are linked by *is*. One is the free relative clause *what they do*, which contains the finite verb *do* and the grammatical subject *they*. The other is a reduced clause *ignore minor crimes*, in which the verb *ignore* has no tense and which lacks a grammatical subject. The lack of tense and a grammatical subject signal the downgrading of the clause and confirm its integration into the construction as the complement of *is*. As we will see in §3.7.2, WH clefts in spontaneous spoken English typically do not evince the reduction and downgrading of the second clause but consist of two complete clauses which may or may not be linked by BE. In, for example, *what they do they ignore minor crimes* they are not linked, but in *what they do is they ignore minor crimes*, they are. Almost all the WH clefts in the Map Task dialogues and the spontaneous conversations are unintegrated.

The third construction, or set of constructions, that will be examined in some detail is the relative clause. In written English the pattern is that the complementizer in relative clauses, whether a WH word or *that*, can be and is omitted when the noun modified by the relative clause has the same reference as the direct or oblique object in the relative clause. Thus, *the book I read* vs. *the book that/which I read*; *the book* has the same reference as the missing direct object of *read*. The close linkage of the relative clause and the matrix clause is shown by the lack of complementizer and the missing noun phrase. Where the noun modified by the relative clause has the same reference as the subject noun phrase in the relative clause, the complementizer is not omitted, as in *I told you about the book that/which surprised me*. Without *that* or *which* the example is incorrect (at least in standard English): **I told you about the book surprised me*. In contrast with written English, the complementizer is typically omitted when the relative clause is inside an existential construction: *There was a student came looking for you* and *I had a student knew several languages*. These examples are correct and typical although the reference of the noun, *student*, modified by the relative clause is identical with the reference of the (missing) subject of the relative clause.

The above examples of relative clauses have simple syntax, but relative clauses may have quite complex syntax. In *the guy that I thought he was going to attack us* the relative clause consists of the clause *I thought* with another clause complementing *thought*: *he was going to attack us*. The complementizer *that* could be omitted, but the salient property of the relative clause is that the grammatical subject is not omitted but is present in the form of the pronoun *he*. In written English we would find (making appropriate changes of vocabulary) *the man who I thought was going to attack us*. The linkage between the relative clause and the modified noun can be even looser, to the extent that there is no noun in the relative clause with the same reference as the modified noun. For example, in *a filing cabinet that you can only open one drawer at a time* there is no noun inside the relative clause that refers to the filing cabinet.

The lack of integration applies to Noun Phrases, not in English but certainly in Russian and Australian Aboriginal languages. In Russian a determiner and a noun, say, may not be adjacent. In *v etom v dome* (in this in house) the determiner *etom* agrees in gender, number, and case with *dome* but is separated from it by the second occurrence of the preposition *v* 'in'. The occurrence of two prepositions makes sense if the syntactic structure is such that it can be glossed as 'in this one—in house', with two Noun Phrases, *this one* and *house*. In *kakie u vas v biblioteke knigi* (what at-you in the-library books), i.e. 'what books do you have in your library?', the WH determiner *kakie* is right at the front of the clause and the noun it agrees with in number and case, *knigi*, is right at the end. This structure can be glossed as 'what-ones at you in the-library books', in which *what ones* and *books* constitute two Noun Phrases. Such an analysis in terms of separate Noun Phrases is not the only possible one; it is possible to think of *kakie* and *knigi* as starting out together as one Noun Phrase in an early stage of a derivation (say in some transformational framework) but being split up by a rule that moves *knigi* to final position in the clause. The data and the analyses will be discussed in detail in Chapter 4.

The lay-out of the chapter is as follows. §3.2 offers a discussion of what clauses are and the semantic interpretation of clauses. An important point, arising out of Chafe's work, is that the syntax of spontaneous spoken language reflects the limited capacity of short-term memory. Complex structures require more processing than simple structures and highly integrated clauses require more unpacking than clauses that are integrated either loosely or not at all. §3.4 examines the distinction between main and subordinate clauses and in particular the types of subordinate clause that are typically not found in spontaneous speech. §§3.5–3.7 examine constructions that are found in spontaneous speech but typically not in writing. It is in this part of the chapter that the integration of clauses is explored.

The major results that will emerge are as follows.

i There are types of clause (finite and non-finite) that occur regularly in formal written language but are absent from our spontaneous spoken data.

76 *Spontaneous Spoken Language*

ii The linking of clauses is much looser in our spontaneous spoken English data than in formal written language. This looseness is manifested in two major ways: speakers may produce a series of main clauses involved in relationships that would be expressed in formal written language by subordinate clauses with appropriate subordinating conjunctions; speakers may produce sequences that look like subordinate clauses but which are free-standing and/or differ from genuine subordinate clauses in word order.

iii Some constructions, particularly relative clause constructions, are very different from their counterparts in written language.

iv Noun Phrases are much simpler in our spontaneous spoken data than in written language, a finding which applies to English, German, and Russian. For Russian the question arises as to whether nouns, determiners, and adjectives are always to be analysed as combining into Noun Phrases. (See Chapter 4 for details.)

v The linking of clauses is on occasion even more tenuous in spontaneous spoken Russian than in spoken English. One regular feature of Russian clause complexes is the occurrence of zero NPs, which are far more frequent in Russian than in English. This connects with a discourse property that will be treated in detail in the chapter on discourse.

vi Syntactic structures that are typical of languages that have no written variety are similar in crucial respects to structures that occur in the spontaneous spoken variety of languages that are both written and spoken.

3.2. Clauses

3.2.1. *Definition of clause*

We come to a crucial question: what is a clause? One answer, which comes out of the discussion of sentences in Chapter 2, is that the clause is the unit that is required in order to handle distributional regularities in a given language. (This is adapted from the definition of 'sentence' in Lyon (1968).) This definition is applicable to written language and much spoken language but it does not explain why the notion of clause can be applied across a large number of languages of very different grammatical structure. Chafe (1988: 3) declares that a clause is a segment of language that consists of a subject and predicate. That is, speakers indicate by way of the subject some entity—person, thing, event, state, abstraction—which is their starting point and add information about that entity, the added information typically being the concept of some event or state. This definition is employed by Lehmann (1988: 182), who treats the clause as a syntagm with a single predication. Halliday (1985) treats the clause as the unit of syntax that is relevant for the analysis of situations and their participants, for the analysis of information structure (subject-predicate, given-new, focus), and for the analysis of linguistic interaction, which he calls 'exchange'; that is, the analysis of the syntactic constructions by means of which speakers can make statements, ask questions, and issue mands (to use the terminology of Lyons 1977). Foley and van Valin (1984: 187ff.) treat clauses as units that have a nucleus corresponding to an event, process, or state, a core corresponding to the principal participants in that event, process, or state, and a periphery corresponding to locations, settings, preceding events, and so on. The nucleus and core are semantically obligatory components and the corresponding syntactic constituents are obligatory.

Following Foley and van Valin (1984) and Lehmann (1988), we take a clause to be a syntactic structure that relates to one state or event and has a nucleus and core (some elements in the core being optional or obligatory depending on the nuclear predicate) and an optional periphery. For example, in *The car crashed into the barrier* the nucleus is *crashed*, signalling that the clause concerns an event of crashing. The major participants are the entities referred to by *the car* and *the barrier*, but the latter noun phrase is optional with this particular verb. Adverbs such as *yesterday morning during the rush hour* can be added to the clause but would belong to its periphery.

The syntactic structure conveys a predication about an entity and is the locus of the densest network of distributional and dependency relationships. (See the discussion of clause and sentence in §2.5.) The entity may be a person, place, thing, abstract idea, or a whole situation. It will be convenient, following Sasse (1987), to recognize a class of thetic clauses which do not express a predication about an entity but state the existence of an entity. For instance, in the example *there was a westerly gale blowing and rain thumping down in sheets*, it is difficult to say exactly what entity is presented as the subject or topic and what might be the predication made of that entity. Rather, the construction introduces an entire situation, and the speaker/writer can go on to pick out entities in that situation and predicate properties of them.

What the foregoing amounts to is that a working definition of clause involves reference to semantic and pragmatic concepts (participants, situations, locations, times, reference, predication, focus, given-new) and to syntactic concepts (distribution of phrases, obligatory and optional constituents). The definition is complex because the clause is a complex concept and is put to work in complex areas of language; it does have the advantage that it is applicable across languages without its application in, say, the Fore language of Papua New Guinea being completely unrelated to its application in, say, Turkish.

78 *Spontaneous Spoken Language*

3.2.2. *Clauses and situations*

Speakers use different clauses to talk about situations that are in sequence or overlap, that are applied to a particular entity, or that function as the argument of a predicate denoting a situation. Consider (1*a*–*d*).

(1) (*a*) When Sheila came home she phoned her son
    (*b*) As he cleared up the broken glass, Torquil worked out a plan of action
    (*c*) Shonaid realized that the sheep had escaped from the pen
    (*d*) Ruaridh shot the stag that was eating the crops

In (1*a*) the event of Sheila coming home precedes the event of Sheila phoning her son; in (1*b*) the event of Torquil clearing up the broken glass is concurrent with the event of Torquil working out a plan of action; in (1*c*) the event of the sheep escaping from the pen is an argument of *realized*, or the clause referring to that event is an argument; in (1*d*) the event of the stag eating the crops, or being involved in that event, is a property of the stag shot by Ruaridh. Events can be described by a series of main clauses: *Shonaid realized—The sheep had escaped from the pen, Ruaridh shot the stag—It was eating the crops*. Events can also be described by more intricate arrangements of clauses whereby one event is chosen as central and the other events are presented as less important. The central event is described by means of a main clause and the events presented as less important are described by means of subordinate clauses: adverbial clauses, as in (1*a*,*b*)— *When Sheila came home, As he cleared up the broken glass*, complement clauses (1*c*)—*that the sheep had escaped from the pen*, and relative clauses (1*d*)—*that was eating the crops*. Events presented as less important can be conveyed by reduced pieces of syntax that are more restricted than the subordinate clauses listed above. They may lack grammatical categories such as tense and mood and constituents such as the subject NP, and they may be more like NPs than predicate expressions with a finite verb.

As observed in the introduction to this chapter, the intricate arrangements of clauses mentioned above are typical of written language, whereas spontaneous spoken language favours a looser arrangement of clauses. This looser arrangement affects relative and adverbial clauses more than complement clauses. In conversation and dialogue it allows main and subordinate clauses to be produced in different turns by the same speaker or by different speakers. In narratives what look like main and subordinate clauses may be separated by long pauses or by other syntactic material. Constructions which are typically highly integrated in written language—as indicated by an ellipted subject or object NP, say—may be less integrated in spoken language. The lack of integration is usually reflected in the juxtaposition of two complete clauses as opposed to the reduction of one clause which is made part of the other. Numerous examples will be given, particularly in §3.7 on WH structures.

3.3. Constraints on Complexity in Spontaneous Spoken Language

Chafe (1987) sums up many years of work with spoken language. His basic working assumption is that people's minds contain very large amounts of knowledge or information, but can focus on, or make active, only a very small amount of this information at any one time. Accepting the hypothesis that the active portion of our knowledge resides in short-term memory, he points to George Miller's theory that short-term memory can hold only seven plus or minus two items. Chafe connects the hypothesis about the capacity to handle information with Halliday's theory that the content of clauses is organized into information units, that speakers choose how to organize the information, and that their choices are reflected in their intonation.

According to Halliday (Halliday 1985: ch. 8), information units are realized as tone groups, which in turn consist of one or more feet. A foot begins with a stressed syllable followed by one or more unstressed syllables. A tone group contains one tonic syllable, that is a syllable that is the site of maximal pitch movement, maximal pitch height, and maximal intensity. The tonic marks the focus of new information and, other things being equal, falls on the stressed syllable of the last major lexical item in the tone group—this is the unmarked focus of information. The tonic may fall elsewhere, signalling a marked focus of information. Halliday correlates the information units directly with tone groups: tone groups may or may not coincide with syntactic groupings—but tone groups typically coincide with clauses.

Chafe incorporates processing constraints into Halliday's theory. He points to the fact that spontaneous spoken language is produced in relatively brief spurts, which he proposes to call intonation units. (Chafe and Danielewicz 1987: 95–7). When speakers speak they verbalize one piece of temporarily active information after another, each such piece being expressed in an intonation unit. Chafe asserts that the prototypical intonation unit is a sequence of words combined under a single, coherent intonation contour, usually preceded by a pause. An intonation unit in English typically contains about five or six words, and new intonation units typically begin about two seconds apart. Chafe takes the latter as indicating that active information is replaced by other, partially different information at approximately two second intervals.

Although the following caveat does not affect the hypothesis that speakers activate and grammatically encode information in small quantities, it must be said that not all researchers have found it straightforward to apply the concept of tone groups to spontaneous spoken language. G. Brown, Currie, and Kenworthy (1980: 138 ff.) discuss the difficulty of recognizing tonic syllables, not just the difficulty that they themselves experienced, but the problems encountered by experienced phonetician-colleagues in assigning tonics under experimental conditions. They propose the use of pause as an indicator of syntactic boundaries. G. Brown and Yule (1983: 159–64) present a revised version of the analysis that recognizes three lengths of pause instrumentally determined. These difficulties with tonics and pauses do not affect the thrust of Chafe's argument, namely that speakers can deal with only a small amount of active information at a time. Indeed, they reinforce Chafe's argument, because the syntactic units that correlate with chunks of activated information are both clauses and phrases—but no unit bigger than the clause. It may well be that most speakers of a given language get by in spontaneous speech with phrases. G. Brown et al. (1984: 17–18) state that 'the spoken language produced by the majority of young people, as indeed by the majority of the population, consists of relatively simple sentence structures—often just phrases and incomplete sentences, strung together'.

3.4. Main and Subordinate Clauses

The incidence of main and subordinate clauses in spoken and written language has excited the interest of various scholars, particularly those concerned with education and the acquisition of literacy. In the light of what we know about the learning of written language in school and about the written output of pupils both in primary and secondary schools (see Perera 1984 and Rosen and Rosen 1973), it is reasonable to suppose that spontaneous spoken language contains fewer subordinate clauses than written language; at least, one perennial classroom task is to persuade children to combine sequences of main clauses into sentences by making some of the main clauses subordinate. Interestingly, this supposition is not unanimously supported by past studies, although the lack of support can be related to the types of data gathered and analysed by researchers. Beaman (1984: 76–91) suggests that in some analyses modality (spoken vs. written) has been confounded with register (degree of formality). The discrepancies in results are neatly exemplified in Poole and Field (1976) and Kroll (1977). The former found that spoken discourse had significantly more subordination, elaboration or syntactic structure, and use of adverbs. The latter found that written narratives contained more subordinate constructions than spoken ones, 35% vs. 14%, but that the converse held for coordinate constructions, 25% in written and 40% in spoken narratives.

Halliday (1989: 76–91) proposes the subtler view that written and spoken language are both complex but in their own ways. Written language is complex in that highly compact but simple syntactic constructions are loaded with many lexical items. Spoken language is complex in having intricate syntactic structure with a considerable proportion of subordinate clauses, but with lexical items spread thinly over clauses, whereby the lexical density of each clause is reduced. Let us briefly say at this point—repeating Chapter 1.3—that the properties of a body of spoken language are determined by the speakers and what they are doing. Narration is different from conversation and task-related dialogues because the narrator has the floor, does not have to manage turn-taking or adjust to contributions from other speakers, and has more planning time. In narration or conversation speakers with more formal education, particularly higher education, produce spoken language that is influenced by their exposure to written language. Narration or conversation in formal circumstances may be supposed to produce more complex language than narration or conversation in informal circumstances, say in the speaker's home or over an informal meal such as beer and pizza (one that does not involve complex dishes or layers of mysterious cutlery and is eaten in the kitchen). Finally, even in formal circumstances the simultaneous performance of a task and production of speech reduces the planning time available for language.

Our databases contain spontaneous spoken language collected in circumstances favouring the production of unforced language. The Map Task dialogues left the participants little time or energy for language production and the free conversation was collected under circumstances (described in Chapter 1) that the participants found congenial and relaxing. The syntax of the data differs significantly from the syntax of written English (especially, but not exclusively, formal written English). We will begin by examining various constructions, many of them subordinate clause constructions, that are missing from the data. Thereafter we will look at the proportions of main and subordinate clauses in our data and in other bodies of data.

3.4.1. *Finite constructions missing from the corpus of spoken language*

3.4.1.1. *Missing subordinate clauses*

There are no adverbial clauses of concession introduced by *although* and no adverbial clauses of reason introduced by *since* or *as*. Speakers use concession clauses in order to concede one point while asserting another. Thus in *although one or two people seem to annoy him, he's usually quite even-tempered*, the speaker concedes that the person concerned has been known to be annoyed, none the less he usually does not become annoyed. The order of the clauses can be reversed so that the speaker makes the positive assertion first and adds the negative point as a concession at the end of the utterance—*he's usually quite even-tempered, although one or two people seem to annoy him*. Concessions are made in our spontaneous spoken data by means of *but* or clause-final *though*. The above example would be phrased as in (2).

(2) (*a*) he's usually quite even tempered but one or two people seem to annoy him
    (*b*) he's usually quite even tempered one or two people seem to annoy him though

The absence of adverbial clauses of reason introduced by *since* and *as* is unexpected; the adverbial clauses of reason that turn up are all introduced by *because* or *cos*.

3.4.1.2. Gapping

There are no examples of gapping in the data. Typical of written English are examples such as (3*a,b*)

(3) (*a*) Sue likes, and Bill hates, crosswords
    (*b*) Celia likes Van Gogh, and Bill—Rembrandt

The analysis of these examples has exercised many generative linguists, and quite rightly, since the structure occurs regularly in formal written English. In (3*a*) the problem is that *likes* and *hates* have the same direct object, *crosswords*, but the latter NP does not seem to belong to either of the clauses *Sue like* or *Bill hates*. If (3*a*) were spoken, most likely in the reading aloud of a written text, *Sue likes* would be followed by a pause; then would come the sequence *and Bill hates*, followed by another pause. Finally the speaker would utter the word *crosswords*. In addition to the pauses, there would be separate intonation envelopes over the three sequences *Sue likes*, *and Bill hates*, and *crosswords*. The difficulty posed by (3*b*) stems not so much from the constituent structure—the verb is ellipted from the second clause *Bill likes Rembrandt*—as from the question of what constraints affect the constituents left behind in the second clause. For example, how acceptable is *Celia put the dog in the kitchen and Bill—the cat in the porch*?

These questions are bypassed both in our spoken data, and indeed in general in spontaneous spoken English; speakers use the constructions in (4*a,b*).

(4) (*a*) Sue likes crosswords and Bill hates them
    (*b*) Celia likes Van Gogh and Bill likes Rembrandt

3.4.1.3. Indirect questions

The indirect question construction is exemplified in (5*a,b*), while (5*c*) is an example of an indirect statement. Both types fall into the more general class of indirect speech constructions.

(5) (a) This is not just a case of whether the two words can combine
    (b) She asked if she could help
    (c) He shouted that he would be down in a couple of minutes

The key properties of indirect speech are these. Instances of someone's direct speech or the contents of a written or spoken message—statement, question, or command—are reported by means of a construction containing a verb of saying or asking followed by a complement clause. A direct statement keeps its word order but changes the tense of the verb from present to past and the person of pronouns from first or second to third. A direct question acquires the word order of declarative clauses and may also acquire a complementizer that was not in the original question. For example, the direct question corresponding to (5b) is *Can I help?* and the question lying behind (5a) is *Can the two words combine?* The statement corresponding to (5c) is *I'll be down in a couple of minutes*.

The indirect speech constructions are required in formal written English but many users have difficulty meeting the requirement. One reason for this is that the classic indirect speech constructions occur very infrequently in spontaneous spoken English. (6) is an example of the classic construction. The speaker is a woman in her mid-twenties.

(6) he said that they didn't even send white policemen down there and he wasn't going to take me

(7) is an example of the typical spontaneous spoken construction in which the speaker purports to reproduce the original's speaker's words. This means that the verb does not change to past tense nor the pronouns to third person. Moreover, the speaker typically changes pitch and/or voice quality to signal where the reported speech begins and ends. The speaker in (7) is an 18-year-old schoolgirl.

(7) Brenda passed the message over to me when I kick you knock the cup into Andrew's face

Speakers produce examples of a mixed construction in which they use, for example, *X said* and/or transpose first into third person, but, that apart, purport to reproduce X's exact words. Cf. (8).

(8) they said if they get us there again they're going to wrap the air-rifle round my neck

A subset of 14 conversations was examined for instances of direct and indirect speech. There are 22 instances of the direct speech construction exemplified in (7), 3 instances of the indirect speech construction exemplified in (6), and 1 instance of the mixed construction exemplified in (8). The indirect speech examples include *we thought he was going away*, which could have been expressed as *we thought—'he's going away'*. Two of the three indirect speech examples are produced by an older speaker, the woman in her mid-twenties from whose narrative (6) has been taken.

3.4.1.4. *Conditional constructions*

Conditional constructions consist of a protasis and an apodosis. The protasis typically consists of a clause introduced by *if* which lays down a condition. The apodosis typically consists of a declarative clause, but may consist of an interrogative clause or an imperative clause. It relates to an event or state whose existence depends on the condition laid down by the protasis. Thus in *If he knew, he would come to help*, *If he knew* is the protasis and *he would come to help* is the apodosis. Examples of apodoses consisting of interrogative and imperative clauses are *If she can't solve the problem, who can?* and *If the bear comes in this direction, lie on the ground and pretend to be dead*.

Conditional constructions do differ from spoken to written English. Our spontaneous spoken data has no examples of the construction in which the protasis is expressed in what looks like an interrogative structure, as in (9a,b).

(9) (*a*) Were you to write to her, she would forgive you
    (*b*) Should you meet him, pass on my best wishes

Such examples are rare in spoken English generally. Some constructions that occur in spoken English do not occur in written English—that is, they are not accepted by the language authorities but are so frequent that it will not be long before they find their way into writing and provoke another wave of letter-writing by perturbed professors of philosophy. The conditional clause in (10*a*) describes an event that has not happened but could happen. The conditional clause in (10*b*) describes an event that can no longer happen.

(10) (*a*) If she came to see things for herself, she would understand
     (*b*) If she had come to see things for herself, she would have understood

In spontaneous spoken English the past tense verb is frequently replaced with *would* + verb, and the pluperfect is replaced by *would* + *have* + participle.

(11) (*a*) (= 10*a*) If she would come to see things for herself, . . .
     (*b*) (= 10*b*) If she would have come to see things for herself

The above constructions are produced by educated speakers and are making their way into standard written English, as is shown by (12), taken from *The Times*.

(12) Suppose further that all Conservative and Labour voters in England would have given the Alliance as their second choice and that Alliance voters would have divided equally between Conservative and Labour.

The standard canon requires *had given* and *had divided*.

Conditional clauses expressing events that can no longer happen also occur with the pluperfect replaced by *had* + *have*, the latter typically in its reduced form *'ve*. The same construction is also found in clauses introduced by *wish*, which likewise present an event as no longer possible. Cf. (13).

(13) (*a*) I reckon I wouldn't have been able to do it if I hadn't 've been able to read music [= hadn't been able]
 (*b*) you wouldn't have got Mark's place if you'd 've come up last year [= had come up]
 (*c*) I wish he'd 've complimented me, Roger [= had complimented]

Quirk *et al.* (1985: §1023) mention protasis clauses with *would*—*I might have married her if she would have agreed*—however the interpretation is not 'if she had agreed' but 'if she had been willing to agree'. They list the example *If I'd have seen her, I'd have told her*, only to say that informal American English speech may have matching modals—here, *would* = *'d*—in both clauses. The construction is clearly not just American English.

3.4.2. Non-finite constructions missing from the corpus of spoken language

3.4.2.1. Accusative and infinitive

There are no instances of the accusative and infinitive construction. The examples in (14) are typical of formal written English but are not found in our data and our impression is that such examples are missing in general from spontaneous spoken English.

(14) (*a*) I considered her to be the best candidate
 (*b*) Celia believes him to be a liar
 (*c*) We know Susan to be the one with the ideas

This construction requires special treatment in Government and Binding theory as involving exceptional case marking; the problem is that, e.g. in (14*a*) *her* seems to be the direct object of *considered* because of the form of the pronoun—*her*. In traditional grammar *to be the best candidate* is said to have an understood subject which is identical with *her*. The Government and Binding model treats *her* as the actual subject of the infinitive. The snag is that *considered* has to be allowed to assign direct object case to the pronoun, although the latter is in a different clause, hence the exceptional case marking. This difficulty too is not relevant to spoken English, in which (14*a–c*) are always expressed by means of the common complement construction, as in (15*a–c*)—replacing *considered* with *thought*.

(15) (*a*) I thought she was the best candidate
 (*b*) Celia believes he's a liar
 (*c*) We know Susan's the one with the ideas

3.4.2.2. Gerunds

Our corpus of spontaneous spoken English contains infinitives, participial phrases, and gerunds, but there are important differences in internal structure and syntactic function between these three structures and their counterparts in formal written English.

Let us begin with gerunds. Examples of the gerund constructions in the conversation corpus are given in (16).

(16) (a) I'm not the easiest person at **making friends** if I'm on my own you know
    (b) how would you go about **asking for permission**
    (c) I can remember **sitting among the ashes**
    (d) but I mean it seems a bit senseless **coming into the school when you know you're going to get into trouble for it**
    (e) but he didnae want to take it with him because with **being old friends** he doesnae like . . .
    (f) **getting over the top**'s the worst part
    (g) but he keeps **applying for jobs**

There are 41 gerunds in the subset of conversations that were examined in detail. Only one occurs in subject position, namely (16f). All the others are either complements of verbs, as in (16c,g) or of prepositions, as in (16a,b,e), or are extraposed, as in (16d). With respect to internal structure, it is worthwhile noting that there are no examples with a possessive pronoun subject, as in (17a), and no examples with an auxiliary, as in (17b).

(17) (a) **His having the book at all** astonished me
    (b) **Fiona's having gone back to university** is a lesson to us all

Examples such as (17a,b) are typical of formal written English, and certainly typical of much theoretical syntactic work over the last thirty years, with the establishment of parallel syntactic structures for finite clauses and gerunds. These parallels are justified for formal written English but it looks as though spontaneous spoken English has a simpler type of gerund in which only the main verb and its modifiers can occur.

3.4.2.3. Participial constructions

Participial clauses occur in our corpus but again there are differences between the spoken structures and the structures of written English. The corpus has no examples in which a present participle clause—a free participle—precedes a main clause, as in (18a) from Quirk *et al.* (1985: 1041) and (18b). There are no examples in which a passive participle clause precedes a main clause, as in (18c). In such examples the participle clause modifies the subject noun of the main clause.

(18) (a) **Reaching for the phone**, he dialled Directory Inquiries
(b) **Sitting at the window**, I noticed a car at the bank
(c) **Covered in confusion**, he apologized

Typical examples from the conversations are given in (19).

(19) (a) and they all ended up in the pub at lunchtime **celebrating**
(b) she just goes about **screaming and doing odd things**
(c) there's only twelve of us the smallest sixth year **ever known**
(d) we ended up **tied to a fence** and things like that
(e) do you want to go and have a look and see if there's anyone **standing outside**

The participial clauses all follow the main clause. They can denote: concurrent states and events, as in (19a)—the state of being in the pub and the event of celebrating; concurrent events, as in (19b)—the event of going about, the event of screaming, and the event of doing odd things. They can denote properties of (sets of) entities, as in (19c,d,e). Note that in (19c,e) the participial clause is embedded in an NP and follows the head noun.

There are grounds for supposing that the positioning of the participial clause is not accidental in parsing or informational terms. With respect to parsing, the main clause is parsed, or at least presented in its entirety to the listener, before the participial clause, a fact that is important when the listener is presented with utterances that have to be decoded instantly. Since the reader decoding a written text has more time to scan backwards and forwards and to pause on particular stretches of text, the ordering of participial clause and main clause is not so important. With respect to information structure, the participial clauses in the above examples carry important information, in some cases the most important information, which is made salient by virtue of being carried by a constituent at the end of the utterance. For instance, in (19a) *celebrating* is important because it often involves unwise consumption of alcohol, and in the event being described that is precisely what happened with serious consequences for the pupils involved when they went back to school in the afternoon. In (19b) *goes about* carries a minimum of information and the important content is conveyed by *screaming and doing odd things*.

3.4.2.4. *Infinitive constructions*

Infinitive clauses occur in our spontaneous spoken data, but none in subject position and none with auxiliaries. That is, examples such as (20a–c) are missing.

(20) (a) **To leave the dog in the car on a hot day** was just stupid
(b) **To demolish the buildings** would cost a large sum of money
(c) She intended **to have left before the police arrived** but they were too quick

3.4.3. Passives

It is worthwhile saying something about the passive clauses in the Map Task dialogues and the spontaneous conversation. It is clear from various studies that the GET passive is the typical passive of spontaneous spoken English but this fact has taken a long time to be recognized. Svartvik (1966) was able to state that the GET passive is infrequent in English and in the process of disappearing, but this comment reflected his particular corpus of data—news broadcasts, radio programmes, and conversations between university lecturers (Svartvik 1966: 7–8). Quirk and Greenbaum (1973: 802–3) were able to say that the GET passive is usually restricted to constructions without an overt animate agent noun; they cite as incorrect *The boy got given a violin by his father*, but examples of this sort do occur regularly. They could also have said that in spontaneous spoken English most instances of the passive, whether with BE or GET, lack the agentive BY + NP constituent. Quirk *et al.* (1985: 161) merely say that GET tends to be limited to constructions without an expressed animate agent, but cite *James got caught by the police* as an example with an agent phrase. They describe GET as BE's only serious contender for the status of passive auxiliary and comment that it is avoided in formal style and is far less frequent than the BE passive even in informal English.

Givón (1990: 620ff.) argues that the GET passive is semantically more active than the BE passive and argues that the patient-subject acts volitionally. He claims that in (21*a*) the rival group acted deliberately, in (21*b*)—the picket acted deliberately.

(21) (*a*) The supporters were deliberately provoked by a rival group
    (*b*) The picket got knocked down deliberately by the security guard

The interpretation assigned to (21*b*) by Givón is also appropriate for (22), which contains a reflexive pronoun.

(22) The picket got himself/herself knocked down by the security guard

Givón claims that GET passives are incorrect with the adverb *accidentally*—as in *the picket got knocked down accidentally*—but implicitly recognizes that such examples occur by stating that the use of *accidentally* in GET passives is sub-standard.

Table 3.1 provides the essential information about passives in our corpus. As it shows, the Map Task dialogues are short on passives (because of the conditions under which the data was collected) but the passives are split equally between GET and BE, 9 of each. In the subset of conversations analysed in detail the BE passive is indeed more frequent than the GET passive—18 to 11, but in the conversations as a whole there are 57 GET passives and 21 BE passives. Similar results were obtained by Suzanne

Clauses: Type, Combination, Integration 89

TABLE 3.1. *Frequency of passive constructions in conversation and Map Task dialogues*

Passive structures	Conversation	Map Task	
		eye contact	no eye contact
BE passive	18	7	2
GET passive	11	9	0
Long passive (with BY NP)	4	0	0
Short passive (without BY NP)	25	16	2

Romaine (personal communication), who recorded a 10-year-old girl talking about her home and friends, her school life, and the television programmes she watched. She used 66 passives, of which only 6 were BE passives.

None of the GET passives in our data involves deliberate action on the part of the patient. Where deliberate action is involved a reflexive pronoun occurs, as in (23).

(23) It's his pal that I mean his pal sort of sits back and eggs him on and of course he gets himself landed into it [conversation]

Moreover, those GET passives that do turn up in written English typically describe situations in which the patient has no say in the matter at all. (24a) is from an advertisement and (24b) is from Graham Greene's novel *The End of the Affair*.

(24) (a) Some gifts get used a dozen or so times a year
(b) He gets the bad reports from clients, but the good ones never get written

The upshot of the above discussion is that, at least in British English, the GET passive is at least as frequent as the BE passive in spontaneous spoken language, and there appears to be no distinction between deliberate and involuntary action on the part of the patient.

3.4.4. *Proportion of main and subordinate clauses*

As will be seen, the proportions of main and subordinate clauses in our data correspond to those in the narratives collected by Macaulay (1991) in people's homes. Let us consider first Table 3.2. Although the total number of clauses is not crucially important for present purposes, note the larger number of clauses (labelled 'no eye contact') in the Map Task dialogues in which the participants could not see each other. The lack of non-verbal communication is accompanied by an increase in the number of clauses but

90 *Spontaneous Spoken Language*

TABLE 3.2. *Percentages of main and subordinate clauses in conversation and Map Task dialogues*

	Conversation	Map Task eye contact	Map Task no eye contact
Total number of clauses	1274	1746	2413
Main clauses as % of total	75%	80%	85.5%
Subordinate clauses as % of total	25%	20%	14.5%

also a decrease in the number of subordinate clauses. The proportion of subordinate clauses is highest in the free conversations, but the participants in the subset of conversations which were analysed in detail were the interviewer (a graduate), two 18-year-old girls, one of whom had been accepted for university and the other of whom was hoping to be accepted, and various minor contributors who were not aiming at university entrance. That is, the major contributors were speakers who had not only been exposed to formal education for at least twelve years but had responded to it. In particular, to achieve academic success, they had to master written language, and the latter, it may be inferred, was influencing the syntax of their spoken language.

What is the significance of these percentages? Consider next Table 3.3(a), showing the percentage of subordinate clauses in different written texts. Various points are noteworthy. As shown by the figures in the column labelled 'GM', the highest proportion of subordinate clauses is in the *Geographical Magazine*, which is the journal of the Royal Geographical Society and contains many articles written by academics. The language of academic texts is notoriously complex, but the leaders and the readers'

TABLE 3.3(a). *Main and subordinate clauses in various written texts*

	GM	JH	PL1	PL2	IT1	IT2
Number of main clauses	64	88	79	68	62	56
Number of finite subordinate clauses	52	29	21	32	38	44
Total number of clauses	116	117	100	100	100	100
Subordinate finite clauses as a % of the total	45	25	21	32	38	44

GM = 'Conflict of Interests', *Geographical Magazine*, Dec. 1990, 18–22
JH = James Herbert, *Lair* (1988), 148–50
PL1 = Penelope Lively, *Judgment Day* (Penguin, 1982), 26–9
PL2 = Penelope Lively, *Judgment Day* (Penguin, 1982), 116–19
IT1 = *The Independent*, 30 Jan. 1996, Editorials
IT2 = *The Independent*, 30 Jan. 1996, Readers' letters

letters in *The Independent* are not far behind. The two extracts from Penelope Lively's novel demonstrate that one and the same writer can write differently in the same text. The higher figure of 32% is well above the 25% for the free conversations but the lower figure of 21% is just the same as for the Map Task dialogues with eye contact. The science fiction novel by James Herbert, at 25%, has practically the same proportion of subordinate clauses as the conversations.

Even where the proportion of finite subordinate clauses is very similar for the spoken and written texts, the language of the latter is still much more complex. Anticipating Chapter 4, we will simply mention in passing that the written texts contain noun phrases with an intricate structure of nouns modified by finite relative clauses, prepositional and participial phrases, and infinitive relatives. Two examples from Penelope Lively are *the less sinister transport aircraft, low-slung and erect-tailed* and *flowing weed, like green hair, with little white flowers blooming just above the water*. What is directly relevant to this section is the occurrence of non-finite clauses of the sort mentioned in § 3.4.2 as not to be found in our texts of spontaneous spoken English: free participles as in *She was hanging up washing, inefficiently,* **dropping things into the dirt and giving them just a quick shake before pegging them out**; attributive participial phrases, as in *a distant cloudbank* **piled up away beyond Spelbury** and *tiny scarlet gnats* **flying in tight formation** (all examples from Penelope Lively).

A second analysis was done of the passages referred to in connection with Table 3.3(a), taking account of the non-finite subordinate clauses. The total number of clauses was counted—main, finite subordinate, and non-finite subordinate. The total number of finite and non-finite subordinate clauses was calculated, and the percentage ratio of this number to the total number of all clauses. The figures are given in Table 3.3(b).

Interestingly, when participial phrases and gerunds are taken into account all the written texts have far higher percentages of subordinate clauses than the spoken texts. Since these non-finite clauses are lacking in the spoken texts, counting their occurrences would make little or no

TABLE 3.3(b). *Finite and non-finite subordinate clauses in written texts*

	GM	JH	PL1	PL2	IT1	IT2
Number of non-finite clauses	62	67	31	49	20	28
Total number of clauses	178	184	131	149	120	128
Total number of finite and non-finite subordinate clauses	114	96	52	81	58	72
Finite and non-finite subordinate clauses as a % of the total number of clauses	62	52	40	54	48	56

difference to the percentage figure for subordinate clauses. We feel confident that the figures for the corpus of spoken language have general validity because they correspond to the figures obtained by Macaulay (1991: 88–92). He collected narratives about their working lives from six middle-class and six working-class speakers in Ayr. The relevant percentage figures are in Table 3.4.

TABLE 3.4. *Percentages of subordinate clauses in Macaulay's data*

	Range	Mean	Median 1	Median 2
Middle class	22.7–45	30.9	30.3	29.5
Working class	15.5–35	22.8	21.6	22.5

The reason for the two median figures, median 1 and median 2, is this. One member of the working-class group had a very low proportion of subordinate clauses—15.5% compared with the second lowest figure of 18.4%. Median 1 is the figure for the group including the lowest percentage and median 2 is the figure excluding it. One of the middle-class group had a very high proportion of subordinate clauses—45% compared with the next highest figure of 32.5%. Median 1 is the figure including the 45% and median 2 is the figure excluding it. The higher mean and median figures correlate with amount of formal education. From the information given by Macaulay we know that the lowest figure in the middle-class group came from a speaker who had left school at age 14, although subsequently working in white-collar jobs, while the highest figure came from a research scientist of working-class origin. Amount of formal education does not necessarily coincide with middle-class status but it does tie in well with complexity of language. The average of the mean figures is 26.8%, which is marginally higher than the figure for our spoken language corpus. The difference could be explained by the fact that Macaulay's corpus consists of narratives as opposed to conversation and dialogue.

Tables 3.5 and 3.6 provide information about the types of finite subordinate clause in our corpus. We will not comment on the tables except to explain that the large number of WH complement constructions in the Map Task no-eye-contact dialogues relates to the use of reverse clefts, as in *that's where you want to be*. (These are discussed in Chapter 6.) The large number of adverbial clauses of time in the Map Task dialogues occur in instructions such as *turn left before you reach the quarry/when you cross the bridge/once you reach the stream*. The adverbial clauses are discussed in §3.6 and the relative clauses in §3.7.1.

The first number in each column relates to the occurrences of the

Clauses: Type, Combination, Integration 93

TABLE 3.5. *Complement clauses in conversation and Map Task dialogues*

Complement clause structures	Conversation	Map Task eye contact	Map Task no eye contact
Total number of complement clauses	97	48	106
TH complement	11/11.3%	2/4.2%	3/2.8%
WH complement	21/21.6%	14/29.1%	75/70.8%
Contact complement	64/66%	28/58.3%	28/26.4%
Complement dependent on an adjective	1/1%	2/4.2%	0
Comment clause complement	0	2/4.2%	0

TABLE 3.6. *Adverbial clauses in conversation and Map Task dialogues*

Adverbial clauses	Conversation	Map Task eye contact	Map Task no eye contact
Condition	19/14.6	33/30.8	48/29.4
Time	51/39.2	39/36.4	79/48.5
Reason	46/35.4	28/26.2	15/7.2
Concession	0	0	0
Result	3	1	2
Purpose	2	6/5.6	8/4.9
Comparison	7/5.4	0	11/6.7
Except	2	0	0
TOTAL	130	107	163

constructions. The second number, to the right of the oblique, gives the number of occurrences as a percentage of the total number of complement structures. That contact complements are most frequent in the conversations and the Map-Task-with-eye-contact dialogues is not surprising. This matches the pattern found in the general analysis of the entire corpus of spontaneous conversations described in Brown and Miller (1982). The very high number of WH complements in the Map-Task-without-eye-contact dialogues was attributed above to the high frequency of reverse clefts in that set of dialogues. It is not yet known what pragmatic and/or discourse factors account for the high frequency of the reverse clefts and the relatively low frequency of the contact complements.

94 *Spontaneous Spoken Language*

The discrepancy between the conversations and the Map Task data in the frequency of conditional clauses is to be explained by the use of conditional clauses for the issuing of commands. (See §3.6.) Like the high incidence of reverse WH clefts, the relatively high frequency of adverbial clauses of reason in the Map Task dialogues with no eye-contact awaits investigation. The higher frequency of adverbial clauses of reason in the conversations can be explained by the fact that in conversations people give reasons why they make statements or, in the course of narratives, why they or others performed particular actions.

3.5. Form and Function: When a Subordinate Clause is not a Subordinate Clause

3.5.1. *English*

The classification of a clause as subordinate may not be straightforward. Consider adverbial clauses of reason introduced by *because*. They can either precede or follow main clauses but have different properties depending on their position. *Because* clauses preceding a main clause have fairly rigid constituent order, whereas *because* clauses following a main clause have a more flexible order. (See examples (36) and (37) in §2.5.3.) Chafe (1984) suggests that preceding *because* clauses signpost what follows and provide reasons for the events described in the main clauses, whereas following *because* clauses provide comment on the preceding chunk of message. Comments are not so closely integrated with the preceding text but behave more like main clauses. In the conversation data there are instances where an adverbial clause of reason is separated from the main clause by a long pause. One speaker may produce the main clause and the second speaker—the adverbial clause of reason as in (25).

(25) LM 49   they go to X now do they not the school?
     LH 43   yeah cos it's indoor

Putting aside degree of integration, we can recognize main clauses and subordinate clauses. Main clauses can, as the traditional formula puts it, stand on their own. For instance, *Angus visited London last spring* is a perfectly good discourse—assuming the hearer knows who Angus is and what London is. It could be the opening contribution to a conversation. In contrast, *because his aunt left him a large legacy* does not stand on its own: the hearer needs another clause to complete the discourse.

Subordinate clauses are subject to certain restrictions that do not affect main clauses. For example, in the main clause *The dog came into the kitchen* can be remodelled as *Into the kitchen came the dog*. Consider now the sentence *When the dog came into the kitchen, it stole a large slice of beef*. The *when* clause is subordinate, and cannot be remodelled to **When into the kitchen came the dog*. The preceding example describes a situation in which two events happened one after the other: event 1—the dog came into the kitchen; event 2—the dog stole a slice of beef. The main event is the stealing, described by the main clause, and the entry into the kitchen, expressed by the *when* clause, is secondary.

Let us turn to another example: *She switched off the light when the dog came into the kitchen*. This could be interpreted as describing two events: event 1—the dog came into the kitchen; event 2—she switched off the light. The order of clauses does not correspond to the order of events but there may be sound discourse reasons for this; the example may be an answer to the question *When did she switch off the light?*, in which case the main clause presents the given information first (the information that has already been uttered) and the adverbial clause presents the new information. (See Chapter 5 for a discussion of given and new information.) In spontaneous spoken English another interpretation is regularly and frequently appropriate; namely, she switched off the light and then the dog came in. In this interpretation the two events are given equal status. The *when* clause looks like a subordinate clause but it does not express a secondary event and it can be remodelled: *She switched off the light when into the kitchen came the dog*.

There is a view held by a number of teachers (an observation based on an examination of corrections made to homework exercises by teachers of English) that the main event should always be expressed by a main clause, the secondary event—by a *when* clause. Furthermore, where the secondary event precedes the main event, the *when* clause should precede the main clause. Thus, one sentence in a 13-year-old's essay, similar to the above example, was not acceptable to the teacher. The child had written *She shone the light along the dark passage when suddenly she saw a big rat*, but the teacher wanted to sentence changed to *When she shone the light along the dark passage, she suddenly saw a big rat*. The problem is that the *when* clause is not a subordinate clause but a main clause and *when* can be treated as a conjunction joining two main clauses—a very common construction in spontaneous spoken English but not one that is in the canon of formal written English.

3.5.2. *Spoken Russian*

The differences between spoken and written English are large, but the data collected by Zemskaja (1973) and her colleagues is even more astonishing.

3.5.2.1. *Free coordination between predicative constructions*

Zemskaja applies the term 'free coordination between predicative constructions' to examples in which one clause is inserted inside another or follows another without any syntactic marking of the clause boundary. Consider (26). (The inserted clause is in bold.)

(26) A čto eto za fil'm **ja pročital** budet?
and what that for film I read will-be
[The speaker is looking at the TV programmes in a newspaper. A film is listed, but its title is not given]

Zemskaja says that *ja pročital* has certain properties.

i It may be unmarked by intonation or it may carry a rising intonation.
ii It may have a faster rhythm than the rest of the utterance.
iii It may occur at the front of the clause, as in *ja pročital/čto eto za fil'm budet* with a break in intonation after the sequence, but the preposed construction is extremely rare.

(27*a,b*) and (28*a,b*) are examples in which one clause follows another.

(27) (*a*) vot na Litejnom **u vas est' takoj magazinčik** ja byl
Focus on Litejnij at you is such shop I was
(*b*) vot na Litejnom u vas est' takoj magazinčik **ja byl**
Focus on Litejnij at you is such shop I was

(28) (*a*) ja včera videla **ženščina nesla vot taki maki,**
I yesterday saw woman carried Focus such poppies,
nu vot takie!
Particle Focus such-ones
(*b*) podaj mne karandaš **/ležit tam**
hand me pencil is-lying there

The first point to make is that such constructions may be grammatically ambiguous. (27*a,b*) contain the same sequence of the same constituents but can be assigned different constructions, as indicated by the different portions in bold. (27*a*) has the interpretation 'ja byl na Litejnom, gde u vas takoj magazinčik' ('I was on Litejnij where you have such a shop'); that is, the portion in bold is a relative clause modifying *Litejnom*, although it contains no relative pronoun. (27*b*) is to be given the interpretation 'u vas na Litejnom est' magazinčik, v kotorom ja byl' ('you have on Litejnij a shop in which I was'; that is, the relative clause is *ja byl* (I was), modifying *magazinčik* (shop). The context determines which interpretation is appropriate.

(28*a*) contains a verb of perception followed by a complement. In literary Russian we would find either (29*a*) or (29*b*). In the former, *videla* is followed by a complement clause clearly marked by the complementizer *kak* (how), while in the latter it has a direct object NP, *ženščinu* (woman), clearly marked by the accusative case inflection and modified by a relative clause clearly marked by the relative pronoun *kotoraja* (who).

(29) (*a*) ja včera   videla, kak ženscina nesla   vot   takie maki
        I yesterday saw   how woman   was-carrying Focus such poppies
    (*b*) ja včera   videla ženščinu, kotoraja nesla   vot   takie maki
        I yesterday saw   woman   who   was-carrying Focus such poppies

(28*b*) contains a piece of syntax *ležit tam* which can be construed as a relative clause or a main clause, although the relative clause analysis is not very plausible given that relative pronouns are typically not ellipted in Russian. If it is to be analysed as a relative clause, it shares with (28*a*) and (27*a,b*) the lack of syntactic marking for the clause boundary. If it is to be analysed as a main clause, it is to be seen as displaying a common feature of non-initial main clauses in Russian texts, namely the lack of an overt referring expression. In (27) the linking of the relative clause to the remainder of the construction is particularly loose given that what is 'missing' is a locative prepositional phrase, whereas what is missing in (28*b*), on the relative clause analysis, is a subject for the relative clause, that is, a relative pronoun in the nominative case. In other words, the clauses in bold in (27*a,b*) and (28*b*) can be seen as having a zero anaphoric subject NP, and zero anaphors are particularly frequent in spoken Russian, and even in written Russian. An example of a passage of literary Russian with an extended sequence of zero anaphors is given in (30), repeated from Chapter 2. The zero anaphors are represented by pairs of square brackets in bold.

(30) Etot portnoj byl   ešče statnyj . . . mužčina
     this tailor   was   still stately   man
     Šest' večerov . . . stojal on . . . , [ ] rezal, [ ] šil,
     six   evenings   stood he   cut   sewed
     [ ] proglažival švy   utjugom
          smoothed   seams with-iron
     [ ] Zarabatyval den'gi.
          earned   money
     Voskresen'e [ ] provodil na ippodrome
     Sunday   spent   at racecourse

To conclude this section we return briefly to the problem raised by (28*b*): does the structure consist of two juxtaposed main clauses or a main clause and a relative clause? Although relative pronouns are not ellipted, at least in written Russian, a case could be made for treating the second clause in (28*b*) as a relative clause, on the ground that highly topical subject NPs are ellipted on a massive scale in spoken Russian. However, a further difficulty is that an ellipsis analysis must posit the ellipsis not just of subject relative pronouns but of oblique relative pronouns, as in (27), and of direct object relative pronouns, as in (31).

(31) v gazete   byla stat'ja **ja čital** [= kotoruju ja čital 'which I was-reading']
 in newspaper was article I was-reading

Since the occurrence of zero direct object anaphors is also typical of spontaneous Russian conversation, an analysis in terms of juxtaposed main clauses may be sufficient, but we cannot exclude the possibility that spoken Russian has a different system of relative clauses, especially in the light of §3.7 on relative clauses in written English and spontaneous spoken English.

3.5.2.2. *Juxtaposition of adverbial clauses*

Sequences of clauses are found in which one of the clauses can be interpreted as adverbial, although there is no conjunction marking the boundary of the clause and its type. Many of the examples given by Zemskaja can be interpreted as adverbial clauses of time, as in (32*a*–*c*), but there is one example of a sequence, in (32*d*), that can be interpreted as an adverbial clause of reason.

(32) (*a*) ja u nego byl **sjuda priezžal**
 I at him was here he-came
 = ja u nego byl, kogda on sjuda priezžal
 'I was at his place when he here came'
 (*b*) tam bystro vysoxnet **doždi končatsja**
 there quickly will-dry rains will-end
 (*c*) im očen' ponravilos' **v Rige byli**
 them very-much pleased in Riga they-were
 (*d*) ne vidno ničego zdes'/ **kraska sterlas'**
 not visible anything here dye has-faded

(32*a*) has the interpretation '. . . kogda on sjuda priezžal' ('when he came here'), (32*b*) 'kogda doždi končatsja' ('when the rains finish'), (32*c*) '. . . kogda v Rige byli' ('when they were in Riga'), and (32*d*) has the interpretation '. . . tak kak kraska sterlas'' ('as the dye has faded').

It is important to remember that a clause having a particular interpretation does not mean that the clause must be of the syntactic type that would normally carry that interpretation in the written language. The relevant syntactic fact is that the ellipsis of subordinating adverbial conjunctions is not a feature of Russian and should not be invoked in order to make the syntax of spoken Russian fit our preconceptions based on written Russian. As with the putative relative clauses above, an alternative, and more attractive, analysis is that the clauses in bold in (32) are not adverbial clauses but main clauses juxtaposed with the other clauses. With respect to the relationship between the clauses in each example, the second clause certainly specifies the time of the event described by the first clause or the reason for the state of affairs described by it, but the interpretation is not sufficient reason to classify the clauses as subordinate and adverbial. What is relevant here, although there is no space to elaborate, is the scheme proposed by Matthiessen and Thompson and others (see Chapter 2) for handling discourse relations that hold between clauses and between sentences in written language. Their approach offers a way of handling relationships between clauses without the clauses being arbitrarily grouped into sentences by the analyst.

3.5.2.3. *Further comments on juxtaposed clauses*

Let us note that a sequence consisting of a main clause and a juxtaposed 'adverbial' clause may be ambiguous. Cf. (33).

(33) Ja na ulice xorošo projdus'
    I on street nice   will-walk
    [= projdus', potomu čto / projdus', esli . . .]
    [= will-walk, because/if . . .]

That is, (33) can be interpreted as *'projdus', potomu čto na ulice xorošo'* ('I will go for a walk because it is nice outside') or as *'projdus', esli na ulice xorošo'* ('I will go for a walk if it is nice outside').

A second point is that simple juxtaposition emphasizes the connection between constituents that would in written Russian be separated. In (34*a*), for example, the close link between *v bol'nicu* and *zub bolit* is highlighted compared with the written Russian version in (34*b*), says Zemskaja.

(34) (*a*) ja v bol'nicu zub   bolit   edu
       I to hospital tooth is-sore am-going
    (*b*) Ja v bol'nicu edu,   potomu čto bolit   zub
       I to hospital am-going because   is-sore tooth

Zemskaja maintains that differences in intonation pattern signal a different link between two juxtaposed clauses (she talks about predicative blocks). Thus the clauses in (35*a*), with a break in intonation pattern signalling an unfinished utterance, are seen by her as a main clause followed by an adverbial clause of reason. In (35*b*), with a break in the intonation patter signalling a completed utterance, she sees two juxtaposed main clauses. An alternative is to treat both examples as consisting of juxtaposed main clauses with the same discourse relationship between them, namely one of elaboration, to borrow a term from Halliday. This of course leaves the question of how to analyse the intonation patterns; one approach is to treat them as indeed signalling whether an utterance is unfinished or not but not to set up a necessary correspondence between utterances and sentences, at least not in spontaneous spoken language.

(35) (a) rozy očen' kaprizny/ za nimi že   očen' trudno   uxaživat'
       roses very capricious for them Particle very difficult to-care
    (b) rozy očen' kaprizny//za nimi očen' trudno uxaživat'

The discourse relations can be quite complex. Zemskaja glosses (36) as 'košelek ležal tut, teper' ego net, i poetomu ja xoču znat', gde že on' ('My purse was lying there, now it is not there, and therefore I want to know where it is') and (37) as 'raz byli, to znaete i možete otvetit'' ('if you have been, you know and can reply').

(36) a   gde   moj košelek **tut   ležal**
     but where my purse   here was-lying

(37) a   čto tam   bogataja mečet' ili net **vy byli/**
     and what there rich   mosque or not   you were

The speaker utters the highlighting question (see Chapter 5) *a čto*, approximately equivalent in this context to *OK then*. The next question is the important one—*tam bogataja mečet' ili net?* ('is there a rich mosque there or not?'). The final part of (37), *vy byli* ('you were (there)') can be interpreted, as Zemskaja's gloss indicates, as conveying the reason why the speaker thinks it appropriate to put this question to his/her interlocutor. The initial chunk *a čto* is a question which the speaker both asks and answers. As we will see in Chapter 5 on discourse, this is a typical way of highlighting a piece of text in spontaneous spoken Russian and indeed in spoken English.

3.6. Order of Main Clause and Surbordinate Clause

The order of main and adverbial clauses is not as reported in other studies of spoken language and the function of the adverbial clauses also differs. In the Map Task dialogues by far the most frequent order is 'main clause'–'adverbial clause' but the spontaneous conversations offer several examples of the order 'adverbial clause'–'main clause'. In the latter sequence, the adverbial clause is typically highly topical, or sets the scene, or provides an explicit contrast. Consider first conditional clauses. In the Map Task dialogues there are 90. Twelve have the order 'conditional clause'–'main clause' and 12 have the order 'main clause'–'conditional clause'. The interesting statistic is that 59 conditional clauses stand on their own unconnected with a main clause and their function is to issue an instruction, a polite command, as demonstrated in (38).

(38) A1   I've also got privately owned fields
     B1   will you hit them if you go through that?

Clauses: Type, Combination, Integration

A2 could well do they are due right of the start and directly below the granite quarry
B2 right if you just g . . . if you're at the top of the . . . right at the top of the adventure playground, just eh almost touching it if you go straight there will you miss them?
A3 yes I will indeed
B3 right **if you go right along there** until you're at the right hand edge of the granite quarry
A4 OK

(38) contains four conditional clauses. *if you go through that* in B1 and *if you go straight there will you miss them* in B2 are prototypical conditional clauses related to a main clause. In B3 the clause highlighted in bold conveys an instruction. There is no main clause it might be related to and the response *OK* in A4 indicates that A took the utterance B3 as a command. (Not to mention the fact that A proceeds to draw the relevant section of route.) The first conditional clause in B2, *if you're at the top of the . . . right at the top of the adventure playground, just eh almost touching it*, is not an instruction to move but could be construed as an instruction to be in the relevant location. Another interpretation is that the speaker is checking whether the other participant is in fact in the proper location. The intonation and rhythm—a pause and a separate intonation contour over *if you go straight there will you miss them?*—rule out an interpretation in which *if you're at the top . . .* combines with the latter; that is, an interpretation in which *if you're at the top . . .* specifies a general condition within which a more particular condition is specified—*if you go straight there*.

In the spontaneous conversation conditional clauses follow and precede main clauses. When they precede, they relate to entities that are topical/given or set

(39) A1 one of them was 18 and they all ended up in the pub at lunchtime celebrating they came back to school and the girl that her eighteenth birthday was on that day was stoned couldnae stand up was sick all over the corridor
B1 and what happened what developed
A2 she got her prefect's badge taken off her
C1 she was deputy head girl
B2 yeah but tell me exactly what happened did someone come in
C2 the whole school knew about it
A3 somebody must have went into the common room
C3 one of the teachers must have gone and reported it
B3 what about your year how are you
C4 we're good girls no so far our eighteenths all start next week so we're going to be good and we're not going to get drunk
A4 no at dinner time anyway

102 *Spontaneous Spoken Language*

    C5   no we're certainly not coming back into the school drunk
    A5   **if they hadn't brought her back** nothing would have been said they brought her back to school instead of taking her home she was really ill

(40) A1   what did they say when you were looking for your screwdriver
       B1   aye, I hadn't been caught I had never talked to them but as they said **if they get us there** again they're going to wrap the air rifle round my neck

In (39) the conditional clause in bold in A5 relates to bringing the drunk girl back to school, which has been the topic of discussion during the previous twelve turns. (40) is preceded by a long story about poaching pheasants and being chased by the gamekeeper and a policeman. *There* in the conditional clause in B1 is the estate where the pheasant poaching was taking place and is highly topical both for the narrator and doubtless for the gamekeeper and the policemen at the time of the actual incident. That is, in both the above examples the conditional clause functions as a link to the preceding text or to the immediate context of utterance and is given. Constituents conveying given information typically precede constituents conveying new information. (See Chapter 5 for a discussion of given and new.)

A scene-setting conditional clause is given in (41).

(41) A1   what what sort of thing do you get disciplinewise in your family
       B1   it's not bad my dad he doesn't say a lot but you know **if I say something** it's always my Dad that'll come and give me a row but he's not that strict really you know I can predict what he's going to say it doesn't bother me that much

The conditional clause in B1 sets the scene for the rest of the narrative in the turn.

The order of main and time clauses is interesting because of differences between the Map Task dialogues and spontaneous conversation. The dialogues have only one instance of a time clause preceding a main clause. The time clause also happens to be the only instance of a clause with *while*, that is a clause that presents the time of one event as included in the time occupied by another event. Cf. (42).

(42) A1   right you've got to take the line down from the start to just . . . vertically . . . to just . . . to the left of burnt forest
       B1   to the left of burnt forest?
       A2   Mhm
       B2   so it's not far down?
       A3   no it's a tiny bit OK and while you're doing that go in to your right a bit but . . . it doesn't really matter

All the other occurrences of time clauses have to do with continuing a section of route up to a certain point—e.g. *till you're underneath the left-hand edge of the adventure playground*—or with executing a manoeuvre at a certain point on the route—e.g. *and then stop when you get to the other side.* The spontaneous conversations have many more examples of time clauses preceding main clauses, and all have to do with setting a scene or with a change of episode in a narrative or discussion. Consider (43, 44).

(43) A1   it's the same chap that takes us hillwalking on Sundays and we had one about a fortnight ago at Comrie and the weather was really bad and we were in a snow blizzard and we didn't know how we were going to get out and we were petrified
     M10   can you ever em did you ever feel when you were on that thing at any time that you were really going to get lost there
     A10   yeah quite often **when we were on the top the top of the hill** there was just about a whiteout you couldn't see where the farm was you were lucky if you saw a foot in front of you and I was convinced we were still going in the wrong direction

(44) A1   I was frightened until I actually got over getting over the top's the worst part **once I was over** it was better

In (43) the time clause in A10 picks up the question about how they felt on top of the hill and is therefore topical. It is also sets the scene for the rest of the narrative: there being a whiteout, being unable to see the farm, having limited vision, being convinced she was going in the wrong direction. In (44) the time clause picks up two previous comments by the same speaker, *until I actually got over* and *getting over the top's the worst part.*

The time clause in (45) introduces a change of episode in the overall adventure.

(45) A1   did they give him his gun back
     B1   aye and they gave me mine but the next day my gun there was something wrong with it and I had to carry a screwdriver with me all the time and I had the screwdriver in my wellies [Wellington boots] and **when the policeman ran after us** it fell out so I went back for it the day after and they got me

The time clause in B1 introduces the episode of being chased by the policeman and being caught and the tale of what happened thereafter.

The Map Task dialogues have no instances of adverbial clauses of reason preceding main clauses. Chafe (1984) describes such reason clauses as signposting an argument, whereas in sequences of 'main clause'–'reason clause', the reason clause typically comments on the proposition expressed by the main clause. Since the Map Task dialogues do not contain extended discussion and argument, their absence is not surprising. More surprising is the fact that out of 29 reason clauses, only 11 are in a clear 'main clause'–'reason clause' combination. Twelve occur on their own in different turns from the main clause they relate to and 4 occur in the same turn but separated from the main clause by other material. Not all the reason clauses relate to a main clause. Some provide the reason why the speaker has uttered a particular question or instruction. Cf. (46).

(46) A1 right . . . my map deviates here so I presume that's why you must have an obstacle . . . so what I want you to do is go west . . . as far left as the sta . . . just the edge of the of this
  B1 Mhm
  A2 then . . . do you have to go up to avoid the . . .
  B2 well . . . if . . . there's a very, very thin line I ca . . . I can go up though . . . yes
  A3 **because that's how this map indicates** . . . so I want you to go up . . . not straight up . . . ehm . . . north west

In (46) the reason clause, highlighted in bold, gives the reason for the question in A2.

There are very few examples of the sequence 'reason clause'–'main clause'; the one example is introduced by SINCE and is part of a structure running parallel to a previous syntactic structure. The first part of the parallel is *If she didn't ask* [conditional clause] *I'd go and do it* [main clause]. The second part begins with a positive reason clause contrasting with the negative one—*since she asks me*. This is followed by a negative main clause contrasting with the positive main clause in the first part of the parallel: *I don't*. The example is given in (47).

(47) A1 you'll not do that now you'll not go near the fire now
  B1 that's because she asks me to go and do it if she didn't ask me I'd go and do it **since she asks me** I don't I'm a bit like that

3.7. WH constructions

Relative clauses and WH clefts are of particular interest because they illustrate in a very obvious fashion the non-integrated nature of the syntax of spontaneous spoken language. We begin with relative clauses, which constitute quite a complex and different system from relative clauses in written English. In the data there are no instances of NPs being moved across more than one clause boundary and there are very few examples even of movement across just one clause boundary. Pied-piping is completely absent, ruled out both by the small number of WH relative clauses and the simple structure of NPs. On the other hand, the Keenan-Comrie hierarchy does not apply because it is circumvented by the use of TH relative clauses with shadow pronouns.

3.7.1. Relative clauses

On the basis of the Map Task dialogues, the free conversation, further informally collected spoken data, and written work by pupils at Edinburgh secondary schools, the following system of relative clause constructions can be postulated. Strictly speaking, it is a system for Scottish English, but there are good grounds for supposing that a similar system operates in all non-standard varieties of British English and to some extent in informal spoken standard English. (Colleagues who work on other non-standard varieties recognize the constructions, and they can be heard in radio discussion programmes.)

3.7.1.1. *Relative clauses in spontaneous spoken English*

The main features of the relative clause system are described below, with references to the data in Table 3.7. It is necessary first of all to distinguish different types of relative clause. Restrictive relative clauses, exemplified in (48), restrict the reference of the noun phrase, helping the listener or reader to pick out the correct referent. They are introduced by *that* or a WH word. In (48), the relative clause *that Angus bought* narrows the reference of *the car*.

(48) The car that/which Angus bought turned out to be rotten with rust

Non-restrictive relative clauses do not restrict the reference of a noun phrase but simply add extra information. They are introduced only by WH words and very often are separated from their head noun by a break in rhythm or intonation. In writing restrictive relative clauses are not separated by a punctuation mark from their head noun, whereas non-restrictive

TABLE 3.7. *Relative clauses in conversation and Map Task dialogues*

Relative clauses	Conversation	Map Task eye contact	Map Task no eye contact
WH relative clauses	0	19	4
restrictive		3	1
non-restrictive		13	3
propositional		1	0
where		2	
TH relative clauses	35	18	10
Contact relative clauses	37	1	9
Headless relative clauses	14	40	54
TOTAL	86	97	81

relative clauses are separated from their head noun by a comma, or even by a dash. (49) is an example of a non-restrictive relative clause.

(49) The car, which Flora didn't want to buy in the first place, turned out to be rotten with rust

The relative clause *which Flora didn't want to buy in the first place* adds extra information but is not intended to help pick out the referent of *the car*.

A third type of relative clause is the type that modifies, not a noun, but an event or proposition, as in (50).

(50) The government imposed a tax on domestic fuel, which did not make them popular

It is not the fuel that made the government unpopular but the act of imposing the tax on domestic fuel. Propositional or event relative clauses are introduced only by *which*.

With these distinctions in mind, we can examine the grammar of relative clauses in our spontaneous spoken data.

a Most restrictive relative clauses are introduced by *that*. All non-restrictive relative clauses are introduced by WH items, mostly *who* or *which*, but there are no occurrences of *whom* or *whose*. In the spontaneous conversation there are no WH relatives, but they do turn up in the Map Task dialogues. Note however that 13 out of 19 in the eye-contact dialogues are non-restrictive and 1 is propositional. Only 3 out of the 19 are restrictive. Restrictive relative clauses may be introduced by *where* or *when*.

b Instead of *whose*, *that* + possessive pronoun is typically used: *the girl **that her** eighteenth birthday was on that day was stoned, couldnae stand up*. This possessive relative is probably a special case of the shadow pronoun construction discussed in (**c**).

c The shadow pronoun is a typical feature of relative clauses, particularly if the relative clause contains a long constituent or another clause:

(51) (*a*) the spikes **that** you stick in the ground and throw rings **over them**
 (*b*) an address **which** I hadn't stayed **there** for several years. (Both examples recorded informally.)

d Prepositions always occur at the end of the relative clause, as in *the shop [I bought it **in**]*, but prepositions are frequently omitted:

(52) (*a*) of course, there's a rope that you can pull the seat back up [ ]
 (*b*) I haven't been to a party yet that I haven't got home [ ] the same night (informally recorded—radio discussion)

With prepositions the examples would be:

(53) (*a*) of course, there's a rope that you can pull the seat back up with
  (*b*) I haven't been to a party yet that I haven't got home from the same night

e *that* is typically omitted in existential constructions:

(54) (*a*) we had this French girl [ ] came to stay
  (*b*) my friend's got a brother [ ] used to be in the school
  (*c*) there's a man in our street [ ] has a Jaguar
     (Informally recorded)

f Non-restrictive relative clauses require further investigation, but are not frequent. There are no non-restrictive relatives with *who*. Of the non-restrictive relatives with *which*, 16 are from the undergraduate Map Task dialogues and none from the two 18 year olds in the East Lothian conversations. In fact the database of spontaneous conversation as a whole offers only 29 non-restrictive relatives—8 from undergraduates, 18 from the 17/18 year olds at the fee-paying Edinburgh school, and 3 from other contributors. These 29 non-restrictive relatives have to be set against 409 TH restrictive relatives, 38 propositional relatives, 32 restrictive relatives introduced by *where* or *when* and 49 restrictive relatives introduced by *which*. That is, the non-restrictive relatives constitute 5.5% of the total number of relative clauses. If we take only the data from the state schools, the adults with a minimum of formal education, and the interviewer, the proportion of non-restrictive relatives drops to 1.5%. Instead of non-restrictive relatives, coordinate clauses occur: *The boy I was talking to last night*—**and he actually works in the yard**—*was saying it's going to be closed down.*

g Grammars of English list infinitival relatives; that is, non-finite clauses containing *to* infinitives which function like the relative clauses examined above. Examples are given in (55).

(55) (*a*) We found a splendid house **in which to spend our holiday**
  (*b*) There is nothing **to read here**

The relative clause in (55*a*) is a WH infinitival relative, the infinitive *to spend our holiday* being preceded by *in which*. The dialogues and the free conversations contain no WH infinitival relatives. They do however contain 2 infinitival relatives, reproduced in (56*a,b*).

(56) (*a*) eh Laurine—question to tell you—eh if you haven't got the volcano—where do you go if you haven't got the volcano
  (*b*) I've got a place to start

(56*a,b*) exemplify two properties shared by the infinitival relatives to be found in the free conversations. A number of instances appear idiom-like and are possibly learned and used as entire chunks: *question to tell* in (56*a*) can be analysed in this fashion, especially as it is simply a phrase and not part of a clause. *Question to ask* and *something to tell / something to say* are relatively frequent phrases in a primary classroom. (56*b*) illustrates the lack of prepositions: we might expect *I've got a place to start at/from*, which is what the context indicates as appropriate. Other examples, with the 'missing' preposition in square brackets, are: *It's not the ideal place to go [to] for teenage drinking, . . . because there's vandals and it's a horrible place to live [in]*.

The free conversations contain 52 infinitival relatives. Two adult informants produced 6 apiece, while 5 came from one informant who also produced a large number of restrictive WH relative clauses. The remaining 35 were distributed over 15 informants. In general, infinitival relatives do not seem problematic in the corpus of informal free conversation. They occur regularly but not frequently; they do not contain prepositions; some of them could be analysed as fixed phrases; and WH infinitival relatives are absent.

3.7.1.2. *The Keenan–Comrie hierarchy and general clause linkage*

The example in (52*b*) above, *I haven't been to a party that I haven't got home the same night* can be regarded as a bridge from relative clauses to more complex non-integrated structures. Relative clauses like those in (**d**) with no shadow pronoun and no relative pronoun are closely linked to their head noun and cannot stand on their own. Clauses with a shadow object pronoun or possessive pronoun certainly follow their head noun but can function as main clauses as they stand, without any changes in word order or the replacement of relative pronouns by ordinary pronouns.

One advantage of these non-integrated relative clauses is that they allow speakers to provide more complex information about the referent of the head noun than they would normally be able to cope with in spontaneous speech, and they allow the listener to cope with that information too. Consider (57*a,b*).

(57) (*a*) I only wear shoes that I'm not thrown forward on my toes
    (*b*) tracking down a person that you would think someone would recognize them

The function of *that* in these examples is to signal a link between the noun and the clause that follows: in information processing terms, the noun tells the listener to open a file for information about the referent, and the *that* instructs the listener to prepare to add to the file the information provided by the following clause. (57*b*) allows the speaker to avoid a structure in which a WH pronoun moves out of the relative clause altogether, as in *tracking down a person who you would think [someone would recognize]*. The square brackets in bold mark the boundaries of the relative clause; *who* is at the front of the next clause to the left.

In (57*a*) the relative clause consists of a short passive construction *that I'm not thrown forward on my toes*. The passive in English (and its equivalent in other languages) is a construction that enables the speaker to use a one-place verb, mentioning only the patient and leaving out any agent or other participant. The data from spontaneous spoken English (and from much written English too) suggest that the passive is typically one-place, with the long or two-place passive being used only in very formal writing. This in turn favours an analysis whereby the link between the main and the relative clause is not to be handled by postulating an empty agent BY NP phrase but by invoking a discourse link between the two clauses. The exact relationship must be pragmatically inferred: the listener knows that the relative clause contains information about the noun *shoes*. The speaker talks about being thrown forward on her toes; shoes affect people's stance and the listener constructs the appropriate interpretation.

The shadow pronoun construction enables speakers to avoid the constraints of the Keenan–Comrie hierarchy. That hierarchy states in essence that languages with relative clauses will have the relative pronoun as subject of the relative clause but not necessarily in any other grammatical function. Languages in which relative pronouns can function as subject and direct object in the relative clause do not necessarily have them functioning as oblique objects or possessives. Conversely, if in a given language relative pronouns can function as oblique objects in the relative clause, they will also function as subject and direct object. As it happens, English—that is, written English—is extremely flexible; its relative pronouns can have any grammatical function in relative clauses, as shown in (58*a–e*).

(58) (*a*) the girl who helped me [relative pronoun as subject]
 (*b*) the girl who I helped [relative pronoun as direct object]
 (*c*) the girl to whom I gave the book [relative pronoun as oblique object]
 (*d*) the girl whose book I borrowed [relative pronouns as possessor]
 (*e*) the book on the pages of which I found these words

The constructions in (58*c–e*) are absent from the corpus of spontaneous English. This indicates that most speakers find these constructions difficult to produce with little or no planning time. Instead, they either use two main clauses or a shadow-pronoun construction: e.g. *the girl that I gave her the book*, *the girl that I borrowed her book*, and *the book that I found these words on its pages*. The essential property of these examples is that the relative clause has the same word order as a main clause and the listener's task is simply to figure out that the relative clause conveys information about the referent of the noun it modifies.

In (57*a,b*) the relative clause does provide information about a property of the noun it modifies, but a number of apparent relative clauses contain information that does not relate directly to the head noun at all. Consider (59), with a TH relative clause:

(59) some people lift the phone that you think you've interrupted a suicide attempt [participant in radio discussion programme]

The relative clause introduced by *that*—*that you think you've interrupted a suicide attempt*—conveys a property of some events of lifting the phone, but there is no slot in the relative clause which might be held to have contained a noun that has been ellipted because it is identical with whatever noun is modified by the relative clause. Compare *the book I bought*, in which *bought* can be analysed as having a direct object noun identical with *book* (or *the book* in the classic transformational account) which is deleted. In (57*b*) the pronoun *them* does at least throw a link back to the head noun *someone* and (57*a*) could be regarded as having a PP *by them* that is deleted but also throws a link back to *shoes*. There is no such link in (59). It should be remembered that relative clauses modifying propositions or events are introduced by *which*. Since the relative clause in (59) is introduced by *that*, it seems not to modify an event or proposition. In fact, it is not at all clear that the clause should be analysed as a relative clause; rather, *that* signals some type of general subordination link, and in this respect the construction is analogous to the structure of (60*a*,*b*).

(60) (*a*) you can leave at Christmas if your birthday's in December to February which I think is wrong like my birthday's March and I have to stay on to May **which** when I'm 16 in March I could be looking for a job
(*b*) cos one other thing which I wasn't sure how far we wanted to go how intelligent to aphasics some of these things are

(60*a*) contains two occurrences of *which*. The first one, *which I think is wrong*, is in a relative clause modifying a proposition—'You can leave at Christmas if your birthday's in December to February'. The second one, *which when I'm 16 in March I could be looking for a job*, is not a relative pronoun. It does not belong to any clause but is followed by an adverbial clause of time *when I'm 16 in March*, combining with a main clause *I could be looking for a job*. The function of *which* is to signal a general link between the material that precedes it and the material following: I have to stay on at school till May—but I'm 16 in March and I could be out looking for job instead of going to school.

This construction is not new in English. It is attested in Dickens's novels—Mr Wegg in *Our Mutual Friend* has a strong line in this *which* construction—and was regularly used in cartoons in *Punch* as a stereotypical feature of uneducated language. *Which* and *that* have similar histories. Both derive from pronouns in Early English, the change in status from pronoun to complementizer being typical throughout Indo-European and other language families. *That* became a complementizer, losing all pronominal features, but *which* kept its status as pronoun, witness the fact that it still forms a system with *who* and *whom* (in literary English). Once *that* became a complementizer, the way was open for it to change into a general conjunction, as in (59), and *which* has also acquired a second function as general conjunction. Example (60*b*) is interesting because, to return to a theme from Chapter 1, it could be analysed as the speaker setting out to say *Cos one other thing **which I wasn't sure of** was how far we wanted to go* . . . That is, its structure could be related to a structure typical of written language, namely a regular relative clause. In context it was clear that there was not a first thing which the speaker was not sure of; the speaker was introducing a new proposition by means of the phrase *cos one other thing* and providing a further link, *which*, between that phrase and the next clause. That is, a more plausible paraphrase is *one other thing I want to say is that I wasn't sure how far we wanted to go*.

3.7.1.3. *Relative clause constructions in other languages*

The various phenomena mentioned above in connection with English are found in other languages, both in spontaneous spoken texts from speakers of languages with a written variety and in texts from speakers of languages that are purely oral and have no written tradition. The relevant features are loose linkage between a relative clause and the noun it modifies, relative clauses that are so loosely linked with their head noun and the preceding clause that the complementizer can be seen as a general discourse linking element rather than a relative pronoun or relative clause complementizer, and the non-integrated syntax enabling speakers to avoid the Keenan–Comrie hierarchy.

3.7.1.3.1. *French*

The data here are taken from Deulofeu (1981). They are from a speaker of non-standard French. (61*a–d*) illustrate the occurrence of shadow pronouns.

(61) (*a*) Il y a   beaucoup   d'appareils
        there-are many   of pieces-of-equipment
        qu'on   s'   en   sert pas tous les jours
        that one self of-them use not all   the days
        'There are many pieces of equipment that are not used everyday'
    (*b*) si vous trouvez des   fosses
        if you find   some ditches
        que les gens   risquent de tomber à   l'intérieur
        that the people risk   to fall   into the interior
        'if you find any ditches that people are in danger of falling into'

(c) vous avez des   feux
    you have some fires
    qu'il faut   appeler les pompiers   tout de suite
    that it is-necessary to-call the fire brigade immediately
    'you have fires in connection with which you have to call the fire brigade immediately'
(d) il y a   des   personnes
    there-are some   people
    qu'   ils   ont   de la répugnance à   le faire
    that they   have   reluctance   to it to-do
    'there are some people who are reluctant to do it'

(61*d*) is interesting because the subordinate clause contains a shadow pronoun in subject position: *ils* in *ils ont* . . . That is, the shadow pronoun construction is employed even for the highest, unmarked position on the Keenan–Comrie hierarchy. This piece of data indicates that the shadow pronoun construction is not just an ad-hoc means for solving on-line syntax planning problems. In contrast, (61*a*–*c*) do involve a simpler syntactic code than the construction demanded in written French. The written version of (61*a*) is . . . *dont on s'en sert tous les jours*, with the possessive relative pronoun *dont* at the front of the clause and therefore removed from its governing verb *se sert*. The written version of (61*b*) is . . . *dans l'intérieur desquelles les gens risquent de tomber*. In this relative clause the noun *intérieur* has been provided with a PP complement *desquelles* [= *de* + *lesquelles*] in which *quelles* is feminine and plural and refers back to *fosses*, which is also feminine and plural. The complement of the verb is moved to the front of the clause, whereas in (61*b*) it directly follows the verb. Moreover, the complement is quite complex, consisting of an NP plus a PP. This example poses problems analogous to those posed by such English examples as *there's a rope with which you can pull the seat back up*. Spontaneous spoken English simply omits the preposition. French requires the PP *à l'intérieur* but omits the pronoun.

The gap between (61*c*) and its written version is different from the sort just described. The relative clause *qu'il faut appeler les pompiers tout de suite* does convey a property of the set of non-specific fires, but there is no shadow pronoun in the relative clause and no place for one. Instead, the adjective *tels* (such) has to be inserted into the NP *des feux* to yield *il y a des feux tels qu'il faut appeler les pompiers tout de suite*. The use of a procedural description is not to be interpreted as approval of an old-style transformational relationship. All we are entitled to say is that one construction in spontaneous spoken French and another construction in written French are equivalent. In the spoken construction the two clauses are not integrated at all but are merely juxtaposed and loosely linked with the general purpose conjunction *que*. In the written construction the subordinate clause is linked to and is part of the NP *des feux tels que* 'fires such that . . .' and any adequate analysis has to show that the subordinate clause modifies *tels*.

3.7.1.3.2. German
Spoken German also has the classic IE relative clause construction with a relative pronoun (based on the definite article) which, as in Russian, agrees with the head noun in number and gender, and takes its case from its grammatical role in the relative clause. These clauses are subordinate, since they have the finite verb in clause-final position, which is the classic property of subordinate clauses in German.

In addition spoken German has an unintegrated construction. It is used in specific contexts, i.e. with certain existential/presentative constructions which perform particular discourse functions, and may add an element of modality.[1]

(62) (*a*) es gibt doch viele Schriftsteller die   haben keine eigene
      it gives Particle many writers   they [DEMPRO] have no own
      Vorstellung von Zeichensetzung
      idea   of   punctuation
     (*b*) und jetzt hat er ein mädchen die   ist alles andere als schön
      and now has he a   girl   she [DEMPRO] is all else than pretty

(62*a*) begins with the existential clause *es gibt doch viele Schriftsteller*. The next clause begins with *die*. This could be a demonstrative pronoun or a relative pronoun. However the finite verb *haben* is in second position in the clause, which indicates that this is not subordinate but a main clause. *Die* must therefore be a demonstrative; here it points to the set of entities established in the discourse by *viele Schriftsteller* and functions to specify the subset of writers the speaker has in mind. The existential construction in (62*b*) is a possessive existential, with *hat*. As in (62*a*), the first word in the second clause, *die*, is analysed as a demonstrative pronoun, for the same reason. The discourse context of (62*b*) is 'in contrast to his previous girl friend'.

3.7.1.3.3. Bengali and Russian: correlative structures
Although they both belong to the Indo-European language family, Bengali and Russian are far removed from each other with respect to geographical location and grammar. What they do share is a correlative construction corresponding to relative clauses in English. The Bengali correlative construction belongs to both spoken and written Bengali, whereas the Russian construction belongs to spontaneous spoken Russian and does

---

[1] Gaertner (1996)—who does not discuss this phenomenon as pertaining to spoken language, implying that it is non-standard—discusses some of the constraints.

not occur in formal written texts. The Bengali construction is exemplified in (63a,b). (Data from Morshed 1986.)

(63) (a) je   cheleta amar bondhu, se esechilo
     WH boy-the my   friend   he came
     'The boy who is my friend came'
   (b) se esechilo, Je   cheleta amar bondhu
       he came   WH boy-the my   friend [=(a)]

The key feature of the correlative construction is that it consists of two clauses, one containing a non-specific deictic (non-specific for the listener), the other a specific deictic. In (63a) the non-specific deictic is *je cheleta* (WH boy) and the specific deictic is *se* (he). The two clauses can occur in either order, as demonstrated by (63b), which contains exactly the same clauses as (63a) but in reverse order. This construction offers the advantage that both clauses have the word order of main clauses, which means that the Keenan–Comrie hierarchy is irrelevant, but still provides a formal marker of the link by means of the indefinite J deictic and the specific deictic.

Srivastav (1991), analysing the very similar Hindi correlative construction, suggests that a J deictic clause to the left of the specific deictic clause, as in (63a), is base generated away from the NP in the latter and has a quantificational function. It appears that (63b) is not a possible structure of Hindi. What is possible is a structure with the J deictic on its own, unaccompanied by any noun, and the J deictic clause can be adjacent to a noun modified by a specific deictic, as in (64a), or at the end of the clause complex, as in (64b). (Cf. Srivastav 1991: 641–2.)

(64) (a) vo   LaRkii lambii hai jo   kharii   hai
        DEM girl   tall   is WH standing is
        'the girl who is standing is tall'
    (b) vo   laRkii jo   khaRii hai lambii hai
        DEM girl   WH standing is   tall   is

Srivastav proposes that the structure of (64a) is derived from the structure of (64b), which enables the analysis to meet the requirement that nouns and their modifiers must be syntactic sisters. Bengali does have a construction like that in (64a,b) but it also has the constructions in (63a,b), which on Srivastav's approach have to be generated as adjacent clauses, precisely the analysis advocated here.

It is not necessary for the J deictic clause in the Bengali correlative construction to contain a full noun, as shown in (65), where the binding is between *Jekhane* and *se baksota*.

(65) Mou Jekhane angti rekheche, se   baksota dekhte sundor
     Mou WHere ring   put-has   that box   looks beautiful
     'The box in which Mou has put the ring looks beautiful'

Furthermore, the Bengali correlative construction is used where English uses, not a relative clause, but a comparative construction. Cf. (66).

(66) Joto   boi   tumi cao, toto   tumi pabe
     WH-many books you want, that-many you get-will
     'You will get as many books as you want'

To escape the constraints of the accessibility hierarchy, Bengali uses a construction partially corresponding to the Hindi example (64*b*). Consider (67).

(67) ami meeTa, Jake   boi diechilam, se   amar bandhobi
     I   girl-the to-whom book I-gave   she (is) my   friend
     'The girl to whom I gave the book is my friend'

The construction looks, prima facie, like an English construction that will be discussed in Chapter 5, in which an NP is followed by a complete clause containing a shadow pronoun, as in *the driver you get a good laugh with him*. In (67) the initial NP *ami meeTa, jake boi diechilam* contains a relative clause, the J deictic being in a separate clause from its head noun, *meeTa*. The core clause in the construction is *se amar bandhobi*, which can stand on its own as a main clause. The Bengali construction solves the encoding and decoding problem by allowing speakers to produce a main clause that picks up the reference of the noun modified by the J clause. That is, there is a complex J clause, but it is not integrated into another clause.

The Russian construction is similar. Let us note first that standard written Russian and formal spoken Russian have a classical Indo-European relative clause construction with a relative pronoun. Prepositions cannot be stranded but always immediately precede the relative pronoun. The relative pronoun either constitutes the first phrasal constituent in the relative clause, as in (68*a*), or is part of it, as in (68*b*), where it is inside the PP *v kotoroj*. Relative pronouns agree with their head noun in number and gender, but take their case from the verb in the relative clause.

(68) (*a*) kniga,   kotoraja   soderžit eti   teorii
           book [FEM, SG, NOM] which [FEM, SG, NOM] contains these theories

     (*b*) kniga,   v kotoroj   ja našel
           book [FEM, SG, NOM], in which [FEM, SG, LOC] I found
           eti   teorii
           these theories
     (*c*) *kniga, kotoroj ja našel eti teorii v

In (68*a*) *kniga* is a feminine singular noun and the relative pronoun *kotoraja* is feminine and singular, in agreement with *kniga*, and also, by virtue of being subject of the relative clause, in the nominative case. In (68*b*) the relative pronoun is feminine and singular, but its case is locative because it is part of an oblique object. (68*c*) is incorrect because the preposition *v* is at

116 *Spontaneous Spoken Language*

the end of the relative clause. That is, the classical relative clause construction of written and formal spoken Russian has a different word order from main clauses, and direct or oblique object noun phrases are in first position, separated from their governing verb.

The correlative construction offers the same advantages as the Bengali one, namely a juxtaposition of two clauses both with main clause word order, as in (69a–d), which are taken from Lapteva (1976).

(69) (a) kotorye vot klienty est' u menja, i tem ja smotrju
WH Particle customers are at me and to-these I look
'I look after the customers who are mine'

(b) kotorye mal'čiki lomajut, on vsex zabiraet
WH boys break he all catches
'He catches all the boys who break things'

(c) Vot tem, kotorye rebjata ne podgotovleny,
Particle to-them, WH boys not prepared
tem prixodilos' tugo
to-them comes-refl. tight
'The lads who haven't prepared properly find themselves in a tight spot'

(d) Ta, kotoraja zdes' stojala lampa, ja ee ne bral
that WH here was-standing lamp, I it not took
'The lamp which was standing here, I didn't take it'

(69a,b) are straightforward correlative structures with an indefinite deictic clause followed by a clause containing an ordinary deictic. The quantification analysis proposed by Srivastav for Hindi applies quite unproblematically to these examples, picking out the subset of customers who belong to the speaker and the subset of boys who are vandals. In (69c) the indefinite deictic clause is in apposition to the deictic *tem*. The clause is not a relative clause because its subject NP is *kotorye rebjata*, in which *kotorye* is a determiner of *rebjata*. (69d) apparently has a *kotoraja* clause in apposition to the deictic *ta*. This *kotoraja* clause too cannot be a relative clause because *kotoraja* is at the front of the clause and *lampa* is at the end. (69d) suggests that *kotoraja* and *lampa* can occur as independent items, an analysis which gains further support from (70), in which the indefinite deictic clause contains only *kotoroe*, without a noun.

(70) A kotoroe v butylkax, ono segodnjašnee?
but WH in bottles it today's?
'But the [milk] in the bottles, is it today's?'

The question of NPs is discussed at length in Chapter 4; what is important for present purposes is the non-integrated nature of the correlative structure and the fact that it turns up in spoken and written Bengali and, perhaps unexpectedly, in spontaneous spoken Russian.

As a postscript to correlative structures it is worthwhile noting Keenan's

(1985: 165) observation that correlative structures are not attested in rigid verb-final languages such as Japanese and Turkish, nor in rigid SVO or verb-initial languages, but are attested in languages such as Warlbiri, with very free word order, and in early forms of Indo-European languages such as Sanskrit and Medieval Russian. As we have seen above, the construction is very much alive in spoken Modern Russian, in exactly the same form with one exception: Keenan, citing data from an unpublished manuscript by John Payne, gives a Medieval Russian example in which both clauses in the correlative construction contain an occurrence of the same noun. In the first clause it combines with KOTORYJ and in the second with TOT ('that'). Cf. (71).

(71) I   kotoruju zvezdu   potrebno bylo nam videt'
     and   WH-ACC   star-ACC necessary was to-us to-see
     tu   zvezdu   zaslonilo tučeju
     that-ACC star-ACC it-covered cloud-INSTRUMENTAL
     'The star we needed to see was covered by a cloud'

Two final comments here. The above example is of course from a written text and is but one instance of how, in many languages, constructions from spontaneous spoken language find their way into early written texts only to be cast out as writers develop a preference for integrated syntax. And we may ask whether spontaneous spoken Japanese and Turkish are quite as rigid in their word order as the written language and have exactly the same syntactic constructions.

3.7.1.3.4. *Australian Aboriginal Languages*

A number of linguists have commented on the non-integrated subordinate syntax of Australian Aboriginal languages. We will draw on the discussions in Macgregor (1988), Morphy (1983), and Austin (1981). The non-integration and lack of complexity manifests itself in two properties: the simple conjoining of main clauses and the existence of a general subordinate construction corresponding to relative clauses and adverbial clauses in English. (The Australian Aboriginal construction is unhelpfully called a relative clause in grammars of Australian languages.) While English does not have a generalized subordinate clause, we have seen that relative clauses range from the classic type such as *the book that I sent you*, through more loosely integrated structures such as *a party that I haven't got home the same night*, to clauses that look like relative clauses but which do not modify the apparent head noun, as in *some people lift the phone that you think you've interrupted a suicide attempt*. And there is the use of what was, and in many of its occurrences still is, a relative pronoun, *which*, to indicate a general link between two chunks of text. In other words, the spontaneous spoken version of English, with a long-established literary tradition and written variety, offers syntactic phenomena similar to those found in a spoken language that has no literary tradition and no written variety.

Examples (72–73) are from Macgregor's paper on Kuniyanti. (72) is an example of conjoined main clauses that can be interpreted as main clause plus relative clause or main clause plus adverbial clauses. It is two different interpretations that are at issue, and the translation into English differs according to which one is chosen.

(72) thangarnti karntiwangurru kurrumpaya yutjiti
word many paper-LOC we-put-it
thangarnti pinarrikmiluna
word I-taught-them
'We put lots of words down on paper and I taught them the words'
'I taught them the words we had put on paper'

(73) is an example of two conjoined main clauses in which the second one corresponds to an infinitive of purpose in English.

(73) Wartji t uwayirra manyi tuwunga
he-went store-ALL food he-got-it
'He went to the store to get food'

Morphy (1983: 127–9) discusses a general subordinate clause introduced by *ngunhi* which can function as complement clause, relative clause, and adverbial clause of time. (74) is an example of the general subordinate clause as complement.

(74) nganpurr guyangi-rr-ny
1-PL-EXCL think-unmarked-prominence
ngunhi yanbi galki wänga Gurrumuru
COMP mistake close place Currumuru
'We mistakenly though that Gurrumuru was close'

(75) is an instance of the generalized subordinate clause that has two interpretations, as relative clause or adverbial clause of time.

(75) danggu-tanggu bathala-ny/
ray big-PRO
ngayi ngunhi nganya nguli buthuwa-ny
3SG-NOM COMP 3SG-ACC IRREAL give-birth-to
ngunhi-yi yutjuwala-n
that-ABS-ANAPH small-ACC
'The big one is danggu-tanggu, which gives birth to the small one'
'The big one is called danggu-tanggu when it gives birth to the small one'

An example of the generalized subordinate clause functioning as an adverbial clause of condition is given in (76).

(76) ngunhi   nhe yurru guku-m
    COMP 2-sing-NOM fut   harass-unmarked
    ngarra   yaka-n   ngatha-ny   batha-n
    1-sing-NOM not-immediacy food+ABS-prominence   cook-unmarked
    'If you harass me, I won't cook food (for you)'

Writing about Diyari, a language of South Australia, Austin (1981: 209) says, 'It is important to note that the Diyari sentence is simply VAGUE as to the semantic connection between the clauses.' There are ways of ensuring a particular reading of a given 'relative clause', but we must remember that languages are designed for use, face-to-face in context, and in context there is often no difficulty in determining which interpretation is appropriate. That is not to say that a purely oral language will not differentiate the various types of subordinate clause recognized in, say, written English. Rather, speakers in context can communicate successfully without resorting to complex syntax and we should not be surprised by these properties of Australian Aboriginal languages.

Neither should we be surprised to find that similar structures are found in spontaneous spoken English. Consider the sequence *I'm looking for the book Ronnie left it on my table yesterday*. Speakers may or may not have a pause between the two clauses but each clause is likely to have its own pitch pattern. The second clause conveys information about the book in question but is not thereby a relative clause and would be treated as a main clause. There is no information available to us at the time of writing as to the frequency of sequences of main clauses in which the second main clause could be paraphrased as a relative clause, and there is no comparison available to Kuniyanti and English spoken texts. None the less the languages are different; English has a recognizable and regularly used relative clause construction (more than one if we count the standard TH and WH constructions and the shadow pronoun construction as three different structures) and many instances are clearly distinguished from complement and adverbial clauses. Kuniyanti does not have a distinct relative clause structure, only a generalized subordinate construction and speakers are obliged to use either the latter or complexes of main clauses.

Spoken Russian also offers sequences of clauses which could be analysed as main clauses or main clause plus relative clause. Cf. (77).

(77) Idi v   vannu,   voz'mi tam   platoček na trube   soxnet
    go into bathroom take   there cloth   on pipe   is-drying
    'Go into the bathroom and bring the cloth that is drying on the pipe'

There are three clauses in (77), two imperative clauses—*idi v vannu* and *voz'mi tam platoček*. The difficulty lies in the third clause—*na trube soxnet*. There is no overt NP, not even a pronoun, but *soxnet* is a third person singular verb form and the person-number suffix is a deictic pointing to a relevant entity—here, the cloth. The lack of overt subject NPs is a typical feature of Russian, both spoken and written. In written texts topical entities are typically referred to by zero NPs across clause boundaries and even across sentence boundaries, as will be shown in Chapter 5. (77) is reproduced without change from the transcription in Zemskaja (1973), which shows that there is no pause at the clause boundaries in the sequence. Since relative clauses, even in spoken Russian, typically have an indefinite deictic KOTORYJ or KTO, this example will be treated as three main clauses. That is, the phenomenon of the spontaneous spoken language having sequences of main clauses where edited written language prefers a main clause and relative clause is not unique to languages which have only a spoken variety.

3.7.2. WH clefts

Another WH construction that displays non-integrated syntax in spontaneous spoken English is the WH cleft. (The discourse function of this construction will be discussed in Chapter 6 and is ignored here.) Quirk *et al.* (1985: 1388) describe the WH cleft—they call it the pseudo-cleft—as a subject-verb-complement construction with a headless relative clause (they call it a nominal relative clause) as subject or complement. Their initial examples are given here as (78*a*) and (78*b*).

(78) (*a*) A good rest is what you need most
    (*b*) What you need most is a good rest

(78*b*) exemplifies the typical WH cleft. Quirk *et al.* proceed to WH clefts which allow the focus to fall on the predication, as in (79*a–d*).

(79) (*a*) What he's done is (to) spoil the whole thing
    (*b*) What John did to his suit was (to) ruin it
    (*c*) What I'm going to do to him is (to) teach him a lesson
    (*d*) What I'm doing is teaching him a lesson

The key points are that the structure is headless relative + BE + predication (Verb Phrase) and that the predication contains a bare verb stem, *spoil the whole thing*, or an infinitive, *to spoil the whole thing*, or a present participle, *teaching him a lesson*. The last construction occurs when the headless relative contains a progressive.

Quirk *et al.* mention a type of WH cleft with a past participle in the predication, as in (80).

(80) What he's done is spoilt the whole thing

They state that the type illustrated in (80) is of doubtful acceptability, and suggest that it can be seen as an ellipted version of *What he's done is ((this): he's) spoilt the whole thing.*

3.7.2.1. *The syntax of the WH clefts in the Map Task data*

Not surprisingly, most of the WH clefts in the Map Task data differ in structure from Quirk *et al.*'s examples. They consist of the WH headless relative, BE and then a complete clause whose syntax mirrors the syntax of the headless relative. If the latter contains the progressive or the simple construction, the clause complementing BE contains, respectively, the progressive or simple construction. (See (82a–d) below for examples of the progressive.) There are two reasons for the lack of surprise. One is that the latter are devised (but natural) examples that could occur in careful speech or in writing, whereas the Map Task examples were produced in real time by speakers engaged in a complex task. The second is that the structure evinced is exactly the structure to be found in the corpus of free conversations (see J. Miller 1984).

The comments that follow take pitch and pausing into account. Only (81) is an indisputable example of a classic WH cleft.

(81) now what you want to do is curve round that wood so

Two properties make (81) a classic WH cleft: there is no pause, and there is a single pitch pattern over the entire utterance. The predication or Verb Phrase contains a bare verb stem, *curve*, and is fully integrated into the construction. In contrast, a number of WH clefts do not have an integrated structure but consist of a headless relative and BE followed by a complete clause as in (82a–e).

(82) (a) what you're going to do is you're going to continue your downward line for about another inch
 (b) cause what you're doin' is you're goin up the side of the allotments
 (c) right, well, what you're doin' is you're drawin' a line
 (d) eh, what you're doing now is you're going along to the right
 (e) A1 ⟨I've got a fast running creek, and canoes/
  B1 Yeah, ok, what you want to do
  A2 and things⟩
  B2 is is you want to be sort of like going up and then curving right round the fast flowing creek

(83) shows the headless relative and the BE complement both with a simple form.

(83) A1 ⟨Yeah. W . . . What you do/
 B2 Right
 A2 you drop . . . you drop down, then you go right⟩

Some utterances look at first sight as though they contain incomplete WH clefts, but this analysis can be maintained only for (84) and (85).

(84) A See what you're . . .
(85) B So, what we—. . . Oh heck, It's quite difficult to explain . . . Right. There's this kind of group of baboons right . . .

These examples look like embryonic WH clefts, but the WH part is itself incomplete, lacking a verb. (86) is interesting because the syntax of the BE complement does not mirror the syntax of the headless relative.

(86) A1 ⟨And then across, but there's a swan pond. Do you have/
     B1 No I don't
     A2 that?⟩ OK, well what you've got to do is moving across to the left, you should be about three inches from the bottom of the page
     B2 Yeah
     A3 Be- Draw a curve up the way about another inch higher . . .

The headless relative is *what you've go to do* and the BE complement is *you should be about three inches from the bottom of the page*. From the maps it is clear that what B has to do is draw a line from right to left. The first segment of the line has to be three inches from the bottom of the page (the accuracy of the estimates is irrelevant for this discussion) and B has to make the line curve up another inch. That is, the WH structure relates not just to the complement of BE but to the instruction in A's next contribution to the dialogue.

The independence of the two parts of the WH cleft is reinforced by the copula, which both links the two parts and helps to keep them free of each other simply by separating the two important parts of the message. The salience of the cleft clause is enhanced by further properties, one phonetic and one semantic. In the dialogue data the WH clause is often phonetically reduced and minimal in content. In the dialogue and the conversation data the WH clause contains the indefinite deictic *what*, verbs low in content such as DO and HAPPEN, and the pronoun *you*. The following clauses are not phonetically reduced, contain major lexical items and can function independently, as pointed out in the examples above. All these properties downgrade the WH clause, increase the salience of the cleft clause and support the view that the main function of WH clefts in the dialogue data is to focus on, i.e. to make salient, the second clause.

In the analysis of particular examples rhythm and pitch play an important role. For instance, the basic transcription of the Map Task dialogues contains (87)–(89), which look like classic clefts. The rhythm and pitch cast doubt on this analysis.

(87) Eh, what you're going to do is go in between the camera shop and the left-hand side of the page, right

(88) Okay. Now what we have to do is sort of v- veer to the left just a wee bit . . .

(89) what we need to do is turn turn right . . . straight right . . .

The difficulty with (87) is that the rhythm and pitch pattern are compatible with the sequence *go in between the camera shop and the lefthand side of the page* being an imperative main clause. The sequence *what you're going to do is* is spoken with a fastish tempo. There is no drop in pitch and amplitude on *is* (contrary to what happens in other examples), but between *is* and *go* there is a short pause, and the vowel of *go* is held so that it is realized as a double vowel with an increase in amplitude.

In (88) the sequence *what we have to do is sort of* is separated by a medium pause from *v- veer to the left*. In (89) the sequence *what we need to do is* is spoken with a fast tempo. That is, in both (88) and (89) the pausing and the tempo suggest an imperative clause analysis for the sequence following the headless relative. It will be seen from the discussion below that this analysis is compatible with other features of the WH clefts.

The final candidate for the status of classic WH cleft is (90).

(90) A1 I've got a gold mine, a totem pole, and then a great rock, a really good bit down
     B1 right
     A2 And then bandit territory right at the bottom
     B2 Right. What you're trying to do is avoid the totem pole

There are no pauses or differences of tempo in the WH cleft, but the word *avoid* is the site of a considerable pitch movement. This movement could be interpreted as contrastive stress, but the context makes this interpretation unlikely, as no suggestions have been made about the route and the totem pole. Another possible interpretation is that the sequence *avoid the totem pole* is an imperative construction. For present purposes the question remains open: the key point is that what looks like a classic WH cleft on paper may turn out to be of doubtful status when suprasegmental features are taken into account.

3.7.2.2. *WH clefts in free conversation*

The examples presented above enable us to establish a continuum with the classic WH cleft construction at one pole, a looser construction—headless relative + BE + complete clause—in the middle, and an even looser construction in which the lexical items in the BE complement clause do not match the lexical items in the headless relative. There are even looser constructions. In (83), for instance, the headless relative is not even connected with the following clause by BE: *What you do—you drop—you drop down*, and the focusing effect of the headless relative in (90) actually extends over several clauses following that excerpt. In free conversation

124 Spontaneous Spoken Language

WH clefts are regularly used either to open a text or to introduce a change of topic or an elaboration of a topic. These discourse functions will be discussed in Chapter 6 but are relevant here because they are often associated with WH clefts whose connection with the following chunk of syntax is even more tenuous than in the examples discussed above. Consider (91)–(93).

(91) What I thought I'd do Chairman: as you all know, the most important issue at the moment is the poll-tax

(92) I'll just give the mixture a little stir first because what happens is things tend to settle a bit

(93) A what are you doing to these
     B what we're doing we're hanging them up to drouth

(91) was uttered by a Member of Parliament addressing a meeting; the headless relative does not tie in syntactically or lexically with the following chunk, and in fact is more of a general please-pay-attention message allowing the audience to concentrate their minds before the important information arrives. The speaker did not outline what he thought he would do, but plunged *in medias res*. Speakers on radio interviews or discussion programmes use examples such as *What I say: the danger from whooping cough is far greater than the danger from the vaccination.* (92) was produced by the resident expert on a TV cookery programme, not in response to questions but simply giving a running commentary on the preparation of a dish. (93) is particularly interesting because it shows a WH cleft arising out of a WH question. A asks *what are you doing to these?* (*these* being herring about to be smoked) and B echoes the question, with appropriate change of person, in *what we're doing*, which is then followed by a main clause *we're hanging them up to drouth* (the last word, meaning 'dry', reflecting the location of the smokery in Arbroath, on the east coast of Scotland).

English and German WH clefts are structurally similar. While we find syntactically integrated examples such as (94), there are also cases where the cleft clause stands on its own as in (95)–(97).

(94) ja   was   ich bei   Bernstein immer besonders   schwierig finde
     yes   what I   with   Bernstein always especially   difficult find
     ist die Tatsache, daß er nicht klar   trennt   zwischen
     is the fact   that he not   clearly distinguishes   between
     linguistischen,   soziologischen   und   psychologischen Variablen
     linguistic,   sociolinguistic and   psychological   variables

Like the preceding English examples, (94) contains a WH clause—*was ich bei Bernstein immer besonders schwierig finde*. As in the classic English WH clefts in (79), this clause is followed by the copula *ist* and its complement, a noun modified by a complement clause—*die Tatsache, daß er nicht klar trennt* . . . It may well be significant that the speaker is clearly a person with higher education, versed in linguistic literature and discussing serious topics. (95)–(97) are more like the unintegrated WH clefts.

(95) was du jetzt angesprochen hast
 what you now referred-to have
 das ist eben dieses klischeehafte krimifilmchen
 that is (MODAL Part.) this clichéd crime-film (diminutive)

(96) und was ja vielfach gemacht wird das wird ja
 and what (MODAL Part.) often done is that is (MODAL Part.)
 gemixt
 mixed

(97) was ich noch sagen wollte ich hab dir das geld da hingelegt
 what I still to-say wanted I have you (Dative) the money there put

(95) is not unlike the Bengali correlative construction discussed in § 3.7.1.3.3. The first clause has an indefinite deictic *was* (see the following section) and the second clause has a definite deictic *das* specifying the referent of the *was* clause. (96) has the same construction, (97) does indeed begin with a WH clause, but the latter is followed by a main clause with no definite deictic. *Was* simply points forward to the main clause and in this respect (97) resembles the English examples in (83), (91), and (93).

3.7.2.3. *WH pronouns as indefinite deictics*

Givón (1979: 217–18) suggests that IT cleft constructions arose historically from a paratactic combination of a copula structure IT BE NP and a headless relative WHO V NP, as in *It was John who did it*. (The relative clause is treated as a presupposition that is added to the focused assertion IT BE NP as an afterthought.) Our data from spontaneous spoken English do not favour Givón's analysis of the IT cleft but do allow his analysis to be extended to WH clefts.

The alternative to Givón's approach has at its centre the view that WH words are indefinite deictics used for pointing at entities not in the immediate situation of utterance because not yet mentioned. This view will be argued for, first, on the basis of English and then on the basis of the corresponding Russian items. Consider the following uses of WH words in English. Speakers either ask for a specification of an entity, as in *Who is going to drive the car?* or provide the specification, as in *I tell you what—you drive the car and I'll take the train* or *I remember what he bought for our first anniversary—a beautiful Chinese watercolour*. In the first example, *you drive the car* specifies *what* and in the second example—*a beautiful Chinese watercolour*. The rationale behind the use of WH words in interrogatives can be reconstructed as the speaker saying, as it were, 'Someone is going to drive the car—specify the person.' The WH pronouns in WH clefts function in the same way. The speaker who utters the sequence *what he did was* points the listeners in the direction of something that is non-specific for them but specific for the speaker. In the expectation that the speaker will provide an appropriate specification, the listener pays attention to what follows.

The Russian equivalents of the English WH words are instructive because they occur in interrogatives and relative clauses and even in constructions akin to headless relatives but are quite clearly non-specific deictics. The interrogative construction is exemplified in (98*a*), the relative clause construction in (98*b*), the headless relative construction in (98*c*). The occurrence of *kto* in conditional clauses is shown in (99), and clear deictic uses are exemplified in (100*a,b*).

(98) (*a*) Kto pozvonil
      Who telephoned?
  (*b*) My priglasili na daču   tex, kto nam pomagali
     we invited to (the) dacha those who us were-helping
  (*c*) kto u vas živet/ včera   k nam zaxodila
     who at you lives yesterday to us came
     'The person who lives in your flat called on us yesterday'

(99) esli kto pridet, skaži, čto vernus' zavtra
    if anyone comes say that I-will-be-back tomorrow

(100) (*a*) kto-to zvonil
      someone phoned
  (*b*) nadejus', čto nam pomožet kto-nibud'
     I-hope that us will-help someone

Let us begin with the obviously deictic uses. In (100*a*) *kto-to* consists of *kto* plus a definite deictic *to*. Speakers who use (100*a*) signal that they can specify the someone, either to the extent of identifying the caller or to the lesser extent of being able to say *It sounded like a woman of 30 or so*. In (100*b*), *kto-nibud'* consists of *kto* plus the non-specific suffix *nibud'*. The latter derives from the combination of the negative *ni* and the imperative form of *byt'* (be): i.e. it has the force of 'let it be anybody'. Speakers producing (100*b*) do not have a specific referent in mind and cannot provide further information.

In (98*c*) *kto* has specific reference and has to be translated into English by 'the one who' or 'the person who', that is, by means of a definite referring expression. The occurrence of *kto* in relative clauses is limited in written Russian to clauses modifying the pronoun TOT (that one), though it occurs in a wider range of relative clauses in spontaneous spoken Russian. In relative clauses *kto* also has specific reference, in that its reference is bound to the entity referred to by the noun modified by the relative clause. The apparently non-deictic usage is in the interrogative in (98a), but even here the speakers know that there is an entity. The speaker's message is 'I know that someone telephoned. Please specify that someone.'[2]

WH clefts can be seen as arising from a combination of two clauses, a headless relative with a WH deictic and a main clause. The WH deictic is non-specific for the listener but specific for the speaker, who can give the listener further information about the referent. It may well be that the discourse conditions that helped the development of the construction are those applying in (93), where one speaker asks a WH question and the second speaker echoes the question before answering it. The main clause following the headless relative can be declarative, as in the examples above, or interrogative or imperative, as in (101).

(101) (a) What I would like to know (is) how did he manage to get that job
 (b) What I want you to do—go down to the office and check the unpaid bills

The distinction between presupposed and focused material still applies. Speakers producing headless relative clauses (as part of the WH cleft construction) take situations or propositions for granted and proceed to ask about one of the entities in the situation or proposition. The non-integrated syntax is typical of spontaneous spoken English; either two clauses linked by BE or two clauses simply juxtaposed. With respect to (101a), note that the written English version is *What I would like to know is how he managed to get the job*, in which the complement of *is* has declarative syntax apart from the WH word in first position. (101a) is the typical indirect question construction in spontaneous spoken English. (See the discussion in §3.4.1.3.) The details of the constructions are not straightforward. The interrogative structure in (101a) occurs as the complement of verbs such as KNOW, ASK, and WONDER. The declarative structure can function as subject (but this is not typical of spontaneous speech) as in *How he managed to get the job puzzled everyone*, and as the object of verbs such as DISCOVER—*We discovered how he managed to get the job*. The historical development of the two indirect question constructions is obscure; the crucial point is that they both rest on the non-specific-deictic nature of WH words.

3.7.2.4. *IT clefts*

We turn now to IT clefts. The examples cited by Givón (1979: 217–18) are reproduced in (102a,b).

---

[2] § 2.5.5.2 contains a discussion of 'condensed relative pronouns'. The analysis there relates to the topic of fragmented syntax in Russian and is relevant to the current topic too. The clauses introduced by *čto* or *čem* are similar to, though not identical with, headless relative clauses in English.

(102) (a) It's John who left
(b) It was John who did it

Givón's analysis is that the clause *It was John*, carrying the speaker's assertion, has added to it a noun phrase containing a relative clause *(the one) who did it*. The first problem with this account is that the IT clefts in our data do not contain WH clauses but contact clauses, as in (103) or (104).

(103) We're we're after everything I mean not not not the phonetics because that's fairly well known anyway em **it's the SYNtax we're after**

(104) Cause I was supposed to we were wanting pictures in dress costume for Viva Mexico you know and there's no costumes and I'm supposed to have it for today and I forgot all about it so I'm not very popular I don't know **I think it's one of the TEAchers is takin photographs** but I hate gettin my picture taken so I'm no very fussy I don't mind

Both examples are from the corpus of free conversation. One noteworthy feature of (104) is the contact 'relative clause' *is taking photographs*. It is surprising that there is no complementizer or relative pronoun because the latter would have been the subject of the clause and subject relative pronouns or nouns are not omissible in written English. (But cf. §3.7.1.1 on relative clauses in spontaneous spoken English.)

Since WH clauses do not occur in the IT clefts in our data, Givón's analysis involving questions and headless relatives is not appropriate. Exactly what analysis is appropriate is unfortunately not clear. The first problem is the nature of what we have been calling the relative clause. Quirk *et al.* (1985: 1386–7, 1406–7) discuss the syntactic differences between ordinary relative clauses and the 'relative clauses' in IT clefts, concluding that the latter are different in certain important respects and should be called annex clauses. Sornicola (1989) shows that the problems posed by the English construction are also posed by the corresponding constructions in other language. (105a,b) illustrate two problems.

(105) (a) It's me that doesn't like polenta
(b) It's me that's kicking himself for not seeing the answer to the problem

In (105a) the NP complement of BE in the first clause is the first person pronoun *I*. Since the 'relative clause' modifies that noun, its verb should also be first person but in fact is third person, *doesn't*. The same remarks apply to (105b), with the additional complication that the reflexive pronoun in the 'relative clause' is also third person. Quirk *et al.* (1985: 1387) observe that the WH forms are rare in IT clefts, and that while *whose* does occur, *whom* or *which* preceded by a preposition are only marginally possible. It is clear that any analysis in which WH forms play a central role is descriptively inadequate.

An alternative analysis of the IT cleft is that it consists of a copula clause in which an NP is highlighted by being the complement of BE, which has a dummy subject IT. The major semantic content, that is, is postponed to the end of the clause to a position that is inherently prominent. The annex clause is not a relative clause but a main clause that was initially juxtaposed with the copula clause and came to acquire a formal marker of the link in the form of *that*, which is still optional. This is advanced as a plausible hypothesis in the light of what we know about spontaneous spoken English and other languages but it receives support from two further types of evidence.

The first is that the annex clause can be phonetically reduced and even missing. Consider first example (106) in which the annex clause is highly redundant with respect to the information it carries. This annex clause is unstressed and the preceding context makes clear what its import is.

(106) A1 see the side where the cliffs are
      A2 go along till go straight along then down till you're about a cm above the picture of the waterfall
      B2 so its the side nearest the CLIFFS i've to go to

A1 mentions *the side* and A2 mentions *go . . . till. I've to go to* is highly given in the context of the map task. This property, together with the self-contained structure of the IT BE X sequence in IT clefts, makes them omissible.

The conversation data yielded 20 examples that are good candidates for analysis as IT clefts with omitted WH clauses. The examples include only IT BE X structures for which the preceding discourse supplies an obvious annex clause, but it is not always easy to distinguish between reduced IT clefts and anaphoric IT BE X structures. Examples are given in (107*a–c*).

(107) (*a*) A1 right come on who was first through that fence come on own up
           B1 nobody was owning up
           A2 yes I **it was me** I think **no it wasn't it was George**
           B2 you didn't own up
           A3 no it was **it was George**
      (*b*) A so when do they start again
           B eh **it's the middle of the month**
      (*c*) A really what did they think had happened
           B well **it was the speed that we went into the toilet at** because you dinnae wander about the corridor soakin wet yeah they thought somebody had broke a leg or something

(107*a*) can be understood as *it was George that owned up*, (107*b*)—as *it's the middle of the month they start again* and (107*c*)—as *it was the speed we went into the toilet at that got them worried*. These copula clauses function like IT clefts in that they activate a particular entity in the set of possible candidates for owning up, the starting date, and the reason why the teachers became alarmed. These examples demonstrate that the copula clause occurs on its own with the same discourse effect as a full IT cleft. Examples such as (108) demonstrate that the copula clause can be followed by a declarative clause.

(108) it was Dave   he suggested we spend that money

And (108) is a possible stepping stone to a construction with the two clauses linked by *that* and then further to a construction in which the subject pronoun of the second clause is ellipted: *it was Dave that suggested we spend that money*.

There is an interesting difference between full and reduced IT clefts. 87% of the full IT clefts in our data have single NP clefted constituents, compared with only 50% of the reduced clefts. However, as their clefted constituent the reduced clefts also have adverbial clauses and sequences of NP + relative clause and NP + complement clause. It appears that longer clefted constituents are only possible in spoken language when the annex clause is omitted, which is not surprising given the less complex and less integrated syntax of spontaneous spoken language.

In addition to IT clefts, our data also has two rare examples of an IT cleft structure where IT is replaced with THAT, as in (109).

(109) that was Stavros who said that

3.7.3. *Headless relative clauses in Russian*

We have looked at headless relative clauses in English in connection with WH clefts and found them to be relatively unintegrated with the complement of BE, as in (82). Of course headless relative clauses can and do occur as well-integrated subjects and objects of matrix clauses, as in (110*a,b*).

(110) (*a*) What you're doing won't please everyone
     (*b*) I reported what he had said

Written Russian does not have an exact equivalent of the English headless relative construction but has instead a construction in which a relative clause modifies a definite deictic, as in (111*a,b*).

(111) (*a*) To, čto   vy delaete, ne   ponravitsja vsem
        that which you are-doing not   will-please to-everybody
    (*b*) Ja soobščil to, čto   on skazal
        I   reported that which he said

In contrast, Zemskaja's corpus of spoken Russian does have headless relative clauses functioning as subjects, direct objects, indirect objects, and oblique objects, but they are poorly integrated into the matrix clause. Examples are provided by Zemskaja (1973: 228 ff.) under the heading of 'condensed relative pronouns' and are discussed in § 2.5.5.2, as mentioned in note 2 above. One of Zemskaja's examples is (112), in which the WH clause in Russian, *kak exat'*, is at the end of the main clause but is so loosely connected with it that it can be analysed as being in apposition to it.

(112) ja ne znaju dorogu (kak exat')
     I not know road (how to-go)

The indefinite deictic clause in (112), *kak exat'*, would in written Russian be replaced by relative clauses; say, *po kotoroj nado exat'* (along which necessary to-travel). Spontaneous spoken English offers similar and frequently occurring constructions. Consider first (113).

(113) (*a*) everyone knows Helen Liddell how hard she works
      (Radio Discussion Programme)
   (*b*) look at his face what they've done to it
      (Script of 'The Bill', ITV)

Each example consists of a main clause followed by a headless relative clause. In (113*a*) the main clause is *everyone knows Helen Liddell* and the headless relative clause is *how hard she works*. In (113*b*) the main clause is *look at his face* and the headless relative clause is *what they've done to it*. The main point conveyed by (113*a*) is how hard Helen Liddell works, by (113*b*)—the extent of the injuries to the man's face. These points could be expressed by means of a single clause containing a WH complement— *everyone knows how hard Helen Liddell works* and *look at what they've done to his face*. The construction in (113*a*) not only enables the speaker to avoid a complement clause but to highlight the principal information. In (113*a*) the main clause re-establishes Helen Liddell as the focus of attention. The headless relative introduces a new property of Helen Liddell, her capacity for work. The listeners can process the main clause, moving Helen Liddell back into their focus of attention, before processing the headless relative clause.[3] (The same commentary, *mutatis mutandis*, can be applied to (113*b*).) A plausible hypothesis is that this strategy enables speakers (and listeners) to cope with the limitations of short-term memory as outlined in the discussion of Chafe's work in Chapter 1.

---

[3] Note examples such as *It's amazing how many books she buys* in which the subject of the main clause is *it* and the clause *how many books she buys* is in apposition (or a relationship not unlike apposition). This is an example of Extraposition and the occurrence of a clause in clause-final position rather than in subject position is not surprising. Frequently, however, examples occur in which the extraposed constituent is not a clause but an ordinary noun phrase: *it's amazing the things he gets away with*. The classic label 'Extraposition' is misleading. It suggests that a constituent moves from one position to another, whereas the approach taken here is that what you see is what the speaker started with.

3.8. Conclusion

The data presented in this chapter does not make easy reading but is essential to the argument that spontaneous spoken language has its own syntactic structures and its own patterns of inter-clause connection. Picking up the point made at the beginning of the chapter, we would emphasize the presence in various languages of similar constructions and the regularity with which they occur. Apart from its relevance to questions of processing, this data (along with the data in Chapters 5 and 6) plays a central role in the discussions of typology in Chapter 7 and of language acquisition and sociolinguistic issues in Chapter 8.

4 Noun Phrases: Complexity and Configuration

4.1. Introduction

Another property that varies between spontaneous spoken language and written language is the structure and complexity of phrases. This observation is not new. For Russian Sirotinina (1974: 79–80) establishes a scale of genres going from formal written language through academic spoken discourse, literary discourse, and informal letters to conversation. She observes that as one moves along the scale from formal writing to spontaneous speech the number of full nouns diminishes as does the number of adjectives. For full nouns she cites figures of 386 per 1,000 words in formal writing but only 142 in conversation; and for adjectives, 152 per 1,000 words in formal writing but only 39 in conversation. Krasil'nikova (1990: 20) also mentions the lack of complex and combined phrases but notes additional properties of NPs in spontaneous spoken Russian; typically only the final noun in an NP has a case affix, and in frequent phrasal combinations of words the case of the first word spreads to the other words (Krasil'nikova 1990: 31).[1]

Hawkins (1969) and Coulthard and Robinson (1968) present studies of English noun phrases ('nominal groups'). Both papers conclude that the structure of noun phrases in written language is more complex than the structure of noun phrases in spoken language, modifiers of all types being rare in the former but typical in the latter. (See the reference to Jucker's recent work in §4.2.2.) Biber (1988: 89, 104–8) establishes what he calls 'Factor 1', related to a textual dimension of involved versus informational production. Involved production has to do with discourse produced under real-time conditions, which typically exclude the time-consuming processes of making precise lexical choices and packing a lot of information into a small amount of text. The latter task requires the use of adjectives, prepositional phrases, and participial phrases, all of

---

[1] One example is *k 20 janvarju* 'by the 20th of January'. In literary Russian *20*—*dvadcatomu* in words—is in the dative case, and the word for January is in the genitive case—*janvarja*. In this example from Krasil'nikova *janvarju* is also in the dative case.

which have a high negative weighting. That is, they are not found in spontaneous spoken English (or indeed Russian, as will become clear from §4.2.2).

This chapter provides linguistic detail to support Biber and demonstrates that English is no different in this respect from Russian or from German (although we only glance briefly at German). We will also consider the structure of NPs in spoken Russian, drawing some comparative data from descriptions of some Australian languages, which are relevant as being only spoken. Whereas the data presented in Chapters 2 and 3 bear on the general properties of spontaneous speech, the noun phrase data to be described here contribute to our understanding of the syntax of spontaneous speech but also relate to controversial topics in current syntactic theory; what constituent should be taken as the head of a noun phrase and indeed what is the structure of a noun phrase? Since the data from spontaneous spoken language yield a different perspective from that found in accounts based on written language, the topic is discussed in §4.6. The central fact is that both spoken Russian and Australian languages possess a 'split' NP construction that poses interesting problems for formal models, and is relevant to the controversy over whether the heads of NPs are nouns or determiners. We will suggest that for Russian (both spoken and written) adjectives and nouns are equally good contenders for the status of head, and that for any given noun phrase the choice depends on context. The main points that will emerge are:

i specific information on the ways in which NPs in spontaneous spoken language are simpler than NPs in written language;

ii interesting structural differences, in some languages, between NPs in spontaneous speech and NPs in writing.

The above data (**ii**) will be discussed in relation to the following theoretical issues:

iii heads and modifiers in noun phrases, including the role of deictics (in particular the deictic suffixes on a class of adjectives in Russian);

iv the contribution of the data to the question of configurational and non-configurational languages, in particular the view that spoken Russian is not necessarily configurational while formal written Russian is;

v the inappropriateness of standard transformational operations such as Scrambling for the split, unintegrated NP structures in the spoken varieties of certain languages.

The relevance of the data and the surrounding theoretical discussion for typology and theories of language acquisition will be considered in detail in Chapters 7 and 8.

4.2. Complexity of Noun Phrases

4.2.1. *Noun phrases in written English*

One striking feature of spontaneous spoken language is the simplicity of noun phrases (NPs) in comparison with the NPs that occur in written language, particularly in the language of formal written texts. Let us remind ourselves that written English (and Russian and German) is not a single homogeneous genre but a collection of many different genres. With respect to noun phrases the general picture is that the most complex structures are found in dense technical texts (such as academic monographs, legal documents, encyclopaedia articles, broadsheet newspapers) with the least complex structures in tabloid newspapers, comics, and books for young children.

What do we mean by 'simplicity'? For written English (and written Russian and written German) a relatively simple noun phrase consists of a noun modified by one or two adjectives, or a numeral/quantifier, or a prepositional phrase, or some combination of these modifiers. The simplest noun phrases consist of just a noun or pronoun. The most complex noun phrases consist of a noun modified by participial phrases or relative clauses, possibly in combination with adjectives, quantifiers, and prepositional phrases. (1*a–g*), from Thubron (1987), exemplify some of the noun phrase structures to be found in serious but not weighty literature.

(1) (*a*) the beautiful marble gates
    (*b*) a perfectly framed backdrop
    (*c*) minutely woven gold thread
    (*d*) a wild apricot tree red on the bare slopes
    (*e*) a bank coaxing investors with a lottery
    (*f*) (the elephants rested on) legs buckled before them in defiance of anatomy
    (*g*) a youth in jeans

(1*a*) contains the noun *gates* and two adjectives, *beautiful* and *marble*. (1*b*) contains the noun *backdrop*, modified by the participial phrase *perfectly framed*. (1*c*) contains a noun modified by a participial phrase, *minutely woven*, and an adjective, *gold*. In (1*d*) the head noun *apricot tree* is itself compound, and is preceded by an adjective, *wild*, and followed by an adjective phrase, *red on the bare slopes*, in which *red* is modified by the prepositional phrase *on the bare slopes*. In (1*e*) the noun *bank* is followed by a participial phrase *coaxing investors with a lottery*, and in (1*f*) the noun *legs* is followed by a participial phrase containing a passive participle, *buckled*. (1g) contains a noun, *youth*, modified by a prepositional phrase, *in jeans*. Other types of NP not exemplified in (1) but common in formal written English are *politicians who do not like change* (noun modified by a relative clause), *three wise men* (numeral, adjective, and noun), *all these interesting books* (quantifier, determiner, adjective, and noun). In general it is taken for granted that nouns can be preceded by a large number of adjectives, in fact an infinite number, limited only by physical constraints of time, memory, and energy. An NP can in principle contain any combination of the modifying structures mentioned above, as in the fabricated example *all three of these wise men, given the good news by a herald and bearing gifts, who journeyed from the East*.

The examples in (1) will not be considered particularly complex by adults who regularly read serious literature; much more complex NPs are not hard to find. Let us briefly look at examples of the most complex English NP structures. They come from articles in *The Guardian* and from an issue of the *Newsletter* produced in the Human Communication Research Centre in the University of Edinburgh. The 39 NPs which were collected were very complex in their syntax (and also in their vocabulary).[2]

i Some NPs contain both a participial phrase and a relative clause, e.g. *the government-backed Alvey Project which aimed for a massive increase in information-technology based resources*. The head of the NP is the compound noun *Alvey Project*. It is preceded by the participial phrase *government-backed* and followed by the relative clause *which aimed for a massive increase in information-technology based resources*. The relative clause in turn contains the complex NP *a massive increase in information-technology based resources*. The head of this second NP is *increase*, which is modified by the adjective *massive* and the prepositional phrase *in . . . resources*. The prepositional phrase contains a complex NP in which the head noun, *resources*, is modified by a participial phrase containing a compound noun, *information-technology based*.

ii In another type of complex NP the head noun is modified by a number of pre-modifiers, each of which is complex. Consider the noun phrase *a garishly vertical jokingly post-modern Holiday Inn*. The head noun, *Holiday Inn*, is modified by two APs both containing an Intensifier and an Adjective, *garishly vertical* and *jokingly post-modern*.[3]

---

[2] The discussion in Chapter 1 can usefully be recalled; the actual numbers of NP tokens are not crucial at this particular point, since we are concerned with the types of structure that were found, not with their frequency.

[3] These NP structures are important both linguistically and socially. Such complex NPs are typical and quite frequent in formal written English. They do not occur in less formal written

Further general points can be made about noun phrases in written English.

iii English quality newspapers and monographs contain complex compound nouns such as *state-owned development bank* and *Queen's Moat House lenders*. In the former compound the core—*development bank*—is modified by a compound participle, *state-owned*; in the latter two noun phrases are compounded—*Queen's Moat* and *lenders*, and the first noun phrase consists of the compound *Moat House* preceded by *Queen's*. These compounds are far more complex than the compounds that occur in spontaneous (or even not-so-spontaneous speech), as will be demonstrated below.

iv Even light literature offers many examples of shorter NPs which are nonetheless quite complex compared with the general run of NPs in spontaneous speech (as will be shown shortly): NPs such as *interrupted silk sutures* and *a shimmering, yellow ocean*, in which the head noun *sutures* is modified by a participle and an adjective. These come from the novel *It Shouldn't Happen to a Vet* by James Herriot, a novel which is generally light and amusing in tone but occasionally throws up NPs that are as complex as the two discussed in the preceding paragraphs. One such NP, which we leave unanalysed, is *a unique combination of born horseman and dexterous surgeon with which I couldn't compete*.

Complexity *per se* is important but complexity also interacts with grammatical function, as mentioned below in connection with Quirk *et al.* (1985), Jucker's work on newspapers, and Thompson's work on English and Chinese cited in §4.2.2. Consider the examples in (2), taken from Haegeman (1991: 382). They demonstrate how complexity interacts with direct and oblique objects; where a clause contains a heavy direct object and a light oblique object, as in (2*b*), the heavy direct object is typically moved to the end of the clause.

(2) (*a*) Jeeves introduced $_{DO}$[the famous detective from Belgium] $_{OO}$[to the guests]
    (*b*) Jeeves introduced $_{OO}$ [to the guests] $_{DO}$ [the famous detective from Belgium]

(2*a*) is considered clumsy because the long direct object NP *the famous detective from Belgium* separates the oblique object *to the guests* from the

English, certainly not in spontaneous speech and not in the writing of most pupils at primary and secondary school. That is, they are typical of the kind of written English that is an indispensable part of higher education and even the later years of secondary edition. They are difficult to understand, never mind produce, and, along with complex sentences, are a central part of the language barrier that has to be crossed, on the way not just to good qualifications and well-paid jobs but to understanding of and participation in social and political developments.

verb *introduced*. The rearrangement of the direct object and oblique object yields (2*b*), which is much more satisfactory. Discussions of heavy NPs do not usually pay attention to subject NPs (infinitives and gerunds in subject position are excluded from the present discussion) and in the linguistic literature examples such as *All the politically active people who received the message came to the meeting* are not treated as having a heavy NP that needs to be repositioned.

The above observation is interesting because, although complex NPs can in principle occur as subjects in English (and Russian and German), examinations of texts have revealed that there is a strong tendency for subject NPs not to be complex. This is true of spontaneous spoken language, as will be shown in §4.3, but it is also true of written texts; of the 39 complex NPs from the *Guardian* articles and the newsletter only 5 were grammatical subjects. The tendency varies according to type of written text; heavy subject NPs are more frequent in academic monographs, broadsheet newspapers, and serious literature such as biography than in detective novels and tabloid newspapers. Jucker (1992), working on British newspapers, collected information on the occurrence of simple and modified NPs as subjects and non-subjects. Quirk *et al.* (1985): 1350–2) proposed a correlation between subject and NPs with no modifiers and between non-subject and NPs with modifiers. Jucker found that the association between simple NP and subject, modified NP and non-subject, was weaker than in the data examined by Quirk *et al.* (1985); 1350–2). For his newspaper texts he calculated the overall percentage of simple nouns appearing in subject position and the percentage of complex nouns appearing in subject position. The relevant figures were 43.4% and 27.5%, which differ by only 15.9 percentage points. The corresponding figures in Quirk *et al.*'s study are 48.4 percentage points for informal speech and 25.2 percentage points for scientific writing. Interestingly, a finer analysis showed that the differences in figures vary according to category of newspaper. For the down-market newspapers the figure is 18.6, for the mid-market papers 16.6, and for the up-market papers 14.6. That is, the up-market papers have a significantly larger proportion of their modified NPs in subject position.

In fact, regardless of subjects and non-subjects, the frequency of nouns with modifiers varies across different types of written text, as does the grammatical function of modified nouns. With his sample of up-market, mid-market, and down-market newspapers, Jucker (1992: 117ff.) demonstrated statistically significant differences in the occurrence of modified and unmodified nouns. The down-market papers had the smallest percentage of modified nouns and the smallest percentage of nouns with more than one modifier; the up-market newspapers had the greatest percentage of both types. The mid-market papers were exactly halfway between the other two groups.

To summarize, as illustrated by the above written-language examples, NPs in written language can potentially contain any number and a large variety of pre-modifying and post-modifying elements. The relevant linguistic literature concentrates on the ordering of NPs rather than the complexities of NPs themselves, and excludes NPs functioning as grammatical subject. This restriction has prevented the development of the interesting hypothesis (which is implicit in the literature) that the avoidance of complex NPs (in spontaneous speech generally and in subject position in less formal writing) and the avoidance of complex direct objects before simple oblique objects can be explained with respect to ease of processing. If this hypothesis is correct it will allow a closer relationship to be established between competence and performance.

4.2.2. Noun phrases in spontaneous speech

The preceding section provides examples of various noun phrase structures that are typical of written English. The contrast between academic or legal texts and light literature is large but it turns out to be minor in comparison with the contrast between spontaneous spoken language and other varieties. With one exception, written English texts will not be examined in detail, since the general characteristics of noun phrases in written English are contained in the lists of properties presented in Biber (1988), are discussed in Quirk *et al.* (1985: 1350–2), and are examined in Jucker (1992) with respect to different types of newspaper. We will however investigate the noun phrases in one written English text and in two spontaneous spoken English texts. The former consists of the readers' letters in one issue of a British broadsheet newspaper and the latter are the narrative entitled 'the great American sandwich' and an extract from spontaneous conversation. We will also present the general results of work on samples of text from a Russian conversation and a mid-market newspaper, with a brief look at a Russian academic monograph (Kubrjakova, Šaxnarovič, and Saxarnyi 1991) and a Russian novel (Voinovič 1976). 'Brief' means that the major properties are mentioned in the discussion, but there are no tables for the monograph or the novel. Three spoken German texts will be considered; a Telephone Conversation (Brons-Albert 1984), a Face-to-Face Conversation (Texte . . .II/3 1975), and a Map Task dialogue.

Before dealing with the specific details of the spoken English texts, it will be helpful to comment on the general properties of NPs in spontaneous speech.

i The number of words in a given set of noun phrases is important; noun phrases with more than one adjective are rare both in the English and the Russian data and in the supplementary set of German data discussed in

§4.5. Even more important is the *structure* of noun phrases and this is what we focus on here: to what extent do NPs contain adjective phrases or prepositional phrases, relative clauses or participial phrases? How frequently do we come across combinations of, say, adjective phrase and relative clause in the same noun phrase, and prepositional phrases or relative clauses embedded inside prepositional phrases which are in turn embedded in a noun phrase? Also important is the grammatical function of complex NPs and the grammatical function of nouns modified by relative clauses and participial phrases. (See the discussion in §4.2.1 of noun phrases in different types of newspaper.)

ii All our spontaneous texts contain relatively high proportions of noun phrases consisting of a personal pronoun. In the spoken English narrative the proportion is 44.9%, in the conversation 48.9%. In contrast, the proportion in the readers' letters is 14.1%. The proportion in the Russian conversation is only 21.9%, but this is almost twice the percentage in the Russian newspaper and academic monograph texts—10% and 12.1%, respectively. It is not however much higher than the figure for the novel, where 16.8% of the noun phrases consist of personal pronouns. In the German telephone conversation single pronoun NPs account for 43.9% of NPs. In the German face-to-face conversation they account for 38.7% and in a Map Task dialogue for 52.4%. In a newspaper text only 6.6% of the NPs were single pronouns.

The relatively low percentage of personal pronouns in the Russian conversation is partly explained by the number of clauses with zero subjects and with impersonal constructions, 172 altogether.[4] An example of zero subject is *priedem v tri časa* 'we-will-arrive at three o'clock'. *Priedem* is a first person plural form of the verb referring to the speaker and one or more other people. An example of an impersonal construction is *menja mutit* lit. 'me makes-sick', i.e. 'I feel sick'. *Mutit* is the third person singular, present tense, form of the verb and *menja* is an accusative case form; that is, *menja* is the direct object of *mutit*. Another impersonal construction consists merely of the neuter form of an adjective and the third person singular of the copula in references to past or future time: *xolodno* 'cold', i.e. 'it is cold'. The low percentage can also partly be attributed to the use of the demonstrative pronoun *tot* where English would have the personal pronouns *he* or *it*.

iii While a high proportion of noun phrases consists of a personal pronoun, an even higher proportion of noun phrases consists of a single constituent. This constituent can of course be a personal pronoun, but also

---

[4] If the 172 zero NPs are included, the percentage of 'pronominal' NPs rises to 29.4, still considerably lower than for the English spoken texts.

a numeral, a demonstrative pronoun, a possessive pronoun (e.g. *mine, yours*), a quantifier (*some left early, each received a present*), a WH pronoun (*who wrote the report?, what did you buy?*). (Proper names, whether one-constituent as in *Bill* or two-constituent as in *New York* or longer, were counted as single items.) The figures for all the spoken texts, English, Russian, and German are high: 64.1% for 'The great American sandwich', 62.5% for the English conversation, and 61.4% for the Russian conversations. The Russian newspaper text has 47.5%, the novel—45.7%, and the academic monograph—23%. The figure for the readers' letters is 26.2%. In the German telephone conversation, 70.9% of the NPs consisted of a single constituent. For the face-to-face conversation, the Map Task dialogue, and the newspaper text the figures are, respectively, 64.3%, 64%, and 19.4%.

iv The data collected by Thompson (1988) and our own data show clearly that speakers avoid heavy (complex) NPs in subject position. In the most formal written English texts complex NPs occur as subject as well as object (direct, indirect, or oblique). In less formal written texts complex NPs tend not to occur as subject. In Thompson's samples of English and Mandarin Chinese speech adjectives tended not to occur in grammatical subject NPs. 45% of her adjectives were in direct object NPs, 19% in oblique object NPs, but none occurred in the subject NPs of transitive clauses. 36% of her adjectives did occur in subject NPs in intransitive clauses. In the English narrative no adjectives occur in a subject NP but seven do in the English conversation. As in Thompson's data, the seven are all in intransitive clauses. The closest we come to an adjective in a subject NP in a transitive clause is an example of the NP-clause structure discussed in Chapter 5: $_{NP}$[*the other laddie*] $_{Clause}$[*he's got a shotgun*]. Similar results were obtained for spoken Russian.

v The English narrative and conversation together contain 42 gerunds. None of them has a subject expressed as a possessive NP, as in (the invented example) *their son's having found a job*, and many of them have only the *-ing* form, with no complements. Two gerunds are in subject NPs; they are given in (3).

(3) (*a*) getting over the top's the worst part
    (*b*) oh aye swearing's one of his favourites
        (in context, = one of his pet hates)

There are 105 infinitives, but not a single one in a subject NP. Similarly in the Russian dialogues there are no infinitives and no gerunds (verbal nouns in *-eniel-anie*) in subject NPs. In fact, the gerunds occur in the written texts but not in the conversation.

vi Noun phrases in spoken and written language differ with respect to the type and structure of modifiers. In spoken English (and spoken Russian) noun phrases containing participial phrases are very rare; there are no examples in our data. In spoken English the vast majority of relative clauses are either contact relatives—e.g. *the book I read*—or TH relatives—e.g. *the book that I read*. Spoken English does offer examples of noun phrases containing prepositional phrases or relative clauses but of very simple structure. (Specific examples will be presented and discussed in §4.3.2.) Finally, spontaneous spoken English (and Russian and German) offer no examples of complex noun phrases, that is, noun phrases in which the head noun is modified by a number of constituents, say an adjective, a prepositional phrase, and a relative clause, which may in turn contain other phrases and clauses. (Examples of such structures will also be given in §§ 4.3.2 and 4.4.)

vii Space precludes a comprehensive analysis but it is important to mention that speakers avoid complex NPs by building up descriptions over a number of clauses and phrases. The spoken English texts present clear examples of this. Properties can be introduced one at a time via copula clauses in which the complement of the copula is either an adjective or a noun phrase containing an adjective. Alternatively, properties may be introduced by means of NPs or adjective phrases which are simply dropped into the discourse independently, unattached to any clause. Consider (4), from the narrative 'The great American sandwich' discussed in §4.3.2.[5]

(4) A well it's a city underground really   it's **an incredible place**
    B New York's **an incredible place**

       ...

       we went through the Bowery ... and we had to keep the windows locked through there   but it's **an incredible city**   it's **mind-boggling**   and the negroes are **fantastic**   the clothes they wear   they are **so magnificently turned out**   flamboyancy that they just seem to carry off   I was very impressed with the way that they dressed ...
       it's **a marvellous city**

Speaker A, referring to a bus station called 'Port Authority', describes it as an incredible underground city. At least, she could have done so in writing, but here she first describes it as *a city underground* and then uses a second clause to introduce the epithet *incredible*: *it's an incredible place*. Speaker B says (this is clear on tape but not from the transcript) that it's not just the bus station but the entire city that is incredible. She repeats A's phrase *'s an incredible place* and slots *New York* into subject position. Two

---

[5] This may partly explain why the spoken English narrative has a much higher proportion of adjectives in BE complement NPs than Thompson's data.

clauses further on she repeats her first clause, substituting *city* for *place*: *New York's an incredible city*.

The next clause brings in another property via a complement adjective: *it's mind-boggling*. Speaker B then changes topic from New York to the black population. One clause introduces one property of the Blacks: *and the negroes are fantastic*, again by means of a complement adjective. This property is specified by means of the next phrase, a noun phrase, which is not part of any clause: *the clothes they wear*. Further specification comes with another independent noun phrase: *flamboyancy that they just seem to carry off*. Note that these two independent noun phrases both contain relative clauses. That is, they are comparatively complex NPs for spontaneous speech but the speaker is freed from whatever processing load is required for the integrating of phrases into a clause.

Speaker B then sums up this topic with the clause *I was very impressed with the way they dressed*—another relative clause, but in an oblique object NP. Finally B returns to the superordinate topic, New York, and produces a variation on one of her earlier clauses, substituting *it* for *New York* and *marvellous* for *incredible*: *it's a marvellous city*. B might have written *New York is a marvellous, incredible, mind-boggling city. I was impressed with the flamboyant, indeed magnificent, clothes worn by the Negroes*. But B was speaking, and who is to deny that her spoken text has a certain elegance and power?

4.3. Spontaneous spoken English

4.3.1. *The data and its coding*

The data examined in this section comes from two samples of spontaneous spoken English; one was a spontaneous narrative told by a woman in her mid-twenties and the other was a spontaneous conversation between a 23-year-old male researcher and two 18-year-old female school pupils. The researcher had completed his undergraduate degree, one of the pupils had been accepted for university, and the other was hoping to be accepted. That is, the researcher had had a long, wide-ranging experience of written language and the pupils had taken written language seriously enough to achieve relative academic success.

A comment is required at this point both as a warning and an apology. In writing up the analysis of the noun phrases in the samples of spoken and written English, Russian, and German we have been obliged to strike a balance between exhaustive treatment of the noun phrase structures, clarity of presentation, and space available. The original analysis of noun phrases draws very fine distinctions: for instance, noun phrases consisting of a single constituent are coded differently depending on whether that constituent is a personal pronoun, demonstrative pronoun, numeral, quantifier, WH word (e.g. *who, which*), and so on. Noun phrases consisting of one or more determiners and a noun receive different codes according to the number of determiners (cf. *the books* and *all the books*) and the type of determiner. Nouns modified by a relative clause are subclassified according to whether they have other modifiers, such as an adjective, two adjectives, a prepositional phrase, and so on.

For this discussion only the major distinctions were taken into account. On the basis of our experience and that of researchers such as Hawkins and Coulthard and Robinson mentioned earlier, these are: does a noun phrase consist of (i) a noun or personal pronoun; (ii) a noun plus a determiner; (iii) a noun plus one or more adjectives; (iv) a noun followed by a prepositional phrase; (v) a noun followed by a relative clause; (vi) a noun followed by a participial phrase? The data from English and other languages gives good grounds for believing that this list of different constructions begins with the most frequent structures in spontaneous speech and ends with the most infrequent. In the various genres of written language one- and two-constituent noun phrases are also most frequent but the frequency of the more complex construction increases.

Because certain structures have been excluded there appears to be a discrepancy in certain tables giving numbers and percentages for various noun phrase constructions in particular bodies of data; namely that the total number of noun phrases exceeds the total numbers listed in the table. This discrepancy merely reflects the exclusion of certain types from the discussion.

NPs can have very intricate structures and certain decisions had to be made about what structures were counted and when. Consider the phrase *the black dog on the lawn*. This contains both an adjective, *black*, and a prepositional phrase (PP), *on the lawn*. On the face of it, *the black dog* could be counted as an NP containing an adjective, *the lawn* as an NP consisting of Determiner and Noun, and *the black dog on the lawn* as an NP containing a PP. Since a PP outranks an adjective in our ordering, it was decided that the important piece of information to be recorded was that the whole phrase is an NP containing a PP. The adjective would be ignored but the NP *the lawn* inside the PP would be counted. If the latter NP were *the damp lawn*, it would be counted as an NP containing an adjective. Similarly, a phrase such as *the black dog on the lawn that had just been mown by its owner* would be counted as an NP containing a relative clause. The sequence *the black dog* would not be counted as an NP but any NPs inside the relative clause would be. Thus, *its owner* is counted as an NP consisting of a possessive pronoun and a noun (a structure which has its own code). A phrase such as *the very black dog with no collar lying on the recently-mown lawn which was still damp after the rain* would be classed as a 'complex NP' and none of the phrases such as *the very black dog, no collar,* or *the rain* would be counted.

The label 'complex NP' applies to structures containing, say, a noun modified by a relative clause, and a participial phrase and an adjective, or a noun modified by several adjectives and several prepositional phrases. The noun phrase cited above from James Herriot's novel, *a unique combination of born horseman and dexterous surgeon with which I couldn't compete*, counts as complex because the head noun combination is modified by an adjective, *unique*, a prepositional phrase, *of born horseman and dexterous surgeon*, and relative clause, *with which I couldn't compete*. Moreover, inside the prepositional phrase are two conjoined nouns, each modified by an adjective.

This method of counting NPs prevents the rapid proliferation of NPs even in spontaneous spoken texts but in one instance it also prevents incorrect decisions. The phrase *which of the books* could be analysed as an NP containing a PP, with the smaller NPs *which* and *the books*. *Which* might be counted as a one-constituent NP. Even if this analysis could be justified in some framework, it is wrong for our purposes; the speaker (or writer) has not produced a one-word NP but a four-word sequence. Interestingly, our approach to the counting of NPs coincides (and it is a coincidence) with an X-bar analysis that has been generally accepted since the mid-1970s whereby *the black dog on the lawn* is assigned two top-level constituents, *the* and *black dog on the lawn*. The latter does not count as a full NP–N″, but as part of an NP–N′.

4.3.2. *The spontaneous spoken narrative*

Let us begin with the narrative called 'The great American sandwich'. (The text consists mainly of the narrative followed by a short piece of dialogue in which the narrator and another participant compare their experiences in the United States.) The title reflects the narrator's experience in spending a night in a hotel in Los Angeles en route from New Zealand to London and attempting to order a 'beef sandwich', which turned out to be very different from the two mouthfuls of bread and meat she was expecting. Tables 4.1–4.6 contain all the examples of the various constructions so that readers can gain an idea of the actual data in one of the texts. In all the tables the relevant part of each example is in bold. For the other spoken texts a general outline of type, number, and relative frequency of noun phrase structures will be given with at most one or two particular examples.

Before looking at specific examples in Tables 4.2–4.6, let us consider Table 4.1, which gives the bare numbers and percentages of the noun phrase structures in 'The great American sandwich'. Remember that 'determiner

146 *Spontaneous Spoken Language*

TABLE 4.1. *Narrative—'The great American sandwich' (woman in mid-twenties)*

	Number of noun phrases	% of total
TOTAL	730	—
1 Personal pronoun	311	44.9
2 Noun	49	7
3 Determiner noun	51	7
4 (Determiner) adjective (adjective) noun	41	5.6
5 (Determiner) noun prepositional phrase	44	6
6 X noun relative clause	23	3.2
7 (Determiner) noun participial phrase	4	0.5
8 Compound noun phrase	30	4.1
9 Complex noun phrase	0	0

noun' covers combinations of definite/indefinite article and noun, but not demonstrative and noun, numeral/quantifier and noun, and not combinations of numeral/quantifier and determiner/demonstrative, as in *all these books*. NPs consisting of just a numeral or quantifier or demonstrative are not listed either.

Perhaps the most striking fact emerging from Table 4.1 is that 51.9% of the NPs contain only one constituent. In fact Table 4.1 does not give the full picture; when we take into account NPs containing only a numeral (*give me two please*), or a quantifier (*I'd like more*) or a WH pronoun, the percentage of one-constituent NPs rises to 64.1. Also striking are the small numbers of noun phrases in rows 4–7; only 5.6% of the noun phrases contain an adjective (with or without a determiner); only 6% contain a noun modified by a prepositional phrase; and only 3.2% contain a noun modified by a relative clause. Seven examples of nouns modified by an adjective are given in Table 4.2.

In §4.2.2 we mentioned Thompson's (1988) observations on the grammatical functions of noun phrases with adjectives; with respect to Table 4.1 note that none of the 41 noun phrases with adjectives is a grammatical

TABLE 4.2. *Examples of (determiner) adjective (adjective) noun*

1 it was **very good Irish coffee**
2 and I counted eight slices of roast beef **hot roast beef**
3 they didn't even send **white policemen** down there
4 it's for **single people**
5 that's **a big fruit cocktail** with
6 it's got **the rough   really rough   salt** round the edge of the glass
7 they don't seem to have **a very good**   what's the word **reputation**

subject; they function as complement of BE, direct object, and oblique object. (See examples (1), (3), and (4), respectively.) One example, (2), does not have a grammatical function but is an elaboration of the preceding noun phrase *roast beef*.

Table 4.3 lists all the examples of noun phrases in which the head noun is modified by a prepositional phrase. Three of the examples, *row of telephones*, *a glass of milk*, and *the middle of the desert* occur twice in the text but are only listed once in the table.

The range of prepositions is small; *with* occurs 3 times, *in* 5 times, *behind* and *for* once each, and *of* 31 times. The noun phrases following the preposition are mostly single nouns; the small number of exceptions consists of the compound nouns *Irish coffee* and *mashed potatoes*, the place-names *LA*, *Salt Lake City*, *Las Vegas*, and *New York*, and the sequences *crushed things* and *something else*. The compound nouns refer to common items in the food and drink of the UK (and presumably the US) and can be considered as being stored and manipulated as single lexical items, as can the place-names. The noun in the sequence *crushed things* has very general content and occurs frequently in conversation, and the final sequence, *something else*, not only contains a pronoun but can be considered almost a fixed phrase. (See the discussion of fixed phrases in § 8.3.6 and in Weinert 1995a.)

In 28 of the 41 noun phrases in Table 4.3 the head noun is either not modified at all or only by a determiner. The exceptions are *three slices, eight slices, three scoops, an enormous glass, a long bottle, the big hotels, the very outskirts, all the sort, the Mormon Cathedral, an awful lot, a high percentage, an early order,* and *tequila and lime. Slices, scoops,* and *glass* function here as measure nouns and are in any case highly predictable; meat and bread, in the situation under consideration, come in slices, ice-cream comes in scoops, and liquids come in glasses or cups. *An awful lot* and *all the sort*, quite apart from the lack of lexical content, are fixed phrases, as is *a high percentage*. *Mormon Cathedral* is a proper name which we can be confident was first heard and then stored as a single item. *Tequila and lime* is almost a proper name; certainly in the context of alcoholic drinks the combination is one of a fixed number of variations on the pattern *X and lime*. *An early order* is an elaboration of the preceding *an order*. Only *a long bottle* and *the big hotels* count as candidates for freely produced sequences.

To sum up, a small percentage of the noun phrases contains nouns modified by prepositional phrases and this small percentage typically contains a simple head noun, the most common preposition *of*, and a very simple structure complementing the preposition. Only three of the noun phrases are subjects—*the driver of the bus* (28), *a friend of mine* (39), and *parts of New York* (38).

The NPs containing relative clauses are shown in Table 4.4. Excluded

148 Spontaneous Spoken Language

TABLE 4.3. *(Determiner) noun prepositional phrase*

1. it's vodka galiano and **fresh orange juice with lots of crushed things**
2. and they had a long bar   about fifty feet long   **with just rows and rows of glasses ready**
3. it comes in **a long bottle with a twig in the centre of it**
4. **one of the barmen** . . . would rush up
5. there was about **twenty of them** behind the bar
6. and start doing **the rigmarole for Irish coffee**
7. it's **tequila and lime with something else**
8. because there's **a row of telephones**
9. they're all connected up with **the big hotels in LA**
10. and I walked up to **this terribly elegant creature behind the desk**
11. **what kind of sandwich**
12. **the chest of drawers**
13. I'll have a roast beef sandwich and **a glass of milk**
14. I have never seen **anything like it**
15. there was **three slices of bread** lying on this plate
16. and I counted **eight slices of roast beef** hot roast beef lying on this plate
17. and **three scoops of mashed potatoes** round the outside
18. **an enormous glass of milk**
19. and **a glass of water**
20. and **all the sort of extra paraphernalia** you know
21. and I had placed **an order** . . . **an early order** . . . **for breakfast**
22. and on **the flight back** there was an American sitting next to me
23. we stayed in some places . . . but never in **the centre of LA**
24. I only stayed in one other hotel on **my travels in the States**
25. did you ever see **any of the other canyons**
26. Bryce or **any of these**
27. **the Mormon Cathedral in Salt Lake City**
28. and **the driver of the bus** said before we got there
29. someone else is losing **an awful lot of money**
30. **rows and rows of them**
31. they reckon breakfast is **the cheapest in Las Vegas**
32. if you try and break in on **one of the machines**
33. did you smell **the smell of chlorine** too
34. there's **a high percentage of chlorine** in the water
35. it's right in **the middle of the desert**
36. it actually comes from a reservoir **somewhere in California**
37. it supplies **all of California**
38. I expect **parts of New York** do
39. **a friend of mine** showed me round New York
40. it was possibly Charlie that was instilling **a sense of fear**
41. he took me to **the very outskirts of Central Park**

TABLE 4.4. *Noun phrases containing relative clauses*

1. any other fascinating drinks **that you tried**?
2. right up to the level **that you would normally have**
3. apart from one when we found an Irish Bar in San Francisco **that was famous for its Irish Coffees**
4. it was the one place **where I had to stay in a hotel**
5. you must remember that for every tourist **that comes to Las Vegas** each one of you is going to lose I think it was 392 dollars per head
6. I couldn't believe it all those machines **everywhere you turn**
7. even in the bus station **where we arrived** rows and rows of them
8. in fact they were cracking jokes about it during one of the shows **we went to see at night**
9. about the little ladies **that wear gym shoes and keep five machines going**
10. and there was thunderstorms following us around **everywhere we'd just been**
11. it was that day **that it just so happened we had a thunderplump**
12. it's the only town in the whole of America **that I saw going twenty four hours a day**
13. but I think it was possibly Charlie **that was instilling a sense of fear** you know
14. the clothes **they wear**
15. they are so magnificently turned out flamboyancy **that they just seem to carry off**
16. I was very impressed with the way **that they dressed**
17. if you don't play the machines someone else is losing an awful lot of money **which is true** because I lost two dollars
18. c31 they reckon breakfast is the cheapest in Las Vegas
    k31 **which is served all day**
19. and in the middle of the night the longest train **I have ever heard in my life** went past the window

from the table (but counted in the overall total) are one headless relative, *from what I could gather*, and the cleft clauses in two IT clefts—*it was 72 that I went*, *and there was about the week after I had been there that they had the big floods*. The second example is problematic because some structure is missing, on the assumption that the speaker was indeed intending to say *it was the week after I had been there that* . . . The IT clefts are excluded because there is some controversy over the exact nature of the cleft clauses. (For the term 'cleft clause' and a discussion of clefts, see Chapter 6. Item 13 in Table 4.4 is an IT cleft but has been included because *that* can be replaced by *who*.)

In Table 4.4 most of the relative clauses modify non-subject nouns. In some examples the noun modified by the relative clause has no grammatical function, since the noun phrase is independent of any verb; consider (6) *all those machines everywhere you turn*, (14) *the clothes they wear*, and (15) *flamboyancy that they just seem to carry off*. Only one of the noun phrases in the above table is a subject, the phrase *the longest train I have ever heard in my life* in (19). Interestingly it is also a relatively complex noun phrase; the head noun *train* is also modified by an adjective, *longest*, and if there were an overt relative pronoun, say *which*, it would be the direct object of the verb *heard* in the relative clause. Such a noun phrase functioning as subject is rare in spontaneous speech. Its occurrence does not go against the tendency (in our data, very strong tendency) for subject noun phrases in spontaneous speech to be very simple, but it raises an important question; what do we mean by 'spontaneous' when we talk of 'spontaneous speech'? The sandwich narrative is spontaneous in the sense that the speaker did not prepare notes and, as far as can be seen from the entire conversation, did not know beforehand that she would be asked to talk about her visit to the States. On the other hand, since her journey to New Zealand and the United States was a major event in her life, we can be certain that she had related the events on previous occasions. It is quite possible that a number of the phrases and clauses used in the narrative had been used before and were not totally spontaneous in the sense of being created on the spot. (Candidates for the status of already-used phrases, in addition to the above noun phrase, are item 10 in Table 4.3, *this terribly elegant creature behind the desk*, and item 9 in Table 4.4, *the little ladies that wear gym shoes and keep five machines going*.)

The relative clauses in Table 4.4 fit the pattern for spontaneous speech set out in the discussion of relative clauses in §3.7.1. Ten are introduced by *that* and five are contact relative clauses. None is introduced by *who*, and there are no occurrences of *whom* or of relative clauses introduced by a preposition plus WH constituent. (In fact, there are none of the latter in the entire 50,000 word corpus of spontaneous conversation.) Two relative clauses are introduced by *where*, which is not unusual, and two are introduced by *which*. One of the occurrences of *which*, in (17), is obligatory because this relative clause modifies the proposition 'if you don't play the machines someone else is losing an awful lot of money' and only *which* relative clauses modify propositions. The other *which* occurs in (18). The clause containing *breakfast* is uttered by one speaker but the other speaker produces the relative clause modifying *breakfast*. In such sequences the second speaker provides additional information, not information designed to help the listener identify the referent. That is, the relative clause in (18) and in all such sequences is non-restrictive. Interestingly, speakers of Scottish English (and possibly speakers of other varieties) do produce (in speech and writing) non-restrictive relative clauses introduced by *that*, but where main clause and relative clause are uttered by different speakers the relative clause is always introduced by a WH word. Our evidence only permits speculation but it is interesting that *which* also occurs in the other examples of such sequencing. Certainly, the substitution of *that* for *which* in

(18) makes the example strange to our ears and we hypothesize that WH pronouns are obligatory in such structures. We also leave for investigation whether this use of *which* is related to the general conjunction use of *which* in (56) in §3.7.1.

Finally, we should note that the structure of the individual relative clauses is simple; they consist mostly of a verb and one temporal or spatial modifier—the exceptions are (11) and (13), which contain direct objects. The complex relative clause in (9) was commented on above but it is worthwhile adding that (8) and (9) occur in that order in the same turn. That is, the speaker produces *they were cracking jokes about it*... and then elaborates *it* by means of (9); this complex relative clause is not integrated into the clause in (8) but is partially independent. The speaker is free of whatever processing load is imposed by the integration of constituents into a clause and can handle the complexity of (9). (Of course, in the light of the above discussion of spontaneity, (9) may be less complex than it appears.) The narrative has six examples of a noun modified by a participial phrase shown in Table 4.5. Four of the examples consist of the classic existential construction with *there*—(2)–(5) and one is a copula construction—(1) and (6) is a subject-verb-direct object clause which has a presentative-existential function. In all cases the participial phrase follows the head noun (and could be treated as reduced relative clauses). The participles are all present participles as opposed to past passive participles; i.e., there are no examples on the lines of *We gazed at the statue recently acquired by the Gallery*, where *recently acquired by the Gallery* contains the past passive participle *acquired* and can also be viewed as a reduced relative clause (= *that had been recently acquired by the Gallery*).

The narrative has only one example of a noun modified by a complement clause—*and they couldn't get over* **the fact that I didn't like ice in whisky**. *Fact* is the most common head noun in examples of this construction and the complement clause has a subject-verb-direct object-locative adjunct structure in which all the noun phrases have only one constituent, *I*, *ice*, and *whisky*.

At the beginning of this section we outlined general properties of noun phrases in written language. One of the properties was the occurrence of

TABLE 4.5. *Noun plus participial phrase*

1	it's for single people or for married men **pretending to be single**
2	there was three slices of bread **lying on this plate**
3	and on the flight back there was an American **sitting next to me**
4	there was a woman **keeping five machines going**
5	and there was thunderstorms **following us around everywhere we'd just been**
6	and I counted eight slices of roast beef hot roast beef **lying on this plate**

TABLE 4.6. *Compound nouns*

1 Harvey Wallbanger
2 vodka gimlet
3 Irish bar
4 Irish coffees
5 a singles bar
6 the hot water tap
7 west coast
8 whisky sourmex
9 the air hostess
10 the limousine and mini-bus service
11 a colour television
12 hot roast beef
13 a roast beef sandwich
14 a steel-covered dinner plate
15 room service
16 the front bell
17 a double room
18 gym shoes
19 their rubber gym shoes
20 the water supply
21 thunderstorm
22 thunderplump
23 a bus window
24 the United Nations building

complex compound noun phrases. The narrative does have examples of compound noun phrases, but they are all rather simple in structure and interpretation. Consider Table 4.6.

Most of the compounds in Table 4.6 consist of just two nouns. The ones that do have more constituents function as proper names—*United Nations building*, refer to objects that are common in the culture—*hot roast beef* (vs. *cold roast beef*), *rubber gym shoes* (now replaced by trainers), or refer to objects typical of hotels and used in hotel advertisements and literature—*limousine and mini-bus service*. *Steel-covered dinner plate* is unlikely to occur in advertisements and literature but does refer to an object typical of hotels and restaurants, especially in connection with food being delivered to guests in their rooms. These facts suggest that these more-complex compounds (like many of the more-complex noun phrases containing prepositional phrases) are learned and stored as wholes. In any case, the narrative offers no compound noun phrases even remotely like the intricate written examples cited at the beginning of this section.

4.3.3. Extract from spontaneous conversation

Table 4.7 presents numbers and percentages for noun phrases in an extract from the corpus of spontaneous conversation. There is only one major difference in the proportions: noun phrases containing determiners constitute 16.9% as opposed to 7% in the narrative. For our purposes this difference is not important; the central fact is the high proportion of noun phrases with one constituent or two constituents, and the low proportion of noun phrases containing adjectives, prepositional phrases, relative clauses, compound nouns (and also participial phrases and complement clauses). The comments made above on the structure of noun phrases in the spoken narrative are equally pertinent to the noun phrases in the conversation. Of the 100 relative clauses, only 17 are introduced by a WH pronoun; of these, only four have *who*, the others having *which* (in relative clauses modifying a proposition, see §3.7.1.1) or *where*. 41 are introduced by *that* and 42 are contact relatives, with no complementizer.[6]

TABLE 4.7. *English conversation (23-year-old male interviewer and two 18-year-old female school pupils)*

	Number of noun phrases	% of total
TOTAL	2,657	—
1 Personal pronoun	1,308	48.9
2 Noun	127	4.8
3 Determiner noun	449	16.9
4 (Determiner) adjective (adjective) noun	159	6.0
5 (Determiner) noun prepositional phrase	135	5.6
6 X noun relative clause	100	3.8
7 (Determiner) noun participial phrase	2	0.07
8 Compound noun phrase	82	3.1
9 Complex noun phrase	0	0

4.3.4. A newspaper text

To provide a contrast with the spoken data we analysed the noun phrases in the readers' letters published in the British broadsheet *The Independent* on 7 August 1996. Note that we worked on the readers' letters and not news

---

[6] One *who* clause is produced by a speaker who speaks Broad Scots, but all the other WH clauses are produced by the interviewer, a university graduate, and an 18-year-old school student who was about to go to university. This pattern fits with our view that the use of *who* and *which* clauses comes principally from exposure to written language and the people most exposed to written language are the academically successful, like the interviewer and the student.

154 Spontaneous Spoken Language

reports, background articles, or leaders; that is, on written texts which were certainly planned and possibly revised before being sent to the editor but which were not written by professional journalists or columnists and not subject to the same degree of sub-editing. We hoped that even the least dense parts of the newspaper[7] would turn out to contain a higher number of more complex noun phrases than the spoken texts. The bare figures for the readers' letters are given in Table 4.8.

TABLE 4.8. Letters to The Independent, 7 August 1996

	Number of noun phrases	% of total
TOTAL	447	—
1 Personal pronoun	63	14.1
2 Noun	68	15.2
3 Determiner noun	40	8.9
4 (Determiner) adjective (adjective) noun	88	19.7
5 (Determiner) noun prepositional phrase	84	18.8
6 X noun relative clause	14	3.0
7 (Determiner) noun participial phrase	5	1.1
8 Compound noun phrase	29	6.5
9 Complex noun phrase	14	3.0

In the readers' letters far fewer noun phrases consist of just a personal pronoun—14.1% compared with over 40% in both the narrative and the spontaneous conversation. We assume that this is because the writers of the letters were not describing events in which they had taken part and were not discussing entities present in the situation of utterance. Participants in the conversations did both, and the narrator in 'the great American sandwich' was describing her experiences. The differing proportions of single nouns and sequences of determiner + noun are not readily explicable; even if an explanation were forthcoming it would probably have little bearing on this discussion. More important are the much greater proportions of noun phrases containing adjectives and prepositional phrases: 19.7% have one or more adjectives compared with 5.6% in the narrative and 6% in the conversation; 18.8% have one or more prepositional phrases compared with 6% in the narrative and 5.6% in the conversation.

The noun phrases containing prepositional phrases are worth a more detailed look. Table 4.3 presents the total of 41 such noun phrases in the spoken narrative; Table 4.9 presents the first 41 (out of 84) such noun phrases in the readers' letters.

[7] Pilot work on The Times in 1991 demonstrated that background articles and leaders tend to have denser and more complex syntax than readers' letters and news reports.

TABLE 4.9. *Letters to* The Independent, *7 August 1996—(determiner) noun prepositional phrase*

1 the national requirement for numbers
2 every member of the population
3 the limits of the numbering range available prior to phONEday
4 the entire code portion of the number
5 every telephone exchange in the country
6 the desire of Oftel to retain the geographic significance of the area code
7 a long-term solution to the problem
8 the everyday constraints to cash flow
9 the additional outlay on new letterheads
10 any phone within the UK
11 25 per cent of short-term business
12 a sad indictment of British industry
13 the importance of shoreline management plans
14 a vehicle for strategic management of the coastline
15 a period of up to a century
16 a minority of cases
17 terms of cost, technical suitability and impact on the environment
18 support for the hard concrete defences of our predecessors
19 the lead role for flood warning
20 those at risk
21 your report on coastline erosion
22 the forces of nature
23 a role in defending the land against the sea
24 this sort of pattern
25 responsibilities for sea defence and flooding
26 an adverse effect on our natural sea defences
27 the system for the granting of licences for dredging
28 total income from licences granted
29 transparency with regard to the financial details
30 the mention of Ned Kelly
31 for the sake of historical accuracy
32 the first of the Victorian police
33 makers of the world's first feature
34 an article on Australian film-making
35 the current celebration of the 'Century of Cinema'
36 today's article by Godfrey Hodgson
37 the relative performance of the US and the nations of the EU
38 a maximum of three competitors per country per event
39 an athletics final of eight competitors
40 three from the US
41 a rise in the A-level pass rate

The spoken narrative offered a small range of prepositions—*of, in, with, behind,* and *for. Of* was by far the most frequent. Table 4.9 shows a much larger range, 15 altogether, including phrases such as *with regard to, for the sake of,* and *prior to* which could be analysed as complex prepositions, see Quirk *et al.* (1985: 669–73). The simple prepositions are *for, of, in, to, on, per, within, up to, at, against, from,* and *by*. The prepositional phrases not included in Table 4.9 also offer *towards, concerning,* and *with*.

The comments on the relevant noun phrases in the spoken narrative mention the minimal status of many of the head nouns, which are measure nouns or quasi-measure nouns. The noun phrases following the preposition typically consist of a single noun. A glance at the noun phrase in Table 4.9 shows that the head nouns are not measure nouns and in many instances are modified by an adjective or a possessive noun. The noun phrases following the preposition are quite intricate, and many of them contain in turn at least one prepositional phrase. Since the structure of noun phrases in written language was discussed in §4.2.1, we here simply draw attention to (3), (6), and (13). In (3) the head noun *range* is followed by an adjective phrase in which the adjective is modified by a prepositional phrase *prior to phONEday*. The adjective phrase can be seen as a reduced relative clause; this is entirely in keeping with the properties of (especially formal) written language, which is characterized by condensed syntactic structure. In (6) the head noun *desire* is modified both by the prepositional phrase *of Oftel* and by the infinitive phrase (or non-finite clause) *to retain the geographical significance of the area code*. In (13) the modifying prepositional phrase contains the three-member compound noun *shoreline management plans*.

In the spoken narrative no adjectives occurred in subject noun phrases. A different and not entirely straightforward picture emerges from the letters. Since Thompson (1988) distinguished between intransitive and transitive clauses for speech, we partly followed suit for the letters. Partly, because copula clauses were kept apart from non-copula transitive and intransitive clauses. Passives were counted as intransitive clauses rather than copula clauses. Thompson (1988) found, for English and for Mandarin Chinese, that 36% of the adjectives in intransitive clauses were in subject noun phrases. None of the adjectives in transitive clauses was in a subject noun phrase. For the letters the corresponding figures are 17.4% and 15%. That is, adjectives do occur in subject noun phrases in transitive clauses, but in small numbers compared to the 78% occurring in oblique objects in intransitive clauses and the 55% occurring in oblique objects in transitive clauses. The picture is complicated by the figures for adjectives in copula clauses; 50% occur in subject noun phrases. The strong tendency to exclude adjectives from subject noun phrases in spontaneous speech can be plausibly explained in terms of processing constraints; complex phrases tend to be postponed in the clause, even in writing, so that they can be processed (for production or comprehension) once the general structure of a particular clause has been determined. (This hypothesis must of course be investigated experimentally.) The postponing tendency is much weaker in written texts, possibly because written texts can be re-read as often as necessary and can be processed in several stages.

The relative clauses in the letters are set out in Table 4.10. In the spoken narrative none of the relative clauses occurs in a subject noun phrase and some noun phrases containing relative clauses had no grammatical function at all. The pattern in the letters is not very different in this respect, since only 2 relative clauses are in subject noun phrases. Compare the 5 in oblique objects, 4 in direct objects, and 3 as complement of BE. The relative clauses differ in type. In the narrative 52.6% of the relative clauses are introduced by *that* and 26.3% are contact relatives. There are no occurrences of *who* nor of a preposition plus WH pronoun. In the letters 64.3% of the relative clauses are introduced by a WH word, including 5 instances of *who*. One relative clause, (4), is introduced by a preposition plus *which*. There are no contact relative clauses.

The structure of the relative clauses in the spoken narrative is typically simple—subject noun phrase + verb + temporal/locative constituent (which may be a complement or adjunct). A glance at Table 4.10 shows that the

TABLE 4.10. *Letters to* The Independent, *7 August 1996—noun phrases containing relative clauses*

---

1 numbers that do follow the subscriber from network to network
2 numbers that are not attributable to one specific land line but can be re-routed to any phone within the UK
3 two associated issues which need highlighting
4 the appalling manner in which the search for the Kelly gang had been organized
5 the Queensland trackers, who he called 'six little demons'
6 those candidates who study a mixture of modular and linear A-levels
7 a linear A-level whereby students are tested in the traditional way at the culmination of their course
8 a rigorous and valid examination on applied economics that consists of three papers
9 the woman pregnant with twins who wishes to abort one of the foetuses
10 those who wish to take up this opportunity
11 a list of 'undesirables' that are now being weeded out before they see the light of day
12 those who, through genetic testing in utero, are told that their child has a 25 per cent chance of being homosexual, or a 50 per cent chance of having an IQ lower than that required to get into the Oxford college of their choice
13 those who might discriminate against people of a particular sexual orientation
14 a woman of 28, single and in straitened circumstances, who already has a child

relative clauses in the letters typically have a more complex structure. Even the simplest ones have direct objects, such as *which need highlighting, who wish to take up this opportunity*. One relative clause has a complex subject, *the search for the Kelly gang*; the relative clauses in (2) and (12) contain coordinated clauses, (12) being especially intricate. In a number of examples the noun modified by the relative clause has other modifiers; these range from *two associated issues which need highlighting* to (14) and (9), in which the head noun is followed by modifiers which are in turn followed by a relative clause—(9) *the woman **pregnant with twins** who wishes to abort one of the foetuses* and (14) *a woman of 28, **single and in straitened circumstances**, who already has a child*.

Table 4.11 shows the noun phrases containing participial phrases. The spoken narrative only has present participles in noun phrases, whereas all but one of the participles in Table 4.11 are past passive participles. The participial phrase in (3) is non-restrictive, not unusual for written language but unknown in typical spontaneous speech. As observed before, such participial phrases can be seen as non-finite clauses resulting from the reduction of relative clauses and as before it is worthwhile commenting that this condensing of syntactic structure is exactly what is typical of written language but untypical of spontaneous speech.[8] Note the complex structure of the participial phrases, which in turn contain prepositional and infinitive phrases.

There are two examples of nouns modified by complement clauses: *Not only is there a perception **that the modular courses are in some sense 'easier'*** and *the claim **that modular A-levels are causing grade inflation***.

Finally we come to the noun phrases that are complex in that the head noun is modified by a number of modifiers or by modifiers, such as

TABLE 4.11. *Letters to* The Independent, *7 August 1996—noun phrases containing participial phrases*

1	a different number at work to that used by my friends to reach me at home
2	the demand on the telephone system and the chaos caused by the continued changes to area codes
3	... 'going to the cinema' ... [has] ... always implied at least one feature-length film on the programme, billed as 'the main attraction'
4	an IQ lower than that required to get into the Oxford college of their choice
5	a magical plant believed to cure anything from gout and sciatica to festering wounds

---

[8] The letters offer an example of a free participial phrase containing three passive participles and one present participle: ***produced, written and directed by the Tait brothers of Melbourne in 1906 and running for 100 minutes**, Kelly Gang was the first feature to be made anywhere in the world*.

participial phrases and relative clauses, which themselves have a complex structure. Such noun phrases are a hallmark of very formal writing but are not found in typical spontaneous speech.[9] The complex noun phrases are listed in Table 4.12 without further comment.

TABLE 4.12. *Letters to* The Independent, *7 August 1996—complex noun phrases*

1   a separate number for my telephone line and my fax machine
2   a different number at work to that used by my friends to reach me at home
3   the limits of the numbering range available prior to phONEday
4   the desire of Oftel to retain the geographic significance of the area code despite the fact that this is already being attenuated
5   the demand on the telephone system and the chaos caused by the continued changes to area codes
6   (about) the additional outlay on new letterheads and informing our customers of our 'new' telephone number
7   numbers that are not attributable to one specific land line but can be re-routed to any phone in the UK
8   the most applicable flood defence option in terms of cost, technical suitability and impact on the environment
9   a rigourous and valid examination on applied economics that consists of three papers
10 at least one feature-length film on the programme, billed as 'the main attraction'
11 the current debate concerning the woman pregnant with twins who wishes to abort one of the foetuses
12 a list of 'undesirables' that are now being weeded out before they see the light of day
13 those who, through genetic testing in utero, are told that their child has a 25 per cent chance of being homosexual, or a 50 per cent chance of having an IQ lower than that required to get into the Oxford College of their choice
14 a woman of 28, single and in straitened circumstances and who already has a child

4.4. Spoken and Written Russian

The noun phrases in four Russian texts were counted and analysed. One of the texts consists of spontaneous conversation taken from Kapanadze and Zemskaja (1979); the other three texts are texts from the newspaper *Argumenty i Fakty* (background articles, not news reports), and an extract from the academic monograph by Kubrjakova, Šaxnarovič, and Saxarnj (1991) *Čelovečeskij faktor v jazyke* 'The human factor in language'.

[9] It is possible that the letters were written by more than one person; for instance, the person who signed the letter might have written a first draft which was then revised by someone else. Such cooperation is merely a special case of the general thesis that written texts are typically planned. Complex structures are made possible by planning and editing time (and by experience of written texts).

4.4.1. *Russian conversation and Russian newspaper text*

The first thing to notice in Table 4.13 is that line 8 is missing. This is because compound nouns were not counted in the Russian texts. The comparison of compound nouns in different types of English text is relatively straightforward; a comparison of compounds in English and Russian texts would have required a general account of compounds in Russian and delicate decisions about the comparability of noun-noun sequences in Russian written as one word and adjective-noun sequences in English. Since such an exercise would have gone far beyond the scope of this chapter, compound nouns in Russian were abandoned. However, the numbering of the lines in the tables has been carried over from the tables for English noun phrases to the tables for Russian noun phrases, and in spite of the lack of compound nouns the figures for the complex nouns are still on line 9.

§4.2.2 presented possible explanations for the low proportion of personal pronouns compared with the English spoken texts. The important point is that there are far more personal pronouns than any other type of NP and that, as commented in §4.2.2, when the tokens of all types of single-constituent NPs are counted, they constitute 61.4% of the NP tokens, a figure comparable to the 62.5% for the English conversations and the 64.1% for the spoken English narrative. Another central point is that, as can be seen by comparing Table 4.13 with Table 4.14 below, the percentage of personal pronouns in the Russian conversation is more than twice the percentage in the Russian newspaper. This is less than the difference for the corresponding English texts but none the less significant.

The label 'prepositional phrase' is not applied in exactly the same way to

TABLE 4.13. *Spontaneous Russian conversation noun phrases*

	Number of noun phrases	% of total
TOTAL	2,310	—
1 Personal pronoun	507	21.9
2 Noun	243	10.5
3 Determiner noun	122	5.2
4 (Determiner) adjective (adjective) noun	127	5.5
5 (Determiner) noun prepositional phrase	72	3.1
6 (Determiner) noun relative clause	20	0.9
7 (Determiner) noun participial phrase	0	0
8 . . .	—	—
9 Complex noun phrase	0	0
10 Split noun phrase	36	1.6

TABLE 4.14. *Newspaper* Argumenty i Fakty *noun phrases*

	Number of noun phrases	% of total
TOTAL	2,019	—
1 Personal pronoun	201	10.0
2 Noun	543	26.9
3 Determiner noun	314	15.6
4 (Determiner) adjective (adjective) noun	319	15.8
5 (Determiner) noun prepositional phrase	232	11.5
6 (Determiner) noun relative clause	26	1.3
7 (Determiner) noun participial phrase	16	0.8
8 ...	—	—
9 Complex noun phrase	35	1.7
10 Split noun phrase	0	0

the Russian data as to the English data. It is indeed applied to examples such as *stul v uglu* '(the) table in (the) corner' containing the prepositional phrase *v uglu*. It is also applied in the analysis of phrases such as *kvartira muzykanta* '(the) flat of (the) musician'. *Muzykanta* is a noun in the genitive case but is used where English would use a possessive form in *'s* or the preposition *of*. It might be thought that, since the genitive case covers both *'s* and *of*, this treatment might yield an inflated number of Russian items labelled 'prepositional phrase'. In fact the percentage of prepositional phrases in the Russian conversation is lower than that in the English narrative or conversation, and much lower in the Russian newspaper text than in the English one.

Line 10 bears the label 'split noun phrases'; this refers to a construction mostly found in spoken Russian which will be discussed in §4.4.2.

Table 4.14 gives the numbers and percentages for noun phrases in the Russian mid-market newspaper *Argumenty i Fakty*. The same general remarks apply to spoken and written Russian as apply to spoken and written English. The noun phrases in the Russian conversation are simpler in structure; nouns typically have only one modifier, prepositional phrases typically do not contain other prepositional phrases, and relative clauses do not contain other clauses. There are no complex noun phrases in the conversation but 35 in the newspaper; there are no participial structures in the conversation but 16 in the newspaper. 5.5% of the noun phrases in the conversation have adjectives, but 15.8% in the newspaper; 3.1% of the noun phrases in the conversation have prepositional phrases, but 11.5% in the newspaper. In spoken Russian subject NPs, as in spoken English, are typically very simple. In the Russian data 19 out of 127 NPs with an adjective function as subjects, but only two are in transitive clauses. Further data is required but it is interesting and possibly significant that these two subject NPs are in clause-final or next-to-clause final position. The examples are given in (5) and (6). The subject noun phrases are in bold.

(5) tebja   kačaet iz   storony v   storonu **malen'kij avtobus**
 you-ACC shakes from side   to side   the-little bus
 'the little bus shakes you from side to side'

(6) potomu čto mne   skazal **glavnyj**   **konduktor**   čto on ostanovitsja
 because   I-DAT said   chief-Nom guard-Nom that it   will-stop
 'because the chief guard told me it would stop'

In fact, (5) is doubtful, because it is interrupted between *storonu* and *malen'kij avtobus* by another participant. From the transcript it is not clear whether *malen'kij avtobus* is supposed to be the subject of *kačaet* or whether it is added as an explanation, the shaking being particularly bad because of the size of the bus.

The example of a participial phrase modifying a noun in (7) gives an idea of the structures of written Russian. (A participial phrase also occurs in (8), which is presented primarily as an example of a complex noun phrase.) The whole noun phrase is in bold and the participial phrase is in bold and italic.

(7) on rešil   napisat' **diplomnuju rabotu,** *osnovannuju na tekstax pesen*
 he decided to-write diploma   work   based   on texts   of-songs
 russkoj   **rok-gruppy**
 of-Russian of-rock group
 'He decided to write a diploma work[10] on the texts of the songs of the Russian rock-group'

Rabotu is a feminine noun and is in the accusative case, as the direct object of *napisat'* 'write'. The participle itself is *osnovannuju*, derived from *osnovat'* 'to base (something on something)'. It is singular, feminine, and in the accusative case, agreeing in these three properties with *rabotu*. Note the two 'prepositional phrases' inside the participial phrase: *na tekstax pesen* and *pesen russkoj rok-gruppy*.

An example of a complex noun phrase from the newspaper text is given in (8) in bold.

(8) poznakomilsja s   **rozovoščekim xudym norvezčem**
 met   with pink-cheeked thin   Norwegian
 priexavšim   **v**   **Rossiju liš'**   **dlja togo,**
 having-come to Russia just for   that
 čtoby uzret' legendarnogo rokera
 to   see   legendary   rocker
 'He met a thin, pink-cheeked Norwegian who had come to Russia just to see the legendary rocker'

---

[10] A 'diplomnaja rabota' is a dissertation written by students in the fifth and final year of their undergraduate degree.

The head noun *norvezčem* is modified by two adjectives, *rozovščekim* (a compound) and *xudym*, and by a participial phrase containing a non-finite purpose clause, *čtoby uzret'* . . . The central participle is *priexavšim*, which is singular, masculine, and in the instrumental case. With respect to the last property it agrees with *norvežcem*, which is assigned instrumental case by the preposition *s*.

Although the newspaper text has complex noun phrases while the conversation text has none, only 1.7% of the noun phrases count as complex. Since it was clear that English academic texts are typically written in very complex language, we examined an extract from the Russian academic monograph cited at the beginning of this section. 10.9% of the noun phrases counted as complex. A typical example is given in (9).

(9) izučenie kognitivnyx, poznavatel'nyx processov,
    study   of-cognitive of-conceptual processes
    a   takže sposobov polučenija,   xranenija i   ispol'zovanija
    and also of-methods of-constructing of-storing and of-using
    struktur   znanija
    of-structures of-knowledge
    'the study of cognitive, conceptual processes and also of the methods of constructing, storing and using knowledge-structures'

The head noun is *izučenie*. It is modified by two conjoined noun phrases. The head of the first one is the noun *processov*, which is genitive plural and is in turn modified by the adjectives *kognitivnyx* and *poznavatel'nyx*. The head of the second conjoined noun phrase is the genitive plural noun *sposobov*, which is in turn modified by three conjoined nouns in the genitive case—*polučenija*, *xranenija*, and *ispol'zovanija*. These three nouns are modified by the noun phrase *struktur znanija*, in which *struktur* is modified by *znanija*, in the genitive case.

Before leaving the Russian monograph, several facts are well worth mentioning. The general structure of the noun phrases in the monograph is more complex than the structure in the newspaper. The ratio of noun phrases to words of texts is a good indicator. The 2,019 noun phrases in the newspaper were gathered from 4,000 words of text. 2,000 words of monograph text yielded 165 noun phrases. (The 2,310 noun phrases from the conversation were gathered from 9,000 words of text!) The samples are not of equal size. The object of the exercise was to obtain approximately the same number of noun phrases from the newspaper and the conversational texts. Only a small sample of academic monograph text was analysed, since it quickly became clear that a very large number of words would be required in order to obtain 2,000 or so noun phrases. It was also clear that for the purposes of the discussion the small sample of monograph text yielded the important properties of noun phrases in this text type. The noun phrases in the monograph are typically much longer than the noun phrases in the newspaper, which are in turn much longer than the noun phrases in the conversation. (It is clear from our overview of different types of English text, plus the evidence in Biber (1988), that similar results would be obtained from English monograph, newspaper, and conversation texts.) It is not just a question of length but of levels of structure. 34% of the NPs in the sample of academic texts contain prepositional phrases, compared with 11.5% of the NPs in the newspaper text. 21.5% of the NPs contained at least one adjective, compared with 15.8% of the NPs in the newspaper text.

4.4.2. *Split noun phrases*

This section examines the relationship between certain modifiers and the nouns they modify in Russian noun phrases. The relationship is of interest because of the occurrence of what can be called split NPs, that is, NPs in which the head noun (or what would be the head noun in writing) is separated from its modifiers by other constituents. This construction is important because, as will be seen in §4.6, it is not typical of formal written Russian and is part of a body of evidence (including the data from Australian languages in §4.6.2) that raises questions about the head of a noun phrase and about the analysis of split noun phrases. (The term itself assumes that the relevant constituents are initially part of an integrated NP which becomes split.) There are three typical cases; in (10) an adjective and a noun are both preceded by a preposition; in (11) adjective and noun are at opposite ends of the clause; in (12) a quantifier/numeral/possessive noun and a noun are in a dependency relationship but are not adjacent.[11] The related adjective/quantifier and numeral are in bold.[12]

(10) Adjective and noun in a prepositional phrase
 živem   v   **novom** v **rajone**
 we-live in new   in quarter
 'we live in a new quarter'

---

[11] Further constructions involve the splitting up of constituents that are traditionally handled as being in a relation of apposition: first name and surname, first name and patronymic, or sequences such as *palata nomer četyre* (ward number four); *v palate ona ležit nomer četyre* (in ward she is number four = she is in ward number four).

[12] These and other relevant data are taken from Zemskaja (1973), Lapteva (1976), and Morozova (1984), together with an analysis of the sample from Kapanadze and Zemskaja (1979) which was the basis of the discussion of noun phrases in conversation in § 4.4.1. Given the censorious and inflexible attitudes displayed by many educated Russians towards any variety that can be seen to differ from formal written Russian, it is worthwhile reminding ourselves that Zemskaja and Lapteva recorded and transcribed the language spoken by educated Russians in informal and relaxed settings.

(11) Adjective and noun
interesnuju prinesi mne **knigu**
interesting bring to-me book
'bring me an interesting book'

(12) Numeral and noun
trista ja nasobiral **značkov**
three-hundred I collected badges
'I collected 300 badges'

In (10) the adjective *novom* modifies the noun *rajone*, with which it agrees in case, number, and gender. In written Russian we would expect to find *v novom rajone*, with a single preposition assigning locative case to the noun, which in turn assigns locative case to the adjective (according to the traditional account). In (10) there are two occurrences of the preposition. (The analysis of this construction is discussed in §4.6.) In (11) the adjective *interesnuju* modifies the noun *knigu*, with which it agrees in case, number, and gender. *Knigu* is the direct object of *prinesi*, and in written Russian we would find *prinesi mne interesnuju knigu* or *interesnuju knigu prinesi mne* or *knigu interesnuju prinesi mne*; different word orders are possible in written Russian but the adjective and noun are typically adjacent. In (12) the numeral *trista* assigns genitive case to *značkov*; in written Russian we would find *ja nasobiral trista značkov*, with numeral and noun adjacent.

Non-adjacent adjectives and nouns are not always at opposite ends of clauses nor does the adjective always come first. Consider (13)–(16).

(13) **zdorovennuju** oni **kanavu** zdes' rojut
huge-ACC-FEM-SG they trench-ACC-FEM-SG here dig-3PL-IMPERF
i ukladyvajut vot **eti** vot **truby**
and lay-3PL-IMPERF look this-PL-ACC look pipe-PL-ACC
'They are digging a huge trench and laying—just look at them—these pipes'

(14) **nekotorye** daže do vos'mi turov delajut **baleriny**
some even to eight turns do-PL-IMPERF ballerina-NOM-PL
'some ballerinas even do up to eight turns'

(15) Kuricu na **bol'šuju** položi **tarelku**
chicken-ACC on big-ACC-FEM put-IMPERF plate-ACC-FEM
'put the chicken on the a/the big plate'

(16) **doma** ne budu stroit' **zimnego**
house-M-GEN not AUX build-INF winter-M-GEN
'I'm not going to build a winter house'

The second clause of (13) and the word order in (15) will turn out to be of particular interest in the discussion in §4.6 of how non-adjacent adjective and noun are to be analysed. Here we simply present the salient structural details. In the first clause of (13) the adjective is in initial position but its noun is separated from it only by the subject of the clause, *oni* 'they'. In the second clause *eti* 'these' and *truby* 'pipes' are separated by the deictic particle *vot*. In more formal spoken Russian (but not written Russian) we would find only *vot eti truby*, with the particle preceding the sequence of demonstrative and noun. The clause-initial constituent in (14) is an adjective, although it is translated into English by a quantifier. The Russian word *nekotorye* agrees with its noun in number, gender, and case and must be analysed as an adjective. In (15) the adjective is not in initial position and is separated from its noun by the verb. *Tarelku*, in the accusative case, is the direct object of *na* (oblique object of *položi*). In (16) it is the noun that is in clause-initial position and the adjective in clause-final position.

(17)–(19) are examples of non-adjacent numeral and noun and non-adjacent possessive noun and noun. In (17) the numeral *tri* follows the main verb *prixodili* 'came' and its noun (modified by an adjective) precedes. In (18) the possessive noun in the genitive case, *Igorja*, is in clause-initial position, while the head noun is in clause-final position. The reverse holds in (19), with the possessive noun *Tamary* at the end of the clause and the head noun *podružki* in second position.

(17) **Ital'janočki moloden'kie** prixodili **tri** k nam v gosti
Italian-girls young came three to us into guests
'three nice young Italian girls came to stay with us'

(18) **Igorja** k nam sobiralas' priexat' **mama**
Igor-Gen to us was-intending to-come mother
Igor's mother was intending to visit us'

(19) kogda **podružki** priedut **Tamary**?
when friends will-arrive Tamara-Gen?
'when are Tamara's friends arriving?'

Variations in word order seldom if ever come free, even in spontaneous speech. Lapteva (1976: 213–23) suggests that the different orders are associated with different intonation patterns and different information structure. She distinguishes two post-posing constructions—'distantnaja postpozicija', and a pre-posing construction. (Terms such as pre- and post-posing carry the presupposition that two items are originally adjacent and then separated, or that the construction in which the two items are adjacent is more basic than the other one.) A distant post-posed adjective may be an afterthought or an important component of the message. As an afterthought, it does not carry focal accent ('dynamic stress') and is spoken at a quicker tempo. As an important component of the message it can carry the focal accent and refers to some property of a given entity that is not objectively new but given in a particular situation. Lapteva remarks that this is typically the case in clauses organized in a sequence of stressed and unstressed constituents in which the rhythm helps the listener to interpret the disjoined adjective and noun. As examples of post-posed adjectives Lapteva gives (20)—an afterthought, and (21)—an important component of the message.

(20) ja tože platok vzjala teplyj
 I too a-shawl took warm
 'I also took a shawl, a warm one'

(21) a zamok-to vstavila novyj
 and lock-particle has-put-in new
 'And has she/you put in a new lock?'

Distant pre-posed adjectives, whether clause-initial or clause-internal, are equal to or more important than the noun with respect to information load. Lapteva's example is (22), in which the adjective *čistoj* carries a falling pitch, there is a sharp rise on *net* and another falling pitch on the noun *rubaxi*.

(22) a u tebja čistoj net rubaxi?
 and at you clean not shirt
 'but haven't you got a clean shirt?'

The afterthought analysis of examples such as (20) has one disadvantage; it does not fit with the fact that these and the other examples cited by Lapteva were produced, according to the transcription, without a pause, yet the typical afterthought, or at least the stereotypical afterthought, is added after a short silence. Alternatively, an afterthought expression has its own intonation envelope. For instance, the English utterance *get me a pizza a small one* sounds peculiar without a pause (even very short) between *pizza* and *a small one* or without a separate intonation pattern over *a small one*. The same holds for Russian, but Lapteva marks only one out of thirty odd examples as having a pause (Lapteva 1976: 213–14). In another example, reproduced here as (23), she indicates a clause break by a comma, but a clause-final post-posed adjective immediately precedes the comma. That is, the adjective is intended to be read as part of the first clause both in intonation and rhythm.

(23) a potom devčonki tak pripustilis' zadnie, tak bežali, užas
 and then the-girls so quickened-pace rear, so ran, horror
 'and then the girls, the ones at the back, quickened their pace so much, ran so fast, that it was terrifying'

In fact, Lapteva's example in (20) is more revealingly set out as in (24) (following the information in Lapteva 1976: 213).

(24) A u menja platok
 at me a-shawl
 'I've got a shawl'
 B ja tože platok vzjala teplyj
 I too a-shawl have-brought warm
 'I've also brought a warm shawl'

168 *Spontaneous Spoken Language*

That is, *platok* is given. Speaker B picks up the words of Speaker A, and adds the information that her shawl is warm. *Teplyj* certainly conveys new information, but whether it is an afterthought is not certain. Clearly there is much work to be done on the position of adjectives in spontaneous spoken Russian; the central point for our purposes is that the word order is not free but controlled by discourse factors.

Only two of the split NPs have the order noun-X-adjective, where X stands for some constituent(s). That is, most of the split NPs with adjective and noun are not to be explained as afterthoughts. Interestingly, there is only one clear example of an afterthought, or at least of problems with the parallel processing of language and the accessing of information in memory. The example is in the extract from the Russian conversations and is in (25).

(25) kak raz popal na etot samyj/ na festival'// Venecianskij
     Particle fell on that very on festival Venetian
     'what should he do but end up at that festival—the Venice festival'

The '//' indicates an intonation contour marking a completed syntactic structure. The adjective *Venecianskij* carries its own intonation contour and constitutes a separate chunk of syntax. The language processing difficulties are signalled by the use of the dummy word *samyj* (equivalent here to the use of *what's its name* by speakers of English, as in *he went to that em what's its name Venice Festival*). *Samyj* is followed by a single oblique marking the intonation pattern 'utterance not finished' and the speaker repeats the preposition *na* along with the appropriate lexical item *festival'*. These are all signs of processing problems, and the intonation signals that the utterance is finished with the word *festival'*. *Venecianskij* really can be interpreted here as an afterthought.

Lapteva's analysis of pre-posed adjectives as carrying a large information load applies to an example of Zemskaja's in which the adjective is separated from the rest of the clause by an intonation break signalling an unfinished piece of syntax. Zemskaja's example is reproduced in (26). The adjective *glazirovannyx* delimits the set of entities that the speaker is interested in; the rest of the utterance specifies what the speaker wishes to know about those entities.

(26) A glazirovannyx/ net u vas syrkov?
     And glazed-GEN-PL not at you cheese-GEN-PL
     'And what about glazed cheese curds? Have you got any?'

In the light of Lapteva's comments, it is tempting to say that the constructions with non-adjacent noun and adjective are either the result of planning problems which lead to constituents being added as afterthoughts or serve a special informational purpose, namely highlighting the adjective. The highlighting is achieved by moving the adjective out of its original position in a noun phrase. None of this explains why spontaneous spoken Russian has them and not written Russian; that is, why the unusual construction with non-adjacent head and modifier is found in the variety that otherwise has much simpler syntax. The answer proposed in §4.6 is that the adjective and noun are linked, as signalled by the inflections, but that the adjective is more accurately seen as an independent noun phrase, the noun constituting another separate NP. That is, in (13) the first clause can be glossed as 'It's a big one they are digging—a ditch'.

This section can usefully be brought to a close with more figures, since Zemskaja and Lapteva do not quantify the occurrences of split NPs. For the extract of conversation analysed for noun phrases in §4.4, Table 4.13 indicates 36 split NPs, constituting a mere 1.6% of the total. Prima facie this is a minute proportion of the total number of NPs which might not be worth bothering about. These first impressions are misleading because there are only 285 candidates for splitting, the 249 items quantified on lines 3 and 4 of Table 4.13 plus the 36 split NPs. That is, 12.6% of the candidates were actually split. This percentage is hardly overwhelming but it does indicate a construction that has to be taken seriously. To put it in perspective, Table 4.13 shows that the number of split NPs is greater than the number of NPs containing a relative clause and half the number of NPs containing a prepositional phrase.

4.5. Noun Phrases in Spoken German

The German data, summarized in Tables 4.15–4.18, offers the same general links between type of NP and type of texts as for English and Russian. Single-proform NPs account for at least 60% of NPs in all the spontaneous

TABLE 4.15. *German telephone conversation*

	Number of noun phrases	% of total
TOTAL	1,030	—
1 Personal pronoun	452	43.9
2 Noun	36	3.5
3 Determiner noun	168	16.3
4 (Determiner) adjective (adjective) noun	34	3.3
5 (Determiner) noun prepositional phrase	9	0.01
6 X noun relative clause	9	0.01
7 (Determiner) noun participial phrase	0	0
8 Compound noun phrase	57	5.5
9 Complex noun phrase	0	0

170 *Spontaneous Spoken Language*

TABLE 4.16. *German face-to-face conversation*

	Number of noun phrases	% of total
TOTAL	235	—
1 Personal pronoun	91	38.7
2 Noun	18	7.7
3 Determiner noun	52	22.1
4 (Determiner) adjective (adjective) noun	13	5.5
5 (Determiner) noun prepositional phrase	0	0
6 X noun relative clause	5	2.0
7 (Determiner) noun participial phrase	0	0
8 Compound noun phrase	22	9.3
9 Complex noun phrase	0	0

TABLE 4.17. *German Map Task*

	Number of noun phrases	% of total
TOTAL	250	—
1 Personal pronoun	131	52.4
2 Noun	4	1.6
3 Determiner noun	63	25.2
4 (Determiner) adjective (adjective) noun	8	3.2
5 (Determiner) noun prepositional phrase	0	0
6 X noun relative clause	5	2.0
7 (Determiner) noun participial phrase	0	0
8 Compound noun phrase	9	3.6
9 Complex noun phrase	0	0

TABLE 4.18. *German newspaper*

	Number of noun phrases	% of total
TOTAL	231	—
1 Personal pronoun	11	4.8
2 Noun	18	7.8
3 Determiner noun	24	10.4
4 (Determiner) adjective (adjective) noun	17	7.3
5 (Determiner) noun prepositional phrase	18	7.8
6 X noun relative clause	8	3.4
7 (Determiner) noun participial phrase	16	6.9
8 Compound noun phrase	101	43.7
9 Complex noun phrase	18	7.8

spoken texts; indeed in transcripts of telephone conversations the proportion reached 70%. In contrast, the proportion of single-proform NPs in written texts was below (in some cases well below) 50%. (Proforms exclude full nouns but do include personal pronoun, numeral, demonstrative pronoun, possessive pronoun (e.g. *mine, yours*) and quantifier (e.g. *some left early, each received a present*).)[13] Spoken German also has zero noun phrases in subject and object position (13, 8, and 4, in the three texts, respectively)—fewer than the Russian texts but more than the English texts.

The difficulty of comparing compound nouns in English and Russian was commented on in §4.4. Likewise it is difficult to compare English and German with respect to compound nouns; compounding is a regular process of word formation in German and the spoken German texts, not surprisingly, have more compounds than the English texts. However, the large majority of compounds consists of two lexemes only (the remaining 5 out of 88 consist of 3 lexemes) and there are large differences between spoken and written German. In the written text compounding is much more frequent than in the spoken texts—*c.*7 compounds per 100 words vs. 1 per 100 words. In the written text, 6 compounds consist of 3 lexemes and 4 compounds of 4 lexemes.

The pattern continues with adjectives and prepositional phrases. The written German text contains more adjectives than the spoken texts, although in both speech and writing noun phrases with two adjectives are also rare. (See the discussion of pre-nominal adjectives in written German in Schecker (1993).) He does not state explicitly that his examples are written, but we may infer this since he refers to the use of commas.) The proportion of NPs containing PPs is much higher in the written German text than in the spoken texts. As in the English texts—see Table 4.3 and Table 4.9—the written text has a wider variety of prepositions and more complex structures. For instance, NPs containing adjectives are embedded in PPs, as in (27), where the NP *das nächste Jahrtausend* is the complement of the preposition *in*.

(27) der Schritt ins   nächste Jahrtausend
     the step   into-the next   millenium

PPs are also embedded in PPs, as in (28).

(28) das Nachdenken PP1[über das Spielen PP2[mit den Spielregeln]
     the thinking   about the playing   with the game-rules

The head noun *Nachdenken* is modified by the PP *über das Spielen mit den Spielregeln*, and *Spielen* is in turn modified by the PP *mit den Spielregeln*. Another difference between the spoken and written texts has to do with the

---

[13] All single demonstrative pronouns in German are DER, DIE, or DAS. There are no cases of DIES. Informal observation suggests that DIES is used exophorically in spoken language. There is a high proportion of demonstratives in the telephone conversation (243/23.6%).

common use of *von* in the spoken data where written German might use genitive possessive pronouns (e.g. the spoken *der verlobte von meiner schwester* 'the fiance of my sister'; *der onkel von ihr* 'the uncle of her' compared with the written *der Verlobte meiner Schwester* and *ihr Onkel*). In the written text NP PP structures also occur in complex NPs.

As in the English and the Russian texts, complex NPs are absent from spoken German but abundant in the written text. In fact, the written German text contains many examples of very complex NPs, including various combinations of participial phrases, prepositional phrases, relative clauses, co-ordination, and genitives. One example is in (29).

(29) die angeblich schwindende Bedeutung von Texten
    The allegedly dwindling   importance of   texts
    gegenüber Bildern in der heutigen Gesellschaft
    opposite   images   in the today   society
    'opposite' = 'as compared with'

In (29) the head noun *Bedeutung* is pre-modified by the present participle *schwindende*, which is itself modified by *angeblich*. *Bedeutung* is post-modified by the prepositional phrase *von Texten gegenüber Bildern*. *Texten* is modified by the prepositional phrase *gegenüber Bildern*. The final prepositional phrase *in der heutigen Gesellschaft* modifies the entire NP with 'Bedeutung' as its head. It is not clear how this relationship can be represented in constituent structure without resort to transformations.[14] Another example of a complex NP, this time containing a relative clause, is given in (30).

(30) alle Produkte des   menschlichen Geistes,
     all   products of-the-GEN human-GEN   mind-GEN
     die   eine kulturelle Funktion besitzen
     which a   cultural   function   possess

In (30) the head noun *Produkte* is modified by the genitive NP *des menschlichen Geistes* (the head noun of this NP is modified by the adjective *menschlichen*), and by the relative clause *die eine kulturelle Funktion besitzen*. This complex NP is not untypical, since the written text contains 21 genitives (13% of all noun phrases). Many of these are part of complex noun phrases including prepositional phrases, as in *die Faszination der Kulturwissenschaft für die Zukunft* (the fascination of-the cultural-studies with the future). *Der* is the genitive singular feminine form of the definite article, *Kulturwissenschaft* being feminine. In contrast, the spoken texts

---

[14] This noun phrase also contains the pre-modifying participle *schwindende*. Tables 4.15–4.18 indicate that there are no such particles in the spoken German data, although they are noticeably present in the newspaper text. Nobody familiar with German journalese will be surprised; particles are common in the dense noun phrase constructions in newspaper language, and are also typical of literary German.

yielded only 6 genitives, all of them simple (e.g. *die hälfte des wegs*, the half of-the-(Gen) way-(Gen)).

The preceding discussion is concerned with constructions that occur regularly in written German but infrequently in spontaneous spoken German. Spontaneous spoken German also offers examples of constructions that are excluded from writing, such as sequences containing noun phrases/prepositional phrases and deictics such as the demonstrative determiners *der*, *die*, and *das*, but also *dies*. Consider (31), taken from Brons-Albert (1984). The sequence of immediate interest is in italics in B's response to A.

(31) A ja   das will ich auch mal   wieder machen
       yes that want I also Particle again   do
       und zwar   beim   sportreferat   gibts   da   gibts   da   so
       and Particle at-the sport-seminar gives-it there gives-it there so
       bewegungsübungen   ne
       movement-exercises Tag
       'yes I want to do that again too—at the gym class you get movement exercises'
     B ach em meins du   *da*   *von* *der frau* *z* *dieses*
       och em mean you there from mrs   z   this
       'oh you mean at that class of Mrs Z's'

Chapter 1 discusses the difficulties of working with a transcription of spontaneous speech but without access to the original recording. (31) is a good example of the problem, since it is difficult to establish the exact intonation from Brons-Albert's transcription. In her notes on transcription conventions she states that they are based on Ehlich and Rehbein (1976). In her own transcription Brons-Albert inserts a comma after *frau z*. Her own list of transcription signals state that intonation is indicated by means of 'normale Interpunktion' (1984: 196), but she does not explain what this 'normal punctuation' indicates. She adds that where this is not possible rising and falling intonation are marked by separate signals. She also marks pauses. Her transcription of B's response in (31) is *Ach, em, meins du da von der Frau Z, dieses?* If *von der frau* and *dieses* were separate, we would, for instance, expect a question mark after *Frau Z*, or a pause. (Ehlich and Rehbein (1976) list commas as indicating a variety of boundaries.) Interpreting the transcription is not helped by the fact that there are commas after *ach* and *em* as well, although we would not expect these items to carry their own intonation envelope. Our informal observation of similar examples, together with the lack of a question mark, leads us to analyse (31) as having no break in intonation after *frau z*, though of course anything more than a statement of possibility would be foolish.

The undisputable fact is that the prepositional phrase *von der frau z* 'of

Mrs Z' modifies the demonstrative pronoun *dieses* 'this one'. If there is a break in intonation as indicated by Brons-Albert's transcription, the sequence is an example of information being spread over constituents that may not make up a single NP—see the discussion of split NPs in §4.6. If there is no break in intonation, the sequence is an example of an NP with a modifying PP preceding the head noun. Neither structure is permitted in written German (except of course in representations of dialogue).[15]

(32)–(35) contain examples with another deictic, DA 'there'. The DSK and Map Task data yield more examples with *da* as focus marker, where it typically follows the NP. (33) and (35) are informally collected examples from informal domestic conversations. (34) is taken from the face-to-face conversation. We make no claims with regard to relative frequency at this point; what is important is that these structures occur regularly in spoken language.

(32) mhm die sache *mit der ödipalen phase da*
     mhm the thing with the oedipal phase there

(33) gibst du mir mal   *da   die schere*
     give you me Particle there the scissors

(34) du Hanna *hier der rock* gehörte wohl der   mutter
     you Hanna here the skirt belonged Particle the-DAT mother

Without going into detail, it can be assumed on grounds of intonation and rhythm that *da* in (32) and (33) is part of the noun phrase in italics. These phrases are produced under one intonation contour, i.e. we are not dealing with two separate constituents. In (32) *da*, at the end of the noun phrase, is used as an attention marker, or focusing device (see Chapter 5) while in (33) *da*, at the beginning of the noun phrase, does not have a focusing function but is simply a modifier. In (34) the two functions of *hier* are difficult to separate, indeed there is no reason why in principle items such as *da* and *hier* should not have more than one function in one and the same utterance.

The *da* item can be more specific, i.e. *da* + preposition (35)

(35) gibst du mir mal   die schraube dadrüben
     give you me Particle the screw   there-over

Examples such as (35) may be considered to be similar to reduced relative clauses such as *the screw on the table* in English. The point is that the modifier following the NP is a deictic. NPs with full prepositional phrases preceding the NP also occur, as in (36). These structures are not found in written German. Again, on grounds of intonation and rhythm *aufm flur* 'in

---

[15] Variations of this structure are *die von Grossmann* 'those from Grossmann', *bei Karstadt die* 'at Karstadt those', i.e. 'those of Karstadt'.

the corridor' is to be analysed as modifying *die birne* rather than as an adverb of place modifying *die birne ist kaputt*.

(36) aufm   flur   die birne ist kaputt
     on-the corridor   the bulb is broken

Noun phrases preceded by demonstrative deictic SO also fit into the above picture as a construction typical of spontaneous spoken German but not written German.

(37) heute abend   kannst du   mir wieder so *salatplatten*   machen
     today evening can   you me again so salad-platters   make

(38) da   war   *so ein schickes shetland kostüm*
     there was   so a   smart   shetland suit

(39) da   gibt's   da   *so bewegungsübungen*
     there gives-it there so movement-exercises

(40) das is   dann auch wieder *so'n   idealer klatschzirkel*
     that is then also again, so-an   ideal   gossip-round

In these examples *so* is unstressed and not to be interpreted as an intensifier (e.g., not as in *we had such a good time* in English). The meaning is more closely rendered by 'like this', i.e. *so* appears to stress the nature and/or existence of the referent. This use approaches the use of *SOLCH* (e.g. *such friends are rare*, or a more likely spoken example, *friends like this/that are rare*). This interpretation would only work for (37), however, where we can presuppose the existence of previous salad platters. In (38)–(40) there is no such presupposition and existence *per se* is stressed. This interpretation is supported by the existential constructions. For instance in (39) *so* can only be said to stress the existence of the referent, since there is no indication or previous mention of exercises which could serve as comparison. Indeed, a reasonable English rendering of (39) might be *there's like stretching exercises*. (See the discussion of LIKE in Chapter 6.) We would argue that *so* is above all a focusing device.

SOLCH can also be used in this way but differs structurally from SO. *SOLCH* occurs after the determiner (e.g. *eine solche kulturwissenschaftliche Ausrichtung* 'a such cultural-scientific orientation', taken from the written text). *So* always precedes the determiner. There is only one example with SOLCH in the spoken text *eine solch grandiose erkältung* (a such grandiose cold), where the ironic, grandiose use of *grandiose* may explain the more formal construction. There are 25 cases with *so* in the same text. *SOLCH* + NP does not occur at all in the three texts. Although the exact structural and functional properties of demonstrative deictic focus markers and modifiers in German noun phrases remain to be investigated in detail, examples like the above occur regularly in spoken German. They add to the growing body of data demonstrating the importance of deictic elements, as well as 'scene-setting' items in general, a point taken up in more detail in Chapters 5 and 6, where it is suggested that the organization of deixis may be quite different in spoken and written German.

In Chapter 1 we drew attention to the important connection between characteristics of speakers, topics of discussion, and the syntax and vocabulary of the texts they produce. This connection is no less important for noun phrases than for clauses, as is shown by the transcripts in Wackernagel-Jolles (1971). Unfortunately the nature of her data makes it impossible to sort out the effect of topic from the effect of educational background: participants such as a labourer and a panel beater discuss, respectively, incidents in daily working life and experiences during the war, while a television director discusses the relative quality of German programmes and programmes from other countries and a professor discusses the problems of the economic development of Berlin. However, there are facts worthwhile reporting. The text produced by the first two contains only 3 instances of a noun modified by a PP, but there are 43 in the text produced by the latter two. The latter two produced all 10 relative clauses and all 6 complex NPs, and a larger number of NPs containing adjectives, 31 as opposed to 20. Exposure to written language exercises a huge and fundamentally important influence on spoken language.

4.6. Split NPs: A Problem for Constituent Structure

We return to spoken Russian to pick up the split NP structure exemplified in §4.4. An important question was not addressed: how should such NPs be analysed? The terminology used by Lapteva, post-posing and pre-posing, suggests an analysis in which the adjective and noun (or quantifier/numeral and noun or possessive noun and noun) are initially combined into a single NP, with the adjective subsequently being moved out of the NP to form a separate constituent. An alternative approach is to treat the adjective (quantifier/numeral) and the noun as independent constituents which have never combined into a single NP. As will be shown, a solid case can be made out for this analysis. The argument takes in the nature of adjectives in Russian, the question of what counts as the head of an NP anyway, even in English, and the existence of 'split' NPs (the term 'split' will be put in inverted commas from now on) in Australian languages. The latter data are particularly interesting because they come from languages that are spoken-only; another part of the analysis being advanced is the hypothesis that the combining of demonstratives, quantifiers, adjectives, and nouns into NPs happens as groups of language users develop written languages. (This hypothesis gains plausibility given the high frequency of very simple NPs in spontaneous speech.)

There are already two major analyses of NPs in English. Following the publication of Abney (1987), the view has spread that the head of an NP is the determiner and not the noun. (See for instance Radford 1988 and Cann 1993.) The discussion below suggests that the determiner-as-head analysis has to be taken seriously in syntax (with the emphasis on syntax, since a distinction has to be drawn between the constituent with the greatest semantic load in an NP, typically the noun, and the constituent that determines the fine syntactic class of the phrase, typically the determiner).

4.6.1. 'Split' NPs in Russian

The central problem arises from the fact that in Russian long adjectives are very noun-like and can function as the sole constituent in noun phrases. Russian adjectives fall into two classes, known as long adjectives and short adjectives. The major difference is that long adjectives occur both attributively and predicatively but short adjectives are only predicative.[16]

The short forms of *INTERESEN* 'INTERESTING' are exemplified in (41).

(41) (*a*) Odin proekt byl interesen
'One scheme was interesting'
(*b*) Odna mysl' byla interesna
'One idea was interesting'
(*c*) Eto opisanie bylo interesno
'This description was interesting'
(*d*) Eti teorii byli interesny
'These theories were interesting'

The short adjective forms—*interesen, interesna, interesno, interesny*—have the same gender and number as the subject noun but have no case inflections. They occur only as the complement of BYT' 'BE'; that is, they never occur inside NPs, nor do they occur as complements of verbs such as KATZAT'SJA 'SEEM', which require their complement to be in the instrumental case.

The long adjective forms are exemplified in (42).

(42) (*a*) interesnyj proekt
'(an/the) interesting project'
(*b*) interesnaja mysl'
'(an/the) interesting idea'
(*c*) interesnoe opisanie
'(an/the) interesting description'

[16] Here again spontaneous spoken Russian differs from written Russian. Spontaneous spoken texts have a much higher frequency of predicative long adjectives than written texts (cf. Zemskaja 1972: 199–216, discussion by E. V. Krasil'nikova), and the frequency is greater yet in what Russian linguists call 'gorodskoe prostore ie' (urban simple-language) and in non-standard dialects. (Cf. Morozova 1984.)

(d) interesnye idei
 '(the) interesting ideas'
(e) v interesnom proekte
 'in (the) interesting project'
(f) avtor interesnogo proekta
 '(the) author (of) (the) interesting project'

The adjective forms in (42) are called 'long' because they consist of the stem plus an affix: *-yj, -ja, -oe, -ogo, -ye, -om*. The long forms take the same number, gender, and case as the noun they combine with and occur both in NPs, as in (12), and as the complement of verbs, including BYT' 'BE'. (The choice of long or short predicative adjectives is a controversial topic in Russian grammar but is not relevant for present purposes.)

The key fact is that the 'long' affixes derive historically from deictic pronouns and are still deictic in Modern Russian. The question *Ty kakoe plat'e kupila?* 'You which dress bought?' can be given a one-word reply: *zelenoe* '(the) green (one)', *šerstjanoe* '(the) woollen (one)'. These one-word replies are also appropriate answers to the question *čto za plat'e ty kupila?* 'What kind of dress did you buy?'. The 'adjective' forms can also function as referring items and as subject, direct object, or oblique object. In, for example, a situation where a number of dresses are on display the speaker can say *Zelenoe dorogo* '(The) green (one)—(is)—too dear' without having previously used the word *plat'e* 'dress'.[17]

The data give rise to an important question: in the above examples, are the long 'adjectives' adjectives as we understand the category in English examples such as *the green dress*, or are they nouns, with the following noun in apposition? That is, should the structure of, for example, *zelenoe plat'e* '(the) green dress' be glossed as 'the green one—dress', where *plat'e* 'dress' provides an intension for the deictic element *-oe*? It will be argued that the answer to these two questions is 'yes'.

Consider now the second clause in (13). The demonstrative *eti* 'these' is both preceded by a deictic particle *vot* and separated from its noun by another occurrence of *vot*. (This particle is treated as deictic because *vot* is in general equivalent to the English 'Look!'.) It is possible to speak or write the corresponding phrase *vot eti truby*, in which *eti* is said to be a demonstrative adjective modifying *truby*. We could see *eti truby* as the source for *eti vot truby* in (13), as an NP that is broken up by *vot*. However, an alternative view, which fits better with the pronominal nature

---

[17] Bulgarian is a Slav language that lost the distinction between long and short adjectives; compare *rokljata e zelena* 'the-dress is green' with *zelena roklja* 'a-green dress'. Bulgarian has developed a definite article from a deictic. The deictic is postposed to the first constituent in a given noun phrase, whether that constituent is a noun or adjective; compare *rokljata* 'the dress' and *zelenata roklja* 'the-green dress'. The structure *zelena + ta* is analogous to the Russian *zelena + ja* (feminine, to match the Bulgarian adjective) or *zeleno + je*, the original Russian neuter adjective.

of *eti* and with previous examples, is that *eti* and *truby* are separate NPs and that *vot* does not break up an NP but occurs before each NP. In context the utterance is quite appropriate. The speaker points verbally—and possibly physically—and says *vot eti* 'look—these ones' and then adds information to make absolutely clear the reference of the deictic: *vot truby* 'look—(the) pipes'. (Since nouns in Russian lack a definite article, a single noun can be interpreted as definite or indefinite depending on context and/or syntax.)

In their ability to be the sole constituent of NPs and to function as referring expressions long adjectives in Russian are not unusual. Demonstratives (such as *eti* in the above paragraph and *tot* 'that one'), quantifiers (such as *vse* 'all' and *každyj* 'each'), and numerals (particularly collective numerals—see the discussion in §4.7.3) can all occur as the sole constituent in NPs. They also function as referring expressions, although their referential power is more dependent on the immediate context of utterance than long adjectives. The details of the relevant constructions would take us too far from the discussion of adjectives. The interested reader will find an excellent discussion of numerals in Corbett (1993*a*).

Finally we go back to example (10) with two prepositions, reproduced here as (43).

(43) My živem v novom v rajone
 we live in new in housing complex
 'we live in a new housing complex'

What syntactic structure should be assigned to (43)? We could say that there is a single prepositional phrase which happens to have two occurrences of *v*. In order to explain the two occurrences a (hitherto unknown) process of preposition spreading could be invoked. The alternative solution is to take the syntactic facts at face value and treat (43) as containing two PPs, the first being *v novom*, and the second being *v rajone*. (NB: Not two PPs with one embedded inside the other, but two PPs in apposition.) Preposition spreading sounds an attractive transformational solution but raises serious questions. What other languages have preposition spreading—or postposition spreading? Case spreading is a familiar phenomenon, not least in Russian; in a phrase such as *v novom rajone* the noun and the adjective agree in case and the traditional view is that the case marking spreads from, or is assigned by, the noun to the adjective. (The traditional direction of case spreading is reversed in the analysis which takes the adjective as head.) This phenomenon is easily handled by transformational and non-transformational grammars, but does not involve the creation of extra constituent structure. (We assume a formalized word-and-paradigm morphology.)

In contrast, preposition spreading involves the use of empty prepositional nodes for the preposition copy to attach to. The use of empty nodes is familiar, but in relation to NPs and the various arrangements of NPs round the central verb. In the Principles and Parameters analysis of active and passive clauses, the verb and all its complement NPs are generated under one node in the initial structure. Higher up the tree there is an empty NP node. Either of the complement NPs can be moved into this empty NP node; if the original subject NP moves, the resulting clause is active; if the original direct object NP moves, the resulting clause is passive.

There is no such rationale for empty preposition nodes. In any case, having empty preposition nodes means having two prepositional phrases, each containing a noun phrase. In other words, a putative preposition-spreading rule leads us to the second analysis proposed below, that *novom* and *rajone* are two juxtaposed PPs and that they themselves are NPs. One gloss of (43) is 'We live in a new one in a housing complex'; it has the merit of bringing out the appositional nature of the relationship between *novom* and *rajone*. A further drawback of preposition spreading is that we postulate more complex structure in order to handle a variety of language in which the syntactic structures are relatively simple. To sum up, the 'split' NP construction and the double-preposition construction provide independent reasons for treating the long adjectives as nouns.

4.6.2. *'Split' NPs in Australian languages*

The adjective-noun construction in spontaneous spoken Russian have their counterpart in Australian languages, which are particularly relevant in that they have (at least, until recently they had) no written variety. It quickly becomes clear from descriptions of these languages that linguists working on them have no inhibitions when analysing 'attributive' adjectives not-adjacent to their nouns. They regard the adjectives and nouns as independent noun phrases. Bowe (1990: 53) observes that in Pitjantjatjara nouns and attributive modifiers combine in two different ways. First of all, either a noun or a modifier can be the sole constituent in a Noun Phrase, as in (44).

(44) (*a*) minyma-ngku-ni   nya-ngu
     woman-ERG-1SG-ACC see-PAST
     'the woman saw me'
  (*b*) wara-ngku-ni   nya-ngu
     tall-ERG-1SG-ACC see-PAST
     'the tall one saw me'

Note that a first person singular direct object is signalled by the clitic *-ni* which attaches to the subject noun. *Minyma* and *wara* can combine to give the NP in (45).

(45) minyma wara-ngku-ni   nya-ngu
     woman   tall-ERG-1SG-ACC   see-PAST
     'the tall woman saw me'

Wara and *minyma* constitute a single NP, witness the single case affix on *wara* but both can carry a case affix and can occur in either order, as in (46a,b).

(46) (*a*) minyma-ngku   wara-ngku-ni   nya-ngu
         the-woman   the-tall-one-me saw
     (*b*) wara-ngku   minyma-ngku-ni   nya-ngu
         the-tall-one the-woman-me   saw

The disjoined nature of the Pitjantjatjara noun phrase is further brought out by the typical relative clause construction as exemplified in (47).

(47) wati-ngku panya   kuka ngalya-kati-ngu
     man-ERG Anaphor   meat back-bring-PAST
     panya   paluru   mutaka palya-ngu
     ANAPH   3SGNOM   car   fix-PAST
     'that man brought the meat back, that one fixed the car'

This construction is strongly reminiscent of the unintegrated clause structures discussed in Chapter 3, especially the Bengali correlative structure. The key property of such structures is that instead of a clause embedded inside an NP, as in the relative clause construction of written English, two clauses are juxtaposed and the relationship between them is signalled by means of deictics—Bowe describes *panya* as an 'anaphoric demonstrative'.

Interestingly, Bowe (1990: 101) says that Pitjantjatjara does have a strategy for forming relative clauses, by which she means a construction that is more integrated in having two verbs and therefore two clauses but only one overt subject NP, as in (48).

(48) wati panya   waru atu-ntja-lu   ngayu-nya u-ngu
     man ANAPH   wood chop-INF-ERG   1SG-ACC   give-PAST
     'the man who chops wood gave me some'

The central features of this construction are the lack of a case marker on *wati* (man) and the presence of a case marker on the verb *atu* (chop). This case marker, according to Bowe, indicates that the head of the relative clause is the transitive subject of the main verb *ungu* (gave). A further feature is the lack of a tense marker on the verb in the relative clause. We can assume that the integrated structure in (48) is not typical of Pitjantjatjara, since Bowe describes it as 'not used very often in narrative'. A reasonable hypothesis (given that conversation is typically not pre-planned whereas narrative is) is that it is not used in conversation either and may be a construction that was used in planned or rehearsed speech. Elsewhere

Bowe (1990: 30) comments that any number of attributives may modify a head noun, although in practice the number is limited—a comment that raises questions about the nature of the data.[18]

We know from spontaneous spoken English and Russian that complex NPs belong to writing, especially formal writing, and in the texts of the Australian languages Diyari and Ngiyambaa included in Austin (1981) and Donaldson (1980) respectively, it is difficult to find a noun phrase containing one adjective let alone three or four. This discrepancy is mentioned by Dixon (1972: 60), who notes that a noun phrase can in principle contain any number of adjectives, although in actual texts few noun phrases involve more than one adjective. The small number of adjectives is actually surprising given that the texts are not conversation but narrative, which allows specific tales to be rehearsed. These narratives do have one special property; they were almost lost before being elicited by the analysts and are not regularly recited in the original language. This circumstance precludes the polishing up and elaboration of texts and would explain the simple syntax. It does raise the question of what intuitions the analysts were tapping into when they found evidence for complex noun phrases.

4.7. Theoretical Implications

4.7.1. *Configurational languages and spoken language*

Zemskaja (1973: 383–93) observes that spoken Russian and what she calls scientific Russian (i.e. the formal written Russian of academic monographs, but also of official documents and serious newspaper discussions) differ in that heads and modifiers are placed adjacent to each other in formal written Russian but are not necessarily adjacent in spoken Russian. As we have seen in §4.4 and §4.6, constituents that would be adjacent in formal written Russian may be at opposite ends of the clause in spoken Russian and the occurrence of split NPs is not a peripheral construction that can be discounted.

Indeed, the examples cited by Zemskaja are relevant to recent attempts to formulate constraints on the positioning of heads and modifiers. Hudson (1990: 117) proposes a 'relaxed Adjacency Principle': 'D is adjacent to H [can be counted as adjacent to H] provided that every word between D and H is a subordinate either of H, or of a mutual head of D and H'. Consider (49).

(49) Kuricu   na **bol'šuju**   položi   **tarelku**
chicken-ACC   on big-ACC-FEM put-IMPERF plate-ACC-FEM
'put the chicken on a/the big plate'

---

[18] Austin (1981: 96) says that examples of two adjectives in a noun phrase are rare but cites one example.

D is *bol'šuju* and *tarelku* is H. These can be counted as adjacent if the word that comes between them is a subordinate of *bol'šuju*, a subordinate of *tarelku*, or a subordinate of some word on which they are both dependent. These conditions are not met, because the intervening word, *položi*, is the head of the clause (in the long-standing verb-dependency tradition within which Hudson works). That is, *bol'šuju* and *tarelku* are both dependents of *položi*, and *položi* itself does not depend on any other word. We offer the hypothesis that constraints on adjacency and head-modifier relationships can be formulated for written langauge but that the choppy nature of syntactic structure in spontaneous speech makes it unlikely that general constraints can be established for all languages.

The Russian data is relevant to the distinction between configurational and non-configurational languages that has been current since the publication of Hale (1983). Formal written Russian is without doubt configurational. Spontaneous spoken Russian is non-configurational, which is to say that heads and modifiers may or may not be adjacent to each other. Of course, Hale was working on an Australian language with a rich system of syntactic linkage, but Russian, spoken or written, has just as rich a system. More important from our perspective is the fact that Hale was working on a spoken-only language; this gives rise to the suspicion that his thesis of non-configurationality rests on the 'untidy' nature of syntax in spontaneous speech. Putting the argument in the Russian context: linguist X working on spoken Russian (and with no access to written Russian texts) might well conclude that the language is non-configurational; linguist Y working on written Russian (and ignoring the spoken language) would certainly conclude that Russian was configurational. The consequences for typology are clear—see the discussion of typology in Chapter 7.

4.7.2. Scrambling and 'split' NPs

One question arises immediately if we ask how 'split' NPs are to be handled in a particular formal model, in particular how agreement between adjective and noun is to be handled. Whatever the formal mechanisms employed in a given model, the central fact of agreement is that a noun and the adjectives modifying it are constituents of a single larger constituent; it is relatively straightforward to ensure that features are spread from noun to adjective (or vice-versa) or that a combination of noun and adjective with different features (usually number, case, and gender) is rejected. The above account proposes that in sequences with 'split' NPs adjective and noun are independent NPs separated from each other by one or more constituents. This proposal handles the data presented in §4.4 and §4.6 but does make agreement between adjective and noun much trickier to handle.

Within Government and Binding or Principle and Parameters the analyst has to treat 'split' NPs as split only in surface syntax and as deriving from a single large NP containing both the adjective and the noun. The 'split' NP construction itself has not actually been tackled in the GB and PP frameworks, but a similar problem does arise with verbs and their complement NPs in German. Consider the German subordinate adverbial clauses in (50).

(50) (*a*) weil   Peter das Buch wahrscheinlich gelesen hat
         because Peter the   book probably   read   has
         'because Peter has probably read the book'
     (*b*) weil   das Buch niemand gelesen hat
         because the book nobody read   has
         'because nobody has read the book'

In (50*a*,*b*) the NP *das Buch* receives a theta role (say, Patient) from the verb *gelesen*. In one account of German (Webelhuth 1989: 328–30) a wellformedness condition ensures that the grammar only generates clauses in which the complement NPs have the appropriate theta roles (and case marking). Webelhuth proposes a general constraint on such wellformedness conditions, namely that they mention only the properties of the two elements involved in the process of syntactic linkage, and that the two elements form a constituent. This general constraint is called the Saturation Constraint, the name reflecting an interpretation of syntactic linkage in terms of variables (such as role and case, number and person, etc.) taking up enough meaning (values for case, role, etc.) to become, so to speak, saturated and unable to absorb any more meaning.

(50*a*,*b*) poses difficulties for the Saturation Constraint; in both the direct object *das Buch* is separated from the role-assigning main verb *gelesen*—in (50*a*) by the adverb *wahrscheinlich* and in (50*b*) by the subject noun phrase *niemand*. Webelhuth (1989: 330) deals with the problem by hypothesizing that no direct object can be generated except as sister to V. A complement that is not adjacent to its head V has been dislocated from its D-structure position leaving a trace. This hypothesis mentions adjacency but not order. (50*a*) can be derived from the underlying structure *weil Peter wahrscheinlich das Buch gelesen hat*, in which *das Buch* and *gelesen* are adjacent, and (50*b*) can be derived from *weil niemand das Buch gelesen hat*.

Scrambling, subject to the conditions postulated by Webelhuth, could be extended to the Russian split NPs. An example such as (11) *interesnuju prinesi mne knigu* could be derived from the underlying structure *prinesi mne interesnuju knigu*. The adjective *interesnuju* would be assigned case, gender, and number by its head noun, *knigu*, and would then be moved by Scrambling to clause-initial position.

The elegance of the formalism conceals difficulties. The first is that Scrambling ignores examples such as (43) in §4.6.1, in which adjective and noun are both preceded by a preposition. The evidence and the semantic interpretation strongly support an analysis of *v novom v rajone* 'in a-new-one in a-district' in terms of two juxtaposed noun phrases, each noun phrase inside a prepositional phrase.

Second, there is the question of complexity. An analysis with Scrambling is more complex than one without Scrambling, and we might expect an example analysed by means of Scrambling to be more complex than one analysed without Scrambling. The difficulty is that Russian split NPs occur in spontaneous spoken Russian, which is precisely where syntactic structures are at their simplest because of lack of planning time. From this viewpoint, the application of a more complex analysis to a simple structure is unappealing. Moreover, it ignores the deictic function of long adjectives in Russian and the availability of anaphoric treatments.

How then can grammars handle examples such as (49), Kuricu na **bol'šuju** položi **tarelku** 'the-chicken on a/the-big-one place a/the-plate?' *bol'šuju* 'big' and *tarelku* 'plate' are syntactically linked but non-adjacent. The first step towards a solution is to note that the problem is not confined to Russian long adjectives. Pollard and Sag (1994) ask how French speakers know to say *elle est belle*, pointing to a table or to a car and using the feminine singular pronoun rather than the masculine singular pronoun *il*, and the feminine singular adjective *belle* rather than the masculine singular *beau*. The relevant French nouns have feminine gender—*table* and *voiture* or *bagnole*—but the example contains no overt full nouns.

Pollard and Sag (1994: 60), working within a unification constraint-based framework, suggest that the feature structure for nominals includes indices relating to three types of agreement: syntactic agreement, involving syntactic objects such as case values; index agreement, which arises when indices are to be token-identical, and pragmatic agreement, which arises when contextual background assumptions are required to be consistent. Furthermore, the indices are not specified as part of syntactic categories but in the internal structure of referential indices. Indices are abstract objects whose discourse function is to keep track of the entities being talked about; for example, in *My neighbour$_i$ thinks she$_i$ is a genius* the subscript 'i' is a third person singular feminine index (Pollard and Sag 1994: 66–7). With respect to the French example above, they propose that the index of the pronoun must coincide with the index of a French common noun denoting the set of entities containing the entity referred to by the pronoun (Pollard and Sag 1994: 79).[19]

---

[19] Pollard and Sag point out that German has the nouns *Haus* (house) and *Hütte* (hut) which are respectively neuter and feminine in gender. They assert that using the second noun rather than the first speakers can indicate their poor opinion of a particular building. They further assert the same poor opinion can be conveyed by using the feminine pronoun *sie* (appropriate for *Hütte*) rather than the neuter pronoun *es*, appropriate for *Haus*. They propose that grammars of German either recognize as many pronouns as there are lexical items or treat

All this is relevant to Russian long adjectives in split NPs. The adjectives agree in gender and number with a noun. As discussed in §4.6.1, the long adjectives consist of a stem and an ending that historically derives from a deictic, and they still function as deictics in Modern Russian. Taking advantage of the proposals in Pollard and Sag (1994), and perhaps taking unfair advantage by (justifiably) not developing an explicit account, we can say that the occurrence of pronouns in Russian, including long adjectives, must make reference to the relevant lexical item.

This approach to the problem is particularly pleasing as it is compatible with the view, outlined at the end of Chapter 1, that the distinction between competence and language production should not be taken to be clear-cut, especially with regard to the syntactic structure of spontaneous spoken language. With respect to (49), the speaker can be thought of as first fixing on the situation to be talked about and then deciding on what is to be referred to first—in this case a property of a particular entity, the plate. The reference is performed by means of a long adjective, *bol'šuju* but, as Pollard and Sag put it, the reference of *bol'šuju* is mediated by the lexical entry for TARELKA, which supplies the information that the noun, and therefore any pronoun, must be feminine. Since there is only one entity, and since TARELKA is not in the class of pluralia tantum nouns, the number is singular.

4.7.3. Functional constituents as heads

The 'split' noun phrase constructions in spoken Russian bear on recent work in which minor grammatical items, and not major lexical items, are given the status of heads of constructions. They are relevant because an argument can be made (with respect to both spoken and written Russian) for taking adjectives to be the syntactic heads of adjective-noun sequences. The fact (let us take it to be a fact) that adjectives and nouns in spoken Russian can occur as independent, non-adjacent NPs lends support to the argument that adjectives play just as important a role as nouns in integrated NPs.

While not agreeing with the entire analysis of particular constructions, Hudson (1987) invokes the criteria laid out in Zwicky (1985). The head of a construction is: the constituent that carries any inflexions in languages with inflectional morphology (the morphosyntactic locus); the constituent that denotes the kind of entity denoted by the construction (*planted potatoes* denotes a kind of planting rather than a kind of potato and *planted* is the head); the constituent that is subcategorized with respect to its sister

---

the referential relation between pronouns and entities as mediated by the lexical entries for the appropriate lexical items. That is, the pronoun *sie* must be able to pick up information that entities referred to by means of NPs containing *Hütte* are presented by the speaker as inferior with respect to entities referred to by means of NPs containing *Haus*.

constituents in the construction (the subcategorizand); the constituent that determines the morphosyntactic form of some sister; (the governor); the constituent that is obligatory; the constituent whose distribution is similar to that of the mother. Hudson rejects one of Zwicky's criteria, concluding that the direction of agreement between constituents is irrelevant. Long adjectives in NPs, 'split' or integrated, meet most of the above criteria. They carry inflexional morphology (as do nouns); in traditional accounts they are subcategorized with respect to the gender, number, and case of the noun; they have similar distribution to nouns, as demonstrated in §4.6.1. The semantic criterion has to do with denotation; the head of a construction denotes the kind of entity denoted by the entire construction. It does not apply unambiguously to combinations of adjective and noun, but the ambiguity itself is significant. The crucial question is this; does a phrase such as *bol'šuju tarelku* 'big plate' denote a kind of big thing or a kind of plate? The answer must be that both denotations are possible depending on context; in rather crude terms, it depends on whether the phrase turns up in a reply to the question *kakaja bol'šaja vešč?* 'what big thing?' or *čto za tarelka?* 'what for a-plate', i.e. 'what kind of plate?'. That is, in Russian, nouns and long adjectives meet the same criteria and both have an equal right to be considered the head of a 'Noun' Phrase.

This analysis of Russian links up with Lyons's hypothesis on the ontogenesis of referring expressions consisting of deictic determiner and noun. (See Lyons 1975, 1991.) We will ignore the part of Lyons's argument based on the generation of referring expressions such as *that dog* and *the dog* in the standard model of transformation grammar, but other parts of the argument are still valid. For instance, Lyons points out that in the English phrases *that dog* and *the dog* the head cannot be *dog* because the singular count nouns cannot be used as referring expressions without some kind of determiner or quantifier. Lyons proposes to analyse *dog* as in apposition to *that* or *the*. The relevance of the noun phrase data from spoken Russian (and spoken English) is this. The high incidence of referring expressions with one constituent, particularly personal pronouns, deictic determiners and quantifiers, reflects the use of language in context. Speakers make, usually justifiably, generous assumptions about what their addressees can pick out from the immediate context of utterance. These assumptions lead to the extensive use of referring expressions that are syntactically simple and light in information. If speakers want to supply extra information, they can add a noun—that is, if they are speaking Russian they can add a noun, but if they are speaking English they have to add a combination of definite article and noun. The point is that historically the construction of definite article plus noun arose from a combination of deictic determiner plus noun, the definite article being a reduced deictic determiner. In spontaneous speech we can still see the type of situation in which a combination of deictic and noun arose and we can see the situational justification for regarding the noun as in apposition to the deictic.

We have argued that split NPs, including long adjective and noun, should not be derived by scrambling from a solitary noun phrase but that the two constituents should be generated in situ. What about the combinations in which long adjective and noun are adjacent? Let us remind ourselves first that the long adjectives are deictic, that, e.g. the adjective *xorošij* ('good') consists of the stem *xoroš-* and the deictic suffix *-ij*. In grammars of Russian these suffixes are described as case affixes, but given that they derive historically from deictics and given that the long adjectives are regularly used deictically, it is reasonable to assume that the affixes have not lost their deictic nature. Just as Lyons suggested that the determiner plus noun structure in English and other languages began with nouns being put in apposition to deictics, so we suggest that the Russian adjective-noun construction arose out of nouns being put in apposition to long adjectives, which are deictic. That is, examples such as *xorošij meč* (a/the-good sword) arose out of a structure that can be glossed as good-that-one a/the sword. The modern Russian phrase is translated into English simply as 'a/the good sword'.

Combinatorial grammar sheds further light on this analysis. Let us begin with a straightforward example. Categorial grammar treats a VP as a category that requires a noun phrase in order to yield a sentence; e.g. *swam in the loch* is merely a verb phrase, but it can be converted into a sentence by the addition of a noun phrase such as *the children, the monster*, and so on. In Montague terms, a VP belongs to the category *t/e*, that is it requires an element belonging to the category *e*—that is, an element referring to an entity—in order to produce an element belonging to the category *t*, the category of elements referring to truth values. Sentences are held to refer to truth values, truth values being assigned to propositions.

We are concerned here with the various categories of elements inside elements of category *e*, that is, inside noun phrases. The starting point is the generally accepted analysis which takes determiners to apply to single nouns or to combinations of adjective and noun. In *the red cup* the determiner *the* picks out a specific entity that is in the set of red things and in the set of cups. As already observed, English common count nouns do not become referential until they have a determiner. A singular common count noun can be treated categorially as an element that requires a determiner in order to become a member of the category *e*. In purely syntactic terms, such a noun allows the addition of a determiner or a numeral or a quantifier, but once the addition has been made no further determiners, numerals, or quantifiers can be added.

How do adjectives appear in this perspective? In English the addition of an adjective to a singular common count noun yields an element still belonging to the category of elements that require a determiner, etc. to become a member of the category *e*. That is, the categorial perspective presents the noun as the head of the adjective-noun structure. The Russian situation is different. A singular common count noun in Russian, say *čaška* (cup) may be referential or non-referential depending on the syntactic construction. The addition of a long adjective yields an expression that is also referential or non-referential depending on the syntactic construction. The major difference between English and Russian is that whereas *red* on its own cannot belong to category *e*, the Russian adjective *kransnaja* can belong to category *e* on its own. In fact, like *čaška* it is referential or non-referential depending on the syntactic construction.

To sum up, the categorial perspective brings out the difference between Russian and English adjectives. The crucial evidence for Russian is the deictic source and nature of the long adjective. On the evidence that adjectives are at least equal in status to nouns in the adjective-noun construction, we propose the adjective as potential head of noun phrases. The appositional structure referred to above has not died out but is alive and well in modern Russian.

5 Focus Constructions

5.1. Introduction

In Chapters 2, 3, and 4 we have examined the differences between spoken and written languages with respect to clauses and noun phrases. In both spontaneous speech and in written language, clauses are organized into larger chunks. In writing, clauses are first combined into sentences and sentences are then put together into texts. In spontaneous speech speakers combine clauses into larger units but, as argued in Chapter 2, it is not fruitful to analyse spontaneous speech in terms of sentences. Writers produce letters, novels, business and legal documents, textbooks, and so on. They typically have time to plan the written text and are able to set it down on paper or computer screen without competition from other writers wishing to make their contribution to the text. When producing spontaneous speech, however, speakers typically cooperate and take turns, especially in conversation and task-related dialogue such as the Map Task data. Both spoken and written texts have devices for organizing the presentation of information; to produce a successful text both speakers and writers have to employ appropriate ways of introducing new information, reintroducing information at a later stage in a text, contrasting one piece of information with another, and concentrating the listener's or reader's attention on the information that is central to the exposition at any given point.

In this chapter we look at the organization of spoken and written texts, concentrating on the devices for highlighting particular constituents and the information they carry. (The term 'highlighting' is explained below.) We will also look at the devices by which constituents can be left unhighlighted. By 'devices' is meant special syntactic constructions, such as the English clefts (discussed below and in Chapter 6), particles, pitch, and word order. The spoken and written varieties of a given language may even differ with respect to which positions in the clause are important. Zemskaja (1973: 382) observes that in literary Russian the end of an utterance is more important for information structure, whereas in spoken Russian it is the beginning of the utterance. (We go further than Zemskaja and suggest that word order by itself is relatively unimportant for highlighting in spoken Russian but does have a role to play in written Russian.) She cites, though with qualification, the view of Kovtunova (1967: 60–1) that word order has a minimum role in signalling information structure (aktual'noe členenie) in spoken Russian because of the role of context, gestures, and intonation.

As before, the differences between spoken and written language are in part made possible by the properties of spoken and written language described in §1.5. The databases used in this and the next chapter are those described in §1.3, supplemented by additional data collected in connection with a typology-of-discourse project.[1]

The additional data falls into two subsets. The first consists of 8 Catalan and 6 Hungarian Map Task dialogues. The second consists of elicited data, obtained by taking cleft constructions from the English Map Task dialogues and using them as the basis of a questionnaire administered orally. (Cleft constructions are described in detail in Chapter 6. Examples of three constructions are *What you need is a mobile phone, it's a mobile phone that you need*, and *That's what you need*.) Certain examples actually occurring in the spontaneous Map Task dialogues were presented to the informants along with a description of the situation with which each example was associated, and the informants were invited to imagine themselves in the situation. Previous analysis of the English Map Task dialogues had established the functions of the cleft constructions (Weinert and Miller 1996) and this understanding shaped the contextual information given to the informants. The latter were not asked to translate the English examples but to imagine what they would have said in the given situation. The Map Task examples were supplemented by other examples of clefts, such as *what I'm going to talk about today is X*, which were included in order to explore different uses of cleft constructions. For each example an appropriate context was devised; for instance, the above example was said to have been uttered by a speaker beginning a talk.

The use of a questionnaire has various disadvantages: it is impossible to determine whether a given informant has properly understood the situation; it is by no means certain that informants consult their intuitions correctly; and the influence of the English examples cannot be discounted. For instance, both the Finnish informant and one of the Hungarian informants produced direct analogues of English WH clefts, as in *what I'm going to do today is talk about X*. The Finnish informant commented that educated Finns with a good knowledge of English can be heard producing the Finnish analogue regularly, although it is not a construction recognized in Finnish grammars. One Hungarian informant felt initially that the Hungarian WH analogue was a possible structure but declared that no native speaker of Hungarian would use it. A similar comment was made by

---

[1] This was the Eurotype project, funded by the European Science Foundation, which ran from January 1990 to December 1994. Jim Miller was a member of Theme Group 1 'The pragmatic organization of discourse'.

the Serbo-Croat informant, who searched through written texts (children's books, academic papers, instructions in crosswords and in magazines) for Serbo-Croat analogues of IT clefts but found none. Consultation with other native speakers of Serbo-Croat resident in Slovenia and Croatia revealed that none of them would ever use a Serbo-Croat analogue of the English IT cleft. Instead, the constituent to be highlighted is fronted. None the less the Serbo-Croat informant insists that an analogue of the English IT cleft is possible and grammatical but that if it were used, say, in a Zagreb tram, heads would turn. Finally, a German speaker who answered the questionnaire and provided German analogues of IT cleft constructions with *es*, as in *it's Fiona who's helping, not Kirsty*, is a specialist in English, while the one German contributor to the German Map Task corpus who provided analogues of English WH clefts had been living in the UK for two or three years.

Another disadvantage is that the Map Task may not generate the contexts in which a given type of cleft appears. For instance, the naturally-occurring German Map Task dialogues, with no WH clefts apart from the exception mentioned at the end of the above paragraph, tempt the analyst to dismiss the WH clefts provided in answer to the questionnaire. They can after all be seen as arising from constant exposure to English. In fact, German does have a WH cleft construction but it has a different function from that of the English WH clefts and occurs mainly in formal conversation. (Note that this disadvantage applies only to languages that have cleft constructions but not the same range with the same discourse functions as English. The languages in our sample that have no cleft constructions at all—Finnish, Hungarian, and Turkish—are unaffected. And for English and German the Map Task data is supplemented by data from corpuses of conversation.)

In spite of the drawbacks, certain pieces of reliable information were obtained. The English examples all involved some type of cleft construction. Informants were influenced by the English to the extent that where possible they provided a natural rendering by means of a cleft.[2] But this brought out clearly the fact that some languages simply do not have cleft constructions, and that other languages have one or two but not the entire range of cleft constructions found in English. A final, but far from negligible, advantage of using Map Task dialogues and questionnaires based on Map Task dialogues is that they yield cross-language data roughly comparable with respect to discourse function.

---

[2] This is a problem noted by Dahl with respect to his tense-aspect questionnaire. See Dahl (1985).

5.2. Concepts for the Analysis of Discourse

Before summarizing the results of the work reported in this and the next chapters and embarking on a detailed analysis, it will be useful to define briefly the major concepts that will be used.

5.2.1. *Focus (1)*

The literature on discourse is filled with the term 'focus', which has a number of applications. Indeed, the theoretical burden carried by 'focus', both as a noun and a verb, is so great that we will not use the term except when reporting the findings of other investigators. Our key assumption is that listeners and readers with adult competence in a given language can recognize when constituents stand out from the surrounding constituents in a clause or sentence. We can ask what devices are available to the speakers and writers of a given language for making constituents stand out; we can ask what means they actually use according to corpus evidence; and we can ask what discourse purposes are served by a particular device. That is, the research supporting this chapter is data-driven.

Since the various concepts of focus will be reviewed in § 5.4, we will say nothing here about 'focus' as a technical term except to remark that every concept of focus has to do with giving prominence to constituents and the information they carry, albeit for different reasons—the introduction of new entities or new propositions, the contrast of one entity with another, 'exhaustive listing' (one particular entity and no other), or non-contrastive prominence. Our strategy is to take as broad a perspective as possible by avoiding any one definition of focus and instead examining the devices which give prominence to constituents, whatever the reason. Consequently, readers should be prepared to come across constructions that are excluded by whatever definition of focus they might be thirled to.

We also believe that the technical burden carried by 'focus' is too great for the term to be employed even in a non-technical sense. It will be necessary to appeal repeatedly to the concept of constituents standing out from the surrounding constituents, whether this is achieved by means of pitch, syntactic construction, word order, or particle. Constituents will be said to be given prominence, made prominent, highlighted, made salient or given salience. Prominence, salience, and highlighting are not technical terms but used in their everyday meaning. The other side of this theoretical coin is that we will also have to look at constituents that are made less prominent—typically because they refer to highly topical entities.[3]

---

[3] In this connection the adjective 'topical' and the noun 'topic' are not connected, in that a noun phrase that is topical is not thereby the topic of a sentence or larger stretch of text.

5.2.2. Deixis

Speakers and writers use deictics to pick out entities without describing them. They do this when they consider the relevant entity to be present in the situation of utterance, either because it is physically present or has been previously mentioned. Personal pronouns such as I, SHE, THEY, etc. pick out respectively the speaker, a female entity other than speaker or hearer, and a number of entities other than speaker and hearer. THIS and THAT are definite deictics, used when the speaker treats an entity as near or remote, respectively. Nearness and remoteness can be judged with respect to the speaker alone or the speaker and hearer together. Thus, if X and Y are in the same room and X turns to Y and asks *Did you notice that car when you came in*, *that* points to an entity remote from both speaker and hearer. In contrast, if X and Y are walking round a car showroom and X stops to look at a particular car C while Y has gone off to look at another car on the other side of the showroom, X can attract Y's attention to C by calling *Have you seen this car?* but not **have you seen that car?*

The above examples illustrate the basic spatial use of THIS and THAT. This spatial use underlies the anaphoric use of deictics in texts (though the extent to which the spatial uses carry over into the anaphoric, textual uses is a matter of debate), but many non-anaphorical occurrences of the deictics cannot be interpreted as literally spatial but rather as metaphorical, reflecting where speakers wish to situate themselves with respect to given entities. For example, the student who asked Jim Miller *Have the answers to that essay of yours been marked yet?* was signalling that he considered the essay remote from himself and near to Jim Miller; the remoteness was not physical but mental and the utterance reflected the student's attitude to the essay and the topic of the lecture course. In the Map Task dialogues utterances such as *that's where you should be* are used by instruction givers to point to locations remote in several senses; the segment of route drawn by the instruction follower has led to a location at some distance from the correct location, and the correct location has been specified in a chunk of discourse through which the participants, so to speak, have travelled and from which they are moving away. In contrast, an utterance such as *this is where you should be* points to a location which is about to be described in the chunk of discourse which the participants are entering.

'Topical' merely indicates that the entity has already been mentioned, possibly several times, in the immediately preceding text. As will emerge from the discussion of Russian in §5.4, defocusing occurs when an entity is deemed by the speaker to be salient in a situation, even without being mentioned. But different languages offer different possibilities for defocusing.

5.2.3. *Theme and thematization*

The starting point for this discussion of thematization is Halliday (1985: 38), who adopts the Prague School concept of theme as the first constituent in a clause, the element which serves as the point of departure of the message. Theme constituents often, but not necessarily, convey given information. Theme constituents also enjoy salience merely by virtue of being in first position in the clause. Final position in the clause is also important, but not the middle position. The major constituent-movement rules move items into clause-first or clause-final position, not to some clause-internal position. Clause-initial position is occupied by constituents that link a particular clause with the preceding text, either because the constituents carry given information or information that links up with the preceding text but is contrastive. In the second clause of *They went into the dining room. There they found an intruder*, *there* provides a bridge to the preceding text by picking up the referent of *the dining-room*. In the second clause of *Celia willingly agreed to help. However Susan refused*, *however* provides a bridge by pointing back to the situation described in the first clause and signalling that a contrast is about to be presented.

As will be seen in Chapter 6, languages without cleft constructions use particles to make constituents prominent but also move constituents into clause-initial position. Moreover, one of the major properties of clefts is that they enable the thematization of elements which would not be theme in uncleft alternatives. Thus, in *What I don't like the Director doing without consulting any of his colleagues is changing the financial plan*, the entire clause *I don't like the Director doing something* has been converted into the theme *what I don't like the Director doing* and the complement of *is*, *changing the financial plan*, specifies *what*. Similarly, the reverse WH cleft construction allows a clause such as *you should do that* to be converted into a two-clause structure in which *that* is theme—*that's what you should do*. Assuming for the moment that *what* in the WH cleft is an indefinite deictic (an analysis that will be argued in Chapter 6), we can regard all the cleft constructions as crucially involving both thematization and deixis.

5.2.4. *Given and new information*

Given information is information that the speaker/writer treats as recoverable by the listener/reader (Halliday (1967: 211)—though Halliday talks about speakers). Speakers/writers treat information as given because the entity is relates to is present in the situation, or has already been mentioned, or because they assume that the entity is present in the background knowledge of listeners/readers or can be inferred by the latter from the situation. G. Brown and Yule (1983: 183) give as an example the following utterance from a spontaneous description of an incident: *there was a car approaching the junction + but the driver didn't stop at the give way sign*. The speaker could not actually see the driver of the car but assumed first that the car had a driver and second that the listener would pick up the reference of *the driver*.

New information is information that the speaker presents as new. It may be objectively new in the sense that it has not been mentioned in the course of the conversation or has never been heard before anywhere by the audience. On the other hand, it may have been mentioned before or be known to the audience, but the speaker chooses to present it as not recoverable from the linguistic or extra-linguistic context. One of the advantages of the Map Task is that the analyst knows what landmarks are physically presented on both maps or on only one of the maps and can investigate discrepancies between the objective status of entities as given or new and the way in which the participants present the entities.

5.3. Results

The main conclusions that will emerge from this and the next chapter are these.

i A major role in highlighting is played by particles. All languages have particles, though some make more use of them than others. For instance, in the spontaneous Map Task dialogues particles were frequent in German, Hungarian, and Catalan, but less so in English. In English particles are typical of spontaneous spoken language, whereas in, e.g. German, Finnish, and Hungarian, particles are typical of both speech and writing.[4]

ii Certain languages have clefts, while others do not. Among the former, only English possesses and regularly uses three cleft constructions. Some languages have clefts in principle but their speakers prefer to use particles— see the discussion of the Catalan spontaneous Map Task dialogues in §6.4. Clefts appear to be a feature of languages spoken on or near the western seaboard of Europe, an area which has to be interpreted liberally in order to include Italian. But, taking Britain as a starting point, the general picture is that clefts become rarer and eventually disappear as one moves north-east, east, and south-east.

iii In languages with cleft constructions, the frequency of occurrence of clefts may differ from spoken to written language. For instance, IT clefts

---

[4] 'Particles' here are not focus particles such as *only* or *even* but particles expressing impatience or surprise, particles signalling that the speaker is about to issue an instruction, particles signalling that a particular constituent is important.

are a regular highlighting device in written English but are rare in our spoken data, both the Map Task dialogues and the spontaneous conversations.

iv Changes in word order, i.e. preserving the construction type but rearranging the words as in *below the castle there's woods* (declarative main clause but locative PP in first position), have to do with the distinction between given and new in that the fronted constituent is given. Where the fronted constituent is to be highlighted, a number of languages, such as Russian and German, often combine fronting with the occurrence of a particle. In the latter two languages the fronting alone highlights a deictic or personal pronoun, while in other languages, such as Hungarian, Greek, Serbo-Croat, and Bulgarian, any fronted constituent is highlighted.[5]

v All the languages sampled have devices for highlighting new (first-order) entities, items such as chairs and tables. In many and perhaps all languages the syntactic coding for new entities ranges from yes–no interrogatives (*have you got a great viewpoint?*) to special existential structures (*there's baboons on my map*). Other devices include special particles, such as the Russian *vot*, but the particles in this function appear to be typical of spoken language.

vi New propositions have their own highlighting devices. In spoken language these are particles or semi-fixed constructions such as the English *the thing is* or *thing is*, or conversational strategies such as speakers asking a WH question and answering it themselves—*what did we do then? we just picked up the phone and called the police, She must be worth—what?—several million pounds*. Written language makes use of special constructions such as clefts—*what I think about this theory is that it has very limited application*—or formulaic expressions such as *Let us now consider the view that, let us turn to the hypothesis that*.

vii Contrastive and non-contrastive highlighting is achieved by means of particles in spoken language but typically by means of special syntactic constructions in written language. For example, IT clefts are a favourite focusing device in written English but are rare in our data, both the Map Task dialogues and the spontaneous conversations. Word order alone is seldom used for contrastive highlighting. It can be so used in VS clauses in Russian,

---

[5] This statement is based on the Map Task data elicited from informants or, in the case of Hungarian, both elicited and occurring spontaneously in Map Task dialogues. Given that informants reporting on their spoken language regularly overlook particles, and given the central role of particles in spontaneous speech (cf. Fernandez 1984), we are entitled to suspect that we would find particles in spontaneous dialogues in Greek, Bulgarian, etc. At the time of writing such data is not available to us.

but even Russian with its very rich morpho-syntax prefers particles (possibly accompanied by changes in word order), overtly contrasted clauses—[NP Predicate] followed by [Predicate NP], and other syntactic devices.

viii Spontaneous spoken language makes heavy use of pitch for highlighting. Written languages can make use of underlining or italic and bold fonts to capture part, but only a part, of the role of pitch.

5.4. Focus (2)

5.4.1. *Overview*

As announced in the third paragraph of this chapter, our approach is data-driven, in that we are interested in devices that highlight constituents/give them prominence/make them salient in the basic sense of standing out from the surrounding constituents in a clause or sentence. How do these devices link in with the various concepts of focus that have been proposed over the last twenty years? The short answer is that all the concepts have something in common; they involve the possible highlighting of a constituent and the information it carries, albeit for different reasons. Highlighting serves contrastive and non-contrastive purposes, and the latter include highlighting for the purpose of fixing new entities, or re-fixing previously mentioned entities, in the listener's attention. In addition, the concept of focus is invoked in accounts of how a given speaker and listener shift attention from one entity to another in a given context, thereby shifting the reference of pronouns, as described in the classic paper by Grosz (Grosz 1981).

The core concept of contrastive focus as employed by Halliday and Chafe turns out to have much in common with the concept of focus as used by Dik, and even with two apparently very different concepts—Grosz and Sidner's, which has to do with referential status, and Vallduví's (Vallduví 1993), which has to do with the transmission of information. In order to accommodate the various concepts in one framework, we add the notion of communicative goal as deployed by Levy (1985) and bring in the further concepts of macro-focus and micro-focus. Macro-focus relates to major, high-level, transitions in a text, and micro-focus relates to minor, low-level transitions. The important notion here is 'transition', which is also at the heart of Grosz and Sidner's work.

5.4.2. *Halliday*

Halliday (1967–1968) posits information units which are realized as tone groups. A tone group contains one obligatory component, a tonic segment, which may be a whole word or part of a word, and at least one optional component, the pretonic segment. One information unit is realized as one tone group, and the number and size of the information units in a given utterance reflect how the speaker has divided the message into blocks of information. Within each information unit the speaker selects a certain element or elements as points of prominence within the message. For example, (1) can be realized as (2*a*) or (2*b*), where the double obliques mark tone group boundaries and small capitals mark the position of the tonic segment.

(1) John saw the play yesterday

(2) (*a*) //JOHN// saw the PLAY YESterday//
    (*b*) // John saw the PLAY YESterday//

'(Information) focus' assigns the function 'new' to what is within its domain. The constituent specified as new is the one marked out by the speaker for interpretation as carrying non-derivable information, either cumulative to or contrastive with what has preceded. In this respect Halliday's notion of information focus is very close to the notion proposed by Valldui (1993)—cf. § 5.4.5 below. Halliday emphasizes that new information is what the speaker chooses to present as new. In a later work (1985: 277) Halliday states that one form of newness frequent in dialogue is

[6] One further important concept employed by Halliday is markedness, one of the classic Prague School concepts. The classic concept relates to oppositions between two items, where one item definitely has a particular property but the other item may or may not have it, i.e. is neutral. For instance, the English lexical items BITCH and DOG are in relation to one another: BITCH can only denote a female canine, whereas DOG may or may not denote a female canine. Halliday distinguishes between unmarked focus and marked focus. With the former, the tonic falls on the final accented lexical item in the clause, assigning the function 'new' to that constituent but not specifying the remainder of the clause as given or new. Any other location of the tonic constitutes marked focus. The focal constituent is assigned the function 'new' and the remainder of the clause (more accurately, information unit) is assigned the function 'given'.

The opposition marked–unmarked applies within many domains in linguistic analysis, not just focus but also syntactic constructions (not to mention the classic applications in phonology and in grammatical categories, which do not concern us here). Consider (*i*).

    (*i*) //John saw the **play** //

The tonic falls on the final accented lexical item in the information unit/clause and the focus is thus marked. The construction itself is among the simplest in English—neutral, active, declarative—and is treated as unmarked, in contrast with (*ii*), which is more complex and draws attention to a particular constituent, *John*. (NB: This effect holds independently of whether the tonic falls on *John* or not.)

    (*ii*) //It was John who saw the **play** //

At the same time the focus is unmarked too, as the tonic falls on the final accented lexical item in the information unit. In (*iii*) the focus is marked, as the tonic does not fall on the final accented lexical item, but the syntactic construction, as in (*i*), is unmarked. In (*iv*), however, the syntactic construction is marked as well, since it is the more complex IT cleft construction, which draws attention to one particular constituent.

contrastive emphasis.[6] This is true, but we will distinguish contrast and newness in order to facilitate our account of expressions that are employed for contrastive salience and expressions that are employed for making new entities salient.

5.4.3. *Chafe: components of contrastiveness*

Chafe (1976) extends Halliday's work by asking explicitly what contrastiveness is. With respect to the example *RONALD made the hamburgers* Chafe spells out the factors involved: (i) background knowledge that a set of hamburgers was prepared; (ii) a set of possible candidates for the cook; (iii) assertion of which candidates is the correct one. Contrastiveness is manifested principally by the placement of higher pitch and stronger stress on the focus of contrast, although IT clefts are an alternative device. Like Halliday, Chafe regards the pitch phenomena as of primary importance and the use of syntactic constructions as secondary, but Chafe limits focus to contrast, unlike Halliday, who regards contrastiveness as only one property of focus—focused, new information can be cumulative to existing information or in contrast with it.[7]

5.4.4. *Dik: extended notion of focus*

Dik (1980: 210–29) extends the concept of focus and presents a taxonomy of focus types. He draws a distinction between shared and non-shared, or new, information—the distinction depending on a given speaker's assessment—and, like Halliday, treats focus as usually, but not necessarily always, marking information as non-shared. In the interests of communication, the non-shared information is made salient, either by intonation, constituent order, focus markers such as particles or special focus constructions. Dik provides a hierarchy of different types of focus—the examples are from Mackenzie and Keizer (1990). All the examples apart from parallel focus are unmarked, the tonic falling on the final accented lexical item, but they all have in common that the speaker uses the tonic to make information

(iii) // **John** saw the play //
(iv) // It was **John** who saw the play //

The above concept of markedness will not be explored further here but it may well provide a measure of highlighting and deserves to be mentioned as an integral part of Halliday's framework which has not been exploited either by Halliday or by other scholars.

[7] Givón (1990) suggests that the various focusing or contrastive devices can be ranked according to contrastive strength, the weakest being neutral syntactic constructions with unmarked focus (Givón uses the term 'neutral') and the contrastive strength increasing as we move from neutral to stress focus, then IT clefts and finally WH clefts. Givón notes that WH clefts are not contrastive unless the nominal predicate carries focus stress.

salient, presenting it as unshared or new. In Halliday's scheme the second and third clauses in Dik's parallel focus example (3*b*) each consist of two tone groups, e.g. //*John*// was *nice*//, with a tonic not just on the final accented lexical item but also on the first lexical item. Dik's hierarchy is given in Figure 5.1. Examples of the different types of focus are given in (3). Obviously, the placement of the tonic is relevant only to speech. Speech shares with written language the syntax of the different types of focus but in speech the syntax might well be reduced; for instance, in (3*c*) a possible spoken retort is simply *coffee*, with the appropriate pitch pattern and an

```
                        Focus
                  ╱            ╲
        completive focus    contrastive focus
                         ╱              ╲
                  parallel focus    counter-presuppositional focus
                              ╲         ╱  │
                               ╲       ╱   └── restricting focus
                            replacing focus
                                  │      │
                           expanding focus  selecting focus
```

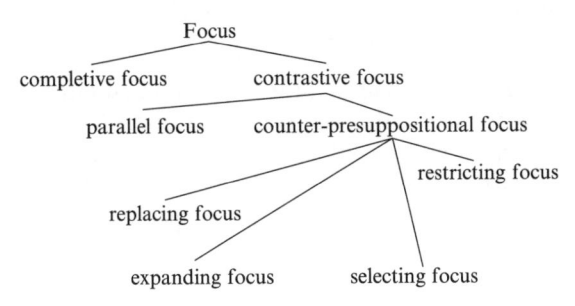

FIG. 1.

appropriate voice quality.[8]

(3) (*a*) **completive focus**
   Where is John GOING?
   He's going to the MARKET / to the MARKET
 (*b*) **parallel focus**
   John and Bill came to see me. JOHN was NICE but BILL was BORING
 (*c*) **replacing focus**
   John bought RICE
   No, he bought COFFEE
 (*d*) **restricting focus**
   John bought coffee and RICE
   No, he only bought COFFEE
 (*e*) **expanding focus**
   John bought COFFEE
   Yes, but he also bought RICE
 (*f*) **selecting focus**
   Would you like coffee or tea?
   COFFEE, please

---

[8] One further point, made by Chafe (1976), is that contrast is not necessarily explicit, as in Dik's examples in (3). The speaker or writer of a text that begins *It was in 1966 that I first went to Moscow* makes *1966* salient and implicitly contrasts it with all the other years that the audience might have in mind.

From Figure 5.1, it is clear that Dik takes Halliday's distinction between cumulative and contrastive focus, draws out the various reasons why a speaker might wish to highlight a constituent and extends the range of devices to be recognized as highlighting.

5.4.5. *Vallduví*

The concept of focus as new has been incorporated into an explicit information-handling model by Vallduví (1993, 1994). Consider (4).

(4) (*a*) What did Sally give Andrew for his birthday?
    (*b*) She gave him a CD of Jean-Michel Jarre

Sentences encode a logico-semantic proposition and an information-packaging instruction. The proposition in (4) is GIVE (SALLY, SOMETHING, ANDREW). The information-packaging instruction indicates what part of a given sentence carries information and where and how that information fits in the hearer's information store. (Strictly speaking, it indicates where and how the speaker thinks the information fits in.) In (4*b*) the sequence *She gave him* is taken to be the ground, which is what is already established in the speaker's information model. 'Being established' is to be understood in terms of a file card having been opened for the relevant entities. *A CD of Jean-Michel Jarre* is the focus; this is information to be fed into the hearer's information model, either by adding information to, or changing information on, a file card—here the card for the entity given to Andrew. In the appropriate circumstances the hearer may have to open a new file card.

Tail elements are ground elements that are not links. The ground consists of a link element and a tail element. The link points to a specific file card in the hearer's knowledge store—in (4*b*) *she* and *him* point to the cards for Sally and Andrew. Link elements are typically pronominal and, in speech, carry low pitch and amplitude. In spoken English the answer to (4*a*) would typically be *a CD of Jean-Michel Jarre*, with a zero link element.

As will be shown in § 5.6, spoken and written language have different devices for indicating what is new, and different devices for signalling new entities as opposed to new propositions, and they both have ways of defocusing or backgrounding entities that are given. The concepts of ground and tail will be important for the discussion of defocusing in Catalan.

5.4.6. *Grosz and Sidner: focus spaces and transition*

Grosz and Sidner (1986) appeal not just to linguistic structure, which pertains to the analysis and representation of utterances, but also to the notions of intentional and attentional structure. The former has to do with the intentions of the speaker in producing a particular discourse or discourse segment and the latter with the salience of entities, properties, relations, discourse purposes, and intentions. We are concerned here with attentional structure, since it, like focus, has to do with salience.

The important concepts are focus space and transition rule. The notion of focus space relates to knowledge bases. Working within an AI framework, Grosz thought of speakers as bringing to every linguistic interaction a collection of facts, a knowledge base, to which facts are added during any interaction. Adult speakers have large knowledge bases, but they do not have all the information at the forefront of their minds all the time. Rather, they have one or two items of information at their centre of attention and these items change as an interaction proceeds. Grosz describes the items at the centre of attention as being 'in focus', and the subset of the knowledge base containing those items is termed a focus space. (Cf. McKeown 1985: 56–81.)

A given focus space is associated with a particular discourse segment and contains representations of entities salient in that discourse segment—i.e., entities that are mentioned explicitly or become salient as speaker and hearer work to produce and interpret utterances.[9] Within focus spaces all the different types of focus described by Dik are relevant, and also the devices mentioned above for introducing new entities and new propositions into focus spaces. Of course, speakers can choose one of these devices or simply use a neutral syntactic construction, as in much of the dialogue analysed by Grosz and Sidner.

As a discourse is built up, speakers pass from one focus space to another and it is here that the concept of transition rule becomes relevant. For present purposes it is not necessary to investigate this concept, but it is important that speakers and writers may choose to make a given transition salient and §5.5 on macro- and micro-focus examines how they do this. It is because the need for saliency or highlighting is shared by all the concepts of focus examined above that the approach here is data-driven and not confined to any one notion of focus.

5.5. Macro- and Micro-Focus

5.5.1. *A text schema*

Levy (1985) extends Grosz and Sidner's work by demonstrating that a given text may contain larger and smaller focus spaces; that is, it may have a

---

[9] For Grosz and Sidner focus spaces include representations of the discourse segment purpose, since they consider conversational participants to be focused not only on what they are talking about but also on why they are talking about it.

general goal containing a number of smaller goals. Salience and transition are relevant both to general goals and to smaller goals. Consider the text schema in (5).

(5) A text schema
    (*a*) I had a lousy day at work

      (*b*) (*i*) Monday is a horrid day anyway.
            (*ii*) When I arrived . . .
            (*iii*) At the second year lecture . . .
            (*iv*) Right in the middle of my afternoon nap . . .
            (*v*) Just as I was leaving . . .
      (*c*) (*i*) At the second year lecture
            (*ii*) the first thing was that the overhead projector was playing up
            (*iii*) then the students hadn't done any reading
            (*iv*) but what bugged me most was . . .

If written, the text schema could be given a title such as *My day*, which would signal a macro-transition from the previous topic, possibly null. Participants in conversation do not use titles, but the opening statement *I had a lousy day at work* signals the new topic and a new focus space just as effectively. Assuming that we have a complete text to work on, it might contain utterances like those in (5*b*), which signal major transitions, albeit inside the text. That is, (5*a*) leads into a major focus space, (5*bi–iii*) signal transitions into less major focus spaces, and within the focus space introduced by (5*biii*), (5*ci–iv*) signal transitions into relatively minor focus spaces. Within each of the latter further transitions are possible into smaller focus spaces if the speaker wants to make salient specific entities or actions.[10]

Of course, what is given above is an ideal text, but speakers (and indeed writers, in spite of their planning time) do not necessarily produce ideal texts and hearers may be left to work out for themselves where a (relatively) major change of topic takes place. Chafe and Danielewicz (1987) maintain that speakers exhibit drops in pitch and pausing at (relatively) major transitions in spoken texts and argue that what is achieved in writing by paragraph layout and punctuation is signalled to some extent at least in speech. G. Brown and Yule (1983: 100–6) also argue that pitch and pausing demarcate units of spoken language corresponding roughly to paragraphs in written language. Chafe and Danielewicz (1987) further suggest that a spoken unit corresponding to the sentence can also be recognized from pitch and pausing, but their view is far from self-evident on the basis of free conversation. Reading written text aloud is a different matter.

---

[10] The expressions marking the transitions are frequently thematic, in Halliday's sense of the term. That is, they occupy first position in the first sentence of the new focus space. Such phenomena are part of the reason why Halliday and others regard sentence- and clause-initial position as important.

5.5.2. Transition and contrasts

The notion of macro-focus relates to transitions to major focus spaces, the sort that in written language entail new paragraphs, sections, or chapters. Micro-focus has to do with relatively low-level transitions, such as are typically signalled by new clauses or sentences in written language. All Dik's examples of focus given in (3) are instances of micro-focus, even replacive and expanding focus that introduce new entities, but words and phrases such as *although, in spite of that, however, in contrast,* and *but,* functioning as conjunctions, are also micro-focusers.

Macro-focus may involve a change of discourse-topic, such as switching from holidays in France to the privatization of water in England and Wales. Of course, there may be some connection between the topics, say the flood of water rushing off the Pyrenees compared with dry river beds in southeast England, but such a switch none the less constitutes a major change of topic which can be signalled by the speaker. As usual, however, speakers have a choice and a major change of topic need not be signalled, except by changes in the entities, places and times under discussion. A major change of topic may be signalled by the introduction of a new entity, and it is typically in such a context that special presentative focusing devices are used.

In the text schema in (5) the text fragments are to be thought of as having occurred at major changes of topic in the putative complete text. This is not to say that all these fragments of text are focusing devices—only 5(*c*)(*ii*) and 5(*c*)(*iv*) are focusing devices—but simply that where they occur there might be focusing devices such as **The first thing was** *when I arrived I had to take a tutorial for a colleague who was ill.* Inside the putative chunk of text introduced by *At the second year lecture* the fragment *it wasn't so much the fact that the students hadn't done any reading that bothered me as their general attitude*, while conveying an overt contrast and indeed containing an IT cleft, would be an instance of micro-focus because there is no general change of topic.

The distinction between macro- and micro-focus is not always easy to draw. Consider what Quirk and Greenbaum (1985: 634–47) call contrastive and discoursal conjuncts, as exemplified in (6)—our examples.

(6) (*a*) The Government might impose a salary cut—**on the other hand** it might close a university

    (*b*) I forgot to write to them—**however**, they were away on holiday and didn't realise that I had forgotten

    (*c*) I've decided to stay at home this year—**incidentally**, did you see that news item about Russian aircraft-controllers being attacked by crowds of angry passengers?

We might decide that the conjuncts in bold in (6*a,b*) are instances of micro-focus, because they continue the topic of conversation—actions the government might take against universities in (6*a*) and not writing to certain people in (6*b*). (6*c*) is trickier. *Incidentally* is often used to signal a digression from the current topic and the digression may be minor or major. In (6*c*) we might decide that it has a major focus function. The first topic—the speaker not going away on holiday—does have a connection with the topic of the second clause, since aircraft controllers choose to go on strike when they can cause the maximum disruption, but the second clause moves attention away from the speaker and the speaker's reasons and plans, a significant shift which the speaker signals by using *incidentally*.

Although a portion of spontaneous spoken Russian will be discussed below by way of further illustration of macro- and micro-focus, we will not devote much discussion to the differences between spoken and written language except to say that the signalling of macro-focus and macro-transitions is generally much better organized in written texts than in spontaneous conversation. As we remarked above, this is partly because written texts are planned and edited and macro-transitions can be highlighted by words and phrases such as *Let us turn now to Y, In connection with X, we should take a brief look at Y, moreover, however, furthermore, in addition*.[11] One of the striking features of the corpus of spontaneous conversation is the absence of such words and phrases. Instead, macro-transitions are signalled by silences or by *what about X?, let's talk about X, speaking/talking of X* or by the various words and syntactic constructions that serve to introduce and highlight new entities. (See § 5.7.)

5.5.3. Macro- and micro-focus in a spoken Russian text

The distinction between macro- and micro-focus can be illustrated from the text in (7), an excerpt from a quasi-narrative transcribed and published in Kapanadze and Zemskaja (1979: 84–6). ('Quasi' because the main speaker A does not have the floor entirely to himself but responds to questions from B, the interviewer.) The contributions are labelled according to speaker and order of contribution. For example, the second contribution from A is labelled **A2**. For convenience, part of the excerpt has been omitted, hence the jump from **A2** to **A5**. For easy reference to items in the text, within each contribution the text is split into smaller chunks labelled **a**, **b**, etc.

---

[11] The latest edition of *The Economist Style Guide* comments that overuse of such expressions makes a text read like a textbook.

(7) **A1 a** No nado skazat' vam čto on ... imel gipnotičeskoe vozdejstvie na drugix//
But must tell you that he had hypnotic effect on others
  b Potomu čto vot Nikolaj Konstantnyča Dmitrieva/
Because Particle N K D
čelovek črezvyčajno zanjatogo/
person extraordinarily busy
  c i uže na poroge togda ... mm ... zvanija akademika/
and already on threshold then ... mm ... of rank of Academician
on zastavil nam čitat' kurs tureckogo jazyka//
he made to us read course of-Turkish of-language
'He (the professor) made Dmitriev give us a course on Turkish'
  d Očen' interesnyj// Iz kotorogo ja massu vynes//
Very interesting from which I mass took-out
'very interesting from which I learned a lot'
  e Pravda ja ne ovladel tureckim jazykom govorit' ne umeju/
Truth I not mastered Turkish language to-speak not know-how
'To tell the truth I didn't master Turkish, I couldn't speak it'
  f no obščee predstavlenie o sisteme jazyka/ ponimaeš'//
but general idea of system of-the-language you-understand
'but [I had] a general idea of the language system you understand'
  g A Nikolaj Konstantinyč Dmitriev on byt tože takoj strastnyj soveršenno/
But N K D he was also such enthusiast altogether
'but NKD was a complete enthusiast'
  h i vot on vse-tak zastavil/ i tam dovol'no dolgo/
and Particle he anyhow made (us) and there quite long/
eto prodolžalos' goda poltora/
that lasted year one-and-a-half
B1 nu da//
yes
A2 a to est' sezona poltora/ zimnix//
that is seasons one-and-a-half winter
Očen' interesnyj kurs lekcij/ vot iz ...
very interesting course of lectures Particle from
  b edinstvennoe/ čto možno bylo postavit' v uprek/
the -one-thing that possible was to put as reproach
eto čto on takoj tureckij starover/ Nikolaj Konstantinyč
it (be) that he such Turkish Old Believer NK
  c On nas zastavil izučat' arabskij nepremenno šrift-to//
He us made to study (the) Arabic absolutely script-that
A5 No on byl takoj/ znaete//
But he was such you-know
B5 A krome togo on ved' indologom byl//
And besides that he you-know Indologist was

The first step in the analysis is to determine the goals and subgoals of the portions of text. A's overall goal is to talk about the referent of *on* in (A1a), one of A's professors when he was a student. This professor has previously been introduced and discussed, and the initial *no* (but) in (A1a) signals a transition from the preceding text. The sub-goal is to talk about this professor's almost hypnotic power over other people, including junior but none the less distinguished colleagues. The sub-sub-goal is introduced by *potomu čto* in (A1b), which can be taken as signalling that A is about to give a reason for making the statement in (A1a). This sub-sub-goal runs from (A1a) to (A5), the latter line being a lexically vague summarizer—'that's the way he was'. This whole chunk exemplifies the professor's hypnotic power. (The referent of *on* in (A5) is again the professor, not the professor's junior colleague who is the object of discussion from (A1b) to (A2c). The sub-sub-goal and the reason are made prominent by the focuser *vot*, which can have either a macro- or a micro-focusing function.

(A1b)–(A1c) introduce this instance of the professor's power. (A1d)–(A1e) constitute an aside about the Turkish course, the fact that A learned a lot from it although not mastering the language to the extent of being able to speak it. (A1f)–(A2c) meet a second sub-sub-goal, to describe Dmitriev's enthusiasm for Turkish and his insistence on teaching the subject as rigorously as he thought necessary.

A at the beginning of (A1g) signals the transition from A's account of his knowledge of Turkish to Dmitriev's qualities. *A* signals a contrast, namely between the great but uncommitted interest of A in Turkish and Dmitriev's commitment to the language and culture. As Wade (1992: 490) puts it, *a* links ideas which contrast without conflicting. *Vot* in (A1h) functions as a micro-focuser, although it signals a small transition from praise of Dmitriev to what becomes a criticism of his insistence on using the Arabic script. The *vot* in (A2a) looks very like a micro-focuser too, but nothing more can be said, as A, realizing that he is digressing and repeating himself, returns to the criticism.

The return is marked by a long pause and a break in syntax from *iz* (from) to *edinstvennoe, čto . . .* The latter begins the process of making the criticism prominent, which is reinforced by the NP–Clause structure: the NP *edinstvennoe čto možno bylo postavit' v uprek* has no predicate phrase combining with it. Instead it is followed by a complete clause with a copula structure. The deictic *eto* recapitulates the NP and combines with another clause—*čto on takoj tureckij starover*. (A2c) explains what is meant by *starover*. There are two micro-focusers, namely *nepremenno* and *-to*. These function to give great prominence to *arabskij šrift*. Neither of these items can function as a macro-focuser.

Both *vot* and *to* are deictics. *Vot* is used in utterances such as *vot idet avtobus* (particle–goes–bus, i.e. 'here comes the bus') or *vot tvoja kniga* (particle–your–book, i.e. 'there's your book'). It is typically accompanied by pointing. *-to* is the deictic *to* as in *to pero* (that pen), pointing to a pen that is relatively remote from both speaker and hearer. At least, that usage is taken here as basic; there are other usages that require more subtle treatments of remoteness. (See the further examples in § 5.7.8.2.2.)

Comment is needed on two points in the last two lines of text. The first concerns *no* in (A5) and *a* in (B5). *No* links a transition between two ideas which are not just in contrast but incompatible and it can function as a macro-focuser, linking say two clauses on either side of a discourse boundary, or as a micro-focuser, simply linking two adjectives. The omission of the relevant text precludes further discussion. As before, *a* in (B5) marks a transition from one topic to another; there is a contrast but the two chunks of discourse are compatible in content. Here the content is that in addition to being a Turkish specialist, Dmitriev was also an Indologist, an unusual combination. (B5) opens up a new sub-goal with the conjunction *krome togo* (beside that).

5.6. Given

Given information is information which the speaker/writer treats as recoverable by the listener/reader. Since given information is recoverable and contrasts with information that is new and not recoverable (cf. the résumé of Vallduví's framework in § 5.4.5), the constituents conveying it are not highlighted and in fact are regularly reduced. In both spoken and written language major phrasal categories are reduced to pro-elements or zero, as exemplified in (8).

(8) (*a*) The players came on to the pitch. They acknowledged the cheers and gathered in the centre circle
    (*b*) Susan passed the exam. Brian didn't.
    (*c*) I was ill yesterday. So was my wife.

In (8*a*) the NP *the players* is reduced to *they* in the second sentence and to zero in the second clause of that sentence, [ ]*gathered in the centre circle*. In (8*b*) *passed the exam* is replaced by *did*—the negative *n't* adds new information—and in (8*c*) *ill* is replaced by *so*. (8*a–c*) are presented as written language and organized into sentences but in structure and vocabulary they are appropriate examples of spontaneous spoken English. This is an important comment, because we will be arguing that ellipsis is far more frequent in spoken language than in written language.

5.6.1. *Ellipsis*

But what is ellipsis? We follow here the account of ellipsis in Quirk *et al.* (1985: 883–913) and the account in Matthews (1981: 38–49). Quirk *et al.* (1985: 884–8) present the following criteria for ellipsis.

(9) Criteria for ellipsis
  (i) The ellipted words are precisely recoverable, as in *she can't sing tonight so she won't [sing tonight]*.
  (ii) The elliptical construction is grammatically 'defective', by which Quirk *et al.* mean that some normally obligatory element of a grammatical sentence is lacking. For instance, *won't* typically has a complement in the shape of a verb stem possibly accompanied by its own complements, but the complement of *won't* can be omitted in coordinate constructions and, importantly, there are specific constraints on what can or cannot be omitted from what sort of structure.
  (iii) The insertion of the missing words results in a grammatical sentence.
  (iv) The missing words are textually recoverable.
  (v) The missing words are present in the text in exactly the same form.

Quirk *et al.* distinguish various types of ellipsis according to how many of the above criteria apply. If all five apply to a given example, such as in (9*i*), the example is said to display strict ellipsis. If all the criteria except (9*v*) apply, the example displays quasi-ellipsis. Quirk *et al.* give as an example *She sings better than I can [sing]*, where the form *sing* is not present in the text, although *sings* is. Another example that occurs regularly in spoken English is the question *Have you done your homework yet*, to which the answer is *I am [doing my homework]*, with a different auxiliary verb and a change of person both in the auxiliary and in the possessive pronoun. If criteria (9*iv*) and (9*v*) do not apply to a particular example, we have a case of situational ellipsis. Quirk *et al.*'s example is *Glad to see you*, the recoverable words being *I am*. A more complex example is *Glad to be here*, where the words to be recovered are determined by the intonation. A question intonation indicates that the missing words are *are you*, but to recover them the listener has to draw on the conventions governing conversation, which preclude speakers from addressing listeners while asking themselves questions.[12]

Quirk *et al.* provide numerous examples of situational ellipsis (ellipted items in bold italics) reproduced below in (10).

(10) (a) *[I] told you so*
   (b) *[do you] want a drink?*
   (c) *[it/the restaurant/the train] seems full*
   (d) *[there] must be somebody waiting for you*[13]

---

[12] Matthews (1981: 42–3) observes that one and the same example may be ambiguous with respect to whether the ellipted words are to be recovered from within the sentence or from outside it. Thus, *I'll fetch it if Bloggs hasn't* could be filled out to yield *I'll fetch it if Bloggs hasn't fetched it*, with the words in bold recovered from inside the sentence, but other restorations could be . . . *if Bloggs hasn't a car* or *if Bloggs hasn't the time*, in which the restored items are recovered from previous discourse, possibly uttered by another speaker.

[13] Quirk *et al.* do say (1985: 900, § 12.52) that there is no clear dividing line between

(e) *[has]* Joanna done her homework?
(f) *[Is the]* television not working?

These examples are all fine, but it is only in the final paragraph on categories of ellipsis, indeed in the section on structural ellipsis, that Quirk *et al.* state that situational ellipsis is characteristic of familiar spoken English (1985: 900). The main thrust of the statement is that structural ellipsis is characteristic of written English. For our purposes this contrast is of primary importance. Quirk *et al.* do mention (1985: 1360) that given information is regularly omitted, as in the question–answer pair *When shall we know what Mary is going to do?—Next week.* The fact that spoken language is involved is taken for granted, given the question–answer pair, but it should be pointed out that the ellipsis of constituents carrying given information can extend over various turns in a conversation. (11*a*) is an excerpt of conversation from the corpus of Scottish English conversations and (11*b*) is the same excerpt with the ellipted constituents in bold and inside square brackets. The boy mentioned in M59 is one Richard, who has been under discussion.

(11) (*a*) M59 what's he going to do, that boy anyway?
       L59 play golf
       A70 be a professional golfer
       M60 is he?
       L60 he would if he could   I think he's applied for a scholarship
       M61 in this country?
       L61 yeah
       M62 they're very few and far between, aren't they   I mean there's millions of them in America, sports scholarships
       L62 that's what he's done   at the moment he's keeping his fingers crossed that he hears about it
       M63 what about the other ones? what are they doing?

   (*b*) M59 what's he going to do, that boy, anyway?
       L59 **[that boy is going to]** play golf
       A70 **[that boy is going to]** be a professional golfer
       M60 is he **[going to be a professional golfer]**
       L60 he would **[be a professional golfer]** if he could **[be a professional golfer]**   I think he's applied for a scholarship
       M61 **[has he applied for a scholarship]** in this country?
       L61 yeah
       M62 they're very few and far between, aren't they   I mean there's millions of them in America, sports scholarships
       L62 that's what he's done at the moment he's keeping his fingers crossed that he hears about it
       M63 what about the other ones? what are they doing?

situational ellipsis and structural ellipsis. *Must be somebody waiting for you* is one example that looks more like an instance of structural ellipsis: given that this is an example of the existential construction, the missing item can only be *there*.

Categorizing the above ellipses is not straightforward. L59 and A70 certainly contain words that occur in the text, but the words are in a different order and in different constructions. M59 contains a WH interrogative structure *what's he going to do* with *is* and *going* separated by the subject NP, and the NP *that boy* is outside that clause. In L59 *that boy* and *is* and *going to* are gathered together in that order inside one clause. This is either a peripheral case of standard ellipsis or a case of quasi-ellipsis. Finding a solution to the problem is not a priority for present purposes, the main point being that situational ellipsis and large-scale elision by means of standard or quasi-ellipsis are typical of spoken English, whereas elision in written English (and also in spoken English) is typical of coordinate structures, non-finite and verbless clauses, and comparative clauses[14] (cf. Quirk *et al.* 1985: 910–13).

5.6.2. *Ellipsis in Russian*

5.6.2.1. *Null subject NPs*

Like spoken and written English, spoken and written Russian differ with respect to types of ellipsis. Written Russian possesses various types of structural ellipsis, including coordinate structures, non-finite clauses, and one type of comparative clause. The details of these elliptical constructions are not relevant here; instead, we will concentrate on the occurrence of null subject and object NPs. Written and spoken Russian both allow null subject NPs on a much wider scale than in English. Consider the passage of English in (12).

(12) David came out of his room and shut the door. He walked quietly down the stairs and unlocked the front door.

There are subject NPs missing before *shut the door* and *unlocked the front door* but there is nothing unusual, since these are examples of structural ellipsis. Written Russian allows zero subject NPs outside coordinate structures, as illustrated in (13).

(13) A ona molčit.
 But she is silent.
 [ ] Idet, ladoški v rukava svitera [ ] sprjatala,
 [She] walks, hands into sleeves of-sweater has-hidden
 i [ ] molčit
 and is-silent.

---

[14] There are two comparative structures in English: cf. *She's taller than me* and *She's taller than I*. The latter has to be treated as ellipsis—*She's taller than I [am]*—otherwise the subject form of the pronoun, *I*, is inexplicable. In the first example the object form *me* indicates an analysis in which *than* is a preposition and in which no ellipsis takes place. The *me* construction is typical of spoken English and the *I* construction is typical of written English. The *me* construction is also found in informal written English and is spreading.

The first sentence has a pronoun subject, *ona*. (The character has been previously introduced and named and is one of the main protagonists in this part of the story.) The second sentence has a null subject NP before *idet*. This verb form is third person singular and does not carry information about the sex of the agent referent, which has to be recovered from the previous sentence. That is, null subject NPs can reach back across sentence boundaries for their referents, but they can also reach back across boundaries between subordinate and main clauses, as shown in (14).

(14) Igral   Šatrov   ploxo . . .   no   smelo
     Played   Šatrov   badly . . .   but   boldly
     [ ]   bralsja za trudnye . . .   vešči,
     [he]   attempted difficult   things
     tak kak [ ]   igral   tol'ko   naedine
     as   [he]   played   only   (when) alone

The subordinate clause is introduced by *tak kak* and the verb *igral* has a zero subject NP. The agent referent has to be sought, not in the preceding clause, but in the initial main clause. Zero subjects can even reach back across paragraph boundaries, as in (15), which is admittedly a special type of narrative, as it is told in the first person.

(15) Lenja ščelkaet nožnicami . . . potom strekočet   mašinkoj
     Lenja clicks   (the) scissors . . . then   makes whirr the little machine
     vzbivaet   volosy   rasčeskoj
     fluffs up (my) hair with the comb
     I   nakonec, snjav s menja prostinju govorit:
     and finally, taking off me   the sheet, says
     -Možete otkryt'
     You can open (your eyes)
     [ ]   Otkryvaju glaza   i vdrug   vižu . . .   devčonku,   ulybajus' ej,
     [I]   open   (my) eyes and suddenly (I) see . . . a little girl (I) smile at her
     i   ona   mne. Ja smejus', Lenja tože.
     and she-at me. I laugh.   Lenja (laughs) too.

(Baranskaja 1989: 25)

There are various null NPs in (15) but only the relevant one is marked by square brackets. This null NP is a zero anaphor reaching back across the paragraph boundary to pick up the entity referred to by *menja* in *snjav s menja prostinju* and by *možete* in *Možete otkryt'*. Since this entity is the writer, who is always present and salient for a given text, the zero anaphor requires no special explanation.

In the above examples the null NPs refer to what Prince (1981) calls textually evoked entities. In spontaneous spoken Russian, as in spoken English, instances of null NPs, referring to situationally evoked entities (instances of situational ellipsis, in Quirk *et al.*'s terms) are frequent. An example is given in (16), which is an excerpt from the spoken texts recorded and transcribed in Kapanadze and Zemskaja (1979).

(16) A1 Včera   [ ] pošla na lekciju Sergeevoj
       Yesterday [I] went to lecture of Sergeeva
       mne   tam   stalo   ploxo
       to me there became bad (= I was taken ill)
       i   ona pobežala posredi   lekcii   v kakoj-to medpunkt
       and she   ran   in middle of lecture to some first-aid point
       I   glavnoe   domoj ne [ ] mogu-u
       And main thing   home not [I] am able
   B1 Oj!
   A2 [ ]   poexala domoj/prjamo [ ] svalilas'/
       [I]   Went   home just   [I] collapsed
       i xorošo [ ] doexala
       and good (that) [I] reached
   B2 Alka/ [ ] s uma   [ ]   sošla/
       Alka   from mind [you] have-gone
       i začem ty   segodnja-to prišla na rabotu?
       and why   you   today have-come to work
   A3 A   ničego   segodnja vot// [ ] prošlo-o
       But nothing today   see [it] has-passed

(Kapanadze and Zemskaja 1979: 154)

In (16) note in A1 the initial null NP reference to the speaker, who along with the listener is situationally salient. The next reference to the speaker is by means of the dative pronoun *mne*; one constraint on the occurrence of null NPs in Russian (and in Polish—cf. the discussion of Flashner (1987) in §5.6.2.5) is that the referential chain is broken by a change of grammatical function and a change of role. The nominative pronoun *ona* in line 3 of A1 refers to a third participant, the person whose lecture the speaker was attending. In the fourth line of A1 the reference returns to the speaker and in spite of the break in the referential chain the speaker refers to herself by means of a null NP: *domoj ne [ ] mogu*. When participant B takes a proper turn in B2, she addresses A by name—*Alka*. The following clause has a null subject—*[S] s uma sošla*, but the next clause contains the pronoun *ty*, although the chain of reference to A is not broken. The reason for the pronoun is not clear; we can only surmise that B wishes to emphasize A's existence as a rational being independently of the action, since B is giving A a row for coming to work that day.

    The verb forms ending in *-la* are past tense, feminine, and singular, but since both participants are women, this information does not help to pick out the referent. In A3 the verb form *prošlo* is neuter singular. The referent is situationally salient and inanimate—whatever illness it was that struck down A at the lecture.

5.6.2.2. *Null object NPs*

Russian differs from English in the frequency of null direct object NPs. In fact, although zero direct object NPs do occur in English they are limited to two constructions. The first is associated with sentences describing habitual actions, and especially actions that in a given culture are institutionalized. Cf. (17).

(17) Kate buys for Marks and Spencer

BUY is listed in dictionaries of English as a transitive verb; (17) is highly marked and only possible in sentences describing someone's occupation. It is not possible to have a zero direct object even in coordinate structures: **Mary didn't want to pay so much for the painting so Kate bought*.

The second construction is associated with sentences describing actions that, within a given culture, apply to one particular class of entities. Cf. (18)

(18) (*a*) I'm reading, and I don't want to be disturbed
    (*b*) They hunt in the autumn

Other verbs that are like HUNT and READ in the above respect are EAT, DRINK, COOK. The difference between this set of verbs and the verb in (17) is that the latter typically has a direct object, whereas HUNT, etc. regularly occur without a direct object. Furthermore, HUNT, etc., can occur without a direct object even in sentences describing a single event. Russian allows zero direct objects both in the above contexts and in others. We begin with examples in which zero direct objects are recoverable in the text, though these are cases of quasi-ellipsis for the good reason that the antecedent may be a subject or oblique object and therefore in a different case from the missing direct object pronoun, which would be in the accusative case. As with zero subjects, the link from elliptted NP to antecedent can cross various syntactic boundaries.[15]

Boundary between coordinate clauses

(19) A   on tol'ko smotrel na nee, no   tancevat' [ ] ne zval [ ]
      But he only   looked at her, but to dance not   [he] invited [her]

(Baranskaja 1989: 27)

[15] The implications for an explicit analysis are that some occurrences of null NPs can be handled by ellipsis within single sentences but that many occurrences cannot be handled by ellipsis, or at least, not by standard treatments, since many null NPs either reach back across sentence boundaries to their antecedents or have no textual antecedents but only extra-linguistic referents.

(20) Nakonec my končaem, šef   blagodarit [ ]
     At last we finish   (the) boss thanks   [me]
     dopolzaem do konca otryvki . . .
     (we) crawl to the end of the excerpt
     no šef   prosit [ ] povtorit' vse . . .
     but (the) boss asks   [me] to repeat everything

(Baranskaja 1989: 25)

Boundary between a main clause and a gerund phrase

(21) Samoograničenie . . . kak by   zapiralo   ego nagluxo
     (the) self-limitation . . . as though was-shutting him up
     v   temuju komnatu
     into   (a) dark room
     otdeljaja   [ ]   ot   mnogoobraznogo i   širokogo mira
     cutting-off [him] from (the) varied   and broad world

(Efremov 1987: 457)

Across sentence boundaries

(22) Krošku   privez?
     Stone chips you-did-bring?
     -Poltora meška, krasivaja,   melkaja
     1½   sacks nice-stuff   small-stuff
     -Me -e-elkaja- peredraznil Vorobej-
     Small-stuff   mimicked   Sparrow
     Tolku-to,   melkaja: promyvat' [ ]   trudnee
     Good sense small-stuff: to wash [it] (is) more difficult

(Kaledin 1989: 219)

(23) Major   prinjalsja osmatrivat' vse karmany,
     (The) major began   examining   all (the) pockets,
     gnezda i   zakoulki
     housings and crannies
     [2 clauses, then complete paragraph]
     -[ ] Našel   [ ]!-
     [I] Have-found [it]
     I   major podal v   ljuk   planšetku
     and (the) major put through (the) hatch (a) map-case

(Efremov 1987: 459)

(24) Vorobej vošel   bez   stuka
     Sparrow went-in without (a) knock,
     emu   možno i   bez   stuka
     to-him possible particle without (a) knock.
     -Vskopal [ ] ja . . .
     Have-dug [it] I

(Kaledin 1989: 218)

In a recent translation of Kaledin's short stories, the translator translates (22) as '... twice the trouble getting it clean'—putting in a direct object pronoun *it*. In translating (24) she deals with the problem of the direct object zero anaphora by not giving a literal translation ('I've dug it') but by using an idiomatic translation instead—'Finished the job!'

(22) and (23) are complex examples in that the ellipsis can be seen as standard/quasi-ellipsis, that is—textual, or as situational. For the reader of the stories the ellipsis is textual in that the entities referred to by the zero direct object NPs have been mentioned in the text. For the participants in the narrated events the ellipsis is situational. The excerpt in (23) follows a passage describing how the major and the writer are looking for a certain document. The major had a hunch that the author of the document had hidden it in the tank he commanded during the war. The mapcase has not been mentioned before; the missing document has, but so far back in the text that the rules of coherent and cohesive written text would require a full NP, not a zero NP.[16]

Similarly, Vorobej in (24) is a grave-digger who has been given the task of digging a particularly awkward grave. The grave has been mentioned in the text and the ellipsis is therefore textual for the reader,[17] but for the

---

[16] Another interesting example is given below of how in written narratives entities may be textually evoked for the reader but situationally evoked for the characters in the story-world. In (*i*) Nina Ivanova is introduced into the text by the writer, but for the character Šarok, who refers to her in thought by means of a null subject NP, she is situationally salient. The first null subject NP, in the second line, is a second mention by the writer; that is, Nina Ivanova is textually evoked. In contrast, the second null subject NP, in the last line, is 'produced' by Šarok and Nina Ivanova is situationally evoked.

(*i*) Rjadom   s   nim   na divane sidela Nina Ivanova
     at-side   with   him   on sofa   sat   Nina Ivanova
     [S] priminala   pjatkami napolovinu   snjatye   tufli.
     was-crushing   with-heels half   taken-off shoes
     ⟨⟨[S] Kupila,   by   dura,   nomerom   pobol'še⟩⟩,—
     bought   should-have   idiot   size   bigger
     podumal   Šarok
     thought   Šarok

(Rybakov, *Deti Arbata*, 30)

[17] The null direct object NP is striking because it refers back over several pages—the grave is very salient not just for the character but for the reader. A similarly striking example from an English novel of a pronoun referring to a situationally salient entity last mentioned several pages previously is to be found in Charles Dickens's *Great Expectations*. Ch. 56 begins: *He lay in prison very ill, during the whole interval between his committal for trial, and the coming round of the Sessions. He* refers to Abel Magwitch, who has not been mentioned since the beginning of ch. 55. The first page of ch. 55 deals with Magwitch, his appearance in the Police Court and his being taken to prison to await trial. There follow $1\frac{3}{4}$ pages on Herbert Pocket and his impending departure for a merchant house in Cairo, $\frac{1}{2}$ a page on Wemmick's news about Compeyson (an old associate of Magwitch), and $2\frac{1}{2}$ pages on Wemmick's wedding (involving Pip, W's aged parent, W's new wife). In spite of the $4\frac{3}{4}$ page gap since the last mention of Magwitch, *he* is possible as the first word in ch. 56 because of the enormous salience of Magwitch in the last quarter of the novel.

participants the ellipsis is situational, since in the narrative they are taking part in the situation as it unfolds. The foreman of the grave-digging squad gives Vorobej his task and leaves him. Vorobej spends a couple of hours digging and then reports to the foreman as narrated above. Neither explicitly mentions the grave but in the narrated situation the grave is salient: there has been a discussion between Vorobej and the foreman, since the grave is not only in an awkward corner of the graveyard but already contains a coffin. A paragraph is devoted to the digging of the grave, which has required all Vorobej's skills. The grave is therefore central to the thoughts and attention of both Vorobej and the foreman, and is similarly central for the reader. Given the limited range of possible referents for the Patient NP of the verb *vskopal* ('dug/have dug'), the probability of the foreman (and the reader) mistaking the referent is negligible. This example is particularly striking, as *vskopal* is perfective and in written Russian perfective transitive verbs generally require an overt direct object.

Zero oblique objects occur in Russian too. By 'oblique object' we mean a noun in a case other than nominative or accusative (i.e. in the genitive, dative, or instrumental case) or a noun governed by a preposition. In (25) the missing oblique object of *Nadoeli* would be the dative pronoun *emu* ('to him').

(25) A   na eto raz ona izmučila ego svoim   molčaniem. . . .
     But on this time she tormented him (with) her silence
     [end of paragraph]
     [ ]   Nadoeli   eti   Jurkiny fokusy.
     [him] Have made fed up these Jura's   tricks—
     'He was fed up with Jura's tricks'

(Ivanov and Karelov 1986: 10)

5.6.2.3. Overview and null NPs

The preceding examples of zero objects are from written narratives, some from the narrative part of the text and some from dialogue. The examples of null subjects were from narrative and spontaneous speech. At this point in the exposition, it will be useful to provide an overview of the occurrence of zero NPs in different grammatical functions—subject, direct object, and oblique object—and in different types of text. Consider Table 5.1.

The central points in Table 5.1 are these.

a The figures relate to equivalent amounts of text from each source: 8 pages from *Deti Arbata*, 4 pages of spoken narrative from Kapanadze and Zemskaja, and 10 pages of dialogue from *Tri devuški v golubom*.

b The incidence of zero NPs is higher in spoken language than in written language.

TABLE 5.1. *Zero subject and objects in different Russian text-types*

Spoken narrative	
zero subject	17[a]
pronominal or full NP subject	57
zero direct object	3
Deti Arbata (novel)	
zero subject	
textual	6
situational	1
zero direct object	
textual	3
situational	1
'Tri devuški v golubom' (Play)	
zero subject	
textual	5
situational	6
zero direct object	
textual	13
situational	2

[a] 2 in coordinate clauses.

c Null subject NPs are far more frequent in spoken narrative than written narrative—17 as compared with 7 in written narrative and 11 in dialogue from a play. Part of the dialogue is narrative but part is conversational exchange.

d Null direct object NPs are equally frequent in spoken and written narrative but the frequency increases significantly (by a factor of 3) in dialogue from a play. Table 5.1 shows 15 null direct object NPs in the extract from the play but only 4 and 3 from the narratives.

e Transcripts of real-life dialogues (what Kapanadze and Zemskaja (1979) call 'micro-dialogues') present the greatest number of null subject and null direct object NPs—cf. (39). Moreover, whereas in spoken and written narrative and in dialogue from plays the null direct object NPs mainly refer to textually evoked entities, in the real-life dialogues they refer to situationally evoked entities. Further examples of zero direct objects will be given in (39), which contains two examples of micro-dialogue.

f In narratives zero subjects occur in episodes involving one and the same principal (topical) participant, who can be the speaker or a third person. Where there is a change of principal participant, or action, or possible confusion of participants, pronouns occur. Zero direct objects typically occur where two or more consecutive main clauses describe events involving the same entity as Patient. The clauses may be placed in the same sentence or in different sentences (in written Russian). The direct object (denoting the Patient) is typically omitted from the second and subsequent clauses—cf. (34)–(36).

5.6.2.4. Further examples of spoken Russian

Let us now consider a further example of spontaneous speech. (26) is a spontaneous monologue interrupted by short questions and comments from the interviewer. A relates how, on his way by train to collect his family from their country cottage, the train failed to stop at his station, although the chief guard had assured him that it would stop. The null-subject verbs come in two sequences describing actions which involve the speaker as Agent. The first sequence, . . . *sxvatil* . . . *dernul*,[18] describes one action followed instantly by another, and the sequence is then linked to a third action (thinking can be an action or a state) involving the speaker as Agent, namely *dumaju*. The second sequence, *sižu* . . . *dumaju*, describes two actions (granted that sitting and thinking can be called actions for present purposes) that take place simultaneously with the same Agent. They are preceded by *šel*, which describes an action occurring just before the sitting and thinking. That is, the null-subject verbs appear to be favoured by a series of actions involving the same Agent, where there is a high degree of action continuity, to use Flashner's term (Flashner 1987: 143).

```
(26) A1   Ja/    tak skazat' ešče . . . možno    skazat' . . . stojal         uže
          I      so  to say  still       possible to say       was standing already
          na     podnožke čtoby  vyxodit'/
          on     step     to     already
          [S]    sxvatil   etot tormoz/ [S] dernul [DO]/i [S] dumaju
          [I]    grabbed   that brake   [I] tugged and    [I] think
          čto    naverno  on ne  zatormozit [DO]
          that   probably he not will brake [it]
          Nado       vse-taki
          Necessary - anyhow
     B1   Nu da     // On  zatormozil [DO]
          Of course He    braked
     A2   On     tak zatormozil [DO]
          He     so  braked     [it]
          čto    vse       poleteli   s       polok . . .
          that   everyone  was thrown from    their seats
          a      ja  sxvatil  svoi  veščicy /
          and    I   seized   my    things
          [S] vižu   kusty   rjadom/ skorej v      kusty
          [I] see    bushes  besides quickly into  bushes
```

---

[18] Many of the examples that follow have both null subject and null direct object NPs. To make clear which is which, the square brackets enclose an **S** or **DO** as appropriate.

B2 V   Smerdi skorej/   da?
    To Smerdi as fast as you could yes?
A3 Tam   [S] sel
    There   [I] sat-down
    i   [.S] sižu   [S] dumaju   čto   budet//
    and   [I]   am-sitting [I] am-thinking what will be

(Kapanadze and Zemskaja 1979: 83)

(27) and (28) illustrate a frequent structure in coordinate clauses describing actions affecting the same Patient. The Patient is referred to by a full direct object NP in the first clause but by a null NP in the second clause. Thus, *snesli* in (27) has a null direct object NP and so has *sxoronila* in (28)—*sxoronila* also has a null subject NP. (29) shows that null direct object NPs, like null subject NPs, can reach back across sentence boundaries to textually evoked entities. (Although the text represents dialogue, it is organized into sentences with capital letters and full stops.) (30)–(32) show a null direct object reaching back across a turn boundary in a conversation.

(27) i   byla ona ... čem-to   primečatel'no,
      and was it [church] with-something remarkable
      esli [S] ostavili ee tut   stojat'
      if   had-left   it there to stand
      ne   snesli   [DO] s lica zemli
      not had-swept   from   face of-earth

(Rybakov 1988: 22)

(28) Fedorovna Ja ničego   ne   skazala,
                I nothing   not   said
                Juzika podobrala,   [DO] [DO] sxoronila
                Juzik   I-picked-up [I] [him] buried

(Petruševskaja 1988: 10)

(29) Fedorovna Kotenok propal.   Ne vy [DO] prikormili?
                Kitten has-vanished Not you [him] has-enticed?

(Petruševskaja 1988: 9)

(30) Svetlana Tat'jan!   My   zabyli.   U nas est' syr ...
               Tat'jana! We   have-forgotten At us is   cheese
               Tat'jana Nesi [DO]!
               Bring [it]!

(Petruševskaja 1988: 15)

(31) A ex/ [S]   ručku   isportili
        Tsk [they]   biro   have-ruined
     B Da net /[S] [DO] ne   isportili //
        No   they it   not have-ruined
        Vy   sxodite gde   u nas ručki činjat
        You   go   where at at us   biros they-mend

(Conversational examples from Zemskaja 1973: 231)

(32) L Tak čto ty Petju-to uvidiš'
 So what you Petja-deictic you-will-see
 M. [S] [DO] Uvižu dumaeš'/ da?
 (I) (him) I-will-see do-you-think-so yes?

(Kapanadze and Zemskaja 1979: 152)

The above data indicate that Nichols's (1985) claim that zero-subject verbs are rare in Russian, at least in narrative, has to be refined. It is true that a third person verb in the first sentence of a narrative will typically have a pronoun subject, but in the following clauses and sentences zero subjects are the rule rather than the exception. A different picture obtains for first and second person verb forms. The narrative in *Nedelja kak Nedelja* is told in the first person, and there are quite large stretches of text with zero subjects/anaphors. Consider the first-person pronouns and zero-subject first person verbs in (33).

(33) I vot s etimi-to sumočkami ja vdrug svoračivaju so svoego puti
 and particle with these bags I suddenly turn from my path

 [S] petljaju meždu domami
 [I] dodge between (the) blocks-of-flats

 i [S] vyxožu k stekljannomukubu parikmaxerskoj.
 and come out to (the) glass cube of the hairdresser's

 U menja ešče dvadcat' minut. [S] Ostrigus'!
 At me still 20 minutes. [I] will have my hair cut!

 Kogda-to mne eto zdorovo šlo
 At-some-time to-me that very-much went
 (I used to love that)

 Očeredi net. Pod svirepuju vorkotnju garderobščika
 Queue is-not Under ferocious grumbling of-the-attendant

 [S] ostavljaju svoi sumki vozle vešalki na polu,
 [I] leave my bags beside the-coatrack on (the) floor,

 [S] podnimajus' naverx
 [I] climb upstairs

 i srazu že [S] sažus' v kreslo
 and right away [I] sit-down in (the) chair

 k molažavoj ženščine s podbritymy brovjami
 to (a) young-looking woman with trimmed eyebrows

 —čto budem delat'?— sprašivaet ona ...
 What will-we do? asks she

 [S] Smotrju v zerkalo.
 [I] look in (the) mirror

(Baranskaja 1989: 24)

(33) demonstrates how runs of zero NPs can be interrupted if there is a change in the syntactic function of a given zero NP. Such interruptions are caused by

the genitive NP *menja* in *U menja ešče dvadcat' minut* and by the dative NP *mne* in *Kogda-to eto mne zdorovo šlo*. All the other null NPs are nominative; that is, an overt NP in the same slot would be in the nominative case. Note that where there is no change of syntactic function and case marking the run of null NPs can continue across a sentence with a different subject NP, as in the last line of (33). The preceding sentence has a null NP subject indicated by the square brackets in front of *sažus'*. The last line begins with the sentence — *čto budem delat'?—sprašivaet ona*, where the subject is *ona* and the second sentence is *[S] Smotrju v zerkalo* with a null NP subject picking up the chain of null NPs from the last but one sentence. Here too, more than one explanation is possible. Either the first (and second) person affixes are so distinctive in form and in reference that incorrect reference is most unlikely (assuming that the deixis does not shift among too many participants), or the writer is salient in the story-telling context, or both explanations apply.

5.6.2.5. *Null and non-null NPs and action continuity*

Having invoked Flashner's concept of action continuity, we should discuss it further, since it is a reminder that the occurrence of zero NPs resulting from standard/quasi-ellipsis (textual ellipsis) is not free but subject to constraints. Analysing spoken Polish narratives, Flashner (1987) describes anaphoric zero as representing what she calls 'continuing theme', which corresponds roughly to what are here called 'topical/salient entities'. (Topical entities are to be understood in Givón's sense as entities that have been at the centre of the speaker's or writer's attention over the preceding chunk of text. Topicality is measured by counting back from a given NP (null or non-null) referring to an entity X to the previous mention of X. If an entity is topical, it has typically been mentioned in the previous clause or sentence.) Non-null NPs—containing pronouns or full lexical items—signal discontinuities arising from contrasts between participants, or from changes of syntax, episode, or scene, the introduction of direct speech or what Flashner calls 'action discontinuity in core event structure' (1987: 143). ('Action discontinuity' can be thought of as a sub-episode inside an episode.)

The first sentence of (34), with two coordinate clauses, presents the typical structure with full lexical NP in the first clause and null NP in the second. Both are subject NPs. The first reference to Blima in the second sentence is by means of a direct object NP. The change of function from subject to direct object, and the change of role from Agent (in the broadest sense) to Patient, lead to the occurrence of the accusative pronoun *ja*. In the second clause of the second sentence the reference to Blima switches back to a subject NP, the role changes from Patient to Agent, and the nominative pronoun *ona* occurs. Further verbs conveying properties predicated of Blima, i.e. with *Blima* as potential grammatical subject, will have null subject NPs, and so on until Blima's role changes again.

(34) Blima była na matematyce
 B was in maths
 i [S] mieszkała w domu akademickim
 and [she] lived in hostel academic
 A pozniej ... Tatus ja spotkał w Saratowie,
 And later ... Daddy her met in Saratov
 i ona pracowała w stołowce
 and she was-working in canteen

(Flashner 1987: 138)

(35) offers two instances of overt contrast between the participants. *ja . . . a one* (I . . . but they) and *one . . . a ja* (they . . . and I)

(35) i tyłko trojka dziewczat idzie,
 and only trio of-girls are-walking
 ja miałam tyłko teczuszke
 I had only small-bag
 a one miały z sobą troche rzeczy
 but they had with them some things
 bo one wyszły ze Lwowa a ja wyszłam z domu
 for they had-come from Lwow but I had-come from home

(Flashner 1987: 147)

5.6.2.6. *Russian examples relating to Flashner*

(36) exemplifies the breaking of a referential chain by a change in grammatical function. The chain begins with the first word *my* and continues to the end of the second sentence via a series of null subject NPs. The chain is broken in the third section by the pronoun *on* as subject referring to the bus, but in any case the next first person plural reference is by means of the dative pronoun *nam* and the possibility of a null NP is cancelled by the change of grammatical function and participant role.

(36) my žili v Nikitskom Sadu//
 we were-living in N S
 i ot Nikitskogo/ [S] doexali do Yalty na avtobuse
 and from N [we] went as-far-as Yalta by bus
 Nu tam [S] pozavtrakali
 Well there [we] breakfasted
 i [S] seli na avtobus baxčisarajskij//
 and [we] got on bus for-Baxčisaraj
 On idet do Baxčisaraja/
 It goes as far as B.
 no nam nado bylo proexat' dve treti puti
 but to-us necessary was to-travel two thirds of way

(Kapanadze and Zemskaja 1979: 89)

Note also in (16) the initial null subject NP referring to the speaker *[S] pošla*... and the subsequent reference to the speaker by means of the dative NP *mne* in *mne stalo ploxo* (to me–became–bad). The concomitant change of role is from Agent to Experiencer.

Changes of syntactic function/role do not necessarily trigger the appearance of pronouns in conversation. In (40) the line *I [GEN] ne bylo* contains a null genitive NP—genitive case being required by the negative. The following line has *[NOM] byla*, with a null, nominative subject NP as required by *byla*. Note further that changes in syntactic function/role do not prevent the occurrence of pronouns or zero anaphors following full NPs. In (37) the first reference to the central actor is by means of his first name and patronymic *Marka Aleksandroviča*, which is a direct object NP. The next reference is by means of the subject NP *on* in the next sentence. The change of grammatical function does not affect the move along the referential chain from full NP to pronoun.

(37) Marka   Aleksandroviča   vyzvali   po   familii.
     Mark   Aleksandrovič   (they) summoned by   surname
     Čerez   komnatu, gde   rabotali   sekretari,
     Through room   where   were-working   secretaries
     on prošel v   zal   zasedanij
     he passed into hall   of meetings

(Rybakov, 1988: 23)

(38) is interesting because of the direct object of *ljubila* and the subject of *poxoronen*, a passive participle: both are null, in spite of the change in grammatical function and the change in role. The referent is Fedorovna's late husband, first mentioned just previously in the conversation.

(38) Fedorovna [S] Ne   ljubila [DO],   kak tol'ko [S] Vadima rodila,
                [I] Not loved   [him]   as-soon-as [I] Vadim   bore
     srazu   ušla   k   Mame.
     immediately went-off   to Mother
     I   gde   [S]   poxoronen,   [S] ne   znaju
     And where [he] (is)-buried [I] not know

(Petruševskaja 1988: 14)

An examination of spontaneous narratives (transcripts as published in Kapanadze and Zemskaja) indicated that the number of zero subjects was tiny compared with the number of full subjects (pronouns or lexical nouns). In contrast, the transcripts of real-life spoken dialogues yield relatively large numbers of null subject and direct object NPs. In conversations, zero subjects and direct objects occur for the same reasons as in narratives—and of course parts of conversations are narrative. More importantly, they also occur because the relevant participants are

situationally evoked. Conversations with references to entities in the immediate situation favour the occurrence of null NPs, as will be seen from some of the dialogues given below. In written conversation—e.g. dialogue in novels—zero subjects and direct objects can be explained on two levels: they are situationally evoked for the characters taking part in the dialogue, but textually evoked for the reader reading the dialogue. In the data examined for this book, most of the zero anaphors referring to situationally evoked entities are subjects.

5.6.2.7. Situational ellipsis of subjects

The null subject NP in (39) requiring comment is *[S] brenčit*. The radio is not referred to linguistically, although it is the referent of the null direct object NP in *vyključila [DO]*. Although not specified in the transcript, it is highly likely that the speakers drew attention to the radio by a hand gesture, by a nod, or by the direction of gaze. It is important to remember that in situated conversation the central linguistic verbal system is supported by various paralinguistic systems which on their own are capable of achieving successful reference, and we suggest that one or more of the paralinguistic systems permits the situational ellipsis of the subject of *brenčit* and the direct object of *vyključila*.

Note the translation of *razmundirivajus'* as 'I'm taking it off' does not indicate a zero direct object. The verb is reflexive, *-s'* being the reflexive suffix, and a gloss that conveys better the force of the Russian verb is 'I am divesting myself (of my coat)'.

(39) A Zin/ eto ja
 Zin this I (= it's me)
 B razmundirivajsja
 Take your coat off
 A **[S]** razmundirivajus'
 [I] am taking-it-off
 A Zin/ **[S]** vyključila **[DO]**/
 Zin [I] have-switched-off [it]
 ja prjam ne znaju
 I really not know
 B **[S]** Brenčit/ da?
 [it] Is-'strumming' yes?
 A Užasno// Ja tak ne mogu
 Terribly I thus not am able (= I can't stand it)

(Kapanadze and Zemskaja 1979: 154)

(40) was commented on above, in connection with the fact that the change from genitive NP to subject NP does not lead to the introduction of a pronoun.

(40) A možno?
       Possible?
       (= 'Can I come in?')
    B da//
       Yes
    A zdrastvyjte
       Good morning
    B zdrastvyjte
       Good morning
    A Neli net u vas?
       Neli not at you?
       'Isn't Neli here?'
    B Net
       No
       'she's not here'
    A I   [GEN]   ne   bylo?
       And   [her]   not was? [bylo = neuter form]
       'And she wasn't here (earlier)?'
    B [NOM] byla// No sejčas net
       [she]   was   But now   not-is [byla = feminine form]
       'She was. But she isn't here now'
    A Davno   [ ]   byla
       Long-time [she] was?
       'Was she here some time ago?'
    B Polčasa   nazad
       Half-an-hour ago
    A [ ]   isčezla
           has-disappeared
       '[she] has disappeared'

                                    (Kapanadze and Zemskaja 1979: 154)

(41) is a piece of dialogue from a play. The interesting feature is not the first null subject, *[S] byl*, which simply refers back to *muž*, but the second null subject, *[S] razošlis'*. Since the verb is plural, it refers, or the speaker is using it to refer, to herself and her husband. Both are very salient by this point in the conversation, textually, via *u tebja* (at you) and *muž* (husband), and situationally.

(41) Fedorovna slusaj, a   u tebja muž   est'?
                listen, and at you   husband is?
     Ira   Da [S]   byl, [S] razošlis'
                Yes [husband] was [we] got divorced

                                           (Petruševskaja 1988: 13)

Finally, (42) offers a different sort of situationally evoked participant. In the scenario of letters to newspapers, for each letter the initial situationally salient entity is the letter-writer. Many of the letters to the paper *Argumenty i Fakty* begin with the formula *slyšal, čto,* or *slyšala, čto* (both = 'I have heard that . . .') if the writer is female. Even a pronoun is unnecessary. Note in (42c), however, that if the writer is not referred to by means of a subject NP, a pronoun or full NP must be used, in this case *u menja*.

(42) (a) [S] slyšal, čto v Moskve . . . rabotaet produktovyj specraspredelitel'
[I] heard that in Moscow is operating foodstuffs special distributor
(= a special distributor of foodstuffs)

(b) [S] Slyšala, čto Bavarija perestala propuskat' . . . graždan
[I] heard that Bavaria has-stopped admitting citizens
iz SSSR
from (the) USSR

(c) U menja troe detej. Muž - seržant milicii -
At me three children. Husband (was) sergeant of police
[S] pogib 2 goda nazad . . .
[he] died 2 years ago
[S] Živu v užasajuščix uslovijax
[I] live in horrifying conditions
Kuda [S] tol'ko ni obraščalas'
Wherever [I] only NEG turned
'No matter where I turned . . .'

5.6.2.8. *Grammaticalization of null subject NPs*

This is an appropriate moment to recall the discussion in Chapter 3 of referring expressions lacking head nouns. Example (28a) is reproduced here as (43)—cf. Zemskaja (1973: 320).

(43) Ja včera videla ženščina nesla vot takie maki
I yesterday saw woman carried Particle such poppies

Zemskaja speaks of 'free coordination between predicative constructions', the latter being *Ja včera videla ženščina* (I yesterday saw woman) and *nesla vot takie maki* (carried Particle such poppies). The second verb, *nesla*, has a null subject—following the conventions used above, the representation could be changed to *[S] nesla vot takie maki*. The point is that whereas the instances of null subjects considered above relate to referential chains crossing clause, sentence and occasionally paragraph boundaries, the null subject in (43) is associated with a single intonation contour over the whole construction. Zemskaja talks of 'free coordination' but were it not for the fact that relative pronouns cannot be dropped, at least in standard written Russian, it would be tempting to interpret (43) as consisting of a main clause and a relative clause. That is, the null subject can be seen not just as a large-scale discourse feature signalling cohesive links over a large number of clauses (and sentences in written Russian) but also as a grammatical link between two clauses. The link is not one of full subordination nor of full coordination; the term that comes to mind is cosubordination. (Cf. Foley and Van Valin 1984: 238–63.)

Zemskaja (1973: 227) cites, among many others, (44)–(46).

(44) moloko [ ]   raznosit/ [ ]   ne   prixodila   ešče?
     milk   [she] brings   [she] not come   yet?

(45) [ ]   s   tranzistorom s   Vami?
     [person] with   transistor   with you?
     (i.e. 'Is the guy/bloke/pain with the transistor with you?')

(46) [ ]   za   dvadcat' dve i   tri   paketa tvoroga
     [thing] for   twenty   two and three cartons of curds
     (i.e. 'a 22 kopeck carton of curds')

Zemskaja draws attention to the fact that each example contains a 'referential block' which lacks the relevant full NP. In (44) we might expect *ženščina, kotoraja moloko raznosit* ('woman–who–milk–delivers'), in (45) *čelovek s tranzistorom* ('person–with–transistor'), and in (46) *paket tvoroga za dvadcat' dve* ('carton–of curds–for–twenty–two'). In these examples there is a clause, in (44), and prepositional phrases, in (45) and (46), but no noun or noun phrase helping the listener to pick out the entities to which these constructions relate. The fact is that such examples are typically used to refer to entities that are salient and situationally evoked. The speakers who produced (45) and (46) might well have used nods or hand gestures to point, but even if they did not we can assume that the person listening to the transistor and the 22 kopeck cartons of curds were present and salient in their respective situations. The woman who delivers milk, referred to in (44), is not herself present but is none the less situationally salient, being a crucial participant in one part of the daily routine. In spite of the bizarre syntax—viewed from the perspective of written Russian, (44)–(46) are merely extensions of the null NP structures.

5.7. Highlighting Devices

The introductory section on focus, §5.4, mentions three types of focus: (1) the traditional concept of focus as involving contrast and extended by Dik; (2) the concept of focus as what is new, as in Vallduví's work; (3) the concept of focus as pertaining to what entity is at the centre of the speaker and listener's attention, as in the work of Grosz and Sidner. We will begin with focus 3 and focus 2.

5.7.1. *Knowledge stores and focus spaces: highlighting entities*

Halliday describes as new any information that the speaker presents as not recoverable from the situation; that is, any information which the speaker supposes that the listener will not be able to recover. Vallduví, following Heim (1982), talks in terms of the listener having a knowledge-store which has to be updated. The knowledge-store is thought of as a set of file cards each carrying the denotation of an entity. When speakers use an indefinite noun phrase they treat the relevant entity as new and the indefinite NP can be thought of as an instruction to the listener to open a new file card for a new entity.

5.7.2. *Existential and existential-possessive constructions*

While the use of definite and indefinite articles is an important part of the treatment of entities as given or new, other parts of the treatment are also worthy of attention. For instance, speakers (and writers) have at their disposal two special constructions in English, the classic existential construction, as exemplified in (47), and the possessive existential construction, as exemplified in (48). (Cf. the discussion in Quirk *et al.* (1985: ch.18) and Givón (1991: ch.17).)

(47) (*a*) There's a Phillips screwdriver in the lefthand drawer
 (*b*) There are three letters for you

(48) (*a*) Fiona has a sister in Berlin. She has invited us to spend a day or two there
 (*b*) We have an old Volvo. It keeps going but it drinks petrol

Even if the speaker/writer uses the existential construction, the distinction between the definite and indefinite article is still crucial. Compare (49*a*,*b*).

(49)   A Who can we get to look after the dogs while we're away?
 (*a*) B There's the girl two doors along. She loves dogs.
 (*b*) B There's a girl at work who's crazy about Labradors

(49*a*) introduces the girl into the conversation, but she is not treated as new. Rather, the listener is reminded of her existence. In Vallduví's terms, the listener is not instructed to create a new file card but to go to an already existing card. Of course, speaker A may have got things wrong. B can reply *Oh yes—I'd forgotten about her*, thereby indicating that he does indeed have a file card for the girl, or he can reply *What girl two doors down?*, which tells A that he has made incorrect assumptions about B's knowledge-store. Note that in informal speech the use of the demonstrative *this* is typical for the introduction of new entities: *There's this girl at work she loves Labradors*. It may be that speakers use THIS in order to bring a new entity right into the foreground; for present purposes the central fact is that THIS in the existential construction signals a new entity, whereas THE or THAT signals that the speaker is reminding the listener of a given entity.

5.7.3. *New entities in written texts*

The above remarks about the definite and indefinite articles in the existential construction apply to both spoken and written language, the THIS construction is spoken language only. It is worth pointing out that written narratives have their own conventions, including the use of definite NPs for completely new entities—the reader is expected to wait and find out, or to work out, who or what the entities are, as in this (carefully chosen) first sentence from the science fiction short story 'It's a Good Life' by Jerome Bixby (in Crispin 1960). Aunt Amy, Bill Soames, the front porch, the highbacked chair, the road, the house, and Bill Soames's bicycle are all split new entities.

(50) Aunt Amy was out on the front porch, rocking back and forth in the high-backed chair and fanning herself, when Bill Soames rode his bicycle up the road and stopped in front of the house

Another problem with written texts is that different genres have different ways of introducing new entities. Cookery books, as observed by G. Brown and Yule (1983: 174–5), set out all the new entities at the beginning of each recipe in the form of a list of ingredients, and possibly a list of required utensils. A similar technique is used in do-it-yourself manuals. For instance, the *Reader's Digest Repair Manual* (p. 161) has a general introduction to roofs in which new entities are introduced by means of plural count noun phrases or singular mass nouns, all without articles. Cf. the noun phrases in bold in (51).

(51) Sloping roofs have **wooden rafters** and **beams** which rest on 4 × 3 in (100 × 75 mm) **softwood beams** at the top of the walls. The roof covering—**tiles, slates, shingles, thatch, corrugated iron, plastic** or **asbestos**—is fixed to **wooden battens** nailed at right angles to the rafters

The reader can grasp the referents of some of these terms from the accompanying diagrams. Pages 160–2 of the manual contain an explanation of how to replace gutter boards. The explanation is preceded by a list of materials (e.g. tongued-and-grooved softwood boarding, galvanized nails) and a list of tools (e.g. cold chisel or crowbar; panel saw). These lists present the essential new entities, which can the be treated as given.

In expository prose the existential and possessive-existential constructions are available, but new entities may be introduced in ordinary declarative constructions, and not necessarily in subject position, but as direct or oblique objects. The example in (52) is from page 32 of *How Things Work* (Paladin, 1979). The noun phrases referring to new entities are in bold.

(52) A distinction is made between **synthetic petrol**, which is produced from coal and other raw materials by chemical processes, and **natural petrol**, most of which is obtained as a substance already present in petroleum (mineral oil).

In fact, expository prose has a range of fixed constructions in which new entities are introduced as direct or oblique objects: *Let us consider now another problem connected with the phoneme*; *I wish to turn to the unit of analysis known as the morpheme*; *Consider the following example*; *It is worthwhile taking a brief look at the branch of phonology called autosegmental phonology*; etc.

5.7.4. New entities in the Map Task dialogues

In spoken English, as in written English, new entities may be introduced by means of direct objects or oblique objects in declarative or imperative constructions and new entities may be introduced in different ways according to the type of text. For example, in the dialogues produced by participants in the map task, which involves one participant describing a route on a map to another participant who has a map with no route, many landmarks are introduced by means of oblique object definite noun phrases, as in (53).

(53) draw a straight line going up right? and curve round the abandoned cottage right?

This is the first mention of the abandoned cottage in the relevant dialogue. It appears that the instruction-giver operates here on the assumption that the abandoned cottage is a landmark on both maps. Note however that the instruction-giver twice says *right?*, with interrogative pitch, and thereby creates an opportunity for the instruction-follower to query the information.

Furthermore, although indefinite referring expressions are more used for first than for second mentions, first mention referring expressions are more likely to be definite. A detailed analysis of four dialogues produced the data in Table 5.2.

Why are there so many first mentions with definite noun phrases? One explanation is that each of the two participants in each Map Task game had maps with similar but not identical landmarks. The participants were told about the maps beforehand but many clearly worked on the assumption that the maps were identical until proven otherwise. That is, the instruction-giver who says *Go down two inches to the giraffes* can be understood as presenting the landmark as recoverable on the assumption that the

TABLE 5.2. *Definite and indefinite NPs and first and second mention*

	Mentions	
	First	Second
Indefinite	59	32
Definite	91	118

instruction-follower has giraffes in the same location on his/her map. In any case, face-to-face interactions carry a very small risk of serious breakdown in communication because listeners can do question statements that seem incorrect or inappropriate and ask for further information.

The classic existential and possessive-existential constructions are exemplified in (49b) and (48) above. These constructions are generally cited as typical devices for introducing new entities into dialogues but in fact the classic existential construction is in a small minority in the Map Task dialogues. Examples of the possessive existential construction are *do you have carved stones, have you got an adventure playground marked on your map, do you have the old temple, do you have Indian Country*. These examples demonstrate three different referential attitudes among the participants. Some participants did not use articles but treated the labels on the maps as proper names—thus *do you have Indian Country?* On certain occasions the remaining participants treated the landmarks as given, hence *do you have the old temple*, or as new, hence *have you got an adventure playground marked on your map*. Where participants used plural nouns with no articles it is impossible to decide whether they are using the label or an indefinite noun phrase, as in *do you have carved stones? do you have baboons, have you got pelicans, don't have springboks*. Where participants use a singular count noun with no article, it is clear that they are using the labels as proper names, as in *have you got level crossing, do you have anything underneath pine grove*. In these constructions the vast majority of the expressions referring to landmarks are indefinite.

5.7.5. SEE and KNOW

The above special presentational constructions are used when the participants in a given dialogue have been reminded, by disagreements as to what landmarks are visible and where, that the maps are not identical. The more cautious participants use the presentational constructions to establish what landmarks are available before formulating instructions about drawing the relevant stage of the route. Two other constructions for presenting or representing landmarks do not occur in written English unless the written text is imitating spoken English. SEE occurs in a number of syntactic structures in the Glasgow Map Task and the Map Task dialogues: *do you see X, can you see X, you'll see X, you see X, see X*. The latter construction might look on paper as though it is an imperative, especially as it occurs most frequently without the subject noun phrase *you*. In fact, the intonation indicates that the construction is interrogative, which analysis is supported by the behaviour of the listeners, who regularly respond with *yes* or *no*. It is worth mentioning that SEE is related to deictics in that it involves visual pointing by the speaker; in contexts other than the Map Task, a question such as *do you see the monument* would probably be accompanied by a manual pointing gesture and/or by a pointing gesture of the head and by the speaker directing his or her gaze at the said monument. In unusual situations, say in adventure films, where neither speech nor manual gestures are possible, one person can draw another's attention to an entity by looking alternately at it and at the second person.

The first two constructions occur with both definite and indefinite noun phrases, the third occurs only with indefinite noun phrases, and the last two occur only with definite noun phrases. Where there is an indefinite noun phrase an entity is introduced into the dialogue and the construction is presentational. One participant injects a note of certainty by using the formula *you'll see a diamond mine on your map, you'll see a graveyard*. The use of WILL reflects this instruction giver's confidence that both maps have these landmarks. Where instruction givers use a definite noun phrase, as in *you see where it says burnt forest, see the pine grove*, and *see where the pebbled shore is*, they are confirming or re-presenting landmarks that have previously been introduced. The reason for the confirmation is to ease the description of awkward pieces of the route by relating the latter to as many well-established points of orientation as possible.

Similar to *(you) see X*, are constructions with KNOW: *you know the windows of the flagship?, you know how you've got Green Bay?, you know where it says secret valley?* The construction in general is interrogative and the direct object of KNOW is always definite. Examples of the construction are found only where the instruction-giver is re-establishing already mentioned landmarks, or referring to details of a given landmark; the participants know that both maps have the landmark and the instruction-giver acts on the assumption that both maps have the same picture associated with the landmark. An example of the latter is *you know the windows of the flagship?* The flagship has already been established as existing on both maps but the windows have not been mentioned.

SEE is regularly used in the spontaneous conversations for introducing entities. The author's intuition is that it can be used for initial introduction of entities and for re-establishing entities for the purposes of making out an argument, but the examples in the corpus of conversation all serve the initial introduction of entities. In the example in (54) SEE also serves to change the discourse topic:

(54) K1　Mr X's too soft
　　　S1　Dr X
　　　W1　Dr X Dr X
　　　K2　stupid name eh doctor
　　　S2　Dr X
　　　K3　you think of doctors being [indecipherable]
　　　S3　he got in America too
　　　W2　beg pardon
　　　S4　he got the doctorate in America　feeble
　　　K4　something to do with the Z　now he's got some
　　　W3　yes he's had something to do with the Z for a few years
　　　S5　**see Mr Y** he's got rid of whatsername the old secretary
　　　K5　hmm
　　　S6　she's not there any more I like her she
　　　K6　she was horrible
　　　S7　ah she's not bad **see the joggers** it's funny Mr Y he's reorganizing the junior school and all the girls in primary five they can go jogging

The two occurrences of the SEE construction are in S5 and S7 and in bold. For both S and K, Mr Y and the joggers are part of the frame; the conversation takes place in their school and concerns people and events in the school. W was a former pupil of the school and knew many of the staff. That is, Mr Y and the joggers are not brand new entities; Mr Y is available to all the participants in the conversation and the joggers are available at least to S and K. *See Mr Y* and *see the joggers* focus the listeners' attention on these entities, foreground them and bring them into the conversation as discourse topics.

The following is an interesting example of the SEE construction.

(55) A　**see those old houses over on the far side** . . . this area was all houses like that right round

In (54) *see Mr Y* is followed by the pronoun *he*, which is the typical pattern of full noun phrase for first mention and pronoun for second mention. *See the joggers* is not followed by any pronoun picking up the referent of *the joggers*, which remain a discourse topic and are not referred to directly again, although the speaker does go on to talk about the primary five girls who can go jogging. In (55) the houses are first mentioned by means of a full noun phrase, *those old houses over on the far side*, but the second mention is also by means of a full noun phrase. This is a good example of information being spread over clauses. A written version of the utterance might be *This area was all houses like those ones over on the far side, all*

236   *Spontaneous Spoken Language*

round the square. Instead of a single complicated clause, the speaker introduces the relevant set of houses in the SEE clause and states his proposition about those houses in the second clause. That is, the single task of communicating the information that the square used to have houses like those ones all round it is broken into two tasks: make sure the houses are salient for the listener and then provide the information about the square, good tactics in conversation, where the listener's attention may be easily exhausted or distracted. The listener's attention is concentrated first on the new entities and then on the proposition.

5.7.6. Highlighting constructions in German

German has a range of highlighting constructions and devices similar to those found in English, including existential constructions, NP-clause (see § 5.7.7), deixis, discourse particles, and cleft constructions. The demonstrative deictics DA and SO are widely used and appear in a variety of constructions and discourse contexts—see § 5.7.7.1 and Chapter 6. Another common focusing device is the sequence *UND ZWAR* which partially overlaps with the function of *LIKE* in Scottish English—see Chapter 6.

5.7.6.1. Existential constructions in German

The construction DA SEIN X (THERE BE X) is frequent in spoken but not in written German. The existential/locative distinction is not always clear. In (56) from the dialogue data A and B are negotiating a mismatch on the maps, A has two view points, B has only one. Note that *da* in A1 and A3 is translated as *there*. The latter is the locative *there* (contrasting with *here*) and not the reduced existential *there* as in *there's a fly in my soup*.

(56) A1   ja   da   ist   noch   einer   aber da   auf der rechten seite
          yes there is   another one   but there   on the right   side
          ist   da   noch   einer
          is   there another one
     B1   nee den hab ich nicht hast du n ostsee
          no   that have I   not   have you an eastlake
     A2   n ostsee   hab ich ja/
          an eastlake have I   yes
     B2   schön
          good
     A3   oh ja   genau   der ostsee   aehm unten in der mitte
          oh yes exactly the eastlake ehm below in the middle
          wenn du   da   ist
          when you there is
          direkt   dadrunter   ist der zweite aussichtspunkt
          directly there-below   is   the second view point

In A1 the first (declarative) DA SEIN X construction, *da ist noch einer*, is existential. The second (interrogative), *ist da noch einer*, could be existential or locative, i.e. 'do you have another one somewhere' or 'do you have another one in that spot I'm talking about' (*auf der rechten seite* 'on the right-hand side'). In A3 *da ist* is locative, *da* referring back to the locative expressions *der ostsee aehm unten in der mitte* 'eastlake ehm below in the middle' and locating the missing feature. As in the English, existential constructions can include either definite or indefinite NPs. In (57a–b) the NP is indefinite—*n brief* and *kartoffeln*, but in (57c) *seine tante* is definite.

(57) (a) da   ist   n   brief für dich
         there   is   a   letter for you
    (b) da   sind noch kartoffeln
         there are   still potatoes
    (c) wer   kümmert sich denn um   ihn
         who cares   self then about   him
         'who looks after him then'
         da   ist   doch   seine tante
         there is   MODAL Part.   his   aunt

Such existential constructions are frequent in informal spoken German.

5.7.7. *NP-Clause*

A very common construction in spoken English consists of a Noun Phrase followed by a complete clause containing a pronoun anaphor of the Noun Phrase. Quirk *et al.* (1985: 1416–17) give the examples below.

(58) (a) This man I was telling you about—well, he used to live next door to me
    (b) The book I lent you—have you finished it yet

Quirk *et al.* suggest that the construction occurs in very loose and informal speech. We would prefer to say that it is typical of spontaneous speech from all sorts of speakers and that it is not confined to English—cf. the discussion of Russian in § 5.7.7.1. Quirk *et al.* say that the disjoined noun phrases—e.g. *the man I was telling you about* and *the book I lent you*—clearly set out the 'point of departure' for the utterance as a whole and that 'it is not uncommon for long noun phrases which are nonfocal to be thus treated in familiar speech, a convenience alike to hearer (in receiving an early statement of a complex item) and speaker (in not having to incorporate such an item in the grammatical organization of his utterance)'.

By 'nonfocal' Quirk *et al.* mean that the noun phrase does not carry the intonation nucleus. None the less the noun phrase is highlighted by being in first position and by not being part of the following clause. Moreover, it may be separated from the clause by a pause. Quirk *et al.* are correct to point out that the construction is a convenience for speaker and hearer, but we suggest that it would be optimistic to expect any other construction to be typical of spontaneous speech. One more comment before examining some of the examples in our data: a common label for the construction is left-dislocation. Like a number of labels that were coined during the classic phase of transformational grammar, this one carries a dynamic meaning; the metaphor is of the noun phrase originating in the clause and being dislocated to leftmost position. This metaphor is entirely inappropriate for the analysis of spontaneous spoken language in which the principal idea is that speakers produce a sequence of short constituents which are interlinked by deixis and by discourse relations (cf. Chapter 1). Rather than devise a complex Latinate label, we will refer to it simply as the NP-Clause construction.

Let us turn now to some examples from the conversations.

(59) A1   well on a Friday night I just do two and half hours   I get a pound and I get tips   which make about one pound fifty and then on Saturday I get three pounds for the whole day and about two pounds tips there   but it's awful hard work
B1   cold as well   eh?
A2   aye   in the snow
C1   what are the people like to work with   the drivers and that
A3   the driver he's really friendly   you get a good laugh with him and the boy that's full time he gives you a lot of laughs and that

A3 has two occurrences of the NP-Clause construction. One important point is that the first NP is short, merely determiner and noun—*the driver*. There is no pause between the NP and initial pronoun in the clause, *he*. That is, there is no indication that the speaker is running into planning problems, a suggestion that is sometimes made, for instance in the first edition of Quirk *et al.* The second occurrence of the NP-Clause construction has a longer NP with a relative clause—*the boy that's full time*. Again, there is no pause between the NP and the clause. This example is, however, consonant with the observation in Chapter 4 that spontaneous speech contains very few noun phrases of any complexity. In this example the complex NP comes on its own.

The complexity of the NP is unlikely, however, to be the essential reason for the construction, since most of the NPs in our examples are simple, like *the driver*. It is more likely that the construction is connected with the spreading of information over syntactic constituents in small doses and in particular with the need to highlight entities being introduced into the discourse. Of course, in (59) *the driver* and *the boy that's full time* could be seen as given, since they link back to *the drivers and that*, but that specific driver and his full time assistant are being mentioned for the first time.

In (60) B3 uses the NP-Clause construction to introduce an entity not connected with any previously mentioned entity or set of entities but none the less known to B and C. The entity is unknown to A, who picks up B's phrase *that technician* and asks about his role in the events being narrated. Moreover the construction allows the NP (at B3) to have its own exclamatory pitch pattern.

(60) A1 so you were how long were you off for?
     B1 four days
     A2 four days oh dear
     B2 it was great fun I I didn't have any appetite so I existed on oranges and I lost about three pounds
     A3 goodness me
     C1 you'll have put it back on by now
     B3 I know start putting it back on again eating a bit more yeah it's unfair that technician I think he ought to be shot
     C2 yeah cause we're getting these films at
     B4 very interesting films with any luck
     C3 sex education
     B5 they're boring at the beginning
     C4 and he must have slept in or something
     B6 and the roads were icy we were late I was late in the car was all over the place
     C5 my Mum was going awful slowly
     A4 so what's this technician got to do with it?

5.7.7.1. *NP-Clause constructions in other languages*

English is far from unique in its NP-Clause construction, both with respect to its syntax and its discourse functions. This is hardly surprising, since NP-Clause constructions result from speakers spreading information over small constituents and from their need to highlight entities which are introduced into the discourse. German too has an NP-Clause construction, and like the English one it reflects the convenient distribution of information over syntactic structure and not the complexity of the NP or planning difficulties. In contrast with English, German uses demonstrative pronouns rather than personal pronouns. Altmann (1981) provides a detailed analysis of such constructions (which he calls left-dislocation/Linksversetzung without adopting a transformational analysis). He distinguishes between left dislocation and similar constructions such as hanging topic/Freies Thema, using criteria such as case-agreement, intonation, pauses, interruptibility by parentheticals, etc. The former he considers syntactically integrated, with the sentence initial slot being filled twice. The latter is considered less integrated, with the first NP having independent status. Although it is beyond the scope of this chapter to discuss this distinction in detail, it is worthwhile drawing attention to the problematic nature of the criteria whereby left dislocation does not allow a pause between NP and co-referential pronoun and requires case-agreement. For instance, in (64) there is no pause between the NP and co-referential pronoun, yet there is no case-agreement. While we agree that certain NP-Clause constructions should be classified as hanging topics, we do not believe that the distinction between hanging topics and left dislocation is categorical. Rather, a scale of more and less syntactically integrated constructions exists. German examples are given in (61)–(64). (63) comes from a transcript of spontaneous conversation and the others—from the German Map Task dialogues.

(61) also   der gelbe   und der rote Fluß die   mmm begrenzen die
     Particle the yellow and the red river they (DEM) mmm border   the
     oberste   linke   Ecke
     topmost   lefthand corner

(62) der Vulkan   der   ist ungefähr auf gleicher Höhe wie der rote Fluß
     the volcano it (DEM) is about   on same   height as the red river

(63) aber auf der anderen Seite eh ein eh
     but on the other   side eh a   eh
     vernünftig erzogene   Kinder
     sensibly   brought-up children
     den   merkt man an wenn sie   etwas   wissen wollen
     to-them (DEM) notices one to when they something to-know want
     'On the other hand eh a eh sensibly brought up children one notices when they want to know something'

In many such examples, including (63) and (64), there are no pauses (prima facie therefore the construction is not necessarily associated with planning problems) and where there are pauses they occur in the clause, between the pronoun and the rest of the clause, as shown by the position of *mmm* in (61). The NP in the NP-Clause construction is in the nominative case in (61)–(62) but can be in, e.g., the accusative case, as in (64), and the anaphor in the clause need not be in the same case as the NP. In (63) *vernünftig erzogene Kinder* is in the nominative or accusative but *den* (which is a phonetically reduced realization of *denen* in (63)) is dative, and in (64) *diesen Flußlauf* is accusative whereas *dem* is dative, since FOLGEN (follow) governs its object in the dative case. If there had been a planning problem leading to an interrupted construction, we would expect either a hesitation after *diesen Flußlauf*, or *diesem Flußlauf*, i.e. an NP in the dative case as object of FOLGEN.

(64) ja und diesen   Flußlauf   dem   folgen wir jetzt
     yes and this-ACC rivercourse it (DEM) DAT follow we now
     'yes and this rivercourse we now follow it'

NP-Clause constructions are much more varied in German than in English. Altmann (1981) discusses among others nominalized subject clauses, headless relative clauses, infinitives, and prepositional phrases. Some of these also occur in written language, however, NPs and PPs are typical only of spoken language.

NP-Clause constructions are much less frequent than NP VP main clauses. They create focus, which is achieved via the separation of the NP and the deictic which follows it and refers back to it. This deictic is particularly important in German, where the phonologically more prominent demonstrative pronoun is used and where other deictics such as DA feature. There are 17 cases in the Map Task data (8 nominative subjects, 6 locative NPs/PPs/headless relative with DA). In the Map Task data NP-Clauses the need to focus on the entities arises out of the importance of or difficulties in establishing locations.

Zemskaja (1973: 239–47) provides the Russian examples (65)–(67), which are similar to the English NP-Clause construction. Speakers use the constructions in (65a,b) to introduce or reintroduce an individual first-order entity into the discourse in order to utter a proposition about that entity. Like the English examples, the NP is followed by a complete clause containing a shadow pronoun that picks up the reference of the NP. Note that the extraclausal NP is in the nominative case, whereas the pronoun can be in any appropriate case. (65a) has the nominative pronoun *ona* (she), the subject of *pridet*, and (65b) has the dative pronoun *emu*, dative case being required by *ravno*.

(65) (*a*) A   Lena/ ona skoro pridet
        But Lena/ she soon will arrive
   (*b*) Miša/ emu   vse ravno
       Miša/ to him all equal
       i.e. 'It's all one to Misa'

Zemskaja does not provide the above examples with a context but we can infer that *Lena* at least is given, since the conjunction *a* indicates a contrast between Lena and someone else, both of whom have been mentioned or are otherwise salient and known to speaker and hearer. The examples in (66a,b) are different in structure, since the initial NP, always nominative, is followed by a complete clause containing the same NP, though not necessarily in the same case.

(66) (*a*) Vasja/Vasja ušel   v   školu
      Vasja/Vasja has gone to school
   (*b*) Cvety/cvetov   ja   ne   pokupala
      Flowers/Flowers I   not have bought

In (66a) the second occurrence of *Vasja* is nominative case, as subject of *ušel*. *Cvetov* is genitive, being the direct object of the negative verb *ne pokupala*.[19] Zemskaja (1973: 244) gives as a typical context for (66*b*) *žal' cvetov u nas net* (It's a pity—we've got no flowers). (66*b*) picks up the given entity with *cvety* and the clause conveys a proposition—I haven't bought flowers. From Zemskaja's comment it can be inferred that the first occurrence of *Vasja* in (66*a*) is also given.

In a third construction the central entity is introduced by a nominative NP, but there is neither shadow pronoun nor repeated NP in the following clause. The initial NP does not introduce a specific entity, but a class of entities.

(67) (*a*) Sobaka vsegda poly grjaznye
Dog always floors dirty
(*b*) Deti/ bez šuma ne obojdeš'sja
Children without noise not you-will-manage

Sobaka in (67*a*) is nominative singular but the meaning is clearly 'when you have dogs, the floors are always dirty', and the interpretation of (67*b*) is 'when you have children/when there are children around, there will always be noise'. Again, it can be inferred from the discussion that dogs and children have already been mentioned. The closest English translations are along the lines of *the thing about dogs/children is* . . ., which brings out the larger function of this construction in picking up a given entity and using that as a bridge to a new proposition.

The final word in this section is that many other languages have the NP-Clause construction with the same function; it occurs in the Hungarian Map Task dialogues, is well attested for French, and is reported for Finnish. For other languages, such as Irish and Turkish, it is not clear whether the construction occurs.

5.7.8. Highlighting new propositions

The participants in the conversation in (60) and in the Map Task dialogues introduce relatively concrete entities into the discourse—individual people, sets of people, landmarks, features of landmarks, sections of route. Other types of entities that are regularly introduced into discourses are properties and propositions. These may be brought in without fanfare but can be made salient both in writing and speech. The written English examples in (68) are typical.

(68) (*a*) X has one interesting/obvious/relevant/important property, namely . . .
(*b*) Another proper of X that must be taken into account is . . .
(*c*) We turn now to a less/more attractive property of X

---

[19] The assignment of case to direct objects of negated verbs is not straightforward. Plural nouns with non-specific reference, like *cvetov* in 66(*b*), mass nouns and abstract nouns are more likely to be in the genitive case than singular concrete nouns.

(d) It is worthwhile remarking at this point that . . .
(e) Consider for a moment the fact that . . .

Spoken English has a variety of constructions that highlight properties and propositions being introduced into a discourse. The devices are not used in written English (unless the writer is devising dialogue) and are relatively short: like SEE, they serve to make a property or proposition salient, to concentrate the listener's attention on it.[20]

5.7.8.1. the thing is

A very common construction is *the thing is*, which can be used to concentrate the listener's attention either on properties or on propositions. An example of a proposition is given in (69).

(69) A What about Edinburgh do the people go up there
     B oh yeah a lot
     C oh aye especially at night they go to the pictures **but the thing is if you go to the pictures if you go to the late show you're you've to run for buses**

This example is interesting in several respects. It is typical of our data in that *the thing is* is never followed by a complementizer, there is regularly a pause between it and the next clause, which has its own pitch contour. These properties are compatible with a loose construction in which *the thing is* and *you've to run for buses* are juxtaposed, just like the constituent parts of the WH cleft discussed in Chapter 3. (69) is yet another good example of information being spread out over clauses in small chunks: a written version might be *if you go to the late show at the pictures you've to run for buses*. The event of going to the pictures is split into two events, going to the pictures and going to the late show, and each smaller event is mapped onto its own conditional clause.[21]

Examples of the construction in its property-introducing function are given in (70) and (71).

(70) A1 . . . and there's my Aunt Mary and Uncle Jim's Stewart, David and Beth and up till last year we've always went our holidays together
     B1 where about?
     A2 up and down the country   Scotland   England
     B2 what? camping or ?
     A3 no no in a flat to begin with . . . but there again you've got all the dishes and everything to wash up   it's just like a home from home out of one sink and into the other

[20] The WH cleft construction is relevant to this task but only one example will be given in this section as the clefts (reverse, IT, and WH) will be dealt with separately in §§ 6.2.5–6.2.7.

[21] There are indications that the *thing is* construction, introducing propositions, is on the way to being grammaticalized. In ***thing is*** *he's watching the man he's not watching the ball*, *thing* has lost its definite article and becomes less noun-like. No other modifiers are possible, unlike the property-introducing structure, which typically contains an adjective modifying THING or a prepositional phrase, as in (70) and (71).

B3   what about   sorry? [addressed to participant C, who tries to take the floor]

C1   I find holidays an awful bore . . . last year we met up with my Mum's cousin and her husband—like they're my Mum and Dad's age too—and I was bored stiff

A4   you were sick   that's all right in my case because Beth's just a year younger than me

C2   and it comes to a point where I spend all week in the nearest pool or something you know trying to keep myself amused

A5   **the only thing with Beth**   Beth'll not spend money   she's mingy   she's really mean   she wouldn't give you two halfs for a one

B4   who's this?

A6   my wee cousin

With respect to the syntactic structure, note that A5 contains a noun phrase, *the only thing with Beth*, followed by a clause, *Beth'll not spend money*. There is no copula; indeed, there is no copula between the noun phrase and the clause in any of the examples of this structure. From a pragmatic perspective what is interesting is that Beth is treated as given by A, although B shows by the statement in B4 that he has lost track of the people introduced into the conversation by A. A has mentioned Beth in A1 and referred to her again in A4. It is not Beth herself that is new in the discourse but the fact that she is tight-fisted. The phrasing is important. *The thing with Beth* is neutral with respect to whether the speaker regards the upcoming property as good or bad, but *the only thing* signals that the speaker is about to mention a property that contradicts previous good impressions—good impressions created in A4 by the statement that A had an easier time on holiday than C because she had a female cousin with her and not just a collection of middle-aged relatives.

In (71) the *thing* phrase is part of a separate clause. The construction is analogous to reverse clefts (discussed in Chapter 6), which serve to halt the progress of an interaction and to sum up the section of dialogue that has just been uttered. (71) is preceded by one of the participants, a first-year university student, relating how she had tried to write an essay the previous evening, had sat down at her desk at seven p.m. but had not put pen to paper till ten p.m. because of people calling in to have a chat and drink coffee. The speaker in (71) sums up this aspect of life in the halls of residence. *That* points back to the interruptions narrated by the previous speaker.

(71)   A   **that's the bad thing about the halls of residence**   there's always people knocking on your door

5.7.8.2. Clefts

WH clefts introduce propositions. The literature on discourse includes classic examples such as *What John painted was the shed*, in which *what* points forward to the noun phrase *the shed* and the particular shed referred to. In the Map Task dialogues and the conversations the WH cleft is used to point forward to, and to highlight, new propositions. Consider (72).

(72) no you had no food attached you got your meal hours of course but // **what you did in the evenings** you carried a /sandwich or two/and you had a little break in between

What points forward to *you carried a sandwich or two*. In this particular example there is a contrast between not being supplied with food (in the pub in which the speaker used to work) and the speaker taking his sandwiches with him. This contrast is accidental; the essential property of the WH clefts is that a clause and the chunk of information it carries are thematized, i.e. put into first position, and the combination of the indefinite WH deictic and the thematization create the highlighting for the new proposition. (See the detailed discussion in Chapter 6.)

(73) is an interesting example from our conversation data of WHAT pointing forwards and highlighting an upcoming proposition but not as part of a WH cleft, simply as the subject of a free relative that is the direct object of a verb.

(73) **I tell you what surprises you em**//as I say . . . it's marvellous how many people stayed in such a really small area.

Let us say first that (73) as it stands is a much shortened and therefore misleading representation of the utterance, but for a reason. The speaker uses a WH pronoun to point forward but without using the WH cleft construction. The stretch *I tell you what surprises you* is syntactically complete but informationally incomplete because of the indefinite deictic *what*. The speaker could have said *what surprises you is how many people stayed in such a really small area*, but this has a tight syntactic link between the free relative and the *how many* clause: one clause is the subject of *is* and the other one is the complement, and the *how many* clause, being a WH clause, is a genuine complement of the copula and not just in juxtaposition to *what surprises you is*. But the speaker opts for the (typically) simpler structure of subject-verb-direct object, *I tell you what surprises you*, and subject-copula-free relative, *it's marvellous how many* . . . This syntactic arrangement also enables the speaker to emphasize the unexpected nature of the area by using *surprises* and then *marvellous*.

In fact the use of *I tell you what surprises you* is even more appropriate in the real utterance, because the speaker does not simply talk about how many people there were but builds up a detailed picture of the area before recapitulating and closing that section of his account with *it's marvellous* . . . Cf. (74).

(74) B uh huh there was huge families stayed in
     A oh yes   I tell you what surprises you   eh as I say   I remember seeing Arthur's Street when I went back from the university like from the gymnasium roof looking over into Arthur Street where you had three open Middle Arthur, East Arthur Place eh Lower what   it three opening off   well in that area when there was hundreds of families   and looking now   well, actually they're rebuilding it   but just before they rebuilt the flats it was hardly any area at all and I don't know how the people ever how many people in such a short
     B uh huh
     A I mean   well   when you're you of course you visualize streets big and long
     B uh huh
     A and when you see it now up you realize they were never nearly as big as you visualized them   and the area itself   it's marvellous how many people stayed in such a really small area

The crux of the matter is that the classic WH cleft is suitable for a relatively small amount of information that is to be highlighted in a well-planned piece of syntax. Not only is planning time very brief in spontaneous dialogue but speakers regularly have large amounts of information to convey, as in the excerpt above. *I tell you what* or *I tell you what surprises you* is an appropriate highlighting device, since it does not require a complement clause, which by its very nature is limited in extent.

One of the points made in Chapter 6 is that WH clefts are not frequent in our data. Far more common as a focusing item is LIKE, which is also discussed separately in Chapter 6, and there are certain alternative clausal constructions that are used instead of the WH cleft. The first one, (75), could occur in written English but the others are typical of spoken English.

(75) we were all in a hurry to get good seats and it turned out **all we got was** listening to questions about the boarding house

The above example is syntactically tight-knit. The main clause has as its subject *all we got*, which contains a relative clause, *we got*. The copula *was* has a complement in the shape of the gerund *listening to questions about the boarding house*. This is a much tighter organization than the WH cleft, in which *was* is followed by a complete clause, and the following example (76), in which *it was* is likewise followed by a complete clause, *he got a Yamaha drum kit*.

(76) aye he had that he had that for a good while even when were going when everybody had their amps just about// **then it was** he got a Yamaha drum kit it was secondhand it cost him £400

This example too illustrates the spreading of information over clauses. There are three pieces of information: he got a Yamaha drum kit, the kit was secondhand, it cost him £400. It would be possible to utter *he got a secondhand Yamaha drum kit for £400*, but this structure does not correspond to what we think is the appropriate pragmatic interpretation. The person who bought the drum kit is seen by the speaker, a member of a band, as an untalented person who has been brought into the same band. This untalented person has had the nerve to buy, not just any drum kit, but a Yamaha. This is the important new proposition that is highlighted by *then it was*. The secondary propositions are that the Yamaha was secondhand and that even so it cost the large sum (for the time) of £400, a sum which is quite out of proportion to the amount of talent residing in the buyer. The major proposition is highlighted and the secondary propositions are assigned to separate unhighlighted main clauses.

The final example of a clausal focusing construction is in (77).

(77) A Well if I went three inches down from the caravan park I would
    B so then
    A you know I'd more or less hit the picket fence
    B right I see **so is that the idea of this then?** so you go straight to where I am instead of going round the picket fence?

Here the highlighting clause *so is that the idea of this then?* is syntactically complete and the proposition that is highlighted is in the following clauses— *you go straight to where I am instead of going round the picket fence*. Note the role of the deictics in the first clause. *That*, which typically points at entities remote from speaker and hearer, here points ahead to the approaching proposition; that is, the speaker metaphorically points away from herself and the instruction-follower to a proposition that is upcoming. The fact that the speaker herself is formulating the proposition is irrelevant, since what is important is how the speaker decides to present the proposition. *This* typically points to entities near the speaker (and hearer), and in this example it points to the suggestion that has just been made by the instruction-follower A as to the route he might draw on his map. Since the suggestion has been articulated, it is closer to the speaker and hearer than a proposition that has not been articulated, hence the use of *this*. Note too that, apart from the noun phrase *the idea*, the nominal and adverbial constituents are all deictic.

5.7.8.2.1. *Clefts in German and French*
Weinert (1995*b*) gives examples of German WH clefts, one of which is reproduced in (78). It comes from spontaneous conversation.

(78) ja   was ich bei Bernstein immer besonders schwierig finde
    yes what I   with Bernstein always especially difficult find
    ist die Tatsache, daß er nicht klar   trennt   zwischen
    is   the fact   that he not clearly distinguishes between
    linguistischen, soziologischen und psychologischen Variablen
    linguistic,   sociolinguistic and psychological variables

The above example is a classic WH cleft, with the free relative *was ich bei Bernstein immer besonders schwierig finde* connected by the copula *ist* with the noun phrase *die Tatsache* . . . The German Map Task dialogues offer examples of unintegrated WH cleft structures, parallel to the spoken English unintegrated WH cleft constructions discussed in § 3.7.2—see (79*a*). Informal German conversation provided examples of a structure that is cleft-like in function but correlative in structure, as in (79*b*).

(79) (*a*) und was   wir für die Route   brauchen ist
and what we for the route   need   is
vom   Start aus geh'n wir über's   Raumschiff
from-the start out go   we   over-the spaceship
(*b*) was du   jetzt angesprochen hast das ist eben   dieses
what you now referred-to   have that is MODAL Part. this
klischeehafte Krimifilmchen
clichéd   crime film (diminutive)

In (79*a*) the free relative clause is *was wir für die Route brauchen*. It is followed by the copula *ist* but the latter does not connect the free relative clause to some noun phrase. Instead, *ist* is followed directly by the clause *vom . . . Start aus geh'n wir über's . . . Raumschiff*. The clause following the copula is independent both syntactically and with respect to the discourse; it contains no constituent linking up with *was*.

In (79*b*) the free relative clause is *was du jetzt angesprochen hast*. The free relative clause could be followed by *ist* and a complement NP *dieses klischeehafte Krimifilmchen*. Instead it is followed by another main clause which could stand alone—*das ist dieses klischeehafte Krimifilmchen. Was* correlates with *das*.

German has a construction analogous to the IT cleft, though examples with *es* (it) are typical of written or spoken German rather than informal spontaneous spoken German. In the latter, clefts with *das* 'that' are more common, as in (80).

(80) das ist doch   die Fiona, die das macht
that is Particle the Fiona who that does

French lacks a free relative construction but Blanche-Benveniste (1991: 59–64) presents examples of IT clefts (under the heading of 'dispositif d'extraction') and what she calls pseudo-clefts ('pseudo-clivé'). French IT clefts allow a wide range of cleft constituents—noun phrases, adverbs, and prepositional phrases, as demonstrated in (81*a,d*). In spontaneous spoken French the IT cleft also allows a clause, as in (81*e*). That is, unlike the English IT cleft, the French IT cleft can be used to highlight propositions.

(81) (a) c'est vraiment à la dernière minute qu'il est mis au point
it is really at the last minute that it is put to-the point
'it's really at the last minute that the final draft is put together'
(b) c'est ainsi qu'il se comporte
it is thus that he himself behaves
(c) c'est que des transistors qu'on fabrique
it is COMP transistors that one makes
'it is only transistors that we make'
(d) c'est elle qui a passé l'examen c'est pas moi
it is she who has sat the exam it is not me
(e) c'est que je ne veux pas le déranger
it is COMP I NEG want NEG him to-disturb
'the thing is; I don't want to disturb him'

(81e) is typically used in situations where the speaker is offering an explanation. Whereas (81c), e.g., is both highlighting and contrastive, (81e) merely highlights the proposition 'I don't want to disturb him'.

5.7.8.2.2. *Highlighting propositions in Russian*

Spoken Russian has a construction which is usually translated into English by an IT cleft. The construction does not occur in formal written Russian but is found in dialogue in novels, which is the source of the example in (82), taken from Baranskaja's novel *Nedelja kak Nedelja*.

(82) Bez četverti šest' zvonit telefon.
without quarter six rings telephone.
Net, eto zvonjat u DVERI.
No that they-are-ringing at door
'At a quarter to six the telephone rings. No, it's the doorbell they're ringing'.

The structure of the Russian construction is unclear. It can be analysed as consisting of a deictic *eto* (this/that) followed by a complete clause. In (82) *dveri* carries a focal pitch. The construction is typically used for contrast, at least in the examples we have found: not X but Y. It can be analysed as a copular construction. In Russian the present tense forms of the copula are typically zero, which allows (82) to be assigned the structure [Deictic–Copula–Clause]. The contrasted constituent in the clause carries focal pitch. The construction can be used to pick out and contrast any participant in a given situation. Thus in (83) Ivan is picked out as the person who is knocking at the door.

(83) Eto IVAN stučit v dveri
that Ivan is-knocking at door

The English equivalent, *It's Ivan that is knocking at the door*, could be analysed as containing a relative clause modifying *Ivan*, though there are certain difficulties with this analysis that lead, e.g. Quirk *et al.* (1985: 1386–7) to talk instead of an annex clause. The important point here is that the Russian construction offers no temptation to talk of either a relative or an annex clause. The deictic (plus zero copula) is followed by a single clause.

Spoken Russian has a number of other constructions that allow speakers to highlight propositions. Examples are given in (84)–(85).

(84) — Leša, slušaj . . . Slyšiš'?
       Leša listen   can you hear me?
    — Nu?
       what?
    — Takoe delo: zabud', čto bezxoz kopal. Ponjal?
       such thing forget that ownerless (grave) (you) dug Got it?
       Normal'naja rodstvennaja mogila, ponjal?
       normal relatives grave got it?
       'This is what: forget you dug that ownerless (grave) Got that? It's an ordinary relatives' grave, got that?'

(Kaledin 1989: 221)

(85) (a) On teper' ved' u nas čto? každyj den' po utram truscoj begaet
         he now you know at us what? each day in mornings at-jog runs
     (b) On čto? Na jug xočet etim letom?
         he what? to south wants this summer
     (c) A vy tuda kak? Električkoj?
         But you there how? By-the-electric-train?
     (d) Nu čto že? Ja momental'no otpravil telegrammu Zorovu
         OK what then I immediately sent telegram to-Zorov

Takoe delo in (84) is reminiscent of *I tell you what surprises you* in (73); both *takoe* and *what* are deictics and point forward. In examples (85a–d) the speakers ask a question which they immediately answer. As mentioned in the discussion of the WH cleft in § 3.7.2, the WH words and their equivalents in other languages are indefinite deictics and the WH words in the above examples, although traditionally classified as interrogative pronouns, are none the less non-specific deictics pointing forward to an upcoming specification. Note the additional focusing item *ved'* in (85a).

Blanche-Benveniste (1991: 124–5) supplies parallel examples from French, both for introducing new entities and new propositions. She gives an example of question and answer produced by different speakers but points out the very close relationship between questions and answers produced by one and the same speaker, especially when they contain the same verb.

(86) et dans les protistes qu'est-ce qu'on trouve
     and in the Protista what-is-it that-one finds
     on trouve les bactéries les champignons et les algues
     one finds the bacteria the fungi and the algae

(87) voyez   à   Grenoble   là   dernièrement
    see-IMP   at   Grenoble   there recently
    il y a   combien   il y a   il y a   huit   jours
    there-is   how-much   there-is   there-is eight   days
    'how long ago—eight days ago'
    il y a   une   dame   elle   était
    there's a   a   woman   she   was

Similar devices can be found in spontaneous spoken English—cf. *she must be what—sixty at least* and *so what did she do? she told him exactly what she thought of him*—and it is probable that the technique whereby one and the same speaker poses a question and answers is widespread as a highlighting device in spontaneous speech.

In Russian, *vot*, like *see* in English, is used to bring new propositions into focus, as in (88).

(88) vse vremja splošnye   povoroty // vot   tebja kačaet / iz   storony v   storonu
     all time   continuous bends   // Particle you   it-rolls / from side   to side

A suitable English translation, one that preserves the simple syntax of the Russian, would be along the lines of *like, you get rolled from side to side* (see the discussion of LIKE in Chapter 6) or *you get rolled from side to side, see*.

(89) oni   očen'   blizko drug k   drugu   podxodjat//
     they [cliffs] very   close   one   to   other   approach
     i   vot   po   kamennomu ložu   tečet reka
     and   Particle along stone   bed   flows river

Vot in (89) could be interpreted as introducing the new entity the river, but the interpretation we prefer is that *vot* concentrates the listeners' attention on the entire proposition, which includes a mention of the river. The speaker is a young woman recounting her adventures with a walking group in the mountains of the Crimea and *vot* can be taken both metaphorically, as a highlighter, and literally, as a linguistic pointer. The speaker invites her listeners to imagine themselves in this awesome canyon which looks as though it has been moulded in one piece and says that in the stone were hollows in which were floating autumn leaves of different hues. Her assertion of this last proposition is given in (90), the important feature being the occurrence of the phrase *vot tak vot* (*tak* = thus), which is described in the transcript as accompanied by a gesture. In this example *vot tak vot* follows the proposition but it is highlighted by the linguistic and physical gestures together.

(90) i   tam v kamne   takie ... mmm ... vpadiny / i   v nix   voda
     and there in (the) stone such   —mmm—   hollows and in them water
     os ... list'ja raznocvetnye/   plavajut/   vot   tak vot
     aut ... leaves different-coloured are-floating Particle so Particle

There are examples in our data of *vot* alone following the proposition highlighted by it. One such instance is (91).

(91) reka tečet/ ona nazyvaetsja Kokkozka //Kokkozka // vot   // gornaja   reka
     river flows it   calls-self   Kokkozka Kokkozka   Particle mountain river

The force of *vot* here is almost 'yes, that's right; that's the name'. The name of the river is repeated too, probably because the river name is unfamiliar both to the speaker and her listeners.

Highlighting can be achieved by simple repetition, as in (92).

(92) Ona etogo ne xotela // ne xotela
     she this   not wanted   not wanted
     i.e. 'She didn't want this at all'.

Finally, one of the first phrases that foreign learners of Russian pick up—because it is so frequently used—is *delo v tom, čto* (thing (is) in that, that, i.e. 'the thing is that'). Like *the thing is* in English, this Russian phrase highlights new propositions.

5.7.8.2.3. *SEE introducing propositions*

We finish this section with a second look at SEE. Our first look concentrated on its property-introducing function; this time we examine its proposition-introducing function. In (93) SEE highlights propositions that are presented as a precondition for success in drawing the next section of route. The propositions are encoded in conditional clauses which are not linked to a main clause. Rather, each conditional clause is highlighted by SEE, and the punch line is encoded, not in a main clause, but in a noun phrase, *that wee bit*. Note that the final part of A's instruction is encoded in a free relative, *where the pilot would go*, likewise highlighted by SEE. Since this use of SEE appears bizarre at first sight to speakers of standard English, it is worthwhile observing that speakers of standard English might well use expressions such as *you see if you come straight down*.

(93) A then you go down to the crashed aeroplane and turn a wee bit
     B which hand side of the crashed aeroplane
     A the the right wing if you look at it the it'll be on your left wing
     B it will be on the right side that's got the b the side that's got the burnt–written
     A right **see if you come down straight down**—right **see if you come round the left of the hills**—right?

B   uh huh
A   **see if you go straight down** but not go straight to the aeroplane right **see where the see where the pilot would go**   that wee bit

In the next example, (94), from the spontaneous conversations, SEE does not have a complement but functions as a general attention-rouser. It is equivalent to 'pay attention; I am about to say something interesting'— interesting, that is, to the speaker. Speakers of standard English could use *you know* (and indeed speakers of Scottish English could equally use *ken*) or expressions such as *I can tell you this*.

(94) A   there's a car park at the Waverley Station in Princes Street
     B   aye the shoppers' car park
     A   aye **see** I hate going in there

Finally, one very common construction should be mentioned—entity-introducing, but also entity-changing: *What about school? Do you enjoy the lessons?* This example was used by the speaker to change the topic of conversation to a new topic which he thought might provoke more discussion. Also common in radio and TV discussions, but not in the HCRC databases, are *As far as X is concerned*, or *As far as X*. The much cited *As for X* is not in the databases and is not frequent in radio and TV discussions.

5.7.8.3. *Particles (micro-focusers)*

In many languages particles play an important role in highlighting. Fernandez (1994*a*) gives a detailed account of particles and the part they play in the organization of spoken discourse. Weinert and Miller (1996) analyse the function of clefts in the English Map Task dialogues. Taking that analysis, and the examples, as a starting point, Miller (1996) investigated the functional equivalent of clefts in a range of languages via an oral questionnaire and also via Map Task dialogues in Catalan and Hungarian. In, for example, Finnish and Hungarian, particles and word order, both jointly and severally, are the major highlighting devices both in writing and speech. In other languages, such as German, particles are abundant in both spoken and written texts, but in French and Russian, for example, particles are more common in spoken texts. In Russian, particles play a much more important role in highlighting than word order, which has more to do with the distinction between given and new constituents. Examples allegedly illustrating the highlighting function of word order typically turn out to contain particles, as in (99) below. English has particles such as *right*, *well*, and *OK* that have to do with the management of dialogue rather than highlighting; the only highlighting particle is *like*, discussed in Chapter 6, unless *see* and *know* are counted as particles. We rejected the latter analysis on the ground that examples such as *see the old mill?* carry interrogative

254 Spontaneous Spoken Language

intonation, are interpreted by the participants as questions, and can easily be analysed as examples of the subject-less interrogative structure that is very frequent in spontaneous spoken English.

Russian has a large number of micro-focusers, whose purpose is to lend local salience to a constituent but without marking a major transition. They can mark Grosz and Sidner's type of transition because they may move the hearer's attention to another entity. In Grosz and Sidner's model this involves a transition from one focus space containing a given collection of entities to another focus space containing a (possibly overlapping but) different collection. Such micro-focusers are *že, kak raz, nepremenno*, and *vot*. The first three are exemplified in (95)–(97).

(95) Ivan často pokidaet kabinet
    Ivan often leaves (his) study
    Petr že nikogda ne pokidaet kabinet
    Peter Particle never not leaves (his) study
    'Peter now, he never leaves his study'

(96) Kak raz segodnja on mne govoril o vas
    as once today he to-me was-speaking about you
    'It was just today that he was speaking to me about you.'

(97) on nas zastavil izučat' arabskij nepremenno šrift-to[22]
    He us made study (the) Arabic absolutely script-that

(96) with *kak raz* is translated by means of an IT cleft but the Russian example does not involve any major restructuring of the basic main clause construction. The time adverb *segodnja* is in theme position, whereby it automatically becomes salient but one very important point is that word order on its own rarely serves to highlight constituents. For instance, Bivon (1972) states that the first constituent in the SVO and OSV orders is occasionally emphatic, but his examples are those in (98a,b).

(98) (a) Imenno doč', mysli o nej, ... dolžny byli zapolnit' pustotu
       Namely daughter thoughts about her were-to fill the-emptiness
    (b) K sožaleniju, imenno takoj xarakter nosit ob"edinenie social-demokratov
       Unfortunately, namely such character bears the-union of-social-democrats

In both the above examples the first NP is modified by the micro-focuser *imenno*. In any case, since SVO is the most frequent and the most unmarked order, it would be strange if occurrence in the S position alone conferred salience on constituents. Another very frequent particle is *vot*, which is a

---

[22] The hyphen connecting *šr:ift* to *to* indicates that the latter is taken to be a clitic. This analysis is supported by the fact that, while it is clearly related in form to the deictic *tot* (masculine), *ta* (feminine), and *to* (neuter), the latter items agree with nouns in gender (also in number and case). *To* in (97) looks like the neuter form but *šrift* is a masculine noun and if *to* were in the independent deictic it would take the form *tot*. Moreover, the form is always -*to* no matter what the case of the noun it follows.

powerful deictic. It is used in contexts in which speakers of English could use SEE or LOOK and is often accompanied by a pointing gesture, as in *vot idet avtobus* (look/see—the/a bus is coming), or as in (99).

(99) vot u mosta u etogo/ u mosta u etogo idet granica
     see at bridge at this/ at bridge at this goes frontier
     'see, the frontier is here at this bridge'

The repetition of *u mosta u etogo* is a second means of giving salience to the bridge but the initial salience comes from *vot*.

Returning to (97), note that in addition to *nepremenno* preceding the highlighted NP there is a deictic item *-to* following *šrift*. Another example of this *-to* is in (100). This Russian example can be appropriately translated into English by means of an IT cleft. Anticipating the discussion of clefts in Chapter 6, we can say that the *-to* in Russian picks out Molčok from the set of relevant individuals in the given situation, namely the set of gravediggers working in the cemetery, and IT clefts perform an analogous function in English.

(100) štatnym   zemlekopom byl   odin   Molčok, brigadir.
      State   gravedigger was alone M.   brigadier
      Na nego-to i   pisalis'   narjady.
      On him-that and wrote-selves orders
      'Molčok, the brigade leader, was the only staff gravedigger. **It was his name that was used for all the paper work.**'

5.7.8.4. *Contrastive highlighting in Russian*

Extra highlighting, particularly in written Russian, comes from the occurrence of a negative in one clause but not the other or from a difference in word order between the two clauses. Consider (101*a,b*).

(101) (*b*) Ne je vinovat, vinovata xolera
           Not I guilty   guilty   (the) cholera
      (*b*) Ne važen   predmet očarovanija,
           Not important object   of-fascination
           važna   žažda byt'   očarovannym [literary]
           important thirst to-be fascinated

In (101*a*) the first clause has SV order, *ja vinovat*, while the second clause has VS order, *vinovata xolera*, with the negative *ne* in the first clause. (101*b*) is different in that both clauses have VS order, *važen predmet* and *važna žažda*, but as in (101*a*) the first clause has the negative *ne*. In (102) both clauses have SV order.

(102) Ne ona brosila—   ja brosil
      Not her abandoned (me)—I abandoned (her)

Since the contrastive highlighting is present no matter what the order of constituents in the two clauses, we may assume that it is the juxtaposition of a negative clause and a positive clause that plays the essential role. In single clauses with intransitive verbs[23] the order VS is typically used when the S is the first mention of the appropriate referent or when the referent is being reintroduced after a certain length of text. We examined four different text-types; journalese, academic monograph, novel, and spontaneous speech, each type being represented by 2,000 words of connected prose (albeit consisting of material from different reports in the case of the newspaper). The main findings are given below.

a The proportion of VS structures in each text type was: newspaper—3.1 per 100 words, novel—1.76, research monograph—1.39, the spoken text—1.3 (the lowest proportion).

b Referential distance[24] is greater for VS. The greatest difference between VS and SV referential distance was in the spoken text (VS—16.8, SV—8/2.5), then the novel (15.5 to 6.5), then the research monograph (18.5 to 10). The smallest difference was in the newspaper texts (20 to 15.7).

c There was a high proportion of pronoun subjects in SV construction but a low one in VS: newspaper texts—20% to 0%, novel—56% to 3%, spoken texts—44% to 27%, research monograph—17.3% to 11%.

d S has more words in VS than SV: the biggest difference was in the research monograph (8 to 4), then the novel (3 to 2.3), then the newspaper texts (2.9 to 2.3), then the spoken texts (2.3 to 1.9).

e VS structures typically introduce the entity that is the discourse topic of the following piece of text, ranging from a sentence or two to a whole paragraph.

The data we have examined suggests that when two clauses are juxtaposed in contrast, VS word order can occur in the second clause even though that order is not justified by any of the properties in **(a)**–**(e)** above. As a further piece of support for this analysis, consider the text in (103).

---

[23] The notion of verb is interpreted somewhat liberally here, but not unjustifiably. If the example had been past tense, the clauses would have contained *byl* and *byla* (both = 'was') respectively. The generally accepted notations SVO, OVS, etc. apply most straightforwardly to transitive constructions in languages such as English, but considerations of word order apply to other languages, such as Chinese, in which the notion of verb is broader than in English, encompassing adjectives, at least with respect to the major distributional frameworks. And it must be extended to take in constructions like the Slavic subject-predicate adjective one in which the copula is present or absent depending on the tense of the clause.

[24] This notion is to be understood as in Givón (1983), the essential point being that the higher the referential distance, the greater the number of clauses between a given mention of an entity and its previous mention.

(103) (i) V časovne daval prokat inventarja   vetxij, bezzubyj djadja Zora
          in chapel   gave hire   of-equipment ancient toothless Uncle Zora
     (ii) xuliganjaščij v   p'janom vide i   tixij tak
          raging   in drunk   state and quiet thus
    (iii) Na vtorom etaže pereodevalis', eli, pili,   spali—žili   zemlekopy
          on second floor changed,   ate, drank, slept—lived (the) gravediggers
     (iv) Vpročem,   oformleny   podsobnymi.
          Incidentally enrolled   as-auxiliaries
      (v) štatnym zemlekopom byl odin Molčok, brigadir. . . .
          Official gravedigger was one Molcok brigade-leader
     (vi) Sam že   on kopal redko, v složnyx   slučajax ili pri zaparke.
          Self Particle he dug rarely in complicated cases or in rush
    (vii) Kopali rebjata-časovnja, da izredka   želajuščie s   xozdvora.
          Dug   lads-chapel   and occasionally volunteers from yard
                                                              (Kaledin 1989)

'In the chapel ancient, toothless Uncle Zora hired out the equipment—he was a devil when drunk but quiet otherwise. On the second floor the gravediggers changed, ate, drank, slept—in short, lived. They were listed as auxiliaries, incidentally. Only Molčok, the brigade-leader, was an official gravedigger. However he himself rarely did any digging—only in complicated cases or when there was a rush on. The lads—the chapel—did the digging and occasionally volunteers from the yard.'

The gravediggers are first mentioned, as a collective, in line (iii); hence, the VS structure. The complement-VS structure in line (v) is not sanctioned by this being the first mention of Molčok, because he has been mentioned seven lines earlier and fifteen lines earlier. The latter mention also contains the information that he is the brigade-leader. It is more likely that the order of constituents is determined by the writer's wish to put the complement *štatnym zemlekopom* in first position to contrast with *podsobnymi* in the preceding sentence. Line (vi) has the expected SV order with a given, pronominal subject. Line (vii) has VS—*kopali rebjata*. Again, the VS order seems to be dictated by the need to provide a contrast with *on kopal*, but also by considerations of syntactic weight, the object-less verb *kopal* being followed by the subject NP *rebjata-časovnja* coordinated with the ellipted clause *da izredka želajuščie s xozdvora*.

The same short story offers the VS structure in (104), where the S is highly salient in the context but the VS order is used to make the adjective prominent. One English translation of (104), by Kelly (1990), is '. . . but they were certainly good 'uns'.

(104) On položil lopatu   na kraj   mogily
      He laid   (the) spade on (the) edge of-the-grave
      i   priporošil   vyrabotannoj   zemlej:
      and covered   (it) with-the-excavated earth
      svoi   ne   svoi,   a   uvedut—
      his (mates), not his (mates) but they-will-remove (it)—
      s   Molčkom, brigadirom,   rassoriš'sja
      with M.,   brigade-leader, you-will-fall-out
      Gde   on lopaty eti   —oficialki —zakazyvaet—odnomu bogu   izvestno
      where he spades these official ones   orders   to-one to-God known
      No   i   verno—xoroši lopatki
      But   and true   —good (the) spades
      'He laid the spade on the edge of the grave and covered it with the earth he had just dug out. Mates or not, the others would steal it and there would be big trouble with Molčok, the brigade-leader. Where he got these spades, "official" ones, God alone knew. But one thing was certain—they were good ones.'

We remarked above that the criteria governing VS order in single clauses do not necessarily apply when two clauses are juxtaposed. This comment is apparently correct but does not go far enough. Invoking Halliday's distinction between unmarked and marked clauses, we can say that for intransitive verbs the order SV is unmarked when S is given, and the order VS is unmarked when S is new, either brand new or simply being mentioned for the first time although present in the context. In contrast, the order VS, where S is given, is marked, and is sanctioned by the need to make the V particularly salient, typically for reasons of contrast.

The examples in (105) and (106) need little commentary. The first has a VS order because the two entities are being introduced—the speaker's nose may seem inappropriate as a new entity but is perfectly understandable in context; the writer is describing how she slowly and with great difficulty comes out of a deep sleep, trying to interpret a noise. The *ne . . . a* construction is perhaps the basic contrastive construction of Russian. (105) is an example of expressive journalistic style but is none the less another striking way of creating contrastive focus: produce a yes–no interrogative and provide the answer in the negative.

(105) vdrug   ja ponimaju: svistit   ne čajnik, a   moj nos.
      suddenly I understand: whistles not kettle but my nose.
(106) Meloč', pridirka? Net, vysokaja trebovatel'nost'
      A-trifle, a-cavil? No, a-high   duty

Finally, contrastive highlighting can be created by using either the fixed structure *ne to čto* + Infinitive followed by another negative clause which enjoys contrastive salience, or by using the fixed structure *malo togo, čto* + clause. In both (107) and (108) a deictic pointing to one event is negated; the general structure is 'not this but that'. Not *vstat'* and not *on sam rabotal* but (only there is no overt adversative coordination) *emu kazalos', čto* . . . and *on i materi s Nastej daval ukazanija*. These two examples remind us how important a role deixis[25] plays in language in general and in focusing constructions in particular, a role that is central to the English cleft constructions discussed in the following chapter.

(107) Ne to čto vstat',
not that (deictic) that (comp) to-stand-up
emu kazalos' čto on ne mozet otkryt' glaz
to-him seemed that he not can open eyes
'Far from standing up, it seemed he couldn't even open his eyes.'

(108) Malo togo, čto on sam rabotal,
Little of-that that he self worked,
on i materi s Nastej daval ukazanija, . . .
he and to-mother with Nastja gave instructions
'Quite apart from working himself, he even gave instructions to his mother and Nastja . . .'

5.8. Russian Word Order

It is worthwhile taking a brief look at word order in Russian. There is interesting interaction between word order and particles or clause combinations that serves to create contrastive focus and there are interesting differences between word order in written and spoken Russian. We can use fully Zemskaja's opinion reported in §5.1 that in written Russian it is

---

[25] Deixis is the key to the way in which a change of entity is signalled in Russian. Continuity of entity is signalled by the use of a pronoun subject or zero subject, the continuing entity being taken by the speaker or writer as firmly established for the listener or reader. In contrast, entity change, which particularly poses problems when a scene involves two or more human participants, i.e. two or more candidates for a given role, must be signalled strongly in order to get the new entity established. In spoken and written Russian that problem is solved by the use of TOT ('that'), one of the Russian demonstratives, as opposed to the neutral personal pronoun ON ('he/she/it').

Russian has two demonstratives: ETOT is neutral between 'close to speaker' and 'close to addressee' and TOT is used to point to entities remote from speaker and addressee. ETOT is translated into English by THIS or THAT, but TOT can only be translated by THAT. Consider the following example.

Val'ka ego rastolkal, i tot podvinulsja
Val'ka him shook and he moved

(*Rebjata ja živ*, 12)

Pursuing the metaphor of a path of continuity, we can regard TOT as pointing to an entity lying away from the path: one path stops and another potential path begins. English THAT cannot be used in this way; either HE is used twice and the reader/listener is left to work out the reference, or a proper name is used: *Val'ka shook him and Jura moved.* (Bolkestein 1991 has drawn our attention to the use of *ille* in Latin texts for change of Agent.)

the final position in an utterance that is important whereas in spoken Russian it is initial position. Table 5.3 indicates further differences.

TABLE 5.3. *Constituent order in written and spoken Russian*

Mainly written		Spoken	
SVO	79%	SVO	42%
OVS	11%	SOV	34%
OSV	4%	OSV	11%
VOS	2%	OVS	3%
SOV	1%		
VSO	1%		

Bivon (1972) gives the data in the column headed 'Mainly written'. The significance of the heading is that the figures relate to the data collected for the Essex Russian Project in the mid-1960s, the materials being mainly written, but the spoken materials being lectures rather than spontaneous discussion. The column headed 'spoken' contains figures relating to 10,000 words of spontaneous spoken Russian extracted from the transcripts published in Kapanadze and Zemskaja (1979).

The main differences lie in the absence of V-initial structures, which in any case constitute an insignificant proportion of the written data, and in the larger proportion of SOV clauses. Both bodies of data contain O-initial clauses but the proportion of OSV is higher for the spoken data whereas the proportion of OVS is smaller. The most frequent order, SVO, has a high percentage of objects that consist of a noun or a noun plus some other constituent. The second most frequent order, SOV, has a large number of objects that are pronouns. That is, the S-first orders occur when S is given (as Bivon maintained for written Russian—in our data from spoken Russian a large number of subject NPs in S-first sequences are pronominal).

The position of the O depends on whether it is pronominal—pronoun Os tend to occur pre-verbally, other Os—post-verbally. The absence of V-initial structures has been mentioned but there is a considerable number of verb-only clauses. The O-first orders occur when the O is given; Bivon says that in O-first structures, S occurs before the verb when it too is given, as in (109) and after the verb when it is new. In this OVS order the S is often a heavy noun phrase, but the two properties are connected, at least in written Russian: writers wishing to provide a considerable amount of information about a new entity can achieve this by means of a heavy noun phrase, whereas given entities are typically referred to by pronouns or other light noun phrases. (As remarked in Chapter 4, NPs in spontaneous spoken

Russian, and English, are typically very simple and the question of syntactic weight is largely irrelevant.)

(109) Etot period svoej žizni Krejn opisal   zatem   v 1897g ...
      this   period of-his of-life Crane described afterwards in 1897

Both *etot period svoej žizni* and *Krejn* are given in context in that they have been mentioned previously, hence the use of the deictic *etot* and the proper name *Krejn*. However, *etot period* . . . picks up a referent in the preceding sentence and is placed first. (Strictly speaking, the writer is not absolutely obliged to use this pattern, but it is accounted good style.)

Examples of OV (S) do occur in which the O is mentioned for the first time, but in the context of housecleaning, in the context built up by the story, the Os are given in that they are a salient part of the physical setting.

(110) Dima vošel,   ulybnulsja:
      Dima came-in, smiled
      'Kakaja ty   ešče   moloden'kaja, okazyvaetsja'—
      how   you still   young   it-appears
      i   vo   vremja užina pogljadyval na menja,
      and during dinner kept looking   at me
      a   ne čital kak obyčno.
      and not read as   usual
      i   **posudu** myl   so   mnoj   vmeste
      and dishes   washed with me   together
      i   daže **pol** podmel sam.
      and even floor   swept   himself
      — Ol'ka,   ty   ved'   sovsem takaja, kak pjat' let   nazad!
        Ol'ka, you (are) you know just   such   as   five   years ago!
      Po   etomy slučaju my zabyli   zavesti   budil'nik
      Because-of this   event   we forgot   to-wind-up   (the) alarm clock

The relevant Os are in bold. Neither *posudu* nor *pol* has been mentioned in this section of the tale, but can be regarded as inferable from the frame, which in any case has occurred in an earlier section. First-mentioned NPs, even if inferable, are not typically put in first position, and the constituent order here produces strong highlighting. *Pol* is further highlighted by the particle *daže* and *posudu* is highlighted by being the first major lexical item in a separate clause introduced by *i* (and). The reason for this powerful highlighting is that Dima, the husband, typically does practically nothing to help with the housework, the cooking, or the two children; his setting the table for dinner is a major event but his washing the dishes and sweeping the floor almost count as miracles.

5.9. Conclusion

In this chapter we have examined a range of highlighting devices; devices for introducing new entities, devices for contrastive highlighting, devices for dealing with already-mentioned, given entities. Spontaneous spoken English (Russian, German, etc.) differ from written English (Russian/German, etc.) and have their own delicate system of discourse organization. What is just as interesting is the fact that the same general devices occur across languages. To be sure, discourse particles do not play the same extended role in English as in other languages (judging by the Map Task data) and English has a richer system of cleft constructions than other languages. That apart, three major sets of structures are widespread; highlighting particles, the NP-Clause construction, and the positioning of constituents carrying given information in clause-initial position. These facts point beyond the scope of this book to the possibility of discourse organization being based on very general cognitive principles of foregrounding and backgrounding—making salient and making inconspicuous.

6 Focus Constructions: Clefts and *like*

6.1. Introduction

Following the overview of general highlighting/focusing constructions in Chapter 5, we will examine in some detail two sets of highlighting devices in spoken English. One set consists of the three cleft constructions (outlined in §6.2) and the other consists of two constructions with LIKE. The cleft constructions occur in both spoken and written English but are relatively rare in our data compared with highlighting particles such as LIKE. The IT cleft is exceedingly rare, while WH clefts function simultaneously as micro- and macro-focusers, highlighting a particular constituent and at the same time signalling a boundary in text. (See §5.5 for micro- and macro-focusing.) LIKE is a micro-focusing item but has two different functions. At the end of a clause it signals that the speaker has uttered the clause in order to counter possible objections to a previous statement. In other positions, it functions as a non-contrastive focuser. LIKE is a particularly interesting item because it is generally assumed that it is a mere pause-filler, enabling the speaker to hold the floor while resolving planning difficulties. Our data from the Map Task dialogues does not support the planning-difficulties hypothesis but shows that the occurrence of LIKE has its own patterns.

6.2. An Overview of the Clefts

6.2.1. *Cleft types*

This section deals with the cleft constructions of English as exemplified in a body of task-related dialogues and in a body of spontaneous conversation. The constructions are the IT cleft, the WH cleft, which has often been termed pseudo-cleft, and the REVERSE WH cleft (henceforth RWH), exemplified in (1)–(3) below:

(1) It's that side you should be on (IT cleft)

(2) What you want to do is curve round that wood (WH cleft)

(3) That's what I've done (REVERSE WH cleft)

Following Hedberg (1990), the subject or complement of the copula will be termed the **cleft constituent** (*that side, what you want to do* and *that* in (1)–(3), respectively). The term **cleft clause** will be applied to the quasi-relative clause in IT-clefts, the reduced clause in WH clefts, and the WH clause in the reverse cleft.

6.2.2. *The main points in the analysis*

The main theoretical points emerging from the discussion are as follows.

i Previous accounts of clefts in terms of focus are too narrow but a model of syntactic focus can be developed which accommodates previous observations.

ii There is no reason to abandon the analysis of clefts as constructions which speakers use to treat certain information as given and to present a novel, maximal instantiation of a variable. However, in text these properties of clefts can retreat into the background or be overridden by the macro function of a given cleft in a given text.

iii The concepts of presupposition, specification, and maximality apply to clefts, but are not necessarily central to their focusing function. Rather, the focusing function of clefts is crucially related to thematization and deixis, and not to the givenness of the WH clause. This view contrasts with that of Declerck (1988), which is discussed in § 6.2.7. These three features mean that a cleft such as *It was John who won the race* is to be interpreted as (1) 'someone won the race', (2) 'this someone was John', and (3) 'John and only John won the race'.

iv In IT and reverse clefts the clefted constituent precedes the WH clause. This suggests that the purpose of these clefts is as much to specify the cleft constituent as to specify the variable in the WH clause.

v The macro-textual function of the clefts is governed by the deictic constituent, TH deictic, IT or WH deictic. The TH items in reverse clefts highlight items from the immediately surrounding discourse or situational context, exerting a braking and consolidating effect on the discourse. The WH items in WH clefts are indefinite deictics pointing to some entity or information which is specific for the speaker but unknown to the listener (or is treated as such by the speaker) and which the speaker is about to elucidate. The nature of the WH deictics propels the discourse forward. The pronoun IT is neutral with respect to direction and is the preferred cleft for indicating contrast and for focusing on subjects.

vi Our data confirm Delin's view (Delin 1989) that various stress patterns are possible in clefts and that WH clefts with primary stress on the cleft constituent and an unstressed WH clause (the typical contrastive pattern) are relatively rare. The distribution of the various stress patterns differs in places in our data. We found clefts with either cleft constituent or cleft head, or both, bearing primary stress, with both or neither bearing secondary stress, and with both unstressed. It turns out that what has been thought of as the typical contrastive pattern is not necessarily contrastive.[1]

6.2.3. Distribution of clefts in the data

At this point a brief overview of the data will be helpful. It must be emphasized that clefts are relatively rare in our data, occurring far less frequently than other focusing devices such as the discourse particles SEE and LIKE (J. Miller and Weinert 1995). The difference in frequency of occurrence is at least partly to be explained by the fact that, because of their complex syntax, clefts have a stronger focusing function and make a bigger impact than the less disruptive discourse particles which slip smoothly into the flow of discourse. Another possible reason is that, for instance, WH clefts have specific discourse functions (see §6.2.6.2) which are required less frequently than the general highlighting function associated with LIKE and the function associated with SEE, which is used to highlight entities treated as given but being mentioned for the first time or being reintroduced into the discourse.

IT and WH clefts are particularly rare. RWH clefts are considerably more common than the others, but even in the adult data (including school leavers), they number only 1 per dialogue and $1\frac{1}{2}$ per conversation, which is approximately 1 per 1,000 words. Table 6.1 shows the number and distribution of clefts in the two types of data and across the age groups in the dialogue data. The figures in brackets for the conversation data indicate the number of conversations. The figure for WH clefts is taken from J. Miller (1984). In addition we will comment on a number of interrogative IT clefts. Their function differs from declarative IT clefts and will be discussed in §6.2.7. Although there are quantitative differences between younger and older speakers, no significant differences in the nature of clefts was found. We will use examples mainly from older speakers.

Examples (1)–(3), from the dialogue data, illustrate the type of cleft constituent typically found in the different cleft constructions. In IT clefts we find mainly full NPs and, more rarely, PPs and adverbials. Phrasal and

---

[1] Primary stress will be indicated by capitals (i.e. THAT), and secondary stress by spaced letters (i.e. t h a t). Further details of the syntactic and prosodic structures of clefts will be provided in §§6.2.5–6.2.7 for each cleft type.

266 *Spontaneous Spoken Language*

TABLE 6.1. *Number of clefts in the dialogue and conversation data*

Age in years	Number	IT	WH	RWH
Dialogues				
7/8	40	—	—	4
10/11	40	1	—	18
13/14	40	3	3	33
16/17	10	—	1	11
17–19	20	1	18	20
Conversations				
17–18		20 (70)	31 (100)	73 (50)

clausal complements are the province of WH clefts. RWH cleft constituents are almost entirely deictic—THAT or THIS. In addition, while the RWH clefts are all uttered under one intonation contour, the structure of WH clefts is loose, with pause or pitch markers separating the two parts of the cleft. We will briefly summarize our discussion presented in §3.7.2.

Example (4) shows the headless relative and the BE complement both with a simple form.

(4) A1 ⟨Yeah. W . . . **What you do/**
 B1 Right
 A2 **you drop . . . drop down**, then you go right⟩

Some utterances look at first sight as though they contain incomplete WH clefts, but this analysis can be maintained only for (5) and (6).

(5) A See **what you're** . . .

(6) B So, **what we**—. . . Oh heck, It's quite difficult to explain . . . Right. There's this kind of group of baboons right . . .

These examples look like embryonic WH clefts, but the WH part is itself incomplete, lacking a verb. Example (7) is interesting because the syntax of the BE complement does not mirror the syntax of the headless relative.[2]

(7) A1 ⟨And then across, but there's a swan pond. Do you have/
 B1 No I don't
 A2 that?⟩ OK, well **what you've got to do is moving across to the left, you should be about three inches from the bottom of the page**
 B2 Yeah
 A3 Be—Draw a curve up the way about another inch higher

---

[2] It might be asked if (7) should be classified as a cleft construction at all, but there are good reasons for this analysis. Although (2) and (7) differ in a number of respects, they both contain a headless relative followed by BE followed by the complement of BE. In both, the headless relative has the same discourse function: it focuses on the BE complement.

The cleft constituent, a headless relative, is *what you've got to do* and the complement BE, the cleft clause, is *you should be about three inches from the bottom of the page*. From the maps it is clear that what B has to do is draw a line from right to left. The first segment of the line has to be three inches from the bottom of the page (the accuracy of the estimates is irrelevant for this discussion) and B has to make the line curve up another inch. That is, the WH structure relates not just to the complement of BE but to the instruction of A's next contribution.

Similarly, apart from the 33 integrated IT clefts, i.e. clefts which contain both a cleft head and a WH cleft clause, there are cases which look like the beginning of IT clefts where the cleft head, instead of being followed by a WH clause, stands independently (e.g. *it was me*, with *who didn't own up* omitted, as in (68)).

6.2.4. Theoretical preliminaries

6.2.4.1. Deixis

Deixis was invoked at various points in Chapter 5; in the discussion of clefts, the SEE construction of English and the VOT construction of Russian. Since they are particularly important for an understanding of the various clefts, we present a further discussion of deictics.

Speakers use deictics to pick out entities without describing them. This is possible when the relevant entity is present in the situation of utterance, either physically present or previously mentioned. Personal pronouns such as I, SHE, THEY etc. pick out respectively the speaker, a female entity other than speaker or hearer, and a number of entities other than speaker and hearer. THIS and THAT are definite deictics, used when the speaker treats an entity as near or remote, respectively.[3] RWH clefts such as *That's where you should be* are used by instruction givers in the Map Task to point to locations remote in the sense that the line representing the route has not led to the appropriate location, which has in any case not previously been specified as pertinent. THIS and THAT have a further emphasizing function, from which IT is excluded, partly because they are longer than IT and partly because they are strongly deictic, are often accompanied by pointing gestures (even for metaphorical deixis) and can carry stress. For instance, to emphasize the purchase of a particular book as opposed to other books a speaker can say *I bought THAT/THIS one* but not *I bought IT*.

For convenience, the following information is repeated from §3.7.2.3. WH words are indefinite deictics used for pointing at entities not in the

---

[3] 'Remote' may be 'remote from the speaker and hearer' or just 'remote from the speaker', and likewise for 'near'.

immediate situation of utterance because not yet mentioned. Speakers either ask for a specification of an entity, as in *Who is going to drive the car?*[4] or provide the specification, as in *I tell you what—you drive the car and I'll take the train* or *I remember what he bought for our first anniversary—a beautiful Chinese watercolour*. In the first example, *you drive the car* specifies *what* and in the second example—*a beautiful Chinese watercolour*.[5]

In WH clefts such as *What you're doing is you're going down the side of the allotments* the indefinite deictic *what* points forward to a specification about to be supplied by the instruction giver. That is, the indefinite deictics in the preceding examples are deictically similar to, for instance, the WH clefts that are used in the Map Task dialogues to signal that a section of discussion has reached its limit and that the instruction giver is going to specify the way forward.

IT clefts contain the pronoun IT which is definite but does not involve proximity, unlike THIS and THAT, and is typically unstressed. It lacks the forward-pointing power of WH clefts and the emphasizing and backward-pulling power of the RWH clefts with THAT or THIS. They are perhaps best analysed as unmarked with regard to the direction of the pointing, functioning as neutral attention markers with no referential function of their own.

6.2.4.2. *Thematization*

We touched on the notion of theme in § 5.2.3 but only to say that the theme is the first phrasal constituent in a clause, the element which serves as the point of departure of the message, and that theme constituents often, but not necessarily, convey given information. Theme constituents also enjoy salience merely by virtue of being in first position in the clause. A—perhaps the—crucial property of clefts is that they make possible the thematization of elements which would not be theme in uncleft alternatives. The theme in clefts is (typically) a deictic which points to, or highlights, entities themselves and their relevance. While we will argue that thematization and deixis are central to the analysis of all clefts, they operate in slightly different ways in the three cleft types. They typically interact in RWH clefts, but they can act independently, and the mere fronting (i.e. thematization) of important entities may motivate the choice of a cleft construction.

WH clefts enable the thematization of complex entities through nominalization in the sentence-initial WH clause and always have a deictic WH element as theme. The complex entities are propositions that are made nominal by being expressed as a headless relative: thus, *I don't like the*

---

[4] The rationale behind the use of WH words in interrogatives can be reconstructed as the speaker saying, as it were 'Someone is going to drive the car—specify the person'.

[5] Cf. §3.7.2.3 on the Russian equivalents of the WH pronouns.

Director doing X without consulting with any of his colleagues converts to *What I don't like the Director doing without consulting any of his colleagues is* and the cleft clause assigns a value to X.

A central characteristic of RWH clefts is thematization, or clause initial highlighting, which plays a major role in distinguishing RWH clefts from other clefts. The grammatical form and function of the cleft head frequently determine cleft choice. The 'point of departure', we argue, is central to the use of RWH clefts, together with the motivation to use THAT (and less frequently THIS). The argument that thematization is central to the choice of RWH clefts will now be developed in relation to unclefted and thematized alternatives.

There are several reasons why RWH clefts are effective where unclefted declarative and thematized alternatives and IT and WH clefts do not work. The large majority of RWH clefts have deictic cleft constituents pointing at constituents which would have been in object position in unclefted declaratives: 100% in the dialogue data, 89% in the conversation data and 86% in a sample of 50 clefts in Delin's data, including 34 written clefts. Moreover, a construction other than the RWH cleft is not possible for the typical examples in the Map Task dialogues. One barrier lies in constraints on the use of THAT and THIS, which apply to declaratives, both neutral and with a constituent thematized by fronting. The second is a consequence of the function of thematized sentences in general in combination with prosodic features. We will discuss each reason in turn below. Consider the RWH cleft in (8a), the corresponding neutral declarative construction in (8b), and the construction with fronting in (8c). (Examples from Delin 1989.)

(8) (a) A spanner is what I need
    (b) I need a spanner
    (c) A spanner I need

Where RWH clefts have *that* or *this* as cleft constituent, analogous triples of examples can be found only where the cleft clause contains *what*: thus, *That's what I need*, *I need that* and *That I need*. Where the cleft clause contains another WH item, straightforward examples corresponding to (8b) and (8c) are not to be found: e.g. *That's where I am* but **I am that* and **That I am*, and similarly for RWH clefts with WHEN, WHY, and HOW. The latter items carry information which THAT (and THIS, and indeed IT) cannot carry without extra lexical material. In other words, RWH clefts are required if there is strong motivation to use THAT, either for its special pointing function, or for its precise identification of referents, or for its summarizing function (see § 6.2.5.3). RWH clefts compensate for the limited content of THAT by providing the essential information in the WH cleft clause.

Another difficulty is that with pairs such as (8a) and (8c)—with the same stress pattern—the fronting construction regularly carries a contrastive reading that is absent from the RWH cleft in the same context. This contrastive reading can relate to the predicate, as in (9) or the subject/ cleft constituent, as in (10).

(9) (a) that's what you're trying to aVOID
    (b) that you're trying to aVOID

Example (9a) implies that other things were mentioned which involved other actions, e.g. *this you're trying to hit, that you're trying to avoid*. Alternatively, (9b) implies *this other thing you were not trying to avoid, but this thing you are trying to avoid*.[6]

Consider also (10):

(10) (a) A Well, I've gone round the forest in mine
     (b) B Right ok aye maybe THAT's what it is then
     (c) Right ok THAT it is then

Here again we get a contrastive reading which is not present in the cleft. The cleft relates the event of having gone round the forest to how the route should be drawn. No other alternatives are considered. The thematized version implies *oh THAT it is, rather than all the other things we have considered*.[7]

---

[6] The above constraints are not only restricted to constructions with *that*. Similar factors are involved in the interpretation of constructions with full NPs. Since we are at this point interested in the function of RWH-clefts, and since the majority of these have *that* heads, we restricted our discussion of thematization in English to this aspect. In a case-inflected language like German, objects in sentence-initial position are much more common and readings are neutral. For instance, (9c) does not have the contrastive reading of (9b) and would in fact be the appropriate translation of (9a) in context, rather than a cleft:

(9c) DAS versuchst du zu verMEIden.

We do not have the space to go into detailed discussion of thematization in English and other languages. However, we would like to suggest the possibility of thematization in English having a more specialized function, i.e. leading to certain contrastive readings of the WH-clause VP, whereas in a language like German, sentence-initial objects do not necessarily result in this kind of contrastive reading. Because thematization in English is more rare and specialized, clefts can take on a thematizing function. J. A. Hawkins (1986: 42) also points out that German encodes more pragmatic relations through word order than English, which has more pragmatically ambiguous constructions.

[7] But if *that* is unstressed, then we get a *that's it finished* reading. That this reading is in fact strongly preferred is indicated by the following exchange:

A right that's it
B so you're at the finish no?

This exchange takes place in the middle of the task when there is no real indication that A could have made a mistake and ended up at the finish. B's *no* indicates that he himself considers this unlikely and that he is puzzled. A in fact means *I've done what you've told me to do, let's move on*. It is in fact important not only to consider general factors which seem to affect language use, but also cases where the use of a particular construction can be explained in terms of undesirable side-effects due to conventionalized meanings of certain constructions involving certain lexical items.

We would like to add that thematization of THAT objects in cases where the WHAT of the

Finally consider example (11).

(11) (*a*) that's what I mean
(*b*) that I mean

Here we also get a contrastive reading in (11*b*) which is absent from the cleft, i.e. *I really mean it this time* or *I might not be serious about other things, but this I really mean*.

Although examples (9)–(11) cover only some of the stress patterns found in the data, we can state that, no matter what the stress pattern, the unwanted contrastive reading emerges regularly. In fact only with the pattern in (12) can we expect to regularly find the same contrastive reading in both the cleft and the thematized equivalent.

(12) (*a*) THAT'S what I mean
(*b*) THAT I mean

Here both (12*a*) and (12*b*) can contrast the cleft head with other alternatives.

The above discussion shows that there are strong constraints on the thematization of THAT objects in English. THAT objects need the WH element for specification in all cases except for WHAT. However, even in cases where it is possible to propose thematized alternatives to WHAT RWH clefts, the alternatives carry undesirable contrastive meanings in all cases in our data except where the cleft head is stressed and the WH clause unstressed.

If RWH cleft heads are almost exclusively deictics and direct or indirect objects, it also appears that the use of THAT objects is restricted to RWH clefts. There are no deictic cleft constituents in WH clefts in our or Delin's data. There are no deictic cleft constituents in spoken IT clefts. Even in written language they are rare—only two examples in Delin's data. This distribution further indicates that the deictic in RWH clefts is used as an attention-drawing device and not simply in an anaphoric or specificational function. The deictic loses this attention-drawing force in WH and IT clefts, and indeed in other structures where it is not sentence-initial.[8]

6.2.4.3. *New information and the cleft constituent*

New information, as discussed in §5.2.4, is information that the speaker presents as new. It may be objectively new in the sense that it has not been mentioned in the course of the conversation or has never been heard before

---

cleft WH clause can be omitted does not always result in acceptable sentences in the context in which the original cleft occurred. However, without further naturally occurring data it is impossible to assert that such cases can never occur.

[8] Other copular structures with initial *that* are also used in our data, e.g. *That's me doubling back, that's us finished, that's the finish.*

anywhere by the audience. On the other hand, it may have been mentioned before or have been known to the audience, but the speaker chooses to present it as not recoverable from the linguistic or extra-linguistic context. Delin (1990) suggests that there is no contradiction in assigning new information to the cleft constituent, which is usually regarded as expressing information that is presupposed or taken for granted. In her account speakers assign new information to the cleft constituent in order to signal that the information is to be treated in a certain way.[9] The material in the cleft clause is asserted, while the material in the WH clause is presupposed and needs to be accommodated by the hearer into his discourse model as such. When the presupposed information is new, i.e. when there has not been a context created in the previous discourse for the presupposition contained in the cleft, hearers have to create one. From there they then move on to the instantiation of the presupposed variable.

Conversely, speakers can present new information as given, as in (13), from Prince (1978: 894).

(13) I've been bit once already by a German shepherd. It was really scary. *It was an outside meter the woman had.* I was reading the gas meter and was walking back out . . .

(13) is not susceptible to explanation in terms of the cleft constituent being anaphoric and the information carried by it being subordinate to the identifying cleft clause (Huddleston 1984), nor in terms of the information being indisputable fact (Prince 1978), nor in terms of the cleft constituent being contrastively emphatic. The most satisfactory current explanation is Hedberg's notion of activation: clefts activate particular entities out of a set of potential participants (animate and inanimate) in a situation. The

---

[9] Delin (1990) suggests a slightly different view of focus in clefts, proposing that focus rests on the *novel* instantiation of the variable in the presupposition. The novel instantiation criterion is best discussed in relation to information structures and the principle of informativeness. As observed by Delin, clefts can contain either old or new information in both the cleft clause and the WH clause, or they can contain old information in both. The novel instantiation criterion is met automatically by any new/old combination. It is needed to account for the informativeness of clefts which contain only old information as in the following example given by Delin (1990: 21).

I know someone won the race, and I saw John a moment ago, but I
didn't know it was John who won the race.

We suggest that this effect derives from the way the principle of informativeness interacts with copular structures in general and which accounts for the informativeness of the following example:

I knew you had a brother and I've known John for a while, but I didn't
know that John was your brother

We suggest that the novel instantiation criterion is a necessary precondition for the construction of informative clefts, rather than a main aspect of their function in discourse.

activation may be direct in the sense that the participant is overtly present or given, or indirect, in the sense that the participant has to be inferred (Hedberg 1990: 149–73). It is also true, as Declerck (1988: 227) states, that the speaker of (13) stresses a relevant point, since if the meter had been inside, the woman could have saved him from the dog. New information in the WH clause makes such clefts predicational in the sense that the whole uncleft subject-predicate structure *the woman had an outside meter* is focused on by means of the cleft structure, with *an outside meter* being more crucial than the WH clause. However, as stated in point (iii) in §6.2.2, the focusing effect is brought about by thematization and deixis and not by the givenness of the WH clause.

Example (13) demonstrates that where the WH clause carries new information, the specificational aspect of clefts can become considerably weakened. IT and RWH clefts become more predicational—that is, serve more to assign a property to an entity rather than to identify that entity. In contrast, WH clefts become topic-introducing, as in (14).

(14) My dear friends, **what we have always wanted to know, but what the government has never wanted to tell us, is what exactly happens at secret conferences like the one you have been reading about in the papers this week**. There is one man, however, who has been present at such conferences himself and who is willing to break the silence. His name is Robert Fox, and he is the man that we have invited as guest speaker for tonight.

As Delin puts it, the hearer does indeed have to create a context for the variable in the presupposition along the lines of *there is something we have always wanted to know*, etc. But this is not so much because this variable is then specified, but rather because creating it is an end in itself. Presenting it in a nominalized form allows it to be the starting point, whence its topic-introducing function. The topic is elaborated in the following discourse. The topic-introducing function of the WH clause in (14) is exactly the property that is adapted in the macro discourse function of WH clefts in the Map Task dialogues; summing up a stretch of discussion and pointing forward to a fresh and important instruction concerning where the route is to be drawn on the map.

6.2.4.4. *Maximality*

The third feature associated with clefts, the exclusiveness/exhaustiveness/ maximality component (cf. (ii) in §6.2.2) also derives from the WH clause. According to Delin the maximality condition 'stipulates that . . . the element in the head of the cleft . . . must be the totality of objects currently in the discourse capable of satisfying the description contained in the predicate (of the wh-clause)' (Delin 1990: 19). This means that in a cleft such as *It was John who came to the talk* (Delin's example), it must be the case that John and only John came to the talk (Delin 1990: 19). Halliday (1985) makes a similar point. We agree with the interpretation of this example, although there are many cases where maximality is trivially present. Such is the case with the specifications of location in time and space in examples (15) and (16) respectively, which can only be unique:

(15) That's where the finish is

(16) That's when it finishes off for me

The element of maximality, like the presuppositional element, derives from the specificity of the WH element,[10] a point also made by Huddleston (1984: 466). Maximality is a feature of specificational sentences in general. Chafe (1976) distinguishes between overt and covert contrast in clefts. We suggest that the maximality component is what makes all clefts, and indeed all specificational sentences, at least covertly contrastive, a point also made by Declerck (1988: 226). This description captures the contribution of maximality to cleft function more adequately than the view that a cleft is used appropriately only if it refers to the only entity specifying the presupposed variable. The idea that contrastiveness is essentially covert is important, because it turns maximality into a background feature rather than a main aspect of cleft function. It will be made clear by the discussion of RWH clefts in §6.2.5 and WH clefts in §6.2.6 that their main function is to slow the discourse in order to emphasize a particular point or to propel the discourse forward, and maximality becomes almost irrelevant.

6.2.5. *RWH clefts*

In this section we will discuss the syntactic and prosodic properties of RWH clefts and their relationship to the discourse function of RWH clefts. We will argue that the use of RWH clefts derives from the motivation to use deictic THAT in its pointing/attention drawing function and to thematize it. We will consider alternative structures such as unclefted and thematized sentences, as well as the other two cleft types. Finally, we will briefly relate the use of RWH clefts in spoken discourse to their use in written language.

6.2.5.1. *Range of cleft heads and WH elements*

The range of RWH clefts in the data as a whole is strikingly narrow. In particular, we found a very narrow range of cleft heads. There are 2 instances of a full NP, 4 instances of IT, and 4 instances of deictic THIS. The vast majority of clefts—149—have deictic THAT as their head.

We believe that the high frequency of THAT heads compared with full

---

[10] 'Specificity' in the sense that the WH item points to an entity that is specific for the speaker and which is about to be made specific for the hearer.

NP heads and pronouns is not an effect of the task, since it has also been reported for other text types by Delin (1989) and Hedberg (1988). The difference between THAT and THIS frequencies, on the other hand, is likely to be related at least partially to differences in their meaning. The important point is the overall frequency of deictic cleft heads and its implication for the analysis of the function of RWH clefts.

The range of WH elements is ALSO narrow at all levels in the data. WHERE, WHAT, WHEN, WHY, and HOW all feature, but WHAT and WHERE are by far the most common. The percentages for WHAT and WHERE are roughly reversed in the two sets of data—67.5% and 22.5%, respectively in the conversational data, 25% and 70%, respectively in the dialogue data. This difference is largely an effect of the nature of the map task which requires speakers to make frequent reference to locations/ directions. WHAT is the most frequent WH element in all text types investigated by Delin (1989).

6.2.5.2. Intonation

In Table 6.2, + and − refer to the presence or absence of primary stress, = to the presence of secondary stress. Throughout the following discussion we will represent primary stress with capitals (i.e. THAT), and secondary stress with spaced letters (i.e. t h a t). By stress we understand a movement in pitch. Primary stress involves higher pitch than secondary stress. The latter can involve a constant pitch or falling intonation, with the highest pitch point being higher than the rest of the clause but lower than the primary stress. We analysed the RWH clefts in all the dialogues and in 20 conversations. Examples of the various stress patterns from the data are given below.

TABLE 6.2. *Distribution of stress patterns in RWH clefts*[a]

Head	WH clause	10 year olds (40)	13 year olds (40)	18 year olds (20) dialogues	conversations	Total
+	+	5	7	8	6	26
+	−	1	3	2	1	7
−	+	0	1	2	3	6
+	=	5	15	6	2	28
=	+	4	4	2	8	18
						85

[a] The data from the 14 year olds contains 4 examples with more complex stress patterns. We have excluded these from our analysis. They do not pose any serious problems for our overall analysis.

THAT must be where the BAY is
THAT's how you go
that's what i MEAN
THAT'S where you finish
that's where you SHOULD have been

Unstressed cleft heads are rare. But clefts where only the head is stressed, i.e. what has often been thought the typical contrastive cleft, are also rare. Analysis of these clefts in context also reveals that they are not necessarily explicitly contrastive. The large majority of RWH clefts have a stressed element in both the cleft head and the WH clause. In the dialogue data the preferred pattern is to have the primary stress in the cleft clause, but in the conversation data the primary stress is preferred in the WH clause. This is consistent with Delin's conversation data, where pattern 3 is the most common. This difference is likely to be task related. The map task requires the precise identification of referents whereas this is not so crucial in casual conversation where there are no specific goals. It may be that in conversation there is more opportunity for using the THAT BE sequence to focus on the content of the WH clause (see (22) below).

The analysis of prosody in RWH clefts shows a wide variety of stress patterns. Prosody and information structure interact in complex ways and it is not possible to associate a particular stress pattern with only one function. Further analysis of which elements in the WH clause are stressed is necessary, which is beyond the scope of this chapter. However, this basic analysis does reveal the important fact that in the large majority of cases both the cleft clause and particularly the WH clause, which has been associated with given or subordinate information, carry important and/or new information.

6.2.5.3. *The discourse function of RWH clefts*

The following example illustrates many of the aspects which are relevant to the analysis of RWH clefts, especially the role of different deictics. It was overheard on a bus travelling at moderate speed past a park. A mother speaks to her child, after a period of silence, while pointing in the direction of the park:

(17) THIS is where ANdrew works in THEre

Previous analyses of clefts in terms of the three characteristics discussed in (iii) in §6.2.2 and §6.2.4.3 would consider (17) in the following way: (17) can be said to presuppose *Andrew works somewhere* and this *somewhere* is identified by the cleft head *this*. There has been no previous discussion of Andrew and his work, which is also indicated by the intonation. The presupposition is likely to be inferable, since the child may well know that

Andrew works somewhere, or even that people have jobs. The givenness status associated with WH clauses may therefore help the child to recover this information. In Huddleston's terms, *where ANdrew works* would be considered subordinate to the cleft head *this*, which is thus in focus.

While we also consider the focus of the utterance to be *this*, our analysis of (17) differs from the above. Specification of the variable in the WH clause is not the central issue. Rather, the sight of the park triggers a connection with *Andrew's work*. The point of the utterance is to say something about the referent of *this*, i.e. the park. Why did the speaker choose the RWH cleft with that particular order? She could have said *Where Andrew works is in here* or simply *Andrew works in here*. A reasonable assumption is that the speaker wanted first to pinpoint the park for the child, given that the bus was moving and would soon have left the park behind. *THIS* and the pointing gesture accompanying the utterance achieve that goal. With this beginning, the speaker then has no choice but to continue with a copulative structure or to change the construction completely.

Although *this* is a deictic whose use signals that the speaker treats its referent as given, the hearer might in fact have difficulty picking out the referent, especially as the hearer is a small child. The mother adds *in THEre* to help the child. Note the contrast in the deictics: *this* is proximate but *there* is remote. *This* is to be explained with reference to the movement of the bus, picking out the place that mother and child have reached as opposed to the places, now remote, which the bus has travelled past or through. Having fixed the present location of the bus, the mother wishes to pinpoint the park as opposed to the actual stretch of road or the adjoining pavement. As the park is separated from the bus by road, pavement, and railings, she treats it as remote, hence the use of *there*. The use of the deictic followed by elaboration to ensure identification of the referent indicates the primary importance of the attention-marking function of these deictics.[11]

The deictic nature of RWH cleft heads is central to their function. It is illustrated particularly well in our example where physical movement calls for action. However, the motivation to point to things also transfers to other RWH clefts which try to hold on to important items in the flow of discourse. We will discuss the motivation to use deictics and to thematize them throughout the following discussion.

The use of THAT in RWH clefts creates a strong link with the preceding discourse. RWH clefts regularly gather up previous discourse, clarify the

---

[11] In *The Pickwick Papers* Dickens recounts Mr Pickwick's adventure during a shooting expedition. The shooting party have a large lunch, Mr Pickwick falls asleep and the others leave him sleeping in a wheelbarrow, intending to come back and collect him later. This plan was thwarted, and Dickens finishes the paragraph with the sentence *And this is what happened*, in which *this* points forward to the next paragraphs recounting Mr Pickwick's misadventure.

present state of affairs and provide a starting point for a following piece of discourse, which often starts with an elaboration of the referent of THAT, as in (17) above. Examples (18–20) are typical of RWH cleft use in our data.

(18) A1 So can you not go round the picket fence and round the old mill? Can you . . . Do you not have to go round the picket fence, no?
B1 I don't think so **THAT'S what we did FIRST of all**

In (18) *that* refers back to part of A1, i.e. *go round the picket fence*.

(19) A1 Follow that bit up vertically, right, till it stops going/vertically.
B1 Uhuh
A2 **THAT'S what I mean**

In (19) *that* refers to the whole of the previous utterance A1 which is a clarification of A's previous instructions which caused B some difficulty. Here we have then a series of instructions which is summarized in A1 in order to clarify it. It is then further summarized in the cleft by *that*, helping B to focus on what A means.

(20) A1 I've got a great viewpoint away up in the top left hand corner
B1 Yeah, **that's what I thought you were TALKING about**
A2 No . . .

In (20) *that* refers to an antecedent nominal—*great viewpoint*—in A's preceding utterance. This follows a lengthy exchange of 13 turns during which A and B talk about two different *points* without immediately realizing this. With the cleft in B1 B explicitly indicates for the first time that there is a problem. A2 then confirms that there is in fact a mismatch and proceeds to explain what she does mean.

In (21) A and B are talking about changes which have taken place in Edinburgh since B was young (*ones* in A1 refers to *changes*).

(21) A1 Which ones do you regret?
B1 Well I regret
A2 Most of them
B3 I regret putting the people out of the south side and central Edinburgh you know i do think especially after the war you know after the war when they started redevelopment and well the authorities more or less made it that everybody was to go outside you know gardens and houses but I would reckon that eighty percent of the people didnae want to go out of the town they didnae want the gardens eh they were quite happy where they were if they'd built houses in the town which they're doing now after aboot thirty years too late so to speak you know **that's what I regret** especially central south Edinburgh uh I would reckon that with takin the people out they've lost the community no community spirit at all I don't think that they've the same spirit in the new housing schemes as you had in the old type of dwellings.

In (21) the cleft serves to clarify what the point of B's contribution is, i.e. to specify what it is he regrets about the changes to housing in Edinburgh. In Hedberg's terms (1988), the RWH cleft reasserts the topic which is first introduced in A1 and repeated in B1 and at the start of B3. The RWH cleft is then followed by further elaboration of the topic.

What is important in all of these examples is the strong anaphoric and attention-marking function of the clefts, due to the pointing function of THAT in initial position. We are dealing here with 'on-the-hoof' spoken discourse where there is a need for the speaker to identify what is crucial to his concerns at a given moment, which is the referent of THAT. In the Map Task data THAT RWH clefts frequently follow a series of turns involving negotiations through a difficulty which can be due to problems with instructions or in establishing a referent. The THAT cleft calls a halt to an exchange which seems to be getting nowhere and by focusing on and resolving the referent of THAT helps to sort things out or to establish a new starting point for further negotiation. In other words THAT RWH clefts signal a need to 'stop and reconsider'. In the conversation data this function is not quite so prominent, but there is usually an equal need to hold on to part of the previous discourse, draw attention to it and specify its import. THAT in cleft-initial position can refer to a variety of constituents such as NPs and PPs, but also larger phrasal and clausal units and discourse chunks, and it can extract and summarize propositions. The use of THAT allows the wrapping up of much lexical material into a small package (which may or may not be unpackaged again after the cleft). Many of the above types of reference are only possible in RWH clefts. For instance, the summarizing function of *that* is illustrated by (21) above, where an unclefted alternative to the cleft in B3 would have to be something like *I regret all of that/all those things (which I have just mentioned)* etc. We will return to this point shortly.

To summarize our initial observations, with THAT the speaker indicates his need to focus on a particular referent. Its pointing function seizes the attention, causing the hearer to look for a referent. Referent resolution is at least in part made possible through the WH clause of the cleft. The RWH cleft construction allows the speaker to use THAT as a focusing device in clause-initial position. Here it is particularly useful in a summarizing or extracting function which is not always possible in other sentence types and sentence positions.[12]

---

[12] RWH clefts are less frequent in written language. Delin (1989) records 38 RHW clefts in the entire LOB corpus (1 million words), compared with 159 RWH clefts in the dialogue and conversation data (150,000 words). This could be due to the fact that written discourse is not ephemeral and does not require as many attention markers for important items. 29 out of Delin's 38 RWH clefts have deictic clause constituents: 13 occurrences of THAT and 16 of THIS. The frequency of THIS, which is infrequent in speech, may be connected with its forward-pointing role, a role performed by WH clefts in our data (cf. §6.2.6.2). About 25% of written RWH clefts have a full NP cleft constituent.

Therefore, to restate our earlier claim, if there is a strong motivation for the use of THAT in a prominent position, the choice of possible constructions is limited and the use of an RWH cleft is often the only option. The specificational aspect of the copula + WH clause structure is in all cases in our data preferable to the contrastive reading of thematized alternatives and in any case retreats into the background. Instead RWH clefts function as attention markers and thematize THAT objects, thereby focusing on an entity which is important at a particular point in the discourse. While RWH clefts do not need to contain deictic heads, we believe that it is significant that the large majority do, across a variety of spoken and written tasks. Even in cases where the cleft head is a NP, RWH clefts are primarily thematizing, given the distribution of object heads and the constraints on thematization in English. In cases where the WH clause carries entirely new information the RWH cleft focuses on the event in the WH clause while at the same time maintaining a link with the preceding discourse, as illustrated by (22).

(22) A1 what about the other ones what are they all doing
 B1 well Alan Richardson wanted to be an officer with a commission in the RAF but they didnae accept him and that put his nose out o joint so **THAT'S when he discovered he had to have a unive rsity qualifiCAtion to do it** so he applied for all the universities and he got rejected by all of them except Surrey

What is important here is not the specification of the exact time of Alan's discovery of X, but the fact that something important happened at the time of *that's when*, i.e. his discovery of X. The hearer has to pay attention to both the WH clause and to the fact that it is related to the preceding discourse.

6.2.5.4. Clefts, fronting, and deixis in German

German RWH clefts are similar in structure to English RWH clefts, as exemplified in (23) and (24).

(23) das ist genau was ich meine
 that is exactly what I mean

(24) das ist das was ich immer sage
 that is that which I always say

(24) differs from English in having, not a free relative clause, but the deictic pronoun *das* modified by a *was* relative clause. This structure is parallel to the *ce que* structure of French mentioned in §5.7.8.2.1. The structural parallels are not accompanied by functional parallels. In particular, the German and English RWH clefts are partly similar in discourse functions but are separated by a major difference, since one important function of

RWH clefts in the English Map Task dialogues is fulfilled by the German fronting construction.

Fronting in English is a construction in which an NP that is not normally in clause-initial position is moved to the front of the clause, as in (25).

(25) This book I really don't like

According to Givón (1990: 705–6), the fronted constituent carries weaker stress than the highlighted constituent in IT and WH clefts, and fronting occurs when the speaker breaks normative expectations; that is, expectations created by listing members of a group who might be expected to receive similar treatment. The example given by Givón is reproduced in (26) (see also our analysis in 6.2.4.2).

(26) She has two brothers, Tom and Jerry. She likes Tom a lot—Jerry she can't stand

Typically the fronted constituent is a direct object. Such fronting occurs regularly in spoken German as in (27), though other constituents can also be fronted.

(27) den   hab   ich auch
     it (DEM) have I   too

The German construction displays subject-verb inversion—the neutral construction without fronting is *ich hab den auch*. The fronted constituent is typically given but, unlike in English fronting, it is not contrasted.

In previous sections we claimed that reverse WH clefts in English have a thematizing function due to restrictions on fronting in English, particularly in relation to deictics.[13] Fronting is very common in our spoken German data and, as suggested earlier, frequently functions like RWH clefts in English. The German RWH clefts themselves actually have a more powerful highlighting effect than English RWH clefts. While there is no space to explore German word order, it must be pointed out that the pragmatic versatility of the English cleft constructions is compensated for by the more flexible word order of German, which encodes a large range of pragmatic relations (as discussed in J. A. Hawkins 1986: 42). For present purposes, we focus on the clefts and will be suggesting that RWH (and WH) clefts in German have more specialized functions than they have in English, where fronting has a more specialized function than in German.

6.2.5.4.1. *Fronted deictic DA*

German has a range of deictics which may be fronted where English has to rely

---

[13] Kirkwood (1969: 96/97) anticipates our exploration of the parallels between German fronting and English RWH clefts in his discussion of the communicative value of word order in the two languages.

on THAT + WH element: DESHALB/DARUM/DESWEGEN (That's why), SO (That's how), plus others which require a variety of English constructions (DA + Preposition: DAMIT, DAVON, DAFÜR, DARÜBER, etc.). German also allows fronting of deictic DAS which was shown to be problematic in English, and has DA. While fronting in German does not always carry the same discourse function as English RWH clefts, the overlap often arises very clearly out of the discourse context. This applies particularly in relation to locations, which naturally feature prominently in the Map Task data: 70% of RWH clefts in the English Map Task data involve WHERE (*c.*1 per dialogue). There are 112 instances of DA as theme in the German Map Task data, excluding combinations of DA with a preposition (8 per dialogue). They are used for four main functions:

i DA SEIN X constructions (the existential/locative distinction is blurred in this data) (32 examples)

ii DA + existential-possessive constructions (17 examples)

iii Fronted DA (32 examples)

iv Fronted DA equivalent to RWH function (31 examples)[14]

Example (28) combines an existential/locative function, DA being a clear reference to a location mentioned by A.

(28) A und jetzt gehst du nochmal drei zentimeter nach unten
        and now go you again three centimetres to below (down)
     B ja **da ist bei mir**   **ein toter Baum**
        yes there is at me (here/on my map) a dead tree

In (29) DA refers back to the location reference in A3 (*Palme*), locating the *Brunnen* of the existential-possessive.

(29) A1 also erstmal beschreiben Startpunkt oben linke Ecke
        right first describe starting-point top left corner
     B1 ja
        yes
     A2 also nich ganz linke Ecke aber/
        that is not completely left corner but
     B2 mhm
     A3 dann folgt eine Palme
        then follows a palm
     B3 nein **da hab ich noch** n brunnen davor
        no there have I in-addition a well there-before

---

[14] We found 34 candidates overall for fronted DA and DAS with RWH cleft function—*c.*1 per 1,000 words, which is the proportion of RWH clefts in the English Map Task data.

In (30) DA refers to *die Steine*. This is followed by a new direction. This fronting construction therefore follows the typical given new flow of information without special focus, but with DA nevertheless clearly pinpointing the important location.

(30) A1 aehm und dann haben wir unter den Bergen die Steine eingezeichnet
ehm and then have we under the mountains the stones drawn
B1 ja
yes
A2 genau und **da gehste jetzt waagerecht aehm links um**
exactly and there go-you now horizontally ehm left around
die nee rechts um die Steine herum
the no right around the stones around

In (31) A6 follows a long explanation where A describes the location of B's missing feature. The final utterance wraps these explanations up with DA in a way similar to RWH clefts. RWH clefts also typically occur at the end of difficult negotiations. In (32) the English native speakers are negotiating a similar problem.

(31) A1 und du hast also rechts keinen Aussichtspunkt mehr
and you have therefore on-the-right no view-point more (no other)
B1 nee
no
A2 weil ich hab nämlich noch einen Aussichtspunkt und zwar
cause I have you-see another view-point Focus Part.
ist der direkt unter der Ostsee
is that directly under the eastlake
B2 ja
yes
A3 und zwar aeh nicht unter dem aehm rechten unterem Zipfel
Focus Part. eh not under the ehm right bottom corner
der Ostsee sondern/
of-the eastlake but
B3 ja
yes
A4 unter dem leicht diagonal höheren
under the slightly diagonally higher-up-one
B4 mhm
A5 oder drunter
or below
B5 ja so ungefähr
yes so roughly
A6 ja **da ist ungefähr der Aussichtspunkt**
yes there is roughly the view-point
'that's where the view point is'

284 *Spontaneous Spoken Language*

(32) A1 right they've obviously not marked the graveyard
 B1 how far to the right of the diamond mine is it
 A2 the graveyard is almost halfway in between do you have carved stones
 B2 I have carved stones at the top followed by a ravine followed by Indian country
 A3 right in between the diamond mine and the carved stones is a graveyard **that's where it should be**

It is not always possible to decide whether German fronting has the same function as RWH clefts in English. Sometimes DA in RWH equivalents receives a considerably higher pitch than in other fronting clauses, but this is not always the case. However, there are no RWH clefts in the German Map Task data and some discourse contexts where fronting occurs are very similar to those where RWH clefts are used in English. For instance, at the end point of the Map Task English speakers use RWH clefts such as *That's where the finish is*. German has fronting equivalents, as in (33).

(33) (*a*) da   ist das Ende
     there is   the finish
 (*b*) da   endest   dann
     there finish-you then
 (*c*) da   ist der Schluß
     there is   the finish
 (*d*) da   ist es   fertig
     there it   is   finished

6.2.5.4.2. *Fronted NPs and pronouns*

Altogether the German Map Task data offers 121 examples with fronted noun phrases. Of these, 59 are full noun phrases and 62 are pronouns—all the pronouns are demonstrative. The fronted NPs occur in three types of construction: existential possessive, locative, and instruction/direction. Examples are given in (34).

(34) (*a*) die Palme hab ich
     the palm   have I
 (*b*) den Zaun   hab ich südost
     the fence   have I   southeast
 (*c*) den Bergsee   passierst du   wieder in Form einer Schleife
     the mountain-lake   pass   you   again in form of-a bow

In almost all cases, particularly existential possessive, English would have SVO order—*I've god the palm, I've got the fence to the southeast*, and *you pass the mountain lake making the shape of a bow*. Fronting relates to the conventions governing the packaging of old and new information packaging, as discussed in § 5.4.4 on Vallduví (1993). Almost all the fronted NPs are definite and given. Indefinite NPs typically occur with SVO order as opposed to the OVS order created by fronting. However, fronting is not confined to the signalling of old information but can interact with stress and deixis to create focus.

6.2.5.4.3. *Fronted deictic DAS*
In the Map Task data there are 12 cases of fronted DAS used in a summarizing function, i.e. referring to clauses or larger stretches of discourse, not to NPs, which is the typical use of THAT in English RWH clefts. Three of these would be RWH clefts in English. Examples (35)–(36) are examples of fronting and fronting equivalent to an RWH cleft.

```
(35) A1 ich    hab   auch  noch        die   hab  ich  auch
          I      have  also  in-addition that  have I    too
          aber ich  habe  noch       den Westsee
          but   I    have  in-addition the westlake
          und zwar        ist der  links von der Ruine direkt   unter der Burg
          FOCUS Part.     is that left   of   the ruin  directly under the castle
          und zwar        kannst du   dir         vorstellen das obere
          FOCUS Part.     can    you  (reflexive) imagine    the top
          aeh die obere Grenze meines Westsees
          eh  the top    border of-my westlake
     B1 mhm
     A2 ist an der unteren Grenze der     Schrift Ruine
          is  at the  bottom  border of the writing ruin
     B2 o  Gott nee nee du  **das hab  ich noch  nicht ganz**
          oh God  no  no  you that have I   yet   not   completely

(36) A1 ja  wunderbar wundervoll so   und jetzt gehst du  nach    links
          yes wonderful wonderful  right and now  go    you towards left
          und zwar          bis   die/
          FOCUS Part.       until the
     B1 ach so        ich mach  den  ich schließe den  Kreis nicht ja
          ah so (I see)  I   make  it    I   close    the  circle not  yes
     A2 nein
          no
     B2 ach so
          I see
     A3 nein nein ach so
          no   no   I see
     B3 ja  **das dachte  ich**
          yes that thought I (that's what I thought)
          ich hatte  jetzt verstanden ich müßte   den Kreis/
          I   had    now   understood  I   had-to the circle
     A4 nee nee
          no  no
     B4 den Kreis schließen
          the circle close
```

A5 nee nee
   no no

While we have not quantified the DSK data, there are also cases of RWH cleft equivalent fronted DAS constructions, e.g. (37).

(37) A1 ja ja das ist also   das Ganze   ist
        yes yes that is Particle the whole(thing) is
     B1 delikate Angelegenheit
        delicate matter
     A2 angrenzend an Kinderei
        bordering on childishness
     B2 ja und **genau das wollte ich ihm nicht sagen**
        yes and exactly that wanted I   him not   to-tell
        'that's what I didn't want to tell him'

        um   ihn nicht zu kränken
        in-order him not   to hurt

6.2.5.4.4. *Deictic SO*

Another German alternative to the RWH cleft structure is the thematization of SO, which is used where English might use an RWH cleft *that's how*.(**das ist wie* . . .), e.g. (38).

(38) A1 und aehm diese diese kleine runde   unterhalb der fliegenden
        and ehm this this small round-thing below   the flying
        untertassen
        saucers
        sieht fast so aus   wie das runde maul von dem was
        looks almost so (like) sep. prefix like the round mouth of that which
        eben   der
        MODAL Part.   the
        Walfisch hat ja   so'n   riesen
        whale   has MODAL Part.   (so) like-a giant
     B1 mhm
     A2 große Oberhälfte und dann so'n   sehr langgezogenes rundes Maul
        large top-half   and then like a very long-stretched round mouth
     B2 ja
        yes
     A3 mit so'ner kleinen Unterlippe
        with like a small   lower-lip
     B3 mm
     A4 und und **so ungefähr sieht sieht der bogen aus**
        and and so roughly   looks looks the curve like
        'that's roughly what the curve looks like'

SO is also used in a forward pointing focus function as in (39)–(40), like

THIS in RWH clefts in English—see n. 11. The copula construction occurs either on its own or is followed by a *daß*-complement clause.

(39) A im   Prinzip   **ist das so**
       in   principle   is   that so (like this)
       daß   die daß die aeh daß man   Einführungen (B: mhm) aeh und
       that the that the aeh that one   introductions   and
       Proseminar   nicht im   gleichen Semester machen sollte
       introductory-seminar   not   in the   same   semester do   should

(40) A **und nun ist es so**
       and   now   it   is   so (like this)
       'and this is what happens'
       ein eckenaufbau aus   diesem material
       a   corner-repair from   this   material
       der hält leider   nie   sehr lange
       that lasts unfortunately   never very long
       warum
       why
       weil   wir kein material haben
       because   we   no   material have
       das   dieser beanspruchung auf der ecke (B: ja) standhält
       which   this   stress   on   the corner   withstands

6.2.5.5. *German RWH clefts*

German does make use of DAS RWH clefts, but there are more structural and functional restrictions. For instance, the equivalents of the common English *that's why* and *that's how* are not acceptable—*das ist wie (that's how), **das ist wann/als* (that's when); ?*das ist warum* (that's why). The usual German equivalent of the latter is *darum/deshalb/deswegen* (all = therefore); when a stronger highlighting is required, *das ist der Grund warum* (that is the reason why) is used instead. The DAS RWH clefts are much rarer than in English (1–1½ per 1,000 words in English; 1 per 30,000 words in German) and create an even stronger focus.

Dyhr (1978) established frequencies for a subset of the FK corpus, a different subset from our subset. His count is of pseudo-clefts which appears to refer to what we call WH clefts and also includes other WH elements and constructions with DER-DIE-(JENIGE). The count does not appear to include what we call RWH clefts. Despite these slight differences, the overall frequencies are very similar, suggesting a combined frequency of WH and RWH clefts of approximately 1 per 10,000 words. RWH clefts are heavily stressed on the deictic and often other constituents. They frequently combine with lexical items which complement the extra focus, i.e. GENAU (exactly), IMMER (always), and modal particles indicating speakers' emotional involvement. Because such clefts are rare, they are difficult to

288 *Spontaneous Spoken Language*

collect. The examples in (41) were collected informally from family members and friends in informal conversation.

(41) (a) das ist genau   was ich meine
        that is exactly   what I   mean
    (b) und das ist das was   ich meine
        and that is that which I   mean
    (c) und das ist das was   ich immer sage
        and that is that which I always say
    (d) das ist doch   genau was ich auch sage
        that is MODAL Part. exactly what I   also say

These clefts occur in emotionally charged contexts where the referent of DAS is very important to the speaker. They indicate 'the crux of the matter'.

Further examples come from the Dialogstrukturenkorpus and the Freilburger Korpus. In the DSK there are no cases of clefts with *wo* (where) and only one instance each of *womit* (where-with) and *worauf* (where-on). We will focus on clefts with *was* (what), since *what* was observed to be the most common WH element in our English conversation data and also in Delin (1989). There are only 8 cases in the entire DSK corpus and only 4 in a subset of the FK corpus (*c.*200,000 words—henceforth FKY).

Example (42) comes from a conversation about sociolinguistics which involves discussion of various theories. Despite the fact that this is an academic topic, the speaker is clearly emotionally involved, indicated not only by his use of language, but also accompanying gestures such as banging on the table. There is a lengthy discussion of the inadequacies of certain theories and the speaker's impatience with overgeneral concepts. He then moves on to his opinion about what type of investigation he advocates.

(42) A1 wichtig   is aeh vor   allen dingen daß wir dann nicht
        important is eh above all things   that we then not
        so ganz   allgemein zum beispiel über sozialisation
        so rather generally for example about socialization
    B1 ja
       yes
    A1 sprechen
       speak
    B2 mhm
    A2 sondern sagen konkret   **was ist das**
       but   say   concretely what is that
    B3 ja aeh
    A2 **was hier an   sprachlichem material**
       which here by-way-of linguistic   material
    B4 jaja

```
A2  vorliegt
    exists
B5  jaja
A3  und  das  ist  ja              das  was    uns  eigentlich
    and that is   MODAL Part.      that which  us   really
B6  mhm ja
A3  interessiert ne
    interests   (tag)
```

This extract consists of three units in which the speaker formulates his opinion as to what constitutes a worthwhile object of sociolinguistic enquiry. A1 spells out what it is not. A2 and A3 spell out what it is by means of two clefts, the first a question which establishes the sociolinguistic question, i.e. the concrete linguistic analysis. The second is a statement which confirms that this question is indeed the desired object of enquiry. This suggestion is taken up by B for 5 turns and then taken up again by A. In one of these turns A talks about 'konrete Ansätze' (concrete approaches) which is followed by the table banging, underlining the importance he attaches to his earlier suggestion expressed in the example above.

The extra focus achieved by RWH clefts in German is not necessarily the result of emotional involvement. In the following examples everything we have said about the function of RWH clefts in English applies: the clefts refer back to the previous discourse, summarize it, and form the basis for moving on. However, the effect is heightened in German RWH clefts. The following example (43) is taken from a picture task. Each speaker has two pictures from a set of four which forms a story. Together they have to establish the correct sequence.

```
(43) Ja  das  ist  das  was    ich  sehe  was   siehst du
     yes that is   that which  I    see   what  see    you
```

This cleft, the only one in the dialogue, follows 16 turns by speaker A and 15 turns by speaker B where A describes the two pictures and B responds only by confirming comprehension (mhm, ja, aha, etc.). It summarizes A's macro-turn, brings it to a close and is used as a basis for handing over to B. It is then followed by B's description and after a few turns by negotiation between the speakers as they try to establish the correct sequence. This use is similar to (21) in the English data.

In (44), which is taken from the same conversation as (42), the cleft highlights the relationship between recent trends in linguistic theory and earlier approaches. It follows a long discussion of the difficulties in specifying social variables. The speaker is speaker B of (42).

(44) das ist ja   eben   genau das wieder was   für Bernstein
     that is MODAL Part. MODAL Part. exactly that again   which for Bernstein
     n problem war
     a problem was
     halt   diese verschiedenen aspekte linguistik und Soziologie
     MODAL Part.   these different   aspects linguistics and sociology
     und psychologie da   so reinzukriegen   ne
     and psychology there so to-get-into (integrate) (tag)

Finally, (45) illustrates the different uses of fronting clauses and RWH clefts where English would, in the light of our data, use RWH clefts in both cases. The topic is the controversial building of a new nuclear power station in Germany which is being discussed at length. At one point in the conversation one of the speakers raises the subject of the possibility of a nuclear power station being built in France very near the proposed German one. Speaker A wants to establish the issue at hand as the question of the German power station. The first two lines of A's utterance are structurally somewhat unclear, but basically mean 'we shouldn't push aside the issue of the German power station' (i.e. by moving on to the French one), 'kulissenschieber' are literally scene-shifters in theatres.

(45) A1 (und wir sollten nicht vorschnell   jetzt wieder
        and we should not   prematurely now again
        kulissenschieber und solche leute   aeh schon)
        scene-shifters   and such   people eh already
        denn   das genau   ist ja   was die Bevölkerung dann
        because that exactly is MODAL Part. what the public   then
        letztlich   uns   gegenüber noch mehr verunsichert
        in-the-end   towards us   still   more makes-insecure
        sondern   wir
        rather   we
        ('makes the public still more suspicious of us')
     B **das hat   ich gesagt**
        that had   I   said ('that's what I said')
     A2 als Politiker   sollten sagen hier steht zur Frage
        as politicians should say   here stands the question
        ob   Whyl gebaut wird   oder nicht
        whether   Whyl built   will be or   not

A1 follows a long discussion of the issues. A is concerned that the main issue is being lost, which he does not want for the reason expressed in the cleft, i.e. the consequence of the public losing faith in the politicians. In contrast, B does not contain such momentous information, or at least the speaker does not consider important the fact that he is of the same opinion as A and has already expressed it. Another cleft here would have been possible, but would have led to a temporary interruption in A's contribution, i.e. a topic shift (what are we talking about   who said what). However, a topic shift is precisely what both speakers want to avoid. This is supported by the fact that after B's comment, A continues with his topic immediately without break in syntax. In fact, from the quite extensive conversation it becomes clear that a number of speakers have collaborated in the construction of B's contribution. What B does is to gather the various contributions together and uses them to steer the conversation back on course.

To summarize, German and English RWH clefts are very similar in the way they gather the preceding discourse and hold onto important items in order to resolve where the discourse has led to. Only then can the discourse proceed. This lock effect is magnified in German, where the RWH has a much greater holding capacity, signalling major topic boundaries, an item of major informational or emotional importance.

6.2.6. WH clefts

The following discussion is based on the dialogue data. Reference will also be made to the conversation data reported in J. Miller (1984) and some informally collected examples. The Map Task dialogues offer 20 examples of WH clefts, the conversation data 31 (out of 100 conversations).

6.2.6.1. *Focus in WH clefts*

§§ 6.2.4.1–6.2.4.3 present an argument that focusing, making a constituent salient, is achieved by a combination of deixis and thematization. In WH clefts the WH clause allows complex syntactic structures to be made theme, and by being theme the WH clause becomes prominent. However, the WH deictic points forward to the cleft clause, which also becomes salient, partly from the deixis and partly from being in final position. The copula also plays a part by separating the two important parts of the message.

In the dialogue data further properties contribute to the salience of the cleft clause. In the dialogue data the WH clause is followed by verb phrases and complete clauses. The WH clause is often phonetically reduced and its content is often minimal. In the dialogue and the conversation data the main verbs in the WH clause are DO, the one exception being HAPPEN. These verbs are low in content. The following clauses can function independently, as pointed out in the examples above. All these properties downgrade the WH clause and increase the salience of the cleft cause and support the view that the main function of WH clefts in the dialogue data is to focus on, i.e. to make salient, the second clause. It goes beyond specifying a variable, since the cleft head always contains new information and could function independently.

The above account of focus applies easily to classic WH clefts such as

What you need most is a good rest, but in spite of their less integrated syntax it also applies to examples such as (46).

(46) cause what you're doin' is you're goin up the side of the allotments

In uttering (46), for example, the speaker has no choice but to presuppose that the addressee is doing something, and specifies what that something is: going up the side of the allotments rather than in some other direction.[15] Note, however, that the presupposition and the exclusiveness component are preconditions to the use of the cleft here. The main import of the cleft is to explain to the hearer what he has to do next by first of all stating explicitly that it is time to do something and then specifying this something. In other words the doing is around in the background during the task and the WH clause in the dialogue data frequently signals when it is time to do something, or to indicate that an instruction is the conclusion of some difficult negotiation. We will return to this point in §6.2.6.2. Below are two further examples which indicate the potentially independent status of the cleft head.

Examples (47)–(49) look like classic clefts, but this analysis is open to doubt.

(47) Eh, what you're going to do is   go in between the camera shop and the left-hand side of the page, right

(48) Okay.   Now   what we have to do is sort of v- veer to the left just a wee bit, . . .

(49) what we need to do is turn turn right . . . straight right . . .

The difficulty with (47) is that the rhythm and pitch pattern is compatible with *go in between the camera shop and the lefthand side of the page* being an imperative main clause. The sequence *what you're going to do is* is spoken with a fastish tempo. There is no drop in pitch and amplitude on *is* (contrary to what happens in other examples), but between *is* and *go* there is a short pause, and the vowel of *go* is held so that it is realized as a double vowel with an increase in amplitude.[16]

In (48) the sequence *what we have to do is sort of* is separated by a medium pause from *v- veer to the left*. In (49) the sequence *what we need to do is* is spoken with a fast tempo, whereas the following sequence *turn turn*

---

[15] In the context of the Map Task there is no contradiction in stating that the speaker specifies what the addressee is doing, because the latter relies on information from the speaker. Depending on the specific context for each example, the progressive can have the force of *what you are doing at the moment—although you don't know it because you haven't got all the details yet* or *what you are about to do*.

[16] The assessments of pause, amplitude, and pitch are intuitive. Two earlier projects on Scottish English, one run by Gill Brown and one run by the author and Keith Brown, independently concluded that three lengths of pause could be recognized. The researchers on Gill Brown's project verified the intuition instrumentally.

right is spoken on a slow tempo. That is, in both (48) and (49) the pausing and the tempo suggest an imperative clause analysis for the sequence following the headless relative. It will be seen from the discussion below that this analysis is compatible with other features of the WH clefts.

The final candidate for the status of classic WH cleft is (50).

(50) A1 I've got a gold mine, a totem pole, and then a great rock, a really good bit down
 B1 right
 A2 And then bandit territory right at the bottom
 B2 Right. *What you're trying to do is avoid the totem pole*

There are no pauses or differences of tempo in the WH cleft, but the word *avoid* is the site of a considerable pitch movement. This movement could be interpreted as contrastive stress, but the context makes this interpretation unlikely, as no suggestions have been made about the route and the totem pole. Another possible interpretation is that the sequence *avoid the totem pole* is an imperative construction. For present purposes the question remains open; the key point is that what looks like a classic WH cleft on paper may turn out to be of doubtful status when suprasegmental features are taken into account.

6.2.6.2. *The discourse functions of the WH clefts*

It will be helpful to distinguish two functions fulfilled by WH clefts: their micro-function inside their immediate clause complex, and their macro-function in larger stretches of discourse. The micro-function, as stated in §6.2.4.2 is to focus on constituents and the information carried by them. The focusing can be overtly contrastive or covertly contrastive (following Chafe 1976): the latter involves merely giving some prominence to the constituents following the headless relative. We have seen that most of the WH clefts in the Map Task data do not fit the classical integrated pattern. One interpretation of this misfit is that the latter construction is a special development of written English. We have already noted that there is a continuum with the classic construction at one pole, a looser construction—headless relative + BE + complete clause—in the middle, and an even looser construction in which the lexical items in the BE complement clause do not match the lexical items in the headless relative.

There are even looser constructions. In (4), for instance, the headless relative is not even connected with the following clause by BE: *What you do—you drop . . . you drop down*, and in (14) the focusing effect of the headless relative extends over several clauses. Two further pieces of information must be introduced here. The first is that speakers regularly use headless relatives to introduce topics. One example provided by a Member of Parliament addressing a meeting is: *What I thought I'd do*

Chairman: as you all know, the most important issues at the moment is the poll-tax. The headless relative does not tie in syntactically or lexically with the following chunk, and in fact is more of a general 'please-pay-attention' message allowing the audience to concentrate their minds before the important information arrives. The speaker did not outline what he thought he would do, but plunges *in medias res*. Speakers on radio interviews or discussion programmes use examples such as *What I say: the danger from whooping cough is far greater than the danger from the vaccination.*

Relevant here are the properties of WH clefts mentioned at the beginning of §6.2.6.1, namely that the headless relative sequence not only has a faster tempo than the following clause but undergoes phonetic reductions. It was suggested that the faster tempo and the phonetic reductions reflect the secondary status of whatever content is carried by the headless relative, whose importance lies precisely in its being a sequence of some sort leading into and giving prominence to the second clause.

With respect to the type of constituent and information focused on by the headless relative, the WH clefts in the Map Task data are limited.[17] Quirk *et al.* (1985) list examples in which the WH clause focuses on a noun phrase: *What John wore to the party last night was his best suit* or [our example] *What she carried the cat in was an old laundry basket.* In such examples the content of the headless relative is indeed important; without it the noun phrases complementing *was* would not be of any great significance, since at the very least the addressee would have to work hard to establish the relevance of *his best suit* or *an old laundry basket*. The Map Task WH clefts focus mainly on complete clauses, but also on verb phrases, which describe an action to be carried out by the addressee. Even without the headless relative, the addressee can interpret the clause or verb phrase, and this, we suggest, is what allows the fast tempo and phonetic reductions on the headless relative.

The WH clefts have a particular macro-discourse function, which is not unlike the textual function of WH clefts recognized by Sornicola (1989). She points out that WH clefts may bring a section of text to a climax, and from her examples it is clear that the climax is also a boundary. In the Map Task dialogues, the WH clefts all occur after a section of negotiation which involves the instruction-giver and the instruction-follower in ascertaining current position, shared and unshared landmarks, and possibly in discussion of the next step to take. The WH clefts serve as a climax to the negotiation in the sense that they express the conclusions arrived at by the instruction-giver on the basis of the negotiation. The WH clefts also lead into the next subset of instructions; that is, they can be seen as both a climax to one section and a bridge to the next.

---

[17] Our data contains only WH clauses with WHAT, which further indicates the low information content of WH clefts.

Focus Constructions: Clefts and like   295

The negotiations can be short (and right at the beginning of the dialogue) as in (51), or more complex, as in (52).

(51) A1 Right. Okay em right, have you got a start point right down near the botto- . . . oh shit . . . down near the bottom of the page which is above crest falls?
   B1 Yeah.
   A2 Right. The start point's about half an inch above it?
   B2 Yeah.
   A3 Okay. Right. Oh. Right **what we need to do right is** like eh . . . above that you've roughly . . . well above and t- a wee bit to the left you've got a s- poison stream. Is that right?
   B3 Eh no . . .

Example (51) begins with two requests for information from A, the instruction-giver—cf. A1 and A2. The requests are answered. The interjections at the beginning of A3—*okay, right,* and *oh!*—can be taken as indicating that A is processing the data. The results of this processing are introduced by the WH cleft *what we need to do is like eh* . . . As it happens, the WH cleft is premature, because A discovers in the next three turns that the two maps are not identical. At that point a second WH cleft introduces the first subset of instructions proper. Example (52) is more complex.

(52) A1 Draw a line about 5 cms opposite way
   B1 Right
   A2 the way the front giraffes and then if you've right have you done that?
   B2 Yeah
   A3 Well draw a line for about 3 cms down just
   B3 Straight down
   A4 Yeah straight down. Have you got a dead tree?
   B4 Yes but that's the opposite way I'm going
   A5 What do you mean? I know you're heading
   B5 Away from the dead tree
   A6 Yeah but see once you're through the desert at the foot of the desert
   B6 I've not got a desert though
   A8 Oh right right
   B8 I've got a stony desert at the top
   A9 That's no it right
   B9 Right
   A10 See *what you do is* know how the dead tree down at the bottom

Example (52) contains a complex negotiation. A1–A3 offer instructions, but the second part of A4, *have you got a dead tree*, opens the way for B to counter A's instruction: *but that's the opposite way I'm going*. At A5, A questions the validity of B's counter and offers an alternative with A6. This leads to more problems, since B does not have the desert to which A refers. A6–B8 enable A and B to arrive at an understanding concerning 'desert' and 'stony desert'. At A10, A embarks on a revised instruction which excludes the original one at A1–3, and this revised instruction is introduced by the WH cleft. As in (51), the WH cleft is premature, since A has still not sorted out the number and location of trees on B's map. That it is premature is irrelevant, since A is signalling: *ignore what has gone before. Here is the proper way to proceed.* This WH cleft can be seen not just as the climax of the negotiations but as strongly contrastive.

This type of negotiation is less common in the conversation data, but the use of WH clefts to focus on the second clause or phrase and to bind together previous discourse and to signpost what is to follow is very similar. WH clefts are regularly used in a context of description or explanation, as in (53) and (54) below.

(53) A1 we were up at the mansion last Tuesday no it was the Friday before Christmas it was and it was a Christmas dance and this punk rock record came on and there was only one guy on the flair and he was on his back jigglin about like a clown
   B a friend of mine does that he gets on the flair and shakes his legs an his hands an everything it looks daft
   A2 **what they do is they balance themselves on one hand and walk sort of** right they can walk round in a circle

In (53) A in A2 uses the cleft both to link up with his own previous utterance and to explain in more detail what jiggling about like a clown involved.

(54) in order to get a good school you've got to involve the pupils and a classic example of the biggest cock-up that we've ever seen in the school I think recently was the Christmas service which was organized entirely by two school chaplains that we did not pick and we have no liking for . . . well **what happened was when the school was opened the chaplains the priests of the other kirk St Barnabas were picked to be school chaplains**

In (54) the WH cleft serves as a starting point for an explanation of why it is a good idea to involve pupils in decisions affecting their school. Informal observation also shows that WH clefts are frequent in spoken discourse where speakers describe and explain their motivation and purposes, as for instance in academic descriptions of their research work. WH clefts are more frequent in the dialogue data—by a factor of 5, presumably because the Map Task involves constant description and explanation.

What emerges from the previous discussions of RWH and WH clefts is that they both share an attention-marking function but differ in the direction of the sign-posting: RWH clefts point backwards whereas WH clefts point forwards. We can conclude this section by indicating another type of cleft which does not contain a WH word, but instead ALL plus headless relative + BE + clause or verb phrase as in (55) below.[18]

(55) A1 Right. **All you're doing is you're sort of doing** . . . see that wee bump you've got over the monastery at the moment?
B1 Yeah
A2 you're sort of doing that in reverse . . .

6.2.6.3. *WH clefts in German*

WH clefts are rare in the German data. There are 4 cases in the Map Task data—3 from one speaker. There are 14 WH clefts in the DSK and 14 in the FKY (5 from 1 speaker giving a lecture). The majority of WH clefts, 18 of them, highlight full NPs, e.g. (57), while the rest highlight complement clauses, unintegrated main clauses or clause complexes. The highlighting analysis proposed for English also applies in general to the German WH clefts but it is important to note that, in spite of the similarities in discourse function, there are some subtle differences. Example (56) is a typical explanatory cleft.

(56) was   sie   hier sehen   ist immer wenn ein Partner zurückkommt und
    what   you   here see   is   always when a   mate   returns   and
    die beiden partner lösen sich zum beispiel bei der brut   ab
    the two   mates   take turns for example with the brooding   Sep. Prefix
    bringt er etwas   mit
    brings he something Sep. Prefix

However, there are no WH clefts with the equivalents of DO and HAPPEN, which suggests that the general topic-introducing explanatory function is not so central. Instead we find a discourse function that is not so common in English, namely the use of WH clefts to expand on topics or to introduce a new topic. Rather than highlighting the content, the WH cleft makes salient the speaker's desire to raise the topic itself. In fact, speakers typically highlight content by means of particles such as NOCH, SONST NOCH, ZUSÄTZLICH, meaning 'in addition'. The combination of WH cleft and particle is rare in the German Map Task dialogues, which afforded only (57); it is more common in informal conversation, from which (58)–(60) were collected.

(57) was   ich **noch zusätzlich**   habe ist eine Wüste
    what I   in-addition (Double marking) have is   a   desert
(58) was   wir **sonst noch**   haben da   von Bernstein n Aufsatz
    what we in-addition (Double marking) have there from Bernstein an essay
(59) was ich noch sagen wollte   ich hab dir das geld   da   hingelegt
    what I   still to-say wanted   I   have you the money there put

---

[18] Geluykens (1988: 832) also includes in his treatment of pseudo-clefts structures such as *the one who did it was John* and *the thing he read first was a book*. We agree that these are indeed similar in function to WH clefts.

(60) was ich dich schon   immer fragen wollte hast du mal
    what I   you for-a-long-time always to-ask wanted have you (MODAL Part.)
    wieder was   von X gehört
    again something from X heard

Examples (58)–(60) suggest something of the meaning of 'that reminds me' or 'and another thing'. What is interesting about the last example is that a likely English translation would be 'There is something I always wanted to ask you . . .'. This is in fact the presupposition carried by the WH clause in the cleft. It seems that this kind of strong highlighting of the content of the WH clause has to be made explicit in English, supporting our analysis of English WH clauses as general attention markers when focusing on clauses.

What these features suggest is that WH clefts create a stronger focus in German, deriving from the notion of additional import triggered by the previous discourse. In other words, there seems to be a relationship between the extra focus in RWH clefts, as discussed in §6.2.5, and that in WH clefts, which relationship is connected with the crucial relevance of the surrounding discourse in relation to a particular important content that the speaker wants to convey. This notion needs to be developed further given our limited data particularly on WH clefts. We might expect to find more evidence for our analysis in informal conversation between familiar speakers.

It appears that German speakers rely on other devices such as explicit explanation (*also ich erklär dir das mal* (right. I explain to-you that MODAL Part. vs. *what you've got to do . . .*)); fronted DA constructions in the Map Task data where a mismatch of features has been resolved and speakers are ready to continue (§6.2.5.4.1); copula definite NP constructions (§6.2.6.4), constructions involving SO (§6.2.5.4.4).

6.2.6.4. *Other focusing devices involving deixis and nominalization*

While clefts are rare in the German data, there are other focusing constructions involving deixis which fulfil similar functions. The mirroring constructions DAS IST DEFINITE DETERMINER NP and DEFINITE DETERMINER NP IST X are backward and forward looking constructions respectively. English has many similar constructions. German also uses nominalized adjectives where English might use WH clefts or 'thing' constructions. Examples of the two constructions are given in (61).

(61) (*a*) das ist das problem
        'that's the problem'
        das problem ist
        'the problem is'
    (*b*) das ist das dumme
        'that's the stupid thing'
        das dumme ist
        'the stupid thing is'

(c) das wichtige ist
'the important thing is', 'what's important is'
(d) das ärgerliche ist
'the annoying thing is', 'what annoys me is'

Examples (62)–(63) are from the Map Task and the DSK, respectively.

(62) B1 ich hab die linie jetzt hier unterhalb der fliegenden untertassen
I have the line now here below the flying saucers
A1 das ist richtig ja
that is right yes
B2 langgezogen nach unten
along-drawn towards below
A2 ja
yes
B3 aeh und dann muß ich sie irgendwie wieder nach rechts ziehen ne
eh and then must I it somehow again towards right draw TAG
A3 ja und ich glaub das ist **das ist die schwierigkeit** jetzt
yes and I think that is that is the difficulty now
weil d- aehm du du aehm bist ja jetzt nach links
because ehm you you aehm have MODAL Part. now towards left
gegangen
gone
B4 mhm
A4 und jetzt muß du eigentlich parallel zu der linie die du nach links
and now must you really parallel to the line which you towards left
B5 ja
A5 gegangen bist parallel wieder zurückgehen
gone have parallel again go-back

A has already used a number of turns in order to describe the route. In B1–B3, B checks her comprehension but is still not quite sure what the route looks like. In A3, A uses *das ist die schwierigkeit* to pinpoint why A and B have had to negotiate this point so extensively.

(63) **die frage scheint mir eigentlich zu sein**
the question seems to-me really to be
machen sie jetzt das erste semester einfach so was ihnen spaß
do you now the first semester simply so (that) which you pleasure
macht
brings
oeh verteilen sie die arbeit also konkret oeh sehen sie auch in die
eh spread you the work that-is concretely eh look you also into the
alte abteilung
old department

The first clause stands independently and is not integrated syntactically, i.e. not 'die frage scheint mir eigentlich zu sein ob sie . . .+ V end'. It is followed by three direct questions.

6.2.7. IT clefts

IT clefts are very rare in the dialogue data, which yield only 5 examples, but are more frequent in the conversations, where we found 28. The range of constituents appearing as cleft head is narrow, with 29 NPs, 2 adverbs, and 2 PPs. The nature of the NPs, on the other hand, is varied, ranging from pronouns to complex NPs with pre-modifiers and one post-modified NP + relative clause. A subset of 17 IT clefts yielded the primary and secondary stress patterns. Table 6.3 summarizes the patterns found.

This distribution is consistent with Delin's (1989) data. IT clefts occur with a variety of patterns and not only the contrastive pattern. Delin also found 26% of pattern 3, which typically indicates an anaphoric cleft head—Declerck (1988) talks of unaccented-anaphoric-focus clefts. We cannot think of an obvious explanation for the fact that this pattern does not occur in our data at all. It is again important to note that pattern 2 is not necessarily contrastive, witness the fact that only 3 of the above 7 were contrastive. Analysis of stress patterns allows us to see that clefts can contain important information in both clauses, but the exact information structure of clefts would have to be studied in conjunction with their discourse context.

IT clefts have a more complex structure than WH and RWH clefts, being genuinely cleft sentences—cf. Huddleston (1984: 462). The cleft clause is a self-contained IT copular structure. IT clefts are the preferred cleft for indicating contrast. While all clefts can be said to express covert contrast, only 2.5% of RWH clefts and 0.5% of WH clefts in our data express explicit contrast, which figure rises to 36% for IT clefts.

Whereas WH clefts typically focus on phrases and clauses and RWH clefts on deictics, IT clefts focus on full NPs and permit larger cleft constituents

TABLE 6.3. *Distribution of stress patterns in IT clefts*

Cleft clause	WH clause	Numbers
+	+	7
+	−	7
−	+	0
+	=	2
=	+	1
		17

than RWH clefts, presumably because of the self-contained IT BE X structure. As mentioned earlier, IT clefts, apart from focusing on direct and indirect objects, also allow subject-focus more readily than RWH clefts.

It clefts are used when identification of the cleft constituent is of primary importance. RWH clefts and IT clefts share the same order of cleft constituent + WH clause but differ in the nature of the cleft constituent. RWH cleft constituents are almost exclusively deictic attention markers (cf. §6.2.5.1) and an exact description is not so important. In IT clefts, on the other hand, the nature of the cleft constituent is important, particularly if the cleft is contrastive. Since it clearly matters what the alternative is, IT clefts typically have fully identified cleft constituents, which means that the use of deictics is severely limited in practice.

IT clefts can be contrastive and non-contrastive as exemplified by (64) and (65), and (69) and (70), respectively.

(64) We're we're after everything I mean not not not the phonetics because that's fairly well known anyway em **it's the SYNtax we're after**

Example (64) contrasts syntax with phonetics.

(65) Cause I was supposed to—we were wanting pictures in dress costume for Viva Mexico you know and there's no costumes and I'm supposed to have it for today and I forgot all about it so I'm not very poplar I don't know I think **it's one of the TEAchers is takin photographs** but I hate gettin my picture taken so I'm no very fussy I don't mind

Example (65) contrasts one of the teachers with a professional photographer.[19]

The information in the WH clause of IT clefts can be more or less redundant, and in (66) is in fact highly redundant. The WH clause is unstressed and from the preceding context it is clear what the import of the cleft clause is:

(66) A1 see the side where the cliffs are
 A2 go along till go straight along then down till you're about a cm above the picture of the waterfall
 B2 so **its the side nearest the CLIFFS** i've to go to

---

[19] The sequence *it's one of the teachers is takin photographs* can be given two syntactic analyses: *it's* + clause or *it's* NP [WH clause]. In all the dialogue and conversational data there is only one instance of IT BE + clause: *then it was he got a Yamaha*. This example gives salience to the latest event in a series of events recounted by the speaker as opposed to describing an event that is not presented as part of a series. The absence of a TH or WH complementizer may seem peculiar, since the NP missing from the putative relative clause is the subject, and in these circumstances English relative clauses generally require a complementizer. In fact, missing complementizers are the rule in relative clauses in presentative constructions: examples from the conversations are *We had a French girl came to stay, there's two pupils have brothers in the school*. The presentative construction is very similar to the IT cleft structure: deictic NP + BE + NP + WH clause. Given this parallel and the frequency of missing complementizers, the analysis of the above example as an IT cleft is very plausible.

A1 mentions *the side* and A2 mentions *go till*. *I've to go* is highly given in the context of the Map Task. This property, together with the self-contained nature of the cleft clause in IT clefts, makes them omissible. The conversation data yielded 20 examples that are good candidates for analysis as IT clefts with omitted WH clauses. The examples include only IT BE X structures for which the preceding discourse supplies an obvious WH clause, but it is not always easy to distinguish between reduced IT clefts and anaphoric IT BE X structures.

There is an interesting difference between full and reduced IT clefts. As shown in Table 6.4, 29 full clefts have single NP cleft constituents, compared with only 9 reduced clefts. However, the reduced clefts also offer as cleft constituent adverbial clauses and sequences of NP + relative clause and NP + complement clause. It appears that longer cleft constituents are only possible in spoken language when the WH clause is omitted. This is not surprising, since spoken language is characterized by a less integrated and less complex syntax generally. Delin (1989) also notes 9 cases of adverbial clause cleft constituents in her spoken data, the unusually high frequency probably being attributable to the speakers being largely academics. Delin also reports figures for written language which are three times as high. Table 6.4 shows the distribution of cleft constituents for full and reduced IT clefts.

Single cleft clauses can identify more or less explicit entities. The majority—65%—are contrastive. The presupposed material for contrastive clefts is usually explicitly and closely present in the preceding discourse, which makes its omission from the WH clause possible. Examples (67) and (68) are contrastive cleft clauses.

(67) A is he the murder?
     B no no **it's the man that owns the garage (that's the murderer)**

TABLE 6.4. *Cleft constituents in full and reduced IT clefts*

	Full clefts	Reduced clefts
NP	29	10
Adverb	2	2
PP	2	1
NP + rc	0	2
NP + cc	0	1
Participle	0	1
Adverbial clause	0	3
	33	20

(68) A1 right come on who was first through that fence come on own up
     B1 nobody was owning up
     A2 yes I **it was me** I think no it wasn't **it was George**
     B2 you didn't own up
     A3 no it was it was George

In (68) A and B relate a story about an outing to a third party. A1 reports the speech of a teacher who wanted to know who had been responsible for a hole in a fence through which sheep were escaping. B1–A3 are then concerned with establishing that somebody owned up and who that person was.

Examples (69) and (70) are both non-contrastive. Example (69) identifies an explicit entity, but the entity identified by (70) needs to be inferred.

(69) A so when do they start again
     B eh **it's the middle of the month**

(70) A   really   what did they think had happened
     B1 well **it was the speed that we went into the toilet at** because you dinnae wander about the corridor soakin wet
     C   yeah
     B2 they thought somebody had broke a leg or something

B in (69) can be understood as *it's the middle of the month they start again*. In (70) we infer something like *it was . . . toilet at that got them worried*.

In addition to IT clefts, our data also has two rare examples of an IT cleft structure where IT is replaced with THAT, as in (71).

(71) that was Stavros who said that

Such examples are rare and space does not permit us to pursue this point further in this chapter. *That* in (71) has a similar function to THAT in RWH clefts, and indeed in other THAT initial constructions (see also note 8).

As indicated earlier, some IT clefts contain new information in the WH clause and appear more predicational than specificational or specifying.

(72) A are there any other laddies from school go up there
     B eh well there's a laddie **it's his UNcle who ORganizes it**

Example (72) follows a discussion of clay pigeon shooting, which B regularly pursues. B is not so much concerned with specifying who organizes the shooting, but with emphasizing what is special about this particular laddie, i.e. he emphasizes the connection between the laddie and the organizer of the shooting. In other words, the topic is the laddie and not the person who organizes the shooting.

There are some examples in our data which contain a mixture of old and new information in the WH clause. Examples (73) and (74) combine a specificational function with a description, thus exploiting the predicational element of IT clefts.

(73) A1 did you do you like these sandals?
B1 aye but they're hurting me actually they're no bad on my feet they're alright but **it's HERE across HERE they CUT** they're really hard

Example (73) is a partly specificational, explicitly contrastive IT cleft. It is also partly predicational, despite the fact that the new element in the WH clause is inferrable. *Cut* receives primary stress and adds some important new information about *across here* but is at the same time inferable from the previous context which includes *hurting* and adds a proposition. In addition to indicating contrast, i.e. *they don't hurt my feet but they hurt across here*, (73) also conveys *they cut across here*. *Across here* therefore both identifies the entity specified by the WH element through inference from *cut* to *hurting*, and is also part of a description which includes *cut*. It takes part in a specificational/predicational double-act. The predicational part may be minor and dependent on the specification, but it is there.

(74) A1 oh God and X pushed her over into the flower beds
B1 that's right yes she went she went spare and ruptured our hooker
A1 she went absolutely spare because Neil Neil Y when she was in the flower bed he picked her foot up and she thought **it was him that tossed tossed her over into the flower bed**

The context of this cleft is that at some point prior to being tossed into the flower bed, Neil Y had picked up her foot, but it was X who had actually pushed her. *Tossed* is inferable from *pushed*, but the different lexical choice clearly matters. It is possible that the speaker decides against a repetition of *pushed* in order to add some spice to the story. Therefore apart from identifying the variable in the relative clause, the cleft adds a new description.

The predicational element can also fall into the cleft clause. Declerck comments on clefts which contain some new information in the WH clause which makes them look predicational. His example is (75):

(75) Was it an INTERESTING meeting that you went to last night?

Declerck maintains that (75) is still essentially a specificational cleft and that the only predicational element is *interesting*. He states that 'The predicational meaning of such IT clefts follows (more or less accidentally) from the fact that the NP specified as value for the variable represents old information except for the adjective modifying the noun head' (Declerck 1988: 178). Declerck suggests that, except for the modifying adjective, the cleft would be specificational. We agree with this interpretation. Delin (personal communication) suggests that there is a syntactic constraint on adjectival cleft constituents, making unacceptable a sentence like *was it interesting that the meeting that you went to last night was*. This is presumably because modifiers cannot be separated from their head nouns. The cases in our data are different from Declerck's example in that the head nouns are not unstressed and not assumed as given, as in (76) and (77).

(76) But they had a lovely pint of beer yes at one time I think **it was WAter a special WAter they had**

(77) Do you think **it is a dangerous AGE that we live in?**

In both these cases the clefts are partly specificational, partly predicational.

There are some cases of clefted WH-questions in our data, exemplified by (78) and (79).

(78) Where is it that you're at the now?

(79) Which part of Leith is it you're from?

J. Miller (1984) suggests a force of 'remind me' for one of his examples. This interpretation also fits (78) and (79).

Our final comment on IT clefts concerns their different uses in spoken and written language. We mentioned earlier that written IT clefts can contain larger cleft constituents, including adverbial clauses. PP cleft constituents are also considerably more frequent than in spoken language, which has more indirect object heads with stranded prepositions in the WH clause. Written clefts also contain more information in the WH clause and indeed clause complexes. Example (80) illustrates how written language can use the IT BE structure to focus on complex information in one condensed sentence. The example is taken from the LOB corpus and quoted by Delin (1989).

(80) It was precisely because the 'primal mythic adventure' could not form the total substance of a novel that Lawrence was driven to invent the paraphernalia of a political and religious movement led by Ramon which Mr. Kessler rightly regards as superficial.

6.2.8. *Conclusions*

In our analysis of clefts we have explored the role of thematization and deixis in combination with the copula structure and in relation to the discourse context of clefts. We have claimed that the sentence initial, i.e. thematized, deictic element *this/that*, WH clause, and *it* in RWH, WH, and IT clefts, respectively, are central to the highlighting function of clefts. The copula structure does not merely serve to instantiate the presupposed variable in the WH clause but identifies why a speaker has chosen to present an entity by means of an attention-marking deictic (RWH and WH clefts), or identifies the entity itself (IT cleft). If the highlighting function of clefts derives from thematization and deixis, highlighting ('focusing' in the usual terminology) can be separated from new information. In other words, clefts can highlight information either given or new.

Because of the different deictics and the different cleft constituents, thematization and deixis operate differently in the three cleft structures. RWH clefts, where the deictic is also the cleft constituent, highlight entities in the immediately surrounding discourse or situation, holding onto important items before the discourse moves away from them and creating a slight backwards pull. The large majority of RWH clefts highlight object NPs, which strongly suggests that they are thematizing constructions.[20] WH clefts highlight clauses and phrases by means of an indefinite deictic WH clause which is low in lexical content. They are forward-pointing and often introduce topics or mark an important starting point for the following discourse. IT clefts operate with the definite deictic IT which is neutral with respect to forwards or backwards pointing. It highlights the cleft constituent, which is typically a full NP. IT clefts are the preferred cleft for highlighting subjects and for expressing overt contrast. We may therefore conclude that the different cleft types fulfil largely complementary functions in our data and that their choice does not merely depend on how well a cleft continues the thematic line of the previous discourse (Declerck 1988). However, what unites all clefts is their highlighting function.

By considering the role of thematization, deixis, the nature of the cleft head and discourse context we hope to have provided a new perspective on the highlighting function of clefts. While previous accounts have tended to concentrate on cleft semantics, we suggest that taking into account the discourse context of clefts in particular has made it possible to view their structure and function in a new light.

6.3. LIKE

The discourse organizing constructions with LIKE have caused us severe difficulties. Most of our colleagues simply assumed that LIKE is a filler item that helps speakers to hold the floor or to avoid awkward silence when dealing with problems of utterance planning and execution. As we said in

---

[20] The data did not include enough RWH clefts with NPs to allow for generalizations. However, the two cases in our data, Delin's written example and some informally recorded examples are consistent with the general analysis for RWH clefts: the NPs have an anaphoric function without the attention-marking function of the deictic. Speakers wish to thematize an important entity which would not be theme in unclefted alternatives.

§6.1, we will argue that LIKE is a non-contrastive focuser. Clause-final LIKE, as in (81), is concerned with countering objections and assumptions and is found only in the spontaneous conversation. (Example (81) is part of (106), which is discussed in §6.3.5.3.) Elsewhere, LIKE is concerned with the elucidation of previous comments and is associated with the game-task moves of instructing, aligning, and checking—that is, with moves in which the instruction-givers enlarge on their explanations or the instruction-followers check the information they have been offered. Examples are in (82).

(81) my wee girl can swim you know—she has her wings **like**

(82) (*a*) right so I'm just **like** below the allotments just now
 (*b*) **like** I go past the collapsed shelter?
 (*c*) **like** that's how you go.

It is worthwhile stating here, before tackling the details of LIKE, that this section makes an important contribution to the question of syntactic differences between informal spoken language and written language, differences which are not observable in every corpus. (Cf. the comments of Biber (1988) reported in Chapter 1.) We will demonstrate that LIKE, which does not appear frequently in written texts and is liable to be seen as a lapse of style when it does (witness the comment in the *OED* reported in §6.3.1), has a systematic role in spoken discourse, and a role which is learned relatively late, apparently after age 10, by native-speaker learners. It has been suggested (Ochs 1979) that the constructions appearing in unplanned adult discourse go back to the constructions acquired early in childhood and that their occurrence in adult unplanned discourse is caused by the large amount of processing time required for instant planning in spontaneous conversation. For the LIKE constructions that account is incorrect.

6.3.1. *Previous accounts of LIKE*

6.3.1.1. *The* OED *and accounts of non-standard English*

This overview of previous accounts of LIKE has two goals—to indicate previous treatments of LIKE in order to bring out what is novel in this analysis, and to demonstrate that the discourse marker LIKE is no late-twentieth-century parvenu but has a recorded history in written English going back to the early nineteenth century. Since words, phrases, and constructions tend to appear in spoken language first and to be slow in gaining entry to writing, it is reasonable to speculate that the discourse marker LIKE has a much longer, though unrecorded, history in the spoken language.

The *Oxford English Dictionary* (*OED*) (1st edition) has an entry for the discourse marker LIKE (without the label 'discourse marker'). LIKE is labelled dialectal and vulgar and is said to be 'used parenthetically to qualify a preceding statement: = "as it were", "so to speak"'. Examples are given from Scott ('Guy Mannering', 1815: *The leddy, on ilka Christmas night . . . gae twelve siller pennies to ilka puir body about, in honour of the twelve apostles **like***), Lytton (1838), De Quincey (1840–1), and E. Peacock ('Ralf Skirl', 1870, *Might I be so bold as just to ax, by way of talk **like**, if . . .*). The *OED* account of the above examples will be challenged in §6.3.5.

The *OED* describes a second colloquial usage of LIKE as a meaningless interjection, as in the following example from 'Black Panther', November 9/4, 1973: *What will be the contradictions that produce further change? **like**, it seems to me that it would be virtually impossible to avoid some contradictions.* While the comment in the *OED* cannot be properly challenged without examining the complete text from which the example is taken, and other texts by the same writer, it is worthwhile anticipating §6.3.4 with the remark that this example has the same 'feel' as similar examples in the spontaneous conversations; that is, *like* appears to be a discourse marker giving salience to what follows. The text following *like* deserves to be salient because the writer is explaining that the initial question presupposes contradictions for the good reason that they seem to be unavoidable.

Wright (1902) provides similar examples, describing LIKE as used redundantly or to modify a statement. Partridge (1984) mentions only LIKE at the end of a phrase or sentence, describing it as 'expressive of vagueness or after-thoughted modification' and glossing it as 'somewhat', 'as it were', 'not altogether', 'in a way'. In current terminology, Partridge treats LIKE as a hedge. Wilson (1915: 98) also glosses LIKE as 'as it were', or 'rather': *I was kind of feared **like*** ('I was somewhat afraid as it were'). Grant and Main-Dixon (1921: 142) state that LIKE is thrown in adverbially to soften an expression, having usually a deprecatory flavour. According to Hedevind (1967: 237), working on Yorkshire English, LIKE is used parenthetically to tone down an expression or a whole sentence without much affecting the meaning, as in *you pile it up **like***, and asserts that this usage is widespread in the North of England. Schourup (1985) demonstrates that the usage is frequent for his North American informants. The works cited above support the *OED*'s contention that the discourse marker LIKE is non-standard. It is attested in the North of England and in Scotland last century, and has been heard by the author in recordings of speakers from Devon. It is unclear to what extent LIKE occurs as a discourse marker in the South-East of England and in the informal speech of standard English speakers but its occurrence cannot be excluded.

6.3.1.2. *Schourup's concept of 'evincives'*

All the above-mentioned sources, except Schourup, concur in the judgement that LIKE is redundant or has a toning-down effect, but this judgement is not compatible with the data on which this chapter is based and is indeed typical of the casual attitude towards informal spoken language displayed by many analysts. Schourup (1985), working on the transcripts of radio talk shows and informal conversations between friends, invokes a category of evincives (see below) and establishes five uses of LIKE, all of which he analyses as evincive. In his explanation of evincives, Schourup starts from the observation that three worlds intersect in a conversation with two participants: the world of the speaker—what Schourup calls the speaker's covert thinking, the world of the hearer, and their shared world—what is on display as talk and other behaviour (Schourup 1985: 7). In the course of conversation speakers correlate the shared world and their private worlds. The processing of information from the private world is not normally manifested in talk, unless speakers want to use talk as a means of sorting out the information and arriving at an analysis. However, the processing of information from the private world regularly affects what is on display, and this 'affect' is signalled by speakers with items such as *oh, well, you know, aha*, and *I mean*. Schourup argues that LIKE has the same function, namely evincive. 'Evincives . . . allow the speaker to call attention to current thought in the private world and to specify . . . the tenor of what is in mind, without placing the details of the speaker's thoughts in the shared world' (Schourup 1985: 35-6).

Schourup (1985: 37-63) distinguishes the following five uses of LIKE.

i Before numeral expressions, as in *I'm* **like** *six feet tall*. He says that such an utterance is not appropriate when precision is called for, since in many such examples **like** is equivalent to *approximately*. LIKE indicates a possible discrepancy between what the speaker is about to say and what the speaker feels ideally might or should be said.

ii Before direct discourse, as in . . . *and she's* **like** *'Come in here and have a beer' you know*. Schourup suggests that in such examples *like* indicates that the direct discourse is not an exact replica of the words uttered but an approximation.

iii After questions, as in:

> EVA When I'm down here I listen to Dayton/When I'm at home I listen to Akron.
> SUE ( ) Yeah but which one **like**
> EVA W. Oh! W.N.X.Q. . . .

Schourup suggests that LIKE indicates a possible discrepancy between the question asked by SUE and the question she thinks ideally more appropriate.

310 *Spontaneous Spoken Language*

iv Equivalent to *for example*, as in: *You know um—besides taking care of groups of people or—um you know uh I'm speaking in **like** a secretarial situation—where you're working for—you know you're you're h- having to— set up your time* . . . Schourup proposes that this use of LIKE signals an accurate but selective representation of what the speaker has in mind. In the above example, the speaker could have referred to various situations but chooses to refer to secretaries.

v LIKE as an interjection: *but I found **like** that helped me a lot*, and *This **like**—This move takes place in 1968*. Schourup suggests that this use of LIKE signals that the material to follow is difficult to formulate appropriately or precisely, that covert thinking is taking place before overt language appears in the shared world.

The comments in the *OED* and Wright, Partridge, Wilson, Grant and Main-Dixon, and Hedevind are limited, as they give no indication of the textual setting of the examples nor of the pitch and rhythm. Schourup's account, while more detailed, relates to a variety of English with a different usage of LIKE from the data treated here and the concept of 'evincive' is too general to be of use. 'Evincives' signal the processing of information from the speaker's private world, but an obvious objection to Schourup is that *aha*, *well*, and *like* are all evincive, though playing quite different roles. For instance, *aha*, depending on intonation, signals that the speaker has caught the previous speaker in an error or, as a result of the conversation, has just understood some point.

6.3.1.3. *The applicability of Schourup's subtypes of LIKE*

Although we have not yet examined data from the Map Task dialogues or the spontaneous conversations, this is a convenient place to ask whether, in spite of the problems with the concept 'evincive', any of the individual functions proposed for LIKE by Schourup are relevant. As will be shown, some are and some are not.

The first, that LIKE before numeral expressions signals that the expressions are approximate, does not fit the Map Task data. Where LIKE co-occurs with a numeral expression there is no indication in the subsequent dialogue that the expression is taken by the instruction-follower as approximate. Moreover, approximations are typically signalled by ABOUT, as in *and then you just slope down to the the left for about an inch and a half* and *now head along +++ beside East Lake and then **about** ++ a centimetre past where it goes up*. LIKE in fact combines with ABOUT as in *I'm just like underneath the telephone box about **like about** fif- fourteen centimetres away from the telephone box*. The last example illustrates another point against adopting Schourup's analysis: LIKE combines with prepositional phrases such as *underneath the telephone box* and with directional and locational adverbs as in *yeah the old mill's **like** + north east of it*. The subsequent dialogue gives no hint that the instruction-follower understands the adverb as 'approximately north east' nor that the instruction-giver intended such an interpretation. In the telephone box example above, such an interpretation would contradict the message signalled by *just*.

The second function assigned to LIKE by Schourup, that it introduces quoted direct speech, is—not surprisingly given the nature of the Map Task data—not found in the Map Task dialogues. More importantly, it is also absent from the spontaneous conversations. The third function, that LIKE at the end of questions signals a discrepancy between the actual question and a more appropriate but unuttered formulation that has occurred to the speaker, is not supported by the Map Task data either. Anticipating §6.3.4, we will simply note here that this use of LIKE has to do with the need for further information from the instruction-giver and that LIKE is an extra piece of coding that, in accordance with the analysis summarized in §6.3, focuses on and makes salient the extra information as in (83) and (84). We should also note that Schourup does not discuss different types of interrogative. In the conversations, most of the YES–NO and WH interrogatives with LIKE have it in final position, as in Schourup's own example, but the Map Task data, though lacking interrogatives with clause-final LIKE, does offer interrogative with LIKE in various other positions, including clause-initial as in (83).

(83) Yvonne er I'm I'm not very sure ++ what I'm supposed to be doing
    Janie em and then you have to go down again
    Yvonne **like** I go past the collapsed shelter?

Example (83) has declarative word order, which occurs in the Map Task data only when the speaker is verifying a previous statement. Example (84) is a YES–NO interrogative with interrogative word order and with LIKE immediately preceding the constituent it relates to.

(84) Yvonne so I just sort of is that + **like** + round the collapsed shelter a line going round?

Schourup's fourth proposal, that *like* can be equivalent to *for example* is supported by 13 of the 83 examples in the conversations but not by any examples in the Map Task data. One instance is given in (85).

(85) [The discussion concerns a male teacher in his 50s—the referent of *he* and *him* and a senior female member of staff—the referent of *she*]
    A1 at the dance . . . he was surrounded by the sixth year girls we were just tormenting him and she was sitting there going 'tsk tsk'
    L1 disapproval—I mean and if we go up and say something to to him she— you know, not really cheeky—but she considers it cheeky and I can see her looking and glaring at you and

        A2 in disapproval and Terry's quite happily standing there taking it all
        L2 **like** you keep telling him to stop smoking
        A3 **like** I walk up to him and say 'How many have you smoked today' and
           he looks very guilty and says 'too many'

While it is true that *like* in (L2) and (A3) introduces examples of saying something not really cheeky (L1) and of what Terry is putting up with (A2), it also serves to give salience to the statement following it. Since introducing examples and giving salience are quite compatible functions, there is no reason to abandon either Schourup's fourth subtype of LIKE or the analysis developed here.[21]

Schourup's fifth proposal is equivalent to the filler hypothesis which was rejected above and will not be further considered here.

The above assessment of Schourup's analysis is as objective as possible, but it must be mentioned in conclusion that many of Schourup's examples are either single lines of dialogue or very short extracts of discourse. In either case it is impossible fully to gauge the discourse role of *like*.

6.3.2. Why LIKE is not a pause filler

One important question is whether *like* is to be treated as having a genuine discourse role or as a filler, an item that serves to hold the speaker's place while thoughts or syntax are being organized. The answer to the question can usefully begin with the caveat that many items can function as fillers in the above sense, from conceptually empty items such as *ehm* and *eh* to phrases with syntactic structure and conceptual content such as *let me see* and *I'm not sure*. Organizational problems are typically manifested by hesitation, false starts, and pauses. There are indeed clear examples of organization taking place, as in (86), uttered at the very beginning of a dialogue by the instruction-giver organizing her first instruction to the instruction-follower and still composing both a strategy for giving instructions and an adequate description of the starting point and the first move.

(86) Ruth 1 right OK ehm ... Right, have you got a start point right down near
              the botto- ... oh shit [relates to something being dropped or spilled]
              down near the bottom of the page which is above a Crest Falls?
     Laura 1 yeah

---

[21] In fact, quite a number of the occurrences of LIKE in the spontaneous conversation are eminently glossable as 'for example'. A plausible hypothesis concerning the historical origin of the discourse marker LIKE—and we advance it simply as a hypothesis—is that the basic sense of LIKE is 'be like/be similar to', that this basic sense gave rise to the 'for example' use and that the latter in turn led to the discourse marker use. Note that both FOR EXAMPLE and LIKE serve to make chunks of discourse prominent in the following example: *Tell me what happened—for example/like, who was driving the car, what other vehicles were around, if the road was dry or greasy, if visibility was good ...*

Ruth   2   right . . . The start point's about half an inch above it?
Laura   2   yeah
Ruth   3   OK right ++tsup hoo [half sung on rising pitch] + right what we need to do is **like** ++ eh above that you've + roughly ++well above and a wee bit to the left + you've got a poison stream ++ is that right?
Laura   3   eh + no I've got nothing above it + I've got an old temple to my right of it
Ruth   4   uhuh + have you got anything to more to the left at all
Laura   4   a footbridge quite a bit over
Ruth   5   right OK right we need to go s [*inbreath*] right what we need to do is **like** [*WH cleft pronounced very quickly, all in one*] see the Crest Falls we need to + go + **like** we start just above it and we move to the + eh + I'll explain it to you right? first
Laura   5   OK
Ruth   6   move to the left about an inch and then drop down + **like** almost at the side of the falls

The dialogue in (86) begins smoothly with both participants agreeing on the existence and location of a starting point. The difficulties begin thereafter as Ruth processes the information on her map in order to describe the first stretch of the route for Laura. The features in (86) indicating, or, to borrow Schourup's term, evincing on-going organizing of thoughts and language are the occurrence of items such as *OK* and *right* in (Ruth 1, 3, 5), and in Ruth 3) the half-sung *tsup hoo* and the WH cleft *what we need to do is like*. The utterance following the WH cleft is not related to it semantically—the cleft mentions doing, but instead of giving instructions Ruth makes a statement followed by a tag question, *is that right?*. Furthermore, the utterance following the WH cleft is not related to it syntactically (as discussed in Chapter 3). Finally, after the hedge *roughly* and the marker *well* in Ruth 3, Ruth utters the main clause conveying the important part of the message with respect to the Map Task. (Ruth 5) presents more indications of on-going organizing in the first two lines, again in the use of the items *right* and *OK* and in the broken syntax, *we need to go* being broken off by an intake of breath followed by *right* and another syntactic construction, *what we need to do is **like***.

Two comments are relevant. The first is that in (86) it is not *like* that evinces the speaker's internal activity but the items mentioned in the foregoing paragraph, the broken syntax and semantics together with the frequent pauses. Far from filling pauses, *like* is integrated with the relevant piece of syntax both in (Ruth 1), *what we need to do right is **like***, and in (Ruth 3), *what we need to do is **like*** and ***like** we start just above it*. 'Integrated' means that there is no pause between *like* and the rest of the construction; indeed, both of the sequences just cited are pronounced very quickly. The transcription notes on the second sequence, *like . . . it*, describe it as 'pronounced in one quick snatch'.

The second comment is that (86) is untypical. Forty instances of discourse LIKE in the undergraduates' dialogue were examined in detail. Only 4 occur in stretches of speech with hesitations and syntactic reformulations or repetitions. Nineteen of the 40 examples are not separated by any pause from the following piece of syntax. The sequences with LIKE also vary with respect to whether the realization of LIKE is reduced. Reduction can involve glottalization of the [k] and/or lowered pitch and amplitude. Table 6.5 summarizes the data on pausing and reduction.

TABLE 6.5. *Pausing and reduction in sequences with LIKE*

Pause	
reduced	6
not reduced	15
No pause	
reduced	9
not reduced	10

The important information in Table 6.5 is that, whereas the numbers of reduced and unreduced forms are equal when there is no pause, the unreduced forms outnumber the reduced ones by 2.5 to 1 when there is a pause. We take this to indicate that LIKE does have an important enough discourse function for it to be realized distinctly. It is worthwhile mentioning that, except for the four examples of hesitations mentioned above, the pauses that do occur are not associated with any of the other signs of difficult on-line processing. Consider *like* in (Sarah 3) in (87).

(87) Sarah   1   do you see a cattle ranch no?
     Danielle 1   nope
     Sarah   2   right em you see that fort?
     Danielle 2   mhm
     Sarah   3   away at the other side right+ you're heading to go under that + but **like** ++ on your way about halfway between the buffalo and the fort + there's a wee blip in your line
     Danielle 3   mhm
     Sarah   4   like you're going over the top of something and then coming back down

Away at the other side in (Sarah 3) modifies *fort*. The following *right* is a tag seeking confirmation from Danielle that she has located the fort on the map—at least, it has interrogative intonation, although Danielle does not reply to the tag. Sarah indicates the relevance of the fort with *you're heading to go under that* followed by a warning that the route between Danielle's current location and the fort is not a straight line. The warning is introduced by *but like*, preceded by a short pause and followed by a medium pause. There is nothing unusual about these pauses, which would have been possible even with *but* alone acting as introduction to the warning. In fact, a typical ploy to attract the listeners' attention to a warning, in all types of spoken language, is to follow it with a pause, even a long pause. That is, in (87—Sarah 3) the medium pause between *but like* and the following chunk of syntax is not necessarily associated with *like*. Furthermore, the rest of the utterance is well integrated, with only a short pause between the adverb of location, *on your way about halfway between the buffalo and the fort*, and the nucleus of the main clause, *there's a wee blip in your line*. We discard the hypothesis that *like* is a filler in favour of the hypothesis that it is a discourse organizer.

6.3.3. *Non-contrastive focus*

Our experience with the Map Task dialogues leads us to follow Mackenzie and Keizer (1990), though with some revisions. Mackenzie and Keizer establish a taxonomy of focus types based on four distinctions which apply in the following order: whether the focused constituent relates to contextually new or contextually given entities; whether the entities are being presented or not— i.e. introduced into the discourse or not; whether the constituent/entity is emphasized or not; and whether the entity/information is contrasted or not.

The first revision we propose is that the terms 'contextually new' and 'contextually given' be abandoned in favour of the simple terms 'given' and 'new', which we interpret along the lines of G. Brown and Yule (1983: 182–8), which represents a revision of Prince (1981). New entities are of two kinds, **brand new** entities assumed not to be known to the hearer, and **unused** entities, assumed to be in the hearer's background knowledge but not in his or her consciousness at the time of utterance. Given entities are also of two major types. The first type are **inferables**, entities which the speaker assumes the hearer can infer from another entity that has already been introduced into the discourse. The second type are **evoked**, and fall into two subtypes. The first subtype are **situationally evoked** entities, which are salient in the discourse context. The second type are **textually evoked** entities, which have already been introduced into the discourse and are being referred to a second or subsequent time. Textually evoked entities in turn fall into two subtypes; **current textually evoked** entities, introduced into the discourse immediately before current **new** entities, and **displaced textually evoked entities**, introduced into the discourse earlier than **current** textual evoked entities.

The second revision affects the number of distinctions and the order in which they apply. For present purposes the distinction of [+/− emphatic] will be put aside, as we have had no reason to invoke it. The remaining distinctions will be reordered. As the major distinction seems to be between focus constructions that introduce entities and those that do not, this will be the first division. The second distinction is between new and given. The third distinction is between contrastive and non-contrastive.

The Map Task dialogues illustrate neatly the need to distinguish between the objective status of entities and their status in the minds of the participants. Consider the data in (88)–(91)

(88) draw a line from the volcano to the crashed spaceship

(89) (*a*) is there a bridge about two inches south east of the cliff?
    (*b*) have you got a bridge about two inches south of the cliff?
    (*c*) can you see a bridge about two inches south east of the cliff?
    (*d*) do you see a bridge about two inches south east of the cliff?

(90) (*a*) do you see the bridge?
    (*b*) can you see the gallows?
    (*c*) you know where the cliffs are?

(91) (*a*) ehm know where the cave is?
    (*b*) see the wee black house at the left hand side of the allotments?

The participants in each Map Task experiment were given certain information before they started. They were told that the maps had certain landmarks, that the instruction-giver's map had a route from a start point to a finishing point, and that the instruction-giver's task was to tell the instruction-follower how to draw the route. They were further told that the two maps might not have identical landmarks. Many of the 8-year-old and 10-year-old instruction-givers in the Glasgow Map Task Corpus treated the landmarks as situationally evoked on both maps and introduced landmarks into the discourse by means of definite NPs in neutral declarative clauses. Example (88) is typical of examples in which entities are introduced into the discourse by means of a definite NP embedded in a clause-final PP. The older school pupils quickly learned not to take for granted the presence of a landmark on both maps. That is, the instruction-givers learned to treat landmarks present on their maps as possibly brand new for the instruction-follower and introduced the landmarks by means of clauses such as (89*a*–*d*), with indefinite NPs in special presentative constructions, either the classic existential with THERE or constructions with HAVE GOT and CAN/DO SEE. The very fact that the entities are introduced by separate clauses makes them salient and fixes them in the listener's attention.[22]

[22] Keenan and Schieffelin (1976: 338) observe that speakers are reluctant to add new information to the discourse if the objects or individuals to which they are referring cannot be established as given. They cite examples where one or more clauses are devoted to the introduction and firm establishment of entities: *Do you remember Tom?*, *Do you remember the*

Focus Constructions: Clefts and like   317

The constructions exemplified in (90) are used to introduce landmarks that the instruction-giver treats as situationally evoked, whereas those exemplified in (91) are used to re-mention landmarks or properties of landmarks that are either situationally evoked or textually evoked but displaced and to put them at the centre of the instruction-follower's field of attention. The syntax of (91)[23] differs from the syntax of (89), (90). Examples (89*c,d*) and (90) are identical in syntax apart from the definiteness of the direct object NP, but (91*a,b*) can have only definite direct object NPs, which ties in with their specific pragmatic function. How are the examples in (88)–(91) to be classified in terms of the revised Mackenzie–Keizer taxonomy? Example (88) is non-introducing, and in Hallidayan terms is an example of unmarked focus. Examples (89*a–d*) are introducing and new; (90*a–c*) are introducing and situationally evoked. Examples (91*a,b*) are introducing and textually evoked.[24]

There are few examples of contrast in the Map Task dialogues, but there is general agreement that IT clefts can signal contrast. For instance, Givón (1990: 705) talks of the speaker inducing contrary expectations, as in *I went through the whole family—mom, dad . . . the lot. It was my great aunt who finally stepped in* and Hedberg (1990: 172–3) agrees that IT clefts can be contrastive, adding that the important factor that determines the contrastive status of a particular IT cleft is whether the information in the cleft clause is activated, that is, within reach of the speaker's awareness. SEE can also have a contrastive function, but is limited to explicit contrast, picking out one from a limited and enumerated set. Thus, Givón's example can be rephrased as *I went through the whole family—mom, dad, . . . the lot. They all refused. But see my great aunt, she gave me the money right away*. In terms of Mackenzie and Keizer, the SEE construction is introducing, situationally evoked and contrastive.

6.3.4. *LIKE as a non-contrastive focuser*

6.3.4.1. *Some arguments and observations*

We argued in § 6.3.2 that LIKE is not to be analysed as a pause-filler. The case must now be put for analysing it as an item that focuses non-contrastively on

guy we met in Paris?, You know those boots we tried on yesterday with the fur lining?, Do you see that chair over there?

[23] On paper (91*a,b*) appear to have imperative syntax but their intonation is interrogative and they evoke responses such as *yes*, indicating that they have been interpreted as a question. It is tempting to derive SEE from DO YOU SEE, but this analysis would not apply to all instances of the SEE construction. SEE can introduce conditions—*see if you just go directly down from that*—and times—*see when you get to that do an angle*, and it is not possible to substitute *do you see* for *see* in the latter examples.

[24] Cf. the discussion in Ch. 5 of proposition-introducing devices in spontaneous conversation: e.g. **thing is** *he's watching the man not the ball*, **the only thing wi' Beth**, *Beth'll no spend money*.

constituents and the entities they refer to. The key questions that require an answer are:

1 Do the instances of LIKE occur randomly?
2 If the analyst feels intuitively that they do not occur randomly but have a discourse function, what arguments can be deployed in defence of that intuition?
3 If LIKE is a focusing item, how does it differ from the focusing constructions discussed in §6.2?

To develop an answer to these questions we can begin with two points stated earlier. The first is simply that any extra coding, whether prosodic or syntactic, lends salience to a constituent. The second is that, if it is accepted that LIKE is not a pause-filler, then, whatever the eventual analysis, LIKE counts as a piece of syntactic code. It is extra, in that it could be omitted—but IT and WH clefts, along with fronting, are equally optional, given the availability of pitch movement, increase in amplitude and increase in duration which can be applied to simple, neutral syntactic constructions.

There are four facts that do not square with the hypothesis that LIKE is generated at random.

i In 32 dialogues, half the fully coded corpus, 76% of the occurrences of LIKE can be paraphrased by a WH cleft. (Some of that percentage can also be paraphrased by an IT cleft.) 8% can be paraphrased by an IT cleft, 4% by a construction with DO YOU MEAN, and 12% are problematic.

ii In the 32 dialogues all the occurrences of LIKE are produced where there has been misunderstanding and argument. LIKE does not occur at the beginning of the first instruction from the instruction-giver in any dialogue nor does it occur in unproblematic sequences of instruction followed by execution of the instruction.

iii All the occurrences of LIKE are associated with only 4 out of twelve possible moves in the game structure, instructing, aligning, checking, and querying.[25]

That is, they are produced by instruction-givers clearing up misunderstanding or contradicting assertions by instruction-followers and by instruction-followers asking for further information or for confirmation of an instruction.

[25] Sixty-four Map Task dialogues are coded for syntax, information structure (first or subsequent mention of an item, acceptance or rejection of information, realization that there is a difference in landmark, and so on), and game structure. The latter consists of the various types of move that participants make in the course of the interaction—cf. Kowtko *et al.* (1992).

iv The occurrences of LIKE are associated, not with landmarks, but with directions, distances, and the shape of the route.

The fact that the LIKE sequences can be paraphrased by WH or IT clefts does not mean that LIKE has exactly the same discourse function as these constructions. The essential point is that the WH and IT clefts lend salience to specific constituents and that the clefts are not appropriate at any and every point in a given discourse. (Readers can demonstrate this for themselves by taking any text of English, including paragraphs of this chapter, and recasting all the neutral declarative or interrogative clauses as WH or IT clefts. The resulting text soon becomes incoherent.) LIKE is not appropriate in any and every clause either, witness the evidence in (ii) and (iii) above.

Accepting that LIKE functions as a focuser, we must ask how it differs from the clefts. LIKE is a non-introducing, non-contrastive focuser that can focus on new or given information or entities. One important difference is that WH items and IT are deictic and LIKE is not. WH and IT clefts, by virtue of the deictic items, point to one item or set of items as being relevant, thereby implicitly excluding other items and they are available for speakers who wish to draw explicit contrasts. (Cf. Hedberg 1990: 163–84.) The actual usage of clefts is more complex. In the Map Task dialogues WH clefts containing an indefinite deictic item are used rather as devices for summing up a discussion and introducing the move indicated by that discussion. Where they draw an explicit contrast, speakers are more likely to use contrastive pitch or an IT cleft. LIKE has neither of these functions.

LIKE is not as powerful a focuser as the IT, WH, or RWH clefts. There is a relationship between certain syntactic properties and degree of focusing power. Considered as transformations of neutral main clauses, the clefts involve a major reorganization of one clause into two clauses (hence the label 'cleft') and the introduction of deictics.[26] In contrast, LIKE is not deictic, its addition to a clause does not entail any syntactic reorganization, and its comparative weakness in these respects accompanies a comparative weakness in focusing power. On the other hand, it enjoys great flexibility, occurring before main and adverbial clauses, NPs, PPs, gerunds, and adverbs—cf. (92).

One final observation concerning the non-random distribution of LIKE and its function as a focuser is that, as Table 6.6 shows, younger participants in the Map Task experiments produced far fewer than the older participants.

---

[26] These comments on transformations are not to be interpreted as hinting at a possible treatment within some generative transformational model.

TABLE 6.6. *Frequency of LIKE by age group*

Age group	Occurrences of LIKE
8 year olds	2
10 year olds	4

The figures relate to the same number of dialogues from each age group, but not to the same amount of dialogue material, because the 13 year olds produced more dialogue than the younger participants. (In turn, the university undergraduates produced much more dialogue than the 13 year olds.) The amount of dialogue is increased primarily by the amount of questions asked (*Have you got a fast-flowing river?* etc.) and by the amount of conversation-management such as checking whether the other participant has understood an explanation or carried out an instruction. As stated in point (iii), many occurrences of LIKE are associated precisely with questioning and conversation management. Since these are lacking in the dialogues from the younger participants, increasing the amount of dialogue from the latter groups would not affect the relative numbers. Interestingly, the younger participants also give instructions, but do not use LIKE there either. The data indicates that LIKE has to be acquired and indeed seems to be acquired relatively late. This may be caused, not by an intrinsic difficulty with the construction, but by the late acquisition of discourse management skills.

6.3.4.2. *Distribution of LIKE*

The examples in (92) illustrate the flexible positioning of LIKE and possible rephrasings as WH or IT clefts.

(92) (*a*) **LIKE + main clause**
  A ⟨I mean and **like** + you've not got any obstacles here have you
  B no
  A between the west lake and the monument?⟩
  [rephrasing: *what I want to ask is—you've not got any obstacles . . .?*]
 (*b*) **LIKE + PP**
  A you go [*inbreath] **like** round it
  [rephrasing: *where you go is round it/it's round it you go*]
 (*c*) **LIKE + PP**
  A so I just sort of is that + **LIKE** + round the collapsed shelter a line going round
  [rephrasing: *is it round the collapsed shelter/do you mean round the collapsed shelter?*]

Focus Constructions: Clefts and like 321

(*d*) **LIKE + PP**
   A and then go straight d- do you have a cattle stockade?
   B right near near the corner?
   A uhuh
   B right
   A go straight down + to the cattle stockade
   B **like** above or below it?
   A below it
   B right OK
   [rephrasing: *is it above or below it?/do you mean above or below it?*]

(*e*) **LIKE + NP**
   A to the lefthand side of East Lake? **like** the very far end of East Lake?
   [rephrasing: *is it the very far end of East Lake I'm going to?*]

(*f*) **LIKE + gerund**
   A I s—don't suppose you've got a graveyard have you
   B ehm no
   A nup ++ right
   B ⟨but a fast running creek + and canoes and
   A ⟨yeah ok what you want to do is
   B things⟩
   A is you want to be sort of **like** + going ++up + and then curving right round the fast flowing creek⟩
   [rephrasing: *where you're going is up and then curving right round the fast flowing creek*]

(*g*) **LIKE + VP**
   A then you want to start + **like** ++ carry on that curve for about four or five inches
   [rephrasing: *what you want to do is carry on that curve for about four or five inches*]

(*h*) **LIKE + adverb**
   A yeah the old mill's **like** + north east of it
   [rephrasing: *it's to the north east of it that the old mill is/where the old mill is is north east of it*]

6.3.4.3. *LIKE: some detailed examples*

The dialogue extracts given in (93)–(97) illustrate the larger contexts in which LIKE occurs. Each example is commented on. With the exception of (93), the examples contain instances of LIKE given in (92).

(93) A1 Right. Can you can you—well can you see the abandoned cottage?
       B1 ⟨Yeah. That's in the middle of my map/
       A2 Uhuh
       B2 right in the middle of the page⟩
       A3 So if . . . mm—so if you go to the old mill and then . . .
       B3 I'd I'd need to go beneath the old mill—right? OK?
       A4 uhuh

B4 ⟨further along to the right and then up about six or seven inches/
A5 Mhm, mhm, mhm
B5 to get to the abandoned cottage. So I I do that, do I—⟩
A6 So you're going to your right—over to your right and then eh straight up to the—round the abandoned cottage right?
B6 OK So I . . . right . . . Well, I've not drawn anything yet. I'll go down from the caravan park, right?
A7 Mhm
B7 and then right?
A8 Is the point still that you . . . it's not so that you d- you avoid that fence or have you got to go by that fence?
B8 I've avoided that fence now.
A9 ⟨Right. You have. Right . . . /
B9 I'm going under the mill. OK?
A10 Uhuh
B10 And up now
A11 No You mu- . . . You're actually meant to go over the mill
B11 Over the mill?
A12 Uhuh. As in . . . on the lefthand side of it. You know what I mean? **Like** going up round it on the map

The extract in (93) is preceded by a dispute about how B might circumvent a Picket Fence that is on his map but not on A's. A further complication is that B's map has a Mill Wheel where A's has an Old Mill. The problems begin at (A4) in this section of the dialogue where she fails to contradict B's statement that he had to go under the Old Mill. The route on A's map goes up and round the Old Mill. (B4)–(A9) deals with general direction and distance of movement and whether B has found a way round the Picket Fence. (B9) contains the announcement that B is going under the mill, and at this point A realizes that B is making a mistake. (A11) states the contradiction in general terms—*You're actually meant to go over the mill*. (B11) picks up this information but questions it (in surprise, as is clear from the pitch) and (A12) provides the necessary detail: *on the lefthand side of it* and *going up round it*. The latter information is important, and is made salient by *like*. Note that by this point A has got her thoughts gathered, has realized the problem and is giving instructions without hesitation.

It is possible to rephrase (A12) as *what you're doing is going up round it* because a contrast is being drawn between B's proposal and the route on A's map, although, as pointed out in §6.3.4.1, contrast is not necessarily signalled by clefts and the element of contrast inherent in WH clefts is often overshadowed by their role in drawing a discussion to an end and pointing to the next general move in constructing the route. Note that (A11) contains an explicit contrast, which is signalled by *no, actually* and by the pitch on *over*. *Like* merely highlights the particular detail—over the mill.

The focusing function of LIKE is even clearer in (94), which is a

Focus Constructions: Clefts and like   323

continuation of the extract in (93) and contains (92b). The numbering of the contributions to the dialogue is continued from (93).

(94) B12 Mhm. Well my Caravan Park is on the lefthand side of the Mill
 A13 Uhuh. So is this. Right. It's it's on the far left, isn't it?
 B13 Yeah. My Caravan Park's on the far left but the Mill Wheel's to the right of it.
 A14 Uhuh. That's fine. So if you . . . You're going to the Old Mill
 B14 First of all?
 A15 Mhm
 B15 It's the very first place I go?
 A16 Uhuh
 B16 Well, I can just draw a line straight between the two then. Right?
 A17 But on my map it's not got that. It's . . . eh . . . you're going in a sort of curve to the bottom of the map, then round the Old Mill.
 B17 Round beneath the Old Mill?
 A18 Uhuh. No—you don't actually go under the Old Mill. You go **like** round it. **Like**, see the side of the steps are? [*sic*]
 B18 Yeah
 A19 **Like**, that's how you go. Just go round the top.

(B12)–(B13) are concerned with the relative positions of the Caravan Park and the Old Mill. (A14)–(A16) establish that the first stretch of route goes from the Start Point to the Old Mill. (A17) counters the suggestion in (B16) that a straight line will be sufficient. (B17) again brings up the possibility of going under the Old Mill—in spite of the discussion in (12). (A18) contains parallel syntactic structures, the first explicitly negating the proposal that the route lies under the Old Mill and the second providing the correct location of the route. The parallel syntactic structures provide a contrast by virtue of the parallelism, and the *like* in the second structure focuses on the correct information: Structure 1: *you don't actually go under the Old Mill*; Structure 2: *You go like round it*.

(A18) continues with more detailed information, namely that the route goes up the side of the steps. A uses the SEE construction exemplified in (91b) to establish the side of the steps in the centre of B's attention, and uses LIKE to focus on the SEE construction: *Like see the side of the steps are?* When B signals that he has located the steps, A uses a reverse cleft to point to them and to convey the information that B has to follow the side of the steps. The reverse cleft is highlighted by LIKE: *Like that's how you go*.

The first *like* in (A18) could be paraphrased as a cleft too. Again there is explicit contrast, but it is expressed by parallel syntactic structures and a further contrastive structure is not necessary. (This does not mean that speakers would never choose a WH cleft at this point.) The second and third occurrences of LIKE in (94) could be paraphrased at a pinch but the paraphrases would be very clumsy and long-winded in themselves and would contravene what seems to be a convention that WH clefts do not occur in a series. A given contrast need only be signalled once, whether by a cleft, by parallel syntactic structure or by pitch. These considerations apart, *like, see the side of the steps are?* in (A18) can in principle by paraphrased by *What I want you to do now is—see the side of the steps are?* In (A19), *Like, that's how you go* can only be given a paraphrase *What you're going to do is (go round them)*, or even *What I'm going to tell you is*, but these paraphrases are again over-long and unnecessary.

(95) contains (92c)
- A   how long do I go along?
- B   ⟨em it's a kind of like a straight/
- A   a straight line?
- B   a straight line + not a str—quite a straight line down down but it's kind of it's vertical anyway⟩
- A   to—about half an inch?
- B   yeah
- A   right
- B   yeah
- A   ⟨right/
- B   and then
- A   so I just sort of—is that + **like** + round the collapsed shelter—a line going round?

About thirty lines before the beginning of the excerpt in (95) A and B discuss whether there is a collapsed shelter on both maps and its exact location. A expresses doubts as to where she is to draw the route. B tells her to draw the route down and at this point A asks for the first time if the route goes past the collapsed shelter.

(96) contains (92h)
- A   well + could you make a line go round it and then ++ is it ++ is it like down and then the old mill's above from it?
- B   yeah the old mill's **like** + north east of it

This example occurs at the end of the long discussion about the old mill.

(97) contains (92a)
- A1   and eh have you got a golf course?
- B1   no I take it you're going round the golf course? just draw a straight line
- A2   ⟨no—the golf course is like nearer the East Lake—below the East lake so/
- B2   oh ah so it is
- A3   so I would be going to the /
- B3   right so see where the monument is?
- A4   lefthand side of the golf course⟩
- B4   ⟨you're going underneath the monument and up—OK? you're curving /

Focus Constructions: Clefts and like 325

A5 ⟨I'm com-/
B5 round the monument⟩
A6 ⟨I'm doing like a I'm drawing a straight line down to the monument and curving r- round/
B6 and go round underneath it
A7 the bottom of it⟩
B7 and curve round the bottom of it uhuh
A8 ⟨I mean and **like** + you've not got any obstacles here have you? below/
B8 no
A9 between the West Lake and the monument?⟩
B9 the West Lake and the monument? I've got a trig point

The relevant occurrence of LIKE is in (A8) and is in a final request for information following a long discussion with interruptions and overlapping speech. The information requested—whether there are any obstacles—is important; the general direction of the route has been established but the exact line of the route is affected by the presence or absence of obstacles.

(A8) could be revamped as *what I want to ask is whether you have any obstacles*, but the WH cleft is inappropriate in a situation where the instruction-follower is expected to ask questions and where the instruction-giver is not expected to avoid answering awkward questions. *What I want to ask* would be perfectly in place coming from an interviewer interrogating a politician, say, where it would function as indicating the next (or first) general stage in the interview. In the middle of an interview the WH cleft would also serve to draw a line under the preceding part of the interview.

Example (98) does not lend itself to reformulation as clefts.

(98) contains (92*h*)
   A   well + could you make a line go round it and then ++ is it ++is it **like** down and then the Old Mill's above from it?
   B   Yeah the Old Mill's **like** + north east of it

WH clefts are complex—*Is where you go down?*, and an IT cleft is not only syntactically infelicitous but focuses too much on the first piece of information at the expense of the second—*is it down that you go and then the Old Mill above from it?* As it stands, (98 A) can be seen as a truncated cleft which has scope over the remainder of the sequence, i.e. applies to both *down* and *the Old Mill's above from it*. In the truncated cleft *like* highlights *down*. Similarly, a cleft would be out of place in B's contribution because B is not contrasting north-east with another direction nor sorting out a disagreement over the route but simply agreeing with A and providing another detail.

6.3.4.4. Focus particle UND ZWAR

A frequent sequence in both the Map Task data and the DSK is UND ZWAR. Its function is in many ways similar to LIKE in its non-clause final use. It can be used to signal exemplification, but has the more general function of elucidating previous comments. Its focusing function may be related to the use of ZWAR as a connector indicating *Einschränkung*, i.e. restriction or narrowing. König and Stark (1991) suggest that UND ZWAR translates into English *and in fact* or *namely*. These translations capture the meaning of some, but not all uses of the particle. The proposed English equivalents are not in fact frequent in spoken English, especially *namely*, although the German equivalent *nämlich* turns up in (99 A2). Our analysis is similar to Granito (1983, 1984). The function of UND ZWAR is illustrated by (99).

```
(99) A1 und du  hast  also       rechts         keinen Aussichtspunkt mehr
        and you have  therefore on-the-right no  view-point           more (no other)
     B1 nee
        no
     A2 weil   ich hab  nämlich  noch einen Aussichtspunkt
        cause  I   have you-see  another    view-point
        und zwar       ist der   direkt   unter der Ostsee
        FOCUS Part.    is  that  directly under the eastlake
     B2 ja
        yes
     A3 und zwar       aeh nicht unter dem aehm  rechten unterem Zipfel
        FOCUS Part.    eh  not   under the ehm   right   bottom  corner
        der      Ostsee    sondern/
        of-the   eastlake  but
     B3 ja
        yes
     A4 unter dem  leicht   diagonal    höheren
        under the  slightly diagonally  higher-up-one
     B4 mhm
     A5 oder drunter
        or   below
     B5 ja  so  ungefähr
        yes so  roughly
     A6 ja  da     ist ungefähr der Aussichtspunkt
        yes there is  roughly   the view-point
```

A is explaining to B where his missing viewpoint is. In A2 *und zwar* signals the forthcoming general location (*direkt unter dem Ostsee*), in A3 it signals a further narrowing down of the location (*nicht unter dem rechten unterem Zipfel sondern dem leicht diagonal höheren*). There are 32 cases of *und zwar* in the 30,000 words of Map Task data, all signalling more specific location or direction. The construction is much rarer in the DSK—only 50 cases in 225,000 words. In this corpus *und zwar* is often used to signal specification of a topic, as in (100).

(100) A wir haben im   moment alle so   n großes problem
       we have at-the moment all Particle a big   problem
   B mhm
   A und zwar   is es die skepsis
      FOCUS Part. is it the scepticism
      die   sich bei uns im   moment so   n bißchen breit macht
      which itself with us at-the moment Particle a little   broad makes
      'which is kind of spreading amongst us at the moment'

In (100) *und zwar* signals the further specification of 'ein großes problem'. *Und zwar* is often similar in function to topic-introducing WH clefts in English, sometimes in combination with a preceding general topic introducer as in (100). In this case possessive existential constructions are often used which then carry a similar function to the WH clause in a WH cleft which presupposes existence of a variable. (See §6.2.4.)

Und zwar also appears to be used as a more general linking device, where the further specification does not always follow on directly as in the above example. There is indeed a scale of more or less integrated examples. In (101) *und zwar* is not followed by the question introduced via the existential possessive. Rather it is used to introduce the description of the whole situation which has led to the question. This is mediated by *hab ich da einen Fall* (have I there a case 'I've got this problem'). The question itself follows later.

(101) guten Tag ich hätt   mal   eine Frage (B: mhm)
       good day I   have (subjunctive) MODAL Part. a   question
       und zwar   hab ich da   einen Fall
       FOCUS Part. have I   there a   case
       mein Bekannter hat jetzt eine Wohnung bekommen...
       my   friend   has now a   flat   got...

In (102) the speaker launches straight into the description without further mediation.

(102) A ich hätte gern   mal   eine auskunft
       I would like (Adv) MODAL Part. a   (piece of) advice
   B ja   bitte
      yes please/go ahead
      und   zwar bin ich sechs jahre   verheiratet
      FOCUS Part. am I   six   years married
      und mein mann   fährt zur see
      and my   husband goes to   sea
      und nun möcht ich gerne   daß er eine landstellung annimmt
      and now would I   like (Adv) that he a   land-job   takes

In some cases *und zwar* functions as a discourse connector and is followed by a main clause without inversion.[27]

6.3.5. LIKE in the spontaneous conversations

6.3.5.1. Contrasts with LIKE in the Map Task dialogues

There are two main contrasts between the Map Task dialogues and the spontaneous conversations. The first is that the occurrences of LIKE + clause (45 instances) far outnumber the instances of LIKE + NP (5) and LIKE + PP (8). The second is that in a considerable number of examples LIKE follows the constituent it relates to—16 instances of clause + LIKE, 5 of NP + LIKE, and 2 of PP + LIKE. Constituent-following LIKE also has a different discourse function from constituent-preceding LIKE; it is used to counter objections and possible false assumptions on the part of the listener. As mentioned in §6.3.1.1, constituent-following LIKE is recorded in the *OED* and early accounts of non-standard English and is treated as having a discourse function. §6.3.1.1 suggested that these earlier analyses are not adequate, but that is irrelevant. The important points are that earlier scholars analysed LIKE not as a pause-filler or a randomly occurring item but as a hedge, and that the construction is clearly not some recent and 'suspect' development of late twentieth-century English but has been in existence for quite a long time.

6.3.5.2. The corpus of spontaneous conversation

Some information can usefully be added concerning the distribution of LIKE over participants in the spontaneous conversations. The data is drawn from two sources, pupils at a fee-paying school as opposed to pupils at state schools and adults who had attended state schools. In approximately similar amounts of conversation, the fee-paying-school informants provided only 17 occurrences of LIKE, whereas the state school informants provided 81 occurrences. It is the latter whose syntactic distribution is summarized in §6.3.5.1.

Table 6.7 gives figures for the informants who produced the largest numbers of *like*. These four informants produced 58 occurrences, the remaining 25 occurrences are distributed over 16 informants, some of whom produced none. The raw numbers distort the picture, because the informants took part in a different number of conversations. To obtain a more accurate picture, a calculation was made of the total number of turns for each informant covering all the conversations in which each informant took part. For each informant an average number of words per turn was

---

[27] Another frequent particle in German is ALSO which awaits detailed analysis. It is even more flexible than UND ZWAR. It shares some functions of LIKE.

TABLE 6.7. *Distribution of LIKE over some participants in the conversations*

Interviewer (male, 24, graduate)	34
Friend of interviewer (male, 31, graduate)	9
18-year-old pupil X (female)	9
18-year-old pupil Y (female)	6

calculated and multiplied by the total number of turns to give a total number of words. For each informant the total number of words was then divided by the appropriate number of occurrences of LIKE to give a ratio of 1 occurrence of LIKE per N words. Table 6.8 shows the value of N for each informant.

The figures are important because they provide evidence against the possibility that the interviewer produced high numbers of *like* in order to identify with the people he was interviewing. It is clear that the interviewer and pupil X are relatively close with respect to the ratio of occurrence of LIKE to number of words, and the male graduate friend of the interviewer produced far more occurrences than the interviewer in a situation very different from that obtaining in the recording sessions with the interviewer and the school pupils. Further evidence comes from another recording session involving the first-named author of this volume, his wife, and five female undergraduates. The recording took place during a meal in the flat belonging to the first-named author and his wife. Two of the female undergraduates produced 12 and 9 occurrences respectively of LIKE, whereas the author and his wife produced one occurrence each. That is, most of the occurrences of LIKE were produced by speakers who were not called on to adjust their speech to make the other participants feel at home—that role belonged to the author and his wife. It is clear that some speakers regularly use LIKE as a discourse organizing device. Furthermore, it is not a feature of immature language, since the Map Task dialogues demonstrate a remarkable increase in its frequency between the dialogues of the 8 and 10 year olds and those of the 13 year olds.

TABLE 6.8. *Words per occurrence of LIKE*

Informant	No. of words for 1 occurrence of LIKE
Interviewer (male, 24, graduate)	567
Friend of interviewer (male, 31, graduate)	428
18-year-old pupil X (female)	652
18-year-old pupil Y (female)	857

While the total number of occurrences of LIKE in the fee-paying-school corpus is relatively small, it is interesting that only two informants out of eight (both 15-year-old females) produced no instances of LIKE. In other words, it seems that most of these informants had the LIKE construction but used it sparingly.

6.3.5.3. *Clause-initial LIKE*

The conversations contain a number of examples in which LIKE occurs in first position, with the entire following clause in its scope. Many of the examples can be analysed in the same way as those in the Map Task dialogues, i.e. as non-contrastive, non-introducing focusers, but examples (103)–(105) illustrate the use of LIKE either to highlight a clause/piece of information that elucidates a previous comment or to ask for details elucidating a previous comment. That is, Schourup's analysis of LIKE as equivalent to FOR EXAMPLE is appropriate—though LIKE cannot simply be replaced by FOR EXAMPLE in the examples below (and cf. the discussion of (85) in §6.3.1.3). (103 B4) asks for an example of A's Dad being very strict. (104 B1) gives an instance of the behaviour that leads to Mr Lindsay's never being slagged by pupils. (105 C2) gives an instance of knowing the number of qualifications required for particular universities and the consequences of knowing the information.

(103) A1 what sort of ehm you know relationship do you have with parents really—disciplinewise and that
   B1 My Dad's very strict
   A2 Is he?
   B2 Aye I keep away from him most of the time—we dinnae get on too well
   A3 really?
   B3 I get on a lot better with my mum
   A4 **like** are there strict rules you know about coming in and all this?

(104) A1 a teachers' bulletin comes out once a month and Mr Y—oh he's got a fantastic sense of humour . . .
   A2 . . . he's got a really brilliant sense of humour and he produced his one at Christmas—it was good
   A3 he'll probably help us because he likes slagging teachers
   B1 yeah and he never gets slagged himself//**like**/you would notice at the Back Marker [a pub] that he was the only one that actually came across and spoke to us

(105) A1 what do you think about the system—university entrance? Do you think it's fair or—do you know how it's done for example?
   B1 well, not really—no—we don't really know much about it you just send in what you've got
   C1 just accept what you get without questioning it

A1 yeah but you must be told something about it because people people with two Highers don't apply and stuff like that
B2 you're told that you need three Highers for university and that's it—even the certain number of qualifications
C2 **like** I knew that I couldnae apply for Edinburgh because I didnae have an O level language—so I just didnae do it

6.3.5.4. Clause-final LIKE

There are 7 declarative clauses and 9 interrogative clauses ending in LIKE. Clause-final LIKE does have some retroactive focusing power but more importantly, it has a rather specific discourse role, which was stated explicitly by Mike Cullen, a temporary research assistant on the syntax and dialogue project. It was known that for some time his father had been suffering from a heart problem. One afternoon Mike announced *he's back in hospital*, referring to his father, and continued with *he's in for observation like*. When it was pointed out to Mike that he had provided another example of *like*, he answered that he had used that construction in order to counter the inference, which he could see from the listener's expressions, that his father was seriously ill again. Inspection of the declarative *like*-final clauses in the spontaneous conversations revealed that they can all be interpreted as countering potential inferences, objections, or doubts. The most general term for the role of LIKE is 'clearing up misunderstanding'. Some examples are given in (106)–(108).

(106) A1 I quite like swimming myself—do you ever go up to the Commonwealth [swimming pool]
    B1 uhuh
    A2 do you like it there?
    B2 aye—it's good
    A3 I think it's a really nice day or afternoon out—sometimes I go there with my family you know—it's really tremendous cos there's a wee kiddies' pool you know where my wee girl can swim you know/she has her wings **like**//she jumps right in you know—she's two and a half and eh—it's a great place . . .

The phrase *she has her wings like* dispels any notion the listener might entertain that A's daughter can swim properly. The absurdity of this notion is made clear by the information that she is only two and a half, information which the listener did not have when A talked of the pool where his daughter could swim.

(107) A1 and there's no way we could get away with the things we would like to put in it [school magazine]
    B1 do you not think that's disgusting to be—it's absolutely disgusting
    C1 sixth year have decided we will produce a new sheet at the end of the year slagging everybody

    A2 that will be interesting
    C2 and that will not be censored by any teacher
    B2 quite right
    C3 just something to leave a memory of us **like**

The phrase *just something to leave a memory of us like* counteracts any potential inferences that the proposed unofficial news sheet is to be big and remarkable. It will be remarkable in being uncensored but otherwise will be a modest production, not a trend-setter but simply a memento from the pupils who are about to leave school.

(108) A1 . . . we just had the Open Day today you know and eh oh there were a lot of people there—I was pleased to see it—you know that all the courses have gone down—all the Social Science and Arts?

    B1 how do you mean 'gone down'?
    A2 they're just no getting the numbers
    B2 oh the intakes **like**—is that right? oh I didnae ken

Like in (108 B2) plays a slightly different role from that played by *like* in (106). B cannot interpret A's statement that the courses have gone down; he does not know what inferences to make, and the statement at A2 enables him to discard all but one.

(109) A1 . . . sometimes a beer got upset and . . . this sort of residue stuff got upset and wouldn't settle and eh the brewers would supply you with finings . . .

    A2 . . . you had a wooden spile—you bored on the top of the barrel . . . and then you had ready a spile, which was a wooden cone about that length . . . and a soft wood naturally was porous and it would help to get this froth to let it work down—you had to be very careful you didn't take it right down **like**/it went flat

The inference being countered by the *like* in (109 A2) is 'Surely the beer would go flat if you bored a hole in the top of the barrel?' A points out that this inference is incorrect because the operation was carried out very carefully precisely to prevent the beer going flat.

All the above examples can be appropriately paraphrased by means of clefts, as in (110), but whereas clause-final LIKE—better constituent-final LIKE—has one special function, the clefts focus on constituents and the focus may be justified by any number of reasons.

(110) A cause there's a wee kiddies' pool you know where my wee girl can swim you know what I mean is she has her wings//she jumps right in
    B all we want to do is leave a memory of us
    C oh it's the intakes you mean//aye/is that right oh I didnae ken
    D you had to be very careful what you didn't do was take it right down

Focus Constructions: Clefts and like   333

LIKE occurs in final position in YES–NO and WH interrogatives, as in (111)–(113). The interrogatives are used to elicit clarificatory details relating to a more general topic. The details help to remove the questioner's astonishment, or to (dis)confirm an inference or assumption made by the questioner: in general, to remove misunderstanding. LIKE occurs in final position only in questions that are asked in response to a statement, never in questions that open a section of dialogue.

(111) A1 do you remember anything that—you know—any sort of tricks you used to get up to when you were—you know—say-in first or second year . . .
   B1 eh we used to eh stick rulers to folk's eh teachers' desks and ask them for a loan of a ruler—they used to try and pick the ruler up
   A2 did you stick it down with Gloy **like**?

(111 A2) asks for information on one point of detail concerning sticking rulers to desks: what substance was used.

(112) A1 how many of these interview or conversation things have you done?
   B1 have I done? I must have done quite a few now actually—I mean I've spent a couple of terms
   A2 maistly in Edinburgh **like**? or—
   B2 at X—I was down at X High School—I had a couple of terms down there—it was good—it was all laid on . . .
   A3 why do particularly go to schools **like**? is it because they are more amenable to getting—
   B3 they're more amenable to getting people—I mean—and you get the same people—it's organized I mean

(112 A2) asks for (dis)confirmation of R's assumption that the interviews are being done in Edinburgh—a reasonable assumption given that M lived and worked in the centre of Edinburgh. M explains that he did the interviews in another town and indeed in its High School. (112 A3) asks about a detail of the interviewing business: why collect the data in schools? There may even be some surprise at the decision to carry out the fieldwork in schools.

(113) A1 got a bairn have you?
   B1 aye—Nicole's eh three
   A2 three?
   B2 aye—I was married young
   A3 aye—you must have been—how old are you **like**

(113 A3), with emphatic stress on *are*, relates to M's exact age, i.e. to the detail that R needs in order to understand the surprising information that M's daughter is three. Note that here, and in (111), the most suitable

paraphrase involves EXACTLY: *why exactly go to schools* and *how old are you exactly?*

6.3.6. Conclusion

The Map Task dialogues and the spontaneous conversations indicate that three properties of focus constructions must be recognized; introducing vs. non-introducing, contrastive vs. non-contrastive and relating to new vs. relating to given entities, with appropriate interpretations of 'new' and 'given'. The two major LIKE constructions—clause-initial and clause-final LIKE—have different discourse roles. In general LIKE is a non-introducing, non-contrastive focuser which may focus on new or given information. In addition, clause-initial LIKE is concerned with the elucidation of previous comments, whereas clause-final LIKE is concerned with countering objections and assumptions. German has clefts but the clefts do not have the same discourse function as their English counterparts and German has other constructions that fulfil the discourse function of, for example, RWH clefts.[28] LIKE is a good example of a particle in English and the nearest German equivalent is also a particle—*und zwar*. At the end of Chapter 5 we remarked that the highlighting/focusing devices in spontaneous speech were organized into a general but delicate system. The discussion in Chapter 6 demonstrates that individual devices are systematic and delicate even when investigated in detail.

---

[28] What English achieves by means of clefts, Russian achieves by means of particles and word order combined. (114*a,b*) give the Russian equivalent of RWH clefts.

(114) (*a*) vot tuda vam nado prijti
look (particle) to-there you-DAT necessary to-come
(*b*) Vot etu knigu vam nado čitat'
look (particle) that-ACC book-ACC you-DAT necessary to-read

Both contain the strong deictic particle *vot* discussed in §§ 5.5.3 and 5.7.8.2.2. In (114*a*) the deictic adverb *tuda* is at the front of the clause immediately after *vot*, whereas the neutral order would be *vam nado prijti tuda*. In (114*b*) the direct object *etu knigu* precedes the verb, but the neutral order is *vam nado čitat' etu knigu*. Russian, that is, resembles German in its use of particles and word order but is unlike it in having no proper cleft construction.

7 Historical Linguistics and Typology

7.1. Introduction

The purpose of Chapters 3 and 4 was to demonstrate, on the basis of data from different languages, that the structure of phrases and clauses in spontaneous spoken language is very different from the structures found in writing. The goal of this chapter and the next is to demonstrate that the spontaneous spoken data and its analysis bear directly on research topics occupying a central position in linguistics. This chapter begins with a note on historical linguistics but focuses on typology, and Chapter 8 is largely devoted to first language acquisition, but ends with a note on the spoken–written dichotomy, non-standard language and education. Educational difficulties affecting speakers of non-standard varieties of a given language are exacerbated by the differences between spontaneous speech and written language.

7.2. Historical Linguistics

It has long been accepted that certain construction-types developed with the elaboration of written varieties of particular languages. For example, both Latin and Greek have a special construction for verbs of fearing in which the verb is followed by a complement clause. This clause is introduced by a negative complementizer and contains a verb in the subjunctive. The closest English construction is the archaic *They fear lest the ship be wrecked*. The force of this example can be conveyed by the two separate clauses *I am afraid* and *Let the ship not be wrecked*. (This paraphrase makes explicit the hidden negative in *lest*.) Gildersleeve and Lodge (1971: 349) discuss the Latin construction in (1).

(1) timeo ne veniat
    I-fear Comp he-come

Veniat is subjunctive and *ne* is overtly negative. The modern English translation is 'I am afraid he will come'. One way of connecting the two constructions is to think of the Latin syntax as spelling out the presuppositions of the English example. If we say that we are afraid that an event is going to happen, our listeners are entitled to infer that we would prefer the event not to happen. The Latin construction developed out of two clauses. One consists of *timeo* (I fear)—or whatever the appropriate form might be in a given context, possibly accompanied by an overt subject noun phrase. The other consists of *ne veniat*, which by itself expresses a wish—'let him not come'. The Latin construction in (1) started as a juxtaposition of the two clauses. This view is supported by the construction used when the speaker expresses a fear that something is not going to happen, as in (2).

(2) timeo ut   amicus veniat
    I-fear Comp friend come
    'I am afraid that my friend is not coming'

The English translation has a negative complement clause, but there is no negative in the Latin equivalent. The explanation is that a literal gloss of the Latin is 'I fear: let my friend come'. The English example licenses the inference that anyone uttering it wants the friend to come; otherwise (assuming sincerity on the part of the speaker) what is the point of combining the proposition that the speaker is afraid with the proposition that the friend is not coming? Speakers of Latin adopted a different convention for such situations; they expressed their fear by means of *timeo* and then expressed a wish that the friend would come—*amicus veniat* (friend let-him/her-come), using the appropriate subjunctive form of the verb. The original Latin syntax, so to speak, spelled out the presuppositions of the English but the original structure was obscured by the development of the integrated verb + complement construction in which the complement is introduced by *ut*. (Main clauses expressing positive wishes were in the subjunctive mood but were not actually introduced by *ut*; on the other hand, main clauses expressing negative wishes were introduced by *ne*.)

The traditional view that hypotactic constructions developed out of paratactic constructions is supported by the data from investigations of spontaneous spoken language; what is often forgotten is that the clausal arrangements of spontaneous spoken language did not stop being paratactic and that the new hypotactic constructions belonged and belong to written language. That is, it is mistaken to talk of languages changing from paratactic to hypotactic; rather, they acquire hypotactic arrangements of clauses in written language and retain the paratactic arrangements in spoken language. (See the discussion of clause linkage in §7.3.5.)

The dating of syntactic developments typically relates only to extant written texts and the earliest appearance in writing of a given construction. For instance, the *Oxford English Dictionary* provides an example of the GET passive dating from 1652, another from 1793 and then an increasing number of instances in the nineteenth century. These dates tell us something about the development of the GET passive, but they tell us much more about its penetration into written English. The construction may well have been in existence for a long time before; indeed, if the passive auxiliary GET is accepted as deriving from the movement verb GET, the dynamic passive can be seen as merely the latest version of a dynamic passive construction built around verbs of movement beginning with WEORðAN in Early English, employing BICOMEN in Middle English and taking over GET in Modern English. (See Miller 1985: 162-91.)

Constructions that belong to the spoken variety of a given language at a given time are not necessarily of recent origin. The use of *which* to connect two sections of discourse—discussed in §3.7.1.2—appears in dialogue in novels by Dickens dating from the 1850s and was used throughout the nineteenth century in *Punch* as a marker of working-class speech. The same construction now has a wider social range of users but is still confined to spoken language; what is important is that its appearance in dialogues and cartoons from the last century shows that spoken-only structures can be durable, and that this particular structure is not just an error resulting from poor syntactic planning.

Spoken language and written language have their own histories. Until the late Middle Ages, Latin was the language of government documents in Western Europe. In England, a special written English for use in government documents was developed by officials of the King's Chancery in the fourteenth and fifteenth centuries. (See Fisher (1977), who describes this variety as an official class dialect.) Keller (1978: 365) describes how the various dialects of German, or at least the written varieties, gradually converged as a result of the documentary language of the imperial chancery and of the larger principalities. Luther claimed that his translation of the Bible employed the Chancery language of Saxony.

In both Britain and Germany further development of the written language was brought about by educated people who wanted to create a written English and a written German fit for the writing of all kinds of literature. Keller mentions the Fruchtbringende Gesellschaft (literally the fruit-bringing society) established in Weimar in 1617; in France the Académie Française and individuals such as Malherbe and Vaugelas strove to codify 'good usage'; in Britain similar efforts towards standardizing the written language were made in the eighteenth century by Samuel Johnson, Bishop Lowth, and Lindley Murray. (See Barrell (1983: ch. 2).) That is, clause and sentence structure and discourse organization in written and spoken language followed very different courses in Britain, Germany, and France, and in general follow very different courses everywhere. Most of the data available on historical syntax relates to written texts.

7.3. Typology

Typology too must take account of the differences between spoken and written language. It is not just that spoken and written language differ with respect to the syntax of phrases and clauses and the organization of discourse; some of the differences are typologically significant. Typologists of necessity work with as large a range of languages as possible. While individual typologists know a number of languages, possibly even a large number, constraints on time and funding oblige them to draw data from grammars, and it is easy to overlook the fact that grammars of languages with written varieties will typically be based on written texts, whereas grammars of languages that have no written variety perforce describe the structure of a spoken variety. In this section we will show that the distinction between spoken and written varieties has consequences for language typology.

7.3.1. *English conditional constructions*

In English a whole range of syntactic constructions are affected. Consider first the conditional. Our spontaneous spoken English data has no examples of the construction in which the protasis is expressed by what looks like an interrogative structure, as in (3*a*,*b*).

(3) (*a*) Were you to write to her, she would forgive you
    (*b*) Should you meet him, pass on my best wishes

These examples not only have interrogative word order in the first clause but contain an auxiliary verb (never DO) and present the situation as remote. Spontaneous spoken English is in fact full of interrogatives functioning as protases, as in (4).

(4) Is he there? In that case I'm not going to the party

Such interrogative protases are yes–no questions with an interrogative pitch pattern. Their role as protases is not marked grammatically but is none the less indisputable once the rhetorical relations between clauses in the discourse are taken into account. If the answer to the question is 'yes' (which the speaker presupposes), the speaker does not go to the party; if the answer is 'no', the speaker does go. In the written language the sequence of yes–no question plus main clause has been grammaticalized; the original interrogative clause retains the interrogative word order but no longer has interrogative pitch pattern. In the spoken language, where no grammaticalization has taken place, we are dealing with a discourse relation.

Where speakers do produce a conditional construction, the tense usage is typically different from the usage in written English. (5a,b) are examples of the written construction and (6a,b) are examples of the spoken one.

(5) (a) If she came to see things for herself, she would understand
(b) If she had come to see things for herself, she would have understood

In spontaneous spoken English the past tense verb is frequently replaced with *would* + verb, and the pluperfect is replaced by *would* + *have* + participle.

(6) (a) (= 5a) If she would come to see things for herself, . . .
(b) (= 5b) If she would have come to see things for herself, . . .

The standard canon requires *came* and *had come*. We should point out that the comments on examples (5) and (6) apply to the written standard in Britain. Readers should not infer that we take written standard English to be exactly the same in every English-speaking country; there are differences, small but unmistakable, between the standard written English of, for example, Britain and the United States. Nor do we assume that the standard written English of Britain is immutable. The constructions in (6a) and (6b) do occur in written texts in the United States and it is quite probable that they will make their appearance in written texts in Britain. As Cameron (1995) observes, at any given time the controls on written texts depend on copy editors. The more written texts appear, the more copy editors are required and the greater the chance of variation among the copy editors or of written texts escaping close scrutiny.

Conditional clauses expressing events that can no longer happen also occur with the pluperfect replaced by *had* + *have*, the latter typically in its reduced form *'ve*. Cf. (7).[1]

(7) (a) I reckon I wouldn't have been able to do it if I hadn't've been able to read music [= hadn't be able]
(b) you wouldn't have got Mark's place if you'd 've come up last year [= had come up]

Quirk *et al.* (1985: §1023) mention protasis clauses with *would*—*I might have married her if she would have agreed*—however the interpretation is not 'if she had agreed' but 'if she had been willing to agree'. They list the example *If I'd have seen her, I'd have told her* only to say that informal American English speech may have matching modals—here, *would* = *'d*—in both clauses. The construction is clearly not just American English and scholars undertaking a typology of conditional clauses will arrive at a misleading view of English if they draw their data from the major grammars

---

[1] The same construction is also found in clauses introduced by *wish*, which likewise present an event as no longer possible.

I wish he'd've complimented me, Roger [= had complimented]

of English (and other languages), which treat primarily the written language.

7.3.2. Participles and gerunds

Similar difficulties attach to participles and gerunds (not to mention ellipsis and oratio obliqua). Free participles as exemplified in (8), are quite untypical of spontaneous spoken English.

(8) (*a*) Sitting at the window, I noticed a car at the bank
 (*b*) Covered in confusion, he apologized
 (*c*) Having shut the window and locked the drawer in her desk, Amanda set off for home

Sirotinina (1974: 95) observes that the corresponding Russian constructions are also not used in spoken Russian and cites a sentence from one of Pushkin's letters to show that he had observed this in the 1820s. In typological work spontaneous spoken English and Russian would have to be classified as not having free participle constructions but the written languages as having them. It is worthwhile repeating the point made in Chapter 1 that while it is essential to distinguish texts according to topic, formality, medium, and so on, it is equally necessary to distinguish informants not just with respect to age and sex but also with respect to their exposure to written language. The latter typically, but not necessarily, is in direct proportion to the amount of formal, especially higher, education. It is also necessary to remember that not all speakers of a given language have equal facility with the structures and vocabulary of the language. This point will be repeated in §7.3.5 on the ways in which relationships between clauses are signalled.

The facts of spoken and written English and Russian in turn raise questions about languages like Turkish, in which subordinate clauses of all types have non-finite verb forms, usually called participles in English-language grammars of Turkish. A sentence of written Turkish can consist of main clause and a large number of clauses with participles which are translated into English by relative clauses, complement clauses, adverbial clauses, and participial clauses as appropriate. It is highly likely that these arrangements of clauses are a property of written Turkish but not of spontaneous spoken Turkish. Indeed Mundy (1955: 291), using different terminology, declares that the more elaborately developed forms of nominal statements (i.e. complements), adjectival statements (i.e. relative clauses), and gerundial or adverbial statements are to be found only in the written language. In another section Mundy (1955: 296) describes spoken Turkish as dominated by short stereotyped sentence forms. (See the discussion of formulae in §8.3.6.) In writing, extra information is supplied via internal elaboration of a given syntactic unit, whereas in speech syntactic units are added to the end of a clause. This contrast is exemplified by (9a,b).

(9) (a) Kayseride doktor olan bir dâmâdi var [**written style**]
Kayseri-in doctor being a son-in-law exists
'He has a son-in-law who is a doctor in Kayseri'
 (b) Kayseride bir dâmâdi var, doktor [**spoken style**]
Kayseri-in a son-in-law-his exists, a doctor

Similarly, not enough is known about all the verb chaining phenomena in languages of Papua New Guinea or about verb forms in Australian languages in which, in sequences of clauses, a switch of referent or a continuation of referent is marked, but not tense, aspect, or modality. These constructions occur in narratives, some of which at least have been given before and are semi-planned, but do they also occur in spontaneous conversation, and are they produced with equal mastery by all adult speakers of a particular language?

7.3.3. Negation

The discussion throughout the book has been mainly based on utterances produced by speakers with at least a secondary education. (As mentioned in §1.4 the link with education is that speakers of non-standard varieties who go through higher education, or are academically successful at secondary school typically adopt a more bookish language, at least in public and formal settings.) Zemskaja's data comes from professional people—university lecturers, doctors, lawyers, and so on. The discussion has so far excluded non-standard data but, for this section only, the exclusion is lifted in order to make an important typological point. As soon as the non-standard varieties of a language are taken into account data appears that is important for typology. It is well known that the Slav languages, for instance, have double negation, in which a negated clause containing a quantifier carries two markers of negation, one preceding the verb and one prefixed to the quantifier, as in (10).

(10) ona ne videl a nikogo
she neg saw neg-one
'she didn't see anyone'

A literal translation into English is *she didn't see nobody*, which would be unacceptable in, for example, English language classes at school or university. It is however the normal construction for many, possibly most, native speakers of English in Britain and North America. The argument against this construction in the classroom is that two negatives cancel each other to give a positive, but the fact is that for speakers of non-standard English the two negatives merely reinforce each other, as they do in Russian. The typological point is that languages are classified with respect to whether they have double negatives or not. English as a whole does not fit the classification, because written English does not have double negatives whereas non-standard spoken English does. Of course standard spoken English does not have double negatives, but this fact proves the general point that typology should deal with varieties of languages and not just languages.

Another rule of written English is that negatives modifying a phrase or word rather than a complete clause immediately precede the relevant constituent, as in (11). (The rule is too crude in this formulation but will do for present purposes.)

(11) (a) Not many people came to the lecture
 (b) Not all the hotels take British guests
 (c) She went away not very happy

Corresponding to (11b,c) spontaneous spoken English, standard and non-standard, has the construction in (12), in which the negative does not precede the word it modifies but is attached to the auxiliary verb DO.

(12) (a) All the hotels don't take British guests
 (b) She didn't go away very happy

A clausal negative is found regardless of whether the quantifier is totalizing, as in (12a), or individuating, as in *It's not very democratic because every member is not consulted on the decision*. (All the above are examples produced spontaneously by native speakers of English, not devised for the occasion.) (11a) is more likely to be rendered by (and here we are relying on our intuitions about spoken English) *There wasn't a lot of people at the lecture* or *there wasn't a lot of people came to the lecture*. A search of the corpus of Scottish English conversation revealed a lack of *many*, *little*, and *few* as quantifiers. Our intuitions suggest that the most neutral spoken equivalent of *many* is *a lot of* and that the equivalent of *little* and *few* is *not a lot of*.

We note in conclusion that English is not peculiar with respect to its written and spoken varieties having different negative constructions. Written French has two-constituent negatives such as *ne . . . pas* and *ne . . . personne*. In spontaneous spoken French the *ne* has been lost. A similar development is reported for Welsh in Payne (1985: 224–5).

7.3.4. Relative clauses

7.3.4.1. Typological overview

We first review the properties relevant for a typology of relative clauses, following Comrie (1981: 131–57), and then examine the various types of relative construction that occur in spoken English. Many of these constructions are not mentioned in the standard grammars of English but are cited in books on sociolinguistics or in accounts of specific non-standard varieties. It is clear where standard written English is located on the typological map of relative clauses, but if 'English' is taken as a cover term for all the varieties of English (say in the UK), then it has various locations on the typological map.

7.3.4.2. *The order of the head NP and the modifying relative clause*

The relative clause can precede the NP, as in Chinese, or follow the NP, as in English. Examples are given in (13) and (14).

(13) nimen yong de   fazi (Chinese)
     you   use Particle method
     'the method that you use'

(14) the book that you are reading

In the Chinese construction the relative clause is separated from the NP it modifies by the subordinating particle *de*; *de* signals that the word, phrase, or clause-like sequence preceding it is a modifier or an attribute and that the subsequent expression is the centre or head of the subordinative construction (Henne, Rongen, and Hansen 1977: 269)

A third possibility is for the head NP to be inside the relative clause. Examples are given in (15)—note that Comrie deals only with restrictive relative clauses.

(15) tye   be   [n ye so   min ye] dyo (Bambara)
     man-the   PRES I PAST house REL see build
     'the man is building the house that I saw'

According to Comrie (1981: 138), the whole clause *n ye so min ye* functions as direct object of the main clause—Bambara has basic SOV word order and (15) has to be analysed as having the constituents Auxiliary (*be*), Direct Object (*n ye so min ye*) and verb (*dyo*).

Languages such as Bengali offer a fourth construction, called a correlative. (As we will see from the discussion in §7.3.5, correlatives are not confined to Bengali and may correspond to other constructions than relative clauses.) Examples of this construction are appropriately translated into English by means of relative clauses, but it is quite different from the constructions exemplified in (13) and (14) above. In the latter, the relative clause and the noun it modifies belong together in one and the same NP; that is, the relative clause is inside the matrix clause containing the head noun, and the matrix clause may be main, as in (16*a*) or subordinate, as in (16*b*).

(16) (a) I approve of the career you chose
    (b) I believe that Mary approves of the career you chose

The career you chose is a single NP. The Bengali correlative construction consists of two clauses, but neither is embedded in the other. Examples are in (17).

(17) (a) je   cheleta   amar bondhu, se   esechilo
         WH   boy-the   my   firend   he   came
         'The boy who is my friend came'
    (b) se esechilo, Je   cheleta   amar   bondhu
        he came   WH   boy-the   my   friend [= (13a)]

(17a) and (17b) consist of the same two clauses, but in different orders. One clause contains the equivalent of a WH pronoun in English, *je cheleta amar bondhu*, while the other contains the equivalent of a personal pronoun deictic, *se esechilo*. The *je* clause picks out a non-specific (for the addressee) person, who is thereby introduced into the conversation and becomes given, while the *se* clause refers to that given person. An idiomatic English translation is *The boy who is my friend came* but a gloss closer in spirit is *the-which boy is friend—he came*. The Bengali construction does the same work as the English one, namely picking a particular entity out of a set of entities, but the goal is achieved by a different syntactic route.

7.3.4.3. *How the head noun is reflected in the relative clause*

In a relative clause structure with head noun and modifying relative clause, the head noun is reflected in various ways in the relative clause.

a The noun may occur unreduced in the relative clause. Comrie (1981: 140) cites the Bambara example in (15) and a Hindi example which is analogous to the Bengali examples in (17) above. As we have seen, this may not be the most appropriate way of describing the Bambara construction, and the Bengali examples are very different from the English relative clause construction, to the extent that it may be misleading to call the WH clause a relative clause. Non-standard English (Trudgill 1983: 41) does offer examples such as *he's a man he likes his beer*, with the pronoun subject of the main clause repeated as the subject of the relative clause, but no examples have been found with the head NP repeated in full inside the relative clause, along the lines of *the house I saw the house was very offputting* (= *the house that we saw was very offputting*).

b The relative clause may contain an ordinary personal pronoun bound to the head noun. An example is given in (18), taken from Comrie (1981: 141):

(18) Persian
   Man zan-i-ra   [ke Hasan be u sibe zamini dad] misenasam
   I   woman-ACC that Hasan to her potato gave   I know
   'I know the woman to whom Hasan gave a potato'

c The relative clause may contain a special relative pronoun, such as the WH pronouns in English, which are different from the ordinary personal pronouns. This structure is also found throughout the Indo-European languages of Europe, as exemplified by the Russian sentence in (19). Written Russian has the classic Indo-European construction in which the relative clause contains a relative pronoun agreeing in gender and number with the head noun while taking its case from the verb in the relative clause.

(19) Mal'čik,   kotoromu ona   pomogla,
   Boy-NOM   who-DAT she-NOM help-PFV-PAST
   okazalsja   neblagodarnym
   turn out-PFV-PAST   ungrateful
   'The boy who she helped turned out to be ungrateful'

In the relative clause *kotoromu ona pomogla*, *kotoromu* agrees with *mal'čik* in having masculine gender and singular number. *Kotoromu* is also in the dative case, which is assigned to it by the verb *pomogala* in the relative clause.

d The relative clause may contain a 'gap'; that is, a verb with a valency of n nouns occurs in a given relative clause with only n-1 nouns. The missing noun corresponds to the head noun modified by the relative clause. This strategy is illustrated by the Tamil examples in (20).

(20) (*a*) taaktar poṉmaṉikku aaspattiriyil   karatiyaal   cooṛu kuṭuttaan
         doctor Ponmani-DAT hospital-LOC spoon-INST rice   give-PAST-3SG
         'The doctor gave rice to Ponmani in hospital with a spoon'
   (*b*) ([ ] poṉmaṉikku   aaspattiriyil   karatiyaal   cooṛu koṭutta) taaktar
            Ponmani-DAT hospital-LOC spoon-INST rice   give-REL doctor
         'the doctor who gave the rice to Ponmani in hospital with a spoon'
   (*c*) (taaktar poṉmaṉikku   aaspattiriyil
         doctor   Ponmani-DAT hospital-LOC
         cooṛu   [ ] koṭutta)   karatiyaal
         rice   gave   spoon
         'the spoon with which the doctor gave rice to Ponmani in the hospital'

(20*a*) is a main clause with the finite verb *kot:uttaan* 'gave' and its four dependent noun phrases. In (20*b*) that main clause has been converted into a relative clause (inside the round brackets in bold) modifying the noun *ṭaaktar* 'doctor'. There is no WH pronoun functioning as subject of the clause; instead there is a gap where (20*a*) had *ṭaaktar*. This gap is marked by the square brackets in bold. In (20c) the main clause has been converted into a relative clause (modifying *karatiyaal* 'spoon' and where the clause in (20a) had an occurrence of *karatiyaal*, (20c) has a gap.

7.3.4.4. English Relative Clauses

The purpose of this section is to demonstrate that the place of English in the typology of relative clauses varies according to what type of English is considered. Formal written English has the classic Indo-European relative clause construction with a special relative pronoun, as in the examples in (21). The English variation in this construction is that preposition and WH pronoun can occur together at the front of the relative clause, as in (21a) or the preposition can be stranded at the end of the relative clause, as in (21b).[2]

(21) (a) the lawyer from whom we received the assurances
 (b) the lawyer who we received the assurances from
 (c) the lawyer whom they consulted
 (d) the department in whose files you found the missing documents

In less formal written English and in much spoken English we find the THAT relative clause construction. This is like the Tamil construction in that there is a relative clause marker, albeit a complementizer and not a special verb form, and the noun identical with the head noun is omitted. The noun phrases in (22) are alternative renderings of the Tamil examples in (20).

(22) (a) the doctor that [ ] gave rice to Ponmani in hospital with a spoon
 (b) the spoon that the doctor gave rice to Ponmani with [ ] in the hospital

In very informal English, constructions such as (22b) do not even have a preposition, (23a) is an example from the Scottish English conversations and (23b) was uttered during a radio discussion.

(23) (a) of course there's a rope that you can pull the seat back up [ ]
 (b) I haven't been to a party yet that I haven't got home [ ] the same night

In more formal English we would expect (23a) to be . . . *that you can pull the seat back up with*, and for (23b) we would expect . . . *that I haven't got home from the same night*. In the most formal English we would expect WH relative clauses; (23a) would be . . . *with which you can pull the seat back up* and (23b) would be . . . *from which I haven't got home the same night*.

Speakers of English use a third construction in which the relative clause is introduced by the complementizer THAT but contains a shadow pronoun. That is, this third construction is analogous to the Persian one exemplified in (18) and also to the relative clause construction of Semitic languages. (24a) is from the Scottish English conversations, (24b) is from a corpus

---

[2] The English data have already been discussed in Ch. 3 but are reproduced here both for convenience and because they are being examined from a different perspective.

collected in Somerset by Ossi Ihalainen, (24c) was noted by Jim Miller during domestic conversation, and (24d)—in a conversation between a shopkeeper and a customer.

(24) (a) the girl that her eighteenth birthday was on that day was stoned, couldn't stand up
(b) would those men I call their names step forward
(c) the spikes that you stick in the ground and throw rings over them
(d) an address which I hadn't stayed there for several years

The relevant parts of the above examples are *that her eighteenth birthday* in (24a) as opposed to *whose eighteenth birthday*, *I call their names* in (24b) as opposed to *whose names I call*, *throw rings over them* in (24c) as opposed to *throw rings over* or *over which you throw rings*, and in (24d) *which I hadn't stayed there* as opposed to *which I hadn't stayed at*. (24d) contains *which* and not *that* but the relevant feature is the occurrence of the shadow pronoun *there*, which is pronominal but not a personal pronoun. The presence of *her* in (24a) contrasts with the absence of *whose*, and the presence of *them* in (24c) contrasts with the absence of *whom*. *Whose* and *whom* are absent from non-standard English and from most spontaneous spoken English. They are a hallmark of formal written English and occur in spoken English only if it is formal and planned, or if the speaker (like many academics and other professional people) has been greatly influenced by written English.

Who uses the constructions in (24)? They are regular constructions in non-standard English, but also occur regularly in the spontaneous speech of educated speakers. Like many other constructions in non-standard English, they are not new but can be traced back to Middle English: the *Oxford English Dictionary* has *that same cock that Peter heard him crow*. The significance of this *OED* examples is twofold; it occurs in a written text and the relative clause is not complex or compound and does not contain a possessive construction. Its occurrence in a written text is important, because it demonstrates both how long the construction has existed in English and that its occurrence is not necessarily associated with complicated syntax during unplanned speech production. (Cf. (51b) in Chapter 3 for an example of a shadow pronoun from modern spontaneous spoken English. The syntax of that example could hardly be simpler.)

The English relative clause constructions discussed above have an overt complementizer but various regularly occurring constructions have no complementizer or WH pronoun. Examples are given in (25).

(25) (a) we had this French girl came to stay
(b) my friend's got a brother used to be in the school
(c) there's a man in our street has a Jaguar

(25a,b) are taken from the corpus of Scottish English conversations and

(25c) was noted in the course of conversation. The key feature is that if a WH pronoun did occur, it would be the subject of the relative clause, as is made clear by the formal English equivalents: *we had this French girl who came to stay, my friend's got a brother who used to be in the school* and *there's a man in our street who has a Jaguar*. The examples are all existential-presentative, either with THERE BE or NP HAVE. The above examples were produced by speakers of Scottish English but the construction is common in spontaneous spoken standard English and examples are to be found in dialogues in novels—the earliest one in Jim Miller's collection coming from an aristocratic character in Trollope's *The Duke's Children*. It is worthwhile emphasizing that this construction occurs freely in spontaneous spoken standard English. Where the missing WH pronoun would be an object of some kind, as in *We had a book everyone wanted to read* or *There is a man in our street everyone detests*, the construction is acceptable in writing. It is unacceptable in writing only when the missing WH pronoun would be the subject of the relative clause.

At this point we make a small detour to comment on relative clause phenomena in spoken non-standard English that have typological relevance. The examples in (24) can be thought of as one step away from the written-language construction, in which a given relative clause is embedded in a noun phrase and integrated with the syntax of the main clause. The reduction in integration is reflected in the fact that the complementizer *that* is followed by a complete clause, that is, by a clause in which the verb has its full range of overt (appropriate) complement NPs. The examples in (24) have ordinary pronominal possessive, direct object, and locational items— *her birthday, their names, them, there*. Trudgill (1976: 41) provides an example of a relative clause with the subject slot filled by an ordinary pronoun and without an overt complementizer. These two properties in conjunction create the strong impression of two clauses merely juxtaposed and with no syntactic integration at all. His example is reproduced here as (26).

(26) He's a man [ ] he likes his beer

Trudgill also gives an example of a non-presentative/existential construction in which the subject slot in the relative clause is empty.

(27) He's a man [ ] likes his beer

Trudgill gives no indication of the geographical spread of the constructions in (26) and (27). There are no examples in the corpus of Scottish English conversation, but (26) and (27) have the loosely integrated or completely unintegrated syntax typical of clause complexes in spontaneous spoken language. In contrast, (28) illustrates the occurrence of a third complementizer, *as*. (28b) demonstrates that *as* can function as the complementizer in complement clauses as well as in relative clauses. The geographical spread of the complementizer *as* is known approximately—southern England.[3]

(28) (*a*) He's a man as likes his beer
(*b*) They say as he's lost his nerve

A fourth complementizer is *what*, as in (29). This complementizer is widespread in Britain, although the boundaries of its distribution are unclear. Cheshire, Edwards, and Whittle (1993: 68), on the basis of a questionnaire issued to teachers and pupils in various urban schools, state that *what* appears to be the preferred relative pronoun in the urban centres of Britain today. Trudgill (1976: 41) provides (29*a*) and (29*b*) is from a detective series set in the northern English town of Newcastle and written by a native of the town. (*What* as a relativizer is not attested in our corpus of Scottish English conversations—collected in Edinburgh and the Lothians—but Macafee (1983: 52) states that it is occasionally found in the West of Scotland.)

(29) (*a*) He's a man what likes his beer
(*b*) Thanks for the letter what you writ
(Newcastle, in *Spender*, BBC 1, Tuesday, 5 Janary 1993)

To conclude this brief overview of relative clauses in spontaneous spoken English we may observe that two constructions cited in many discussions of relative clauses are very rare in spontaneous speech, namely non-restrictive relative clauses and infinitival relative clauses; when they do occur in speech it is typically in the discourse of people who spend much time working with written English. The alternative to non-restrictive relatives is simply the insertion of one clause in the middle of another. The inserted clause is introduced by *and* but is not smoothly coordinated with the matrix clause. The dashes in (30) represent the typical pause before and after the inserted element and the separate pitch pattern over the latter.

(30) The boy I was talking to last night—and he actually works in the yard—was saying it's going to be closed down

The second rare construction is the infinitival relative clause. There are very

---

[3] An equivalent construction, using the third complementizer, has been noted in spontaneous spoken Finnish (both in the urban standard and in several dialects). The polysemic conjunction *kun* (the reduced *kuin* 'as' falls together with the temporal *kun* 'when') serves as a relativizer, as in:

naapurin   tyttö   kun   toi   minulle . . .
neighbour-GEN girl-NOM   Comp brought   I-ALL . . .
'the neighbour's girl as brought me . . .'

The structure is discussed in Fernandez (1982: 220–30). With respect to information structure this relativizer has been shown to share several of the characteristics of the pragmatic particles—cf. Ch. 5. It is a clitic, is prefixed to the initial constituent of a clause, and is a thematizer.

few in the Scottish English Corpus and the Map Task dialogues. There are no WH infinitival relatives—*I'm looking for a place in which to set up the factory*—and the ones that do occur are like spoken finite relative clauses in having no preposition in final position where one would be required in written English. Examples are given in (31), with the slot for the 'missing' preposition enclosed in square brackets in bold.

(31) (a) eh Laurine—question to tell you—eh if you haven't got the volcano—where do you go [ ] if you haven't got the volcano
 (b) I've got a place to start [ ]
 (c) It's not the ideal place to go [ ] for teenage drinking
 (d) because there's vandals and it's a horrible place to live [ ]
 (e) Saxone's is a very good place to work [ ]
 (f) can I have a mat to put the pizza down on

Note that (31f), with preposition, was produced by a university graduate. These examples are interesting because the noun modified by the infinitival relative is *place*, and *place*, *way*, and time nouns such as *day* and *week* do not require a preposition in dependent relative clauses even in written English. Thus, *Edinburgh is a good place to live*, *Do you remember the place/the day we met Angus* are both acceptable in writing, though people on their best writing behaviour will produce *the place in which/where we met Angus* or *the day on which we met Angus*.

WH pronouns are not typical of relative clauses in spontaneous spoken English but *which* does occur regularly in a construction that can be interpreted as a development from its relative pronoun use. The path of development, from pronoun to complementizer, is generally accepted as the source of the complementizer *that* from the pronoun *that*. (Demonstrative pronouns are a typical IE source of complementizers.) *Which* is taking the same route, witness *which [B]* in (32), from the Scottish English conversations.

(32) you can leave at Christmas if your birthday's in December to February which [A] I think is wrong like my birthday's March and I have to stay on to May which [B] when I'm 16 in March I could be looking for a job

The construction in (32) occurs in Dickens—e.g. in the speech of Mr Wegg in *Our Mutual Friend*—and was used throughout the second half of the nineteenth century in the humorous journal *Punch* as a marker of lower-class characters. Its principal characteristic is that *which* functions to connect two chunks of discourse and to signal that the second chunk relates to the first.

What then is the English relative clause typologically? We must first recognize that the term 'English relative clause' is merely a label for a set of constructions with the same function. We must also recognize that the

English variant of the classical Indo-European relative clause construction belongs to written English. (This is not to deny that it occurs in speech; it occurs in planned formal spoken texts such as lectures, sermons, political speeches, and in the unplanned speech of highly educated people.) In spontaneous spoken English and in non-standard English the typical relative clause construction is like the Persian or Semitic constructions, with an invariant complementizer. The clause following the complementizer may be like the Tamil construction in lacking a noun phrase that would occur were the clause a main clause, or it may be like the Persian and Semitic constructions in having a shadow pronoun.

7.3.4.5. *Relative clauses in Russian*

Like standard written English, standard written Russian possesses the classic IE relative clause construction with a WH relative pronoun. Prepositions are never stranded but occur at the front of the relative clause preceding the WH pronoun. The latter agrees with the head noun in number and gender, but takes its case from the verb in the relative clause. In (33) *kotoraja* is feminine and singular, agreeing in these properties with *kniga*. It is nominative, a property assigned by *soderžit*.

(33) kniga,   kotoraja soderžit eti   svedenija
 (the) book, which   contains this information

(34*a*) is an example of fronted preposition and WH pronoun, and (34*b*) is an example of an incorrect relative clause with a stranded preposition.

(34) (*a*) kniga,   v kotoroj ja našel eti   svedenija
  (the) book, in which   I found this information
 (*b*) *kniga, kotoroj ja našel eti svedenija v

Informal spoken Russian possesses a relative clause construction analogous to the Bengali construction in (17). That is, it is more a correlative construction, consisting of two juxtaposed clauses. The first clause contains a WH form, *kotorye* and the second clause contains a definite deictic, *tem* and *vsex*. The key to this construction is that the WH forms are indefinite deictics, that is, deictics that point to entities that are specific for the speaker but non-specific for the listener. Speakers use them to point to and introduce a set of entities into the discourse. (The set may contain one or more members.) The entities are known to the speaker but not to the addressee. The speaker introduces them by means of the first clause and assigns a property to them by means of the second clause. Consider the examples in (35), which are taken from Lapteva (1976: 144).

(35) (a) kotorye vot   klienty   est' u menja,
       which Particle customers are at me
       i   tem ja smotrju
       and these I look-to
       'I look after the customers who are mine'
    (b) kotorye mal'čiki lomajut,
       which boys break
       on vsex zabiraet
       he all catches
       'He catches all the boys who break things'

The first clause in (35a) introduces the set of customers 'belonging' to the speaker by means of *kotorye . . . klienty est' u menja*, and the second clause picks up the reference by means of *tem* and assigns the property 'I look after them'. (35b) is interpreted analogously, although the pronoun in the second clause is *vsex* (all) and not *tem*. (36) is an example of a one-member set being introduced by the first clause, with the reference being picked up by means of an ordinary personal pronoun in the second clause.

(36) Ta, kotoraja zdes' stojala   lampa,
     that which   here was-standing lamp
     ja ee ne bral
     I it not took
     'The lamp which was standing here, I didn't take it'

(37), also from Lapteva (1976: 144), demonstrates the use of the Russian WH forms as independent pronouns.

(37) A   kotoroe v butylkax, ono segodnjašnee?
     but which   in bottle   it today's?
     'But the [milk] in the bottles, is it today's?'

To sum up, written Russian has the classic Indo-European relative clause construction; spontaneous spoken Russian has a construction that can be analysed as analogous to the correlative construction of Bengali. The correlative construction consists of two clauses linked by the occurrence of a WH pronoun in one and a definite deictic in the other. The linkage is looser than in the classic IE relative clause construction, but spoken Russian offers examples of a relative clause construction with an even lower degree of cohesion. In (38) there are three clauses. The first clause is imperative—*Idi v vannu*, the second clause is also imperative—*voz'mi tam platoček* and the third clause looks like a main clause—*na trube soxnet*. This third clause has no subject NP but this is typical of spoken Russian and, to a lesser extent, of written Russian. The 'missing subject' is *platoček*, and the information conveyed by this clause relates to the cloth. There might be no intonation break between the second and third clauses, in which case the intonation can be taken as signalling cohesion between them, but the third clause could equally well have its own intonation envelope.

(38) Idi v   vannu,
     go into   bathroom
     voz'mi tam   platoček na trube soxnet
     take   there cloth   on pipe   is-drying
     'Go into the bathroom and bring the cloth that is drying on the pipe'

To sum up: spontaneous spoken English has a relative clause construction analogous to the relative clauses of Persian and Semitic languages, and spontaneous spoken Russian has a relative clause construction analogous to the correlative construction of Bengali (and Hindi). (These types of English and Russian also have other types of relative clause.) In contrast, written English and written Russian have the classic Indo-European construction with WH pronouns. Written English also has the *that* relative clause structure but without shadow pronouns.

7.3.5. *Clause combining*

A number of linguists have drawn attention to the desirability of establishing typological parameters for the combining of clauses into larger structures. The discussions show two things; for languages with written and spoken varieties, the differences in syntactic organization are not taken into account, and analysts dealing with languages lacking a written variety overlook the possibility that the syntactic structures of such languages might have properties in common with the syntactic structures of spontaneous spoken Eurasian languages (to use Heath's term—see the discussion below).

According to J. Heath (1985: 97), discussing the Australian language Ngandi, in that language 'Although there are some clause types which we can describe as subordinated, . . . such clauses in Ngandi are structurally like main clauses; we find no close parallels to the tightly embedded complement clauses (infinitive, for-to) or nominalizations of English and other Standard Average Eurasian languages.' While Ngandi is grammatically very different from English, some of its syntactic properties are similar to syntactic properties of spontaneous spoken English. As discussed in Chapter 3, texts from spontaneous spoken English have a high proportion of main clauses and a lower proportion of subordinate clauses than written or planned spoken texts. In the spoken texts on which this book is based, certain kinds of subordinate adverbial clause are missing (see §3.4.1); speakers can and do encode their messages in sequences of main clauses. (Allowance must also be made, as argued in Chapter 1, for differences in competence among informants, and for different degrees of exposure to formal education.)

While spoken English does contain infinitives and gerunds, these are of the simplest type (see §3.4.2). Of course, Ngandi appears to lack any construction even approximately analogous to infinitives and gerunds in English, but what does Heath mean by 'nominalizations'? If he has in mind examples such as *Fiona's having gone back to university is a lesson to us all* (see §3.4.2.2), it is important to point out that such structures do not occur in our data and are generally rare in spontaneous spoken English. Other nominalizations such as *the destruction of the city by the barbarians* are also missing from our data and are also generally rare in spontaneous spoken English. That is, the general differences between Ngandi clause syntax and English clause syntax are sharper and more extensive with respect to written English than with respect to spontaneous spoken English.

Another comment by Heath is even more interesting. He states (1985: 107) that 'Ngandi presents a type of discourse structure which seems to a westerner to be highly fragmented and unpredictable. Often a linguist cannot easily decide where to posit clause boundaries or even how many clauses to recognize in a given textual segment,' and (1985: 103) that

Frequent intrusive pauses give the syntax a choppy, fragmented character in which various constituents have little or no obvious surface relationships to each other (fixed order, fixed types of intonational contour, etc.). On the other hand, two clauses (or two clause kernels each containing a predicate) may be run together in a single breath. It is presumptuous to view these simply as low-level performance features overlaid on a more crystalline deep structure with clear clause boundaries. Fragmentation of surface structure is a basic feature of Ngandi which differentiates it from English and many other languages (including free-word-order languages with sharp clause boundaries).

Again, we do not wish to deny that Ngandi clause syntax (and therefore the organization of longer stretches of text) is quite different in detail from that of English. The passage in (39), taken from Heath (1985: 104), illustrates a grammatical property that has a powerful effect on text, namely the occurrence of classifier-like morphs on pronouns and verbs. The classifiers are in bold in (39) and one advantage they confer is that once the speaker has introduced an entity the reference can be maintained by means of the appropriate classifier.

(39) (i) *nana-ja-wanda-ric   nar-udu-ni   **gu**-lerelere*
1PL-EXCL now-track-seek 1P-LEXCL-go-Present   GU-shrub species
'we look for tracks (of emu birds); we go along and see the lerelere bush;'
(ii) *nar**gu**-na-cini   ma-burunburun nar-ga:-karu-ni*
1PL-EXCL GU-see-PRES MA-vine   1PL-EXCL-around-chase-PRES
***ma**-burunburun -bic*
MA-vine-Pergressive
'We see the burunburun vine; we go around through where the burunburun vine is;'

Historical Linguistics and Typology 355

(*iii*) nar-udu-ni nar-ic- a-cini *a-ja-nawk*
1PL-EXCL-go-PRES 1PL-EXCL-mind-hear-PRES A-now-speak
'we go along; we think hard; they are making noises;'

(*iv*) nar*a*-ja-ya -garu-ni na-ci-n-u
1PL-EXCL A-now-voice-chase-PRES that-way
'we follow their noises that way'

In line (*iii*) the classifier *a-* in *a-ja-nawk* picks up the reference to the emus, although there the previous explicit reference to the emus is more distant than line (*i*). Line (*iii*) also exemplifies the occurrence of main-clause structures where even spoken English could have participles: the literal gloss of line (*iii*) is 'we go along; we think hard'; both *nar-udu-ni* and *nar-ic-a-cini* contain Agent markers and tense markers. A speaker of English might produce two main clauses—*we're going along we're concentrating*—but could also produce *we're going along concentrating (on the noises)*. The participle *concentrating (on the noises)*, in combination with GO, is quite typical of spontaneous spoken English.

Consider now Heath's comment that two clauses may be run together in a single breath. This is not unusual in spontaneous spoken English, as illustrated in (1) in Chapter 2. The relevant part of the example is reproduced in (40).

(40) Blackford something or other it's actually an extension of Dick Place but it's called Blackford something or other it shouldn't be it's miles away from Blackford Hill

The sequence in (40) is spoken without pause and contains a phrase and four clauses: *Blackford something or other* is the phrase and the clauses are *it's an extension of Dick Place, but it's called Blackford something or other, it shouldn't be,* and *it's miles away from Blackford Hill.* Spoken English does not usually present a problem with respect to clause boundaries because they can be decided on the basis of verb valency and context, but it is not always clear when a sequence is to be analysed as a finite clause with ellipted constituents or as a participial phrase or as a noun phrase. The text in (41) is taken from the transcript of a speaker telling the story contained in a series of pictures. The speaker is a normal adult native speaker of English.

(41) Ah yes, two people presumably arranging a dinner party . . . making telephone calls to the guests . . . ah yes cooking the meal for the dinner party with the salmon on the table and the third one is laying the table for a dinner party . . . and the last one sitting round the table having a pleasant conversation at the end of the party

The sequences that are problematic are *making telephone calls to the guests, cooking the meal for the dinner party.* Are *making . . .* and *cooking . . .* finite clauses from which the subject noun phrase—*two people* or *they*—has been ellipted, or are they gerunds, i.e. a types of noun phrase, or are they participles? Note that the first line does not contain a finite clause either: *ah yes, two people presumably arranging dinner*. In the later lines we find *laying the table* and *sitting round the table*. Are these noun phrases or participles? What is the relationship between *the third one is* and *laying the table*? Does *laying the table* function here as a gerund, as in *laying the table was simple* or as the title of picture, as in *'Laying the table' is X's masterpiece*? Or does the sequence result from ellipsis, the source structure being, say, *the third one is they are laying the table*? None of these questions can be given a definite answer and it is not clear what evidence can be brought to bear. This is unsatisfactory, but is the sort of problem that Heath treats as a feature of Ngandi syntax. The problem appears to be not a peculiarity of Ngandi but of spontaneous spoken language.[4]

Without going into details again, we will merely note that the difficulty of deciding the relationship between pieces of syntax also arises with respect to the Russian examples given in §3.5.2 and in (38) in the preceding section. The fragmentation of surface structure, its choppy, fragmented character may look bizarre to linguists accustomed to the languages spoken in Western Europe, as Heath claims, but that is because linguists are accustomed to working on written data and not spontaneous spoken data. The properties described by Heath are not typologically significant, except for a typology of written and spoken language.

Macdonald (1988) discusses complement clauses in Tauya, a language of Papua New Guinea. The section on complement clauses is introduced by the statement that complement clauses function as noun phrases within the higher sentence and may take any of the case suffixes which are possible for lexical nouns (Macdonald 1988: 230). She gives, *inter alia*, the example in (42).

(42) amo foi - a - na - ni   ?utine - a - ?a
    tree wet-3SG-SUB-INSTR fall 3SG IND
    'because the tree was rotten, it fell'

foi is a verb denoting a state; *a* signals third person singular; *na* signals that the verb form occurs in a subordinate clause and *ni* is the instrumental case affix. From the discussion of noun phrases in Chapter 4, it is clear that this noun phrase is very complex for spontaneous spoken language. Another unexpected feature is the order of the reason clause and the main clause. The order in the spontaneous spoken data we have examined is 'main

---

[4] Relevant at this point is the discussion of examples (41) and (42) in Ch. 2. (41) illustrates a regular phenomenon of spoken English whereby the speaker accommodates what could be a complex noun phrase by putting part of the noun phrase at the end of the first clause, the rest of the noun phrase in a phrase in apposition and conveys the remaining information by means of a second clause containing pronouns. (42) is an example of syntactic structure that has genuinely broken down.

clause'–'reason clause', whereas the reverse order is typical of planned speech or of written language. As mentioned in Chapter 3, Chafe (1984), working on English, demonstrates that adverbial clauses preceding main clauses function as signposts to the upcoming discourse. Adverbial-clause signposts are a feature of planned text, which is why this ordering is typical of writing. Chafe describes adverbial clauses following main clauses as expressing afterthoughts; while it is true that they sometimes have this function, it is by no means their most frequent function. What is certain is that after main clauses they do not function as discourse signposts.

The puzzling feature is that Tauya is spoken but not written, yet the data displays properties that, admittedly on the basis of data from Indo-European languages, we expect to find in written texts. We could be accused of arrogance in finding it difficult to believe that a langauge such as Tauya could be more complex than spoken English. Such an accusation would be completely unfounded, but in any case two further pieces of evidence indicate that our puzzlement is justified. In a footnote Macdonald explains that 'My principle [*sic!*] consultant was the councillor of Tauya Village, a man between 40 and 50 years old who takes great delight in the complexities of his language'. That is, the data would appear to have been collected mainly from one informant, moreover from one who is aware of syntactic structure and enjoys exploring and exploiting his language. The informant was also a village councillor, which means that he was used to speaking in public, to planning ahead and using the language appropriate to public ceremonials. From the information about the informant we could reasonably infer that the complement constructions are indeed possible in Tauya but are typical of planned, formal speech and are possibly not typical either of spontaneous speech of the majority of speakers. (See the discussion in Chapter 1 of differences among both texts and speakers.)

This inference is supported by further data. Macdonald discusses a construction which she labels 'left-dislocated complement clause' (1988: 237–9). An example is given in (43).

(43) amo foi - a - na   ?i - ni   ?utine - a - ?a
     tree wet 3SG SUB PRO INSTR fall 3SG IND
     'the tree was rotten, that's why it fell'

The term 'left-dislocated' is unfortunate. It could be intended to have a dynamic interpretation in which the notion of movement is central; it could be a label indicating that the complement clause is embedded in the structure assigned to (42), which is taken as the base construction, but is to the left of the second clause in the structure assigned to (43), which is taken as derivative from (42); or it could be a conventional label replaceable by, e.g., 'Construction X'. Since Macdonald does not say how she intends the label to be understood, we will merely remark that if it is intended to reflect the second interpretation above, in which (43) is derivative on (42), it is misleading. An alternative hypothesis, which accords better with the facts of spoken and written language, is that (43) is the typical construction of spontaneous spoken language and that (42) is the integrated structure of planned, formal spoken language.

In (43) the first clause is *amo foi-a-na* and the second clause is *?i-ni-?utine-a-?a*. The grammar of (43) is not entirely clear because the first clause still contains the morph *na* glossed as marking subordination. In what sense is the clause subordinate? Macdonald (1988: 228) explains that clauses with *na* share neither the mood nor the tense of the following final clause. She gives an example in which the complement clause has future tense while the second clause has what is labelled an 'aorist tense'. These remarks indicate that complement clauses are relatively independent of the second clause and that the crucial property of (42) is that the complement clause is embedded in the second clause, as indicated by the case suffix *ni* attached to the complement clause. In (43) the clause appears not to be embedded in the second clause, and the translation indicates two independent clauses (assuming that the translation has been deliberately chosen for this effect). It may be that (43) is an instance of what Foley and Van Valin (1984) call co-subordination. What is important for present purposes is that the first clause gives the reason for the event of the tree's falling and is not integrated with the second clause, witness the pronoun *?i*. The context can be reconstructed thus: it is known to speaker and hearer that the tree fell—this event may have been mentioned along with some guess as to why it fell. The utterer of (43) states what he sees as the reason and drives the point home by means of the second clause. (In the light of the discussion of such clefts in Chapter 6 it is interesting that Macdonald uses a reverse WH cleft in her translation.) The structure in (43), unlike that in (42), does meet our expectations of what syntactic constructions occur in spontaneous speech.

Lehmann (1988) presents proposals for typology of clause linkage which are open to serious objection. For example, he declares that 'The aim of this contribution is to give a survey of the most important aspects of complex sentence formation in the languages of the world. They will emerge as generally applicable parameters of clause linkage' (Lehmann 1988: 181). As demonstrated in Chapter 2, the sentence is best discarded in the analysis of spontaneous spoken language because there are no constant properties marking the boundaries of sentences. Sentences are appropriate in the analysis of written language because the teaching of written language includes the organization of clauses into sentences. Any written text comes divided into sentences which reflect organizational choices by the writer. In spontaneous spoken language, clauses can be recognized and clusters of clauses connected by discourse relationships, such as the protasis relationship between yes–no interrogatives and main clauses discussed above. There are no analogous constant distinguishing properties for sentences.

Lehmann (1988: 219, fig. 6) proposes a set of six continua relating to the elaboration of grammatical and lexical information into separate clauses as opposed to the compression of such information into constituents of clauses. One continuum concerns the downgrading of clauses. Consider the examples in (44)–(47).

(44) **English**
I was trimming a boomerang and you came along

(45) **Walbiri**
ngatjulu-lu lpa-na   kali   tjantu-nu
I-ERG   PAST-SUBJ boomerang trim-PAST
kutja-O-npa   ya-nu-nu   njuntu
SUB-AUX-SUBJ2 walk-PAST-hither you
'I was trimming a boomerang when you came up'

(46) **Latin**
quei ager ex   privato in publicum commutatus est,
any land from private to public   converted   is
de eo   agro siremps   lex esto
of that lang in-the-same-way law it-shall-be
'For any land that has been converted from private to public, to that land the law shall apply in the same way'

(47) **Latin**
Telebois   jubet   [sententiam ut dicant suam]
to-the-Teleboans he-orders [opinion that they-say their]
'He orders the Teleboans to give their opinion'

In (44) the two clauses are equal in status and independent of each other except insofar as the coordination leads us to infer a connection between the two events. (45) offers an example of what Lehmann calls an adjoined clause. It has to precede or follow the main clause, it cannot be embedded or have a syntactic function in the main clause, and in this example it contains a deictic item, glossed as 'hither', which points to the event in the main clause and marks the link between the two clauses. (46) shows what Lehmann calls a correlative diptych in which the relative clause introduced by *quei* is subordinate but not embedded and the connection between the clauses is again signalled by means of a deictic item—here *eo* 'that'. In (47) the second clause is embedded in the first as the object of *iubet* 'orders'. The form of the verb in the embedded clause is partly governed by *iubet*. The verb must be in the subjunctive mood and the embedded clause must be introduced by *ut*.

One of the continua proposed by Lehmann is expansion vs. reduction. This has to do with whether subordinate clauses are reduced and the degree to which they are reduced. As an example of severed reduction Lehmann gives the sentences in (48).

(48) (*a*) She objected to [his constantly reading magazines]
    (*b*) She objected to [his constant reading of magazines]

In (48*a*) the subordinate clause is only partially nominalized; it takes a direct object and is modified by the adverb *constantly*. In (48*b*) the subordinate clause is completely modified; *reading* is a noun that has to be linked to the following noun by a preposition, and it is modified by the adjective *constant*. Both (48*a*) and (48*b*) are typical of written English and quite untypical of spoken English, even of planned spoken English. The typical construction for spoken English is *She objected to him constantly reading magazines*, in which *constantly reading magazines* is highly verbal and is probably to be analysed as a participial phrase modifying *him*. (The adverb would not be *constantly* but *always*—at least for a speaker of standard English.) The information that is available for English is unfortunately not available for other examples of compression cited by Lehmann— the Latin accusative and infinitive construction, Japanese and Quechua complement constructions.

Another of Lehmann's continua is the degree to which two clauses, and the propositions they express, are interlaced. One type of interlacing is gapping, illustrated in Lehmann's example (49).

(49) ut ager . . . sine   cultura   fructuosus esse   non potest, sic sine
    as a-field   without cultivation fruitful   to-be not can   so without
    doctrina   anima
    teaching the-mind

The central point is that the two clauses in (49) express propositions that share a predicate and the syntactic constituent expressing this predicate— *fructuosus esse non potest*—is omitted from the second clause. (Actually, if the predicate were expressed, the complement of *esse* would be *fructuosa*, which is the feminine form agreeing with the feminine noun *doctrina*.) Gapping is a written construction par excellence, at least in English, and there is no reason to suppose that Latin was different, given that Cicero, from one of whose texts the example is taken, is famous for his edited, polished, and highly integrated syntax.

A different aspect of interlacing is what Lehmann calls syntagmatic interweaving, as exemplified in (50).

(50) Viden   me [ut   rapior]?
    don't-you-see me [that I-am-being-abducted
    'Don't you see how I'm being abducted?'

Lehmann (1988: 208) states that the subject has been taken out of the noun clause and made directly dependent on the verb. That is, *me* 'me' is the direct object of *viden* but the construction in (50) derives from the base construction exemplified in (51), in which *ego* 'I' is the subject of *rapior*.

(51) Viden [ut ego rapior]?

Lehmann comments that the transformation of the structure of (51) into the structure of (50) bisects the subordinate clause. Now (50) is taken from a play by Plautus, who not only is an early writer but one who is generally recognized as capturing the grammar and vocabulary of spoken Latin. (50) is a construction of spontaneous spoken Latin, whereas (51) is a construction of written Latin. The suggestion that the structure of (51) is basic does not square with the status of written Latin as emerging slowly over several centuries as writers developed an integrated syntax and a complex vocabulary. On this view, (50) is perfectly natural in spontaneous speech given that human beings are typically the most salient entities in events; the speaker first draws attention to one of the salient humans, himself, and then to what is happening to that salient human. Lehmann's analysis does not fit the syntactic facts of spoken language but it does accord with the stylistic imperatives of written language, which prescribe elegant, smoothly integrated clauses and proscribe the rough juxtaposition of clauses as in (50) in which *ut rapior* could be seen as a second direct object of *viden* but also as in apposition to *me*. (50) and (51) can be considered logically equivalent but they are far from equivalent pragmatically, that is, with respect to what the speaker treats as most salient. (This analysis also applies to the spoken English construction exemplified above by *She objected to him constantly reading magazines*. The obligatory and central part of the main clause, *she objected to him*, refers to the salient humans, and the participial phrase conveys information about the reason for her attitude.) Examples giving similar salience to a human participant are cited by Palmer (1975: 79). Consider (52) and (53).

(52) viden   tu   hunc   [quam inimico   vultu
     don't-you-see you this-man how   with-hostile with-expression
     intuitur]?
     he-is-looking?
     'don't you see that he is looking at us with a very hostile expression?'

(53) qui   noverit   me [quis ego sum]?
     who has-recognized me [who I   am]
     'Who has recognized who I am?'

An exactly analogous construction occurs in spoken English but is not allowed in written English. Examples are in (54) and (55).

(54) every one knows Helen Liddell how hard she works [radio discussion]
Cf. 'everyone knows how hard Helen Liddell works'
(55) look at his face what they've done to it [ITV play]
Cf. 'look at what they've done to his face'

In both (54) and (55) the speaker draws attention to a salient human entity (Helen Liddell) or part of a salient human entity (his face) and then adds information about a property of (part of) that entity. This same construction is found in the Authorized Version of the New Testament, where however it is a direct rendering of the New Testament Greek construction in (56). The relevant point is that the Greek is also spoken language and the Authorized Version does have, although possibly by chance, a translation that uses a contemporary spoken English construction.

(56) katamathete ta   krina tou   agrou, pos auksanousin
     consider   the lilies of-the of-field how they-grow

(Matt. 6: 28)

Interestingly, the Good News Bible and the Revised English Bible have both opted for integrated syntax of written English: the former has *Look at how the wild flowers grow* and the latter *Consider how the lilies of the field grow*.

Lehmann (1988: 219) concludes with the declaration that

Comparative linguists have always felt that the prevalence of such a construction type may characterize—together with other features—a given language. For instance, the prevalence of the correlative diptych is characteristic of Hittite; the strongly nominalized adverbial clause is typical for Quechua and Tamil. Future research will ascertain which features tend to cluster, what are the principles intrinsic to the model of Figure 6 that account for such clustering.

This future research is indeed essential, but its success depends on the recognition that spontaneous spoken language differs from written language. We demonstrated earlier that different types of relative clause are typical of spoken and written English and Russian. The correlative diptych that Lehmann describes as characteristic of Hittite is found in spontaneous spoken Russian, as in (57), and in spontaneous spoken English, as in (58).

(57) A   kotoroe v butylkax, ono segodnjašnee?
     and which   is bottles it today's
     'is the stuff (milk) that is in bottles today's'?
(58) see where the pilot would go? you go round there

The correlative pairs are *kotoroe* and *ono* in (57) and *where* and *there* in (58). The natural rendering of (57) in spontaneous spoken English is *the stuff in bottles—is it today's?* This is not a classic correlative structure, which requires a WH item in one clause and a TH item in the other, but there is a correlation between the two definite deictics *the* and *it*. The syntagmatic interweaving that Lehmann illustrates from Latin (he does not claim that it is unique to Latin) is found in a number of other languages. Given the pragmatic forces behind such examples, as mentioned in the discussion of (50) and (51), it would not be surprising to find analogous constructions in the spontaneous spoken varieties of many languages.

7.3.6. Subject-prominent and topic-prominent languages

Zemskaja (1973: 314–17) and Krasil'nikova (1990: 27) both refer to Li and Thompson (1976), who draw a typological distinction between languages that are subject-prominent and languages that are topic-prominent. (59a,b) are examples of topic-comment constructions from languages that Li and Thompson (1976: 462) hold to be topic-prominent.

(59) (a) **Mandarin**
Nèi-chang huǒ xingkui xīaofang-duì laí de kuài
that-CL fire fortunate fire-brigade come particle quick
'That fire, fortunately the fire-brigade came quickly'
(b) **Japanese**
Gakkoo-wa boku-ga isogasi-kat-ta
school-TOP I-SUB busy-PST
'School (topic), I was busy'

Li and Thompson list the properties distinguishing topics and subjects.

(60) (i) Topics are always definite; subjects may be definite or indefinite.[5]
(ii) A Topic need not be an argument of the predicate in a given clause; a subject is always an argument.
(iii) In a given clause the verb determines which noun—Agent, Patient, Experiencer—becomes the subject.
(iv) Topics have one and same functional role in every clause: they limit the applicability of the main predication to a certain restricted domain . . . the topic sets a spatial, temporal or individual framework within which the main predication holds (Chafe 1976: 50).
(v) Topic-predicate agreement is rare; subject-verb agreement is common.
(vi) Topics typically, perhaps always, occur in sentence-initial position.
(vii) Subjects, but not topics, play a prominent role in reflexivization, passivization, control of infinitives, and the formation of imperatives.

Li and Thompson (1976: 466–71) list properties of topic-prominent languages as in (61).

(61) (i) Topic-prominent languages may also have subjects, which play a role in

---

[5] Jim Hurford points out that subjects in Arabic must be definite, and it is now well known that, although there is no rule excluding definite subject NPs in English, some 96% of subject NPs in written and spoken texts are definite. Topic and subject are regularly difficult to distinguish in a number of languages.

certain grammatical processes. There is always surface coding for the topic (sentence-initial position or morphological marker) but not for the subject.

(ii) Topic-prominent languages typically lack a Passive construction, whereas subject-prominent languages typically have a Passive.
(iii) Dummy subjects may be found in subject-prominent languages but not in topic-prominent ones.
(iv) Topic-prominent languages have 'double-subject' constructions, as in the Mandarin *Nèike shù yèzi dà* (that tree leaves big, i.e. 'That tree, the leaves are big').
(v) In topic-prominent languages the topic and not the subject controls co-reference, as in (62).

(62) Nèike shù yèzi   dà   suǒyi wǒ bu xīhuān
     that tree leaves big so   I   not like (it = the tree)

(vi) In a topic-prominent language the topic-comment construction belongs to the language's repertoire of basic constructions.

According to Li and Thompson, Indo-European languages, along with other families such as Niger-Congo and Semitic, are subject-prominent, and languages such as Chinese and Lahu (Lolo-Burmese) are topic-prominent. They recognize a set of languages, such as Japanese and Korean, which are both subject- and topic-prominent, and another set, such as Tagalog and Ilocano, which are neither subject- nor topic-prominent. Zemskaja and Krasil'nikova suggest that the structures discussed by Li and Thompson are very like a construction in spoken Russian. Some of the examples given in §5.7.7.1 are repeated in (63).

(63) (a) Miša/   emu   vse ravno
         Miša   to-him all equal
         i.e. 'It's all one to Miša'
     (b) Sobaka/ vsegda poly   grjaznye
         dog   always floors dirty
         i.e. 'With a dog the floors are always dirty'

Another example from Zemskaja is in (64).

(64) u   nas jantar'/ brošečka odna skol'ko   stoit
     at us amber   brooch   one how-much costs
     'Here, amber, how much does a brooch cost?'

The nouns *Miša, sobaka* and *jantar'* have some of the properties of topics. They are definite—*sobaka* in the sense that it refers to the class of dogs and *jantar'*—to the substance in general; they delimit the application of the following clause—being indifferent, the floors being dirty, and the cost of just a brooch have to do with Miša, dogs, and amber. The construction was described in Chapter 4 as consisting of a noun phrase followed by a clause, the noun phrase being outside the clause. This analysis was adopted for two reasons. The noun phrase is not involved in relations of agreement or government with any constituents in the clause (this is another property of topics): for instance, in (64) *odna* agrees with *brošečka* in number, gender, and case and *stoit* agrees with *brošečka* in person and number, but none of these words is syntactically connected with *jantar'*. In written Russian we would expect to find *odna brošečka iz jantarja* (one brooch from amber), in which *brošečka* is connected with *jantarja* by the preposition *iz* (from), but that is not the structure in (64). The second reason for the analysis is that the referent of the initial noun phrase can be picked up by a pronoun, as in (63*a*), where the referent of *Miša* is picked up by *emu*, an ordinary personal pronoun (as opposed to a relative pronoun). That is, the clause is complete without the initial noun phrase. As a result of this analysis, we cannot describe the topic nouns as being in sentence-initial (better, clause-initial) position but they do always precede the clause. In (64) *u nas* could be taken as a topic, because it sets the field of application for *jantar'/brošečka odna skol'ko stoit?*, while *jantar'* sets the field of application for *brošečka odna skol'ko stoit?*

Spoken Russian, then, has a topic construction—perhaps it could even be called a topic-comment construction. However, Russian only has one of the properties that Li and Thompson say are typical for topic-prominent languages, namely it has no dummy subject construction. It does have a Passive and it does not have a double subject construction. On the other hand, the NP-Clause construction belongs to the set of basic constructions in spoken Russian. Li and Thompson (1976: 471) say that when they classify the topic-comment construction as basic they mean that it is not derivative, marginal, marked, or otherwise unusual and they employ the definition of basic sentence offered by Keenan (1976: 307), which runs: 'a syntactic structure x is *semantically more basic than* a syntactic structure y if, and only if, the meaning of y depends on that of x. That is, to understand the meaning of y it is necessary to understand the meaning of x.'

Keenan's definition is not easy to apply. We content ourselves with two observations. The first is that the NP-Clause structure is not marginal, marked, or otherwise unusual in spoken Russian, though it may well appear to have all these properties when viewed from the perspective of written Russian. The second is that for (63*b*) and (64) any candidate replacement constructions are longer and more complex and do not have exactly the same meaning. An unpacking of (63*b*) could use a time clause—*when you have a dog*—or a conditional clause—*if you have a dog* or even *as far as dogs are concerned*. Similarly it is not obvious what a more basic sentence than (64) might be. *Brošečka iz jantarja odna skol'ko stoit* (brooch from amber one how-much costs) looks like a paraphrase, but *jantarja* no longer limits the application of the clause to amber; instead a comment is made about amber brooches.

Should Russian be included in the set of languages that are both subject- and topic-prominent? While it has the topic-prominent, topic-comment NP-Clause construction, it lacks most of the properties stated by Li and Thompson to be typical of topic-prominent languages whereas there is no doubt whatsoever that it is subject-prominent. Interestingly, topic-prominent constructions are found in languages which have none of the topic-prominent properties. Spontaneous spoken English offers many examples of the sort discussed in § 5.7.7—*the driver he's really friendly you get a good laugh with him* and *that technician I think he ought to be shot.*—and Blanche-Benveniste (1991: 81) cites the examples from spoken French given in (65).

(65) (a) cette histoire de lentilles je m'en souviens encore
     this story of lentils I self of-it remember still
     'that business with the lentils, I still remember it'
  (b) la voiture j'y ai passé une bonne partie de ma vie
     the car I there have spent a good part of my life
  (c) présenter les choses ainsi moi ça me plaît
     to-present the things thus me that me pleases[6]

What is important is that the NP-Clause construction belongs to spoken Russian, English, and French, and other languages. (Our data includes German examples.) If typology is carried out via the existing grammars of these languages, this construction will not be taken into account—the grammars describe the written varieties, from which the construction is missing. If spoken varieties are included in typology, Li and Thompson's four sets of languages can remain, but the assignment of languages to sets will be less straightforward. It will have to be recognized that the spoken varieties of languages may have topic-prominent constructions that are not found in the written varieties, but that the presence of these constructions does not make the languages topic-prominent. Further, as with all classificatory systems, any set of items contains good central members and poor peripheral members. Russian could be classified as a peripheral member of the set of languages that are both subject- and topic-prominent.

7.3.7. *Noun phrases*

Munro and Gordon (1982) suggest that the number of Noun Phrases allowed in a given clause may be important typologically. Discussing the lack of agentive (full) passives in Chickasaw and Choctaw, they say

---

[6] Jim Hurford (personal communication) cites a slogan from a poster seen during a French presidential election: *La France, nous, on l'aime* (The France, we, we it love). This is very much a spoken-language structure that was used in writing to achieve a specific effect: among other things, conveying the message that the politicians responsible for the poster speak the people's language. There are two topic NPs preceding the clause—*La France* (France) and *nous* (we/us). The clause contains two pronouns; since *on* (one) is only used with reference to human beings, it is clear which of the topic NPs is coreferential with *on* and which with *nous*.

Historical Linguistics and Typology 367

The notion of classifying languages typologically according to their possession or lack of a Passive rule which allows for the expression of an Agent might have a certain amount of interest; but we think that, in some cases at least, the lack of an agentive Passive may be related to a more basic typological feature, something which may represent a more valid basis for differentiating languages of the familiar Indo-European type from languages like Chickasaw and Choctaw; we refer to NP density, or the allowable number of NP's [sic] per clause. (Munro and Gordon 1982: 109)

They give an English example of a verb with seven nominal arguments, reproduced in (66).

(66) The duckling was killed by the farmer for his wife with the hired man at dawn in the barnyard with a .357 Magnum.

In contrast they say that in Chickasaw very few clauses contain more than three noun phrases. On the face of it the facts of Chickasaw do look different from the facts of English, but the matter is not so straightforward. To begin with, an examination of the spontaneous English conversation and the spontaneous Russian conversation (see Chapter 1) shows that no clauses contain more than three NPs. (As discussed in Chapter 4, many of the noun phrases are very simple in structure.) Why should Chickasaw appear very different from English from one viewpoint but not different at all from another?

As discussed in Chapter 1, and in §7.3.5, much depends on the type of data; (66) is an example of written English, indeed, not just written English but a special subvariety that might be labelled 'examples produced and manipulated by linguists'. Chickasaw does not have a written variety and it is when spoken English and spoken Russian are addressed that Chickasaw turns out to be very like these languages with respect to the number of noun phrases per clause. This is not to deny that (66) is a legitimate English clause; the question is—and no clear answer is available at the time of writing—whether our intuitions that are satisfied by (66) are in fact intuitions about written language and whether the possible number of noun phrases per clause in spoken language is highly constrained, which is just what the English and Russian conversational data lead us to believe.

In another respect Chickasaw appears rather different from English and Russian. Consider (67) and (68)—Munro and Gordon's (74*a*) and (76*b*), in which the verb has a single noun phrase modifier. Note that the work of English prepositions, and Russian prepositions and case affixes, is assigned in Chickasaw to a verb affix, glossed as LOC in (67) and INS in (68).

(67) chin-chokk-ak   ish-aa-impa-tok
     2s.III-house-NS 2s.l-LOC-eat-PAST
     'you ate at home'

(68) aboha-anõ'k-akõ to'wa' isht-aa-chokoshkomo-li
    house in-NS   ball   INS-LOC-play-1s.I
    'I'm playing with a ball in the house'

In (67) 2s.III indicates the second person singular form of a verb belonging to class III. NS indicates that the noun to which it is attached is not a subject. The highest number of arguments in a single clause found by Munro and Gordon was four—the Chickasaw example corresponds to the English *I gave him the medicine with a spoon in the house*. Interesting constraints emerge when we move on to examples such as (69)—Munro and Gordon's (79).

(69) top-ak tiwwa-li-kat   sa-hotolhko-tok
     bed-NS lie-1s.I-SBR.SS   1s.II-cough-PAST
     'I was coughing in bed'

The essential fact is that while the English verb *coughed* can be modified by a Locative argument, in Chickasaw *top-ak* cannot be a Locative argument of the verb *hotolhko* 'cough' but must occur in a subordinate clause where it modifies a locational verb, here *tiwwa* 'lie'. Munro and Gordon (1982: 111) cite various examples consisting of several clauses and exactly the same verb in each clause apart from the verb prefix.

(70) ashila tiwa'sh-li-kat   alhponi'-ak   aa-tiwa'sh-li-kat
     soup   sitr-1s.I-SBR.SS   kitchen-NS   LOC-stir-1s.I-SBR.SS
     folosh ish-tiwa'sh-li-tok
     spoon   INS-stir-1s.I-PAST
     'I stirred the soup in the kitchen with a spoon'

According to Munro and Gordon, such examples demonstrate that the crucial factor is the number of noun phrase arguments permitted in each clause. The corresponding English example is perfectly acceptable as a clause of spontaneous spoken English, but it would be interesting to know whether speakers typically produce that example or examples such as *I was in the kitchen stirring the soup with a spoon, I was in the kitchen—I used a spoon to stir the soup, I was in the kitchen stirring the soup—I used a spoon*. The point of these examples is that each verb has no more than two arguments; in the first one the speaker refers to his/her location by means of a main clause and relegates the description of the event of stirring to a free participial clause. In the second and third, the speaker produces two main clauses but distributes the arguments differently. Similarly, it would be interesting to know whether speakers of English actually do produce examples such as the English translation of (69) or whether they prefer examples such as *I was lying in bed coughing*, which is closer to the Chickasaw structure, with *in bed* as an argument of the location verb *was lying* and *coughing* as a free participle without any argument. Of course, speculation does not constitute argument and the above musings about which examples occur (more frequently) in spontaneous spoken English are intended merely as a reminder that even with respect to restrictions on the type of verb that is required for certain types of argument, Chickasaw may turn out not to be so very different from English, even though it has strict restrictions where English is more flexible.

7.3.8. *Word order*

Word order is a central topic in typology. Two hypotheses proposed in the recent literature merit reconsideration given the syntactic and discourse properties of spontaneous spoken language described in Chapters 3–6. One hypothesis offers an explanation for word order in terms of language processing by language-users and the other relates to whether given or new information is presented first in clauses.

The first hypothesis, linking word order and language-processing, has been developed by Hawkins (1990, 1994). It is called the Early Immediate Constituents Hypothesis (EIC); its central proposal is that word and constituent orders are determined by the need for syntactic groupings and their immediate constituents to be recognized and produced as rapidly and efficiently as possible in language performance (Hawkins 1994: 57). Hawkins's method of calculating rapidity and efficiency need not be described in detail here; it rests crucially on the ratio of immediate constituents to words, a ratio of three immediate constituents to four words, for example, being much better than one of three to eleven words.

Clear examples of the EIC in operation are the examples in (71).

(71) (*a*) Joe looked up the number
 (*b*) Joe looked the number up
 (*c*) Joe looked the number of the ticket up
 (*d*) Joe looked the number that Mary had forgotten up

The further the particle *up* is from the verb, the less acceptable the sentence and the more words required to determine the immediate constituents of the verb phrase. The more words required, the less acceptable the structure and the less frequent in English texts. Extraposition, as in (72), is similarly motivated.

(72) (*a*) That Bill was frightened surprised Mary
 (*b*) It surprised Mary that Bill was frightened

In (72*a*), the long subject noun phrase *that Bill was frightened* delays access to the verb phrase *surprised Mary*, whereas in (72*b*) the first two words give access to the subject noun phrase *it* and the verb phrase. (See Hawkins 1994: 65.) Hawkins's evidence comes from psycholinguistic experiments using alternative orders of constituents, text frequency counts of alternative orders, native speaker acceptability judgements, and the grammaticalized constituent orders of the world's languages (Hawkins 1994: 64). Hawkins does not give details of the psycholinguistic experiments but his text frequency counts were all performed on written texts—see Hawkins (1994: 129–214).

In English complementizers introduce complement clauses, whereas in Japanese they conclude complement clauses. Consider (73).

(73) (*a*) [Kinoo   John-ga kekkonsi-ta to]   Mary-ga it-ta
         yesterday John   married   that Mary   said
    'Mary said that John got married yesterday'
    (*b*) Mary-ga [kinoo John-ga kekkonsi-ta to] it-ta

In (73*b*) the complement clause has been centre-embedded in the main clause. The centre-embedding affects the structure adversely. Only a subset of categories in an utterance will trigger mother node construction (those that are unique to the mother's category). It is the categories in this subset that need to be close together for optimal parsing, but in (73*b*) the NP and VP that trigger the construction of an S node are at either end of the sentence. Hawkins (1994: 8) points out that the structure of (73*b*) is acceptable and grammatical in Japanese, although the text-frequency counts (for written Japanese) show a preference for (73*a*). This preference is interpreted by Hawkins as indicative of the processing problems. We agree with this interpretation and would add only that the occurrence of (73*b*) in written Japanese is typical of written texts in any language; complex constructions are allowed because the reader has time to reread difficult stretches of text and work out their syntax and their meaning.

Hawkins's hypothesis is very plausible for written language, but it is not at all clear why it is required for spontaneous spoken language. This is worrying; spoken language developed before written language; many communities have no written language but their languages none the less have word order. The relevant facts from spontaneous speech are these: the large majority of noun phrases have one, or at most two, constituents; the large majority of clauses have a small number of constituents, typically the core subject–direct-object–predicate, and possibly one adjunct/complement of time or place. Moreover, the fact that spoken communication originally took place (and typically still does) face-to-face and with respect to limited contexts is one reason for the well-attested phenomenon of listeners not waiting for utterances to be completed before they seize their turns as speaker. Examples such as (72*a*) with complement clauses as subject do not occur (or at least very rarely). Ease and speed of constituent-recognition does not appear to be a major problem in such language usage, but it is in precisely such usage that the various word orders found in natural languages emerged.

The second hypothesis is that some languages have a word order that is pragmatically-based, and in which the first constituents in a clause convey new information and given information is conveyed by the later constituents. (See Mithun 1987: 304–7; and Payne 1992: 145.) This runs counter to the classic Prague School thesis that in clauses given information generally precedes new information. The hypothesis of pragmatically-controlled word order raises various questions. None of them can be explored within the limits of this chapter, but we offer the observation that the effect of spontaneous spoken language should be investigated.

The investigation will be complicated by the fact that the Prague School thesis has been developed mainly on the basis of Indo-European languages spoken in Western Europe, and these are very different in grammatical structure from the native languages of the United States and Central America on which Mithun and Payne base their hypothesis. Mithun observes that the ordering new–given is particularly common in languages in which the finite verb in each clause contains affixes (called bound pronouns by Mithun) cross-referring to all the core arguments: glossed in English, a typical clause-structure is *he-saw-it Tom the-snake*. If the basic clause order is VSO, then one way to highlight a new piece of information is to move a constituent to the front of the clause. A pragmatic explanation would be that the most urgent task is to draw the listener's attention to a new entity and the second task is to predicate a property of that entity. The pragmatic explanation sits very happily with the facts of syntactic structure in the above-mentioned languages.

But how different are these languages from, say, English, Russian, and German? In written texts in those languages new topics are introduced before anything is said about them: run-of-the-mill examples are *The subject of today's talk is the recent election in Russia*, or *We turn now to the state of the economy*, or *In contrast, consider the latest security measures*. Speakers introduce entities by means of structures such as *Look who's coming up the path!* or *Angus McCrindle! What's he doing going into Fiona's house!* (spoken by a person looking out of the window) or (an actual example) *see when we get into the gardens can we go up the tower*. In the last example the speaker introduces the new entity, their entering the gardens, by means of the *see* construction discussed in Chapter 5. Similar constructions are used in Russian and German. The crucial point is that the urgent task, introducing the new entity, is performed first, and then the predication of a property takes place. The constituents conveying information about the new entity occur fist in the utterance, but typically in the form of a clause. In spoken language, speakers have the choice of simply uttering a phrase, as in the Angus McCrindle example. Mithun *et al.* worked on spoken data, while work using the Prague School thesis is typically based on written data. The examples above indicate that even on this basis the hypothesis of pragmatically-controlled versus grammatically-controlled word order has to be extended and refined. The differences might be much smaller were the comparison based entirely on samples of spontaneous speech.

7.4. Conclusion

It has long been recognized that languages whose history is well known are precisely languages with written varieties. It is also recognized, although sometimes forgotten, that the history is based on written texts and that, except for the occasional glimpses of spontaneous speech in formal letters or plays, we do not have much certain knowledge of the syntax of spoken English, Russian, or German at earlier stages in their development. The distinction between spontaneous spoken language and written language is not normally made, or at least is not made explicitly, in typological work. The preceding discussion shows that the distinction is crucially important, because the spontaneous spoken variety of a given language may differ in certain typological respects from the written variety.

8 Written Language, First Language Acquisition, and Education

8.1. Introduction

In the light of the demonstration in Chapters 2–6 that spoken language differs from written language in syntax and discourse organization, we turn now to the major topic of language acquisition. In addition to the differences in syntax and discourse organization, the key facts in the discussion are that, whatever their native language, children learn spoken language before they learn written language, they learn spoken language in context, and the learning of written language is very different from the acquisition/learning of spoken language.

8.2. Chomsky's Theory of Language Acquisition

The essentials of the Chomskyan theory of language acquisition are set out in N. Chomsky (1986: p. xxvii). What Chomsky calls Plato's problem is to explain how we know so much, given that the evidence available to us is so sparse. Applied to language, the problem is how children learn their native language from the allegedly meagre, degenerate data to which they are exposed. The statement below admirably sums up Chomsky's working assumptions from his 1965 book *Aspects of the Theory of Syntax* to his 1989 book *Barriers*.

A consideration of the character of the grammar that is acquired, the degenerate quality and narrowly limited extent of the available data, the striking uniformity of the resulting grammars, and their independence of intelligence, motivation, and emotional state, over wide ranges of variation leave little hope that much of the structure of language can be learned by an organism initially uninformed as to its general character. (Chomsky 1965: 58)

In Chomsky (1986: 7–8) it is further asserted that 'without instruction or direct evidence, children unerringly use computationally complex structure-dependent rules rather than computationally simple rules that involve only the predicate "leftmost" in a linear sequence of words'.

Using as an example various languages, in the mathematical sense of sets of strings of symbols, Atkinson (1990: 2–6) discusses the impossibility of deducing the properties of certain strings without explicit information to the effect that certain strings are incorrect. On this condition it is impossible to correctly identify the languages, and the same holds for human language. But speakers of a given language are able to make judgements about sentences that they have never heard before and are even able to make subtle judgements about the relative acceptability of such sentences; the examples that Atkinson gives are *Who did John wonder whether kissed Mary*—highly unacceptable—and ?*Who did John wonder whether Mary kissed?*—not completely acceptable but much better than the first sentence.

Atkinson (1993: 1914) points out that mathematical work on the learnability of language is based, *inter alia*, on two 'empirically plausible' assumptions. One is that far from being presented with contrasting data explicitly labelled grammatical or ungrammatical, children are faced with data containing ungrammatical intrusions that are not labelled as such. The second is that, for any given linguistic interaction, children do not have access to the full range of data presented to them before that occasion. The way out of the difficulty is to assume that children bring knowledge to the task of language acquisition, knowledge which limits the hypotheses they can entertain about the properties of the language they are exposed to. To specify this knowledge is the goal of linguists working on English and other languages within Chomsky's principles and parameters framework in an attempt to formulate Universal Grammar (henceforth UG).[1]

The position elaborated here is that various assumptions made by Chomsky (and mentioned by Atkinson) are incorrect; with respect to written language it is not true that children are exposed to meagre degenerate data; the assumption about the lack of access to previously presented data is not true of written language either. A further assumption about children receiving no overt instruction in the use of language is also not true of written language (and as will be argued, with respect to spontaneous spoken language, the incidence of ungrammatical structures has been greatly exaggerated and the absence of overt instruction exaggerated). An overly narrow view has been taken of what counts as instruction. (See §8.3.5.) The structures of spontaneous spoken language are, as demonstrated in Chapters 2–4, much less complex than the structures of written language. This is significant with respect to theories of first language acquisition because the properties attributed to the language acquisition device are based on properties developed to enable formal models of grammar to exclude ungrammatical sentences, and also to enable a choice to be made

---

[1] Atkinson (1990: 24–6) points out that it is quite reasonable to assume both that significant aspects of children's development are genetically determined and that maturation and learning have roles to play.

between competing models. The data on which the development is based is not just complex written data but written data produced by highly sophisticated users of written language playing intricate games with the grammatical code out of context. The properties thus elaborated are not relevant to the acquisition of the structures of spontaneous spoken language.

Finally, it is an open question as to how much of spontaneous spoken language is to be handled by means of productive grammatical rules and how much by the lexicon in which are stored not just individual words but phrases and even clauses or pairs of clauses. (See §8.3.6.) We are not suggesting that first language acquisition is just a matter of rote learning; it is quite clear that children play an active part in making hypotheses about syntactic constructions and extending them beyond their input data. Interestingly, the most daring hypotheses concern not syntax alone but the interrelationship between syntactic constructions and lexical items. Furthermore, first language acquisition typically takes place in a rich social environment but in a relatively limited universe in which referential tasks are initially severely limited in scope. In the context of work on spontaneous spoken language the hypothesis of a rich innate set of principles is too extreme; we would like to replace it with a theory that mixes hypothesis-formation, rote-learning, and social interaction, although the nature of the mix is the subject of future work. (Our position is broadly similar to that advocated in chapter 1 of Hurford 1987.)

8.3. A Critique of Chomsky's Theory

8.3.1. *Introduction*

We will argue that the differences between spoken and written language that we have described make it interesting and essential to examine the assumptions on which the Chomskyan theory rests. Is it true that children acquire their native language from meagre, degenerate data? Is it true that all children acquire their native language to the same extent regardless of intelligence and motivation and emotional state? Do children learn without instruction or direct evidence? How complex are the rules that children are required to develop?

We begin our discussion with the work by linguists on generative grammars,[2] not specifically Principles and Parameters, because much of

---

[2] Mainly English, unfortunately, and even analyses of other languages bear a close resemblance to those of English. This is not surprising, since one danger of a rich and well-developed formal model such as Principles and Parameters, coupled with the assumption that languages share essential and universal properties, is that analyses developed for English are applied to other languages. In this framework centre stage is occupied by the ramifying formal model and differences between languages are smoothed out.

what we have to say relates to all models of generative grammar and even neo-traditional grammars such as Quirk *et al.* (1985). In the Principles and Parameters perspective the constraints developed in the course of work on English and other languages are taken to be the constraints innately available to children.[3]

8.3.2. *Magnasyntax vs. the syntax of spontaneous spoken language*

But what data serve as input to formal models? At this point we appeal to the concept of magnasyntax, based on the concept of magnavocabulary introduced by Ong (1982: 103–8). A national written language like English has been worked over, as Ong puts it, for centuries. Ong suggests that the elaboration of English began in the chancery of Henry V and has been continued up to the present by dictionary makers, writers developing new genres and new styles, normative grammarians, and so on. There are massive collections of printed texts (and nowadays electronic texts and, better late than never, spoken texts). The texts cover centuries of output and thousands of authors (in the broadest sense). The researches by dictionary makers over the last two and a half centuries are embodied in modern dictionaries such as the *Oxford English Dictionary* and *Webster's Third New International Dictionary*. The contents of these dictionaries are what Ong calls a magnavocabulary.

This magnavocabulary of English is not the property of any one speaker—the most erudite scholar would be hard put to it to have even a passive command of 20% of the contents of the *OED*. The *OED* contains a large amount of Greco-Latinate vocabulary, and it is known from primary and indeed secondary schools that school pupils command very little of it. Gropen *et al.* (1989) report that no Latinate dative verbs were used in the speech of the parents talking to the children taking part in the experiments—not even verbs such as *donate*, *explain*, and *demonstrate*, which seem pretty tame to highly educated speakers of English. The fact is that a small minority of speakers of English control the Greco-Latinate part of its vocabulary, and that part includes just the more common words. A smaller number, specialists in scientific and medical fields, control in addition the Greco-Latinate technical terms in their specialism. Anticipating the argument below, we should recognize that the Greco-Latinate vocabulary is typically learned from written texts and is taught at school and university.

We wish to suggest that analogous to magnavocabulary is magnasyntax. Over the centuries written English has been codified and documented and

---

[3] One complaint is that the details of what is innately available to the child change as the formal model changes. This is no ground for complaint. The formal model is a hypothesis constantly being revised as more data is investigated and what is innate is also hypothetical and subject to change.

handbooks of English grammar have been published. These grammars set out the morphology and syntax of written English and include word-, clause-, and phrase-constructions from texts produced last century and this. The latest comprehensive grammar, Quirk *et al.* (1985), describes constructions that are current in speech and writing, constructions that are current only in formal writing, and constructions that are rare even in formal writing. When linguists set themselves the task of writing rules that generate all and only the correct sentences of a language, what they are tackling is this magnasyntax, which is not the syntax of any particular speaker of English or of any particular genre of current English or even of the English of any particular period, but the set of every syntactic construction that has been recorded in written (and spoken) English since 1800 or 1600, depending on the grammar. This is clear from the arguments in, say, Radford (1988), which draws on a range of quite disparate constructions in order to establish the constituent structure of NPs; everyday neutral examples such as *your red pencil and his* are side-by-side with highly formal, rare examples such as *honest politician though he is*.

It is our assertion that generative grammar, considered globally, deals with magnasyntax. The data taken into account ranges from (devised) spoken data (including non-standard structures, which some analysts handle systematically and some do not) through data that is neutral between spoken and written to data that is literary and even archaic. We will not develop this theme here since it is presented in more detail in the following sections, but it is important to point out that generativists do not see themselves as dealing with magnasyntax. A central role in generative work has always been played by the intuitions of individual speakers, but a major difficulty is that the speakers whose intuitions have been consulted are typically professional linguists, or postgraduates studying linguistics, or undergraduate students. These are all classes of people who work constantly with complex written language, who are used to playing language games and whose intuitions are based on written language. It is also the case (see the discussion of grammaticality judgements in §8.3.10) that the skill of making judgements of grammaticality is to some extent taught to students of linguistics.

Suppose someone objects (as did a colleague of ours) that a native speaker can and does judge examples like *honest politician though he is* . . . to be grammatical. How strong is this objection? It is true that some native speakers of English, those with a good command of the written language, will recognize the construction and interpret the example but it is an open question whether other native speakers would do the same. Even if they did, what interpretation could be placed on their judgement?: that they reckoned on balance that the construction was 'correct'?; that they managed to interpret the example from the occurrence of *though*?; that they simply made a guess? Most presentations of grammaticality judgements in the generative literature include no discussion of how the judgements were collected; whether the examples were presented in different orders, whether they were incorporated in a text or presented singly; whether the grammatical judgement test was preceded by other tests requiring the subjects, say, to fill in gaps, to complete sentence fragments, or to take the five words *is, politician, though, honest,* and *he* and arrange them into a clause.

Bard *et al.* (1996) is instructive. They address the problem of eliciting acceptability judgements, drawing a careful distinction between grammaticality and acceptability and extending their net to take in relative grammaticality and relative acceptability. They emphasize the need to collect judgements from different groups of subjects to validate results by cross-modal matching, and to collect judgements from the same group of subjects on different occasions, changing the order of the elicitation items. Finally, the results are subjected to statistical tests of significance. Very little, if any, of the published work in generative grammar meets these criteria; the only exception being the body of work in the Principles and Parameters framework on the acquisition of language by children. A final interesting point in relation to Bard *et al.* is that although they used different groups of subjects, the latter were either undergraduates or 'experienced linguists'; that is, all the subjects were people with a good command of written language.

How do the above considerations relate to the Chomskyan theory of grammar and language acquisition? In Chomsky (1986) a distinction is drawn between I-language (internalized language) and E-language (externalized language). I-language is the internalized grammar of speakers, the set of innate principles and parameters enabling speakers to acquire any human language and specifying the boundaries on the formal properties of human languages. E-language has been defined as pairing of sentences and meanings (Chomsky 1986: 19). Chomsky has declared that the proper study of linguistics is I-language. To return to the line of argument in §8.2, the difficulty is simply that many of the principles and parameters of I-language have been proposed on the basis of the complex syntax of written language and on the ability of highly educated users to manipulate the symbolic (grammatical) code. Complex written language is not obviously relevant to the early stages of first language acquisition, as will be argued in the following section.

8.3.3. *Magnasyntax and the goals of generative grammar*

The aim of any generative grammar is to generate the set of all and only the correct sentences of a language. The route to this goal is to write rules that handle a small number of constructions and then to test the output of the grammar against the intuitions of native speakers, who are asked to judge whether particular sentences are acceptable, or to grade sentences for acceptability relative to each other. We will return below to the subject of intuitions and sentences but the immediate question concerns the interpretation of such generative grammars (and all types of generative grammar are affected, whether transformational, phrase-structure, or lexical-functional). If the grammar is conceived as a tool for handling and bringing out the major syntactic (and indeed morphological and lexical) patterns in a given language, it is open to objections about the method of data-collection (How good are people's intuitions?) and about the range of data (Are spoken and written language distinguished? Are formal and informal registers distinguished, rare, archaic constructions and everyday structures, and so on?). That is, fundamental questions about what a language is need to be addressed.

Of course, generativists can take the view that they are trying to handle the magnasyntax, but this would be rather unusual. Instead, general constraints on the magnasyntax have been established, such as subjacency, binding conditions, and the empty category principle, and these properties are projected onto speakers of languages. The argument runs thus: no human languages have sentential constructions that disobey the constraints; no speakers of any language produce sentences that disobey the constraints; no speakers of any language are exposed to the range and quality of data, with correct or incorrect structures clearly marked as such; the only way to explain why speakers do not produce sentences that break, say, subjacency, is to suppose that the speakers, including very young children learning their native language, have innate knowledge of these constraints.

The syntactic constructions described in Chapters 2–4 bear on the above argument. The properties and constraints established over the past thirty years by Chomskyans are boundary conditions in the sense that no sentential construction will break through the boundaries and remain acceptable; in fact, sentences breaking through the boundaries occur neither in speech nor in writing. But the examples that come closest to the boundaries all occur in writing, and many of these occur as examples in work on syntax. As their first language children do not acquire the written variety of their native tongue but the structures and vocabulary that they hear in the spontaneous speech around them. Anticipating the discussion below of possible mechanisms of acquiring first language, we ask at this point whether it makes sense to think of children as acquiring a grammar that will generate all and only the correct sentences of their native language, including its written variety, when their task is to develop rules for the structures of spontaneous spoken language.

The force of this comment can be brought out if we return to the concern of generative linguists with the set of all and only the correct sentences of a given language.[4] As will be argued in §8.3.10 in connection with intuitions, it is not at all clear whether all sentences can be judged acceptable or not, or even whether speakers have intuitions about all sentences. (The previous sentence is a very inaccurate statement about the current situation, since very few speakers of English, the most intensively examined language in generative grammar, have been asked about their intuitions, and those that have consulted their intuitions have done so for a tiny set of examples.) From the viewpoint of magnasyntax sentences are extendable in various ways; by the addition of another clause or phrase preceded by *and* as in *We visited Chartres and Reims and Metz and Strasbourg and . . .*; by the embedding of another clause inside an existing structure, as *We visited the house that had been designed by the architect who trained with the woman who set up the practice that . . .*; by the insertion of another adjective inside a noun phrase, as in *the desolate moor, the desolate purple moor, the desolate purple rolling moor*, and so on.

Suppose the object of research is spontaneous spoken language. Suppose too that the goal is not to generate all and only the correct sentences of a given spoken language but to generate the typical sentences. For the spoken English and Russian examined in Chapters 2–4, the extendability and complexity of clauses and phrases can be severely limited. Examples are:

i A subject NP contains at most one out of the set {determiner, quantifier, numeral} together with a full noun; alternatively, a subject NP contains a pronoun.
ii Other NPs may contain at most a determiner/numeral/quantifier two adjectives and a noun. The noun may be followed by a prepositional phrase or a relative clause.
iii A main clause may be preceded or followed by only one adverbial clause.
iv The main verb in a main clause may be followed by only one complement clause.
v Subordinate clauses are not embedded in other subordinate clauses.

The above list is not exhaustive but were we to incorporate these constraints in a set of phrase-structure rules, the latter would potentially generate over 95% of the structures in our corpuses. ('Potentially', because the rule would have to be adequately formulated with respect to many other details. The essential point is that from what we know of the data in our corpus, we are confident that there are very few clause complexes—sentences having been abandoned as per Chapter 2—exceeding the limits laid down above. The figure of 95% results from our awareness that corpuses of data can throw

---

[4] By 'sentences' is meant not just linear sequences of words, phrases, and clauses but the hierarchical X-bar structures assigned to such sequences and the semantic and phonological interpretations associated with them.

up unexpected and surprising examples, but a good number of the surprises can be treated as fixed phrases—cf. the discussion of noun phrases in Chapter 4.)

Of course there will be structures not covered, such as one example of a noun phrase with three adjectives or a relative clause embedded inside a noun phrase inside a relative clause. The view taken here is that such structures comes from written language, that they are initially learned as whole chunks and that children begin to develop a more complex grammar of English as they are exposed to written texts, either hearing them read or reading them for themselves. The crucial point is that children are exposed to spontaneous spoken data and their task is to master the structures of that data. One argument for the Chomskyan position is that the complexity of syntactic structure in natural language and the alleged lack of negative evidence make it essential to abandon hypotheses that permit a role to learning and instead to invoke innate constraints that, by virtue of being innate, are not learned. In the context of the simple structures of spontaneous spoken language, hypotheses based on learning from positive examples become plausible and attractive and the drive towards innate constraints is far from compelling. (For instance, the structures are so simple that subjacency is not required and they lend themselves to the sorts of acquisition mechanisms discussed by Bowerman (1988)—see the account in §8.3.11. As we will see in §8.3.8, the attractiveness and compellingness of innate constraints with respect to written language is greatly reduced by the way in which written language is *taught* and by the length of time required.

8.3.4. *Misuse of magnasyntax in discussions of first language acquisition*

Generative discussions of children acquiring language regularly mix up spontaneous spoken language and written language and are invaded by magnasyntax. Pinker (1994: 16) declares that writing is an optional accessory and that the real engine of verbal communication is the spoken language 'we acquired as children'. Clearly this is true, because spoken language is ontogenetically prior to written language and no community of human beings lacks a spoken language, although many still lack a written language. Pinker's assertion does however need qualification with respect to literate members of literate societies. Stubbs (1980) gives a cogent account of the pre-eminent place occupied by written language in such societies, and we should certainly not accept Pinker's further declaration (1994: 18) that language is no more a cultural invention than upright posture and is not a cultural artefact that we learn the way we learn to tell the time. The processes whereby humans handle sequences of symbols can certainly be regarded, in Pinker's words, as a distinct piece of the biological make-up of our brains, but the various genres, registers, and their corresponding syntax and vocabulary are cultural artefacts, having been consciously developed and elaborated by users of written language and developed in different ways in different cultures.

According to Pinker (1994: 22) virtually every sentence that a person utters or understands is a brand-new combination of words appearing for the first time in the history of the universe. Elsewhere (1994: 85) he urges readers to go into the Library of Congress and pick up a sentence at random from any volume. The chances are, he says, that no matter how long they continue to search thereafter readers will fail to find an exact repetition. Estimates of the number of sentences that an ordinary person is capable of producing are breathtaking; a limit of twenty words on the length of sentences would be too severe, a proposition which Pinker supports with a sentence from George Bernard Shaw that is one hundred and ten words long. The matter of exact repetitions and brand-new formulations will be taken up in the section on formulas; what must be pointed out here is that Pinker's discussion concerns written language, and a very formal and complex variety of written language. Sentences of spontaneous spoken language, as demonstrated in Chapter 2, are rather short; indeed it was argued that the sentence is a quite inappropriate unit of analysis for spontaneous spoken language.

In a discussion of long-distance dependencies Pinker (1994: 96) uses as examples an anecdotal sentence obviously devised by an ingenious adult and in his discussion of language structure he asserts that NPs can also have subjects, as in *the guitarist's destruction of the hotel room*. The noun phrase is fine, but this construction does not occur in spontaneous spoken language, certainly not in our corpus.[5] Pinker does recognize in passing that written language is acquired later than spoken language but he severely underestimates the quantity of constructions that are acquired or learned relatively late in children's lives. He maintains (1994: 273) that it is safe to say that all languages are acquired with equal ease before the child turns 4, except for constructions that are rare, are used predominantly in written language, or are mentally taxing, such as *The horse that the elephant kicked kissed the pig*. (That this example is difficult is expected in the light of the discussion of noun phrases in Chapter 4, where it was demonstrated that subject noun phrases typically exclude adjectives, prepositional phrases, and relative clauses.) The general difficulty with

---

[5] It was observed in Chapter 3 that gerunds with subject nouns in *'s*, such as the *guitarist's destroying his hotel room*, are untypical of spontaneous spoken language. Of course, *'s* N-*ing* sequences do occur, as in *I hate my Dad's singing* but *singing* here denotes the sounds produced rather than the activity. Compare *I hate my Dad's writing/spelling*, which are analogous to *I hate my Dad's singing*, and *I hate my Dad when he sings* or *I hate when my Dad sings*, which are not analogous.

Pinker's phrasing is that the syntax learned after the age of 4 is presented as an exception, but the exception is enormous. It includes the structures cited in §3.4, and these include not just gapping and accusative-and-infinitive but WH relative clauses, certain types of adverbial clause, such as clauses of concession, and the large numbers of Greco-Latinate verbs with their peculiar syntax.

Horrocks (1988: 154) provides an example of how the pervasive influence of magnasyntax leads to inappropriate adult data being cited in connection with children's language acquisition, e.g. *Graball found a new set of clients to fleece* and *Jimbo seemed to us to like himself*. The latter gives rise to the unacceptable example **Jimbo pleaded with us to like himself*. The set of children under 5 who will pay attention to examples like these, far less produce them, is null.

Even worse, magnasyntax allows Manzini (1990) to contribute a paper to a volume on language acquisition in which she says nothing specifically about language acquisition and discusses examples such as *John and Peter like each other's pictures* and *John and Peter thought that each other's pictures were on sale*. These are central examples for a grammar that purports to handle the syntax and semantics of *each other* but this is not a construction that older children use, far less young children. (This is not to deny that children do use *each other*, but in examples such as *we don't like each other*. The examples that young children hear are on the lines of *they're very like each other*, with *each* and *other* adjacent, not in possessive constructions and not in a separate clause from their antecedent.)

8.3.5. *The non-degenerate nature of spoken language*

The main point to which the discussion has been leading is that children learn informal spoken language with its own simple structures. They do not learn written language, as argued in detail in the next section. (The irony is that the theory of grammar which has had the greatest impact on theories of first language acquisition is based largely on written language, and not just on the written language of children's stories but on the complex written language of well-educated adults.) Moreover, the language of the various corpuses of informal conversation is not degenerate. Occasionally speakers do make slips of the tongue, but only once in the 50,000 words of the Scottish English Corpus of spontaneous conversation is there a serious breakdown of syntax—interestingly, at a point where the speaker is trying to express a complex set of conditions by means of relatively complex syntax. Labov (1972: 203) goes so far as to say that the ungrammaticality of everyday speech seems to be a myth. In the empirical studies that he conducted 75% of utterances corresponded directly to well-formed sentences. That figure rose to 98% when cases of ellipsis were excluded, along

384 *Spontaneous Spoken Language*

with instances of stammering and false starts.[6] Labov says that a great many other linguists have confirmed his view that when non-academic speakers are talking about subjects they know well, such as personal experiences, only 10% of utterances need to be edited in order to qualify as corresponding to well-formed sentences.

8.3.6. *Computationally complex structure-dependent rules, formulas, and imitation*

A central tenet of Chomskyan generative grammar is that children acquire computationally complex structure-dependent rules. An alternative view is that much of language is formulaic and that imitation, combined with the learning and manipulation of formulas, plays an important part in first language acquisition (and indeed in second language acquisition). This alternative view is supported by three developments in recent work: research into the acquisition of language that highlights the role of imitation and formulas; recent syntactic research focusing on the power of lexical items and the central position of the lexicon in generative models; and recent syntactic research focusing on units that are larger than single words but have to be analysed, and learned, as single units. That is, while not denying the marvellous nature of language acquisition, we can see routes by which children can work their way towards mastery of syntax.

One of the difficulties inherent in a polemic is that the supporters of the winning side tend to see the opposing point of view as completely vanquished. This is exactly what happened in the polemic between Chomsky and Skinner, with behaviourism disappearing from the arsenal of linguistic theory. This disappearance has had the unfortunate consequence that linguists, whether of the generative persuasion or not, have tended to underestimate the number of fixed expressions that occur in all varieties of English and the role of memorization and repetition in mastering the language (in mastering any language).

However, there have always been pockets within linguistics, sociolinguistics, and applied linguistics which have suggested that ready-made chunks of unanalysed language are as important as productive rules. (See Bolinger 1976; Coulmas 1979, 1981; Van Lancker 1975; Widdowson 1984, 1990;

---

[6] Can children 'know' how to exclude false starts, stammers, etc.? If so, how do they do it? These questions are relevant to both the Chomskyan theory of first langauge acquisition and the position advocated here. We may guess (and it is just a guess) that the language addressed to young children, because of its very simple content, presents very few if any false starts and reformulations. Of course children eventually come across false starts; it is reasonable to suppose that by the time they do they have good exposure to smooth delivery and can recognize awkward places in the stream of speech. Likewise children normally know from their own performance and from the performance of the surrounding adults that stammering is an abnormal form of speech delivery.

Yorio 1980: Peters 1983; Nattinger and DeCarrico 1992). Lyons (1968: 416) writes: 'There is a good deal of our everyday use of language which is quite properly described in "behaviourist" terms, and can be attributed to our "acting out" of particular "roles" in the maintenance of socially-prescribed, "ritualistic" patterns of behaviour.' Pawley and Syder (1983) argue that any speaker of English has stored in memory a large number of phrases and clauses. That is, speakers possess many lexicalized expressions that possess certain properties: their meaning is not entirely predictable from their form, they behave like minimal units for certain syntactic purposes, and they are a social institution. By the latter, Pawley and Syder (1983: 209) mean that the expression is a conventional label for a conventional concept. They suggest that the ordinary, mature English speaker probably knows several hundreds of thousands of sentence-length expressions: examples are *I thought better of it*, *It doesn't bear thinking about*, *Think twice before you* VP, *I (just) can't think straight*, and so on (Pawley and Syder 1983: 213). Pawley and Syder observe that such prefabricated patterns are easily encoded and permit the speaker to attend to the task of constructing the larger discourse. Equally, they lessen the decoding burden for listeners.

In the field of second language acquisition and teaching, a growing number of linguists are coming round to the view that much spoken language (specifically, spoken English) is formulaic. McCarthy (1991: 122) maintains that view, adding that native speakers have the advantage of possessing a larger number of formulas than non-native learners. Nattinger and DeCarrico (1992) develop the notion of 'lexical phrases', essentially prefabricated chunks of language which come partially or completely assembled but are none the less open to analysis by grammatical rules. Wong Fillmore (1976) discovered that children of primary school age learning English as a foreign language adopted the technique of repeating whole clauses until they could not only produce the whole clause appropriately but employ pieces of it to construct different clauses.

It is worthwhile taking special note of Nattinger and DeCarrico's assertion that lexical phrases which come partially or completely assembled are none the less open to analysis by grammatical rules. This opens the question of compositionality. If lexical phrases have syntactic structure specifiable by syntactic rules, perhaps part or all of their meaning is compositional and can be handled by rules for composing the meaning of a large syntactic unit out of the meanings of its constituent parts. Nunberg, Sag, and Wasow (1994) argue convincingly that many idioms—which are one type of lexical phrase—can be handled compositionally. They propose that in, for example, *spill the beans*, *spill* can be assigned the interpretation 'divulge' and the interpretation 'information' only when the two are in combination. (The combination can of course be given a literal interpretation depending on the context.) Other idioms require a different treatment;

for instance, the idiomatic interpretation of phrases such as *kick the bucket* (to die) and *saw logs* (to sleep) cannot be split into smaller parts which can be distributed over the constituents of their syntactic structure.

Nunberg *et al.* remark that many linguists have confused conventionality and compositionality. Idioms are conventional in that their meaning or use cannot be entirely predicted from the conventions that determine the use of their constituents in isolation from each other (Nunberg *et al.* 1994: 492). The relevant convention need not apply however to an entire phrase but can be broken up into conventions applying to the individual constituents of the phrase (Nunberg *et al.* 1994: 499).

Finally (for present purposes) Nunberg *et al.* (1994: 499–503) provide a number of examples demonstrating that idioms are not as inflexible in their syntax as is normally supposed. Parts of idioms can be modified by adjectives or relatives (*leave no legal stone unturned, Pat got the job by pulling strings that weren't available to anyone else*), parts of idioms can be quantified (*That's the third gift horse she's looked in the mouth this year*), parts of idioms may be topicalized (*Those strings he wouldn't pull for you*), and so on.

The case presented by Nunberg *et al.* bears indirectly on the case presented here but does not constitute a direct counter-argument. Let us note first that while Nunberg *et al.*'s examples of flexible syntax in idioms are possible, they are at the limits of acceptability and take us to the topics of creativity and differing degrees of competence, discussed in §§ 8.3.7 and 8.3.9, respectively. Cruse (1986: 37–48) provides a counterbalance to Nunberg *et al.*, not by arguing that the syntax of idioms is completely frozen but by showing that idioms have very limited syntactic flexibility. They are not easily interrupted by adverbs—Cruse cites *?Arthur has a chip, apparently, on his shoulder* and *We took them, after a shaky start, to the cleaners*, with the question mark indicating uncertainty (shared by the authors) as to whether the examples are fully unacceptable or merely very unusual; a WH cleft highlighting an entire idiom is fine—*What John did was pull his sister's leg*—but a WH cleft highlighting the object of *pull* will not do—*What John pulled was his sister's leg*. The latter example is of course quite acceptable in its literal interpretation.[7]

A second problem with Nunberg *et al.*'s data is that their examples of syntactically flexible idioms are not taken from spontaneous conversation and many of them are not taken from real texts either. A good number do come from real texts, but from newspapers.[8] That is, they come from one

---

[7] Interestingly, the existence of potential controversy over the status of the syntactically transformed idioms emerges in a subpart of Nunberg *et al.*'s paper in which they point out that judgements of the acceptability of certain syntactically-transformed Italian idioms made by Cinque (1990) were rejected by other native speakers of Italian.

[8] Nunberg *et al.* (1994: 521) refer to a database of the texts of 53 American newspapers. The corpus is of the order of a billion words.

very specific genre of written language; one which is produced by writers skilled (or at least highly practised) in the composition of condensed and highly integrated syntax (to meet the constraints on space) and of unusual and even novel prose (to keep the attention of the reader). Skilled newspaper writers with planning and editing time produce a text quite different in complexity from spontaneous speech and far more creative (in the sense in which that word is used in §8.3.7) in its exploitation of syntax and vocabulary.[9]

The idea that language may not be entirely rule-governed and produced afresh each time it is used is not new. Idioms, for instance, have long been considered a problem for Chomskyan grammar—see Chafe (1968) but also Nunberg *et al.* (1994), who argue that Chafe's view is wrong. Yorio (1980) provides an extensive classification of formulaic conventionalized phenomena in native language use, as separate from other linguistic conventions, including large stretches of memorized discourse in songs and prayers, routine greeting formulas, proverbs, euphemisms, idioms, and collocations. Linguistic studies have begun to show that ready-made language sequences which cannot easily be accounted for in terms of an economic system of generative rules may be more pervasive than generally acknowledged. Native-like selection includes the ability to select the preferred sequence from a number of grammatically acceptable variants but native speakers do not appear to make use of all the productive possibilities of rules available in their language. Rather in many contexts particular functions are realized by particular forms, suggesting a much closer link between forms and usage. (See Church and Hanks 1989; Kennedy 1989; Nattinger and DeCarrico 1992; Pawley and Syder 1983; Williams 1988.) All the above-cited studies suggest that the phenomenon of formulaic language is far from marginal.

There is some evidence for the psychological reality of formulaic language in terms of storage and production (Chafe 1979; Crick 1979; Goldman-Eisler 1968; Guillaume 1973; Peters 1983; Simon 1974; Van Lancker, Canter, and Terbeek 1981). Pawley and Syder (1983) consider native-like fluency one of two puzzles for linguistic theory. In view of the limitations on processing capacity compared to storage (Crick 1979), a plausible explanation for the fluency is that speakers rely, wherever possible, on ready-made memorized sequences in language use rather than novel generation from rules. Pawley and Syder (1975, 1976) and Chafe (1979) provide evidence to suggest that the largest unit of novel spoken discourse is one clause or information unit consisting of 8–10 words.

---

[9] Nunberg *et al.* (1994: 522 n. 365) investigated the occurrence of *take Adjective advantage* in the newspaper corpus and found that in 66% of nearly 6,000 occurrences the Adjective was *full* while in a further 7% it was *unfair*. No other word appeared with a frequency greater than 0.4%. They conclude that some speakers have lexicalized *take full advantage of* and *take unfair advantage of* as idiomatic verbs. In this point at least Nunberg *et al.* arrive at the same conclusion as we do.

It is suggested that spoken production is subject to the same short-term memory constraints which limit the number of individual units which speakers can hold to $c.7$ $(+/-2)$ (G. Miller 1956). Simon (1974) and Chafe (1979) suggest that these units need not be discrete items.

There is some evidence from first language acquisition research for the involvement of formulaic language. There is some evidence for parallel processes of creative construction and formulaic language use and for formulas being analysed and extended (e.g. R. Brown 1973; Cazden 1968; R. Clark 1974; Cruttenden 1981; Hickey 1993; Iwamura 1980; Snow 1981; Peters 1983; and Vihman 1982 provide comprehensive overviews).

Imitation and formulaic language are also widely-documented phenomena in second language acquisition (e.g. Wong Fillmore 1976; Hakuta 1974; Hanania and Gradman 1977; Hatch, Peck, and Wagner-Gough 1979; Huang and Hatch 1978; Kenyeres and Kenyeres 1938; Raupach 1984; Schmidt 1983; Vihman 1982; Wagner-Gough 1975). This ranges from 'amazingly complex sentences' (Haung and Hatch 1978: 131) and 'prefabricated routines' with open slots (Hakuta 1974: 287), to smaller chunks 'which are not always recognized as units in linguistic analysis' (Bolander 1989: 81). There is at present renewed interest in and debate surrounding the role of prefabrication in L2 use and learning. Weinert (1995a) suggests that it may be necessary to abandon the notion of a homogeneous grammatical competence as separate from language use. It is possible to integrate the study of formulaic language into a larger theoretical framework which includes both a linguistic and a learning perspective and which sees learning, knowledge, and production as closely related.[10]

Work on computational linguistics makes crucial use of formulas. The formulas relate primarily to situations and sequences of actions but are designed to enable computers to handle texts associated with given situations. Frames are data-structures representing stereotyped situations like going to a birthday party (cf. Minsky 1975: 212), while scripts represent a predetermined stereotyped sequence of actions that defines a well-known situation (cf. Schank and Abelson 1977: 44). Many scripts are associated with the formulaic language used in simple situations such as buying books, train, bus, or plane tickets, ordering meals, and asking for directions, but also for more complex situations such as doctor–patient interactions, which may follow a highly stereotyped pattern. It is the association of formulaic situations with formulaic language that makes possible the use of foreign-language phrase-books and the teaching of foreign languages partly in terms of the necessary phrases and clauses for dealing with a range of situations.

Neurological evidence is at least consistent with the view that rote and

---

[10] For an extensive discussion of the problems surrounding the definition/identification of formulaic language, see Weinert 1995a.

rule processes may interact (Danesi 1988; Wray 1992). Krashen (1981) argues that formulas are processed in the right hemisphere and are therefore not part of central language processes, which are located in the language-dominant left hemisphere. However, both Danesi and Wray suggest that the available data is consistent with a greater involvement of the right hemisphere in language tasks than hitherto acknowledged, and stress the interactive functioning of the two hemispheres. Danesi reviews the literature on left and right hemisphere involvement in relation to questions of language pedagogy. He suggests that the left and right hemisphere handle analytic and synthetic tasks respectively, in a *combined* fashion. Quoting Levy (1985) he states that 'it is impossible to educate one hemisphere at a time'. The importance of moving away from a simple analytic/synthetic dichotomy towards an integrated view of hemispheric functioning is eloquently and precisely expressed by Wray (1992: 31–3).

There is reason to believe that language needs to be seen as a continuum of the formulaic/creative (Bolinger 1976; Bolinger and Sears 1981; Langacker 1987; Nattinger and DeCarrico 1992; Pawley and Syder 1983; Wood 1981). The case is put most powerfully by Langacker (1987: 46), who asserts that

The grammar lists the full set of particular statements representing a speaker's grasp of linguistic convention, including those subsumed by general statements. Rather than thinking them an embarrassment, cognitive linguists regard particular statements as the matrix from which general statements (rules) are extracted. . . . Speakers do not necessarily forget the forms they already know once the rule is extracted, nor does the rule preclude their learning additional forms as established units. . . . Out of this sea of particularity speakers extract whatever generalizations they can. Most of these are of limited scope, and some forms cannot be assimilated to any general patterns at all.

This view allows formulaic language to become a more central phenomenon with a firm place in linguistic theory. It has led some researchers to question the notion of a homogeneous grammatical competence and to postulate different types of units of language knowledge and use, e.g. disjunctive associations over short or even long distances *a___ago*; *X is unlike Y in that Z* and 'mini grammars' for frames with limited productivity (*a TIME PERIOD ago*) (Nattinger and DeCarrico 1992).

In order to open up the way for a revised model of language use and learning, where the investigation of the possibilities of an integrated knowledge/usage based language theory is given new impetus, it is necessary to give serious thought to the definition/identification of formulaic language. We do not claim that our suggestions below solve all the problems, but they show that there is already substantial potential for future work in a variety of current approaches.

All approaches to the study of formulaic language stress the importance of their *functional* aspect, i.e. the fact that certain language sequences have conventionalized meanings which are used in certain predictable situations. Pragmatic approaches to the study of formulaic language therefore provide a very important basis for their identification and categorization (Coulmas 1981; Bahns, Burmeister, and Vogel 1986). However, this perspective needs to be complemented by psycholinguistic approaches, given that almost all studies invoke *processing* terminology. For instance, Bolinger (1976: 2) suggests that 'speakers do at least as much remembering as they do putting together'; Wong Fillmore (1976: 296) argues that 'A stored repertory of stock phrases . . . reduces the amount of verbal activity which must be created anew for each speech occasion'; and Pawley and Syder (1983: 205) talk of 'strings . . . which . . . are recalled as wholes'. Most studies do not state explicitly what *produced or recalled as wholes* means.

This notion is not a straightforward one. First of all it raises the question of the internal organization of such wholes in mental representation and actual use. Given the temporal aspect of production, the minimal interpretation is that it involves recall or production of the linear surface order of its syntactic constituents and phonological units. Recall/production need not itself be unidirectional, given the observed 'bathtub' effect of lexical recall, whereby the beginning and ends of words are more prominent (Aitchison 1987).

Alternatively, formulaic language may be a 'bundle', organized in various ways, including linear or non-linear arrangements, tied by a particular meaning, function, or situation. There is, of course, no reason to assume that all formulaic chunks are organized in the same way. However, addressing the issue of internal organization seems to us crucial to the empirical verification of formulaic language. The comparison with lexical items suggests a methodology for its investigation. Peters (1983) reports on errors resembling lexical blends (*He was breathing down my shoulder*) which indicate that some multi-word sequences are stored as units in the same way as individual lexical items. Van Lancker, Canter, and Terbeek (1981) have worked on sequences which have a literal and an idiomatic meaning (e.g. *he didn't know he was skating on thin ice*). When asked to produce the two versions, speakers were found to insert longer pauses between words in the literal version while running them together in the idiomatic version.

Another question is how a string acquires formulaic status. With respect to language development Peters (1983, 1985) suggests that formulaic language is the result of segmentation of the input, whereby units larger than morphs or lexical items are extracted and used by learners for specific functions. Iwamura (1980) produces examples of children's neologisms which are the result of fusion, including the lexicalization of syntactic strings where grammatical functions have been removed (*a down-to-the-*

floor dress → *a down-floor dress*). More problematic is the notion that strings may become formulaic through frequent production (Olson 1973; Langacker 1987) where linguistic rules can account for the data. While this notion is generally taken to apply to adult native language use, it applies equally to native and non-native learning, i.e. the status of forms in developed language may be due to the way they were learnt (Langacker 1987).

There is a long tradition in both psychological and second language acquisition research which assumes a distinction between automatic and controlled processes (J. R. Anderson, 1983; Bialystok and Sharwood-Smith 1985; Levelt 1989; McLaughlin 1987). Givón (1989) suggests that grammar is a partly automatized processing system where repetition, frequency, and predictability are necessary for routinization and hence faster processing. Experimental study in this area is in its infancy (Givón 1989) but there is a growing body of data on L2 temporal variables (Cook 1988*a*; Dechert, Möhle, and Raupach 1984; Towell 1987) which are taken to support the controlled/automatized distinction. Most studies assume that it is the application of rules which becomes automatized but the question arises as to how circularity of argument can be avoided. (See Klatzky 1980.) How does one decide whether a fluently produced sequence is recalled as a whole, or is the result of highly automatized hierarchical processes of rule application? Is there a qualitative change and, if so, how does it take place? For instance, MacWhinney and Anderson's 'composition', i.e. collapsing several rules into one allows for both quantitative and qualitative change (MacWinney and Anderson 1986).

Other work suggests that fluent language use is not based on rules at all, as has been claimed for other expert performances (Dreyfus, Dreyfus, and Athanasiou 1986). Wray's focusing hypothesis (1992: 6) is similar in its claim that, while 'language can be and often is processed according to analytic strategies . . . analytic processing of language does not usually occur'. However, her model assumes that the development of holistic mechanisms depends on prior rule formation. This view does not accord with the L1 and L2 acquisitional data which shows that learners may initially operate with unanalysed units which later become analysed. Wray is careful to acknowledge that there is no primary evidence in support of her hypothesis. What she does claim is that available psycholinguistic and neurolinguistic research is set up in a way to preclude any demonstration of holistic processes. She considers finding appropriate experimentation for the investigation of holistic processes a major challenge for future research.

The investigations and hypotheses reported in the preceding paragraphs are certainly compatible with the way in which many (probably most) speakers of a given language normally coast along, certainly in informal conversation and even in relatively formal exchanges: the businessmen or scientists who use words and phrases ('jargon') in radio or television interviews are also coasting.[11] Pawley and Syder's observations suggest that the use of large (and to some extent unanalysed) stretches of syntax is much more widespread in language learning and use than Lyons thought. Their observations also accord with the comments by G. Brown *et al.* (1984) quoted in Chapter 1 to the effect that speakers are happiest producing single phrases which are loosely strung together to form a text. (This is also one explanation for the many examples of utterances produced by English commentators, managers, and coaches during the 1990 World Cup competition: *They are a very difficult team to beat by anybody, Cameroon will not be an easy team to beat by England.* The construction can be seen as BE ADJ N TO V with BY NP tacked on paratactically. The unkind linguist might say that this sort of discourse can in any case be handled as the concatenation of a limited number of set phrases with a limited number of paradigmatic choices.)

The notion of formulas is invoked by Blanche-Benveniste *et al.* (1991) with respect to the French pronoun *lequel*, which can function as an interrogative or a relative pronoun. Examples are in (1).

(1) (*a*) Tu choisiras lequel?
    you will-choose which-one?
  (*b*) vous avez une canalisation de gaz sur laquelle il y a un doute
    you have a pipe of gas on which there-is a doubt

Examples such as (1*b*) are said by Blanche-Benveniste *et al.* to be used by speakers who are highly educated and/or used to public speaking. Most speakers, however, use the pronoun in a small set of formulas built round a small set of lexical items. Cf. (2).

(2) (*a*) le milieu, le groupe, dans lequel je vis
    the milieu the group in which I live
  (*b*) la mentalité, l'ambiance, dans laquelle il a été élevé
    the outlook, the ambiance in which he was brought-up
  (*c*) la raison pour laquelle il le fait
    the reason for which he it is-doing
  (*d*) le secteur dans lequel il intervient
    the sector in which he is-intervening

It is worthwhile pointing out that the view that many chunks of syntax are learned and used as wholes does not mean that these chunks are idioms.

---

[11] The advantage offered by formulas has long been recognized in Homeric scholarship, who long ago established lists of set phrases, studied their function in the *Iliad* and *Odyssey*, and proposed that the formulas could be explained if the poems were originally oral texts, partly held in the memory of skilled reciters and partly created anew at each reciting. Lord (1960) was able to lend substance to this hypothesis by recording and studying the performances of (illiterate) oral bards in Yugoslavia. The bards, although holding enormous passages of text in memory, did not produce the same text at different recitals, and different bards produced different texts of one and the same tale. What each bard carries (or carried?) in memory is a set of themes or formulas out of which all tales could be constructed.

Many idioms are non-compositional and all have a highly conventional interpretation, but the examples cited by Pawley and Syder fall into different subsets. *Who do you think you are?*, *What does she think she is?*, *What kind of report does she think this is?* can be seen as variations on a basic theme—WH + pronoun/NP–DO–Pronoun/NP–*think*–Pronoun/NP–BE. The variations consist of changes in the tense of DO, or changes in the Pronouns or NPs. The meaning of the whole construction is compositional but the construction has a special conversational use: it implicates that whatever the thought entertained by the relevant person, that thought is mistaken and absurd. Pawley and Syder (1983: 211) suggest that the construction can be thought of as a recurrent sentence stem: since syntagmatic variations are possible but only within limits, it is not freely generated by the syntax. At the other end of the spectrum are sentences such as *A stitch in time saves nine*, which they describe as an institutionalized sentence—that is, it is an idiom, with fixed syntax and fixed lexical items.

In this connection, Fillmore, Kay, and O'Connor (1988: 504) draw attention to 'things which are larger than words, which are like words in that they have to be learned separately as individual whole facts about pieces of language, but which also have grammatical structure, structure of the kind that we ordinarily interpret by appealing to the operation of the general grammatical rules'. They analyse the LET ALONE construction, as in *He won't even hold the baby, let alone bath it*, showing that it has a range of idiosyncratic syntactic, semantic, and pragmatic properties which have to be treated as belonging to the construction rather than being assigned by the general principles and parameters of the grammar. If Fillmore, Kay, and O'Connor are correct, the concept of construction needs to be reintroduced into generative grammar alongside general rules, and quite a large amount of structure may turn out either to be generated by highly specific rules or simply stored as whole chunks into which the speaker/writer inserts appropriate lexical items.

Peters (1983: ch. 2) points out that children are good at remembering and reproducing fairly long chunks of speech. Exactly what chunks particular children remember varies from culture to culture, as a function of attitudes to and beliefs about the appropriate way for adults to interact with children. Drawing on observations by Nelson, she observes that most work on first language acquisition has been carried out on children from middle-class homes and with highly educated parents. Especially with the oldest child in a given family, such parents focus on reference to entities and encourage the child to learn single words. The younger children in such families, and children in other cultures, do not have their attention focused on single words and on reference but pick up larger chunks of language and use them expressively; that is, they use them to interact with others, to have doors opened, toys retrieved, and so on. It must be emphasized that Peters does not assign children to two mutually exclusive classes of referrers and expressers: rather, she emphasizes that the referential route with its concentration on single words is not the only way into English and that children routinely learn phrases and indeed whole clauses as single units.

The facts reported in this section should lead us to regard with caution and doubt statements such as Pinker (1994) makes on the linguistic creativity of human beings. Following the Chomskyan line, he asserts that 'virtually every sentence that a person utters or understands is a brand-new combination of words, appearing for the first time in the history of the universe' (1994: 22). On the contrary, it is fairly certain that utterances of spontaneous spoken language will contain phrases and even whole clauses that speakers store and use as wholes. Notice that we are not saying that the entire set of spontaneous spoken utterances consists of prefabricated chunks and nothing else; only that they contain a proportion of prefabricated chunks that ease the encoding and decoding load. It is certainly true that speakers replace single words in the prefabricated chunks in accordance with the situation of utterance, and it is true that these chunks are interspersed with bits that are constructed on-line. It is also true that the combinations of prefabricated chunks differ, but the marvellous creativity of human speakers typically manifests itself in planned utterances, spoken and written.

To sum up: the hypothesis that computationally-complex structure-dependent rules play a major role in language acquisition and in the competence of native adult speakers of any human language is not supported by data from researchers in first and second language learning, and a range of alternative models is available for development. We can aptly close this section with another reference from Peters (1983: 86), this time to work by Crick (1979: 219). Peters says: 'Recent neurological evidence about the human brain suggests that it has a great deal of memory capacity and powerful information-handling capabilities, but is severely limited in processing speed.' She comments that 'redundant forms of storage that would save processing time seem particularly adaptive for such an organ'. While not wishing to deny that children learn to handle structure-dependent rules—the evidence from subject-auxiliary inversion, WH fronting (in single clauses) cannot be denied—it is none the less the case, if Peters's remarks are accurate, that language-acquisition models in which structure-dependent rules play a major part are not viable.

8.3.7. *Creativity*

We must emphasize that none of the views expressed here excludes the idea that children make up rules and that they use language creativity. Pre-school children experiment with the basic patterns of their native language, syntactic, morphological, and lexical. Even such a fundamental construction as, say, the English WH interrogative is only grasped by dint of creative experimentation and practice. Pre-school children do not produce or receive the complex syntactic constructions typical of work in theoretical syntax—see the discussion of Crain and Nakayama in §8.3.8. At what point do children typically begin to demonstrate their creativity with such complex syntax? In the light of the discussion of the syntax of spontaneous speech, it is not surprising that the answer for spontaneous spoken language appears to be 'very late, and possibly never'.

But what about the writings of young children in school? What sort of creative efforts are manifested in them? Certainly creative efforts at syntax take place, though not of a sort discussed in theoretical syntax (whether generative or not). Children learn about and practise setting out main clauses as separate sentences signalled by capital letters and full stops and they learn how to combine a main clause and a subordinate clause. A more exciting sort of creativity among children comes when they learn to observe and describe scenes for themselves, some experimenting with metaphor, alliteration, and rhyme, others giving plain but effective accounts. In the written work of children of 10 and 11 the last sort of creativity is far more in evidence than the creation of complex sentences containing more than a main clause and one subordinate clause. (This sort of creativity is not and should not be the concern of any grammatical model. The point is that such models focus on creativity in one area of language whereas children's creativity is applied to other areas.) Consider the examples (3) and (4) taken from Rosen and Rosen (1973). They are all simple in syntax but very complex in choice of vocabulary. The original spelling is preserved.

(3) The lonely little ant hurrys and scurrys over my desk. He worrys and hurrys away from the edge. Its hard black back looks like a dot on my page. Its helplessness is very great, so when I poke him with my pencil he goes rolly polly unto my ink well. He can't get out so I put my finger down towards him. He crawls quickly and hurriedly over my finger on to the desk and away.

Denise, 10 years (Rosen and Rosen 1973: 120)

(4) The clashing and the grinding
The clicking and the shuttling
Are soothing to her ears,
Filling her arms with rhythm
Her head with daydreams

Anthony, 11 years (Rosen and Rosen 1973: 106)

Denise uses alliteration and coordination as in *hurrys and scurrys* and *worrys and hurrys*. She has two noun phrases, both subjects, containing two adjectives—*the lonely little ant* and *its hard black back*. She has only one subordinate clause, *when I poke him with my pencil*, but it is embedded inside a *so* sequence.[12] Anthony's poem about the woman at work is syntactically complex. There is an adjective phrase in which the adjective is modified by a prepositional phrase—*soothing to her ears*, and there is a gapping construction with a participle as pivot—*Filling her arms with rhythm, Her head with daydreams*. Note that Denise is 10 and Anthony 11. The slow process of learning written language will be discussed in §8.3.8.

8.3.8. *How long do children take to acquire their native language?*

There is a general consensus that normal children have mastered much of the grammar of their native language by age 4. Some researchers, witness the passage from Pinker referred to in §8.3.4, consider that normal 4-year-old children have mastered most of the grammar. We certainly do not dispute the proposition that children have acquired a large range of syntactic structures and vocabulary by the time they are 4, but assertions of this proposition are typically not accompanied by caveats about the vast range of written syntax, derivational morphology and vocabulary that children still have to master. Pinker does mention them, but treats them as trivial exceptions to the general grammar. Our position is that they constitute a large mass of material that children learn over a number of years, that children acquire the material at different rates, that children typically do not command it until the final year of secondary education or the first year of higher education or even later, and that many children do not acquire a command of it at all.

This position is not new. Long ago Carol Chomsky (1968) observed that it was commonly assumed by students of child language that children had mastered the syntax of their native language by about age 5. C. Chomsky (1968: 2) went against this assumption by declaring that comprehension tests revealed several areas in which children's knowledge of syntactic structure fell short of adults' knowledge. In particular control structures were acquired late. The constructions exemplified by *John is easy to see* and *John promised Bill to go* were acquired, by C. Chomsky's subjects, between the ages of 5.6 and 9 and were known by all the children aged 9 years or more. The construction in *John asked Bill what to do* was imperfectly known by some children even at age 10. The structure of *He knew that John was going to win the race* was acquired fairly uniformly at about age 5.6 (C. Chomsky 1968: 120). Note that the structure acquired at age 10 or later, *John asked Bill what to do*, is a classic written construction; one

---

[12] This account assumes that *so* is a coordinating conjunction.

corresponding spontaneous-speech construction is *John asked Bill what do I do*, with direct speech. Carol Chomsky's results are like those obtained by Crain and Nakayama and discussed below; the I-language specialist can of course ignore the results on the ground that they relate to E-language, but the same objection can be made as in §8.3.2, namely the principles embodied in theories of I-language are based on data which is typical of written language but untypical of spoken language. Children acquire spoken language but learn written language.

It is worthwhile reminding ourselves at this point in the discussion that the grammatical relationships between written and spoken language are complex. As shown in Chapters 2–4, while many constructions appear in written language but not in spontaneous speech, equally a large number of constructions do occur in spontaneous speech but not in written language. There is a further subtlety. In the straightforward case an entire construction is missing, such as the NP-Clause structure exemplified in *the driver you get a good laugh with him*, which is simply excluded from writing (except for written representation of speech). In other cases the general construction is present—as with noun phrases, which occur both in speech and writing—but certain arrangements of constituents typical of written noun phrases are either absent from spontaneous speech—e.g. the sequence Determiner-Adjective-Noun-Relative Clause exemplified by *the large dog that we fed*—or (surprisingly) rather rare—e.g. the sequence Determiner-Noun-Prepositional Phrase exemplified by *the book on the chair*. Obviously under-5s come across phrases such as *the man in the Moon* but they may well, as Peters suggests, learn this phrase as a proper name without analysing it. Once they go to school, children come across phrases in the classroom—*the boy at the back, the table at the door*—and in their reading. None the less, the infrequence of this structure in the data we have examined, both English and Russian, suggests that it would be profitable to investigate its occurrence in children's reading and writing in the early years of school.

We would expect to find that children do not at first use the written-language structures that are missing from spontaneous spoken language, and this expectation is met. Perera (1984: 88–158, 223–47) gives an excellent overview, whose main points are reproduced here; the major finding is the number of constructions that are not mastered until age 7 or much later:

i Studies have shown that only half of a set of 10 year olds could accurately interpret the structure Subject–Verb–Second Object–Direct Object as in *We showed her the book*;
ii 11 year olds regularly use adverbs in verb phrases, as in *have been always trying*, but 6 year olds rarely do;
iii the sequence Determiner–Noun–Prepositional Phrase is rare between ages 5 and 12;

- iv the ability to handle a range of pre- and post-nominal modifiers is only reached about age 15 or 16;
- v apart from set phrases such as *mum and dad*, coordinated Noun Phrases are not used extensively before age 5 and only become frequent between the ages of 8 and 13; not surprisingly, the earliest coordinated Noun Phrases function as Direct Object;
- vi concealed negatives are difficult—only 44% of a sample of 7 year olds understood the sentence *Tom's mother was anything but pleased*, only 58% understood *If only David had known, the dog was quite tame*, and only 38% understood *Mary's dress was neither new nor pretty*;
- vii the full passive appears late in children's speech—one study found that only 30% of a sample of 11 year olds used a full passive;
- viii children under 11 do not use finite or non-finite clauses as Subject;
- ix WH complements of indirect speech may have the word order of interrogatives as in *I can't remember what was it about*—as opposed to *I can't remember what it was about* (Perera treats this as an error, but it is the regular construction in spontaneous spoken language from adults);
- x the verbs that take finite complement clauses belong to a limited set— mainly TELL, KNOW, SHOW;
- xi in one study free relative clauses after verbs like ASK, as in *Ask Helen which book to read*, were misunderstood by 30% of a sample of 19 year olds;
- xii adverbial clauses of time, reason, and condition are found in children's speech, but adverbial clauses of result, place, manner, and concession are much rarer;
- xiii even when children can use various adverbial clauses of time, they do not always understand the relationship between the main clause and adverbial clause;
- xiv one study found that only 40% of a sample of 9 year olds used relative clauses in subject noun phrases;
- xv primary schoolchildren generally do not use relative clauses introduced by *whom, whose*, or preposition plus a relative pronoun, as in *the shop in which we bought it*.

The above list is a selection of points from Perera's discussion. Since lists are lifeless, we cite a further two examples of schoolchildren's writing from Rosen and Rosen (1973: 137–8), not stories or poetry but reports of work done in the classroom. Humphrey (aged 7) wrote the text in (5).

(5) A sundial
   I thought it would work in the night because sometimes the moon is very bright so it could make a shadow. Mrs Nethacott brought one to school. The electric all most makes it go.

Language Acquisition and Education 399

I made my timer with a flat piece of wood for the bottom of it and then I had to cut some wood about a foot long and then I asked Mr Lear for the nails and then I hammered the pieces of wood together and painted then let it dry and then I took it to Mr Lear and he drilled four holes through then I could wire the bottle on. Then Mrs Nethacott and I had a lot of trouble making it work. I had to put plasticine in the top and make a hole with a pin. When I was having my dinner it dripped $3\frac{1}{2}$ inches in 1 hour it dropped $4\frac{1}{2}$ inches.

Humphrey's syntax is good for a 7 year old. (Indeed, we have seen written work from 13 year olds that was far inferior to Humphrey's in range of structure—not on one occasion of writing but consistently throughout the school year.) He has a complement clause, albeit a contact one—*it would work in the night*, an adverbial clause of reason, *because sometimes the moon is very bright*, and an adverbial clause of time, *When I was having my dinner*. The bulk of the report however consists of clauses coordinated with *and*. With respect to the sequence *because sometimes the moon is very bright so it could make a shadow* it is not clear whether Humphrey is aiming at a result clause construction, in which case he should have written *the moon is so bright that it could make a shadow*, or whether he has simply produced a main clause *because sometimes the moon is very bright* followed by another main clause introduced by *so*. He has two complex noun phrases—*a flat piece of wood for the bottom of it* and *some wood about a foot long*. In this context the interpretation of the latter is 'pieces of wood each about a foot long'. Anticipating the discussion of degrees of competence below, let us say that since Humphrey's language bears the hallmarks of a child who is encouraged to read at home, the presence of complex noun phrases is not unexpected, but it is quite possible that these noun phrases were produced by Mrs Nethacott or Mr Lear in discussion of the sundial.

Andrew, aged 11, wrote the account in (6).

(6) Spring Balance
The aim of my project is to weigh objects on a spring. I found by experimenting that the spring stretchs [*sic*] five and a half inches when you put a pound in the bucket. Then by splitting up the five and a half in half I got half a pound. I split that up and kept splitting the pieces up till I had sixteen pieces I marked off the ounces and made another card until it weighed five pound. This spring balance will weigh objects accurately if you use a rule and look at it from the side.

The details of Andrew's experiment are not entirely clear but his syntax is more complex than Humphrey's. He has a complement clause—*that the spring stretches*, two adverbial clauses of time—*till I had sixteen pieces, until it weighed five pounds*, and two coordinated adverbial clauses of condition—*if you use a rule and look at it from the side*. There are various simple gerunds—*experimenting* and *splitting up*—both governed by the preposition *by*. The noun phrases are all simple.

8.3.9. Degrees of competence and literacy

The introduction quotes Chomsky's belief that adults' grammars acquired in childhood are strikingly uniform and independent of intelligence, motivation, and emotional state. This belief is consistent with Chomsky's theory of language; the properties of magnasyntax are interpreted as setting the limits on possible syntactic constructions in human languages; the properties are assumed to be a property of the species, and since human beings are not exposed to sufficient evidence when young to enable them to deduce the properties, it is further assumed that the properties are innate and, far from being acquired, actually control the process of language acquisition. This theory is alluring, but one difficulty pointed out in §8.3.3 is that the properties postulated as universal are the properties of magnasyntax. In contrast, most human beings use mainly spoken language and, assuming that English, German, and Russian are not exceptions, spontaneous spoken language has simple syntactic constructions in which juxtaposition and deixis-anaphora play a large role. The boundary conditions are not relevant to this kind of data.

The assumption that the boundary conditions are a property of the human species and that they are innate in humans makes it possible to say that children's grammars are strikingly uniform in that they all obey these properties. All the children acquiring, for example, English as their native language will have uniform grammars insofar as they will share a number of central English structures, such as Determiner–Noun, or 'Noun Phrase–Verb–Noun Phrase'. In both respects the proposition that children have strikingly uniform grammars is true but trivial and misleading. The fact is that any kindergarten nurse or infant-school teacher is well aware that children do not possess the same linguistic competence, far less the same linguistic performance skills. All normal children with English as their native language acquire some minimum central set of constructions. However, it is a fact—unpalatable, but none the less a fact—that children come to school with different degrees of competence in syntax and vocabulary. Children who have been read to regularly and who are encouraged to take part in conversation are not just more skilled performers but have a greater linguistic knowledge than children who are not read to and who are discouraged from participating in family conversation. Moreover, even if we desist from glib talk of 'intelligence', it is equally clear that children from similar social backgrounds do not necessarily acquire the same skills of language-use or language-interpretation.

Glimpses of variation in performance can be found in discussions of psycholinguistic experiments. For instance, Crain and Nakayama (1987) ran an experiment in which children were invited to convert declarative sentences containing subject relative clauses into interrogative sentences. The method used was to get the children to put a question to a puppet character. The spoken instruction given was, for example, *Ask Jabba if [the boy who is watching Mickey Mouse is happy]*. The six sentences used in the experiment are set out below.

1 The boy who is unhappy is watching Mickey Mouse
2 The dog that is sleeping is on the blue bench
3 The ball that the girl is sitting on is big
4 The boy who is watching Mickey Mouse is happy
5 The boy who is being kissed by his mother is happy
6 The boy who was holding the plate is crying

One group, Group I, consisted of fifteen children between the ages of 3;2 and 4;7, with a mean age of 4;3. A second group, Group II, consisted of fifteen children between the ages of 4;7 and 5;11, with a mean age of 5;3. The percentage of each group who gave *incorrect* answers is shown in Table 8.1.

Approximately five out of the fifteen children in Group I could not deal (on this occasion) with (1) and (2), seven or eight could not deal with (3), and twelve or thirteen could not deal with (4)–(6). There were failures in the older group too, though only one child out of the fifteen for (1)–(2), and five were unable to deal with (6). On the basis of the figures it is not legitimate to claim that all the children have acquired the WH relative clause construction. On what basis could we claim that a group of children *had* mastered it, i.e. had it in their competence? Teachers of second languages look for consistent correct performance over a number of occasions and over examples of varying complexity. On the basis of one experiment we can say nothing about the competence of any individual child, and even if we had the relevant information we would still need to know whether the child came from a 'reading and writing' home or not

TABLE 8.1. *Percentage of incorrect answers*

Sentence	Group I	Group II
1	33	7
2	38	7
3	50	27
4	80	13
5	80	27
6	83	36

before we could make even tentative claims about when children in general have the WH construction in their competence. (Note the singular *construction*; with respect to language acquisition the plural might be more appropriate, as signalling a range of WH structures from *the girl who was happy* to *the man by whose dog we had been chased*.) Perera's data indicate that the age could well be greater than has been supposed.[13]

Of course these skills, this knowledge, relate both to spoken and written language. Written language is immensely important, not just because of its social, political, and economic significance, but because it is the repository of complex syntax and complex vocabulary. The range of syntax and vocabulary in the spontaneous spoken language of individuals depends on how much exposure to written language they have received, which in turn typically, though not necessarily, depends on the amount of education they have had, especially on whether they have received higher education. But even at the age of 6 or 7 exposure to written language is important. Indeed at the time of writing (October–November 1994) there has been a discussion in the British press of how girls are outperforming boys at school, and there is evidence, summed up in the programme 'Panorama' broadcast on BBC 1 on Monday, 24 October, that the reasons for the superior performance lie in the practice that girls have in talking to their mothers and to other girls and in the amount of reading that they do at home.

Differences in the linguistic competence of schoolchildren are recognized by teachers in primary and secondary school—and are recognizable too in the teaching experience of university staff. Note that the distinction between standard and non-standard English has not been invoked, although it is another part, and a large one, of a very intricate pattern. Nor is there any doubt that speakers who control only some variety of spoken and non-standard English can entertain thoughts on abstract concepts or have striking insights into the human condition or from time to time express themselves with originality, but they will not do so using complex syntax. Sampson (1980: 115–16) observes that even among university students, who represent a narrow and relatively well-educated segment of the population, there are differences in the ability to speak, write, and even understand complex English.[14]

---

[13] This discussion does not affect the discussion and interpretation of the data by Crain and Nakayama, who were pursuing a quite different point.

[14] There are even more fundamental problems than gender-related differences in educational achievement. One reason for the adult literacy programme set up in Britain in the late 1970s was the realization that a not insignificant proportion of the adult population cannot understand complex written language (neither when spoken nor written). Moreover illiteracy is not a new phenomenon connected with the upsurge of television and computer games, because in both the First and the Second World War it emerged that, in the British Army at least, a significant number of soldiers were unable to read letters from home or to write replies. There is no reason to think that illiteracy is a peculiarly British phenomenon or that it is confined to countries with written languages based on an alphabet.

Blanche-Benveniste *et al.* (1991) distinguish two French constructions with *en* as in (7*a,b*).

(7) (*a*) j'en   prendrai   une
I of-them will-take one
'I'll take one of them'
(*b*) j'en   attends   l'arrivée
I of-him am-awaiting the arrival

Blanche-Benveniste *et al.* (1992: 207) comment that examples such as (7*a*) are acquired by all speakers before school age—which is 6 in France—but that examples such as (7*b*) (and the construction has variations which we omit here) are acquired with greater or less control throughout the lives of speakers of French, and many speakers never acquire them.

It can be objected that the above remarks do not affect the Chomskyan position directly, since they mention language skills, that is—performance, whereas Chomsky is concerned with the largely unconscious knowledge called competence. That is correct, but what is the evidence in support of the hypothesized competence? In answering the question we must avoid obscuring two issues. One has to do with the distinction between performance and competence; let it be clearly stated that that distinction is not under attack. What is under attack is the nature of competence. The Chomskyan notion is based on written language, whereas what children learn in the first five years is informal spoken language, with different and simpler syntax, simpler morphology, and simpler vocabulary. The Chomskyan position invokes the notion that the data children are exposed to is limited in range and degenerate. The position argued here is that different children are exposed to different quantities and quality of data and that, *ceteris paribus*, such differences are reflected in different degrees of competence. The degenerate nature of informal spoken language is exaggerated and the extensive presence of formulaic expressions is ignored, and written data is neither degenerate nor ephemeral. None of these remarks goes against the notion that children make up rules and go beyond the original data to which they are exposed.

8.3.10. *Grammaticality judgements*

The question of grammaticality judgements is important because it relates to speaker competence. How can speakers make judgements about the grammaticality of novel sentences unless they have access to a body of principles that cannot be deduced from their individual and limited experience of a given language? We can assume that some examples are easily judged to be acceptable or not: *She came unfortunately in, these blue two dresses* (word order), *blamed Harry about the noise, bequeathed them with a small fortune* (choice of preposition for a given verb), *we was in the pub* (verb-agreement—a tricky area as the example is unacceptable only for standard English but is the norm in many non-standard varieties). Difficulties arise with the sorts of example that are intended to probe subjacency or bounding—examples such as the ones cited from Atkinson (1990: 4) at the beginning of this chapter: *Who did John wonder whether Mary kissed?* and *Who did John wonder whether kissed Mary?* Atkinson states that native speakers of English have little difficulty in agreeing that the first example is considerably better than the second but this statement requires heavy qualification. It is significant that native speakers are not asked to make grammaticality judgements with respect to such complicated examples. Informants are typically (always?) students in Linguistics classes or at least students at some institute of higher education. Even with this restriction, it is significant that undergraduate students have to be inducted into the practice. It is our experience, and the experience of colleagues in various universities, that on first being confronted with asterisked sentences, or with sentences to be asterisked, many students are puzzled. After some practice, they cease to be puzzled, because the linguistics course has taught them to make judgements. That is, making grammaticality judgements is a learned skill.

Even once the skill is learnt two obstacles remain. Confronted with a number of examples, any group of speakers of the relevant language will probably produce conflicting judgements. These divergences can be accommodated by invoking, let us say, different settings of parameters, but this is analogous to papering over cracks in a wall without investigating what is causing the cracks and how deep they go. Moreover, experience of teaching generative grammar and courses in spoken and written language has shown that students typically have quite unreliable intuitions about spoken language. For instance the sentence *there was only one person came to see the show* exemplifies a normal construction in spoken English; the sentence as a whole is an existential construction, *there was . . .*, which contains a relative clause. If the relative clause contained a relative pronoun it would be *who*, which would be the subject of *came to see the show*. The rules for written English prohibit a subject relative pronoun from being omitted, but the rule does not apply to relative clauses inside the spoken-language existential construction. (Other examples are given in §3.7.1.1.) The construction is the norm in spoken English—and not just spontaneous spoken English—but students typically judge sentences like the above example and the ones in §3.7.1.1 to be unacceptable, and when told that such examples occur frequently they deny ever having heard anything similar. The problem is this. Statements about the ease of making acceptability judgements are usually based on examples from written language and it is taken for granted that the statements apply *a fortiori* to spoken language. This is not correct, and the difficulties experienced by students raise further questions about acceptability judgements and intuitions about grammaticality, which seem to be based on written language.

This particular problem does not apply to languages with no written variety but questions of an even more fundamental sort come up. In the preface to his grammar of Dyirbal, Dixon (1972) remarks that the mingling of cultural and grammatical knowledge was unavoidable when obtaining acceptability judgements. He cites the Dyirbal sentence translated as *the man is building the mia-mia*, which was rejected on the ground that men do not build huts. Similar anecdotes have been reported by anthropologists working with native Americans. Furthermore, Dixon comments that he collected much of his data from only a couple of informants, the ones who proved capable of furnishing judgements on acceptability/grammaticality. There is no reason to assume that differences in the ability to make such judgements are not to be found among urban inhabitants in Britain.

A final difficulty with acceptability/grammaticality judgements was noted, quirkily but effectively, by Matthews (1979). The technique of obtaining judgements rests on the assumption that the grammar of a given language is determinate and that its users do have clear intuitions that they can tap. Matthews showed that any language has areas of grammar which are simply not susceptible to a generative account requiring determinacy and about which users do not have determinate intuitions. For instance, various nouns can be converted to verbs taking complement clauses with *that*, as in *He cabled that he would be arriving on Tuesday*. Other verbs are *phoned* and *radio'd*. But what about *lettered, telegrammed, messaged*, and *wirelessed*. Matthews found *wirelessed* worse than *radio'd*, although he at that time used the noun *wireless* rather than *radio*. About the three other verbs he stated that *messaged* seem peculiar but an occurrence had been noted in an American news magazine. *Lettered* was quite unacceptable; *phoned* and *telegrammed* seemed better than *lettered*, but it was quite unclear whether he would actually use the verb with a complement clause. Certainly Jim Miller's usage is *he phoned/telegrammed to say that* . . . (see Matthews 1979: 25–31).

Matthews gives further examples relating to word formation—e.g. *puceness* is quite intelligible but which speakers of English would use it?—and countability. *Linoleum* is a mass noun and is quite acceptable in the example *Linoleum isn't used much these days*. *Carpet* seems at first glance to be a count noun: *We bought a carpet/two carpets on Saturday*. But is the sentence *Carpet is widely used* unacceptable, and what about *Carpet is used much more than linoleum*?

Jim Hurford (personal communication) has pointed out that while collecting data and grammaticality judgements as part of a typological study of noun phrases containing numerals he came across various examples which caused severe difficulties for native speakers of the languages concerned. One was the German equivalent of the English phrase *three hundred and one woman*. The German phrase *dreihundertundeine Frauen* was problematic because of the juxtapositioning of *eine* and the plural noun *Frauen*; substituting the singular noun *Frau* produced a phrase in which the combining of *dreihundert* and the singular noun was problematic. Several native speakers of German proved unable to provide a definite statement of acceptability. During an investigation of stative verbs in English many years ago Jim Miller found that senior undergraduate students were unable to judge the acceptability of examples such as *You'll soon be owning all the land round here* or *I'm not understanding a thing he says*. Both examples had been collected by Jim Miller from spontaneous speech, the first from a play on television and the second from domestic conversation. The examples had been uttered but other native speakers could not make up their minds whether they were acceptable or not.

8.3.11. *Mechanisms of language acquisition*

It is not our purpose to examine in detail the literature on language acquisition mechanisms and the literature on language acquisition that adopts the idea of innate constraints on hypotheses about possible human languages. Rather we wish to direct attention to properties of spontaneous spoken language that may indicate new lines of attack on the problem of first language acquisition. In this exercise the distinction between spontaneous spoken language and written language is central, since spontaneous spoken language is what young children are exposed to first and what they set about uttering themselves.

The conception advocated here is this. There is a spoken language [s] and a written language [w]. (As mentioned in Chapter 1, this is a gross and misleading distinction which ignores the existence of different spoken genres and written genres, but it is sufficient for present purposes.) Many syntactic constructions occur both in s and w, but some constructions occur only in s and others only in w. That is, s and w intersect but w has a large number of complex constructions, complex vocabulary items, and complex fixed phrases that are unknown in s. Control of w, contrary to the Chomskyan position, depends on social and intellectual factors. The acquisition of s is much less dependent on social and intellectual factors and is acquired to a large extent unconsciously. Much (but not all) of s is acquired in the first four or five years, but the huge extra component that turns s into w is acquired later and over a number of years, from age 5 to age 17 or 18 and beyond. In accordance with the position set out in §8.3.8, this conception does not require a commitment to the idea that all speakers acquire s and w to the same degree.

Colleagues have objected to the conception of spoken and written language as two partially overlapping sets of syntactic and morphological constructions and vocabulary items. Why not have a list of constructions with each construction flagged as to whether it is spoken, written, or both? Clearly if we wanted to discuss the distinction in computational terms it would be sensible to list structures or rules in that way, but that is not our aim. We want to find a concrete image for our conception of spoken language as basic and central with speakers moving out from that into written language, at different rates and to different extents.

Continuing this line of thought, it is assumed that speakers who wish to use **s** and **w** where appropriate have to code-switch. For instance, a lecturer might begin the morning talking to her family then go off to work, where she gives a lecture and attends a high-level committee meeting. The lecturer switches codes to the extent that at home she uses constructions such as those exemplified in Chapters 3–5 but once giving the lecture may drop constructions peculiar to informal spoken language and certainly brings in constructions and Greco-Latinate vocabulary appropriate to formal written language that her children do not yet understand. Of course, the lecturer speaks her lectures or contributions to the committee meeting, but she will utter constructions and vocabulary that are typical of formal written English.

Implicit in the preceding paragraphs is the notion of a non-Chomskyan core. Chomsky's core constructions are the ones that obey constraints such as subjacency. The notion of core invoked here has nothing to do with such constraints. Currently it does not enjoy universal popularity among theoretical linguists, but it is a very old idea and it does play an important part in certain linguistic practices. It is the notion lying behind expectations among teachers as to the syntax and vocabulary to be expected from children on entry to primary school; it drives the writing of many books for very young children (which does not mean that the language is bland and unoriginal); and it determines the constructions and vocabulary taught to learners of foreign languages. (See Perera 1984 and in §8.3.8 for observations on the syntax and vocabulary typically used and understood by children at certain ages.) This notion of core is based on frequency as well as simplicity, and although in the past the correlation with frequency has been impressionistic rather than rigorously statistical, current work (cf. Macaulay 1987 and Perera 1984) bears out the traditional impressions.

Can the core be defined? We could say that the core consists of all the constructions and vocabulary used and understood by normal children on entry to primary school. Or we could define the core as the constructions and vocabulary found in the informal speech of teenage pupils—say age 16—or of adults who have no higher education. (The lack of higher education is specified in order to reduce as far as possible the effect of schooling.) There is a classical boundary problem. We can recognize syntax and vocabulary that are definitely in the core, and others that are definitely outside, and in between there is a grey area. A broader definition of core—say, making reference to 16 year olds—is compatible with the view that not all speakers learn the core to the same degree. On the narrow view—with reference to children entering primary school—all speakers do have to be seen as learning it to approximately the same degree, but thereafter social and intellectual factors play a part. The core is not just an ever-extending list of items: it is clear from existing corpuses that there is a shared body of syntax whose properties can be specified in terms of degree of clause embedding, degree of clause combination, proportion of finite subordinate clauses to main clauses, the absence of certain constructions.[15]

The child cracks the relevant linguistic code via exposure to the spoken language of older people (adults or older children). Major properties of spontaneous spoken language are that, apart from telephone or radio conversations, it is produced in context, with the participants face to face, and the verbal components of interactions are supported by various components of non-verbal communication—facial expressions, body stance, and gestures with arm and hand. Feyereisen and de Lannoy (1991: 49-70), reviewing the relevant literature, conclude that there is much evidence demonstrating a close connection between gesture and the organization of speech production but (1994: 71-103) are more cautious about the role of gesture in the communication of content. In contrast, McNeill (1987) argues convincingly that gesture does play a central role in the communication of information, not just supporting the verbal component but in narratives replacing it.[16] Parents of young children, and adults who have found themselves trying to communicate with a very shaky knowledge of a foreign language, know how much can be achieved by gesture, even if the experimental or naturalistic evidence on video is not yet available. This is not to say that for adults gestures can replace words but that where only a few words are available part of a message can be communicated in words and part by gesture.

---

[15] It might be objected that many of the differences we propose between core and extended grammar are quantitative; e.g. only one adjective in an NP, only one level of subordination. This runs counter to the Chomskyan position that grammars never use quantitative information and that such differences are necessarily matters of performance. Our view, as argued earlier in this chapter, is that the Chomskyan position relates primarily to setting boundaries on patterns in syntactic codes and that the transfer of properties from codes to users is not self-evidently correct and lacks explicit justification in the literature. With respect to magnasyntax, or even just the syntax of written English, it is true that exact boundaries are hard to establish but it is also true that the Chomskyan position rests on assumptions, also not self-evidently correct, about lack of constraint on self-embedding; cf. the discussion of *the rat the cat the dog chased killed* in N. Chomsky (1957).

[16] McNeill's ideas are gaining support from experimental studies being carried out in the University of Pennsylvania. The source of this information is a talk given by Dr Justine Cassell in the Human Communication Research Centre, Nov. 1994.

The relevance of non-verbal communication is that parents use it with young children long before the latter understand or produce language: pointing to body parts, waggling toes and fingers, pointing to items, holding out a hand to be held, gesturing that the children should come, or take something to somebody or into another room, and so on. These gestures are typically accompanied by appropriate utterances and help children to break into their native language. Let us make it absolutely clear that we are not suggesting that children passively receive information via gestures and utterances. They have to work to establish similarity between different occurrences of the same gesture just as they have to recognize different occurrences of the same word, and they have to recognize the different patterns of word and gesture combination and interpret them. The gestures are merely a helping hand into the first stage of language acquisition.

Children interpret and produce utterances in an immediate context, and while context itself requires interpretive work it is none the less much easier dealing with language in context than out of context. The role of context is not generally mentioned in Universal Grammar theories of language acquisition, but much attention is given to structures of various sorts: syntactic, lexical-conceptual, argument, phonological, and logical. This approach has a long history. Since the late 1940s, much syntactic theorizing has focused on establishing a stock of items and on describing the arrangements in which they occur. The Item and Arrangement approach (IA) has its roots in the behaviouristic and positivistic ideas of the period from around 1920 to 1950, according to which good scientific practice consisted of working with the maximum of observables and the minimum of constructs. In the case of Harris (1946) the minimum of constructs meant dispensing with the word as a primitive unit, working instead only with morphemes and their arrangements. Within the behaviourist-positivist framework, linguists such as Bloomfield, Wells, and Harris developed constituent structure analysis, which eschewed all appeals to semantics and attempted to work only with units and arrangements of units that could be established on distributional grounds.

In his review of Skinner (N. Chomsky 1959), Chomsky demonstrated the inadequacy of the behaviourist approach, and in his early work on generative grammar (Chomsky 1957, 1964) he demonstrated the inadequacy of positivism as a basis for the construction of linguistic theories. It is curious that while Chomsky supplied linguistics with an exceedingly rich metatheory and theory of language acquisition, he has kept Item and Arrangement representations of syntactic structure and has returned to them in the treatment of morphology. It has been demonstrated by various scholars that the Item and Arrangement analysis is highly problematical for certain types of language, particularly inflecting languages of the Indo-European sort. (Cf. Hockett 1954; Matthews 1972; Dressler 1985.) In spite of this, Chomsky (1986) can be read as a rigorous Item and Arrangement analysis of morphology and syntax.

The question is: what justification is there for taking Item and Arrangement not just as a suitable basis for linguistic analysis but for theories of language acquisition? Language acquisition includes reference and coreference, and while constituent structure is involved in coreference relations other concepts such as salience, topicality, and accessibility are ignored, along with the contribution of other models such as Discourse Representation Theory. This is not to say that Universal Grammar precludes pragmatics or that its practitioners fail to recognize the achievements of pragmatics, but few current UG discussions of language acquisition give it a role. This is regrettable, not just because of the work of scholars such as Ariel (1988, 1994), H. Clark (1992), Givón (1983), and Kamp and Reyle (1993) is neglected but because the UG language acquisition theory purports to be the whole story. Another objection arises out of the discussion of clauses and sentences in Chapter 2, where it was argued that spoken language is organized into small, loosely-linked units such as phrases and clauses and not into the large, integrated sentences that are the objects of analysis in generative grammar (and not just Chomskyan generative grammar). One consequence of the organization of spoken language is that coreference cannot be handled in terms of single sentences embracing several clauses but must be handled by a discourse model.

A second objection relates to the observation above that children learn their native language initially in very restricted contexts which are only gradually extended. Consider the sentence *Graball found a new set of clients to fleece*, which is used as an example by Horrocks (1987) in his discussion of first language acquisition. Horrocks states:

Without any prior knowledge of principles of interpretation it is difficult to see how the correct interpretation would necessarily be extracted from sentences of this sort by all children, or how, if they got it wrong, they would know that they had got it wrong, and correct themselves. In any case, can it really be true that every two year old has gone through a conscious process of working out what sentences of this sort might mean in principle and then discounting all but the correct interpretation?

Horrocks is concerned with how children might learn that Graball is understood as the subject of *fleece* and the clients as the object (alternatively, Agent and Patient). His concern is misplaced. The set of 2 year olds who would pay any attention to his example is null. They do however hear examples such as those in (8).

(8) (*a*) Here is a car to put in the garage
    (*b*) Oh—you've found a block to put on top of the tower
    (*c*) Here is biscuit to give to the doggie

The important property of these examples is that the interpretation is heavily supported by the extra-linguistic context. We remarked above that young children, certainly children making their first steps in language, have a small world and talk about events as they are ongoing—often driving parents mad by stating the obvious, over and over. Children quickly learn that toy cars go into garages and that they do not go into the garages by themselves but have to be pushed in. Blocks can be put one on top of the other to form towers, and the child or its carers have to manipulate the block. Biscuits are edible, and dogs eat biscuits. That is, children can call on their knowledge of the extra-linguistic world to interpret examples such as those in (8). Even if a given child does not understand the syntax, it can pick up the crucial items *car*, *garage*, *block*, *tower*, *biscuit*, *doggie*. In the child's world, the relationship between the relevant entities is clear-cut. If it is not, the carer will demonstrate the relationship, and from these small beginnings the child will eventually come to examples like Horrocks's one—but probably not before age 8 or later, depending on a given child's reading experience.

Horrocks discusses two more examples: *Jimbo seems to us to like himself* and **Jimbo pleaded with us to like himself*. He asks 'Have we all been taught the principles of pronominal interpretation and reflexive distribution, or determined them on the basis of our experience?' (Horrocks 1988: 155). Here there is the shifting of ground mentioned in connection with magnasyntax. The initial stage in the argument has to do with children learning their native language, but the examples are not typical of children's language. SEEM is indeed a verb that children learn (how early?) but they use it in simple constructions such as those exemplified in (9).

(9) (*a*) Daddy seems angry
    (*b*) The fish fingers seem funny

We should note first that such examples may well belong to the set described by Pawley and Syder as learned whole. (See §8.3.6.) Parents use examples with SEEM and it would be surprising if children did not pick up whole phrases with SEEM. Even if this is not the case, the typical SEEM construction is one in which SEEM is followed by an adjective. The occurrence of a TO phrase, as in *seems to us*, the first of Horrocks's examples, is a feature of formal written English. The kind of utterances from which children learn to interpret and use reflexive pronouns are, for example, *did you hurt yourself?*, *Teddy's hurt himself*. These are straightforward sequences in which the interpretation of the reflexive pronoun is transparent in context. By the time children come across examples like Horrocks's—indeed by the time they pay attention to such examples—they are almost certainly reading, and can work out the interpretation from the context of the story.

The obvious comment to make on Horrocks's second example, *Jimbo pleaded with us to like himself*, is that PLEAD is not a verb that occurs in everyday conversation. Children are most likely to come across it in stories, and will either ignore the word because they understand from the pictures or the narrative what is happening, or will ask the carer to explain. The explanation will be on the lines of: 'Jimbo asked us very nicely to like him. He said "Please, please like me"', and so on. In this case, there is some overt explanation, and either the narrative or the narrative plus the explanation enable the child to understand who is pleading, and who is to like whom. Horrocks asserts that his two examples have exactly parallel syntax, but PLEAD is a different lexical item from SEEM, and requires a different preposition, WITH instead of TO. To sum up, the occurrence of the reflexive with SEEM, in the kind of example that children meet, is quite regular and supported by the extra-linguistic context. The PLEAD example is a special case—a special lexical item from storytelling. Children may learn the syntax of PLEAD as a whole, by memorizing chunks of story which they can use themselves in their own writing at school, and they never hear the PLEAD example with a reflexive pronoun.

As a final example from Horrocks, consider his discussion of coordination (Horrocks 1988: 156):

Is it because they have worked it out for themselves that questions such as *Who do you love me and, Mummy?* are odd? It is not enough to say that there are no examples of this sort for the child to imitate and that therefore they are not employed, because forms such as *goed* and *hitted* do not occur in adult speech but regularly occur in the speech of children who are in the process of mastering English.

This argument is specious. Since past tense forms in *-ed* are frequent in adult speech, children fit all past tense forms to the general pattern and learn the irregular verbs individually. Some children try to generalize particular strong verb patterns: Jim Miller's eldest child tried *slope* for *slept* and *ote* for *ate*. From a pragmatic perspective there is good reason not to end utterances with *and*. *And* sets up an expectation that more information is to follow: the carer who breaks off an utterance on *and* is probably going to say something else, or has changed his/her mind, and the child who finishes an utterance with *and* will be asked to supply the extra information. We do not need to look for purely syntactic constraints that require a LAD: there is a perfectly good pragmatic reason for children to learn that utterances should not finish with *and*. *And* arouses the expectation that further information is about to be conveyed; when it is not forthcoming, listeners display annoyance and impatience. It may be that this sort of pragmatic constraint is eventually subsumed under a general constraint which declares that conjoined constituents must be adjacent. (This is a general pragmatic constraint that applies, at least in the child's world, both extra- and intra-linguistically and would rule out *Who do you love and me?*—an example suggested by Nigel Vincent.) It may be doubted whether children under 5 would tackle the coordinate interrogative structure anyway but would convey the information either by a series of questions—*Do you love me? Who else do you love?*—or by a declarative construction—*You love me and who else?*

Of course the above discussion does not provide an explicit and general account of the role of context and is certainly open to questions such as: what would be counter-evidence to a pragmatic account? Does the pragmatic approach ever provide criteria for ruling out one analysis in favour of another? Can pragmatic analyses be falsified? The answer to these questions is that pragmatic analyses are perhaps not falsifiable in a clear-cut fashion but two or more analyses can be compared and one chosen as the best currently available. Making a choice is not as simple as analogous choices might seem in syntax, since it involves comparison of interactions, preferably controlled interactions involving people carrying out the same task, and comparison of the syntactic structure, information structure, and game structure to see if there are correlations holding across all the interactions. An example of such a set of interactions is described in A. Anderson *et al.* (1991). Whether falsifiability is an appropriate criterion is doubtful—not that it should be thrown away, but even in generative grammar the choice of one analysis over another typically involves, not a demonstration that one is false, but rather that one analysis has sections that could be improved, or does not obviously extend to some further set of examples, or contains some element that is stipulated by the analyst instead of deriving from the basic general principles of the theory.

Questions about scientific methodology and criteria for testing theories and analyses do not alter the fact that human beings produce and interpret utterances in context and make heavy use of context. This fact is recognized by a large number of researchers in areas such as tense and aspect, mood, discourse, and artificial intelligence. Indeed it is worthwhile remarking that the researchers whose work requires them to be absolutely explicit and to aim at producing testable products, namely AI folk, are precisely the people who find themselves having to pay most attention to context, including tricky items such as the beliefs of speaker and hearer. One last comment is in order. A distinction must be drawn between researchers, who aim to produce accounts that meet certain standards of scientific respectability, and ordinary users/acquirers of a language who are not looking on from the outside but are in the thick of events in the language arena (to borrow a term from H. Clark 1992). The insistence on arrangements of items arose from a particular set of philosophical assumptions and predilections which were useful to analysts but need not be attributed to naïve users of a given language.

Of course context is only one part of the business of language acquisition and we suggest it, along with non-verbal communication, as facilitating children's entry into language. Children still have to acquire the syntax, morphology, and vocabulary of their native language, but the discussion of spontaneous spoken language allows us to entertain the hypothesis that the structures and vocabulary are limited and relatively simple. One perspective that accords with this hypothesis is that of Peters (1983: ch. 3), who argues that the task facing children is not just to combine single words into larger units but to extract smaller units from the larger chunks of syntax learned as wholes. Peters discusses various procedures by which children can segment chunks, and comments that such segmenting need not, and typically does not, take place all in the first five years. She also reviews various pieces of research demonstrating how children can produce sequences consisting of independent structures which become fused to form more complex pieces of syntax (Peters 1983: ch. 4). Peters's proposals are all the more attractive when coupled with the idea that children learn the simple, paratactic syntax of spoken language, and a large amount of fixed or semi-fixed syntax.[17]

The relatively simple structures and limited vocabulary of spontaneous spoken language suggest revisions to the review of language learning mechanisms in Bowerman (1988). Much of this review deals with vocabulary, including the set of Dative verbs such as GIVE and DONATE, causative movement verbs as in *They dropped the stone into the well*, and resultative expressions such as *She combed her hair smooth*. Various pieces of research need to be undertaken. Bowerman (1988: 86) cites a number of movement verbs that are causativized: DROP, LOWER, SINK, TOPPLE, RECLINE, DIP, TILT, EXUDE, LIFT, LEVITATE, TRANSFER, WITHDRAW, FILTER, PERCOLATE, RETRACT. At this point in her paper Bowerman is discussing the semantic subsets of verbs established by Pinker and not addressing directly data from children, but the discussion relates to the mechanisms by which children might learn this vocabulary and associated syntax and it is important to sort out ages and type of language. Out of the above list, only DROP, LIFT, and SINK are typical of spontaneous spoken English. The other items are typically learned (and not by every child) from written English or from spoken language heavily influenced by written English such as is heard in classrooms and lecture theatres.

---

[17] Hurford (1987: ch. 5) argues that children understand expressions such as *five bricks* before they understand the expression *five*. This is a good example of children working with larger expressions before splitting the expressions into smaller constituents. Hurford also argues convincingly that the activity of collecting objects is prior to the activity of counting, and that the activity of collection and of exploring collections lays the basis for counting. This is a pleasing parallel to our argument that the activity of using a grammatical code to communicate is typically preceded by intense practice at communicating by non-verbal gestures and by non-linguistic sounds.

There is no evidence that the learning of vocabulary is other than fragmented and historical studies show clearly how vocabulary items change not just their meaning but their syntax, and how there is a large amount of variation in pattern among adults. We are not happy with *donated the museum the picture, attributed this painting Raphael* and *forwarded Susan the letter*, but we have come across a noticeable number of students who are. Of one group of about twenty students consulted by Jim Miller in the course of a tutorial half reckoned these examples were acceptable. Consider too the following examples from Dickens's novel *Martin Chuzzlewit*.

(10) (a) But the young lady evincing no surprise, curiosity or alarm, whispered her, with many thanks for her solicitude and company, that she would remain there some time longer;

    (b) Mr Pecksniff glanced at the volume she held, and whispered Mrs Lupin again: if possible, with increased despondency. 'Yes, ma'am,' he said, 'it is a good book . . .'

For us WHISPER only fits the pattern WHISPER X TO Y, but there it is in print, albeit one hundred and fifty years ago, in the other pattern, WHISPER Y X.

Verbs such as SUPPLY fit two syntactic patterns—SUPPLY X TO Y and SUPPLY Y WITH X. BEQUEATH does not fit the latter pattern, according to the standard canon of English, but cf. (11a). Neither does PARACHUTE, but cf. (11b). CIRCULATE for me fits only the pattern CIRCULATE X TO Y, with TO Y optional, but cf. (11c). INTIMIDATE in the standard canon fits the pattern INTIMIDATE X (possibly with INTO DO-ing SOMETHING), but cf. (11d).

(11) (a) It is odd that the whiskered traffic managers of the LNER and LMS [railway companies nationalized in 1948] have bequeathed Scotland with her most pronounced token of nationhood and reclaimed Berwick for Scotland as she should be

        (Peter Clarke, 'A sporting chance for Scottish Tories', *The Scotsman*, 13 Aug. 1993)

    (b) —if it's a severe winter we'll have to parachute the island with food supplies like Bosnia

        (*Scotland on Sunday*, 24 Apr. 1994)

    (c) would be a member of Technical Committee circulated with all agendas but not expected to attend

        (Excerpt from minutes of a meeting in the Human Communications Research Centre, University of Edinburgh)

    (d) They intended to intimidate them from telling their stories

        (Radio broadcast)

Now these are one-off examples, at least in our experience, but the fact that three of them are in writing is a good indication that these verbs are changing their syntax. The reason they change is that the major pattern typically spreads to all verbs in a set, either among all speakers of a given language or among a subset of speakers. The change can be quite unexpected. PLUG and ZIP are verbs that take the reversative *un-*, giving the lexical items UNPLUG and UNZIP. One of Jim Miller's children, when around age 3, said *zip me out*, asking to have his anorak unzipped, and just recently one of Jim Miller's friends, certainly a lot older than 21, announced *I'll plug out the telephone*. The syntax of individual verbs is far more unstable than literate people like to think, and this should be taken into account in language acquisition. Major patterns spread but some verbs are highly resistant. Exceptions arise—indeed the dictionaries of any language are littered with exceptions. Why should we expect children's acquisition of vocabulary to be any better regulated?

The syntax and vocabulary of spontaneous spoken language raise interesting possibilities for Braine's discovery procedures and for the competition model (Bates and MacWhinney 1987) in which the forms that are regularly activated gain in strength and the forms that are over-regularized are activated only rarely and gradually die off. If either of these models were applied to the task, not of handling the entire magnasyntax and magnavocabulary but just the structures and vocabulary of spontaneous spoken language, we could be much more confident about their eventual success than Bowerman was able to be.

We have discussed the acquisition of spoken language, what we called **s**, much of which is learned in the first four or five years of the normal child's life. What about **w**, the written language? We suggest that **w** is at least partly learned and that its learning/acquisition takes place in a very different fashion. We can suitably start with Chomsky's statement that children learn their native language from meagre degenerate data. This statement was shown to be doubtful with respect to spoken language and it is certainly quite wrong for written language. Children learn written language by reading. If they do not read, they do not gain control of written language, and schoolteachers are well aware of the enormous gaps that open up between young primary school children who read and those who do not. Not only does the lack affect the power of expression but it affects power of understanding. Children with a poor knowledge of written language cannot easily acquire information and labour under a handicap in every subject in secondary school, from mathematics to history.

It is necessary here to deviate briefly from the main line of argument. We probably stand in danger of being accused of having undesirable social attitudes, either on the ground that we assume, as Guy (1988: 55) puts it, that anyone in their right mind would want to move out of the working class, or that we do not value the riches Labov, for instance, has found in Black Vernacular English. Neither of these putative accusations is correct.

Regardless of class, written language in literate societies is the key to political, economic, and social power, and also to the indispensable and all-powerful tool of modern technological societies, the computer. Black Vernacular English, like Scots, is a vehicle for trading friendly insults, telling stories, creating poetry, but, like Scots, it does not have the vocabulary and the complex syntax in which matters intellectual and political are discussed. Of course both Black Vernacular English and Scots could develop the necessary vocabulary and syntax (like standard English, they might simply use Greco-Latinate vocabulary) but powerful social, economic, and political reasons have prevented that development in the past and will probably continue to do so in the future. In any case, we must be concerned with the children at school now and not with what children might be able to do in an alternative possible world at some indefinite future time.[18]

Except for a certain proportion of personal letters, written data is not degenerate and not meagre. Texts for public consumption are carefully checked and changed where necessary by copy editors, and material for children is edited with special care. A given writer may not have a felicitous style, but the text will conform to the canons of standard written English, will have no hesitations or anacolutha and will be set out coherently. Written texts are not evanescent; they stay on the page and they can be consulted again and again.

And children do read their favourite stories again and again and when they are very young they have their favourite stories read again and again—but not in homes where no reading takes place. Children do not have just one sighting of a piece of interesting text but many sightings. Stories and poems lodge in children's memories and can be and are reproduced in part or whole. Children are encouraged to read at school. Texts they find difficult are explained to them and they construct dictionaries containing the words they have not understood or have been unable to spell. There is a lot of instruction and feedback, both for a given child and for the other children in the class, and the feedback is not the unfocused feedback directed at very young children but comments targeted at inappropriate syntax or vocabulary or style. While it is true that younger children typically do not ask for feedback, older pre-school children do, and children of school age certainly do, both in school and at home.

---

[18] We must also state unequivocally that we have nothing to do with Bernstein's *de-haut-en-bas* views on members of the 'working class' nor with any notion of a language deficit. Every child has to work to cross the gap from spoken to written language, regardless of social class, and regardless of social class, children from homes with books and who are encouraged to read have a large advantage. Having a computer with CD Roms and interactive learning programs does not solve the difficulty. The language in which all these activities take place is not spontaneous spoken English (or French or Russian) but written, in the sense that the syntax and vocabulary come from the written varieties.

Not all school pupils are given procedures and labels for parsing and analysing sentences but teachers do draw their attention to special constructions, encouraging them to combine clauses into the complex sentences that attract praise, and they do discuss vocabulary, especially the prized body of Greco-Latinate derivatives.

What are we to make of the oft-repeated assertion that children in their early years do not learn from instruction, which is generalized to such statements as 'It seems that children can and usually do develop their linguistic capacity without the aid of instruction or correction' (Lightfoot 1982: 19)? Such statements presuppose that children have developed their linguistic capacity by the time they go to school, but it has been argued here that the data from investigations of spoken English and of children's spoken and written language in school indicate that the presupposition is wrong.

This error is compounded by another mistaken generalization: the resistance of children to overt language instruction is extended from their early years to their entire childhood. Lightfoot (1982: 18) comments that in certain communities there are haphazard attempts at instruction. His examples are the use of *shall* and *will*, and the use of *who* and *whom*. He observes that this kind of correction comes very late and that children are notoriously impervious to it, which is why teachers repeat these drills in every generation. The bare comments are correct, but Lightfoot's interpretation of them is quite unacceptable. First, the drills have to be repeated because the teachers are trying to inculcate the canons of standard written English, which is not anybody's native variety of English. Second, the examples chosen by Lightfoot are the typical sort of morphosyntactic shibboleth which various groups of speakers are sensitized to: educated speakers precisely because they are considered as hallmarks of 'good' English, and non-standard speakers because the forms, being quite distinctive, are considered hallmarks of a language and culture which is being imposed on them. Third, some children do learn from the instruction, but they are children who have ready access to books, who read books regularly, and who do not see the standard written variety as an imposition to be resisted. These children are also the ones who learn the complex syntactic constructions of written English on which much of generative grammar (and indeed general syntactic theory) is based.

We have not proposed a coherent alternative mechanism of language acquisition, partly because that is too big an enterprise and partly because it is not central to the topic of the book. We have however made out a case for re-examining key parts of the Chomskyan theory of language acquisition. The source of the principles in the Principles and Parameters model needs to be given thought, in particular the step from properties of the magnasyntax of English and other languages to linguistic abilities of the human species, and from that to the linguistic abilities of particular speakers. The reliability of intuitions about acceptability/grammaticality cannot be taken for granted, and neither can the determinacy of all areas of the grammar of a given language.

It is crucial to distinguish between the acquisition of spontaneous spoken language and the acquisition of written language. The syntax, morphology, and vocabulary of the latter is relatively limited and is processed in context with non-verbal communication and context as facilitators in getting children started in their linguistic careers; the syntax, morphology, and vocabulary of written language is vast and complex, but the data is good and permanent and the learning of written language is helped by directed instruction and feedback. Finally, the proposition that children acquire grammar at the same rate and to the same extent regardless of external circumstances only makes sense at the lofty level of hypotheses about the boundary conditions on human languages but makes no sense at all to people whose life is spent dealing with young children at nursery and primary school.

Atkinson (1986) divides the child-acquisition-of-language world into SHARPS, who adopt a theory-driven approach to the problem, and FLATS, who work from the data upwards. (This sounds like a polemical ploy to exaggerate the differences.) He suggests that FLATS might find the dole queue waiting just round the corner because of the theoretical vacuity of their work (a suggestion that sounds very implausible given the proposals presented in MacWhinney (1987) and reviewed in Bowerman (1988)) but also worries about the SHARPS' theories resting on untested assumptions about the primary data. On the basis of our work on spoken and written language we suggest that there is everything to play for; the relevant data has not been determined and described and the theory is far from solid. Both FLATS and SHARPS are assured of full employment for some time to come.[19]

8.4. Language Processing by Humans and by Computer

One of the major reasons advanced for the special syntactic structures of spontaneous spoken language is that it is produced online with little or no time for planning. Much if not all current research into language processing makes use of syntactic structures that are either neutral between speech and writing or are typical of written language and it is not clear that researchers in this area are aware of the special nature of spontaneous spoken language.

---

[19] The term SHARPS is unfortunate given the use of the term in medical and dental establishments for sharp items of metal or glass that might turn up in unexpected places and do serious mischief to the innocent visitor.

Even some who have come across examples of spoken structures do not handle the data appropriately. For instance, Pinker (1994: 221–2) uses the example (devised for the occasion, it seems) *that's the guy that you heard the rumour that Mary likes him* to complain gently that while the construction eases the burden on listeners 'the clumsy extra pronoun' imposes a processing cost on the speaker. Given the widespread occurrence of shadow pronouns, either as part of standard spoken and written relative clauses as in Semitic languages or, more interestingly, in relative clauses with more complex syntax than normal (cf. the discussion in §3.7), the question arises as to why the construction is so frequent in conditions where speakers normally look for the simplest encoding of a message. Is there really a processing cost or is Pinker speculating on the basis of his intuitions about elegant language?

Levelt (1989) examines the processes that speakers undertake in order to produce utterances that can be interpreted by hearers. One process involves building a piece of syntactic structure, and choosing lexical items suitable both for what the speaker wants to say and for the syntactic structure. (Clearly speakers might choose verbs first and allow the verbs to determine the choice of syntactic structure, but that is another matter.) Levelt's examination is based on speakers building up a sentence structure; from what we have seen of spontaneous spoken language, a realistic model will have to take account of speakers working with clauses not necessarily integrated into sentences, with clauses that appear to be subordinate but are not accompanied by main clauses, with noun phrases that are not part of a clause. The various restrictions on syntactic complexity and range of lexical items (discussed in §8.3.2) could be taken as indicating a small, fast-operating syntax-builder and lexeme-chooser for spontaneous speech, with larger and slower components for planned speech and writing.

There is an interesting parallel between the automatic parsing of language and studies of first language acquisition. In §8.3.2 we introduced the concept of magnasyntax in order to bring out what we consider a weakness in the Chomskyan theory, namely that it is based on magnasyntax. The difficulty is that no speaker knows the magnasyntax in its entirety and many speakers come into contact only with its simplest structures. The position of magnasyntax on the syntactic centre stage has caused difficulties for researchers engaged in the development of automatic parsing systems. Two principal problems confront the researchers. With respect to written language, the task of writing programs to handle, say, general English syntax, is not feasible at present and many programmers now put their efforts into writing parsing programs for particular sets of texts. These parsing programs do contain rules that relate to syntax but a large component consists of dictionaries where information about individual lexical items is listed. With respect to spoken language, programmers have found that, quite apart from the daunting problems of analysing speech waves, current generative work is of no help because it does not deal with the unintegrated structures of spontaneous speech. There are two subproblems—sequences of clauses that are not organized into sentences (cf. the discussion in Chapter 2) and sequences of phrases and clauses, as in *what you do you go up past the allotments* and *the driver, you get a good laugh with him*. The frustration of programmers (misplaced, let it be said, because generative grammarians have never claimed to be dealing with spoken language) is summed up in the title of a conference paper by a Japanese researcher in Artificial Intelligence, 'Why I do not care for grammar formalism' (*sic*).

8.5. Literacy and Education

In the discussion of language acquisition the point was made that written language is acquired from written texts, that the texts constitute good-quality and relatively permanent data, that discussion and teaching of written language take place in school and that school-age children receive, both at school and at home, directed feedback about their utterances. It was also pointed out that, putting spoken language on one side, children do not all acquire written language to the same extent. We asserted that acquiring a control of written language is essential for participation, even if just as an informed observer, in political, economic, and social activities, and indeed is essential for the learning of any subject in the school curriculum. In spite of predictions in the media, the central position of written language in literate societies is not going to be eroded by the advent of CD Roms and multimedia systems, because they use the syntax and vocabulary of the written variety of English, French, German, and so on.[20]

Exposure to written language at school does not achieve much without support at home in the form of reading materials, writing materials, and adults who regularly read and write. Since the mid-1980s changes in Scottish and English schools have exposed the severe difficulties that a significant proportion of the school population have with written English. The comments that follow relate to Scottish schools but they apply to English schools too and indeed to schools in any education system that aims to have all or most of the school-leavers obtaining some qualification.

In 1962 13% of the relevant cohort of secondary school pupils gained one

---

[20] These observations are quite compatible with the arguments presented in, e.g., Street (1995) that to understand the role of literacy in a given society it is more useful to talk of literacy practices and to recognize that there may be many literacies within a single society. With respect to the UK, for instance, our remarks apply to the learning of standard written English but also to the learning of formal written Urdu, Hindi, Punjabi, Welsh, Scots Gaelic, and so on.

subject at Higher level in the Scottish Leaving Certificate, the examination being taken in the fifth year of secondary education, at age 17. The percentage gaining enough subjects for university entry was far smaller. The remaining 87% of the cohort sat no formal public examinations at all. 1965 saw the introduction of a new examination, taken by a larger percentage of pupils (but by no means all) in the fourth year of secondary education. This examination was revised in the mid-1980s, and every school pupil now has to sit this examination, although there are three levels of difficulty and pupils are assigned to level of difficulty according to their academic performance. One major barrier preventing pupils from gaining good qualifications in this examination and indeed in the fifth year examination is a lack of control of written English, both in reading it and writing it. An appreciation of the large differences between spoken and written language would be useful to the many teachers in secondary school who do not realize the difficulties facing their pupils, especially those pupils, the majority, from homes where reading and writing are not everyday activities and where reading materials are sparse.[21]

There is a bigger problem. Over the past ten years a number of organizations, such as the Confederation of British Industry, prominent academics, and politicians have stated publicly that the standard of literacy among school-leavers has declined alarmingly. These statements are never supported by data to demonstrate what is meant by illiteracy, and no data is cited to support the view that standards have declined. There is no such data, for two reasons. One is the tiny proportion of pupils who sat formal examinations even in the early 1970s, and the other is the changing demands of jobs coupled with changed expectations of pupils. In 1962, for instance, many female school-leavers went into jobs in shops or factories, which required little or no use of written English. (Cf. Heath (1982) on the non-use of written English by the workforce in the Trackton mills.) The corresponding pupils in 1994 are looking for jobs as secretaries and the pupils who formerly looked for jobs as secretaries now look for jobs as, for example, computer operators. Not only do jobs in shops and supermarkets now call for more use of written English, secretarial and computer jobs require a good command of written English. But the pupils who would have become computer operators in 1962, had the jobs been available, are now going into higher education and their place is taken by pupils who have no

---

[21] Jim Miller's wife teaches mathematics in a secondary school in Edinburgh. This statement is based on the experience of his wife and her colleagues over a number of years. Corroborative evidence that there is a problem comes from changes in the wording of problems in the Scottish Leaving Certificate Mathematics papers, simplifying the syntax, and from the fact that the mathematics advisory service in Lothian Region, which will have vanished as part of local government reorganization by the time this book is published, is putting on a course to show mathematics teachers how to write course material and examination questions in 'plain English'. The problem, however, is not peculiar to mathematics but affects every subject.

poorer a command of written English than the corresponding pupils in 1962 but whose lack of command is exposed in the conditions of 1994. The linguistic situation has not got worse, as some people would have it; the situation is the same, but no longer concealed. Public use of written language is demanded of a much larger proportion of the general population than ever before; that is the crux of the problem.

As a reaction to the perceived decline in standards of literacy, changes in the curriculum have been introduced, one component of which is the testing of children at age 7, 10, and 14. The conditions have been relaxed to take account of different rates of learning and maturation and teachers are allowed to test children when they think the children are ready, but a major part of the testing relates to the control of standard written English. Given the enormous gap between spoken and written English and the time required to gain some control over the latter, testing at age 7 will typically prove straightforward for children from homes where reading materials are readily available and used by adults, and will prove troublesome for children from homes without reading material or where such material is sparse. The tests are supposed to be disguised by being part of the classroom routine but pupils will recognize them as tests. Children in a given class know who performs well academically and who does not and they talk. Children who see themselves as failures at an early age will continue to see themselves as failures. Testing at age 7 flies in the face of what we know about spoken and written language.[22]

The discussion of language by British linguists has typically taken no account of the differences between spoken and written language and tended to play down the advantages offered by a command of written English. This may partly be a reaction to the work of Bernstein (1971), who put his finger on the grammatical and lexical differences between spoken and written English, and also on the different modes of presenting information—highly personal as opposed to impersonal, but attributed these differences to social class. (The position of the authors is that everyone, regardless of social class, has to learn the syntax and vocabulary of written language and has to learn by constant practice the impersonal style of presentation.)

Trudgill (1976: 133–8) makes the point that what Bernstein called 'elaborated code'—the complex syntax and vocabulary of written English—is an essential component of the educational process only by convention and that no cognitive deficiencies attach to what Bernstein called 'restricted code'—which we can now think of as the syntax and vocabulary of spoken language. Of course Trudgill is correct to talk about a convention,

---

[22] Many children face a double barrier. Not only do they have to move from spoken to written language but they also have to move from some non-standard variety of English to the standard language, or to a variety that is much closer to the standard. This affects not just written language but the spoken language of the classroom.

but the fact is that nobody is going to rewrite all the texts that have the grammar and vocabulary of written English. People are not going to stop producing such texts, and nobody is going to produce newspapers, textbooks, novels, and so on in the grammar and vocabulary of spontaneous spoken English. The equivalent assertion in China would be that it is only by convention that Chinese is written in ideographs and not an alphabet.

Trudgill refers to what he described as Labov's convincing example of the way in which working-class children can manipulate abstract concepts very skilfully. In fact Labov demonstrates only that some working-class children can do this, and we would add that only *some* middle-class children can manipulate abstract concepts. There is a difficulty with the excerpt of conversation in which a Black teenager talks about God as being white or black, and that is that we simply do not know whether he had heard adults expressing this view or had arrived at his point of view by himself. Another problem is that, compared with conversations with working-class teenagers in Scotland that Jim Miller took part in when a teenager himself, the passage cited by Labov is not marvellous. On the other hand, it was worthwhile citing and discussing it in a time and place when many educationists assumed that people speaking non-standard English suffered from a cognitive deficit.

Trudgill comments that working-class children are not 'linguistically deprived'. They are less willing or less used to employing a more formal style than middle-class children. This does not suggest linguistic deprivation—stylistic variations are generally held to be equivalent ways of saying the same thing. Working-class children have a narrower range of stylistic options, but this is compensated by verbal skills such as joke-telling, narrating, insulting. Trudgill suggests that 'there are probably certain options open to them which are not available to middle-class children'.

On the same lines, Hudson (1980: 215–19), 224–30) talks about the poor performance of working-class children at school possibly being caused by the type of vocabulary favoured in testing—the intellectually oriented vocabulary favoured by schools. He argues that no information is available on the *total* vocabulary of a given child and that given the lack of knowledge it would be safer to assume that there are no significant differences in the overall size of vocabulary of lower- and upper-class children.[23]

While we reject the notion that normal children come to school with hardly any language, it is important to scrutinize the assertions of Trudgill and Hudson. Counter-assertions can be advanced. The differences at stake are not just stylistic variations but range of syntax and range of vocabulary;

---

[23] The second of Hudson's book, published in 1996, does not refer to the total vocabulary of a given child but does recognize large differences between the vocabulary of the classroom and the out-of-school vocabulary of many children.

some lexical items are cognitive synonyms but it is generally accepted that there are no complete synonyms, that there is always some difference to do with register or speaker's attitude. Many lexical items are related in meaning but are not cognitive synonyms, and written language does use a much larger range of vocabulary than spoken language. Hudson's argument about the total vocabulary of a child also fails to hold up given what we know about the range of vocabulary in writing and speech. And what is wrong with acquiring some intellectually oriented vocabulary, particularly if it opens sources of information, not to mention improving job prospects?

Why is poor command of written language offset by verbal skills such as joke-telling, narrating, and insulting? Middle-class children also tell jokes and recount narratives; in some cultures they also indulge in friendly insults. But since these activities have quite different functions from reading and writing it is unlikely that they compensate at all for poor competence in the written language. Trudgill and Hudson play down the fact that written language has to be learned by children of all social classes and they do not mention the importance of exposure to written materials and writing practices. They overestimate the significance (in a literate society) of the syntax and vocabulary of spoken language and underestimate the importance and scope of written language. Most worrying of all, they do not recognize written language as an indispensable tool for central activities in any literate society.[24]

[24] These comments also apply to Labov's discussion in 'The logic of non-standard English'.

Epilogue

Our exploration of spoken and written language has covered a number of different areas within linguistics and associated disciplines. The details presented in Chapters 2–6 demonstrate that spontaneous spoken language has its own regular characteristics of grammar and discourse organization; not just English but other languages. Certain topics, such as LIKE and WH constructions, are discussed in detail in order to overcome possible reluctance to accept that spontaneous spoken language has regular patterns of syntax and discourse organization. The details and the analytical problems are interesting in themselves, and clearly have implications for theories of constituent structure in spontaneous speech. Chapters 7 and 8 constitute an argument for the view that the distinction between spontaneous speech and written language is directly and centrally relevant to other areas of theory. Chapter 8 concentrated on first language acquisition but the book raises questions for, e.g., the study of online processing and the modelling of the processes involved in the production and understanding of spoken utterances. Given the typical participant in psycholinguistic experiments—university students—and the social classes from which university students are drawn, it is inevitable that such experiments are biased in terms of social class and in terms of literacy and the influence of written language. Models of speech production, such as the one presented in Levelt (1989), are based on analyses of the syntax of written language; the basic syntactic unit is the sentence. The sentence may indeed be a relevant unit for speakers with a large exposure to and mastery of written language but research has yet to be carried out on speakers of languages that have no written variety or on speakers who are only weakly literate. These are major topics, but many questions arise concerning historical change and central sociolinguistic issues such as standard and non-standard language and language and education. Our hope is that this book will encourage scholars to take up these questions.

References

ABNEY, S. P. (1987), 'The English Noun Phrase in its Sentential Aspect', Ph.D. thesis (Massachusetts Institute of Technology).
AITCHISON, J. (1987), *Words in the Mind* (Oxford: Basil Blackwell).
AKINNASO, F. NIYI (1982), 'On the differences between spoken and written language', *Language and Speech*, 25: 97–125.
ALTMANN, H. (1981), *Formen der 'Herausstellung' im Deutschen. Rechtsversetzung, Linksversetzung, Freies Thema und verwandte Konstruktionen* (Tübingen: Niemeyer).
ANDERSON, A. H., BADER, M., BARD, E. G., BOYLE, E., DOHERTY, G., GARROD, S., ISARD, S., KOWTKO, J., MCALLISTER, J., MILLER, J., SOTILLO, C., THOMPSON, H., and WEINERT, R. (1991), 'The HCRC Map Task Corpus', *Language and Speech*, 34(4): 351–66.
ANDERSON, J. R. (1983), *The Architecture of Cognition* (Cambridge, Mass.: Harvard University Press).
ARIEL, MIRA (1988), 'Referring and accessibility', *Journal of Linguistics*, 24: 65–87.
—— (1994), 'Interpreting anaphoric expressions: A cognitive versus a pragmatic approach', *Journal of Linguistics*, 30: 3–42.
ARMSTRONG, S. L., GLEITMAN, L. R., and GLEITMAN, H. (1983), 'What some concepts might not be', *Cognition*, 13: 263–308.
ATKINSON, MARTIN A. (1990), 'The logical problem of language acquisition', in Roca (1990), 1–31.
ATKINSON, M. (1992), *Children's Syntax: An Introduction to Principles and Parameters Theory* (Oxford: Blackwell).
AUSTEN, JANE (1953), *Emma* (Glasgow and London: Collins).
AUSTIN, P. (1981), *A Grammar of Diyari, South Australia* (Cambridge: Cambridge University Press).
BABBY, LEONARD H. (1986), 'The locus of case assignment and the direction of percolation', in R. Brecht and J. Levine (eds.), *Case in Slavic* (Columbus, Oh.: Slavica), 170–219.
—— (1987), 'Case, prequantifiers and discontinuous agreement in Russian', *Natural Language and Linguistic Theory*, 5: 91–138.
BAHNS, J., BURMEISTER, H., and VOGEL, T. (1986), 'The pragmatics of formulas in L2 learner speech: Use and development', *Journal of Pragmatics*, 17: 693–723.
BARANSKAJA, N. (1989), *Nedelja kak Nedelja* (Columbus, Oh.: Slavica).
BARD, ELLEN, ROBERTSON, DAN, and SORACE, ANTONELLA (1996), 'Magnitude estimation of linguistic acceptability', *Language*, 72: 32–68.
BARRELL, JOHN (1983), *English Literature in History 1730–80* (London: Hutchinson).
BARTON, D. (1984), *Literacy* (Oxford: Blackwell).
BASHAM, E. (1971), *The Wonder that was India* (London: Fontana-Collins).
BATES, ELIZABETH, and MACWHINNEY, BRIAN (1987), 'Competition, variation and

language learning', in Brian MacWhinney (ed.), *Mechanisms of Language Acquisition* (Hillsdale, NJ: Lawrence Erlbaum), 157–93.

BEAMAN, K. (1984), 'Coordination and subordination revisited: Syntactic complexity in spoken and written narrative discourse', in D. Tannen (ed.), *Coherence in Spoken and Written Discourse* (Norwood, NJ: Albex), 45–80.

BEHAGEL, O. (1927), 'Geschriebenes Deutsch und gesprochenes Deutsch', in *Von deutscher Sprache: Aufsätze, Vorträge und Plaudereien* (Lahr), 11–34.

BERNSTEIN, B. (1971), *Class, Codes and Control*, i. *Theoretical Studies Towards a Sociology of Language* (London: Routledge & Kegan Paul).

BIALYSTOK, E., and SHARWOOD-SMITH, M. (1985), 'Interlanguage is not a state of mind: An evaluation of the construct for second-language acquisition', *Applied Linguistics*, **6(1)**: 101–17.

BIBER, DOUGLAS (1988), *Variation across Speech and Writing* (Cambridge: Cambridge University Press).

—— (1990), 'Methodological issues regarding corpus-based analysis of linguistic variation', *Literary and Linguistic Computing*, **5(4)**: 257–69.

BIVON, R. (1972), *Element Order in Russian* (Cambridge: Cambridge University Press).

BLANCHE-BENVENISTE, CLAIRE (1991), *Le Français parlé: Etudes grammaticales* (Paris: Editions du Centre National de la Recherche Scientifique).

BLOOMFIELD, L. (1935), *Language* (London: Allen and Unwin).

BOLANDER, M. (1987), 'On the acquisition of word order rules in Swedish as a second language', Paper given at AILA 1987, Sydney, 16–21 August.

—— (1989), 'Prefabs, patterns and rules in interaction? Formulaic speech in adults learners' L2 Swedish', in K. Hyltenstam and L. Obler (eds.), *Bilingualism across the Lifespan: Aspects of Acquisition, Maturity and Loss* (Cambridge: Cambridge University Press), 73–86.

BOLINGER, D. (1976), 'Meaning and memory', *Forum Linguisticum*, **1**: 1–14.

—— and SEARS, D. (1981), *Aspects of Language* (New York: Harcourt Brace Jovanovich).

BOLKESTEIN, A. M. (1991), 'The treatment of topical entities in Dutch and Classical Latin', Paper delivered at November meeting of Eurotype Theme Group 1, University of Bremen.

BOWE, H. J. (1990), *Categories, Constituents and Constituent Order in Pitjantjatjara* (London: Routledge).

BOWERMAN, MELISSA (1988), 'The "no negative evidence" problem', in John A. Hawkins (ed.), *Explaining Language Universals* (Oxford: Basil Blackwell), 73–101.

BRESNAN, J., and MCHOMBO, S. A. (1987), 'Topic, pronoun and agreement in Chichewa', *Language*, **63**: 741–82.

BRONS-ALBERT, R. (1984), *Gesprochenes Standarddeutsch. Telefondialoge. Studien zur deutschen Grammatik 18* (Tübingen: Gunter Narr).

BROWN, E. K., and MILLER, J. E. (1980), *The Syntax of Scottish English*, Final Report to the Social Science Research Council on Grant HR5152.

—— —— (1982), 'Aspects of Scottish English syntax', *English World-Wide*, **3(1)**: 1–17.

BROWN, G., and YULE, G. (1983), *Discourse Analysis* (Cambridge: Cambridge University Press).

—— Currie, K. L., and Kenworthy, J. (1980), *Questions of Intonation* (London: Croom Helm).
—— Anderson, A., Shillcock, R., and Yule, G. (1984), *Teaching Talk: Strategies for Production and Assessment* (Cambridge: Cambridge University Press).
Brown, R. (1973), *A First Language* (London: Allen and Unwin).
Cameron, Deborah (1995), *Verbal Hygiene* (London: Routledge), 33–77.
Cann, R. (1993), 'Patterns of headedness', in Corbett *et al.* (1993*b*), 44–72.
Cazden, C. B. (1968), 'The acquisition of noun and verb inflections', *Child Development*, **39**: 435–48.
Chafe, W. (1968), 'Idiomaticity as an anomaly in the Chomskyan paradigm', *Foundations of Language*, **4**: 109–26.
—— (1976), 'Givenness, contrastiveness, definiteness, subjects and topics', in Li (1976), 27–55.
—— (1979), 'The flow of thought and the flow of language', in T. Givón (ed.), *Syntax and Semantics*, xii. *Discourse and Syntax* (New York: Academic Press), 159–81.
—— (1980), 'The deployment of consciousness in the production of a narrative', in W. Chafe (ed.), *The Pear Stories: Cognitive, Cultural, and Linguistic Aspects of Narrative Production* (Norwood, NJ: Ablex), 9–50.
—— (1982), 'Integration and involvement in speaking, writing, and oral literature', in D. Tannen (ed.), *Spoken and Written Language: Exploring Orality and Literacy* (Norwood, NJ: Ablex), 35–53.
—— (1984), 'How people use adverbial clauses', in Claudia Brugman and Monica Macaulay (eds.), *Proceedings of the Tenth Annual Meeting of the Berkeley Linguistics Society* (Berkeley: Berkeley Linguistics Society), 437–49.
—— (1987), 'Cognitive constraints on information flow', in R. S. Tomlin (ed.), *Coherence and Grounding in Discourse* (Amsterdam: John Benjamins), 21–51.
—— (1988), 'Linking intonation units', in Haiman and Thompson (1988), 1–27.
—— and Danielewicz, J. (1987), 'Properties of written and spoken language', in R. Horowitz and S. J. Samuels (eds.), *Comprehending Oral and Written Language* (New York: Academic Press), 83–113.
Cheshire, Jenny, Edwards, Viv, and Whittle, Pamela (1993), 'Non-standard English and dialect levelling', in J. Milroy and L. Milroy (1993), 53–96.
Chomsky, Carol (1968), *The Acquisition of Syntax in Children from 5 to 10* (Cambridge, Mass.: MIT Press).
Chomsky, Noam Avraam (1957), *Syntactic Structures* (The Hague: Mouton).
—— (1959), Review of B. L. Skinner, *Verbal Behavior, Language*, **35**: 26–58.
—— (1964), *Current Issues in Linguistic Theory* (The Hague: Mouton).
—— (1965), *Aspects of the Theory of Syntax* (Cambridge, Mass.: MIT Press).
—— (1986), *Knowledge of Language: Its Nature, Origin and Use* (New York: Praeger).
—— (1989), *Barriers* (Cambridge, Mass.: MIT Press).
Church, K., and Hanks, P. (1989), 'Word association norms, mutual information, and lexicography', *Proceedings of the 27th Annual Meeting of the Association for Computational Linguistics*, Association for Computational Linguistics, 76–83.
Cinque, Guglielmo (1990), *Types of A' Dependencies* (Cambridge, Mass.: MIT Press).

CLARK, HERBERT H. (1992), *Arenas of Language Use* (London: University of Chicago Press and the Center for the Study of Language and Information).
CLARK, R. (1974), 'Performing without competence', *Journal of Child Language*, 1: 1–10.
COMRIE, B. (1981), *Language Universals and Linguistic Typology* (Oxford: Blackwell).
COOK, V. (1988), 'Cognitive processing and second language learning', *Polyglot*, 9, microfiche 2.
CORBETT, GREVILLE G. (1993a), 'The head of Russian numeral expressions', in Corbett *et al.* (1993b), 11–35.
—— FRASER, NORMAN M., and MCGLASHAN, SCOTT (1993b), *Heads in grammatical theory* (Cambridge: Cambridge University Press).
COULMAS, F. (1979), 'On the sociolinguistic relevance of routine formulae', *Journal of Pragmatics*, 3: 239–66.
—— (1981) (ed.), *Conversational Routine* (The Hague: Mouton).
COULTHARD, R. M., and ROBINSON, W. P. (1968), 'The structure of the nominal group and elaboratedness of code', *Language and Speech*, 11(4): 234–50.
CRAIN, STEPHEN, and NAKAYAMA, MINEHARU (1987), 'Structure dependence in grammar formation', *Language*, 63: 522–43.
CRICK, F. H. C. (1979), 'Thinking about the brain', *Scientific American*, 9: 219–32.
CRISPIN, E. (1960), *Best SF 4* (London: Faber and Faber).
CROOKES, G. (1990), 'The utterance and other basic units for second language discourse analysis', *Applied Linguistics*, 11(2): 183–99.
CRUSE, DAVID A. (1986), *Lexical Semantics* (Cambridge: Cambridge University Press).
CRUTTENDEN, A. (1981), 'Item-learning and system-learning', *Journal of Psycholinguistic Research*, 10: 79–88.
CRYSTAL, D. (1987), *The Cambridge Encyclopaedia of Language* (Cambridge: Cambridge University Press).
DANESI, M. (1988), 'Neurological bimodality and theories of language teaching', *Studies in Second Language Acquisition*, 10: 13–31.
DECHERT, H., MÖHLE, D., and RAUPACH, M. (1984), *Second Language Productions* (Tübingen: Gunter Narr).
DECLERCK, R. (1988), *Studies on Copular Sentences, Clefts and Pseudo-Clefts* (Leuven: Leuven University Press, Foris Publications Holland/USA).
DELIN, J. L. (1989), 'Cleft Constructions in Discourse', Ph.D. thesis, No. 34 (Centre for Cognitive Science, University of Edinburgh).
—— (1990), 'Accounting for cleft constructions in discourse: A multi-layered approach' (Research paper, HCRC/RP-5, University of Edinburgh: HCRC Publications).
DENNY, J. (1991), 'Rational thought in oral culture', in D. R. Olson and N. Torrance (eds.), *Literacy and Orality* (Cambridge: Cambridge University Press), 66–89.
DEULOFEU, J. (1981), 'Perspective linguistique et sociolinguistique dans l'étude des relatives en français', in *Recherches sur le français parlé 3* (Aix-en-Provence: Université de Provence, Service des Publications).
DIK, S. C. (1980), *Studies in Functional Grammar* (London: Academic Press).

DIXON, ROBERT M. W. (1972), *The Dyirbal Language of North Queensland* (Cambridge: Cambridge University Press).
DRESSLER, W. U. (1985), *Morphonology: The Dynamics of Derivation* (Ann Arbor, Mich.: Karoma).
DREYFUS, H., DREYFUS, S., and ATHANASIOU, T. (1986), *Mind over Machine* (New York: Free Press).
Duden Grammatik (1995), 5th edition (Dudenverlag).
DYHR, M. (1978), *Die Satzspaltung im Dänischen und Deutschen* (Tübingen: Gunter Narr).
EFREMOV, I. (1987), 'Zvezdnye Korabli', in A. I. Stepin (ed.), *Ivan Efremov* (Kišinev: Štiinca), 456–500.
EHLICH, K., and REHBEIN, J. (1976), 'Halbinterpretative Arbeitstranskriptionen (HiAT)', *Linguistische Berichte*, 45: 21–41.
ENKVIST, NILS-ERIK (1982), 'Impromptu speech, structure and process', in N.-E. Enkvist (ed.), *Impromptu Speech: A Symposium* (Åbo: Åbo Akademi Foundation), 78: 11–32.
FERNANDEZ, M. M. J. (1982), *Le Finnois Parlé par les Sames Bilingues d'Utsjoki-Ohcejohka (Laponie Finlandaise): Structures contrastives, syntaxiques, discursives* (L'Europe de Tradition Orale, 1; Paris: SELAF).
—— (1984), 'Verbo-nominalisations et scripturarisation d'une énonciation à tradition orale: Les Semi-propositions du same comparées à celles du finnois', *Actes de la Table Ronde sur L'Opposition verbo-nominale dans diverses langues du monde*, in N. Tersis-Surugue (ed.), *Modèles Linguistiques*, 6(1): 181–92.
—— (1994a), *Les Particules énonciatives* (Paris: Presses Universitaires de France).
—— (1994b), 'Oralité et écriture', Paper presented at the Eurotype Plenary Conference, Le Bischenberg, Strasbourg, 27–31 March.
FEYEREISEN, PIERRE, and DE LANNOY, JACQUES-DOMINIQUE (1991), *Gestures and Speech: Psychological Investigations* (Cambridge: Cambridge University Press and Paris: Editions de la Maison des Sciences de l'Homme).
FILLMORE, C. J. (1988), 'The mechanisms of "construction grammar"', *Proceedings of the Annual Meeting of the Berkeley Linguistics Society*, 14: 35–55.
—— KAY, P., and O'CONNOR, C. (1988), 'Regularity and idiomaticity in grammatical constructions', *Language*, 64: 501–38.
FISHER, JOHN H. (1977), 'Chancery and the emergence of standard written English in the fifteenth century', *Speculum*, 52: 870–99.
FLASHNER, V. (1987), 'The grammatical marking of theme in oral Polish narrative', in R. Tomlin (ed.), *Coherence and Grounding in Discourse* (Amsterdam: John Benjamins), 131–56.
FOLEY, W. D., and VAN VALIN, Jr., R. D. (1984), *Functional Syntax and Universal Grammar* (Cambridge: Cambridge University Press).
Forschungen zur gesprochenen Sprache und Möglichkeiten ihrer Didaktisierung (1970), Protokol eines Werkstattgesprächs des Goethe-Instituts am 10. und 11. Dezember 1970. (Goethe-Institut München).
GAERTNER, H.-M. (1996), 'Are there V2 relative clauses in German?', Unpublished manuscript, Berlin.
GELUYKENS, R. (1988), 'Five types of clefting in English discourse', *Linguistics*, 26: 823–41.

Gesprochene Sprache (1973), Bericht der Forschungsstelle Freiburg = Forschungsberichte des Instituts für Deutsche Sprache. Bd. 7 (Mannheim).
GILDERSLEEVE, B. L., and LODGE, G. (1971), *Latin Grammar* (London and Basingstoke: Macmillan, St Martin's Press: New York).
GIVÓN, T. (1979), *On Understanding Grammar* (New York: Academic Press).
—— (1983), *Topic Continuity in Discourse* (Amsterdam: John Benjamins).
—— (1989), *Mind, Code and Context: Essays in Pragmatics* (Hillsdale, NJ: Lawrence Erlbaum).
—— (1990), *Syntax: A Functional-Typological Introduction* (Amsterdam/Philadelphia: John Benjamins).
GOLDMAN-EISLER, F. (1968), *Psycholinguistics: Experiments in Spontaneous Speech* (London: Academic Press).
GOODY, J. (1977), *The Domestication of the Savage Mind* (Cambridge: Cambridge University Press).
GRANITO, M. (1983), 'Nämlich, Und Zwar: Étude syntaxique et sémantique (premiere partie)', Cahiers D'Études Germaniques, No. 7, Université de Provence, Centre d'Aix, Aix-en-Provence.
—— (1984), 'Nämlich, Und Zwar: Étude syntaxique et sémantique (deuxieme partie)', Cahiers D'Études Germaniques, No. 8, Université de Provence, Centre d'Aix-en-Provence.
GRANT, W., and MAIN-DIXON, J. (1921), *Manual of Modern Scots* (Cambridge: Cambridge University Press).
GREENBAUM, SYDNEY (1991), 'The development of the International Corpus of English', in Karim Aijmer and Bengt Altenberg (eds.), *English Corpus Linguistics: Studies in Honour of Jan Svartvik* (London and New York: Longman), 83–91.
GROPEN, JESS, PINKER, STEVE, HOLLANDER, MICHELLE, GOLDBERG, RICHARD, and WILSON, RONALD (1989), 'The learnability and acquisition of the dative alternation in English', *Language*, **65**: 203–57.
GROSZ, B. J. (1981), 'Focusing and description in natural language dialogues', in A. K. Joshi, B. L. Webber, and I. A. Sag (eds.), *Elements of Discourse Understanding* (Cambridge: Cambridge University Press), 84–105.
—— and SIDNER, C. L. (1986), 'Attentions, intentions, and the structure of discourse', *Computational Linguistics*, **12(3)**: 175–204.
GUILLAUME, P. (1973), 'First stages of sentence formation in children's speech', in C. A. Ferguson and D. Slobin (eds.), *Studies of Child Language Development* (New York: Holt, Reinhart & Winston) (originally published 1927).
GUIRAUD, P. (1963), *Le Moyen français* (Paris: Presses Universitaires de France).
GÜNTHNER, S. (1993), '"... weil—man kann es ja wissenschaftlich untersuchen"— Diskurspragmatische Aspekte der Wortstellung in WEIL-Sätzen', *Linguistische Berichte*, **143**: 37–59.
GUY, G. (1988), 'Language and social class', in F. J. Newmeyer (ed.), *Linguistics: The Cambridge Survey*, iv. *Language: The Socio-Cultural Context* (Cambridge: Cambridge University Press), 37–63.
HAEGEMAN, L. (1991), *Introduction to Government & Binding Theory* (Oxford: Blackwell).
HAGÈGE, CLAUDE (1982), *La Structure des langues, 'Que sais-je?'* 2006 (Paris: Presses Universitaires de France).

HAIMAN, J., and THOMPSON, S. A. (1988) (eds.), *Clause Combining in Grammar and Discourse* (Amsterdam: John Benjamins).
HAKUTA, K. (1974), 'Prefabricated Patterns and the Emergence of Structure in Second Language Acquisition', *Language Learning*, **24**: 287–97.
HALE, K. (1983), 'Warlpiri and the grammar of non-configurational languages', *Natural Language and Linguistic Theory*, **1**: 5–47.
HALFORD, B. (1990), 'The complexity of oral syntax', in B. Halford and H. Pilch (eds.), *Syntax gesprochener Sprachen* (Tübingen: Gunter Narr), 33–43.
HALLIDAY, M. A. K. (1967), 'Notes on transitivity and theme in English: Part 1', *Journal of Linguistics*, **3**: 37–81.
—— (1985), *An Introduction to Functional Grammar* (London: Edward Arnold).
—— (1989), *Spoken and Written Language* (Oxford: Oxford University Press).
HANANIA, E., and GRADMAN, H. (1977), 'Acquisition of English structures: A case study of an adult native speaker in an English-speaking environment', *Language Learning*, **27**: 75–92.
HARRIS, Z. S. (1946), 'From morpheme to utterance', *Language*, **22**: 161–83. Reprinted in M. Joos (ed.), *Readings in Linguistics 1* (Chicago: University of Chicago Press), 142–53.
HATCH, E. (1978), *Second Language Acquisition: A Book of Readings* (Rowley, Mass.: Newbury House).
—— PECK, S., and WAGNER-GOUGH, J. (1979), 'A look at process in child second language acquisition', in E. Ochs and B. Schieffelin (eds.), *Developmental Pragmatics* (New York: Academic Press), 269–78.
HAVRÁNEK, B. (1932), 'Ukoly spisovného jazyka a jeho kultura', in B. Havránek and M. Weingart (eds.), *Spisovna Čeština a Jazyková Kultura* (Prague).
HAWKINS, J. A. (1986), *A Comparative Typology of English and German* (London: Croom Helm).
—— (1990), 'Explaining language universals', in J. A. Hawkins (ed.), *Explaining Universals* (Oxford: Blackwell), 3–28.
HAWKINS, PETER (1969), 'Social class, the nominal group and reference', *Language and Speech*, **14(4)**: 125–35.
HEATH, J. (1985), 'Discourse in the field: Clause structure in Ngandi', in J. Nichols and A. C. Woodbury (eds.), *Grammar Inside and Outside the Clause* (Cambridge: Cambridge University Press), 89–110.
HEATH, SHIRLEY BRICE (1982), *Ways With Words* (Cambridge: Cambridge University Press).
HEDBERG, N. A. (1988), 'The discourse function of cleft structures in spoken English', Linguistic Society of America, unpublished conference paper.
—— (1990), 'Discourse Pragmatics and Cleft Sentences in English', Ph.D. dissertation (University of Minnesota).
HEDEVIND, B. (1967), 'The dialect of Dentdale in the West Riding of Yorkshire', *Societas Anglistica Upsaliensia*, **5** (Uppsala: University of Uppsala).
HEIM, I. (1982), *The Semantics of Definite and Indefinite Noun Phrases* (Amherst, Mass.: Graduate Linguistics Student Association, University of Massachusetts).
HEINZE, H. (1979), *Gesprochenes und geschriebenes Deutsch* (Düsseldorf: Pädagogischer Verlag Schwann).

HENNE, HENRY, RONGEN, OLE BJORN, and HANSEN, LARS JUL (1977), *A Handbook on Chinese Language Structure* (Oslo, Bergen, and Tromsö: Universitetsforlaget).
HICKEY, T. (1993), 'Identifying formulas in first language acquisition', *Journal of Child Language*, **20**: 27–41.
HOCKETT, C. (1954), 'Two models of grammatical description', *Word*, **10**: 210–31. Reprinted in M. Joos (ed.), *Readings in Linguistics I* (Chicago and London: University of Chicago Press, 1957), 386–99.
HORROCKS, G. (1987), *Generative Grammar* (London: Longman).
—— (1988), *Generative Grammar* (London: Longman).
HOVY, E. (1990), 'Unresolved issues in paragraph planning'.
HUANG, J., and HATCH, E. (1978), 'A Chinese child's acquisition of English', in E. Hatch (ed.), *Second Language Acquisition: A Book of Readings* (Rowley, Mass.: Newbury House), 118–31.
HUDDLESTON, R. (1984), *Introduction to the Grammar of English* (Cambridge: Cambridge University Press).
HUDSON, RICHARD A. (1980), *Sociolinguistics* (Cambridge: Cambridge University Press).
—— (1987), 'Zwicky on heads', *Journal of Linguistics*, **23**: 109–32.
HUDSON, R. H. (1990), *English Word Grammar* (Oxford: Blackwell).
HUNT, K. W. (1966), 'Recent measures in syntactic development', *Elementary English*, **43**: 732–9.
HURFORD, JAMES R. (1987), *Language and Number* (Oxford: Basil Blackwell).
HYAMS, N. M. (1986), *Language Acquisition and the Theory of Parameters* (Dordrecht: D. Reidel).
IWAMURA, S. G. (1980), *The Verbal Games of Pre-School Children* (London: Croom Helm).
JACKENDOFF, R. (1983), *Semantics and Cognition* (Cambridge, Mass.: MIT Press).
JÄGER, K.-H. (1976). *Untersuchungen zur Klassifikation gesprochener deutscher Standardsprache*, Linguistische und didaktische Beiträge für den deutschen Sprachunterricht, Veröffentlicht vom Institut für deutsche Sprache Mannheim und vom Goethe-Institut München (München: Max Hueber).
JESPERSEN, O. (1927), *A Modern English Grammar on Historical Principles*, iii. *Syntax* (Copenhagen: Ejnar Munksgaard). (Reprinted London: Allen and Unwin, 1974.)
JUCKER, A. H. (1992), *Social Stylistics: Syntactic Variation in British Newspapers* (Berlin–New York: Mouton de Gruyter).
KALEDIN, S. (1989), 'Smirennoe Kladbišče', in I. A. Dedkova (ed.), *Poslednij Etaž: Sbornik Sovremennoj Prozy* (Moscow: Knižnaja Palata), 216–66.
KAMP, HANS, and REYLE, UWE (1993), *From Discourse to Logic* (Dordrecht: Kluwer).
KAPANADZE, M., and ZEMSKAJA, E. O. (1979), *Teksty* (Moscow: Nauka).
KARELOV, E., and IVANOV, A. (1986), 'Rebjata ja živ', in O. I. Sokolov (ed.), *Mir Priključenij* (Moscow: Detskaja Literatura), 3–124.
KEENAN, EDWARD L. (1976), 'Towards a universal definition of subject', in Li (1976), 305–33.
—— (1985), 'Relative clauses', in T. Shopen (ed.), *Language Typology and Syntactic Description*, ii. *Complex Constructions* (Cambridge: Cambridge University Press), 141–70.

KEENAN, E. O., and SCHIEFFELIN, B. B. (1976), 'Topic as a discourse notion: A study of topic in the conversations of children and adults', in Li (ed.), *Subject and Topic* (New York: Academic Press), 337–84.
KELLER, RUDOLF E. (1978), *The German Language* (London: Faber).
KELLY, C. (1990) (trans.), *Sergei Kaledin: The Humble Cemetery and Other Stories* (London: Collins Harvill).
KENNEDY, G. (1989), 'Collocation: Where grammar and vocabulary teaching meet', Paper presented at the RELC Seminar, Singapore.
KENYERES, A., and KENYERES, E. (1938), 'Comment une petite hongroise de sept ans apprend le français', *Archives de Psychologie*, 26: 321–66.
KIRKWOOD, H. W. (1969), 'Aspects of word order and its communicative function in English and German', *Journal of Linguistics*, 5: 85–107.
KLATZKY, R. L. (1980), *Human Memory* (San Francisco: W. H. Freeman and Company).
KÖNIG, E., and STARK, D. (1991), 'The treatment of function words in a new bilingual German–English dictionary', in W. Abraham (ed.), *Discourse Particles* (Amsterdam: John Benjamins), 303–28.
KOSTER, J. (1979), 'Some remarks on language learnability', Paper presented to the Paris Conference on Learnability.
KOVTUNOVA, I. I. (1967), 'Principy slovoraspoloženija v sovremennom russkom jazyke', in N. Ju. Švedova (ed.), *Russkij Jazyk: Grammatičeskie Issledovanija* (Moscow: Akademija Nauk), 96–146.
KOWTKO, J. C., ISARD, S. D., and DOHERTY-SNEDDON (1992), 'Conversational games within dialogue' (Research Paper, HCRC/RP-31; Human Communication Research Centre, University of Edinburgh).
KRASHEN, S. D. (1981), *Second Language Acquisition and Second Language Learning* (Oxford: Pergamon Press).
KRASIL'NIKOVA, E. V. (1990), *Imja suščestvitel'noe v russkoj razgovornoj reči* (Moscow: Nauka).
KRESS, G. (1979), 'The social values of speech and writing', in R. Fowler, B. Hodge, G. Kress, and T. Trew, *Language and Control* (London: Routledge & Kegan Paul), 46–62.
—— (1982), *Learning to Write* (London: Routledge & Keagan Paul).
KROLL, B. (1977), 'Combining ideas in written and spoken English: A look at subordination and coordination', in E. Ochs Keenan and T. L. Bennett (eds.), *Discourse across Time and Space* (Southern California Occasional Papers in Linguistics, 5; Los Angeles: University of Southern California), 69–108.
KUBRJAKOVA, E. S., ŠAXNAROVIČ, A. M., and SAXARNYJ, L. V. (1991), *Čelovečeskij Faktor v Jazyke: Jazyk i Poroždenie Reči* (Moscow: Akademija Nauk).
LABOV, W. (1972), 'The logic of nonstandard English', in P. P. Giglioli (ed.), *Language and Social Context* (Harmondsworth: Penguin), 179–215).
LANGACKER, RONALD W. (1982), 'Space grammar, analysability and the English passive', *Language*, 58: 22–80.
—— (1987), *Foundations of Cognitive Grammar*, i. *Theoretical Prerequisites* (Stanford, Calif.: Stanford University Press).
LAPTEVA, O. A. (1976), *Russkij razgovornyj sintaksis* (Moscow: Nauka).
LATHAM, R. (1978), *The Illustrated Pepys* (London: Bell and Hyman).

LEECH, GEOFFREY (1991), 'The state of the art in corpus linguistics', in Karin Aijmer and Bengt Altenberg (eds.), *English Corpus Linguistics: Studies in Honour of Jan Svartvik* (London and New York: Longman), 8–29.

—— MYERS, GREG, and THOMAS, JENNY (1995), *Spoken English on Computer* (Harlow and New York: Longman).

LEHMANN, C. (1988), 'Towards a typology of clause linkage', in Haiman and Thompson (1988), 181–225.

LESKA, C. (1965), *Vergleichende Untersuchungen zur Syntax gesprochener und geschriebener deutschen Gegenwartssprache. In Beiträge zur Geschichte der deutschen Sprache und Literatur*, Halle 87, 427–61.

LEVELT, WILLEM J. M. (1989), *Speaking: From Intention to Articulation* (Cambridge, Mass.: MIT Press).

LEVY, J. (1985), 'Right Brain, left brain: Fact and fiction', *Psychology Today*, 19: 38–44.

LEWIS, G. L. (1953), *Teach Yourself Turkish* (London: Hodder and Stoughton).

LI, CHARLES, N. (1976) (ed.), *Subject and Topic* (New York: Academic Press).

—— and THOMPSON, SANDRA A. (1976), 'Subject and topic: A new typology of language', in Li (1976), 459–89.

LIGHTFOOT, D. (1982), *The Language Lottery* (Cambridge, Mass.: MIT Press).

LINELL, P. (1988), 'The impact of literacy on the conception of language: The case of linguistics', in R. Saljö (ed.), *The Written World* (Berlin: Springer), 41–58.

LORD, A. B. (1960), *The Singer of Tales* (Harvard Studies in Comparative Literature, 24; Cambridge, Mass.: Harvard University Press).

LYONS, J. (1968), *Introduction to Theoretical Linguistics* (Cambridge: Cambridge University Press).

—— (1975), 'Deixis as the source of reference', in Edward L. Keenan (ed.), *Formal Semantics of Natural Language* (Cambridge: Cambridge University Press), 61–83. Reprinted in Sir John Lyons, *Natural Language and Universal Grammar* (Cambridge: Cambridge University Press, 1991), 146–65.

—— (1977), *Semantics 1* (Cambridge: Cambridge University Press).

—— (1991), *Natural Language and Universal Grammar* (Cambridge: Cambridge University Press).

MACAFEE, G. (1983), *Glasgow* (Amsterdam and Philadelpha: John Benjamins).

MACAULAY, R. K. S. (1987), 'A microlinguistic study of the dialect of Ayr', in A. R. Thomas (ed.), *Methods in Dialectology* (Clevedon: Multilingual Matters), 456–63.

—— (1991), *Locating Dialect in Discourse* (New York and Oxford: Oxford University Press).

MCCARTHY, M. (1991), *Discourse Analysis for Language Teachers* (Cambridge: Cambridge University Press).

MACDONALD, LORNA (1988), 'Subordination in Tauya', in Haiman and Thompson (1988), 227–46.

MCGREGOR, W. B. (1988), 'Mood and subordination in Kuniyanti', in P. Austin (ed.), *Complex Sentence Constructions in Australian Languages*, 37–67.

MACKENZIE, J. L., and KEIZER, M. E. (1990), 'On assigning pragmatic functions in English', in M. Hannay, J. L. Mackenzie, and M. E. Keizer (eds.), *Pragmatic Functions: The View from the V.U.* (Working Papers in Functional Grammar, 38; Amsterdam: Free University of Amsterdam).

McKeown, K. R. (1985), *Text Generation: Using Discourse Strategies and Focus Constraints to Generate Natural Language Text* (Cambridge: Cambridge University Press).
McLaughlin, B. (1987), *Theories of Second Language Learning* (London: Arnold).
McNeill, David (1987), *Psycholinguistics: A new approach* (New York: Harper Row).
MacWhinney, B., and Anderson, J. (1986), 'The acquisition of grammar', in I. Gopnik and M. Gopnik (eds.), *From Models to Modules* (Norwood, NJ: Ablex), 3–23.
Mann, W. C., and Thompson, S. A. (1987), 'Rhetorical structure theory: A theory of text organisation', ISI/RS-87-190 (Marina del Rey, Calif.: Information Sciences Institute).
Manzini, Rita (1990), 'Locality and parameters again', in Roca (1990), 137–56.
Matthews, P. (1972), *Inflectional Morphology: A Theoretical Study Based on Aspects of Latin Verb Conjugation* (Cambridge: Cambridge University Press).
—— (1981), *Syntax* (Cambridge: Cambridge University Press).
Matthews, P. H. (1979), *Generative Grammar and Linguistic Competence* (London: Allen and Unwin).
Matthiessen, C., and Thompson, S. A. (1988), 'The structure of discourse and subordination', in Haiman and Thompson (1988), 275–329.
Miller, George (1956), 'The magical number seven, plus or minus two: Some limits on our capacity for processing information', *Psychological Review*, **63**: 81–97.
Miller, Jim (1972), 'Towards an account of quantifiers in Russian', *Edinburgh Working Papers in Linguistics*, **1**: 73–91.
—— (1984), 'Discourse patterns in spoken English', *Sheffield Working Papers in Linguistics*, **1**: 10–39.
—— (1985), *Semantics and Syntax: Parallels and Connections* (Cambridge: Cambridge University Press).
—— (1988), '*That*: A relative pronoun? Sociolinguistics and syntactic analysis', in J. M. Anderson and N. Macleod (eds.), *Edinburgh Studies in the English Language* (Edinburgh: John Donald), 113–19.
—— (1989), 'Dependency relations and constituent structure in spoken language: Numerals, demonstratives and adjectives in Russian', Unpublished manuscript, Department of Linguistics, University of Edinburgh.
—— (1993), 'Spoken and written language: Syntax and language acquisition', in R. Scholes (ed.), *Literacy and Linguistic Analysis* (Hillsdale, NJ: Lawrence Erlbaum), 99–141.
—— (1996), 'Clefts, particles and word order in languages of Europe', *Language Sciences*, **18**: 111–25.
—— and Weinert, Regina (1995), 'The function of LIKE in spoken language', *Journal of Pragmatics*, **23**: 365–93.
Milroy, James, and Milroy, Leslie (1985), *Authority in Language: Investigating Language Prescription and Standardisation* (London: Routledge & Kegan Paul).
—— —— (1993) (eds.), *Real English: The Grammar of English Dialects in the British Isles* (London: Longman).
Minsky, M. (1975), 'A framework for representing knowledge', in P. Winston (ed.), *The Psychology of Computer Vision* (New York: McGraw-Hill), 211–77.

MITHUN, MARIANNE (1987), 'Is basic word order universal?', in Russell S. Tomlin (ed.), *Coherence and Grounding in Discourse* (Amsterdam: John Benjamins), 281–328.
MOROZOVA, T. S. (1984), 'Nekotorye osobennosti postroenija vyskazyvanija v prostorečii', in E. A. Zemskaja and D. N. Smelev (eds.), *Gorodskoe Prostorečie* (Moscow: Nauka), 141–62.
MORPHY, F. (1983), 'Djapu, a Yolngu dialect', in R. M. W. Dixon and B. Blake (eds.), *Handbook of Australian Languages* (Canberra: Australian National University Press), 1–188.
MORSHED, A. K. M. (1986), *Relativization in Benagli* (Dhaka: University of Dhaka Press).
MÜLLEROVÁ, O., HOFFMANNOVÁ, J., and SCHNEIDEROVÁ, E. (1992), *Mluvená Čeština v Autentických Textech* (Prague: H&H).
MUNDY, C. S. (1955), 'Turkish syntax as a system of qualification', *Bulletin of the School of Oriental Studies*, **17**: 277–305.
MUNRO, PAMELA, and GORDON, LYNN (1982), 'Syntactic relations in Western Muskogean: A typological perspective', *Language*, **58**: 81–115.
NATTINGER, J., and DECARRICO, J. (1992), *Lexical Phrases and Language Teaching* (Oxford: Oxford University Press).
NEIDLE, C. (1988), *The Role of Case in Russian Syntax* (Studies in Natural Language and Linguistic Theory, 10; Dordrecht: Kluwer).
NICHOLS, J. (1985), 'Grammatical marking of theme', in M. Flier and R. Brecht (eds.), *Issues in Russian Morphosyntax* (Columbus, Oh.: Slavica).
—— and WOODBURY, A. C. (1985), *Grammar Inside and Outside the Clause* (Cambridge: Cambridge University Press).
NUNBERG, G. (1978), *The Pragmatics of Reference* (Bloomington: Indiana University Linguistics Club).
—— SAG, IVAN A., and WASOW, THOMAS (1994), 'Idioms', *Language*, **70**: 491–538.
OCHS, ELEANOR (1979), 'Planned and unplanned discourse', in Talmy Givón (ed.), *Syntax and Semantics*, xii. *Discourse and Syntax* (New York: Academic Press), 51–80.
OLSON, D. R. (1973), 'What is worth knowing and what can be taught', *School Review*, **82(1)**: 27–43.
—— (1991), 'From utterance to text', in M. Minami and B. P. Kennedy (eds.), *Language Issues in Literacy and Bilingual/Multicultural Education* (Cambridge, Mass.: Harvard Educational Review), 151–76.
ONG, WALTER (1982), *Orality and Literacy Education* (London: Methuen).
OOSTDIJK, N. (1988), 'A corpus linguistic approach to linguistic variation', *Literary and Linguistic Computing*, **3(1)**: 12–25.
PALMER, L. R. (1954), *The Latin Language* (London: Faber and Faber).
PARTRIDGE, E. (1984), *A Dictionary of Slang and Unconventional English*, ed. Paul Beale, 8th edn. (London: Routledge & Kegan Paul).
PAYNE, JOHN E. (1985), 'Negation', in Timothy Shopen (ed.), *Language Typology and Syntactic Description*, i (Cambridge: Cambridge University Press), 197–242.
—— (1993), 'The headedness of noun phrases', in Corbett *et al.* (1993*b*), 114–39.
PAWLEY, A., and SYDER, F. (1976), 'The one clause at a time hypothesis', Paper read to first Congress of N.Z. Linguistic Society, Auckland, August.

—— —— (1983), 'Two puzzles for linguistic theory: Nativelike selection and nativelike fluency', in J. C. Richards and R. W. Schmidt (eds.), *Language and Communication* (London: Longman), 191–226.

PERERA, K. (1984), *Children's Writing and Reading* (Oxford: Basil Blackwell).

PESETSKY, D. (1982), 'Paths and categories', Ph.D. thesis (MIT).

PETERS, A. (1983), *The Units of Language Acquisition* (Cambridge: Cambridge University Press).

PETRUŠEVSKAJA, L. S. (1988), 'Tri devuški v golubom', in L. S. Petruševskaja, *Pesni XX Veka* (Moscow: Sojuz Teatral'nyx Dejatelej RSFSR), 9–66.

PINKER, STEVEN (1994), *The Language Instinct* (Harmondsworth: Allen Lane, Penguin Press).

POLLARD, C., and SAG, I. A. (1994), *Head-Driven Phrase Structure Grammar* (Stanford: Center for the Study of Language and Information, Chicago and London: University of Chicago Press).

POOLE, M. E., and FIELD, T. W. (1976), 'A comparison of oral and written code elaboration', *Language and Speech*, **19**: 305–11.

PRICE, G. (1971), *The French Language: Present and Past* (London: Edward Arnold).

PRINCE, E. (1978), 'A comparison of WH-clefts and IT-clefts in discourse', *Language*, **55**: 883–906.

—— (1981), 'Topicalization, focus-movement, and Yiddish-movement: A pragmatic differentiation', *Berkeley Linguistic Society*, **7**: 249–64.

QUIRK, R., and GREENBAUM, S. (1973), *A University Grammar of English* (London: Longman).

—— —— LEECH, G., and SVARTVIK, J. (1985), *A Comprehensive Grammar of the English Language* (London: Longman).

RADFORD, A. (1988), *Transformational Grammar: A First Course* (Cambridge: Cambridge University Press).

—— (1993), 'Head-hunting: On the trail of the nominal Janus', in Corbett *et al.* (1993*b*), 73–113.

RAUPACH, M. (1984), 'Formulae in second language speech production', in H. Dechert, D. Möhle, and M. Raupach (eds.), *Second Language Productions* (Tübingen: Gunter Narr), 114–37.

ROCA, IGGY M. (1990) (ed.), *Logical Issues in Language Acquisition* (Dordrecht: Foris).

ROMAINE, S. (1981), 'Syntactic complexity, relativisation and stylistic levels in Middle Scots', *Folia Linguistica Historica*, **2**: 56–77.

ROSEN, C., and ROSEN, H. (1973), *The Language of Primary School Children* (Harmondsworth: Penguin).

RYBAKOV, A. (1988), *Deti Arbata* (Taškent: Izdatel'stvo Literatury i Iskusstva Imeni Gafura Guljama).

SAMPSON, GEOFFREY (1980), *Making Sense* (Oxford: Oxford University Press).

SASSE, H. J. (1987), 'The thetic/categorical distinction revisited', *Linguistics*, **25**: 511–80.

SCHANK, G., and SCHOENTHAL, G. (1983), *Gesprochene Sprache* (Tübingen: Niemeyer).

SCHANK, R. C., and ABELSON, R. F. (1977), *Scripts, Plans, Goals and Understanding* (Hillsdale, NJ: Lawrence Erlbaum).

SCHECKER, M. (1993), 'Zur Reihenfolge pränominaler Adjektive im Rahmen einer kognitiv orientierten Grammatik', in Vuillaume *et al.* (1993), 105–29.

SCHIFFRIN, DEBORAH (1987), *Discourse Markers* (Cambridge: Cambridge University Press).

SCHLOBINSKI, P. (1988), 'Über die Funktion von nicht-eingebetteten *daß*-Sätzen im gesprächstherapeutischen Diskurs: Eine Pilotstudie', *Linguistische Berichte*, **113**: 32–52.

SCHMIDT, R. W. (1983), 'Interaction, acculturation and the acquisition of communicative competence: A case study of an adult', in N. Wolfson and E. Judd (eds.), *Sociolinguistics and Language Acquisition* (Rowley, Mass.: Newbury House).

SCHOURUP, L. C. (1985), *Common Discourse Particles in English Conversation* (New York: Garland Publishing).

SCHULZ, GISELA (1973), *Die Bottroper Protokolle: Parataxe und Hypotaxe* (Munich: Max Hueber).

SIMON, H. (1974), 'How big is a chunk?', *Science*, **183**: 482–8.

SIROTININA, O. B. (1974), *Sovremennaja razgovornaja reč' i ee osobennosti* (Moscow: Prosveščenie).

SNOW, C. E. (1981), 'The use of imitation', *Journal of Child Language*, **8**: 205–12.

SORNICOLA, R. (1981), *Sul Parlato* (Bologna: Il Mulino).

—— (1988), 'It-clefts and Wh-clefts: Two awkward sentence types', *Journal of Linguistics*, **24**: 343–79.

SRIVASTAV, V. (1991), 'The syntax and semantics of correlatives', *Natural Language and Linguistic Theory*, **9**: 637–86.

STEGER, H. (1967), 'Gesprochene Sprache: Zu ihrer Typik und Terminologie', in *Satz und Wort im heutigen Deutsch* (Düsseldorf: Sprache der Gegenwart Bd. 1), 259–91.

—— (1970), 'Über Dokumentation und Analyse gesprochener Sprache', in *Zielsprache Deutsch*, Heft **1**: 13–21 and Heft **2**: 51–63.

STREET, B. V. (1995), *Social Literacies* (London and New York: Longman).

STUBBS, MICHAEL (1980), *Language and Literacy: The Sociolinguistics of Reading and Writing* (London: Routledge & Kegan Paul).

SVARTVIK, JAN (1966), *On Voice in the English Verb* (The Hague: Mouton).

—— and QUIRK, RANDOLPH (1980) (eds.), *A Corpus of English Conversation* (Lund Studies in English, 56; Lund: Gleerup).

ŠVEDOVA, N. JU. (1983) (ed.), *Russkaja Grammatika* (Moscow: Nauka).

TANNEN, D. (1982), 'Oral and literate strategies in spoken and written language', *Language*, **58**: 1–21.

TARPLEE, C. (1989), 'Confirmation and repair: An interactional analysis of redoing sequences in child–adult talk', *York Papers in Linguistics*, **14**: 279–96.

TAYLOR, JOHN R. (1989), *Linguistic Categorization: Prototypes in Linguistic Theory* (Oxford: Clarendon Press).

Texte gesprochener deutscher Standardsprache i, ii, iii (1971, 1974, 1975), Erarbeitet im Institut für deutsche Sprache Freiburg i.Br. (München Heutiges Deutsch Reihe II).

THOMPSON, SANDRA A. (1988), 'A discourse approach to the cross-linguistic category "adjective"', in John A. Hawkins (ed.), *Explaining Linguistic Universals* (Oxford: Basil Blackwell), 167–85.

THUBRON, C. (1987), *Beyond the Great Wall* (London: Heinemann).
TOWELL, R. (1987), 'A Discussion of the Psycholinguistic Bases for Communicative Language Teaching in a Foreign Language Teaching Situation', *British Journal of Language Teaching*, **25**(2): 91–101.
TRUDGILL, P. (1983), *Sociolinguistics: An Introduction* (Harmondsworth: Penguin Books).
VACHEK, J. (1939), 'Zum Problem der geschriebenen Sprache', *Travaux de Cercle Linguistique de Prague*, **8**: 94–104.
VALLDUVÍ, ENRIC (1993), 'Information packaging: A survey', University of Edinburgh: Human Communication Research Centre, Research Paper HCRC/RP-44.
—— (1994), 'Catalan right-detachment and information packaging', *Journal of Pragmatics*, **22**: 573–601.
VAN DER AUWERA, J. (1985), 'Relative *that*—a centennial dispute', *Journal of Linguistics*, **21**: 149–79.
VAN LANCKER, D. (1975), 'Heterogeneity in language and speech: Neurological studies', *UCLA Working Papers in Phonetics*, No. 29.
—— CANTER, G. J., and TERBEEK, D. (1981), 'Disambiguation of ditropic sentences: Acoustic and phonetic cues', *Journal of Speech and Hearing Research*, **24**: 330–5.
VIHMAN, M. M. (1982), 'Formulas in first and second language acquisition', in L. Menn and L. Obler (eds.), *Exceptional Language and Linguistics* (New York: New York Academic Press), 261–84.
VOINOVIČ, V. N. (1976), *Ivan'kiada* (Ann Arbor: Ardis).
VUILLAUME, M., MARILLIER, J.-F., and BEHR, I. (1993) (eds.), *Studien zur Syntax und Semantik der Nominalgruppe* (Tübingen: Gunter Narr).
WACKERNAGEL-JOLLES, B. (1971), *Untersuchungen zur gesprochenen Sprache: Beobachtungen zur Verknüpfung spontanen Sprechens* (Göppingen: Alfred Kümmerle).
WADE, TERENCE (1992), *A Comprehensive Russian Grammar* (Oxford: Blackwell).
WAGNER-GOUGH, J. (1978), 'Excerpts from comparative studies in second language learning', in E. Hatch (ed.), *Second Language Acquisition: A Book of Readings* (Rowley, Mass.: Newbury House), 155–71.
WEBELHUTH, G. (1989), 'Syntactic Saturation Phenomena and the Modern Germanic Language', Ph.D. thesis (Amherst, Mass.: University of Massachusetts).
WEINERT, R. (1995*a*), 'The role of formulaic language in second language acquisition', *Applied Linguistics*, **16**(2): 180–205.
—— (1995*b*), 'Focusing constructions in spoken language: Clefts, Y-movement, thematization and deixis in English and German', *Linguistische Berichte*, **159**: 341–69.
—— and MILLER, JIM (1996), 'Clefts in spoken discourse', *Journal of Pragmatics*, **25**: 173–202.
WEISS, A. (1975), *Syntax spontaner Gespräche. Einfluß von Situation und Thema auf das Sprachverhalten* (Düsseldorf: Sprache der Gegenwart Bd. 31).
WIDDOWSON, H. (1990), *Aspects of Language Teaching* (Oxford: Oxford University Press).
WIESE, R. (1984), 'Language production in foreign and native languages: Same or different?', in H. Dechert, D. Möhle, and M. Raupach (eds.), *Second Language Production* (Tübingen: Gunter Narr), 11–25.

WILSON, Sir JAMES (1915), *Lowland Scotch as Spoken in the Lower Strathearn District of Perthshire* (London: Oxford University Press).
WONG FILLMORE, L. (1976), 'The Second Time Around: Cognitive and Social Strategies in Second Language Acquisition', Ph.D. thesis (Stanford University).
WOOD, M. (1981), *A definition of Idiom* (Manchester: Centre for Computational Linguistics).
WRAY, A. (1992), *The Focusing Hypothesis* (Amsterdam: John Benjamins).
WRIGHT, J. (1902), *The English Dialect Dictionary* (London: Henry Frowde).
WUNDERLICH, H. (1894), *Unsere Umgangssprache in der Eigenart ihrer Satzfügung* (Weimar: Berlin).
YORIO, C. (1980), 'Conventionalized forms and the development of communicative competence', *TESOL Quarterly*, **14(4)**: 433–42.
YOUNG, G. M. (1982), 'The elaborated code: A new formulation within a functional framework', *Language and Speech*, **25(1)**: 81–93.
ZEMSKAJA, E. A. (1973), *Russkaj razgovornaja reč'* (Moscow: Nauka).
—— and SMELEV, D. N. (1984), *Gorodskoe prostorečie* (Moscow: Nauka).
ZWICKY, A. (1985), 'Heads', *Journal of Linguistics*, **21**: 1–30.

Index

academic language 90–1, 136–7, 159, 163–4, 407
Académie Française 337
acceptability judgements 378, 405–6, 419
accusative and infinitive 85, 360, 383
acquisition *see* first language acquisition
  second language acquisition
action continuity 220, 223–4, 224–6
activation 272–3
adequacy:
  of data 10–14
  of expression in spoken language 423–5
Adjacency Principle, relaxed 182–3
adjectives:
  in categorial grammar 188–9
  complement clauses dependent on 93
  German 169, 170, 171
  independent adjective phrases 142–3
  pre- and post-posed 166–8, 176
  Russian 160, 161, 164: long, (deictic function) 134, 185, 186, 188, 189, (nominal nature) 176, 177–9, 180, 186, 188, 189, (in split NPs) 164, 165–6, 176, 179–80, 183–6; short 177
  see also under noun phrases
adverbial clauses 93, 94
  Australian languages' equivalent 117, 118–19
  combining relationships 31
  dependency relations 53
  in IT clefts 265, 302, 305
  late acquisition 383
  looser arrangement in spoken language 78
  order of main clause and 56–7, 100–4, 356–7
  Russian, not overtly linked to main clause 74, 98–9
  separation from main clause 103–4
  types confined to written language 73, 81–2
  see also following types of clause: concession; conditional; purpose; reason; time
adverbs 18
affect and Involved Production 19
afterthoughts 12, 166, 167, 168
agreement, syntactic, index, and pragmatic 185
ALL clefts 297
already-used phrases 150
amplitude 22

annex clauses 128, 129, 249–50
apodosis 84
apposition, and Russian adjective-noun combinations 188
Arabic 44
Arbroath smokies 124
Argumenty i Fakty (Russian journal) 43–4, 159, 227–8
articles:
  definite 187–8, 230, 231, 232–3
  indefinite 230
artificial intelligence 413, 420–1
as complementizer 348–9
as far as X (is concerned) 253
attachment, bi-directional 40
attention markers 16–17, 24–5
  deictics 174, 271
  WH clefts 293–4, 296, 298; reverse 271, 279, 280, 296
attentional structure 202–3, 229
Austen, Jane 42
Australian Aboriginal languages 2
  narratives 182
  non-integrated subordinate syntax 72, 117, 118–19
  NPs 75, 134; split 176, 180–2
  relative construction 117–20
  verb forms in sequences of clauses 341
automatic/controlled processes 391
automatic parsing systems 420–1

backgrounding 262
Bambara 343, 344
because clauses 56–7, 94
behaviour/system distinction 29–30
behaviourism 409, 384, 385
Bengali correlative structure 113–15, 125, 181, 343–4, 351, 353
Biber, D. 14, 15, 18–19, 20–1, 133–4
Bible translations 337, 362
binding conditions 379
Black Vernacular English 416, 417
Bloomfield, L. 4, 49–50
boundaries *see under* clauses; culture; ellipsis; pausing; Russian; sentences
boundary conditions, Chomskyan 379, 400
Bulgarian 197

case spreading 133, 179

Catalan 191, 196, 253
categorial grammar 188–9
CD Roms 417 n., 421
ceremonial language 3
Chafe, W. 5, 11, 17, 20
  on adverbial clauses 57, 356–7
  on focus 198, 200
  on short-term memory 79
  on units of spoken language 33–4, 37, 76, 204
Chancery language 337, 376
Chickasaw 366–9
child language acquisition *see* first language acquisition
Chinese, Mandarin 156, 343, 363, 364
Choctaw 366
Chomsky, Carol 396–7
Chomsky, Noam:
  first language acquisition theory 2, 373–5; critique of 5, 375–419
  Item and Arrangement approach 409–10
  and Skinner 384
  written language as basis of theories 4, 378, 403
chunks of language, learning of 381, 392–3, 411
  segmenting 414
  see also formulas
Cicero, M. Tullius 360
clausal focusing constructions 246–7
clause complexes 6, 12, 28, 31, 32–3
  degree of integration 73–4, 76
  and discourse rules 32, 57
  and sentences 33, 44–5
clauses 28–71, 72–132
  acquisition 31
  apparently subordinate, actually free-standing 76, 94–100
  as basic unit in spoken language 28, 30–1, 32
  boundaries 355–6; relations across 12, 43, 52–3, 54, 213, 215–16, (deixis) 43, (Russian null subject/object NPs) 62, 213, 215–16
  combining 23–5, 31–2, 33, 72, 78–9, 353–63
  complexity constraints 1, 22, 79–80
  constructions possible in main and subordinate 56
  cross-linguistic data 72, 73, 76, 77
  definition 76–7
  dependency relations 50–5, 77
  discourse rules and relationships between 32
  distribution 56–8, 73, 77, 100–4
  inserted 96
  juxtaposition 76, 78–9, 95–100, 336

  main and subordinate 56, 80–94; order 100–4
  non-finite 85–7, 91–4
  in non-spontaneous spoken language 16
  nucleus, core and periphery 77
  rhetorical relationships between 31
  Russian 62–3, 76, 95–100
  situation and 78–9
  in spontaneous dialogue 22, 46–9
  subordinate, developed from parataxis 336
  word order in main and subordinate 56, 76, 94–5, 113, 116
  in written language 17–18, 22, 28, 31, 353; types confined to 1, 72, 73, 75, 81–7, 91–4, 353
  see also individual types of clause and clause complexes
clefts 263–306
  activation function 272–3
  ALL 297
  cleft clause 264
  cleft constituent 264, 265–6, 271–3
  contrast 269–70, 274, 293, 300; IT clefts 264, 300, 301, 303, 306, 317
  deixis 195, 264, 267–8, 273, 305–6; IT clefts 264, 268, 306; reverse WH clefts 268, 271, 276–80, 306; WH clefts 125–7, 268, 306
  distribution 265–7
  French 248–9
  and fronting 281
  German 236, 247–8, 281; IT, analogues of 192, 248; reverse WH 280–7, 287–91, 298; WH 124–5, 247–8, 297–8
  given information 264
  headless relatives 120, 266–7, 268–9, 293–4
  highlighting 190, 196–7, 244–53, 265, 291–3, 297, 300–1
  LIKE as less powerful focuser 319, 321–5
  macro-functions 264
  maximality 264, 273–4
  and new information 264, 271–3, 297–8
  predicational function 273
  presupposition 264, 272
  pseudo-, French 248–9
  specificational function 264, 273, 304–5
  stress patterns 265, 284–5; IT clefts 300, 301; reverse WH clefts 269–70, 275–6; WH clefts 265, 292–3
  thematization 195, 264, 268–71, 273, 280, 291, 305–6
  in written language 196–7
  see also IT clefts; WH clefts; WH clefts, reverse
coasting 391–2
code-switching, written/spoken language 407
coherence relations 47

combinatorial grammar 188
combining relationships 31
commands 56
  conditionals used for 94, 101
comment clause complement 93
communicative goals 198
comparison, clauses of 93
competence 26, 353, 373, 400-3, 421
competition model 416
complement clauses 93, 94
  clause combining 16, 54, 78, 356-8
  contact 19, 93
  dependency relations 51-2, 54
  distribution 56, 57-8, 73
  embeddedness 31, 54
  German 37, 38-9
  Japanese 360, 370-1
  NPs 151, 153, 158
  position of complementizer 370-1
  Quechua 360
  reported speech 54-5
  written language 54, 73
complementizers 51-2, 53, 74-5, 111
  development from pronouns 110-11, 350
complexity 3
  constraints on 79-80, 380
  educational level and 92
  formality and 16, 81, 133
  German 37-8
  postponement of 141, 156-7, 161-2
  syntactic, and lexical density 18, 81
  written/spoken differential 1, 17-18, 31, 37-8, 81, 370, 380
  see also under noun phrases
compositionality 385-7
compound NPs 15-16, 146, 151-2, 153, 156, 160
  German 169, 170, 171
computers 388, 413, 417, 420-1, 426
concession, clauses of 16, 32, 73-4, 81-2, 93, 383
conditional constructions 53, 93
  command function 94, 101
  inferred 73-4
  interrogative protases 338
  order of clauses 100-2
  tense usage 338-40
  types absent from spoken language 84-5
  typology 338-40
Confederation of British Industry 422
configurational/non-configurational languages 134, 182-3
conjunctions:
  absence in unintegrated syntax 23
  which and *that* as general 110-11
constituent structure 3, 6, 23, 409
context 22, 23, 419

and acquisition 373, 375, 408-9, 411-13, 419
and determining head of NP 187
and highlighting 191
incomplete syntax comprehensible in 28, 119
situational ellipsis permitted by 226
continuity, action 220, 223-4, 224-6
contrast 193, 199, 200, 205-6
  fronting constructions 269-70
  see also under clefts; focus
controlled/automatic processes 391
conventionality 386
conversational data 7-8, 9, 10, 81
cookery books 231
coordination 17, 22
  instead of relative construction 107
  between Russian predicative constructions 228
  see also juxtaposition
copula
  clauses, preferred to complex NPs 142
  contractions in Involved Production 19
copula definite NP constructions, German 298
core, language 407-8
coreference 32, 410
correlative structures 16, 113-17
  Bengali 113-15, 125, 181, 343-4, 351, 353
  diptych 359, 362
  German 248
  Hindi 114, 353
  Russian 115-17, 351-3, 362
  Sanskrit 117
  Warlbiri 117
cosubordination 229, 358
creativity 375, 387, 388, 389, 394-5, 395-6, 403
cross-linguistic data 2, 6
  from languages with no written variety 76
  see also individual languages
culture
  language as artefact of 382
  influence on acceptability judgements 405
  sentence unstable across boundaries 42-5, 71
Czech linguistic scholarship 5

DA (German) 236-7, 281-4, 298
Danielewicz, J. 5, 33-4, 37, 204
DAS (German) 270 n., 285-6, 287-8
daß (German) 37, 38-9
data 6-14
  adequacy 10-14
  coding 9, 10, 12, 13-14, 143-5
  conversational 7-8, 9, 10, 81
  effect of different types 18

446 *Index*

data (*cont.*):
  English, German and Russian 7–10
  quality of analysis 11
  size of corpus 10–11, 14
  size of samples 10
  sound recordings 12
  syntactic analysis 13–14
  transcription 11, 12, 173
  see also Map Task Corpus
dating of syntactic developments 336–7
degeneracy, alleged:
  data 373, 374, 403, 416, 417, 419
  spoken language 383–4
deictics and deixis 22, 194
  attention markers 174, 271
  definite 125, 130, 194, 267
  definite article as reduced 187–8
  demonstrative 173–6, 236
  fronting 197, 281–4, 285–6
  German 125, 173–6, 236, 281–7, 298–300
  indefinite 43, 48, 267–8; Russian 49, 64–5, 67–71, 120, 126–7
  interaction with stress and fronting 284–5
  NPs with 134, 173–6, 187
  personal pronouns as 194, 267
  Pitjantjatjara 181
  Russian; contrastive 258–9; definite 130, 249–50; indefinite 49, 64–5, 67–71, 120, 126–7; long adjective suffixes 134, 178, 185, 186, 189; particle *vot* 178–9, 208–9, 254–5
  specific/non-specific, in correlatives 114, 116
  see also under clefts
Delin, J. L. 265, 272, 273
denotation 187
dependence, syntactic *vs* discourse 37–8, 39
dependency relations 44, 50–5, 77, 382
Dickens, Charles 110, 337, 350, 415
dictionary makers 376
digression 205, 206
Dik, S. C. 198, 200–2, 229
discoursal conjuncts 205–6
discourse links 109, 111
discourse model of coreference 410
discourse organization 1, 3, 262, 426
discourse relations between clauses 32, 57, 99, 100
Diyari 119, 182
do-it-yourself manuals 231
downgrading of clauses
  Lehmann's continuum 359
drama 218–20, 227
dummy words 168
Dyirbal 405

E-language 378

Early Immediate Constituents Hypothesis 369–71
editing, opportunities for 22
  see also planning time
education:
  effect on spoken language of formal 1–2, 2–3, 13, 19–20, 21, 81, 340, 402
  complexity of NPs 176
  non-restrictive relatives 107
  subordinate clauses 90, 92, 353
  WH clefts 125
  examination and testing system 421–2, 423
  factors in first language acquisition 406, 408
  implications of study for policy 421–5
  Russian speakers' not reflected in spoken syntax 21, 28
elision 212
ellipsis of given information 209–12, 212–29
  quasi- 210, 212, 217
  Russian 212–29
  null object NPs 215–18, 219, 221–2
  null subject NPs 212–15, 219, 220–1, 228–9
  situational, of subjects 226–8
  in spontaneous speech 220–3, 211–12
  situational 210–11, 212, 216, 217–18, 226–8
  standard 212, 217
  strict 210
  textual 217–18
  over turn boundaries 211–12, 221–2
  in written language 218–19
embeddedness 31, 54
employment 422–3
entities:
  deictics mark change of 259 n.
  highlighting of 197, 198, 202, 230, 231–3, 233–6, 238, 239
  see also situationally *and* textually evoked entities
error, performance 23, 28, 72
evincives 308–10
evocation *see* situationally *and* textually evoked entities
examination and testing system 421–2, 423
except clauses 93
exclusiveness component in clefts 273, 292
exhaustive listing 193
existential constructions 107, 197, 230–1, 233, 236–7
  possessive 230–1, 231, 233, 284, 326
expansion-reduction continuum 359–60
explanation, explicit
  focusing device 298
expository prose 231–2

Express, L' (French journal) 42–3
extendability of spoken language 380
eye contact 22, 89–90, 93, 94, 105, 106

facial expressions 22
fact with complement clauses 151
false starts 384
fearing, Greek and Latin verbs of 335–6
FEEL 19
Finnish 191
  NP-clause construction 242
  particles 27, 196, 253
  relative clauses 349 n.
first person verb forms 222–3
first language acquisition 4, 5, 19–20, 373–425, 426
  Chomskyan theory of 2, 373–5
    critique of 5, 375–419
  clauses 31
  competence varies 373, 400–3, 421
  contextual information 373, 375, 408–9, 411–13, 419
  and core 407–8
  creativity 375, 388, 394–5, 403
  degeneracy of data denied 373, 374, 403, 416, 417, 419
  feedback 381, 417, 421
  formulas and chunks of language 375, 381, 384–94, 403, 411, 414
  French 403
  idioms 385–7
  imitation 388
  inappropriate application of adult data 383, 410–11
  instruction 374, 418
  late childhood 307–8, 319–20, 328, 329, 382–3, 396
  magnasyntax and 381–3, 400, 420
  mechanisms 406–19
  memorisation 384, 393–4
  non-verbal communication 408–9, 419
  over-generalization of strong verb forms 412
  parents' influence through input 393–4
  and pragmatics 412–13
  repetition 382, 384
  restricted contexts 375, 410–11
  spoken language 4, 5, 19–20, 373, 406–16
  time taken 396–400
  vocabulary 376, 414–16
  WH relative clauses 383, 401–2
  of written language 4, 5, 20, 373, 381, 406–7, 416–19, 421, 425
    sentence structures 31, 41
    support at home and 417, 421, 422, 423
fixed phrases 147, 258–9
  acquisition 381, 397, 411

see also formulas
Flashner, V. 220, 223, 224–6
fluency 387
focus 190–262
  and attentional structure 229
  and communicative goals 203–4, 207–8
  contrastive 199, 200, 202, 229, 315, 316, 334
  cumulative 199, 202, 229
  definition 193
  extended notion of, Dik's 200–2, 229
  given information defocused 202, 209–29, 315, 316–17, 334
  information-handling model 202, 229
  introducing/non-introducing 315, 316–17, 334
  macro- and micro- 198, 203–9, 253–5
  new information 197, 198, 229, 230–1, 232–4, 242–59, 315
  non-contrastive 193, 315–17, 317–28
  and referential status 203–4, 229
  scholarship on 198–203
  and transitions 198
  see also highlighting
    salience
    theme
focus spaces 203, 204, 230, 254
foot 79
foregrounding 262
form-usage link 387
formality 2, 3, 15–17, 18, 81, 133
  and relative clauses 346, 351
formulas:
  and computational linguistics 388
  and creativity 389
  and first language acquisition 375, 381, 384–94, 403, 411, 414
  and fluency 387
  genesis 390–1
  and highlighting 197, 243–4, 253, 258–9
  and oral composition 392 n.
  storage 387
fragmented syntax *see under* syntax
Freiburg corpus 5–6, 37
French 2
  acquisition 392, 403
  clefts 248–9
  en construction 403
  highlighting 248–9, 250–1, 253
  index agreement 185
  intonation 24
  lequel 392
  linguistic scholarship 5
  negation 342
  NP-clause construction 242, 366
  Old 45
  pronoun agreeing with implicit noun 185

448 Index

French (*cont.*):
  relative clauses 111–13
  sentences 42–3, 45
  written language 42–3, 45, 337, 342
fronting 197, 269–70, 394
  German 280–7, 290–1, 298
  see also theme
Fruchtbringende Gesellschaft 337
functional properties 3

gapping 44, 82, 345–6, 360, 383
gender-related competence differences 402
generalization of forms, children's 412
generative grammar 2, 377, 378–81, 384
genres 2, 14–22
  written 135, 218–20, 231–2, 256–9
  and NP complexity 136–7, 138, 163–4
Geographical Magazine 90–1
German 2
  Chancery language 337
  complexity 37–8
  copula definite NP constructions 298
  corpus 10
  correlative construction 248
  deictics 125, 173–6, 236, 281–7, 298–300
  existential constructions 236–7
  focus and highlighting 236–7, 247–8, 298–300
    particles 196, 197, 236, 253, 326–8, 334
  fronting 280–7, 290–1, 298
  index agreement 185–6 n.
  linguistic scholarship 5–6
  nominalization 298–300
  NPs 76, 134, 140, 169–76, 184
  NP-clause construction 236, 239–41
  participles 172 n.
  particles 196, 197, 236, 253, 297–8
  questions 37
  relative constructions 113, 248
  sentences 35–9
  signalling of relationships between clauses 23–4
  thematization 270 n.
  word order 113, 281
  written language 37–8, 172 n., 337
  see also under clefts
gerunds 72, 141, 216, 354, 382 n.
  typology 73, 86, 340–1
gesture 22, 25, 226, 408–9
  highlighting 191, 251, 255, 267
GET passives 13, 88–9, 336–7
given information 195–6, 315
  in clefts 264
  defocusing 202, 209–29, 315, 316–17, 334
  fronting 197, 284–5
  German 284–5
  Russian 241, 242, 258

  see also ellipsis of given information
Givón, T. 88, 125, 128, 281, 317, 391
Glasgow 8
goals, communicative 203–4, 207–8
Government and Binding Theory 85, 183–4
grammar:
  normative 376–7, 376
  and psycholinguistic component 27
  uniformity of adult 373, 400
grammaticality judgements 377–8, 380, 403–6, 419
Greco-Latinate vocabulary 376, 383, 407
Greek:
  Classical 51–2, 53, 197, 335
  New Testament 362
Grosz, B. J. and Sidner, C. L. 198, 202–3, 229, 254
GUESS 19

habitual actions 215
Halliday, M. A. K. 18, 79, 81, 195
  on clauses and clause complexes 28, 31, 32, 77
  on focus 198–200, 230
hanging topic 239–40
Hawkins, J. A. 369–71
HCRC Map Task Corpus 8
heads 23, 134, 164, 176, 177, 186–9
Heath, J. 27, 353–6
Heinze, H. 36–7, 37–8, 39
Herbert, James 90, 91
Herriot, James 137, 145
highlighting 190, 193, 229–59
  clausal focusing constructions 246–7
  clefts 122, 190, 196–7, 244–53, 265, 291–3, 297, 300–1
  contrastive 197–8, 249–50, 255–6, 258–9
  deictics and 174, 175, 197, 249–50, 255, 258–9, 298–300
  devices 229–59
  of entities 197, 198, 202, 230, 231–3, 233–6, 238, 239
  existential constructions 230–1
  Finnish 253
  focus spaces and 230
  formulaic phrases 197, 243–4, 253, 258–9
  French 248–9, 250–1, 253
  by fronting 197, 269–70, 284–5, 394
  German 174, 175, 236–7, 247–8, 253, 298–300
  by gesture 191, 251, 255, 267
  Hungarian 253
  intonation 190, 191, 198, 200, 232, 243, 249
  KNOW 234, 253
  LIKE 246, 253, 265, 306–34
  new information 197, 198, 229, 230–1, 232–4, 242–59, 315

NP-clause construction 237–42
particles 190, 195, 196, 197, 200, 251–2, 253–5
propositions 197, 242–59
questions 16–17, 100, 197, 250–1
relatives 131, 248, 252
repetition 252
Russian; contrastive 197–8, 249–50, 255–9; contextual 191; particles 197–8, 251–2, 253, 254–5; propositions 249–52; split NPs 168–9; word order 190–1, 197–8, 253, 255–61
SEE 233–6, 252–3, 253–4, 265
the thing is 243–4, 252
transitions 254
word order 190–1, 195, 197–8, 200, 253, 255–61, 371–2
written language 190, 196, 197, 231–2, 256–61
see also theme and thematization
Hindi correlative structures 114, 344, 353
historical linguistics 335–7, 347
Hittite 362
holistic processes 391
Homeric formulae 392 n.
Horrocks, G. 383, 410–13
How Things Work 232
Hudson, R. A. 186–7, 424–5
Hungarian 191, 196, 197, 242, 253
hypotaxis *see* subordination

I-language 378
idioms 385–7, 392–3
illiteracy 402 n.
Ilocano 364
imperatives 56
  conditionals used as 94, 101
impersonal constructions, Russian 140
incidentally 205, 206
Independent, The (newspaper) 90–1, 153–9
independent communicative function 36
index agreement 185
indirect speech *see* reported speech
Indo-European languages 2, 364
  classic relatives 113, 115, 345, 351, 353
inference in interpretation of unintegrated syntax 28, 58–9, 60–1, 73–4
infinitives 72, 87, 354
  extending 65
  German 241
  indefinite deictic 65–6, 70
  in NP-clause constructions 241
  in NPs 141
  and relatives 64–6, 107–8, 349–50
  Russian 65–6, 66–7, 70
information:
  juxtaposed blocks of 60, 61

packaging constructions 27
spread across syntactic constituents 22, 46, 235–6, 238, 239, 243, 246
structures 87, 166–7, 191, 276
units, Halliday's theory of 79
see also context
informational and involved production 19, 133–4
information-handling capabilities 394
information-handling model of focus 202, 229
informativeness, principle of 272 n.
inserted material 59–60, 96
instantiation 272 n.
institutionalized actions 215
instruction, language 374, 418
instruction/direction constructions, German 284
intelligence, grammars as independent of 373, 400
intentional and attentional structure 202–3
interlacing of clauses 360
International Corpus of English 12
interrogatives:
  conditional clause protases 338
  WH words as indefinite deictics in Russian 126
  see also questions
intonation 23–4, 25
  clefts 121, 122–3, 265, 266, 275–6, 292–3, 294
  and conditional clauses 101
  and focus 200
  French 24
  highlighting 190, 191, 198, 200, 232, 243, 249
  and insertions 96
  juxtaposed clauses 99–100
  narrative 35, 78
  non-restrictive relative clauses 54
  Russian 34–5, 166–7, 191
  and sentence boundaries 34–5, 36, 47
  split NPs 166–7
  units, prototypical 34, 79
  see also pausing; pitch; rhythm
involved and informational production 19, 133–4
Irving, John 42
IT clefts 125, 128–30, 300–5
  adverbial clauses 265, 302, 305
  annex clauses 128, 129
  cleft constituents 265
  cleft head with no WH clause 267
  and contrast 264, 300, 301, 303, 306, 317
  deixis, neutral direction 264, 268, 306
  described 263
  French analogues 248–9

IT clefts (*cont.*):
  frequency 197, 265, 266
  full and reduced 130, 302
  German analogues of 192, 248
  highlighting 196–7, 248–9, 265, 300–1
  information content 264, 300, 301–2, 303–4
  in narrative 149
  participial phrases in 265, 302, 305
  predicational element 304–5
  specificational function 264, 304–5
  stress patterns 300, 301
  subject focus 264, 301, 306
  THAT replacing IT 130, 267, 271, 303
  thematization 306
  WH forms omitted 128, 129–30
  written language 196–7, 305
Italian 5, 26, 28, 58–9, 196
Item and Arrangement approach 409–10

Japanese 117, 363, 364
  complement construction 360, 370–1
jargon 391
Johnson, Samuel 337
judgements *see under* acceptability
  grammaticality
juxtaposition 60, 61, 95–100, 360–2
  negative/positive contrast 255–6
  preferred to subordination 76, 78–9, 95–100, 336
  relativization by 181, 348

Keenan-Comrie hierarchy 104, 109, 111, 112
KNOW 234, 253
knowledge, world 28
knowledge bases 203
Korean 364
Kuniyanti 118–19

Labov, William 383–4, 416, 424
Lahu 364
Lapteva, O. A. 5, 9, 166–9, 176
Latin, Classical 43, 44–5, 335–6, 337, 359, 360–1
left-dislocation 237–42, 357–8
Lehmann, C. 76–7, 358–63
lequel 392
LET ALONE 393
letters to newspapers, readers' 153–9
Levy, J. 198, 203–4
'lexical phrases' 385
lexicon:
  acquisition 414–16
  changing meaning and syntax 415–16
  density 18, 81
  in generative models 384
  Greco-Latinate 376, 383, 407
  spoken/written differences 5, 18, 23, 81

  see also vocabulary
LIKE 7, 306–34, 426
  acquisition, late childhood 307–8, 319–20, 328, 329
  clause-final 307, 331–3, 334
  clause-initial 330–1, 334
  clefts give stronger focus 319, 321–5
  constituent-following and -preceding 328, 334
  conversational use 307, 328–33
  discourse functions 307, 312–13, 318, 319, 320, 326, 330–1, 334
  distribution 308, 320–1, 328–30
  flexibility 319, 320–1
  as focus device 246, 253, 265, 315–17, 319, 321–5
  as hedge 308, 328
  Map Task data 307, 310–28 *passim*, 333
  pause filler interpretation refuted 312–15
  previous accounts 307–12
  with questions 309, 311, 318, 320, 332–3
  Schourup's account of 308–12
  UND ZWAR as parallel 326–8, 334
  in written language 307
literacy, standards of 400–3, 422–3
literate and oral societies 3
Lively, Penelope 90, 91
locative constructions 284
Lolo-Burmese (Lahu) 364
London-Lund Corpus 10, 11, 13, 19
Lothian 7–8
Lowth, Bishop Robert 337
Luther, Martin 337
Lyons, Sir John 4, 385

Macaulay, R. K. S. 8–9, 11, 89, 92
Macdonald, L. 356–8
macro-focus and micro-focus 198, 203–9, 253–5
magnasyntax 376–83, 400, 420
magnavocabulary 376
Malherbe, François de 337
Map Task Corpus 8, 10, 13–14, 19, 81, 191–2
markedness 199 n.
Matthews, P. 49–50
maximality 264, 273–4
memorisation in acquisition 384, 393
memory, short-term 22, 27, 79, 131–2, 388, 394
methodology 38, 191–2
  see also data
Middle English 347
modality/register confusion 18, 80
mood 51, 52, 53
mother node construction 370
multimedia systems 417 n., 421
Munro, P. and Gordon, L. 366–9

Murray, Lindley 337

names, proper 147, 152, 397
narrative 18, 81
  Australian languages 182
  intonation 35, 78
  NPs 142–3, 145–52; Russian null 218–20, 222–3, 225–6
  relative clauses 146, 147, 149–51
  in spontaneous conversation 29
  structure 18, 29, 35, 78
negation 341–2
negative and positive clauses juxtaposed 255–6
negative evidence in acquisition 381, 417, 421
neurological information 388–9, 394
  see also memory, short-term psycholinguistics
new information, highlighting of 229, 230–1
  in clefts 264, 271–3, 297–8
  definitions 193, 196, 199, 200
  entities 197, 198, 202, 238, 239, 315
  in Map Task dialogues 232–4
  pragmatically-controlled word order hypothesis 371–2
  propositions 197, 202, 242–59
  by see 371
  Russian contrastive 258
  written language 202
newspapers 159, 172 n., 227–8, 386–7
  NPs 136–7, 138, 153–9, 161–3
Ngandi 353–6
Ngiyambaa 182
Niger-Congo languages 364
nominalization 241, 298–300
non-finite clauses 91–4, 340–1
non-spontaneous spoken language 16–17
non-standard language 17, 341–2, 344, 377
non-verbal communication 25, 408–9, 419
  see also gesture
noun phrases 133–89
  adjectives in
  and formality 133, 139–40, 153
  German 169, 170, 171
  grammatical function 141, 146–7, 156–7
  more than one in phrase 139–40, 171
  Russian 156–7, 160, 161, 164
  written/spoken use 133, 139–40, 153, 154, 156–7, 161, 164, 169, 170, 171
  Australian languages 134
  -clause construction 236, 237–42, 364–6, 397
  complement clauses modified by 151, 153, 158
  complexity 133, 135–43, 163–4
  avoidance 142, 161, 238, (in subject NPs) 138, 141, 150

postponement to end of clause 141, 156–7, 161–2
  in written language 76, 135–9, 141, 142, 158–9, 161, 162–4, 169, 170, 172–3, 176
compound 15–16, 146, 151–2, 153, 156, 160, 169, 170, 171
and configurationality 134
deictics 134, 173–6, 187
demonstratives as sole constituents in Russian 179
determiners 146, 153, 154, 160, 177
German 134, 169–76, 184, 284–5
gerunds 141
heads 23, 134, 164, 176, 177, 186–9
independent 142–3, 149–50
infinitives 141
in narrative 142–3, 145–52
  Russian null 218–20, 222–3, 225–6
in newspapers 153–9, 161–3
nouns in 62–3, 133, 146, 154
number allowed in given clause 366–9
number of words 139–40
numerals as sole constituents 179
participial phrases 140, 142, 146, 151, 153, 158, 160, 161, 162
personal pronouns 140, 146, 160, 187
prepositional phrases: in spoken language 142, 153, 160–1, 169, 171–2, 173–6, (narrative) 146, 147, 148
  in written language 154–6, 161, 164, 170, 171–2
quantifiers as sole constituents 179, 187
relative clauses 74–5, 140, 142, 146, 147, 149–51, 153, 157–8, 160, 181, 343–4
  Russian 76, 133, 134, 141, 159–69
  academic language 163–4
NP-clause construction 237, 241–2, 364–6
null subject/object 215–18, 219, 220–1, 225–6, 228–9
split 160, 161, 164–9, 176, 177–80, 182–3, 184–5, 186
single-constituent 140–1, 146, 153, 169, 170, 171, 176, 179, 187
split 164–9, 176–82, 183–6
  adjectives in 164, 165–6, 176, 179–80, 183–6, (pre- and post-posing) 166, 167, 168, 176
  afterthought interpretation 166, 167, 168
  Australian languages 176, 180–2
  constituent structure 176–82
  and formal models 134, 182–9
  headship issues 176, 186–9
  highlighting 168–9
  numerals 164, 166–9
  possessive nouns 164, 166–9
  Russian 160, 161, 164–9, 176, 177–80, 182–3, 184–5, 186

452   Index

noun phrases (*cont.*):
  and Scrambling 134, 183–6, 188
  in spontaneous speech
    data 143–59
    general properties 133, 139–43, 160–1
    structure 134, 140
    subject 62, 138, 141, 147, 156–7, 161–2
    typology 366–9
    written data 153–9, 161–4
    zero 23, 62, 120, 171
novel instantiation criterion 272 n.
novels 90–1, 218–20
NPs *see* noun phrases
nucleus with satellite structure 32
numerals:
  acceptability judgements on 405–6
  LIKE before 309, 310–11
  sole-constituent Russian NPs 179
  in split NPs 164, 166–9
Nunberg, G., Sag, I. A., and Wasow, T. 385–7

objects, direct and oblique 137–9
OED *see* Oxford English Dictionary
Ong, W. 376
online processing of language 426
oral composition 392 n.
oratio obliqua 15

Papua New Guinea 341, 356–8
parasyntactic phenomena 39–40
parataxis in spoken language 22, 49, 336, 414
  see also juxtaposition
parsing 87
  automatic 420–1
participial clauses 86–7, 91
participial phrases:
  discourse-dependence 48
  free, confined to written language 73
  in IT clefts 265, 302, 305
  non-restrictive 158
  in NPs 140, 142, 146, 151, 153, 158, 160, 161, 162
  past passive 121, 158
  as reduction of relative clauses 158
participles 121, 172 n., 340–1
particles:
  German 196, 197, 236, 253, 297–8
  highlighting 190, 195, 196, 197, 200, 251–2, 253–5
  management of dialogue by 253
  Russian 197–8, 251–2, 253, 254–5
  show relationships between clauses 23–4, 27
passives 13, 88–9, 109, 336–7
pausing:
  and left-dislocation 240

  LIKE not a pause filler 313–15
  and syntactic boundaries 47, 54, 78, 80
  and transitions 204
  WH clefts 121, 122–3
Pawley, A. and Syder, F. 385, 387, 392, 393
Pepys, Samuel 41–2
perception, participants 316
performance:
  /competence distinction 26, 403
  error 23, 28, 72
Persian 345, 346–7, 351, 353
persuasion strategies 24–5
phrase-books, foreign-language 388
phrases 1, 22, 28
  already-used 150
  fixed 147, 258–9, 381, 397, 411
  in spontaneous speech 22, 23, 80
  succession of juxtaposed 60, 71
  without nouns, Russian 62–3
  see also individual types of phrase
Pinker, S. 381–3, 394, 396, 420
pitch 22, 30–1
  highlighting 190, 198, 200, 232, 243, 249
  phonemes 49
  and transitions 83, 204
  WH clefts 121, 122–3, 292–3
Pitjantjatjara 180–2
planning problems 168
planning time 2, 18, 22, 47, 419
  and complexity 71, 81, 109
  Involved vs. Informational Production 19
Plato's problem 373
Plautus 360–1
please, distribution of 49
Poole, M. E. and Field, T. W. 17–18, 20
positivism 409
possessive nouns 164, 166–9
post-rheme elements 25
pragmatics 77, 390, 410, 412–13
Prague School 4, 195, 371
predicational function of clefts 273, 304–5
predicative constructions 96–8
prefabrication 388
prepositional phrases:
  with deictics 173–6
  German 169, 170, 171–2, 173–6, 241
  in NP-clause constructions 241
  in NPs: in spoken language 142, 153, 160–1, 169, 171–2, 173–6, (narrative) 146, 147, 148; in written language 154–6, 161, 164, 170, 171–2
  Russian 160–1, 164
prepositions:
  complex 156
  empty prepositonal nodes 23–5, 179–80
  and relative clauses 16; omission 106–7, 108

spreading 179–80
  in split NPs 164, 165, 179–80
present tense in Involved Production 19
presupposition 264, 272, 292
Principles and Parameters model 183–4, 376, 418–19
processing 14, 369–71, 419–21
  controlled/automatic 391
  difficulties 79, 156–7, 168, 387, 394
product/process distinction 14
proficiency 340
  see also competence
progressives, WH clefts with 120, 121
prominence *see* focus
  highlighting
  theme
pronouns 23
  complementizers developed from 110–11, 350
  demonstrative 113, 239
  German 239; fronting 284–5
  indefinite 49, 125–7
  interrogative 49
  personal 19, 140, 146, 160, 187, 197; deictic use 194, 267
  reflexive 411
  relative 43, 49; Russian 49, 97, (condensed) 64–71, 127 n., 131
  shadow, in relative clauses 104, 106, 109, 111–13, 346–7, 351, 420
  see also individual instances
proper names 147, 152, 397
properties, linguistic 15, 22–3
propositions 197, 202, 242–59
  see also relative clauses (propositional)
protasis 84
psycholinguistics 2, 22, 27, 390, 426
  see also memory; processing (difficulties)
Punch 110, 337, 350
purpose, expression of 65, 93
Pushkin, Alexander Sergevich 340

quantifiers 179, 187, 342
Quechua 360, 362
questions:
  dependence 37
  highlighting devices 16–17, 100, 197, 250–1
  indirect 82–4
  with LIKE 309, 311, 318, 320, 322–3
  tag 49, 56
Quirk, R., Leech, G., and Svartvik, J. 33, 120–1, 128, 209–11, 212, 237
Quran 44

radio talks 16–17
reason, clauses of 56–7, 81–2, 93, 94, 98–9, 103–4

recordings, sound 12
reduction 78–9, 209, 314
  /expansion continuum, Lehmann's 359–60
  in WH clefts 74, 122, 291, 294
referential status, focus and 203–4, 229
referring expressions 23, 187–8
register 18, 80
relative clauses:
  adjective phrases as reduced 156
  as complementizer 348–9
  Australian languages 117–20, 181
  classic Indo-European 113, 115, 345, 351, 353
  complementizer omitted 74–5
  complex 151, 157–8
  conjoined main clauses interpreted as 118–20
  contact 105, 128, 142, 150, 153, 157
  coordinate clauses replacing non-restrictive 107
  cross-clause dependency relations 52–3, 54
  cross-linguistic data 111–20
  deictics, indefinite 120, 126
  discourse linkage 109, 111
  distribution 56
  embedding and combining relationships 31, 54
  event 106
  existential constructions omitting *that* 107
  eye contact and types used 105, 106
  Finnish 349 n.
  formality and variation in 346, 351
  free 245, 248, 252
  French 111–13
  gapping 345–6
  German 113, 248
  headless 62–3, 64, 68, 105, 241, 347–8; in clefts 120, 266–7, 268–9, 293–4; Russian 126, 130–2
  historical development 347
  Indo-European 113, 115, 345, 351, 353
  infinitival 64–6, 107–8, 349–50
  juxtaposed main clauses as 181, 348
  and Keenan-Comrie hierarchy 109, 111, 112
  loosely or un-integrated 74–5, 78, 108–11, 113, 348
  Middle English 347
  in narrative 146, 147, 149–51
  in non-spontaneous spoken language 16
  non-restrictive 40, 48, 54, 105–6, 106–7, 150–1, 349
  NPs 74–5, 140, 142, 146, 147, 149–51, 153, 157–8, 160, 181, 343–4
  order of head and 343–4
  participial phrases as reduction of 158
  passives in 109

454 *Index*

relative clauses (*cont.*):
  Persian 346–7, 351, 353
  planning time 109
  prepositions 16; omission 106–7, 108
  pronouns; demonstrative 113; shadow 104, 106, 109, 111–13, 346–7, 351, 420
  propositional 105, 106, 110–11, 153
  range 346–51
  reflection of head noun in 344–6
  restrictive 48–9, 105–6, 106–7
  Russian 52–3, 113–14, 119–20, 126, 130–2, 160, 351; correlative structure 115–17, 351–3; headless 126, 130–2; possible different system 97–8; written language 115–16, 345, 351
  Semitic languages 346, 351, 353
  subordinate construction, generalized 117, 118–19
  Tamil 346
  THAT 105, 106, 107, 150, 153, 346, 353; with shadow pronoun 104, 106, 109, 111–13, 346–7, 351
  types 105–6
  and typology 342–53
  unintegrated 74–5, 78, 108–11, 113, 348
  WH 48–9, 105–20, 150, 153, 157; acquisition 383, 401–2; infinitival 107, 108; preposition + WH 16; *what* 349; *when* 106; *where* 105, 106, 150; *which* 110–11, 150–1, 153, 157, 350; *who* 153, 157
  word order 113
  written language 76, 130; classic construction 115–16, 153 n., 346, 351, 353; informal, THAT type 346, 351, 353; restrictive/non-restrictive punctuation 105–6; Russian 115–16, 345, 351; types exclusive to 73, 106, 107, 108
  see also correlative structures
repetition 24–5, 252
  in acquisition 382, 384, 385
reported speech 82–4
  complement clauses 54–5
  direct reporting of speaker's words 15, 54–5, 83
  oratio obliqua 15, 82
result clauses 93
reverse WH clefts *see* WH clefts, reverse
rhetorical relations model 12, 31, 47, 73–4
rhythm 22
  and conditional clauses 101
  clauses run together in single breath 354, 355
  insertions 96
  LIKE 313–15
  WH clefts 121, 122–3, 292–3, 294
Romance languages, early 45
rote processes 388–9

Royal Society 45
rule processes 388–9
Russian 2
  academic language 159, 163–4
  case spreading 133
  compound nouns 160
  configurational and non-configurational 134, 182–3
  corpus 9
  cross-boundary relations 50–1, 52–3, 55, 62, 213, 215–16, 221–2
  drama 218–20, 227
  gapping construction 44
  impersonal constructions 140
  infinitive constructions 64–6, 66–7
  information structure 166–7, 191
  intonation 34–5, 166–7
  juxtaposed clauses 96–100
  macro- and micro-focus 206–9
  mood in subordinate clauses 51
  newspapers 43–4, 159, 227–8
  nouns omitted 62–3
  participles 340
  predicative constructions 96–8
  processing difficulties 168
  pronouns: personal 140, 160; *see also* pronouns (relative)
  reason, clauses of 98–9
  topic- and subject-prominence 364–5
  unintegrated syntax 28, 61–71, 75, 76
  written language 21, 212, 256–9, 259–61
  zero anaphors 97, 98
  zero noun phrases 23, 120, 140
  see also under adjectives; adverbial clauses; correlative structures; education; ellipsis; narrative; noun phrases; particles; prepositional phrases; pronouns; relative clauses; sentences; word order

salience 122, 193, 195, 262
  and goals/sub-goals 203–4
  see also focus; highlighting
Sami 24–5
Sanskrit correlative structures 117
Saturation Constraint 184
scholarship, present state of 4–6
Schourup, L.C. 308–12
Scottish English 7–8, 19, 150
Scrambling 134, 183–6, 188
second language acquisition 385, 388, 401
SEE 233–6, 252–3, 253–4, 265, 317, 371
segmentation criteria 37, 38, 39
Semitic languages 346, 351, 353, 364, 420
sentences 6, 28–71
  acquisition 31, 41
  Bloomfield's definition 49–50
  boundaries 37–40; difficulty of determining

in speech 12, 30, 32, 33, 40; intonational criteria 34–5, 36, 47; relations across 12, 31–2, 43, 44, 50, 55, 62, 213, 216
changing concept 41–5, 71
clause complex as basis of 33, 44–5
cultural variation in concept 41–5, 71
dependency relations 50–5
discourse rules on relationships between 32 and distribution 56–8
French 42–3, 45
intuitions about, in spoken language 35–41
Latin period 44–5
length 382
in planned spoken language 71
relative clauses as separate 43
Russian 43–4, 62, 213, 216
spontaneous speech data 29–32, 46–9
and syntactic analysis 49–55
text-sentences in spoken language 34–45
Turkish 44
as unit of linguistic analysis 32–4, 46–71; inappropriate for speech 22, 46–9, 50, 358, 426; written language 28, 31, 32, 41–5, 71
verbless sequences functioning as 44
in written language 28, 31, 32, 41–5, 50, 71
Serbo-Croat 192, 197
Shaw, George Bernard 382
Sirotinina, O. B. 9, 133, 340
situationally evoked entities 213–14, 219, 225–6, 229, 315, 316–17
Slav languages
  double negation 341
SO (German deictic) 286–7, 298
sociolinguistics 2, 17
Sornicola, R. 5, 26, 28, 58–9, 60, 71, 128–9
specificational function of clefts 264, 273, 304–5
spoken language *see aspects throughout index*
sports commentators 392
stammering 384
standard, language 337, 339
stress *see under* clefts
strings becoming formulas 390–1
subjacency 379, 381, 404
subject-and topic-prominence 363–6
subjective/objective status of entities 316
subordination:
  Australian generalized construction, relativizing 117, 118–19
  co-subordination 358
  juxtaposition preferred in speech 76, 78–9, 95–100, 336
  origin in parataxis 336
  Turkish non-finite verbs 340–1
substitutability 37
Survey of English Usage 20–1

Svartvik, J. 88
  see also Quirk, R.
syntactic/parasyntactic phenomena 39–40
syntagmatic interweaving (Lehmann) 360–2
syntax 3, 5
  complexity, and lexical density 18, 81
  condensed, in written language 156, 158
  fragmented 17, 22, 23, 25–7, 28, 58–71, 78–9, 354, 356; inference needed to understand 28, 58–9, 60–1, 73–4; Russian 28, 61–71
  reduced, and focus 201
  theoretical 4, 5
  see also individual aspects
system, language 29–30

Tagalog 364
Tag Questions 49, 56
tail, ground and 202
Tamil 346, 362
Tauya 356–8
telephone conversations 169, 171
text types, examples of 15–17
text units 30
textually evoked entities 213–14, 226, 315, 316–17
TH complement clauses 93
THAT:
  definite deictic 194; in IT-type clefts 130, 267, 271, 303; reverse WH clefts 264, 266, 267, 271, 274, 277–80; WH clefts 271
  deletion 18–19
  non-anaphorical, metaphorical uses 194
  pronoun to complementizer development 110–11, 350
  spatial and anaphoric uses 194
  see also under relative clauses
theme and thematization:
  in clefts 195, 264, 268–71, 273, 280, 291, 305–6
  continuing 223
thetic clauses 77
(the) thing is 197, 243–4, 252
THINK 19
THIS 194, 230–1, 264, 266, 267, 274, 276–7
time, clauses of 56, 92, 93, 102–3
tone groups 33, 79–80, 198–9
tone unit 33
tonic and pretonic segments 198–9, 200–1
tonic syllable 79, 80
topic introduction 273, 293–4, 306, 326
topic movement 40
topic-prominence 363–6
topicality 193, 223
transcription 11, 12, 173
transitions 198, 203–4, 205–6, 254

456 Index

transitive/intransitive clauses 141, 156
Trollope, Anthony 348
Trudgill, P. 348, 349, 423–5
Turkish 44, 117, 340–1
turns, conversational 33, 54, 78, 211–12, 221–2
types of construction, written/spoken language 1, 3, 31
typology of spoken language 2, 338–72
  clause combining 353–63
  conditional constructions 338–40
  gerunds 340–1
  negation 341–2
  NPs 366–9
  participles 340–1
  relative clauses 342–53
  subject-and topic-prominence 363–6
  word order 369–72

UND ZWAR (German) 236, 326–8, 334
unification constraints 185
United States written standard English 339
Universal Grammar 374, 410
usage and forms
  link 387
utterance 33

Vallduví, E. 198, 202, 229, 230
variation, personal 19, 20, 340, 353, 400–3
Vaugelas, Claude Favre de 337
verb chaining 341
verbless sequences functioning as sentences 44
verbs:
  causative movement 414
  children generalize strong forms 412
  complementizer selection 51–2, 53
  with implicit object 215
  mood selection 51, 52, 53
  present tense in Involved Production 19
vocabulary
  Greco-Latinate 376, 383, 407
  size of individuals' 424–5
  see also lexicon
vocatives, Russian indefinite deictics as 70
voice quality 15, 22, 83
  see also intonation
  pitch
vot (Russian particle) 197, 208–9, 251–2, 254–5

Warlbiri 117, 359
wellformedness conditions 184
Welsh 342
WH clefts 26–7, 40–1, 120–30, 263, 291–8, 426
  attention marker 293–4, 296, 298
  classic and apparently so 265, 291, 292–3
  cleft clause: salient 122, 291; standing alone 123–5
  cleft constituents 265–6
  cleft head as potentially independent 292
  contrast 293, 300
  deixis 125–7, 268, 306
  discourse functions 264, 293–7, 297–8, 306
  exclusiveness component 292
  focus 291–3
  forward-pointing 268, 296, 306
  frequency in data 265, 266
  German 124–5, 247–8, 297–8
  headless relatives 268–9, 293–4
  highlighting 122, 244–6, 247–8, 291–3, 297
  intonation 121, 122–3, 265, 266, 292–3, 294
  introduce propositions 244–6
  loose constructions 74, 123–5, 292, 293–4 n.
  with participle 121
  particle combined with, German 297–8
  presupposition 126–7, 292
  reduction 74, 122, 291, 294
  Russian 126–7
  salience of cleft clause 122, 291
  syntactic integration of clauses 74
  THAT 271
  thematization 195, 268, 291, 306
  topic-introducing function 273, 293–4, 297–8, 306, 326
  unintegrated 74, 123–5, 292, 293–4
WH clefts, reverse 40–1, 92, 93, 94, 274–91
  anaphoric function 279
  attention-marking 271, 279, 280, 296
  backward-pointing 296, 306
  braking and consolidating function 264, 279, 289–91
  cleft constituents 266, 274–5
  contrastive function minor 269–70, 300
  deixis 268, 271, 276–80, 306
  described 263
  discourse function 264, 276–80, 280–7
  frequency in data 265, 266
  German 280–7, 287–91, 298
  information structure 264, 276
  intonation 266, 269–70, 275–6
  THAT 264, 266, 267, 271, 274, 277–80
  thematization 195, 268, 269–71, 280, 306
  the thing is construction similar to 244
  THIS 264, 266, 267, 274, 276–7
  in written language 279 n.
WH constructions 93, 104–32
  see also WH clefts
  WH clefts, reverse
  and under relative clauses
what about? 253
which 110–11, 337, 350, 415

see also under relative clauses
while 102–3
WHISPER 415
word length 19
word order:
   complement clauses 370–1
   Early Immediate Constituents Hypothesis 369–71
   German 113, 281
   highlighting 190–1, 195, 197–8, 200, 253, 255–9, 259–61, 371–2
   inversion as strategy of persuasion 24–5
   permissible, within different types of clause 56
   rigidity, and correlative structures 117
   Russian 113, 116; and highlighting 190–1, 197–8, 253, 255–9, 259–61
   subject-auxiliary inversion 394
   subordinate clauses 76, 94–5, 113, 116
   and typology 369–72
   see also fronting
World Cup competition (1990) 392
would + *have* conditionals 84, 85

written language 4–6, 69
   code-switching with spoken 407
   creativity in 394, 395–6
   dating of syntactic developments by 336–7
   educational policy questions 421–5
   effect on speech of exposure to 20, 71, 81, 90, 143, 153 n., 176, 340, 402
   importance of control of 381–2, 416–17, 421, 423–5, 423
   sentence as analytical unit 28, 31, 32, 41–5, 50
   standardization 337
   theories based on 4, 377, 378
   typology based on 338–72
   see also individual aspects throughout index

Zemskaja, E. A. 5, 9
   on clauses 95–100
   educational level of informants 21, 341
   on fragmented syntax 61–71
   on focus 190–1, 259–60
   on NP-clause constructions 241–2
   on subject- and topic-prominence 363, 364